SUNDAYS AND SEASONS

YEAR A 2011

Sundays and Seasons
2011, Year A
Guide to Worship Planning

Related resources

Worship Planning Calendar, 2011, Year A (AFP 978-0-8066-9521-1)

Words for Worship, 2011, Year A (AFP 978-0-8066-9523-5)

Acknowledgments

Susan R. Briehl, *Holden Prayer Around the Cross* (Augsburg Fortress, 2009): blessings for Advent, Christmas, Lent (alt.) and Summer; declaration of forgiveness for Summer; opening sentence for Autumn.

Evangelical Lutheran Worship (Augsburg Fortress, 2006) and *Evangelical Lutheran Worship Pastoral Care* (Augsburg Fortress, 2008): seasonal texts for the Three Days (except invitations to communion and prayers after communion); confession and forgiveness (Lent, from Sending of Holy Communion and from Corporate Confession and Forgiveness); offering prayers; prayer after communion (Lent); prayers at the sending of communion; blessing (Autumn, from Morning Prayer); and dismissals (except Autumn).

Book of Common Prayer: prayer after communion, alt., for Vigil of Easter and Easter season.

Susan R. Briehl, *Come, Lord Jesus: Devotions for Advent, Christmas, Epiphany* (Augsburg Fortress, 1996): blessing of the Advent wreath; lighting the Christmas tree.

Libro de Liturgia y Cántico (Augsburg Fortress, 1998): Fiesta de las posadas, trans. Sara Calderon.

This Far by Faith: An African American Resource for Worship (Augsburg Fortress, 1999): The Way of the Cross.

Evangelical Lutheran Worship Occasional Services for the Assembly (Augsburg Fortress, 2009): Recognition of Ministries in the Congregation, Thanksgiving for Baptism, Welcoming People to Communion, Blessing and Sending for Mission, Farewell and Godspeed, General Order of Blessing, Remembering Those Who Have Died.

Annual and seasonal materials

Annual essays: Christian Scharen, Craig A. Satterlee, Kyle T. Fever

Preparing for the Season: Clint A. Schnekloth, Robert Buckley Farlee

Seasonal Worship Texts: Martin A. Seltz

Seasonal Rites: Melissa Moll, Susan Langhauser, Roger Gustafson, Nadia Bolz-Weber, Jennifer Moland-Kovash

Weekly materials

Introductions to the Day: Craig Mueller

Introductions to the Readings: Ralph Klein, Richard Carlson, Mark Allen Powell

Prayers of Intercession: Kevin Shock, Marda Messick, Craig Mueller, Miriam Schmidt, Christine M. M. Nessel, Gwenn A. Bazajou, Kimberly Groninga, Chris Duckworth, D. Foy Christopherson

Ideas and Images for the Day: James Armentrout, David A. Berg, Sarah E. Bolick-Lang, Nadia Bolz-Weber, Richard Bruxvoort-Colligan, Mark Buchan, Anne Edison-Albright, Justin J. Lind-Ayres, Carey Gardiner Mack, Joy L. McDonald Coltvet, Joel Nau, Christine M. M. Nessel, Monte Smith Peterson, Blake Rohrer, Rebecca L. Schlatter, Michelle Timm, Dena Williams

Music materials

Hymns for Worship: Daniel E. Schwandt

Choral: Zebulon Highben

Children's Choir: Brian R. and Barbara Larson

Keyboard/Instrumental: Arletta Anderson

Handbell: Carolynne Mathis

Praise Ensemble: Mark David Johnson

Global: Lorraine Brugh

Art and design

Cover art: Nicholas Wilton

Interior art: Joel Nickel, Margaret Adams Parker, Robyn Sand Anderson, Margaret Bartenstein Bussey, M. P. (Paula) Wiggins

Book design: Laurie Ingram, Jessica Hillstrom

Development staff

Suzanne Burke, Andrew DeYoung, Norma Aamodt-Nelson, Carol Carver, Robert Buckley Farlee, Martin A. Seltz

INTRODUCTION

ADVENT

CHRISTMAS

TIME AFTER EPIPHANY

LENT

THE THREE DAYS

EASTER

TIME AFTER PENTECOST — SUMMER

TIME AFTER PENTECOST — AUTUMN

TIME AFTER PENTECOST — NOVEMBER

INDEX OF SEASONAL RITES

Lectionary Conversion Chart

Time after Pentecost, Year A, 2011

If today is . . .	. . . it falls within this date range.	The "lectionary" number assigned to this date range in *Evangelical Lutheran Worship* is . . .	. . . which is equivalent to "proper ___" in other printed lectionaries.	In 2011, this Sunday is the "_____ Sunday after Pentecost."
Sunday, June 26	Sunday between June 26 & July 2	Lectionary 13	8	2nd
Sunday, July 3	Sunday between July 3 & 9	Lectionary 14	9	3rd
Sunday, July 10	Sunday between July 10 & 16	Lectionary 15	10	4th
Sunday, July 17	Sunday between July 17 & 23	Lectionary 16	11	5th
Sunday, July 24	Sunday between July 24 & 30	Lectionary 17	12	6th
Sunday, July 31	Sunday between July 31 & Aug 6	Lectionary 18	13	7th
Sunday, August 7	Sunday between Aug 7 & 13	Lectionary 19	14	8th
Sunday, August 14	Sunday between Aug 14 & 20	Lectionary 20	15	9th
Sunday, August 21	Sunday between Aug 21 & 27	Lectionary 21	16	10th
Sunday, August 28	Sunday between Aug 28 & Sept 3	Lectionary 22	17	11th
Sunday, September 4	Sunday between Sept 4 & 10	Lectionary 23	18	12th
Sunday, September 11	Sunday between Sept 11 & 17	Lectionary 24	19	13th
Sunday, September 18	Sunday between Sept 18 & 24	Lectionary 25	20	14th
Sunday, September 25	Sunday between Sept 25 & Oct 1	Lectionary 26	21	15th
Sunday, October 2	Sunday between Oct 2 & 8	Lectionary 27	22	16th
Sunday, October 9	Sunday between Oct 9 & 15	Lectionary 28	23	17th
Sunday, October 16	Sunday between Oct 16 & 22	Lectionary 29	24	18th
Sunday, October 23	Sunday between Oct 23 & 29	Lectionary 30	25	19th
Sunday, October 30	Sunday between Oct 30 & Nov 5	Lectionary 31	26	20th
Sunday, November 6	Sunday between Nov 6 & 12	Lectionary 32	27	21st
Sunday, November 13	Sunday between Nov 13 & 19	Lectionary 33	28	22nd
Christ the King, November 20	Sunday between Nov 20 & 26	Lectionary 34	29	Last

Lectionary Color Chart
Year A, 2011

Advent

Nov 28	First Sunday of Advent	Blue
Dec 5	Second Sunday of Advent	Blue
Dec 12	Third Sunday of Advent	Blue
Dec 19	Fourth Sunday of Advent	Blue

Christmas

Dec 24/25	Nativity of Our Lord	White
Dec 26	First Sunday of Christmas	White
Jan 2	Second Sunday of Christmas	White
Jan 6	Epiphany of Our Lord	White

Time after Epiphany

Jan 9	Baptism of Our Lord	White
Jan 16	Second Sunday after Epiphany	Green
Jan 23	Third Sunday after Epiphany	Green
Jan 30	Fourth Sunday after Epiphany	Green
Feb 6	Fifth Sunday after Epiphany	Green
Feb 13	Sixth Sunday after Epiphany	Green
Feb 20	Seventh Sunday after Epiphany	Green
Feb 27	Eighth Sunday after Epiphany	Green
Mar 6	Transfiguration of Our Lord	White

Lent

Mar 9	Ash Wednesday	Purple
Mar 13	First Sunday in Lent	Purple
Mar 20	Second Sunday in Lent	Purple
Mar 27	Third Sunday in Lent	Purple
Apr 3	Fourth Sunday in Lent	Purple
Apr 10	Fifth Sunday in Lent	Purple
Apr 17	Sunday of the Passion	Scarlet/Purple
Apr 18	Monday in Holy Week	Scarlet/Purple
Apr 19	Tuesday in Holy Week	Scarlet/Purple
Apr 20	Wednesday in Holy Week	Scarlet/Purple

Three Days

Apr 21	Maundy Thursday	Scarlet/White
Apr 22	Good Friday	None
Apr 23/24	Resurrection of Our Lord	White/Gold

Easter

May 1	Second Sunday of Easter	White
May 8	Third Sunday of Easter	White
May 15	Fourth Sunday of Easter	White
May 22	Fifth Sunday of Easter	White
May 29	Sixth Sunday of Easter	White
June 2	Ascension of Our Lord	White
June 5	Seventh Sunday of Easter	White
June 12	Day of Pentecost	Red

Time after Pentecost

June 19	The Holy Trinity	White
June 26	Lectionary 13	Green
July 3	Lectionary 14	Green
July 10	Lectionary 15	Green
July 17	Lectionary 16	Green
July 24	Lectionary 17	Green
July 31	Lectionary 18	Green
Aug 7	Lectionary 19	Green
Aug 14	Lectionary 20	Green
Aug 21	Lectionary 21	Green
Aug 28	Lectionary 22	Green
Sept 4	Lectionary 23	Green
Sept 11	Lectionary 24	Green
Sept 18	Lectionary 25	Green
Sept 25	Lectionary 26	Green
Oct 2	Lectionary 27	Green
Oct 9	Lectionary 28	Green
Oct 10	Day of Thanksgiving (Canada)	Green
Oct 16	Lectionary 29	Green
Oct 23	Lectionary 30	Green
Oct 30	Reformation Sunday	Red
Oct 30	Lectionary 31	Green
Nov 6	All Saints Sunday	White
Nov 6	Lectionary 32	Green
Nov 13	Lectionary 33	Green
Nov 20	Christ the King (*Lect. 34*)	White/*Green*
Nov 24	Day of Thanksgiving (USA)	Green

INTRODUCTION

The beginning of a new year brings with it the opportunity to look with fresh eyes on old friends: festivals and seasons, commemorations, the lectionary, hymns and songs, old and new prayers, the simple pattern of gathering around the word, the font, and the table. Worship leaders and planners can look with fresh eyes on these stable structures of the church's worship life through the particular vision of the lectionary readings and through the changing experiences of the assembly gathered for worship each Lord's Day.

Christian worship is marked by a pattern of gathering; proclaiming and responding to the word of God, praying for the world and the church; preparing the table, offering thanksgiving, and sharing the meal; receiving God's blessing and departing for service in the world. These basic elements constitute the center of the church's worship. Or, to say it more fully, this center is "an open and participating community gathered on the Lord's Day in song and prayer around the scriptures read and preached, around the baptismal washing, enacted or remembered, around holy supper, and around the sending to a needy world" (Gordon Lathrop, *Central Things: Worship in Word and Sacrament* [Minneapolis: Augsburg Fortress, 2005], p. 14).

Sundays and Seasons is intended for those who help the assembly worship at this center in word and gesture, song and prayer. With various skills and talents many members of one community prepare and assist at worship on a weekly or seasonal basis. In *Sundays and Seasons* readers will find a rich treasure of information and suggestions that strengthen worship around the scriptures, the baptismal bath, and the holy supper.

How to Use this Resource

At its best worship planning is done by a team (including musicians, preachers and presiding ministers, visual artists, educators, altar guild members, writers, and persons concerned with outreach) gathered on a regular basis (seasonally or monthly) to reflect on the lectionary readings and the meaning of the seasons.

A pattern for this regular meeting may include common reading and shared reflection on (at least) the gospel readings of the season; discussion of the seasonal liturgical practices, customs, and music unique to this community;

review of congregational resources for seasonal use in the home; consideration of appropriate means to welcome newcomers, visitors, and strangers to the seasonal worship of this community; and assignment and preparation of responsibilities regarding worship such as texts to be written, congregational/ensemble/instrumental music, environment and visual media, and specific liturgical ministries.

Even though some of the sections in this volume may appear to be geared toward a particular liturgical ministry, the contributors to *Sundays and Seasons* have worked with the understanding that many of the sections may and will be used by all who participate in worship preparation. Likewise, portions of this resource will benefit those who participate in congregational ministries that flow from worship: education, evangelism, stewardship, and social ministries.

Sundays and Seasons is not a "ready-made" worship planner, nor does it prescribe worship practices. Rather, it offers suggestions for those who prepare worship in a particular community of faith according to the distinctive needs and abilities of that community. This resource does, however, presume the use of the lectionary, the calendar, and the essential elements of worship within the Lutheran tradition.

Contributors

As this resource has been prepared for publication, we have welcomed the work of church musicians, preachers and biblical scholars, artists and designers, parish pastors, educators, and writers with various expertise. Their work, offered out of various and varied contexts, is a gift to all worship planners and to the wider church. All of them deserve our thanks.

Visual images

Joel Nickel of Salem, Oregon, works as an artist/theologian and has been creating ecclesiastical art for more than 40 years (seasonal images). **Margaret Adams Parker** of Alexandria, Virginia, explores biblical themes through her art; teaches at Virginia Theological Seminary; and writes about art and the church; www.margaretadamsparker.com (Advent–Transfiguration). **Robyn Sand Anderson** of New Ulm, Minnesota, does illustration and commission work for individuals, businesses, and churches, specializing in watercolor and acrylic paintings; www.robynsandanderson.com (Ash Wednesday–Day of Pentecost). **Margaret Bartenstein Bussey** of Minneapolis is in love with movement, music, color, and light, and uses drawing, painting, and printmaking to say what she sees (Holy Trinity–Lectionary 22). **M. P. (Paula) Wiggins** of Cincinnati, Ohio, has been an illustrator and fine artist for over 25 years. She gets her inspiration from art, music, and nature (Lectionary 23–Christ the King).

Seasonal materials

Clint A. Schnekloth, pastor of East Koshkonong Lutheran in Cambridge, Wisconsin (reflections on preparing for the season). **Melissa Moll**, director of music at First English Lutheran in Appleton, Wisconsin; **Susan Langhauser** and **Roger Gustafson**, pastors of Advent Lutheran in Olathe, Kansas; **Nadia Bolz-Weber**, pastor of House for All Sinners and Saints in Denver; and **Jennifer Moland-Kovash**, pastor of All Saints Lutheran in Palatine, Illinois (seasonal rites).

Prayers of intercession

Kevin Shock, pastor of St. Mark Evangelical Lutheran in Pleasant Gap, Pennsylvania; **Craig Mueller**, pastor of Holy Trinity Lutheran in Chicago; **Christine M. M. Nessel**, pastor, wife, and mom of two living in Woodbury, Connecticut; **Gwenn A. Bazajou**, pastor of New Hope Lutheran in Alvarado, Minnesota; **Miriam Schmidt**, pastor of First Lutheran in Plains, Montana; **Marda Messick**, pastor of St. Stephen Lutheran in Tallahassee, Florida; **Chris Duckworth**, pastor of Resurrection Lutheran in Arlington, Virginia; **D. Foy Christopherson**, pastor of Central Lutheran in Minneapolis; and **Kimberly Groninga**, who teaches in the English Department at the University of Northern Iowa and is a member of her congregation's worship teams.

Ideas and images for the day

David A. Berg, pastor of Good Shepherd Evangelical Lutheran in Rochester, Minnesota; **Nadia Bolz-Weber** (see above); **Richard Bruxvoort-Colligan**, freelance musician in northeast Iowa; **Mark Buchan**, a Lutheran pastor who lives and works in Columbia, South Carolina; **Anne Edison-Albright**, pastoral candidate completing a year of CPE residency in Park Ridge, Illinois; **Justin J. Lind-Ayres**, pastor of Bethany Lutheran in Minneapolis; **Carey Gardiner Mack**, a pastor in the Southeast Michigan Synod; **Joy L. McDonald Coltvet**, director of vocation and recruitment at the Lutheran School of Theology at Chicago; **Joel Nau**, pastor of St. Paul Lutheran in Winterset, Iowa; **Blake Rohrer**, assistant to the bishop for the South-Central Synod of Wisconsin; **Michelle Timm**, former pastor, current choir director, married to a pastor/guard chaplain, and mother of three young daughters in Red Wing, Minnesota; **Dena Williams**, pastor

in the Rocky Mountain Synod, currently on leave from call; **James Armentrout**, pastor of Holy Trinity Lutheran in Lynchburg, Virginia; **Sarah E. Bolick-Lang**, pastor of Grace Evangelical Lutheran in Boone, North Carolina, and Lutheran campus pastor for Appalachian State University; **Christine M. M. Nessel** (see above); **Monte Smith Peterson**, a mom, writer, and baker currently living in Hong Kong; and **Rebecca L. Schlatter**, pastor of Lutheran Church of the Good Shepherd in Reno, Nevada.

Music suggestions

Daniel E. Schwandt, cantor at the Lutheran School of Theology at Chicago (hymns); **Zebulon Highben**, choral conductor, church musician, and composer in East Lansing, Michigan (choral); **Brian R. Larson**, cantor at Trinity Lutheran in New Smyrna Beach, Florida; and **Barbara Larson**, minister of music at Emmaus Lutheran in Orange City, Florida (children's choir); **Arletta Anderson**, associate in ministry and cantor at Queen Anne Lutheran in Seattle (keyboard/instrumental); **Carolynne Mathis**, director of worship and music at Faith Lutheran in Coon Rapids, Minnesota, and adjunct professor of handbells at Concordia University, St. Paul (handbell); **Mark David Johnson**, musician in St. Petersburg, Florida (praise ensemble); and **Lorraine Brugh**, associate professor of music and director of chapel music at Valparaiso University, Indiana (global).

Additional Resources

Sundays and Seasons is integrally related to other worship resources: *Lectionary for Worship Year A*; *Evangelical Lutheran Worship*; *Psalter for Worship Year A*, Evangelical Lutheran Worship Edition; *Worship Planning Calendar 2011*; SundaysandSeasons.com online worship planning tool; and *Words for Worship 2011, Year A*.

Sundays and Seasons, even after fifteen years, is a work in progress that relies on the response of its users in order to enhance its quality and usefulness in the future. Many thanks to all who have written, called, or spoken with us in person to share concerns, praise, ideas, and suggestions for future editions. The Worship and Music team at Augsburg Fortress is eager to hear from you—and perhaps put your gifts to use as a future contributor.

Be welcome, then, to this resource that points us to that merciful place of encounter where God comes to abide among us in the holy gospel and the sacraments of grace: the worshiping assembly. Be welcome to the words, music, and images through which we may mark the Sundays and seasons in the year of salvation, 2011.

Suzanne K. Burke, general editor
burkes@augsburfortress.org or 800.426.0115

Preparing the Prayers of Intercession Locally

In the summer of 2009 I was visiting relatives and joined them for worship on Sunday morning. The small 100-year-old church was quite full for a Sunday in July. The service started in a delightful way as a twelve-year-old girl offered special music at the start of the service. The congregation celebrated a baptism, and the service was well-led throughout. The assisting minister, with white alb and calm presence, led his parts alongside the pastor. Perhaps because of the warmth and distinctiveness of the service as a whole, and my general unfamiliarity with this practice, I was a bit shocked when the prayers of intercession were read by the assisting minister straight out of the *Celebrate* insert, with the assembly mostly reading along with their copy, conveniently inserted in the bulletin.

The prayers on that particular July Sunday were lovely; well-crafted and clear petitions for the church, the world, the nations, the sick, and so on. Yet I couldn't help the overwhelming feeling that these were not actually the prayers of the people—not *this* people, and not *today*. They are, in fact, prayers written for any place and for a day in the liturgical calendar. Their use in some particular place in the midst of the ebb and flow of a week necessarily highlights that temporal and spatial gap between writer and praying community. This brief essay is written in hopes that some will share this concern and find ways to foster prayer practices in your congregation that can draw on the suggestive prayers written for *Sundays and Seasons* while moving a step or two towards locally prepared prayers of intercession.

Of course, dear reader, you might do much worse than simply using the prayers prepared carefully and well by those writers working with *Sundays and Seasons* and then reprinted in the *Celebrate* inserts. In his little book *When You Pray* (Wipf & Stock, 2003), theologian Douglas John Hall worries that prayer in North America too easily becomes another tool for self-cultivation—with "a view to becoming more fulfilled, acceptable, interesting, beautiful, psychically stable, integrated, irenic, healthy, happy, satisfied, or positive people." And turning to locally written prayers of the people might open the door to half-baked theology of just this sort. When we pray, we are certainly not simply lifting our hopes for personal or national self-improvement or safety skyward. Rather, the whole biblical witness shows us a God who comes near, who hears our cries, and who seeks to work healing, reconciliation, and renewal for all creation. If we draw on Christian faith in our praying, Hall says, we portray "nothing more nor less than the God-given courage to be in the world intentionally and without reserve."

A congregation might consider the prayers faithfully prepared by the writers of *Sundays and Seasons* as help getting where you need to go. They are solid and clear steps on the way to being "in the world intentionally and without reserve." Yet by design they cannot get all the way down the stairs to your congregation, your neighborhood, your particular set of concerns on this day, and for this place. I venture to guess that the practice of praying generic prayers of intercession without local adaptation goes without much notice or comment, seemingly without offense but also without the particular spice that would make them stand out and taste particularly good or bitter in our mouths. Martin Luther argues in the little pamphlet *A Simple Way to Pray*, written at the request of Master Peter, his barber, that if a prayer is so generic that one can't remember it afterwards, we may as well have just babbled heavenwards. Rather, he suggests, even when meditating on the Lord's Prayer, take pause after each petition and add in the daily concerns of your heart, congregation, and town.

In suggesting a way of moving towards such locally prepared prayers of intercession, I recommend two possible moves. They are, in order of my discussion, use of *Sundays and Seasons* for adaptation and for inspiration. Adaptation is a relatively easy practice and ought to be accessible to anyone using these prayers. In fact, the printed prayers I write about above did include the line: "Here other intercessions may be offered." And the assisting minister did add one petition for those returning from a mission trip and for those serving in the military. Yet adding a petition is not yet adaptation. Each petition may be slightly adapted to speak with more clarity about local circumstances. For example, here is one petition prayed that day in July:

Righteous Judge, guide those who serve in governments throughout the world. Give them wisdom to administer justice and to strive for peace in our troubled world.

Were it to be prayed this week, the week this essay is being written, one might adapt it thus:

Righteous Judge, guide those who serve in governments throughout the world, especially those now gathered at the U.N. Summit on Climate Change in New York. Give them wisdom and courage to be decisive, leading all peoples and nations to urgent action on behalf of your beautiful, yet troubled world.

While this does not take much work, it does move the prayer from anytime to now, a crucial shift in the work of "being in the world intentionally and without reserve."

A second possible move toward locally prepared prayers of intercession might be to use the *Sundays and Seasons* prayers as inspiration. That is, we might see them for what they are—a thoughtful and inspired framework rooted in the scripture texts for a particular week. We might simply take them petition by petition, writing fresh versions of each one that are like jazz improvisations on a theme, or better, like flesh on a skeleton. For example, here is another petition prayed that day in July:

Merciful God, we pray for all your children, for the innocent who suffer, and for all who find themselves in the valley of the shadow of death.

Psalm 23, echoed in this petition, was indeed the assigned psalm for the day and thus provides inspiration for how to integrate the scripture texts with the petitions. Taking that petition as a starting place, but considering today's concerns about a lingering bad economy, worries about the fall flu season, and particular people who are ill and dying, one might do something like this:

Gentle Shepherd, you promise to care for us in all circumstances. For those who have lost jobs (especially), be a staff of stability. For those who are ill (especially), anoint them with your comforting presence. For those under the shadow of death (especially), take their hand and lead them day by day.

This version, inspired by the general tenor of the petition, moves to say something more particular about God but also something more particular about the suffering people are in fact dealing with now. It is still somewhat general, as it must be if the prayers are to serve an assembly and not just one person. But naming those things many have on their minds, along with the practice of leaving space for people to name those they know aloud or silently, will draw them into the prayers in a more direct way. We do not regularly leave enough silence in our worship and prayer. How then do we expect people to join their prayers as one? Word requires silence to speak.

How might such a practice of adaptation or inspired revision be done in a local congregation? It is not a task to take lightly. The Ministers Edition of *Lutheran Book of Worship* says "Preparation of the prayers is no less important than preparation of the sermon" (p. 28). This strong claim for the prayers of intercession has sat in my craw ever since I first read it decades ago. The Leaders Edition of *Evangelical Lutheran Worship* says: "Because the prayers of intercession balance the needs of the whole world with those of a particular community and occasion, the preparation of these prayers is a responsibility of the local assembly" (p. 21). Taking these recommendations as a common grounding, let me close by offering a few hints about getting started.

First, one ought to have worship planning teams in place who look ahead to the next seasons, study the lectionary texts, and set the stage for hymn choices, sermon themes, and imagery for prayers. Setting up this kind of planning team is not hard, and the discipline of carrying through with it offers spiritual nurture for all those who participate.

Second, build a team of worship assistants who can participate in worship planning team meetings. Invite them also to pray for one another. Host a retreat once a year, at least, to discuss some substantial theological literature and to engage in creative writing exercises. As an example of the latter, one could ask people to pick an animal, then list everything that they associate with the animal, and then create a simple prayer that calls upon God in relation to that animal (O God, like a dog awaiting a juicy bone, you await our return to you in humility, seeking your mercy for our waywardness). These exercises can be silly, hilarious, and also quite profound. Most of all, though, such exercises expand the imaginative range of our writing. When we come back to scripture and do the same exercise (picking a passage of scripture to work with rather than an animal) each person feels more free to play with the language in compelling ways.

We can, unfortunately, go to sleep in our weekly patterns of worship. This is not lost on visitors who come but find no life, no creative spark, in our midst. My plea is that as far as is possible, we would strive always to be a believable church, one that speaks honest words near to our heart, touching on those things that matter, embodying the infinite creativity of the God who in Jesus Christ is making all things new.

Christian Scharen
Assistant Professor of Worship and Theology
Luther Seminary, St. Paul

Helpful Reading

- Walter C. Huffman, *Prayer of the Faithful: Understanding and Creatively Leading Corporate Intercessory Prayer*, revised edition. Minneapolis: Augsburg Fortress, 1992.
- Michael Kwatera, *Preparing the General Intercessions*. Collegeville, MN: The Liturgical Press, 1996.

Affirming Christian Vocation

"We welcome you into the body of Christ and into the mission we share," we say when someone is baptized. "Join us in giving thanks and praise to God and bearing God's creative and redeeming word to all the world" (*Evangelical Lutheran Worship*, p. 231). Joined to Christ's death and resurrection in the waters of baptism, the Holy Spirit calls and empowers us to share in Christ's priestly ministry (Heb. 9:11; 1 Peter 2:9). According to *The Use of the Means of Grace*, "Christians profess baptismal faith as they engage in discipleship in the world. God calls Christians to use their various vocations and ministries to witness to the Gospel of Christ wherever they serve or work" (Principle 52).

The Use of the Means of Grace teaches that "God's Word and the church help us to discover ways to carry out our calling" (Background 52A). Worship is the way the church most closely relates the Christian faith to the daily lives of the vast majority of practicing Christians.

Evangelical Lutheran Worship includes a rite of "Affirmation of Christian Vocation" (p. 84). Using language found in other prayers provided in *Evangelical Lutheran Worship*, worship planners can effectively focus this part of the sending rite to intentionally lift up particular occupations as Christian service in the world at various times during the year—teachers and students in the fall, health professionals during flu season, and accountants and bankers at tax time, for example. By incorporating elements from these prayers into the common rite, congregations can lift up both unique contributions of particular vocations and the common vocation all Christians share.

On the page after "Affirmation of Christian Vocation," for example, we find a prayer for emergency workers (p. 85). Using language from this prayer, the presiding minister might address emergency workers, saying:

[Sisters and brothers]/[name/s], as you work in danger, rush in to bring hope and help and comfort when others flee to safety; as you seek and save, serve and protect, both your work and your rest are in God. Will you endeavor to embody the protection of the Good Shepherd, in gratitude to God and in service to others . . . ?

The prayer on page 84 then might be emended:

Almighty God, by the power of the Spirit you have knit these your servants into the one body of your Son, Jesus Christ. Look with favor upon them in their commitment to serve in Christ's name. Give them caution and concern for one another, so that in safety they might do what must be done, under your watchful eye. Support them in their courage and dedication that they may continue to save lives, ease pain, and mend the torn fabric of lives and social order. Strengthen us all in our Christian vocation of witness to the world and of service to others; through Jesus Christ our Lord. Amen.

Evangelical Lutheran Worship includes prayers for those in civil authority, courts of justice, those in the armed forces, those who work the land, teachers, commerce and labor, prisons and correctional institutions, those entering retirement, those who care for children, caregivers, and health care providers. By pairing these recognitions with appropriate times during the year, congregations can strengthen the connection between faith and daily life and work. Some congregations might consider undertaking to affirm every interested member's vocation during the course of a year.

Craig A. Satterlee
Professor of Homiletics, Dean of the ACTS Doctor of Ministry in Preaching program
Lutheran School of Theology at Chicago

THE YEAR OF MATTHEW

This liturgical year we focus on the gospel according to Matthew. This gospel is commonly referred to as "the church's gospel." Matthew is the only gospel narrative that contains the Greek word *ekklesia*, which commonly is translated "church" (16:18; 18:17). In addition, only Matthew has an extended discourse on "church discipline" (18:1-35). Now, on the one hand, Matthew is no more and no less "the church's gospel" than Mark, Luke, or John. They all address, we presume, already existing groups of believers—they are for the church. But, on the other hand, Matthew focuses more than the others on shaping and challenging disciples to active discipleship. In Matthew many themes complexly weave together into one of the longest gospel narratives, and the task is to understand how Matthew puts these together, how his mosaic is not Mark's. At times it is easy to focus on individual scenes at the risk of losing sight of the bigger picture Matthew paints of Jesus, the gospel, and discipleship. But, like a puzzle or mosaic, Matthew's gospel narrative is best experienced and understood with all of the pieces in view. When we do this, each Sunday can find its place within the big picture of God's purposes, and our lives of worship will begin to take shape as God speaks to us.

Reading Strategies

The Revised Common Lectionary does not cover all of Matthew. It also reorders many scenes. In light of Matthew's purposes, it is important to keep in mind two helpful points as we listen to and experience Matthew's gospel this year. First, Matthew's primary audience is an already existing community of disciples. Put another way, Matthew's gospel is not intended to be read as a first-time presentation of the life and works of Jesus. It does not attempt to "prove" anything about Jesus or God to people who have not heard or who do not believe the gospel. Rather, Matthew is communicating the significance of Jesus, his words, and his actions in order to encourage and challenge disciples in their present contexts. Rather than present the "gospel message," Matthew assumes it, builds on it, and explains it to move people into deeper faith. Much of what is in Matthew's narrative does not place specific emphasis on certain well-worn topics: God's love, how one gets saved, how Jesus forgives

sin, or why Jesus commands his people to baptize disciples. This is not to say that these are not important for Matthew; they are just not new points of understanding. Matthew assumes his readers get these points.

A second important reading strategy is that Matthew's gospel should be read *backwards*. That is to say, Matthew 28:16-20 should be a guide for reading the rest of the story. This is of course related to the first reading strategy: Matthew is written to existing disciples *in order to* encourage and challenge them in making disciples of all people. Taking Matthew 28:16-20 as a cue for reading the rest of the narrative gives us parameters for interpreting various scenes within the narrative, which are written to communicate the significance of this Jesus and his teaching, which is to be shared with all people. The call to Matthew's audience is discipleship and making disciples; the framework and paradigm for this is Jesus' proclamation and life.

A Call to Watchfulness

This liturgical year begins and ends with passages from Jesus' "end times" discourse in Matthew 24–25. This is a fitting way to bracket the year of Matthew, since Matthew is written to a community of disciples to encourage greater discipleship. In this discourse Jesus emphasizes watchfulness and being busy at work while awaiting his return. As we begin the year with Matthew 24:36-44, we are called to *watch*—Jesus' return is unexpected. At the end of the year we are given, in the parable of the sheep and goats (25:31-46), a story of *how* we should "watch" and wait: service to humanity. Not only that—working within this theme of watching—the story of the sheep and the goats, read in the context of Matthew as a whole, reminds us of what the rest of the world should see from Jesus' disciples during this time of watchfulness. It sums up the general nature of our call in the world.

While the lectionary gives us these "bookends," Matthew's gospel presents its own parameters for understanding the gospel narrative. This is best understood in terms of a "presence" theme. In Matthew 1:23 (Advent 4), we learn that in Jesus "God is with us" (or Jesus is "God with us"). This phrase explaining the name Emmanuel is an addition by Matthew from Isaiah 8:10 to a citation from Isaiah

7:14 ("and shall name him Immanuel"). The point is that Jesus is the one in whom God is made present and known. After his resurrection, we read that Jesus has "all authority in heaven and on earth" (Matt. 28:18) and that this Jesus is now "with" his disciples (28:20). There are two important points to observe in light of the "with us" language in 1:23 and 28:20. As the risen Lord, (1) Jesus is now "with" his people just as God was "with" Jesus. That is, we, commissioned and empowered by Jesus, are the vehicle through which God and God's kingdom are seen and experienced in the world, just as Jesus was the one in whom God was made known to the world; (2) Jesus' ongoing presence among his people both enables and encourages them to be his witness to the world. Discipleship is not our endeavor; it is evidence of Jesus' presence in and among us—"with" us.

In the readings from Advent through the time after Epiphany, we learn important things about Jesus and his mission. One significant point is that his coming is related to the proclamation of the kingdom of heaven. The first words of John the Baptist's proclamation concern the nearness of the kingdom (3:2), and this is the same for Jesus (4:17). The last two readings in Advent contrast Jesus with the current king: Herod. The point is not just christological—it is about two kings and two different spheres of living (kingdoms): Jesus and the kingdom of heaven, and the earthly king and the kingdom he represents, which are in this context Herod and Rome. Since Jesus' mission is about the kingdom, Jesus' description of his works in Matthew 11:2-6 also relates to the kingdom. It is characterized by healing, wholeness, restoration. In addition, Jesus' description recalls prophetic expectations of God's salvation and renewal for God's people (Isa. 26:19; 29:18; 35:3-10; 61:1).

A Greater Righteousness for the World

The work of Jesus described in Matthew 11 looks back onto Jesus' teaching and activity in previous chapters of the narrative (5–9), where Jesus teaches about and models the alternative life of the kingdom. The lectionary takes us through the Beatitudes (5:1-12) and Antitheses (5:21-48) in the Sermon on the Mount, where Jesus gives shape to this "upside-down" way of living: happiness in poverty, joy in weeping, reward in suffering. The ethical demand in the Antitheses is high indeed, culminating in the statement "be perfect, therefore, as your heavenly Father is perfect" (5:48). The way that the lectionary brackets this set of readings with Matthew 3:13-17 (Baptism of Our Lord) and 17:1-9 (Transfiguration) is quite appropriate for our understanding. It draws attention to and reminds us of the fact that this Jesus who teaches these things is no less than God's Son, and we are to listen to him (3:17; 17:5). For this

Jesus, God's Son, has taken on human flesh and has himself demonstrated this kingdom life.

One of the great challenges of Matthew's gospel, especially to typical Lutheran theology, is this demand of "works" brought out in these readings. The Sermon on the Mount both makes this demand clear and clues us in to its purpose: "Let your light shine before others, *so that* they may see your good works and give glory to your Father in heaven" (5:16). Our works are not intended to earn God's favor, but to make God favorable to people. In other words, our good works, according to Matthew's gospel, are not of us or for us, they are the evidence of the presence of the Lord in us for the world, that the world may see and know God the Father and the Lord Jesus Christ. One of the most difficult challenges in Matthew is in the story of the sheep and the goats in 25:31-46. However we might interpret the details of this scene, one thing is clear: the good deeds to which Jesus calls his disciples are ones that benefit the world—the poor, the hungry, the stranger, the naked, the sick, the imprisoned. In all of this, Matthew's gospel presumes the "with us" point—with us to enable, encourage, and forgive. The witness of the kingdom is possible because Jesus is present among his disciples.

Through the rest of the year, we encounter various parables and stories about Jesus' life. The parables remind us of the way we should think about the kingdom that Jesus proclaimed and embodied. It is a great treasure—worth selling everything for (13:44-46; Lectionary 17). God has entrusted this valuable treasure to us to share with others (25:14-30; Lectionary 33). The kingdom of heaven calls for workers, not passive believers (20:1-16; 21:23-32; Lectionary 25, 26). In Matthew, one key characteristic of the people of the kingdom is forgiveness (18:21-35; Lectionary 24). These parables and stories point to this: as disciples of Jesus, we are those in whom Jesus is present, and this presence should be patently clear to the world through our works of love, forgiveness, and justice. All of this is not an end in itself, but is central to the kingdom of heaven: "the kingdom of heaven is like this. . . ."

This year Matthew calls us to watchfulness. This is no passive waiting. The gospel according to Matthew calls disciples to *be disciples*: active workers for the kingdom of heaven, proclaiming its message, not only of forgiveness of sins and eternal life, but also of God's salvation and restoration, of an alternative pattern of living where God's will is done "on earth as it is in heaven" (6:10).

Kyle T. Fever
Adjunct Professor of New Testament

ADVENT

PREPARING FOR ADVENT

Weary?

It is not good to begin the year weary. Although we are often encouraged to receive the cycle of the church year as a gift, it seems likely that many church leaders and members may enter into a new liturgical year's rhythms with world-weariness and apathy, rather than faith and hope. When time begins to seem like "one damn thing after another," even a way of keeping time as beautiful as the liturgical year can lose its luster. Ecclesiastes may be our text for this feeling, where it recognizes that although there is a "time for every matter under heaven" (3:1-8), it also laments that "of making many books [even books like *Sundays and Seasons*] there is no end" (12:12). Psalm 80, appointed for the fourth Sunday of Advent, also gives utterance to this concern: "O Lord God of hosts, how long will you be angry with your people's prayers?" At the beginning of this year, God may be calling us to honest testimony to our despair and dread.

Further contributing to this weariness may be the phenomenon of cultural Christmas. The secular marketing season begins early, often before Halloween, and so the launch of Advent is kind of old news, rather than good news. It is old, however, only if we frame it and plan it as if it were simply a continuation or recapitulation of Christmas shopping and partying. By contrast, the actual texts for Advent offer another vision, surprising and renewing, even shocking and challenging. For those of us who have grown weary, maybe especially for those leaders who have preached on these texts for decades, Advent presents an opportunity to re-visit the idea that the church year is not a never-ending cycle, but rather a deepening spiral, God hallowing and blessing time itself. Consider the witness to this in some of the hymnody in *Evangelical Lutheran Worship:* "Mark that miracle of time, God's own sacrifice complete" (#347); "O day full of grace, O blessed time, our Lord on the earth arriving" (#627); or, to anticipate a central theme of the Advent season, not Christ's first coming but his second: "For lo! The days are hastening on, by prophets seen of old, when with the ever-circling years shall come the time foretold, when peace shall over all the earth its ancient splendors fling, and all the world give back the song which now the angels sing" (#282)[1].

Visible Words

Advent is a fresh and powerful season to give attention to visible words. Augustine, for example, thought of the liturgy as "visible speech." The liturgy, and especially the material aspects of the liturgy, like the confession and forgiveness, and the sacraments of baptism and communion, are forms of visible speech that declare Christ's death and resurrection. The Advent lectionary texts offer some of the most resounding declarations of the coming Christ. They are vivid and noisy, designed to wake hearers and those in the grip of death and despair. "*Keep awake*" (Matt. 24:42). "The voice of one *crying* in the wilderness" (Matt. 3:2). "Go and tell John what you *hear* and *see*: the blind receive their sight, the lame walk, the lepers are cleansed, the deaf hear, the dead are raised, and the poor have good news brought to them" (Matt. 11:4-5). "The wilderness and the dry land shall be *glad*, the desert shall *rejoice* and blossom" (Isa. 35:1).

So take time, a good long while, and attend to the visible words in your place of worship. Sit down in the pews or chairs and look around. Walk to every corner. Climb into all the lofts. What do you see and hear? What has been dormant or asleep far too long? What needs to be changed so that the gathered community might hear and see good news? What will gladden hearts and make the assembly rejoice? Think of the sanctuary as like a desert in which new flowers are about to bloom. Then do what needs to be done.

This likely means getting rid of or changing faded banners. It also means being proactive, inviting artists in the congregation and community to create new art with Advent themes. Maybe even a series of banners that illustrate the blind seeing, the lame walking. Or mounting photographs of desert landscapes in full bloom. Do not fear to get rid of lots of old and bring in new. Many sanctuaries have become parched places that need the water of the coming Christ.

However, the most important visible words are the sacraments. Where is your font? What is the condition of the water in it? It needs to be fresh. It needs to be splashed, played with, and spilled. There should be a lot of it. It needs to be brought front and center, if possible.

---

[1] See *Keeping Time: The Church's Years* (Minneapolis: Augsburg Fortress, 2009) pages 3–18, for further insight into time and worship.

What is the condition of your table and place settings? Many households keep special plates and silverware for the holiday season. Why not take your cue from this and make sure the table is set well for communion during Advent. Examine the paten, chalice, napkins, cloths, and table. Finally, what kind of bread and wine are you serving? Anything stale? Does it taste like bread? Is it a feast of well-aged wine strained clear? This is the table of the Lord. It is supposed to be set in such a way that sleepers will be awakened and faith restored.

Introduce new and simple art; find fresh ways to lift up the sacraments; instead of putting up walls to the secular energy around the Christmas season, find ways to dig deep into the energy of the season. Look within, rather than protecting from without.

Matthew

Good commentaries are invaluable companions for preaching throughout the year. It is especially worthwhile to select a new commentary specific to the calendar year—in this case, Matthew's gospel, year A. The options for commentaries on the gospels are almost overwhelming, but for the purpose of preaching and teaching on the text, maybe a theological or homiletical commentary is best. Stanley Hauerwas's *Matthew* in the Brazos Theological Commentary series, and Frederick Dale Bruner's *Matthew: A Commentary* (Eerdmans, 2004), stand out.

One of the gospel readings for Advent comes from the five sermons of Jesus found in Matthew's gospel. Those sermons—the Sermon on the Mount (chaps. 5–7), the mission discourse (chap. 10), a collection of parables (chap. 13), instructions for the community (chap. 18), and finally teaching concerning the future (chaps. 24–25)—are the places Matthew has organized and strategically placed Jesus' teaching within the overall structure of the gospel. The reading for the first Sunday of Advent, Matthew 24:36-44, emphasizes Christ's call to the church to wake up. It is worth considering that Matthew's gospel is the only gospel of the four that mentions the church as such (chap. 18, *ekklesia*). Bruner, in his two-volume commentary on the gospel, calls the second half of Matthew, chapters 13–28, the "churchbook." He calls this section of Matthew the churchbook because in it Matthew shifts the emphasis from Jesus teaching the disciples who he is, to teaching the disciples primarily what the church is.

So we begin year A learning from Jesus what the church is. Chapters 24 and 25 of Matthew are focused on the future and teach hope. What does a church do, or what *is* a church that lives by hope? The *Lutheran Study Bible* (Augsburg Fortress, 2009) offers a simple explanation: "What watching and being ready mean is surprisingly simple. Faithfully carry out the tasks set before you

(24:45-51), and use the gifts God gives you wisely and fruitfully (25:1-30)" (*LSB*, 1648).

The three remaining gospel readings function as a sort of triptych. Imagine three carved or painted panels, hinged together and folded. On the left is John the Baptist in the wilderness, proclaiming a single word, "Repent!" or a phrase, "Prepare the way of the Lord!" He wears clothes of camel's hair with a leather belt, and in one hand he holds his lunch, locusts and wild honey. With his other hand, he points towards the central panel of the triptych.

The right-hand panel, by contrast, shows John's disciples asking Jesus, "Are you the one who is to come?" Jesus, by way of answer, points one hand toward a group of people—lepers who have been healed, blind folk who have received their sight, dead men walking, and poor women rejoicing in good news. With the other hand, he points back to the left hand panel, to John the Baptist, the messenger who has gone ahead of him.

The center panel is the most familiar scene. It is the nativity, the infant born of the Holy Spirit and a virgin. His parents, Joseph Son of David, and Mary, stand on each side. Above the outer shoulder of Joseph hovers an angel. Above the outer shoulder of Mary hovers a dove. Taken as a whole, the triptych focuses inward to Jesus in his incarnation, but all the other figures, including the older Jesus himself, point inward to the depiction of the birth of the Messiah. Imagine inviting an artist or group to make this triptych. Then preach it so clearly that it will live in the minds of hearers as visible words.

O Come, O Come, Emmanuel

"O come, O come, Emmanuel" (ELW 257) can serve as a foundational text and hymn for worship and prayer throughout the Advent season. It is a popular "cross-over" carol, sung as part of the secular holiday repertoire during the lead up to Christmas, but also an authentic (possibly the preeminent) Advent hymn. Furthermore, it has appropriate theological connections to the Gospel of Matthew, emphasizing as it does the fulfillment of Israel's hopes through the appearing of the Son of God. It also happens to link through a hymn text the readings from Isaiah and Matthew. It is really spectacular.

Consider focusing all the musical and creative energies of choirs, ensembles, and music leaders on this hymn through the Advent season. Declare an "O come, O come, Emmanuel" festival. Sing the first stanza throughout the Advent season. Sing stanza 3 in connection with Isaiah 2:1-5. Sing stanzas 2 and 4 in connection with Isaiah 11:1-10. Find other creative links between stanzas, readings, and prayers.

Finally, "O come, O come, Emmanuel" is a lyrical paraphrase of the "O antiphons," traditionally sung during vespers in connection with Mary's *Magnificat* December 17–23. *Evangelical Lutheran Worship* gives indication of this pattern following the stanzas for hymn #257. Although Advent is a busy season for many, this final week leading up to Christmas can be a tremendous opportunity to offer some of the daily prayer offices. If "O come, O come, Emmanuel" has functioned as a central hymn for Sunday worship, it also offers a way to link the daily prayer office to Sunday worship. Alternatively, offer families and members a devotional booklet for these seven days. Invite members of the congregation to write short devotional essays on each of the O antiphons.

Each antiphon is a name of Christ, attributed in scripture. The names are: Sapientia (Wisdom), Adonai (Lord of Might), Root of Jesse, Key of David, Oriens (Dayspring), King of Nations, and Emmanuel (God with us). These antiphons emphasize the importance of naming God appropriately in our prayers. Make use of these antiphons, by way of comparison, to evaluate prayers currently prayed during worship. How are pastors, song leaders, and assisting ministers naming God in their prayers? Craft prayers appropriate to the season that celebrate God as Wisdom, Lord of Might, Root of Jesse, Key of David, Dayspring, King of Nations, and Emmanuel. Use the O antiphons as guide and inspiration.

Seasonal Checklist

- Order candles and greens for the Advent wreath. Consider ordering wreaths for Sunday school classes, small-group gatherings, or as table settings for Advent season meals.
- Purchase and begin reading a commentary on the Gospel of Matthew. Consider acquiring and reading a resource on the whole church year, like *Keeping Time: The Church's Years*, by Gail Ramshaw and Mons Teig (Augsburg Fortress, 2009), or Philip Pfatteicher's *New Book of Festivals and Commemorations* (Fortress, 2008).
- Arrange a day and time before the first Sunday of Advent (Nov. 28) to place the Advent wreath and seasonal decorations. Plan a subsequent day and time to decorate for Christmas, and solicit volunteer help.
- Look ahead to the checklists for Christmas and Epiphany of Our Lord.
- Use the Kyrie. Omit the hymn of praise. Try a new setting of the liturgy if you have been with the same one for quite some time. Return to a familiar setting if you have been experimenting.
- Use the Nicene Creed.
- At evening prayer December 17–23, use the O antiphons of Advent.
- See other suggestions in the body of this essay.
- See the Advent wreath blessing and other seasonal worship texts for Advent (pp. 22–24).

WORSHIP TEXTS FOR ADVENT

Confession and Forgiveness

All may make the sign of the cross, the sign marked at baptism,
as the presiding minister begins.
Blessed be the holy Trinity, ✛ one God,
who does great things in every generation,
who lifts up the lowly,
who keeps promises forever.
Amen.

Let us come to the river of life, confessing our sin.

Silence is kept for reflection.

Righteous and merciful God,
we confess that we have strayed from your ways
and walked our own paths.
We fall asleep to the needs around us,
yet our anxieties jar us awake.
We are bound up in systems
of unrighteousness and injustice.
Restore your people, O God;
renew your creation;
and have mercy on us,
for the sake of Jesus Christ,
our Savior and Lord. Amen.

Listen to what God is saying,
speaking peace to those who turn their hearts:
The night is far gone, the day is near.
All who have a fearful heart,
be strong, do not be afraid!
God comes in ✛ Jesus Christ and forgives your sin.
The Spirit of holiness fill you with wisdom and might,
that you may delight in God's ways.
Amen.

Greeting

Beloved of God,
who are called to be saints:
grace and peace be with you all.
And also with you.

Offering Prayer

God of abundance,
we bring before you the precious fruits of your creation,
and with them our very lives.
Teach us patience and hope as we care for all those in need
until the coming of your Son, our Savior and Lord.
Amen.

Invitation to Communion

God fills the hungry with good things.
Come with joy to the feast.

Prayer after Communion

In this meal of goodness and mercy, O God,
our mouths have been filled with laughter
and our tongues with shouts of joy.
Now send us to gather the harvest of righteousness,
that all those who sow in tears
may come again to you in joy;
through Jesus Christ, our Savior and Lord.
Amen.

Sending of Communion

Gracious God,
whose mercy endures from generation to generation:
As Mary set out to visit Elizabeth
before she gave birth to her son,
bless those who go forth to share your word and sacrament
with our sisters and brothers who are
sick/homebound/imprisoned.
In your love and care, nourish and strengthen
those to whom we bring this communion,
that through the body and blood of your Son
we may all know the hope of your promised coming
in Jesus Christ our Lord.
Amen.

Blessing

The holy Three, holy One
increase your hope,
strengthen your faith,
deepen your love,
and ☩ grant you peace.
Amen.

Dismissal

Go in peace. Remember the poor.
Thanks be to God.

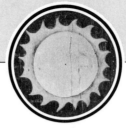

The Advent Wreath

One of the best known customs for the season is the Advent wreath. The wreath and winter candle-lighting in the midst of growing darkness strengthen some of the Advent images found in the Bible. The unbroken circle of greens is clearly an image of everlasting life, a victory wreath, the crown of Christ, or the wheel of time itself. Christians use the wreath as a sign that Christ reaches into our time to lead us to the light of everlasting life. The four candles mark the progress of the four weeks of Advent and the growth of light. Sometimes the wreath is embellished with natural dried flowers or fruit. Its evergreen branches lead the household and the congregation to the evergreen Christmas tree. In many homes, the family gathers for prayer around the wreath.

Lighting the Advent Wreath

Use this blessing when lighting the first candle.
Blessed are you, O Lord our God, ruler of the universe.
You call all nations to walk in your light
and to seek your ways of justice and peace,
for the night is past, and the dawn of your coming is near.
Bless us as we light the first candle of this wreath.
Rouse us from sleep,
that we may be ready to greet our Lord when he comes
and welcome him into our hearts and homes,
for he is our light and our salvation.
Blessed be God forever.

Use this blessing when lighting the first two candles.
Blessed are you, O Lord our God, ruler of the universe.
John the Baptist calls all people to prepare the Lord's way
for the kingdom of heaven is near.
Bless us as we light the candles on this wreath.
Baptize us with the fire of your Spirit,
that we may be a light shining in the darkness
welcoming others as Christ has welcomed us,
for he is our light and our salvation.
Blessed be God forever.

Use this blessing when lighting three candles.
Blessed are you, O Lord our God, ruler of the universe.
Your prophets spoke of a day
when the desert would blossom
and waters would break forth in the wilderness.
Bless us as we light the candles on this wreath.
Strengthen our hearts
as we prepare for the coming of the Lord.
May he give water to all who thirst,
for he is our light and our salvation.
Blessed be God forever.

Use this blessing when lighting all four candles.
Blessed are you, O Lord our God, ruler of the universe.
In your Son, Emmanuel,
you have shown us your light
and saved us from the power of sin.
Bless us as we light the candles on this wreath.
Increase our longing for your presence,
that at the celebration of your Son's birth
his Spirit might dwell anew in our midst,
for he is our light and our salvation.
Blessed be God forever.

From *Come, Lord Jesus: Devotions for Advent, Christmas, Epiphany* (Augsburg Fortress, 1996).

Midweek Prayer during Advent
Magnificat: My Soul Magnifies the Lord

During Advent, we hear of Gabriel's startling announcement to Mary and her resounding song of praise. The Magnificat echoes through the ages, reminding us of the greatness, justice, and promises of God.

Overview

Week of Advent 1: Nothing will be impossible with God
God's redeeming power surprises us anew. Who are we to doubt the impossible?
Week of Advent 2: My soul magnifies the Lord
Mary responds to Gabriel's message with an ecstatic song of praise. How do we respond to God's call?
Week of Advent 3: God has brought down the powerful and lifted up the lowly
God's sense of justice overturns our human constructs. In a world dominated by power and privilege, what does this "overturned justice" mean for us?
Week of Advent 4: According to the promise
God's promises are trustworthy and sure. Do we have the faith to watch and wait for the promise to be fulfilled?

Opening Dialogue

In this Advent time of waiting and watching,
the words of the angel Gabriel break into our world:
"Greetings! The Lord is with you.
Do not fear, for nothing will be impossible with God."
We respond with Mary to the angel's message:
"Here am I, the servant of the Lord;
let it be with me according to your word."
We join with Elizabeth to greet the mother of our Lord:
"Blessed are you among women,
and blessed is the fruit of your womb."
We echo Mary's song of praise:
"My soul magnifies the Lord,
and my spirit rejoices in God my Savior."
In this Advent time of waiting and watching, let us pray:
Gracious God, you come to us in new and surprising ways.
You make the impossible possible.
Help us, like Mary, to answer your call,
that the light of Christ may spread to all the world.
In Jesus' name we pray. Amen. *(Based on Luke 1:28-47)*

Hymn of Light

The Advent wreath may be lit during the singing of the hymn.
Week of Advent 1: Creator of the stars of night   ELW 245
Week of Advent 2: The King shall come   ELW 260
Week of Advent 3: As the dark awaits the dawn   ELW 261
Week of Advent 4: Light one candle to watch for Messiah
ELW 240

Psalmody or Reading

Week of Advent 1: Psalm 138 or Zechariah 8:1-8
Week of Advent 2: 1 Samuel 2:1-10
Week of Advent 3: Psalm 113 or Job 5:8-16
Week of Advent 4: Psalm 85 or Jeremiah 33:14-16

Song

Magnificat   ELW 236

Reading

Week of Advent 1: Luke 1:26-45
Week of Advent 2: Luke 1:46-49
Week of Advent 3: Luke 1:46-53
Week of Advent 4: Luke 1:46-55

Reflection

The reflection may include a brief commentary, nonbiblical readings, or interpretation through music or other art forms.

The reflection may conclude:
The one who testifies to these things says, "Surely I am coming soon."
Amen. Come, Lord Jesus! *(Rev. 22:20)*

Gospel Canticle: The *Magnificat*

Week of Advent 1: My soul proclaims your greatness
ELW 251
Week of Advent 2: My soul now magnifies the Lord
ELW 573
Week of Advent 3: Canticle of the Turning   ELW 723
Week of Advent 4: My soul does magnify the Lord
ELW 882

Prayers

Each portion of the prayers ends with these or similar words.
O God for whom we long,
show us your mercy.

Lord's Prayer

Blessing

Let us bless the Lord.
Thanks be to God.
The God through whom all things are possible
grant you grace, mercy, and peace.
Amen.

Sending Song

Week of Advent 1: The angel Gabriel from heaven came
ELW 265

Week of Advent 2: Unexpected and mysterious   ELW 258

Week of Advent 3: Signs and wonders   ELW 672

Week of Advent 4: Blessed be the God of Israel   ELW 250

Additional resources
Selected nonbiblical readings and poetry on the *Magnificat*, annunciation, and Mary

- Donne, John. "Annunciation," from *Chapters into Verse: A Selection of Poetry in English Inspired by the Bible from Genesis through Revelation*. Oxford University Press, 2000. ISBN 9780195136760.
- Kaan, Fred. "Magnificat Now!" from *The Hymn Texts of Fred Kaan*. Hope Publishing Company, 1985. ISBN 9780852496442.
- Marian Poetry Index, from the University of Dayton: http://campus.udayton.edu/mary/resources/poetry/poetry.html.
- McDonnell, Kilian. "In the Kitchen," from *Swift, Lord, You Are Not*. Collegeville: St. John's University Press, 2003. ISBN 9780974099200.

- Merton, Thomas. "The Annunciation," from *The Collected Poems of Thomas Merton*. New Directions Publishing Corporation, 1980. ISBN 9780811207690.
- Norris, Kathleen. "Virgin Mary, Mother of God," from *Amazing Grace: A Vocabulary of Faith*. Riverhead Books, 1998. ISBN 9781573227216.
- Troeger, Thomas. "Startled by a Holy Humming," from *Borrowed Light: Hymn Texts, Prayers, and Poems*. Oxford University Press, 1994. ISBN 0193859424.
- Yeats, W. B. "The Mother of God," from *Chapters into Verse: A Selection of Poetry in English Inspired by the Bible from Genesis through Revelation*. Oxford University Press, 2000. ISBN 9780195136760.

Keyboard settings of the *Magnificat*

- Bach, J. S. *Meine Seele erhebt den Herren*, BWV 648. Bärenreiter. BA 5171.
- Dupré, Marcel. "Magnificat 1–6," from *Fifteen Pieces for Organ Founded on Antiphons*, Opus 18, Book III. H. W. Gray Publications. GB 00188.
- Pachelbel, Johann. *Fugues on the Magnificat*. Dover Publications. ISBN 0486250377.
- Scheidemann, Heinrich. "Magnificat I–VIII" from *Orgelwerke*, vol. 2: *Magnificatbearbeitungen*. Bärenreiter. BA 5480.

Vocal/choral settings of the *Magnificat*

- Dyson, George. "Magnificat," from *Evening Service in C Minor*. Choral Public Domain Library.
- Hopson, Hal. "Canticle of the Turning." 2/3 pt treble vcs, solo. MSM 50-1500.
- Jennings, Carolyn. "A New Magnificat." SATB, org, sop solo. AFP 9786000175511.
- Kemp, Helen. "Magnificat and Nunc Dimittis." U, pno, C inst, hc, hb. CG CGA954.
- My soul proclaims the greatness of the Lord. ELW 234.
- Pelz, Walter. "Magnificat." AFP 9780800677350.
- Schram, Ruth Elaine. "Magnificat." AFP 9780800676681.

Advent Lessons and Carols
Savior of the Nations, Come:
The World Prepares for Christ's Birth

In this Advent season of hope and expectation, the whole world awaits the coming of the Savior. We hear the words of the prophets. We sing of God's promises. We place our hope in God. The carols in this service draw from a variety of countries, cultures, and traditions. The dialogue, response following the lessons, responsive prayer, and blessing/dismissal are based on passages from Isaiah.

Gathering Song

Rejoice, rejoice, believers   ELW 244

Dialogue

Hear, O heavens, and listen, O earth.
Let the earth hear, and all that fills it.
The wilderness and the dry land shall be glad,
the desert shall rejoice and blossom.
They shall see the glory of the Lord,
the majesty of our God.
Nations shall come to your light,
and kings to the brightness of your dawn.
This is the Lord for whom we wait;
let us be glad and rejoice in the salvation of God.

Opening Prayer

The Lord be with you.
And also with you.
Let us pray.
O Lord our God, you break into our world with messages of comfort, peace, and joy. Renew our strength as we wait for your coming. Shine your light for those who live in darkness. Establish your peace throughout the earth. Prepare our hearts for the birth of your Son, Jesus Christ, the Savior of us all.
Amen.

Lessons and Carols from Around the World

Lesson: Isaiah 60:1-3, 19-20
Following a brief silence for prayer and meditation:
I will wait for the Lord,
and I will hope in God who saves us.
Carol: Lost in the night   ELW 243

Lesson: Isaiah 11:1-9
Following a brief silence for prayer and meditation:
I will wait for the Lord,
and I will hope in God who saves us.
Carol: Come now, O Prince of peace   ELW 247

Lesson: Isaiah 40:1-5
Following a brief silence for prayer and meditation:
I will wait for the Lord,
and I will hope in God who saves us.
Carol: Comfort, comfort now my people   ELW 256

Lesson: Isaiah 40:9-11
Following a brief silence for prayer and meditation:
I will wait for the Lord,
and I will hope in God who saves us.
Carol: Come, thou long-expected Jesus   ELW 254

Lesson: Isaiah 61:1-4, 8-11
Following a brief silence for prayer and meditation:
I will wait for the Lord,
and I will hope in God who saves us.
Carol: He came down   ELW 253

Lesson: Luke 1:26-38
Following a brief silence for prayer and meditation:
I will wait for the Lord,
and I will hope in God who saves us.
Carol: The angel Gabriel from heaven came   ELW 265

Lesson: Luke 1:68-79
Following a brief silence for prayer and meditation:
I will wait for the Lord,
and I will hope in God who saves us.
Carol: Light one candle to watch for Messiah   ELW 240

Responsive Prayer

O Lord our God, be gracious to us;
we wait for you.
Dispel the darkness,
that all nations may come to your light.
Establish your peace on the earth;
join our voices to sing your praise.
Comfort the sick and weary;
renew their strength and power.
O Lord our God, come to us,
that the earth may behold your glory.
Amen.

Lord's Prayer

Blessing and Dismissal

Thus says the Lord: Maintain justice, and do what is right,
for soon my salvation will come,
and my deliverance be revealed.
Savior of the nations, come!
Almighty God, Father, ✚ Son, and Holy Spirit,
bless you now and forever.
Amen.

Sending Song

Savior of the nations, come   ELW 263

Blue Christmas / Longest Night
A service of longing and hope on or near the winter solstice

Pastoral sensitivity to the emotional state of those in the community who have recently lost loved ones or who are living with life-altering circumstances calls us to provide a time and place of solace during the often frenetic days surrounding the celebration of Christmas. Not everyone feels like celebrating. Grief, illness, aging, depression, loneliness, unemployment, and loss are magnified. Even those who are not struggling with losses may feel the stress of preparations and expectations around Christmas.

In the Northern Hemisphere, December 21 is the longest night, the winter solstice, which means literally "standing still." It marks the shortest day of the year, the official start of winter, when the sun is the farthest distance from the earth. Tradition says that nature and all her creatures stop and hold their breath to see if the sun will turn back from its wanderings, if the days will lengthen and the earth will once again feel the sun's warmth.

In the gathering darkness of December, we anticipate the coming again of the Light of the world. It may only be the hope that marks Advent's waiting that keeps us looking toward the coming of Christ. It may also be that the blue of the Advent season (which symbolizes hope) is the very remedy we need for what makes us feel "blue" at Christmas.

If December 21 seems too close to Christmas to hold this service in your setting, it could be offered anytime during the Advent season, or during the week between Christmas and New Year's.

Pattern for Worship

Consider using the basic pattern for Evening Prayer to organize the service (see Evangelical Lutheran Worship, pp. 296–297). The musical setting for Evening Prayer in Evangelical Lutheran Worship (pp. 309–319) or Holden Evening Prayer might be used.

Psalms and Readings

Psalm 27
Psalm 46
Psalm 121
Isaiah 9:2-7
Isaiah 40:1-11
Isaiah 40:28-31
Isaiah 43:1-3a
Matthew 5:14-16
Matthew 11:28-30
John 1:1-5, 10-14
John 8:12
Romans 8:31-35, 37-39

Prayers

Specific prayers for healing may be included. Prayer requests may be received before the service begins. Make sure to allow ample time for silence before, during, and after each petition. If candle lighting, laying on of hands, anointing, or some other physical activity will be included, provide clear instructions for worshipers.

Prayer stations with different suggestions for prayers may be provided in the worship space or gathering area for use before, during, and/or after the service. Prayer ministers may be available for worshipers who desire individual prayers.

Evangelical Lutheran Worship pew edition pages 76–83, 276–278 and Evangelical Lutheran Worship Pastoral Care are sources for many prayers appropriate to a service of this kind.

Examples

Merciful God, in the stillness of our souls we listen for your voice to know again that you are God. Quiet our restless hearts with the knowledge that you stand with us in the shadows, keeping watch over your own. Rekindle our faith and light the lamp of hope within our hearts. Then deal with us as seems best to you, for where you lead we can confidently go with Jesus Christ our Lord.
or
O Lord our God, you see and know and feel the pain of the world. Look upon us when we feel alone, and enfold us with your love, that in the midst of pain we may know your presence; through Jesus Christ, our Savior and Lord.

Hymns and Songs

Consider limiting or eliminating Christmas carols and choose hym-nody reflecting the themes of lament, longing, hope, and light in the darkness. Many hymns in the Advent section of Evangelical Lutheran Worship *reflect these themes. Also check the Heal-ing, Hope/Assurance, and Lament sections. Keep in mind that it may be difficult for some worshipers to participate in assembly song during difficult times. Thoughtful placement of instrumental music (harp, flute, strings), especially during an extended time of prayer, may be welcomed by many worshipers. Hymns with less familiar tunes might be offered by a solo voice or small ensemble.*

Opening

O come, O come, Emmanuel   ELW 257
Come, thou long-expected Jesus   ELW 254
My faith looks up to thee   ELW 759
Come now, O Prince of peace   ELW 247

Around the Prayers

Wait for the Lord   ELW 262
Healer of our every ill (refrain)   ELW 612
Hear our prayer   ELW 178
O Lord, hear my prayer   ELW 751
The Spirit intercedes for us   ELW 180

Other Hymns and Songs

Lost in the night   ELW 243
Each winter as the year grows older   ELW 252
Unexpected and mysterious   ELW 258
How small our span of life   ELW 636
I heard the voice of Jesus say   ELW 611
Healer of our every ill   ELW 612

Closing

As the dark awaits the dawn   ELW 261
The King shall come   ELW 260
Silent night, holy night!   ELW 281
Abide with me   ELW 629
Precious Lord, take my hand   ELW 773

Worship Environment

Use candles, and keep the lighting as low as is practical. If the worship space is dressed for Advent, light the appropriate number of candles on the Advent wreath. If you have already decorated for Christmas, utilize additional candlelight.

If your expected attendance is small and you have flexible seat-ing, consider creating a more intimate space for worshipers than might be afforded by the full worship space. Place chairs in a circle, or, if your seating is not moveable, use lengths of cloth to block off a section of seating, if desired.

A hollowed-out cross filled with sand for the placing of candles within, or other sand-filled containers, may be used during a period of extended prayer. Individual tapers may be distributed to worshipers as they arrive, or may be placed in baskets near the sand containers. Candles may be individually lighted and placed in the sand during the prayers, or used at the end of the service. If anointing will be offered, place shells or small bowls of oil at the stations where this will happen.

NOTES ON THE SERVICE

This service may be advertised to the public, especially if prayers for healing will be included. It would also be appropriate to send special invitations to those whose loved ones were named in worship on All Saints. For many, this will be the first Christmas since their loved one died. Keep in mind that some worshipers may choose to attend this service instead of a Christmas Eve service. Throughout the service, be attentive to the presence of guests, and give clear instructions as needed.

If a spoken form of reflection is included, the following themes may be particularly meaningful at this service: hope, waiting, antici-pation; Christ's own knowledge of suffering; the gifts we receive from God and God's people, especially during times of sadness, sickness, loneliness, and depression; Emmanuel, God with us.

Some helpful Web sites: www.gbod.org/worship (United Methodist Church worship site; search "Blue Christmas"); www.textweek.com; www.wikipedia.org (search "winter solstice").

November 28, 2010
First Sunday of Advent

The new church year begins with a wake-up call: Christ is coming soon! In today's readings both Paul and Jesus challenge us to wake from sleep, for we know neither the day nor hour of the Lord's coming. Isaiah proclaims the day when God will gather all people on the holy mountain and there will be no more war or suffering. Though we vigilantly watch for the promised day of salvation, we wait for what we already have: Christ comes among us this day as the word and meal that strengthens our faith in the promises of God.

Prayer of the Day

Stir up your power, Lord Christ, and come. By your merciful protection save us from the threatening dangers of our sins, and enlighten our walk in the way of your salvation, for you live and reign with the Father and the Holy Spirit, one God, now and forever.

Gospel Acclamation

Alleluia. Show us your steadfast | love, O Lᴏʀᴅ,*
and grant us | your salvation. *Alleluia.* (Ps. 85:7)

Readings and Psalm
Isaiah 2:1-5

The visionary message presented in this reading focuses on a future day when God establishes a universal reign of peace. Divine decisions will make war obsolete, and the worshiping community responds: "Let us walk in that light of that Lord now!"

Psalm 122

I was glad when they said to me, "Let us go to the house of the Lᴏʀᴅ." (Ps. 122:1)

Romans 13:11-14

Paul compares the advent of Christ to the coming of dawn. We live our lives today in light of Christ's coming in the future.

Matthew 24:36-44

Jesus describes his second coming as a sudden, unexpected event that will bring salvation or judgment upon people caught up in the usual affairs of daily life. He urges people to be alert and expectant.

Preface Advent

Color Blue

Prayers of Intercession

The prayers are prepared locally for each occasion. The following examples may be adapted or used as appropriate.

Waiting for the fulfillment of our hope in Christ's promised coming, we pray for the church, those in need, and all of God's creation.

A brief silence.

Holy and faithful God, you have given your people the gift of salvation. Renew us, and make us good stewards of all that you give. Proclaim your life-giving Word through the lives of your people. Lord, in your mercy,

hear our prayer.

You show your glory through the wonders of your creation. Build sound homes and create safe havens for every living thing. Bring provision to places where there is little, especially in barren seasons, so that all who hunger may be fed. Lord, in your mercy,

hear our prayer.

You call all nations into the unity and light of Christ. Establish strong and lasting justice in every land, and draw us into the peace you alone can give. Lord, in your mercy,

hear our prayer.

You soothe the weary and lift up the lowly. Extend your gracious care to those who are troubled by loneliness and despair and to those who question your presence with them (*especially*). Ease their fear and worry by your abundant mercy. Lord, in your mercy,

hear our prayer.

You are a healing balm to people in need. Calm the stress and anxiety of those who are troubled during holidays. Bring comfort where there is pain and wholeness where there is loss. Lord, in your mercy,

hear our prayer.

Here other intercessions may be offered.

You provide an eternal home for all the saints. As we remember their witness, reveal to us again the abundant grace shown in your Son, and remind us always of your great promises. Lord, in your mercy,
hear our prayer.
Into your hands, O God, we commend all for whom we pray, trusting in your mercy, through Jesus Christ our Savior.
Amen.

Ideas and Images for the Day

In the person of Jesus, the reign of God has come into the world, and signs of its presence are abundant. The season of Advent, and today's gospel, remind us that Christian discipleship calls us to be constantly awake to signs of Jesus' activity in our lives. The dominion in its fullness, a glimpse of which is given in today's Isaiah reading, will come in God's time. Until then, we are called upon to live lives of faithful obedience, ready for encounters with the risen Christ when we least expect them.

1. Centering prayer, sometimes called "the prayer of the heart," teaches practitioners to focus their minds on God, to the exclusion of more worldly concerns. Advent, with its focus on watchfulness, could be a good time to explore this spiritual discipline more deeply. With a long tradition in the Eastern church, centering prayer has become much better known in Western Christianity in recent decades, thanks to Thomas Keating, Basil Pennington, and other proponents. For information go to http://www.kyrie.com/cp/.

2. In our anticipation of the advent of Christ, we recognize "the rapture" of recent fiction as foreign to a Lutheran theology of God's grace. On his CD *The Grateful Ed Live* (Fly-By-Night Music, 2004) the singer, storyteller, and folk theologian Ed Kilbourne introduces his song "What Will Jesus Do?" with a story about following a high-end automobile that bears the bumper sticker "In case of the rapture, this car will be driverless." Ed fantasizes about saying to the driver: "In case of the rapture, can I have your car?" Go to http://www.edkilbourne.com/lyrics.html and scroll down to read the song lyrics.

3. Have the children look around the worship space and count the number of images of Jesus they see (or crosses or other biblical image appropriate to your setting), then have them point them out to the group. Tell the children that Advent is a time that reminds us to look around every day for signs of Jesus' love in the world and to keep our eyes open for ways to share Jesus' love with others.

4. The season of Advent coincides with the holiday season of popular culture, a time of intense commercial activity and secular celebration. Amid this busyness, Advent can be an especially challenging time for us to be alert for encounters with Christ and ways to share his love. The congregation is a crucial connection to the devotional aspects of Advent. Ideas for observing Advent in church and at home are available at http://www.elca.org/Growing-In-Faith/Worship/Planning/Advent.aspx.

Hymns for Worship
Gathering
Wake, awake, for night is flying   ELW 436, LBW 31
O Lord, how shall I meet you   ELW 241, LBW 23
Rejoice, rejoice, believers   ELW 244, LBW 25

Hymn of the Day
Savior of the nations, come   ELW 263, LBW 28
  NUN KOMM, DER HEIDEN HEILAND
Each winter as the year grows older   ELW 252, WOV 628
  CAROL OF HOPE
Lo! He comes with clouds descending   ELW 435, LBW 27
  HELMSLEY

Offering
He came down   ELW 253, TFF 37
O come, O come, Emmanuel   ELW 257, sts. 1, 2;
  LBW 34, sts. 1, 2

Communion
Wait for the Lord   ELW 262
My Lord, what a morning   ELW 438, TFF 40, WOV 627
The King shall come   ELW 260, LBW 33

Sending
Soon and very soon   ELW 439, WOV 744, TFF 38
Hark! A thrilling voice is sounding!   ELW 246, LBW 37

Additional Hymns and Songs
I want to be ready   TFF 41
The advent of our God   LBW 22
O Savior, rend the heavens wide   LBW 38

Music for the Day
Psalmody and Acclamations
Ferguson, John. *Gospel Acclamations for Advent–Transfiguration.*
Harbor, Rawn. "Let Us Go Rejoicing (Psalm 122)." TFF 17.
Hobby, Robert A. "Psalm 122" from PWA, Evangelical Lutheran Worship Edition.
Long, Larry J. "Psalm 122" from PSCY.

Choral

o Bach, J. S. "Savior of the Nations, Come" from *Bach for All Seasons*. SATB, org. AFP 9780800658540.

o Hobby, Robert A. "Each Winter As the Year Grows Older." 2 pt mxd, kybd, inst. AFP 9780800679323.

   McNair, Anne. "Come Quickly, Lord." SATB, kybd. AFP 9780800664305.

   Nelson, Ronald A. "A Vision of Peace." SAB, pno. GIA G-7007.

   Paxson, William T. "We Are Waiting." SATB, cant, opt assembly. AFP 9780800676643.

   Poole, David E. "Creator's Peace." SATB, kybd, fl, perc. AFP 9780800664350.

Children's Choir

   Cool, Jayne Southwick. "Lumen Christi." U, kybd. CG CGA1098.

   Patterson, Mark. "Advent Prayer" from *ChildrenSing*. U, kybd, opt hb/hc. AFP 9780800677695.

   Simon, Julia. "Three Advent Songs for Young Children." LE, U, kybd. AFP 9780800679149.

Keyboard / Instrumental

o Dahl, David P. "Nun komm, der Heiden Heiland" from *Hymn Interpretations for Organ*. Org. AFP 9780800658243.

o Distler, Hugo. "Nun komm, der Heiden Heiland" from *Augsburg Organ Library: Advent*. Org. AFP 9780800658953.

o Henkelmann, Brian. "Nun komm, der Heiden Heiland" from *Chorale Preludes for the Liturgical Year*, vol. 1. Kybd, fl. CPH 97-7227U1.

o Raabe, Nancy M. "Helmsley" from *Day of Arising: A Tapestry of Musical Traditions*. Pno. AFP 9780800637460.

Handbell

   Behnke, John. "The King Shall Come" from *Chime In—Advent and Christmas*. 2-3 oct hc, L1+. AGEHR AG23034.

o Nelson, Susan. "Lo, He Comes with Clouds Descending." 3-6 oct hb, opt 3-4 oct hc, L3+. HOP 2253.

o Wissinger, Kathleen. "Savior of the Nations, Come." 3-5 oct hb, opt 1 oct hc, L2+. LOR 20/1399L.

Praise Ensemble

• Farrell, Bernadette. "Christ, Be Our Light." OCP. ELW 715.

• Haugen, Marty. "Awake! Awake, and Greet the New Morn." GIA. ELW 242. Various editions.

• Jabusch, Willard. "The King of Glory." W&P 136. Various editions.

• LeBlanc, Lenny. "There Is None Like You." INT.

• McGee, Bob. "Emmanuel." C.A. Music. W&P 36.

• Story, Laura. "Indescribable." WT/Sixsteps Music.

Global

   Farrell, Bernadette. "Word of Justice" from *Agape: Songs of Hope and Reconciliation*. 2 pt. Lutheran World Federation. AFP 9780191000133.

o denotes suggestions that relate to the hymn of the day.
• denotes songs that are available on iTunes®.

Maraschin, Jaci. "Come to Be Our Hope, O Jesus" from *Global Songs 2*. U. AFP 9780800656744.

Tuesday, November 30

Andrew, Apostle

Andrew was the first of the Twelve. He is known as a fisherman who left his net to follow Jesus. As a part of his calling, he brought other people, including Simon Peter, to meet Jesus. The Byzantine church honors Andrew as its patron and points out that because he was the first of Jesus' followers, he was, in the words of John Chrysostom, "the Peter before Peter." Together with Philip, Andrew leads a number of Greeks to speak with Jesus, and it is Andrew who shows Jesus a boy with five barley loaves and two fish. Andrew is said to have died on a cross saltire, an X-shaped cross.

Friday, December 3

Francis Xavier, missionary to Asia, died 1552

Francis Xavier (SAYV-yehr) was born in the Basque region of northern Spain. Francis's native Basque language is unrelated to any other, and Francis admitted that learning languages was difficult for him. Despite this obstacle he became a missionary to India, Southeast Asia, Japan, and the Philippines. At each point he learned the local language and, like Martin Luther, wrote catechisms for the instruction of new converts. Another obstacle Francis overcame to accomplish his mission work was a propensity to seasickness. All his travels to the Far East were by boat. Together with Ignatius Loyola and five others, Francis formed the Society of Jesus (Jesuits). Francis spoke out against the Spanish and Portuguese colonists when he discovered their oppression of the indigenous people to whom he was sent as a missionary.

Saturday, December 4

John of Damascus, theologian and hymnwriter, died around 749

Born to a wealthy family in Damascus and well educated, John left a career in finance and government to become a monk in an abbey near Jerusalem. He wrote many hymns as well as theological works. Foremost among the latter is a work called *The Fount of Wisdom*, which touches on philosophy, heresy, and the orthodox faith. This summary of patristic theology remained influential for centuries.

December 5, 2010
Second Sunday of Advent

At the heart of our Advent preparation stands John the Baptist, who calls us to repent and make a new beginning. As the darkness increases we turn toward the light of Christ's coming. For Christians he is the root of Jesse, the righteous judge who welcomes all, especially the poor and meek of the earth. We wait with hope for that day when the wolf will dwell with the lamb, and there will be no more hurt or destruction. From the Lord's table we are sent in the spirit of John the Baptist to proclaim that in Christ the kingdom of God has come near.

Prayer of the Day

Stir up our hearts, Lord God, to prepare the way of your only Son. By his coming nurture our growth as people of repentance and peace; through Jesus Christ, our Savior and Lord, who lives and reigns with you and the Holy Spirit, one God, now and forever.

Gospel Acclamation

Alleluia. Prepare the way | of the Lord.* All flesh shall see the salva- | tion of God. *Alleluia.* (Luke 3:4, 6)

Readings and Psalm

Isaiah 11:1-10

In today's reading the prophet describes the ideal ruler who will come in the future as a green shoot springing from a dead stump (David's royal line) of Jesse (David's father). Gifted by the Spirit, this messiah will seek justice for the poor, and the reign of this monarch will be experienced as paradise regained.

Psalm 72:1-7, 18-19

May the righteous flourish; let there be an abundance of peace. (Ps. 72:7)

Romans 15:4-13

God's promise to include Gentiles within the circle of God's blessed people has been fulfilled in Jesus Christ. Christians live out their unity by welcoming and encouraging each other just as Christ has welcomed them into God's family.

Matthew 3:1-12

Just before Jesus begins his public ministry, John the Baptist appears, calling people to mend their ways and speaking of a powerful one who is to come.

Preface Advent

Color Blue

Prayers of Intercession

The prayers are prepared locally for each occasion. The following examples may be adapted or used as appropriate.

Waiting for the fulfillment of our hope in Christ's promised coming, we pray for the church, those in need, and all of God's creation.

A brief silence.

Holy and blessed God, build unity in the body of Christ. Give harmony to our voices of praise and yearning, so that all peoples may know your abundant goodness. Lord, in your mercy,

hear our prayer.

Renew your creation, and establish peace throughout lands and seas. Give cleansing waters and nourishing soil to plants and animals, and make ecosystems thrive under your care. Lord, in your mercy,

hear our prayer.

Defend the cause of those who live in poverty. Extend your righteousness to all nations. Let no one be neglected or denied the opportunity to live in dignity. Lord, in your mercy,

hear our prayer.

Shower your grace upon all who long to receive your mercy. Deliver those who are bound by extended illness, grief, loneliness, or oppression (*especially*). Lord, in your mercy,

hear our prayer.

Send your Spirit of reconciliation to families, those victimized by crime, those addicted to drugs and alcohol, and all who know conflict. Give them the peace which you alone can give. Lord, in your mercy,

hear our prayer.

Here other intercessions may be offered.

As we remember the lives of the saints, sustain us also by your Spirit until we receive in full the promises that have joined all generations to you through Christ. Lord, in your mercy,
hear our prayer.
Into your hands, O God, we commend all for whom we pray, trusting in your mercy, through Jesus Christ our Savior.
Amen.

Ideas and Images for the Day

For the baptized, repentance and forgiveness are characteristics of daily life. During Advent, John the Baptist's call to repentance carries a challenge for us to rid ourselves of everything that is unfruitful in our lives. His proclamation is filled with images of cleansing: straightening paths, cutting down useless trees, and burning away chaff. Undistracted even by thoughts of our own worthiness, our focus is to be on the coming of Christ. John points to Jesus, never to himself, and in so doing becomes a model for discipleship.

1. In his Youth Leadership workshops, Tiger McLuen teaches church leaders a two-step process for working with youth and their families: first, get their attention; second, point them to Christ (and get out of the way). John the Baptist was gifted in both these skills. In the relationships they form with children and youth, skilled adult youth leaders follow John's example of preparing the way of the Lord. Find more on youth work at http://www.youthleadership.org/.

2. Artists throughout history have depicted episodes in the life and death of John the Baptist, lifting up various aspects of his character, from fierce preacher to devoted worshiper of Christ. Leonardo da Vinci gives us a sweetly smiling John, with one finger pointing upward toward a cross he carries, and beyond. If Leonardo's John draws our attention in a different way than the John of scripture, his goal is the same. See this and other images of John at http://www.textweek.com/art/john_the_baptist.htm.

3. Anne Lamott specializes in writing stories about Jesus' activity in her life and the lives of those around her. In the story "Overture: Lily Pads," from her collection *Traveling Mercies* (New York: Anchor Books, 1999), Lamott describes her conversion to faith, which began with visits to a local church. She tells of a mystical recognition of Jesus after months of resistance, precipitated by the constant witness of the pastor and congregation.

4. Gather the children in a circle at the baptismal font. Make sure to splash around a little. Have the children take turns dipping a finger into the font and drawing a wet cross on each others' foreheads as a reminder (or preview) of their baptism. Remind the children that baptism means that God loves and forgives us, that God's love and forgiveness is a free gift, and that we can always count on it.

Hymns for Worship
Gathering
Hark! A thrilling voice is sounding! ELW 246, LBW 37
Blessed be the God of Israel ELW 250, WOV 725
Comfort, comfort now my people ELW 256, LBW 29

Hymn of the Day
On Jordan's bank the Baptist's cry ELW 249, LBW 36
  PUER NOBIS
O day of peace ELW 711, WOV 762 JERUSALEM
There's a voice in the wilderness ELW 255 ASCENSION

Offering
He came down ELW 253, TFF 37
O come, O come, Emmanuel ELW 257, sts. 3, 4;
  LBW 34, sts. 1, 3

Communion
There's a voice in the wilderness ELW 255
Come now, O Prince of peace ELW 247
Each winter as the year grows older ELW 252, WOV 628

Sending
Come, thou long-expected Jesus ELW 254, LBW 30
O day of peace ELW 711, WOV 762

Additional Hymns and Songs
Isaiah the prophet has written of old NCH 108
The King of glory W&P 136
Herald, sound the note of judgment LBW 556

Music for the Day
Psalmody and Acclamations
Ferguson, John. *Gospel Acclamations for Advent–Transfiguration.* "Hail to the Lord's Anointed." ELW 311.
Hobby, Robert A. "Psalm 72:1-7, 18-19" from PWA, Evangelical Lutheran Worship Edition.
Mummert, Mark. "Psalm 72," Refrain 2, from PSCY.

Choral
Cool, Jayne Southwick. "A Prayer for Peace." U, opt two-pt, kybd, opt assembly. AFP 9780800664114.
Jean, Martin. "Advent Hymn." SATB. AFP 9780800656621.

Monteverdi, Claudio. "On Jordan's Bank the Baptist's Cry." SAB, cont, 2 insts. GIA G-2834.

Nelson, Ronald A. "A Vision of Peace." SAB, pno. GIA G-7007.

Proulx, Richard. "His Name Is John." 2 pt mxd, hb. AFP 9780800656386.

Children's Choir

Hopson, Hal. "Dance and Sing, For the Lord Will Be With Us." U/2 pt, kybd, opt perc. CG CGA749.

Patterson, Mark. "Light One Candle" from *Young ChildrenSing*. U, LE, kybd, opt hb/hc/xyl. AFP 9780800676803.

Sleeth, Natalie. "The Lion and the Lamb." U, kybd. CG CGA296.

Keyboard / Instrumental

○ Benson, Robert A. "Ascension" from *A Lovely Rose*. Org. AFP 9780800675714.

○ Callahan, Charles. "Jerusalem" from *Six Postludes on English Hymn Tunes*. Org. MSM 10-316.

○ Miller, Aaron David. "Puer nobis" from *Piano Plus*, vol. 1. Pno, inst. AFP 9780800638542.

○ Organ, Anne Krentz. "Puer nobis" from *Be Thou My Vision*. Pno. AFP 9780800678524.

Handbell

○ Afdahl, Lee. "O Day of Peace." 3-5 oct hb, 3-5 oct hc, L3. AGEHR AG35236.

○ Moklebust, Cathy. "That Easter Day with Joy Was Bright (On Jordan's Banks)." 2-3 oct, L1. CG CGB281.

Organ, Anne Krentz. "Three Advent Settings." 3 oct hb or hc, L3. AFP 9780800674915.

Praise Ensemble

● Espinosa, Eddie. "Change My Heart, O God." VIN. ELW 801.

● Jabusch, Willard. "The King of Glory." W&P 136. Various editions.

● Kendrick, Graham. "God of the Poor." INT/Make Way Music. W&P 17. Various editions.

● Peterson, Hans/Larry Olson. "All Are Welcome" from *Work of the People*, vol. 1. Dakota Road Music.

● Smith, Martin. "Did You Feel the Mountains Tremble?" WT/Curious? Music UK.

● Walker, Tommy. "Prepare Ye the Way." Doulos.

Global

Feliciano, Francisco. "Who Will Set Us Free?" from *Sound the Bamboo*. U. GIA G-6830.

Lee, Geonyong. "Come Now, O Prince of Peace/Ososo" from *Global Songs 2*. SATB. AFP 9780800656744. ELW 247.

Monday, December 6
Nicholas, Bishop of Myra, died around 342

Though Nicholas is one of the church's most beloved saints, little is known about his life. In the fourth century he was a bishop in what is now Turkey. Legends that surround Nicholas tell of his love for God and neighbor, especially the poor. One famous story tells of Nicholas secretly giving bags of gold to the three daughters of a father who was going to sell them into prostitution because he could not provide dowries for them. Nicholas has become a symbol of anonymous gift giving.

Tuesday, December 7
Ambrose, Bishop of Milan, died 397

Ambrose was a governor of northern Italy and a catechumen when he was elected bishop of Milan. He was baptized, ordained, and consecrated a bishop all on the same day. While bishop he gave away his wealth and lived in simplicity. He was a famous preacher and is largely responsible for the conversion of Augustine. He is also well known for writing hymns. On one occasion, Ambrose led people in a hymn he wrote while the church in which they were secluded was threatened by attack from Gothic soldiers. The soldiers turned away, unwilling to attack a congregation that was singing a hymn. Ambrose is credited with authorship of three hymns in *Evangelical Lutheran Worship*, including "Savior of the Nations, Come" (ELW 263).

○ denotes suggestions that relate to the hymn of the day.
● denotes songs that are available on iTunes®.

36

December 12, 2010
Third Sunday of Advent

A note of joyful expectation marks today's worship. Isaiah announces that the desert shall rejoice and blossom. Jesus points to signs of God's reign: the blind see, the lame walk, lepers are cleansed, the deaf hear. We wait with patience for the coming of the Lord, even as we rejoice at his presence among us this day: in word and holy supper, in church and in our homes, in silent reflection and in works of justice and love. We pray that God would open our eyes and ears to the wonders of Christ's advent among us.

Prayer of the Day

Stir up the wills of all who look to you, Lord God, and strengthen our faith in your coming, that, transformed by grace, we may walk in your way; through Jesus Christ, our Savior and Lord, who lives and reigns with you and the Holy Spirit, one God, now and forever.

Gospel Acclamation

Alleluia. I am sending my messen- | ger before you,* who will prepare your | way before you. *Alleluia.* (Matt. 11:10)

Readings and Psalm

Isaiah 35:1-10

The prophet describes the return from the Babylonian captivity as a joyous procession to Zion. God's coming reign will bring a renewal of creation in which health and wholeness will be restored. There is no need for fear, for God is coming to save.

Psalm 146:5-10

The LORD lifts up those who are bowed down. (Ps. 146:8)

or Luke 1:46b-55

My spirit rejoices in God my Savior. (Luke 1:47)

James 5:7-10

In anticipation of the Lord's coming, Christians are called upon to cultivate patience rather than discontent.

Matthew 11:2-11

John the Baptist expects the Messiah to bring God's judgment upon the earth. From a prison cell, he wonders whether Jesus is the one who will do this.

Preface   Advent

Color   Blue

Prayers of Intercession

The prayers are prepared locally for each occasion. The following examples may be adapted or used as appropriate.

Waiting for the fulfillment of our hope in Christ's promised coming, we pray for the church, those in need, and all of God's creation.

A brief silence.

Holy and righteous God, be present now in the gifts you have given through Christ. Lead us to proclaim the glory of all we hear, see, smell, taste, and touch in our gathering. Lord, in your mercy,

hear our prayer.

Reveal to all people the glory evident in your creation. Open our eyes to see the wonder of your works in every blooming plant and in each vibrant animal. Lord, in your mercy,

hear our prayer.

Raise up leaders in the church and beyond who will boldly point people toward your justice. Make them instruments of your work, and bring an end to inequality, poverty, and prejudice. Lord, in your mercy,

hear our prayer.

Send your blessing to people who are broken in body, mind, or spirit (*especially*). Give them wholeness in their communities through Christ's ongoing work of reconciliation. Lord, in your mercy,

hear our prayer.

Bless all caregivers and others in helping professions. Ease their burdens, and let them receive compassion, even as they give it freely to people who are in need. Lord, in your mercy,

hear our prayer.

Here other intercessions may be offered.

Remembering the lives of the saints, grant us patience as we await Christ's coming. Show us signs of your reign until the day when our rejoicing will be endless. Lord, in your mercy, **hear our prayer.**

Into your hands, O God, we commend all for whom we pray, trusting in your mercy, through Jesus Christ our Savior.
Amen.

Ideas and Images for the Day

In this season of Advent we stand in the discomforting quiet of waiting for the salvation of the Lord while simultaneously seeing that very salvation breaking into the world around us. Like John the Baptist we ask Jesus "are you here, or should we still wait?" The new life promised by the coming of a savior is both realized and still to come. As believers, our hope does not rest in the efforts of our piety or in the comfort of the hereafter. Rather, our hope is in the promises of a gracious, faithful God; promises fulfilled before our eyes and those not yet seen. We long for the day in which, like Isaiah's vision of what will be, the blind see and the lame leap like deer. The day is here and yet still we wait.

1. See a free Quicktime video on waiting at http://thecomplexchrist.typepad.com/WaitingQT.mp4. This image has the word "wait" at the top with split-screen images of a train station in which passengers are actively waiting. Consider using this as a film loop as people are assembling for worship. Then start a few minutes later than normal to give people the feeling of anticipation that goes with this season. They are assembled. The time has come—and yet is not here.

2. A lovely litany to use as an entrance rite, along with a host of creative, free liturgical resources for congregations, is available at: http://www.laughingbird.net/Seasonal.html. Sample:
   Your Word is conceived within us,
   and we grow heavy with hope,
   eagerly awaiting the day when all creation
   will be delivered into your glorious freedom.
   Send your Holy Spirit
   to call us by name and lead us home.

3. The following quote from Martin Luther can be used in your bulletin or as a sermon starter: "This life therefore is not righteousness, but growth in righteousness, not health, but healing, not being but becoming, not rest but exercise. We are not yet what we shall be, but we are growing toward it, the process is not yet finished, but it is going on, this is not the end, but it is the road. All does not yet gleam in glory, but all is being purified" (From "Defense and Explanation of All the Articles [1521]," *Luther's Works*, vol. 32 [ed. George Forell, Minneapolis: Fortress, 1958]).

4. Ask children to draw stick figures of themselves as babies, who they are now, and who they will be as adults. Then talk about how who they were has made them who they are now and how who they are now is creating who they will become. Relate this to God's promises. God has fulfilled them, is fulfilling them and will fulfill them in the future!

Hymns for Worship
Gathering
Awake! Awake, and greet the new morn   ELW 242, WOV 633
Prepare the royal highway   ELW 264, LBW 26
Hark, the glad sound!   ELW 239, LBW 35

Hymn of the Day
Prepare the royal highway   ELW 264, LBW 26
   BEREDEN VÄG FÖR HERRAN
Let streams of living justice   ELW 710   THAXTED
Comfort, comfort now my people   ELW 256, LBW 29
   FREU DICH SEHR

Offering
He came down   ELW 253, TFF 37
O come, O come, Emmanuel   ELW 257, sts. 3, 4;
   LBW 34, sts. 1, 4

Communion
Light dawns on a weary world   ELW 726
Lost in the night   ELW 243, LBW 394
All earth is hopeful   ELW 266, WOV 629

Sending
People, look east   ELW 248, WOV 626
The Lord now sends us forth   ELW 538

Additional Hymns and Songs
O promised one of Israel   ASF 18
Stir up your power   DH 51
Lift up your heads   W&P 88

Music for the Day
Psalmody and Acclamations

Ferguson, John. *Gospel Acclamations for Advent–Transfiguration.*

Haugen, Marty. "Psalm 146," Refrain 3, from PSCY.

Hobby, Robert A. "Psalm 146:5-10" from PWA, Evangelical Lutheran Worship Edition.

Makeever, Ray. "Sing unto the Lord (Psalm 146)" from *Dancing at the Harvest.*

"My Soul Proclaims Your Greatness." ELW 251.

Shute, Linda Cable. "Luke 1:46b-55," Refrain 1, from PSCY.

Witte, Marilyn. "Luke 1:46b-55" from PWA, Evangelical Lutheran Worship Edition.

Woehr, Roland. "Luke 1:46b-55," Refrain 1, from PSCY.

Choral

o Ferguson, John. "Comfort, Comfort." SATB, opt insts. AFP 9780800646356.

o Hopson, Hal H. "Prepare the Royal Highway." U or 2 pt, kybd. MSM 50-0301.

Jennings, Carolyn. "A New Magnificat." SATB, org, solos, opt assembly. AFP 9780800652555.

Mendelssohn, Felix/arr. Ronald A. Nelson. "Then Shall the Eyes of the Blind." SAB, pno. CG CGA-927.

Children's Choir

Bedford, Michael. "Come, Lord Jesus" from *Seasonal Songs for Young Singers.* U, kybd, opt 3 bells. CG CGA1160.

Holck, Lois. "Get Ready" from *LifeSongs.* U, LE, kybd.

o Hopson, Hal. "Prepare the Royal Highway." U/2 pt kybd. MSM 50-0301.

Keyboard / Instrumental

o Busarow, Donald. "Freu dich sehr" from *With Music Crowned.* Org, 2 inst. CPH 97-7324U1.

o Cherwien, David. "Thaxted" from *Organ Plus One.* Org, inst. AFP 9780800656188.

o Farlee, Robert Buckley. "Thaxted" from *Augsburg Organ Library: Autumn.* Org. AFP 9780800675790.

o Manz, Paul O. "Bereden väg för Herran" from *Augsburg Organ Library: Advent.* Org. AFP 9780800658953.

Handbell

o Afdahl, Lee. "Prepare the Royal Highway." 3-5 oct, L3. AFP 9780800655778.

Honoré, Jeffrey. "Two for Advent." 2-3 oct, L2. AFP 9780800658939.

o Mazzatenta, Michael. "Prepare the Way, O Zion." 2-3 oct, L2-. GIA G-7443.

Praise Ensemble

• Agnew, Todd. "Magnificat (Mary)." Ardent/Koala Music.

• Byrd, Marc/Steve Hindalong. "God of Wonders." New Spring Music/INT.

• Evans, Darrell. "Let the River Flow." VIN/INT.

• Mark, Robin. "Days of Elijah." Daybreak Music/INT.

• Mullins, Rich. "Awesome God." BMG Songs, Inc.

• Tomlin, Chris/Jesse Reeves/Ed Cash. "How Great Is Our God." WT/Sixsteps Music.

Global

Bena tune, arr. Austin C. Lovelace. "Christ the Savior Has Appeared" from *Set Free: A Collection of African Hymns.* SATB. AFP 9780806600451.

Perera, Homero R. "Tenemos esperanza" from *Pave the Way: Global Songs 3.* U. perc. AFP 9780800676896.

Monday, December 13
Lucy, martyr, died 304

Lucy was a young Christian of Sicily who was martyred during the persecutions under Emperor Diocletian. Apparently she had decided to devote her life to God and her possessions to the poor. Beyond that, however, little is known for certain about Lucy. However, her celebration became particularly important in Sweden and Norway, perhaps because the feast of Lucia (the name means "light") originally fell on the shortest day of the year. A tradition arose of a girl in the household, wearing a crown of candles, bringing saffron rolls to her family early in the morning on the day of Lucia.

Tuesday, December 14
John of the Cross, renewer of the church, died 1591

John was a monk of the Carmelite religious order who met Teresa of Ávila when she was working to reform the Carmelite Order and return it to a stricter observance of its rules. He followed Teresa's lead and encouraged others to follow her reform. He was imprisoned when he encountered opposition to the reform. His writings, like Teresa's, reflect a deep interest in mystical thought and meditation. In one of John's poems, "The Spiritual Canticle," he cried, "Oh, that my griefs would end! Come, grant me thy fruition full and free!"

---

o   denotes suggestions that relate to the hymn of the day.

•   denotes songs that are available on iTunes®.

December 19, 2010
Fourth Sunday of Advent

Today Isaiah prophesies that a young woman will bear a son and name him Emmanuel. The gospel is Matthew's account of the annunciation and birth of the one named Emmanuel, God-with-us. During these final days of Advent we pray, "O come, O come, Emmanuel," a beloved hymn based on ancient prayers appointed for the seven days preceding Christmas. On this final Sunday in Advent we prepare to celebrate the birth of the one born to save us from the power of sin and death.

Prayer of the Day

Stir up your power, Lord Christ, and come. With your abundant grace and might, free us from the sin that hinders our faith, that eagerly we may receive your promises, for you live and reign with the Father and the Holy Spirit, one God, now and forever.

Gospel Acclamation

Alleluia. The virgin shall conceive and ¹ bear a son,* and they shall name ¹ him Emmanuel. *Alleluia.* (Matt. 1:23)

Readings and Psalm
Isaiah 7:10-16

An Israelite and Aramean military coalition presented a serious threat to King Ahaz of Judah. In response, Ahaz decided to secure his throne and kingdom by seeking refuge in Assyrian help. Isaiah reminds Ahaz that human attempts to establish security will fail. The prophet gives the sign of Immanuel that is the only source of true safety: God is with us!

Psalm 80:1-7, 17-19

Let your face shine upon us, and we shall be saved. (Ps. 80:7)

Romans 1:1-7

Most of the Christians in Rome do not know Paul. In this letter's opening he introduces himself as an apostle divinely appointed to spread God's gospel. The gospel's content is the promised coming of Christ, and Paul's mission is to bring about the obedience of faith among all nations, including his Roman audience.

Matthew 1:18-25

Matthew's story of Jesus' birth focuses on the role of Joseph, who adopts the divinely begotten child into the family of David and obediently gives him the name Jesus, which means "God saves."

Preface   Advent

Color   Blue

Prayers of Intercession

The prayers are prepared locally for each occasion. The following examples may be adapted or used as appropriate.

Waiting for the fulfillment of our hope in Christ's promised coming, we pray for the church, those in need, and all of God's creation.

A brief silence.

Holy God of promise, stir up in your people great anticipation for every good thing you are about to do. Teach us to recognize your Son dwelling among us. Lord, in your mercy,

hear our prayer.

Cause all of creation to shout with joy at the coming of your Chosen One. Let every mountain and stream, all the birds of the air and animals of the land, bear witness to your goodness. Lord, in your mercy,

hear our prayer.

Come swiftly to establish justice throughout the world. Bring joy to the lowly and humility to the proud. Lead all peoples into the unity and peace of your reign. Lord, in your mercy,

hear our prayer.

Shine your face upon all who are troubled, especially those who find no joy in this season. Aid those who are sick and suffering (*especially*). Restore them to wholeness. Lord, in your mercy,

hear our prayer.

Give your boundless hope and joy to expectant parents. Bind young children and new parents in love, and reveal your life-giving promises through the witness of families. Lord, in your mercy,

hear our prayer.

Here other intercessions may be offered.

Join our voices to those of all the saints, as we see the promises of salvation unfold in our midst. Increase our faith in your steadfastness, while we await the coming of Emmanuel, God with us. Lord, in your mercy,
hear our prayer.
Into your hands, O God, we commend all for whom we pray, trusting in your mercy, through Jesus Christ our Savior.
Amen.

Ideas and Images for the Day

Names are powerful makers of meaning both in the scriptures and in our lives. The texts for the fourth Sunday of Advent invite us to explore the name "Emmanuel." "Look, the young woman is with child and shall bear a son, and shall name him Immanuel" (Isa. 7:14). And he shall be called "Emmanuel," *God with us.* In his very name, the Son of God proclaims just how "with us and for us" God really is. This fulfillment of prophetic promise offers us a delicate and dramatic reality: God has slipped into skin and walks among us in a totally new way, offering us life and salvation.

1. Highway video is a great resource for worship films. They may be purchased individually or as a package. This example costs $20 and explores the names of Jesus: http://www.highwayvideo.com/Names-of-Jesus-P1175.aspx. Used as a visual meditation during gathering or communion, the video can help worshipers experience the many, yet still limited, ways to speak of the one who has come into the world.

2. In Sunday school have young people share their name and what it means. Either have a dictionary of names on hand (a new mother may have a few to offer!) or an Internet connection so you can help them look it up. Then have them share what hurtful names they have been called. Finally have them share/write down the names God has for them. This is a great way of exploring the power of names!

3. Have stacks of name tags (ideally the "My name is" kind) along with markers out in the gathering space. Ask worshipers to write "Child of God" and wear it for the service. This is a light way to make the point that we too are named and claimed by God in baptism and walk daily in that baptismal journey as God's beloved.

4. In 2009 Beliefnet ran a five-week series on the names of Jesus. This resource is a simple and useful meditation on the ways in which the different names for Jesus invite us into different aspects and attributes of God. Access the series at http://blog.beliefnet.com/contentfeeds/praying-the-names-of-god/.

Hymns for Worship
Gathering

Savior of the nations, come   ELW 263, LBW 28
Of the Father's love begotten   ELW 295, LBW 42
My soul proclaims your greatness   ELW 251, WOV 730

Hymn of the Day

O come, O come, Emmanuel   ELW 257, LBW 34
   VENI, EMMANUEL
O Lord, how shall I meet you   ELW 241, LBW 23
   WIE SOLL ICH DICH EMPFANGEN
Canticle of the Turning   ELW 723, W&P 26
   STAR OF COUNTY DOWN

Offering

He came down   ELW 253, TFF 37
O come, O come, Emmanuel   ELW 257, sts. 7, 8;
   LBW 34, sts. 1, 5

Communion

Unexpected and mysterious   ELW 258
As the dark awaits the dawn   ELW 261
The angel Gabriel from heaven came   ELW 265, WOV 632

Sending

Love divine, all loves excelling   ELW 631, LBW 315
Fling wide the door   ELW 259, LBW 32

Additional Hymns and Songs

Mary, woman of the promise   NCH 123
Sing of Mary, pure and lowly   WOV 634
Gentle Joseph, Joseph dear   NCH 105

Music for the Day
Psalmody and Acclamations

Ferguson, John. *Gospel Acclamations for Advent–Transfiguration.*
Hobby, Robert A. "Psalm 80:1-7, 17-19" from PWA, Evangelical Lutheran Worship Edition.
Wold, Wayne L. "Psalm 80," Refrain 1, from PSCY.

Choral

○ Cooney, Rory. "Canticle of the Turning." SAB, assembly, pno, insts, opt gtr. GIA G-3407.
   Johnson, Ralph. "The Hills Are Bare at Bethlehem." SATB, wind chimes. EAR.
   Nygard, Carl J. "Emmanuel!" SATB, kybd. AFP 9780800664312.
○ Organ, Anne Krentz. "Come My Light." 2 pt (mxd or SA or TB), pno. AFP 9780800675813.
○ Paxson, William T. "We Are Waiting." SATB, cant, opt assembly. AFP 9780800676643.

○ denotes suggestions that relate to the hymn of the day.
● denotes songs that are available on iTunes®.

Children's Choir

Horman, John. "Psalm 80" from *ChildrenSing Psalms*. U, kybd. AFP 9780800663872.

Patterson, Mark. "Advent Prayer" from *ChildrenSing*. U, kybd. AFP 9780800677695.

Walker, Christopher. "Stay Awake and Be Ready" from *LifeSongs*. UE, U, kybd.

Keyboard / Instrumental

○ Culli, Benjamin. "Wie soll ich dich empfangen" from *A Voice Is Sounding*. Org. CPH 97-7012U1.

○ Harbach, Barbara. "Star of County Down" from *Come Join the Dance*. Org. AFP 9780800678760.

○ Organ, Anne Krentz. "Veni, Emmanuel" from *Advent Reflections for Piano and Solo Instrument*. Pno, inst. AFP 9780800657284.

○ Raney, Joel. "Veni, Emmanuel" from *Christmas for 4-Hand Piano*. Pno duet. HOP 8194.

Handbell

Biggs, Susan. "Come, Thou Long-Expected Jesus." 3 oct, L2. AFP 9780800659875.

○ Garee, Betty. "God with Us for All Time." 5 oct, L4. FLA HP5099.

○ Roberts, Philip. "O Come, O Come, Emmanuel." 3-5 oct, L2. GIA G-7555.

Praise Ensemble

● Batya, Naomi/Sophie Conty. "King of Kings." MAR.

● Cain, Patricia. "Jesus, Name Above All Names." Doulos/INT. W&P 77

● Founds, Rick. "Lord, I Lift Your Name on High." MAR. ELW 857

● McGee, Bob. "Emmanuel." C.A. Music. W&P 36.

● Moody, Dave. "All Hail King Jesus." WRD. W&P 3. Various editions.

● Tomlin, Chris/Louie Giglio. "Holy Is the Lord." WT/sixsteps Music.

Global

Bell, John L. "Carol of the Advent" from *Innkeepers and Light Sleepers: Seventeen New Songs for Christmas*. SATB. GIA G-3835.

Taulé, Alberto. "All Earth Is Hopeful/Toda la tierra." U. ELW 266.

Monday, December 20
Katharina von Bora Luther, renewer of the church, died 1552

Born to an impoverished nobleman, when Katharina (Katie) was five her mother died and she was sent to live in a convent. She later took vows as a nun, but around age twenty-four she and several other nuns who were influenced by the writings of Martin Luther left the convent. Six children were born to Katie and Martin. Though initially Luther felt little affection for Katie, she proved herself a gifted household manager and became a trusted partner. She was so influential that Luther took to calling her "my lord Katie."

CHRISTMAS

PREPARING FOR CHRISTMAS

Festivals and Commemorations

The festival of the nativity of the Lord spread rapidly, in large measure because it focused attention not simply on the work but most of all on the person of the God-man, and the celebration of his incarnation would express liturgically the Catholic faith defined at Nicea, that Jesus Christ had two natures, divine and human, but was one person.[1]

Christmas has such gravity in the current North American cultural context that it is hard to believe that no state in the United States considered Christmas a holiday until Alabama declared it one in 1836. Thirteen more states made it a holiday during the Civil War. Christmas as a national holiday is a relatively recent invention, and we do well to remember this in our preparations.

Even in the patristic era, Christmas, though established as a feast, was overshadowed by Epiphany and other holidays. In the Christian East, Jesus' birth was celebrated as a part of the Epiphany season, together with his baptism. In the Middle Ages, Christmas finally rose to a level of prominence comparable to its place in our own culture. Caroling became popular in this era, for example. Because of its cultural prominence, many are endlessly fascinated with the development of Christmas as an institution, and worship leaders and preachers preparing for the season might read the Wikipedia entry on Christmas.

As churches plan worship and preachers write sermons for these high attendance, "make or break" services, there is a natural inclination to drift toward sentiment and relevance, and away from the doctrine of the incarnation. This is understandable. It is natural for congregations to strive to connect with their members and visitors, especially at services where the percentage of visitors is higher. So take the time to review all your congregational worship practices, and make sure that bulletins, art, projection, announcements, and all aspects of the Christmas service connect to and are understandable to visitors. Then make sure and continue those practices year round. Making connections should not just be reserved for high-attendance holidays.

Remember that Christmas has risen to prominence as a feast on a level with Easter and Pentecost for a reason.

It is the liturgical expression of the Incarnation, specifically as defined at the Council of Nicea. Christmas is not Christmas because there is a cute baby and mangy animals. It is Christmas because there is a God-man. The church traditionally offers three masses or services on Christ-mass because of the importance of this claim.

In fact, Christmas may be the perfect opportunity to revisit your congregation's celebration of festivals and commemorations throughout the year. Why, other than its importance as a holiday in North American culture, does your congregation celebrate Christmas at all? If you do celebrate Christmas because it is the festival of the Nativity of Our Lord, it may be worthwhile to celebrate other festivals that the church has, over time, recognized and established. Consider finding ways to celebrate John, Apostle and Evangelist (Dec. 27), The Holy Innocents, Martyrs (Dec. 28), Stephen, Deacon and Martyr (transferred this year to Dec. 29), and Name of Jesus (Jan. 1).

The Nativity of the Lamb of God

Isaiah proclaims, "A child has been born for us, a son given to us" (Isa. 9:6). Isaiah proclaims this son as light, savior, Wonderful Counselor, Prince of Peace. But the surprising, impossible to comprehend claim of Isaiah—this son is also Mighty God (9:6). Central to the New Testament proclamation is the establishment and clarification of this claim. Luke tells the story by giving an account of Christ's birth. John tells the story as the Word made flesh. Both attend to the issue that comes to the center of the church's attention throughout the patristic era—how can this one be both fully human and fully God? Or, as the author of Hebrews expresses it, the son as the "exact imprint of God's very being" (Heb. 1:3).

Although most worship leaders do not have the time and resources to review all the ecumenical councils of the early church as preparation for Christmas, they might consider reading a good recent book on the subject. Sergius Bulgakov's *Lamb of God* (Eerdmans, 2008) traces the development of christology, especially in the period when this was the focus of the patristic writers. His book, which is in some ways a radical representation of Russian Orthodox

[1] Philip Pfatteicher, *New Book of Festivals and Commemorations: A Proposed Common Calendar of Saints* (Minneapolis: Fortress, 2008), p. 623.

theology, also illustrates how this is still a doctrine of the church that is developing, an ongoing opportunity for theologians and Christians to rejoice in the dialectic of Jesus Christ as both Son of Man and Son of God. Exploration of this theme and doctrine cannot but improve the church's preaching and liturgy.

The Orthodox tradition is especially powerful in portraying the nativity in its iconography. In many icons of the nativity of the Lord, the infant Jesus is shown wrapped not in swaddling clothes but in a burial shroud, and placed in a coffin rather than a manger. This stone coffin, located in front of the opening of a dark cave, represents the historical reality that the birthplace of Jesus may indeed have been something like a cave. It offers the juxtaposition of Christ's birth and death, Jesus in his nativity already portrayed as the Lamb of God, crucified, died, and buried. China Miéville's *The City & The City* (Random House, 2009) is a contemporary evocation of this artistic juxtaposition, where two realities exist overlaid, and it takes the willfulness of the viewer or reader to not perceive both simultaneously.

So, in addition to the various manger scenes and depictions of the nativity erected in your church during the Christmas season, consider erecting a small prayer station in the narthex or gathering space for people to view and pray near an icon of the nativity. Offer a meditation, during worship or on a small bulletin stacked near the icon, on the connections between Christ's birth and his death, the manger (Luke 2:7) and the rock-hewn tomb, the swaddling clothes and the linen cloth (Luke 23:53).

Christmas Lament

The holidays are difficult for many. The reality of family and celebration seldom lives up to the hype, and the pressures of the season can be immense. It is a time when we are at risk of singing too many happy songs to a heavy heart. Moderate the joy of Christmas with opportunities to sing out lament as well.

The flow of the lectionary reflects the highs and lows of the holiday season, for the first Sunday after Christmas includes a reading of Matthew 2:13-23, the death of the holy innocents and martyrs at the hands of Herod. The lectionary provides an opportunity for the festivity of carols and Christmas hymns one week, and then the very next provides an opportunity to sing songs of lament, recognizing the presence of grief even in the face of, maybe precisely because of, celebration. Consider songs from the healing and lament sections of the hymnal, such as "In all our grief" (ELW 615). Or imagine Joseph and Mary singing "How long, O God" (ELW 698) while refugees in Egypt. This Sunday is also a powerful opportunity to lift up in prayer refugees, immigrants, and all who suffer unjust, unwarranted, and shocking persecution or violence.

Many churches capitalize on the holidays as high-attendance seasons and offer topical preaching immediately after Christmas or Easter. Experiment with this practice if you have never done so. It might be the case that publicizing a sermon series that takes place on the Sundays after Christmas could lead to continued attendance by those who visit on Christmas proper. If this is already your congregational practice, consider selecting a sermon series that lifts up this theme in an appropriate manner. Adam Hamilton's *Unleashing the Word* (Abingdon, 2003) offers guidance on planning sermon series throughout the year and especially at times that are high-outreach opportunities.

Epiphany: Just Do It

Although Epiphany is just two short weeks after Christmas, it is an incredibly important feast in Christian tradition and deserves to be celebrated on its own day. Consider using Kent Gustavson's *Mountain Vespers*, and especially his Processional and Evening Hymn, for a special Epiphany Vespers service on January 6 (http://www.kentgustavson.com/mountainvespers.shtml). Or use the familiar *Holden Evening Prayer,* or a more traditional setting of vespers such as the one found in *Evangelical Lutheran Worship*. The opening service of light for evening prayer connects well with the overall theme of Epiphany and is an opportunity to introduce or reinforce the daily prayer offices sung in the church.

However, a special Epiphany celebration may also be an opportunity to offer a full eucharist midweek. If this is planned, it can be a chance to energetically transform the worship space, removing paraments and other decorations indicative of the Christmas season, and lighting up the worship space with decor that accentuates Israel as a light to the nations and Jesus as the light of the world. Epiphanize the place!

Here's how to do it. First of all, notice that Epiphany is *missional*. The Epiphany texts emphasize the mission of God. This is a theme that courses throughout the Old and New Testaments, but is highlighted in an especially clear way in the Isaiah text: "Nations shall come to your light" (60:3). The sons and daughters of Israel, once in exile, will reassemble (60:4). The nations that assemble around this light will bring with them gifts, wealth, water, camels. Epiphany is therefore a celebration of abundance, new life, and mission—not mission as something Israel or the church is supposed to go out and do in order accomplish something for God, but rather Israel's participation in the mission of God, which is a mission to gather the nations.

This gathering of the nations is anticipated in the arrival of the magi to visit the infant Jesus. Already at his birth, the nations are arriving, bearing gifts, attracted to the light. Even the darkness of Herod that hovers so near cannot snuff out this attraction, for it is God's mission at work, which will be accomplished.

Paul also proclaims this logic of God's mission in his letter to the Ephesians. He understands that the Gentiles have now been made co-heirs and are caught up in Christ's body, the church, so that "through the church the wisdom of God in its rich variety might now be made known to the rulers and authorities in the heavenly places" (Eph. 3:10). God has designed all of this not so that the church might just quietly gather and celebrate a beautiful light off somewhere, secluded and alone, but that through the celebration of the light the church makes known the wisdom of God to the world.

Keep that in mind as you prepare an Epiphany celebration. How might the assembly participate in the mission of God? Maybe gather for the feast of Epiphany in a public place, like a park, school, or mall. Make use of the Blessing of the Home and Chalking of the Doors ritual in order to bless the place where you gather, but then send home with folks a resource so they can bless their own homes and chalk their own doors.

Sing Epiphany hymns that are accessible and illustrate Jesus as a light to the nations. For example, "Shine, Jesus, shine" (ELW 671), "This little light of mine" (ELW 677), "We are marching in the light" (ELW 866), or "You have come down to the lakeshore" (ELW 817).

Seasonal Checklist

- Prepare materials for Christmas flowers/poinsettias sponsorship.
- Locate any decorations that are in storage from previous years for the Christmas tree, crèche, the chancel, and other interior or exterior areas. Repair or replace decorations as needed.

- If handheld candles are used by worshipers on Christmas Eve, determine how many candles and holders can be used from previous seasons and how many new candles and holders will be needed. Make sure fire extinguishers and detectors are up to date.
- As many communities enter flu season, consider making antibacterial wipes or gel available.
- Publicize Christmas services in local newspapers and on your church Web site.
- Order special bulletin covers if needed for services on Christmas Eve, Christmas Day, and Epiphany.
- Design service folders for Christmas worship that guests will be able to follow easily, including specific instructions for communion distribution.
- Determine communion distribution procedure for services with large numbers of communicants, and make sure sufficient communion elements and communion vessels are available. Rehearse communion assistants if necessary.
- Make arrangements for adequate seating, along with additional worship books and service folders for larger assemblies on Christmas Eve.
- Determine whether Epiphany decorations are needed.
- Consider sites for an off-campus worship service for Epiphany of Our Lord.
- Arrange for removal of Christmas decorations following January 6.
- Use the hymn of praise ("Glory to God"). In addition to the form in the communion setting, see options in the service music section of *Evangelical Lutheran Worship*, #162–164.
- Use the Nicene Creed.
- Consider especially thanksgiving at the table III in *Evangelical Lutheran Worship*.

WORSHIP TEXTS FOR CHRISTMAS

Confession and Forgiveness

*All may make the sign of the cross, the sign marked at baptism,
as the presiding minister begins.*
Blessed be the holy Trinity, ✚ one God,
the Maker of heaven and earth,
the Word made flesh,
the Lord and giver of life.
Amen.

Let us confess our sin in the presence of God
and one another.

Silence is kept for reflection.

God of glory, God of peace,
**we confess that we have shunned the light
that reveals the truth about us.
We cling to worldly things
rather than sharing the gifts of this earth.
We trust ourselves above all.
Save your people, O God;
sustain the rivers and trees that sing your praise;
and free us to live boldly
in the light and truth of Jesus, our Savior.
Amen.**

The grace of God shines upon us,
bringing salvation to the whole world.
We are saved, our sins are washed away,
not because of anything we have done,
but according to God's mercy in ✚ Jesus Christ.
Renewed by the Holy Spirit, let us live in hope and joy.
Amen.

Greeting

Today Christ is born: Alleluia, alleluia!
The grace of our Lord Jesus Christ,
the love of God,
and the communion of the Holy Spirit be with you all.
And also with you.

Offering Prayer

Good and loving God,
we rejoice in the birth of Jesus,
who came among the poor to bring the riches of your grace.
As you have blessed us with your gifts,
let them be blessing for others.
With the trees of the field, with all earth and heaven,
we shout for joy at the coming of your Son,
Jesus Christ our Lord.
Amen.

Invitation to Communion

The bread of God comes down from heaven
and gives life to the world.
Come, eat, and live.

Prayer after Communion

Great and saving God,
you have gathered your scattered people
around gifts of grain and wine,
the body and blood of our Savior Christ.
As we, like the shepherds, return on our way,
may we proclaim all we have heard and seen,
praising you in word and loving deed
for the gift of Jesus, our Savior and Lord.
Amen.

Sending of Communion

O God,
whose grace and truth are revealed
in the Word-made-flesh,
bless those who go forth to share your word and sacrament
with those who are *sick/homebound/imprisoned*.
Nourish and strengthen
those who receive this holy communion,
that through the body and blood of your Son
all may rejoice at his birth
and in his presence among us now and forever.
Amen.

Blessing

The holy Three, holy One
increase your hope,
strengthen your faith,
deepen your love,
and ✝ grant you peace.
Amen.

Dismissal

Go in peace. Christ is with you.
Thanks be to God.

SEASONAL RITES FOR CHRISTMAS

Lighting the Christmas Tree

Use this prayer when you first illumine the tree or when you gather at the tree.

God our Creator,
we praise you for this Christmas tree.
It is a sign of your everlasting, evergreen presence.
It is a sign of the reign of heaven,
sheltering the creatures of the earth
under its open arms.
It is a sign of the cross,
shining with the light of your grace and mercy.

Gracious God,
let your blessing come upon us
as we illumine this tree.
Send us your Son,
the tender shoot of Jesse,
who brings us light and life.

May all who stand in its light
eagerly welcome the true Light which never fades.
We ask this through Christ our Lord.
Amen.

From Come, Lord Jesus: Devotions for Advent, Christmas, Epiphany *(Augsburg Fortress, 1996).*

A Parish Christmas Decorating Event

Many congregations offer a blessing for the hanging of the greens, but since the date for decorating churches varies widely depending on the traditions of each community, a gathering early in December might be a way to get everyone into the "spirit of the season" without abandoning the richness of observing the Advent season. With this event, new traditions can be created while retaining those that have been lovingly shared over the years.

Choose and adapt activities for your local context from the suggestions that follow. Most people will have more invitations than they can accept during the busy holiday season. Publicize your gathering well in advance and communicate clearly about items participants will be asked to create, furnish, or contribute, so that they are able to plan and participate fully.

Opening Prayer

Lord, you have called us together as your people
and given us this new day.
Bless us as we gather to share fellowship
with you and each other.
Thank you for the creative presence of your Holy Spirit
within and among us.
Amen.

Scripture and Song

Accompany each activity with a scripture text and a hymn or song, if desired. Invite participants to tell about their favorite Advent or Christmas song. Sing some traditional carols as you complete your activities; many children do not hear them outside of a church setting. Make full use of the resources already in your church: hymnals, songbooks, Sunday school booklets with Christmas songs, books for carolers, etc. Read from the Christmas story in Luke 2, then add some of Matthew's gospel to hear from Joseph and those wise men!

Blessing of Paraments and Seasonal Art and Environment

Gather paraments and other items (banners, hangings, greens, candles, plants, etc.) that will adorn the worship space at Christmas. Have a member of the altar guild, worship environment team, or artists explain what will be used and why it has been chosen.

A leader may offer a prayer in these or similar words.

Gracious God,
we offer to you
these *items that will beautify our worship space,*
which have been inspired by our love for you.
Accept our grateful thanksgiving for what you have given us
in the Word made flesh,
and bless our Christmas worship
as we announce once again the coming of your Son,
Jesus Christ, our Savior and Lord.
Amen.

Blessing of Nativity Scenes

If your church's nativity scene is sturdy and easy for children to handle, invite children to unpack it and place each figure on a common table. Encourage them to tell what they know about each piece. Then invite others to tell what they know about the set (Was it donated? Did it come from another country? Does it have some other special significance?). Invite participants to bring in their own nativity scenes and have a brief "show and tell."

A leader may offer a prayer in these or similar words.

Jesus, you are coming again at Christmas.
We take this moment in our daily lives
to stop and think about how your birth as a little baby
changed our lives.
Because of your love for us, we know your Father.
Thank you for this time to learn and live your story.
Amen.

Blessing of Ornaments

Invite each household to create an ornament or chrismon to be hung on the church Christmas tree. Plain glass balls could be provided ahead of time (send them home in paper drinking cups and a zipper bag to prevent breakage) and provide some uniformity of color and shape, if that is desired. This blessing, or one like it, may be used when all the ornaments are gathered, before they are hung.

Lord Jesus,
you are the light of the world,
and we remember that light as we decorate this tree
that you have provided from your creation.
When we see this tree,
remind us that we are all part of your family,
and that even though we are all different,
you love each of us as a precious child.
Amen.

Christmas Cookie Exchange

Whatever activities you choose for this gathering, do include refreshments! Ask everyone to bring two dozen of their favorite cookies or bars. Allow one dozen for eating and one dozen for sharing, so that everyone takes home a plate of treats.

Closing Prayer

Loving God, you have gathered and enlightened us,
and you give us the gift of creativity.
We give you our thanks and praise
for this community of faith
and ask your blessing on our witness in the world.
May this space and our lives be invitations to others
to experience the love you have so freely shared with us.
We pray in the name of the babe of Bethlehem,
our Lord Jesus.
Amen.

The Feast of Las Posadas

In Mexico, the Christmas festivities begin on December 16 with the feast of Las Posadas ("Lodgings"), a Latin American Christmas festival that dramatizes the search of Joseph and Mary for lodging. The tradition of Las Posadas started in the sixteenth century with St. Ignatius of Loyola, who suggested having the special prayers repeated for nine consecutive nights.

The activity starts with participants gathering at the church, where they depart in a procession or simply walk toward one of the church members' homes. The assembly may sing hymns and carols. They also bring a crèche or nativity set (according to each country's traditional representation), carried or lifted by adults, youth, or children.

Once at the entrance of the selected home the assembly sings appropriate stanzas of "En nombre del cielo" ("In the name of the heavens," LLC 284) and "Entren, santos peregrinos" ("Come in, pilgrim saints," LLC 286). All enter the home and the nativity set is placed under the Christmas tree. It remains there for the rest of the night, where the procession will resume the following night toward the next home. In this manner the nativity set travels night after night, from home to home.

After placing the nativity set in its place, the fiesta may continue with singing of other carols and Christmas songs. The breaking of a piñata is also a customary part of the celebrations.

On the ninth and last night the procession may either depart from the home with the nativity set to the church for the celebration of a traditional Christmas Eve service, or the nativity set may remain at the last home, where they will celebrate the end of the festivity with a traditional Christmas meal. The crèche or nativity set will stay either at the church or the particular home until January 6.

From *Libro de Liturgia y Cántico* (Augsburg Fortress, 1998), p. 150; trans. Sara Calderon.

December 24, 2010
Nativity of Our Lord
Christmas Eve

On a long winter evening we gather to proclaim the coming of the light. Isaiah announces that the people who walked in darkness have seen a great light. Paul reminds us that the grace of God has appeared, bringing salvation to all. In the familiar account of Christ's birth, the evening sky is bright with the heavenly host singing, "Glory to God in the highest." Amid our broken world we proclaim that the prince of peace is born among us. God comes to us in human flesh—in Christ's body and blood—so that we may be bearers of divine light to all the world.

I
Particularly appropriate for Christmas Eve

Prayer of the Day

Almighty God, you made this holy night shine with the brightness of the true Light. Grant that here on earth we may walk in the light of Jesus' presence and in the last day wake to the brightness of his glory; through your Son, Jesus Christ our Lord, who lives and reigns with you and the Holy Spirit, one God, now and forever.

Gospel Acclamation

Alleluia. I am bringing you good news of great joy for ⁱall the people:* to you is born this day in the city of David a Savior, who is the Messi-ⁱah, the Lord. *Alleluia.*
(Luke 2:10-11)

Readings and Psalm
Isaiah 9:2-7

This poem promises deliverance from Assyrian oppression, a hope based on the birth of a royal child with a name full of promise. While Judah's king will practice justice and righteousness, the real basis for faith lies in God's passion for the people: The zeal of the Lord of hosts will do this!

Psalm 96

Let the heavens rejoice and the earth be glad. (Ps. 96:11)

Titus 2:11-14

The appearance of God's grace in Jesus Christ brings salvation for all humanity. Consequently, in the present we live wisely and justly while also anticipating the hope of our Savior's final appearance.

Luke 2:1-14 [15-20]

God's greatest gift comes as a baby in a manger. Angels announce the "good news of great joy" and proclaim God's blessing of peace.

Preface Christmas

Color White

Prayers of Intercession

The prayers are prepared locally for each occasion. The following examples may be adapted or used as appropriate.
Filled with wonder and joy that God's gift of grace has been given in the Son born for us, let us pray for the church, the good creation, and the needs of all.
A brief silence.
Everlasting God, let your radiance shine forth and renew in your people an eager desire to proclaim the good news of salvation to those who still wait in darkness. Hear us, O God.
Your mercy is great.
Creating God, on this blessed night the heavens and the earth rejoice. Make us ever mindful of our calling to be faithful stewards of all you have given us, so that generations to come may flourish and praise you. Hear us, O God.
Your mercy is great.
Peacemaking God, we pray for those nations where your peace does not yet reign (*especially*). Have mercy on our enemies, and deliver those who are caught in cycles of violence. Hear us, O God.
Your mercy is great.

Wonderful Counselor, shelter those who seek refuge and safety but find no welcome. Help those who are homeless, hungry, unemployed, without health care, and all who are in any need or distress (*especially*). Hear us, O God.
Your mercy is great.

Mighty God, watch over those who travel to join loved ones, and those who are lonely or grieving. Bless all who seek you, and open our hearts to receive the gift of your love. Hear us, O God.
Your mercy is great.

Here other intercessions may be offered.

We give thanks for the faithful who treasured the gospel in lives of witness and service. We wait in hope to join the multitude of the heavenly hosts in praising and glorifying you forever. Hear us, O God.
Your mercy is great.

Into the manger of your love, holy God, we lay our prayers, trusting in your promise made known to us in Jesus the Christ, our brother and Savior.
Amen.

Ideas and Images for the Day

To maintain the machinery of empire, people must be counted; not to be valued as individuals, but to assess tribute. It is the census. Lists of family members, and decisions about them, must be made. As your life, family, and records are audited, so also is your future decided. What sacrifice will be required for the glory of Rome? Shepherds, however, cannot expect to be counted. While the rest of the world is engaged in the games of empire, they watched their flocks, unnoticed by census-takers. But they were not unnoticed by God. Beyond the view of the watchful eye of Caesar, God was doing a new thing, forging true peace to upset the sham *pax* of imperial domination, a new kingdom whose only army is that of angels singing, rank upon rank, of God's saving work. It all begins with the unforeseen birth of a child and the wonder of a mother. We, like shepherds, stand in awe at God's gracious surprise. There is glory enough for all.

1. In the opening ceremonies of the 2004 Summer Olympic Games in Athens, the final parade was full of the pomp of humanity's accomplishments. But how does it end? After the fanfare, a pregnant woman walks onto a pond by herself. Her belly glows as the parade encircles her. The hope of the whole pageant is this child in her womb. Could she be Mary, aglow with the light of Christ?

2. Eclogue IV of the Roman poet Virgil proclaims a new era of prosperity at the birth of a child, thus earning the title "Messianic Eclogue" (Virgil, *The Eclogues*, London: Penguin, 1984, pp. 56–59). While Virgil was most likely referring to a possible future dynasty from the marriage of Marc Anthony and Octavia, the eclogue reveals the depth of human longing for lasting peace. We find that longing fulfilled in Christ.

3. Luther said about Mary that she could not have conceived had she not believed. Meister Eckhart made it more personal: "What good is it that Mary gave birth to Christ so many years ago if we do not give birth to him today?" As those who see all creation in the throes of labor, our acts of discipleship point to this new reality. We, like Mary, do not fully understand it all, but are left with plenty to ponder and treasure in our hearts.

4. With the children share a story, personal or otherwise, of how a family prepared a room for the arrival of a baby. How were colors and decorations chosen? What efforts were made to welcome the baby? Retell the story of Mary and Joseph searching for a place to give birth to Jesus. Since Jesus wants to be born in our hearts, how do we prepare for him? How do we make room for the baby?

Hymns for Worship

Gathering

Hark! The herald angels sing   ELW 270, LBW 60
On Christmas night   ELW 274
Angels we have heard on high   ELW 289, LBW 71

Hymn of the Day

From heaven above   ELW 268, LBW 51   VOM HIMMEL HOCH
O little town of Bethlehem   ELW 279, LBW 41   ST. LOUIS
It came upon the midnight clear   ELW 282, LBW 54   CAROL

Offering

Midnight stars make bright the skies   ELW 280
Your little ones, dear Lord   ELW 286, LBW 52

Communion

Peace came to earth   ELW 285, WOV 641
Away in a manger   ELW 277/278, LBW 67, WOV 644
I am so glad each Christmas Eve   ELW 271, LBW 69

Sending

Joy to the world   ELW 267, LBW 39
Silent night, holy night!   ELW 281, LBW 65

Additional Hymns and Songs

A stable lamp is lighted   HS91 728, LBW 74
Night of silence/Silent night   W&P 101, HS91 732
Before the marvel of this night   WOV 636

Music for the Day
Psalmody and Acclamations

Ferguson, John. *Gospel Acclamations for Advent–Transfiguration.*

Harbor, Rawn. "Let the Heavens Rejoice (Psalm 96)." TFF 10.

Shute, Linda Cable. "Psalm 96," Refrain 4, from PSCY.

Wetzler, Robert. "Psalm 96" from PWA, Evangelical Lutheran Worship Edition.

Choral

○ Benson, Robert A. "From Heaven Above to Earth I Come." SATB, org. AFP 9780800675851.

Highben, Zebulon M. "My Heart Rejoices." SATB, children's choir, org, hb, vla, assembly. AFP 9780800664152.

Kadidlo, Phil. "Jesus, What a Wonderful Child." SAB, kybd, solo, opt gtr. AFP 9780800679316.

Lasky, David. "Alleluia! Christ Is Born." SATB, org, opt brass qt. AFP 9780800664145

○ Schulz-Widmar, Russell. "Bethlehem." SATB, org. AFP 9780800679484.

Children's Choir

Bedford, Michael. "Hodie Christus Natus Est." U/2 pt, kybd. CG CGA421.

Burkhardt, Michael. "Love Came Down at Christmas." U/2 pt/3 pt, orff, kybd. MSM 50-1112.

Nelson, Ronald A. "Wake, O Shepherds." U, kybd, vln, opt vc or bsn. AFP 9780800675967.

Keyboard / Instrumental

○ Lind, Richard A. "Carol" from *Christmas Lullabies and Carols for Piano.* Pno. AFP 9780800677626.

○ Maynard, Lynette. "St. Louis" from *Sing We Now of Christmas.* Pno. AFP 9780800677619.

○ Pelz, Walter L. "Vom Himmel hoch" from *Augsburg Organ Library: Christmas.* Org. AFP 9780800659356.

○ Sedio, Mark. "St. Louis" from *Let Us Talents and Tongues Employ.* Org. AFP 9780800655723.

Handbell

○ Bartsch, John. "It Came Upon a Midnight Clear." 4-5 oct hb w/org or orch, L3. National Music NMHB303 (HB). NMHB303A (orch). NMHB303B (org reduction of orch). NMHB303FS (full score).

○ Eithun, Sandra. "O Little Town of Bethlehem." 3-5 oct hb, opt 3 oct hc, L2+. CG CGB601.

Helman, Michael. "Christmas Meditation." 3-5 oct, L3+. AGHER AG35126.

Praise Ensemble

● Baloche, Paul. "Offering" (with Christmas lyric). INT.

● DeShazo, Lynn. "More Precious than Silver." INT.

● Redman, Matt. "The Heart of Worship." Thankyou Music.

● Rice, Chris. "Welcome to Our World." Clumsy Fly Music.

● Smith, Henry. "Give Thanks." INT.

● Tomlin, Chris. "We Fall Down." WT.

Global

Kwami, Robert M. "Drismas dodzi vo/Christmas Time Is Here" from *World Carols for Choirs.* SATB. OXF 019353231X.

Liang, Qi-fang. "Midnight Stars Make Bright the Skies/Mingxing canlan ye wei yang" from *Sound the Bamboo.* U. GIA G-6830. ELW 280.

○ denotes suggestions that relate to the hymn of the day.
● denotes songs that are available on iTunes®.

December 25, 2010

Nativity of Our Lord
Christmas Day

On this Christmas morning the people of God gather to celebrate the birth of the Word made flesh, Christ our Lord. Luke recounts the familiar story of shepherds and angels; John's gospel tells of the Word that dwells among us, full of grace and truth. The meaning of Christmas is made clear: the light shines in the darkness. It is in the liturgy that we encounter the Word made flesh—in the people of God gathered together as the body of Christ, and in the meal around the holy table. We go forth to be bearers of light as we proclaim this good news to all the ends of the earth.

II

Particularly appropriate for Christmas Day

Prayer of the Day

All-powerful and unseen God, the coming of your light into our world has brightened weary hearts with peace. Call us out of darkness, and empower us to proclaim the birth of your Son, Jesus Christ, our Savior and Lord, who lives and reigns with you and the Holy Spirit, one God, now and forever.

Gospel Acclamation

Alleluia. A holy day has dawned upon us. Come, you nations, and a- | dore the Lord.* For today a great light has come up- | on the earth. *Alleluia.*

Readings and Psalm

Isaiah 62:6-12

The prophet invites the people to give God no rest until God reestablishes Jerusalem. In turn, they will receive names full of promise: Holy People, the Redeemed of the Lord, a City Not Forsaken.

Psalm 97

Light dawns for the righteous, and joy for the honest of heart. (Ps. 97:11)

Titus 3:4-7

God saves us not because of what we do. Rather, God is a God of mercy and salvation who graciously cleanses us in baptism and renews our lives through the Holy Spirit.

Luke 2:[1-7] 8-20

The world's deep night is shattered by the light of God's new day. The glory of God is revealed to poor shepherds, who share the good news with others.

III

Particularly appropriate for Christmas Day

Prayer of the Day

Almighty God, you gave us your only Son to take on our human nature and to illumine the world with your light. By your grace adopt us as your children and enlighten us with your Spirit, through Jesus Christ, our Redeemer and Lord, who lives and reigns with you and the Holy Spirit, one God, now and forever.

Gospel Acclamation

Alleluia. I am bringing you good news of great joy for | all the people:* to you is born this day in the city of David a Savior, who is the Messi- | ah, the Lord. *Alleluia.* (Luke 2:10-11)
or
Alleluia. A holy day has dawned upon us. Come, you nations, and a- | dore the Lord.* For today a great light has come up- | on the earth. *Alleluia.*

Readings and Psalm

Isaiah 52:7-10

A messenger races home to Jerusalem with the marvelous words: "Your God reigns!" In comforting the people, God proves to be the best brother or sister (redeemer) they have ever known. Everyone will witness the victory (salvation) of God.

Psalm 98

All the ends of the earth have seen the victory of our God. (Ps. 98:3)

Hebrews 1:1-4 [5-12]

This letter opens with a lofty declaration of Jesus' preeminent status as the Son through whom God created the world and through whom our sins are cleansed. God speaks to us now through the Son, who is exalted even above the angels.

John 1:1-14

The prologue to the Gospel of John describes Jesus as the Word of God made flesh, the one who reveals God to be "full of grace and truth."

Preface   Christmas

Color   White

Prayers of Intercession

The prayers are prepared locally for each occasion. The following examples may be adapted or used as appropriate.

Filled with wonder and joy that God's gift of grace has been given in the Son born for us, let us pray for the church, the good creation, and the needs of all.

A brief silence.

You have come to dwell with us and in baptism you give us power to become your children. Send out your church to embody your saving presence in a world yearning for peace. Hear us, O God.

Your mercy is great.

You called all things into being and created us to be stewards of life on earth. Restore your creation from the smallest cell to the shining stars, that the universe may praise your name. Hear us, O God.

Your mercy is great.

You give light to all the ends of the earth. Deliver those in the darkness of war, poverty, and oppression (*especially*). Strengthen those who work for justice, human rights, and the welfare of children. Hear us, O God.

Your mercy is great.

You send hope to the suffering. Comfort those who are sick, lonely, grieving, in prison, or destitute (*especially*). Sustain those who are giving birth, dying, or caring for others. Hear us, O God.

Your mercy is great.

You guide this congregation in serving the neighbor. Make us generous givers of your loving-kindness, and prosper the ministries of this and every congregation, that your goodness may shine in and beyond this community. Hear us, O God.

Your mercy is great.

Here other intercessions may be offered.

You have shown us your glory, full of grace and truth. We give thanks for those who have testified to the light in every generation. May their witness continue to enlighten the world. Hear us, O God.

Your mercy is great.

Into the manger of your love, holy God, we lay our prayers, trusting in your promise made known to us in Jesus the Christ, our brother and Savior.

Amen.

Ideas and Images for the Day

"The light shines in the darkness." The prophet Isaiah employs images of the battlefield, of war and captivity, to describe the darkness. We know the darkness, too—even in the merriment of Christmas we need not travel far to see it. Our daily headlines remind us of today's darkness, which Henri Nouwen says "is so visible and tangible, so concrete and specific, that it is often difficult to believe that there is much to think, speak or write about other than our brokenness" (*Life of the Beloved*, New York: Crossroad, 1992, p. 69). But the light shines in the darkness, and the darkness does not overcome it. We wrestle with the paradox that the world did not recognize its own light by which it sees, or its own life from which it has life. Yet we also treasure the wonder by which we have been granted eyes to see and ears to hear. At Christmas we perceive the light in infancy, but, grace upon grace, he is a trace of joy given for us.

1. In the story "Traveling Mercies" by Anne Lamott (*Traveling Mercies*, New York: Anchor, 1999, pp. 106–114), a traveler shares her misadventures with someone who happens to work for the Dalai Lama. In response to her complaints he suggests that "something big and lovely . . . is trying to get itself born—and that this something needs for you to be distracted so that it can be born as perfectly as possible." This is good news for us distracted folks at Christmas!

2. Parker Palmer, in *The Promise of Paradox* (San Francisco: Jossey-Bass, 2008), retells the famous story of Loren Eiseley's "star thrower," who daily walks upon the shore to throw beached starfish back into the sea. In like manner, the story of Christmas is about "a God who threw the stars and throws them still" (p. 41), who reaches out to a parched humanity, only to bathe it with new life in the birth of the Christ child.

3. Bring in a collection of Christmas crèches, preferably from different cultures. Note the similarities and differences. How does each one retell the birth of Jesus in its own style? What stands out in each as important? If we were to create one, what would we want to place in it? How do we make the Christmas story our own?

4. In his poem "Ash Wednesday" (http://www.american poems.com/poets/tseliot/372), T. S. Eliot ponders the relation between our words and the Word, as well as the need for silence: "And the light shone in darkness and / Against the Word the unstilled world still whirled / About the centre of the silent Word. . . . / Where shall the word be found, where will the word / Resound? Not here, there is not enough silence."

Hymns for Worship
Gathering
O come, all ye faithful   ELW 283, LBW 45
Once in royal David's city   ELW 269, WOV 643
Let all together praise our God   ELW 287, LBW 47

Hymn of the Day
Of the Father's love begotten   ELW 295, LBW 42
    DIVINUM MYSTERIUM
Word of God, come down on earth   ELW 510, WOV 716
    LIEBSTER JESU, WIR SIND HIER
Hark! The herald angels sing   ELW 270, LBW 60
    MENDELSSOHN

Offering
Jesus, what a wonderful child   ELW 297, TFF 51
In the bleak midwinter   ELW 294

Communion
That boy-child of Mary   ELW 293, TFF 54
Lo, how a rose e'er blooming   ELW 272, LBW 58
Let our gladness have no end   ELW 291, LBW 57

Sending
Go tell it on the mountain   ELW 290, LBW 70, TFF 52
Good Christian friends, rejoice   ELW 288, LBW 55

Additional Hymns and Songs
For all people Christ was born   DH 52
Emmanuel   W&P 36
Break forth, O beauteous heavenly light   PH 26

Music for the Day
Psalmody and Acclamations
Anderson, Mark. "Psalm 98," Refrain 2, from PSCY.
Ferguson, John. *Gospel Acclamations for Advent–Transfiguration.*
Hesla, Bret. "Shout unto God (Psalm 98)" from *Justice, Like a Base of Stone.* AFP 9780800623562.
"Joy to the World." ELW 267.
Roberts, William Bradley. "Psalm 97," Refrain 2, from PSCY.

Shepperd, Mark. "Psalm 97" from PWA, Evangelical Lutheran Worship Edition.
Wetzler, Robert. "Psalm 98" from PWA, Evangelical Lutheran Worship Edition.

Choral
Bach, J. S. "Break Forth, O Beauteous Heavenly Light" from *Bach for All Seasons.* SATB. AFP 9780800658540.
Mayernik, Luke. "O My Child." SATB. GIA G-7195.
McRae, Shirley. "Bell Carol." 2 pt, pno. AFP 9780800664053.
o Thomas, Andre. "Walk in the Light." SATB, pno. CG CGA-1063.

Children's Choir
Bailey, Lynn. "Today a Savior Is Born." U, kybd. CG CGA1161.
Burkhardt, Michael. "Awake! Arise!" 2 pt/3 pt, kybd, opt hb, xyl. MSM 50-1425A.
Christopherson, Dorothy. "Psalm 98." U, kybd. AFP 9780800663872.

Keyboard / Instrumental
o Bach, J. S. "Liebster Jesu, wir sind hier." Org. Various editions.
o Held, Wilbur. "Divinum mysterium" from *Augsburg Organ Library: Christmas.* Org. AFP 9780800659356.
o Maynard, Lynette. "Divinum mysterium" from *Sing We Now of Christmas.* Pno. AFP 9780800677619.
o Nelhybel, Vaclav. "Mendelssohn" from *Festival Hymns and Processionals.* Br. Conductor score HOP 750.

Handbell
o Gramann, Fred. "Change Ring Prelude on *Divinum Mysterium.*" 3-6 oct, L3+. LOR 20/1239L.
o Mallory, Ron. "Of the Father's Love Begotten." 2 oct, L2+. HOP 2188.
o Wissinger, Katheeen. "Hark! The Herald Angels Sing." 3 oct, L1. HOP 2406.

Praise Ensemble
• African American trad. "Jesus, What a Wonderful Child." Pilgrim Press. ELW 297.
• Avery, Brad/Mac Powell/David Carr/Mark Lee/Tai Anderson. "Born in Bethlehem." Consuming Fire Music.
• Coomes, Tommy/Mike Fay. "As We Gather." MAR.
• Crowder, David. "O Praise Him." WT/Sixsteps Music.
• Doerksen, Brian. "Come, Now Is the Time to Worship." VIN.
• Tomlin, Chris. "We Fall Down." WT.

Global
Bell, John, arr. "I Am for You" from *Heaven Shall Not Wait.* SATB. GIA G-3646.
Witt, Tom, arr. "Go Tell It on the Mountain" from *Global Songs 2.* SATB. AFP 9780800656744. ELW 247.

o denotes suggestions that relate to the hymn of the day.
• denotes songs that are available on iTunes®.

December 26, 2010
First Sunday of Christmas

As we celebrate the Twelve Days of Christmas, our gospel today confronts us with the death of innocent children at the hands of Herod. The birth of Christ does not remove the power of evil from our world, but its light gives us hope as we walk with all the "holy innocents" of past generations and today who have suffered unjustly. In our gathering around word and meal, God continues to redeem us, lift us up, and carry us as in days of old.

On December 26 the church remembers Stephen, deacon and martyr. The lesser festival of St. Stephen's day may be observed this year on December 29.

Prayer of the Day

O Lord God, you know that we cannot place our trust in our own powers. As you protected the infant Jesus, so defend us and all the needy from harm and adversity, through Jesus Christ, our Savior and Lord, who lives and reigns with you and the Holy Spirit, one God, now and forever.

Gospel Acclamation

Alleluia. Let the peace of Christ rule ˡ in your hearts,*
and let the word of Christ dwell ˡ in you richly. *Alleluia.*
(Col. 3:15, 16)

Readings and Psalm
Isaiah 63:7-9

God does not delegate divine intervention to a messenger or angel. God's own presence brings salvation. The prophet and all who read these words join in celebrating God's gracious deeds. God trusts that God's people will not act falsely.

Psalm 148

The splendor of the Lord is over earth and heaven.
(Ps. 148:13)

Hebrews 2:10-18

Through Jesus' suffering and death, the trail to eternal salvation has been blazed for us. We do not fear death, because he has conquered the power of death. Thus Christ, our merciful and faithful high priest, has the final say over the destiny of our lives.

Matthew 2:13-23

Matthew relates the slaughter of babies in Bethlehem as one example of evil in the world. Jesus has been born into this world to manifest God's presence and save his people from their sins.

Preface   Christmas

Color   White

Prayers of Intercession

The prayers are prepared locally for each occasion. The following examples may be adapted or used as appropriate.

Filled with wonder and joy that God's gift of grace has been given in the Son born for us, let us pray for the church, the good creation, and the needs of all.

A brief silence.

O God, strengthen your church in times of testing and trial, and give courage and vision to bishops, pastors, lay leaders, teachers, and all who minister in your name. Hear us, O God.
Your mercy is great.

O God, save all species in danger of extinction because of human neglect and greed. Restore your creation from the smallest cell to the shining stars, that the universe may praise your name. Hear us, O God.
Your mercy is great.

O God, in your love and compassion carry the children of the world to safety. Protect the young and vulnerable in every nation (*especially*), and console the families of children lost to war and violence. Hear us, O God.
Your mercy is great.

O God, have mercy on those who cry out to you in any distress. We lift to you our sisters and brothers who are sick, grieving, troubled, hungry, cold, in pain, or without joy (*especially*). Hear us, O God.
Your mercy is great.

O God, make this congregation a sanctuary of acceptance for all, that together we may share your dream of peace. Bless those gathered here, those who are absent, and those we have yet to welcome. Hear us, O God.
Your mercy is great.

Here other intercessions may be offered.

O God, we thank you for the saints who were tested and witnessed boldly to the gospel (*especially Stephen, deacon and martyr*). Uphold us as we follow Christ, that with them we may behold the fullness of your glory. Hear us, O God.
Your mercy is great.

Into the manger of your love, holy God, we lay our prayers, trusting in your promise made known to us in Jesus the Christ, our brother and Savior.
Amen.

Ideas and Images for the Day

On the one hand, the celebration praise of Christmas continues. The psalmist sings of the Lord present in all creation—and conversely all creation reveals a Creator worthy of praise. On the other hand, the distress present in a dangerous and unjust human society presses in. Human sin severs our relationships with God and one another. In the midst of our distress, Jesus comes in flesh and blood and is proclaimed in today's readings to be fully human, even vulnerable, as we are. Yet the Christ child also is Lord and Savior. Joseph moves from place to place, guided by dreams, to save his family. God saves us and all creation through the one born in Bethlehem's manger.

1. The psalm is a song of praise proclaimed by God's whole creation: sun, moon and stars, weather, plants, animals and insects. "Mystic Christ," by Father John Giuliani (http://www.bridgebuilding.com/narr/gmyc.html), shows many aspects of creation within the one body of Christ, linking together in one image the praises of the psalmist with our continuing celebration of Christmas—God with us.

2. The writer of Hebrews lifts up repeatedly the humanity of Jesus. Artists have drawn and painted Jesus in many ways; forensic anthropologists have crafted this image of Jesus: http://www.popularmechanics.com/science/research/1282186.html. Bring a variety of pictures of Jesus from various cultures (search the Web for "face of Jesus") and invite children to create a collage of the face of Jesus, who comes among us to save us. For an example see http://www.pghupperroom.com/main/wp-content/uploads/2009/04/jesus_collage.jpg.

3. In today's gospel we remember the slaughter of the innocents, the children who died because of an oppressive ruler's rage and fear. In this story from Matthew, this tragedy is a foreshadowing of Jesus' own death—the fate he escapes as a child, he will later face when he dies to overturn sin and death. One of the ways children lose their lives and innocence today is when they are conscripted as soldiers. "I would like you to give a message. Please do your best to tell the world what is happening to us, the children. So that other children don't have to pass through this violence" (http://www.child-soldiers.org). How might these children's voices be lifted up in worship today as we remember all those whom Jesus came to save?

4. "While suns and stars spin endlessly through depths of cosmic space, / while aeons roll and ages pass, you hold us in your grace." —Herman G. Stuempfle Jr., "How small our span of life" (ELW 636, st. 2).

Hymns for Worship
Gathering

All my heart again rejoices   ELW 273, LBW 46
Hark! The herald angels sing   ELW 270, LBW 60
Angels, we have heard on high   ELW 289, LBW 71

Hymn of the Day

Let all together praise our God   ELW 287, LBW 47
    LOBT GOTT, IHR CHRISTEN
Peace came to earth   ELW 285, WOV 641   *SCHNEIDER*
Away in a manger   ELW 277/278
    AWAY IN A MANGER/CRADLE SONG

Offering

Peace came to earth   ELW 285, WOV 641
From heaven above   ELW 268, sts. 1-3, 12-14,
    LBW 51, sts. 1-3, 12-14

Communion

'Twas in the moon of wintertime   ELW 284, LBW 72
Your little ones, dear Lord   ELW 286, LBW 52
The bells of Christmas   ELW 298, LBW 62

Sending

Good Christian friends, rejoice   ELW 288, LBW 55
Cold December flies away   ELW 299, LBW 53

Additional Hymns and Songs

I wonder as I wander   WOV 642, TFF 50
Holy child   DH 54
Oh, sleep now, holy baby   WOV 639

Music for the Day
Psalmody and Acclamations

Ferguson, John. *Gospel Acclamations for Advent–Transfiguration.*
Krentz, Michael. "Psalm 148" from PWA, Evangelical Lutheran Worship Edition.
Makeever, Ray. "Praise and Exalt God (Psalm 148)" from *Dancing at the Harvest.*

Mummert, Mark. "Psalm 148," from PSCY.
"Praise the Lord! O Heavens." ELW 823.

Choral

Edwards, Malcolm V. "Hymn of the Poor." SA, pno. Alliance Music
  Publications 0462.
Ferguson, John. "Unto Us Is Born God's Son." SATB, org. AFP
  9780800652398.
Gelineau, Joseph. "Psalm 148." 2 pt mxd, org. GIA G-2245.
Sedio, Mark. "The Coventry Carol." 2 pt mxd, org. SEL 405-234.

Children's Choir

Hispanic folk tune. "Oh, Sleep Now, Holy Baby" from *LifeSongs*. LE,
  U, kybd.
Makeever, Ray. "Holy Child" from *Dancing at the Harvest*. U, kybd.
West Indies carol. "The Virgin Mary Had a Baby Boy" from *Life-
  Songs*. UE, U, kybd.

Keyboard / Instrumental

o Buxtehude, Dietrich. "Lobt Gott, ihr Christen." Org. Various
     editions.
o Lovelace, Austin. "Away in a Manger." Org. CPH 97-5915U1.
o Mahnke, Allan. "Lobt Gott, ihr Christen" from *Thirteen Pieces for
     Treble Instrument and Organ*. Org, inst. CPH 97-6030U1.
o Maynard, Lynette. "Away in a Manger" from *Sing We Now of Christ-
     mas*. Pno. AFP 9780800677619.

Handbell

o Dobrinski, Cynthia. "Away in a Manger." 3 oct, L3. HOP 1213.
   Mathis, William. "Three Favorite German Carols." 4-5 oct, opt C
     inst, L3. AFP 9780800674939.
o Rogers, Sharon Elery. "Infant Holy in a Manger." 2-3 oct, L2.
     AFP 9780800674878.

Praise Ensemble

• Bullock, Geoff. "The Power of Your Love." WRD/MAR.
• Carpenter, Kelly. "Draw Me Close." Mercy/VIN.
• Fielding, Ben/Reuben Morgan. "Mighty to Save." Hillsong.
• Haynes, Timothy/Joe Beck. "I Will Do the Same." MAR/Doulos.
• Ruis, David. "You're Worthy of My Praise." MAR.
• Tomlin, Chris/John Newton/John Rees/Edwin Excell/Louie Giglio.
     "Amazing Grace (My Chains Are Gone)." WT.

Global

Grau, Alberto, arr. "Ni o lindo/Lovely baby" from *World Carols for
  Choirs*. SATB. OXF 019353231X.
Loh, I-to, arr. "Child of Christmas Story" from *Sound the Bamboo*.
  U. GIA G-6830.

o denotes suggestions that relate to the hymn of the day.
• denotes songs that are available on iTunes®.

Monday, December 27

John, Apostle and Evangelist

John, the son of Zebedee, was a fisherman and one of the
Twelve. John and his brother James once made known their
desire to hold positions of power in the kingdom of God.
Jesus' response showed them that service to others was the
sign of God's reign in the world. Tradition has attributed
authorship of the gospel and the three epistles bearing his
name to the apostle John. John is a saint for Christmas
through his proclamation that the Word became flesh and
lived among us, that the light of God shines in the darkness,
and that we are called to love one another as Christ has
loved us.

Tuesday, December 28

The Holy Innocents, Martyrs

The infant martyrs commemorated on this day were the
children of Bethlehem, two years old and younger, who were
killed by Herod, who worried that his reign was threatened
by the birth of a new king. Augustine called these innocents
"buds, killed by the frost of persecution the moment they
showed themselves." Those linked to Jesus through their
youth and innocence encounter the same hostility Jesus
encounters later in his ministry.

Wednesday, December 29

Stephen, Deacon and Martyr (transferred)

Stephen was a deacon and the first martyr of the church. He
was one of those seven upon whom the apostles laid hands
after they had been chosen to serve widows and others in
need. Later, Stephen's preaching angered the temple authorities, and they ordered him to be put to death by stoning,
with Saul (later Paul) as one of the observers. As he died, he
witnessed to his faith and spoke of a vision of heaven.

Saturday, January 1, 2011

Name of Jesus

The observance of the octave (eighth day) of Christmas has
roots in the sixth century. Until the recent past, Lutheran
calendars called this day "The Circumcision and Name of
Jesus." The emphasis on circumcision is the older emphasis.
Every Jewish boy was circumcised and formally named on
the eighth day of his life. Already in his youth, Jesus bears the
mark of a covenant that he makes new through the shedding
of his blood on the cross. That covenant, like Jesus' name, is a
gift that marks the children of God. Baptized into Christ, the
church begins a new year in Jesus' name.

January 2, 2011
Second Sunday of Christmas

Within the gospel reading's profound words lies the simple message that God is revealed in a human person. Though we may try to understand how the Word existed with God from the beginning of time, the wonder we celebrate at Christmas is that the Word continues to dwell among us. Christ comes among us in the gathered assembly, the scriptures, the waters of new birth, and the bread and the wine. Through these ordinary gifts we receive the fullness of God's grace and truth.

Today is the commemoration of Johann Konrad Wilhelm Loehe, renewer of the church, who died in 1872.

Prayer of the Day

Almighty God, you have filled all the earth with the light of your incarnate Word. By your grace empower us to reflect your light in all that we do, through Jesus Christ, our Savior and Lord, who lives and reigns with you and the Holy Spirit, one God, now and forever.

or

O God our redeemer, you created light that we might live, and you illumine our world with your beloved Son. By your Spirit comfort us in all darkness, and turn us toward the light of Jesus Christ our Savior, who lives and reigns with you and the Holy Spirit, one God, now and forever.

Gospel Acclamation

Alleluia. All the ends | of the earth* have seen the victory | of our God. *Alleluia.* (Ps. 98:3)

Readings and Psalm
Jeremiah 31:7-14

God promises to bring Israel back to its land from the most remote parts of exile. In Zion Israel will rejoice over God's gift of food and livestock. Young women will express their joy in dancing; God will give gladness instead of sorrow.

or Sirach 24:1-12

The figure of Wisdom played a major role in early discussions of christology. Wisdom is the divine word, coming from the mouth of God, and ruling over all of creation. Wisdom, created at the beginning of time, made her dwelling place in Jerusalem among God's people.

Psalm 147:12-20

Worship the Lord, O Jerusalem; praise your God, O Zion. (Ps. 147:12)

or Wisdom 10:15-21

We sing, O Lord, to your holy name. (Wis. 10:20)

Ephesians 1:3-14

In Jesus, all of God's plans and purposes have been made know as heaven and earth are united in Christ. Through Jesus, we have been chosen as God's children and have been promised eternal salvation.

John 1:[1-9] 10-18

John begins his gospel with this prologue: a hymn to the Word through whom all things were created. This Word became flesh and brought grace and truth to the world.

Preface   Christmas

Color   White

Prayers of Intercession

The prayers are prepared locally for each occasion. The following examples may be adapted or used as appropriate.

Filled with wonder and joy that God's gift of grace has been given in the Son born for us, let us pray for the church, the good creation, and the needs of all.

A brief silence.

Holy Wisdom, gather and deliver your people. Guide your church according to your will in the coming year. Mend our divisions and unite the baptized, that the world may know the light of Christ. Hear us, O God.

Your mercy is great.

Divine Mystery, you spoke and the world was created. Breathe restoration and healing upon the damaged earth; preserve the life of endangered creatures; cleanse the skies and seas; and make all things new. Hear us, O God.

Your mercy is great.

Radiant Light, bring hope to those who struggle for justice in every nation (*especially*). Where there is war and violence, establish your peace; where there is famine or disaster, send swift relief. Hear us, O God.
Your mercy is great.

Abiding Spirit, you are near to all in need. Console those who are grieving, lonely, isolated, or far from home (*especially*). Bless them with your tender care and turn their mourning into joy. Hear us, O God.
Your mercy is great.

Gracious Giver, enrich this congregation with grace upon grace in the new year, and sustain us as we are living out our baptismal calling. Open our hearts to welcome all people into life with you. Hear us, O God.
Your mercy is great.

Here other intercessions may be offered.

Lover of souls, we praise you for the faithful who have gone before us as witnesses to your goodness (*especially Johann Konrad Wilhelm Loehe, renewer of the church*). Grant that we also might receive our inheritance as your children. Hear us, O God.
Your mercy is great.

Into the manger of your love, holy God, we lay our prayers, trusting in your promise made known to us in Jesus the Christ, our brother and Savior.
Amen.

Ideas and Images for the Day

In sharp contrast to the image of Jacob, who wrestles with an angel and prevails, in today's first reading the Lord redeems Jacob from hands too strong for him. Jacob does not always prevail. We too are reminded this day that it is not our own strength but God's power that blesses, strengthens, fills, gives, and grants peace. God has the power to bring together and to scatter. God creates family not because we are God's blood relatives but through adoption. In baptism we are claimed, redeemed, and forgiven. We receive wisdom and are lavished with grace. We are marked with the seal of the Holy Spirit. We receive an inheritance. Through God's powerful gift, we are gathered up, become children of God, and receive grace upon grace.

1. A children's choir could be taught in advance this joyful canticle which conveys nearly the whole text of Jeremiah 31 in song: "Listen! you nations" (LBW 14).

2. In many ways, these texts are like previews of themes in the coming Sundays. Ephesians helps us remember our baptism before we celebrate the baptism of Jesus. The Gospel of John points to Jesus—the Word who became flesh and dwelt among us—as the light of the world before we begin marking the days after Epiphany. Use the thanksgiving for baptism or create a ritual to remember God's gracious adoption of all of us. You may wish to ask adoptive families in your congregation for their ideas and resources that could be adapted for use in worship to remind the assembly that we are all adopted. See http://www.elca.org/lifetransitions/adoption.

3. "People still wonder today in the church if God could love so many different types of people and so many different types of families. The answer continues to be Yes!" From *Weaving God's Love Across Cultures: Transracial Adoption and Faith*, ed. Mary Lindberg (Evangelical Lutheran Church in America, 2004), p. 43. Book available at http://www.augsburgfortress.org.

4. This image is an artist's rendition of the Word becoming flesh in Jesus. "Image of God" is written on his forehead; "word" is on his mouth. See http://easterpeople.files.wordpress.com/2009/07/jesus_bible_names.jpg.

Hymns for Worship
Gathering
Angels, from the realms of glory   ELW 275, LBW 50
Joy to the world   ELW 267, LBW 39
Love has come   ELW 292

Hymn of the Day
Let our gladness have no end   ELW 291, LBW 57
  NARODIL SE KRISTUS PÁN
The bells of Christmas   ELW 298, LBW 62
  DET KIMER NU TIL JULEFEST
O come, all ye faithful   ELW 283, LBW 45   *ADESTE FIDELES*

Offering
What child is this   ELW 296, LBW 40
Jesus, what a wonderful child   ELW 297, TFF 51

Communion
Of the Father's love begotten   ELW 295, LBW 42
Word of God, come down on earth   ELW 510, WOV 716
What feast of love   ELW 487, WOV 701

Sending
Hark! The herald angels sing   ELW 270, LBW 60
Let all together praise our God   ELW 287, LBW 47

Additional Hymns and Songs
From east to west   LBW 64, H82 77
Holy child within the manger   WOV 638
The hills are bare at Bethlehem   LBW 61

Music for the Day
Psalmody and Acclamations

Ferguson, John. *Gospel Acclamations for Advent–Transfiguration.*

Hobby, Robert. "Psalm 147:12-20" from PWA, Evangelical Lutheran Worship Edition.

Pavlechko, Thomas. "Wisdom 10:15-21," from PSCY.

Sedio, Mark. "Wisdom 10:15-21" from PWA, Evangelical Lutheran Worship Edition.

Woehr, Roland. "Psalm 147:12-20," from PSCY.

Choral

Hovland, Egil. "The Glory of the Father." SATB. WAL W2973.

Pelz, Walter. "And the Word Became Flesh." SATB, org, ob. AFP 9780800620172.

Powell, Rosephayne. "The Word Was God." SATB. Gentry Publications (HAL) JG2323.

o Sedio, Mark. "Let Our Gladness Have No End." SATB div, hp or kybd, vln. MSM 50-1209.

Children's Choir

Berthier, Jacques. "Gloria" from *LifeSongs.* U, kybd.

Thomas, Andre. "Walk In the Light." U/2 pt, kybd. CG CGA-1062.

Young, Phillip. "When Christ, the Son of Mary." 2 pt, kybd. AFP 9780800656409.

Keyboard / Instrumental

Dahl, David P. "Nordic Aria" from *A Scandinavian Suite for Organ.* Org, C inst. AFP 9780800678432.

o Demessieux, Jeanne. "Adeste fideles" from *Augsburg Organ Library: Christmas.* Org. AFP 9780800659356.

o Sedio, Mark. "Narodil se Kristus Pán" from *Six Slovak Hymn Improvisations.* Org. MSM 10-833.

o Wasson, Laura E. "Adeste fideles" from *A Christmas Season Tapestry.* Pno. AFP 9780800657253.

Handbell

o Buckwalter, Karen Lakey. "Bells of Christmas." 4-5 oct hb, opt 3 oct hc, opt fl or vln, L3. BP HB240.

Moklebust, Cathy. "Sing We Now of Christmas." 3-5 oct, perc, L4. CG CGB591 (HB). CGB590 (full score, perc).

o Tucker, Sondra. "Let Our Gladness Know No End." 3-5 oct hb, opt 3 oct hc, opt tamb, L3+. BP HB336.

Praise Ensemble

• Avery, Brad/David Carr/Mac Powell/Mark Lee/Tai Anderson. "O Come, All Ye Faithful." Consuming Fire Music.

• Grant, Amy/Michael W. Smith. "Thy Word." Meadowgreen Music/WRD. W&P 144.

• Green, Melody. "There Is a Redeemer." Birdwing Music. W&P 140.

• Millard, Bart/Pete Kipley. "Word of God, Speak." Simpleville Music.

• Park, Andy. "Only You." Mercy/VIN. Various editions.

• Tomlin, Chris/Daniel Carson/Ed Cash/Jesse Reeves. "Jesus Messiah." WT/Sixsteps Music.

Global

Bell, John, arr. "Word of the Father" from *Come, All You People: Shorter Songs for Worship.* SATB. GIA G-4391.

Radford, Jeffrey, arr. "Jesus, What a Wonderful Child." SATB. ELW 297.

Sunday, January 2

Johann Konrad Wilhelm Loehe, renewer of the church, died 1872

Loehe (approximate pronunciation: LAY-uh) was a pastor in nineteenth-century Germany. From the small town of Neuendettelsau, he sent pastors to North America, Australia, New Guinea, Brazil, and the Ukraine. His work for a clear confessional basis within the Bavarian church sometimes led to conflict with the ecclesiastical bureaucracy. Loehe's chief concern was that a congregation find its life in the holy communion, and from that source evangelism and social ministries would flow. Many Lutheran congregations in Michigan, Ohio, and Iowa were either founded or influenced by missionaries sent by Loehe.

o denotes suggestions that relate to the hymn of the day.
• denotes songs that are available on iTunes®.

January 6, 2011
Epiphany of Our Lord

Epiphany means "manifestation." On this day we celebrate the revelation of Christ to the Gentiles—that is, to all nations. Some Christian traditions celebrate three great epiphanies on this day: the magi's adoration of the Christ child, Jesus' baptism in the Jordan River, and his first miracle, in which he changes water into wine. The word and sacraments are for us the great epiphany of God's grace and mercy. We go forth to witness to the light that shines brightly in our midst.

Prayer of the Day

O God, on this day you revealed your Son to the nations by the leading of a star. Lead us now by faith to know your presence in our lives, and bring us at last to the full vision of your glory, through your Son, Jesus Christ our Lord, who lives and reigns with you and the Holy Spirit, one God, now and forever.

or

Almighty and ever-living God, you revealed the incarnation of your Son by the brilliant shining of a star. Shine the light of your justice always in our hearts and over all lands, and accept our lives as the treasure we offer in your praise and for your service, through Jesus Christ, our Savior and Lord, who lives and reigns with you and the Holy Spirit, one God, now and forever.

or

Everlasting God, the radiance of all faithful people, you brought the nations to the brightness of your rising. Fill the world with your glory, and show yourself to all the world through him who is the true light and the bright morning star, your Son, Jesus Christ, our Savior and Lord, who lives and reigns with you and the Holy Spirit, one God, now and forever.

Gospel Acclamation

Alleluia. We have observed his star ' at its rising,* and have come to ' worship him. *Alleluia.* (Matt. 2:2)

Readings and Psalm
Isaiah 60:1-6

Jerusalem is assured that nations will make a pilgrimage to her, because the light of God's presence is in her midst. The bountiful food of the sea and the profits of international trade will come streaming to Jerusalem and thereby declare God's praise.

Psalm 72:1-7, 10-14

All kings shall bow before him. (Ps. 72:11)

Ephesians 3:1-12

What had been hidden from previous generations is now made known through the gospel ministry of Paul and others. In Christ both Jews and Gentiles participate in the richness of God's promised salvation.

Matthew 2:1-12

God's promise shines bright in the night as magi follow a star to honor a new king. Strangers from a faraway land, they welcome the long-awaited messiah of Israel.

Preface   Epiphany of Our Lord

Color   White

Prayers of Intercession

The prayers are prepared locally for each occasion. The following examples may be adapted or used as appropriate.

Filled with wonder and joy that God's gift of grace has been given in the Son born for us, let us pray for the church, the good creation, and the needs of all.

A brief silence.

You are the radiant God of glory. We pray that through the church your wisdom may be revealed. Warn us when we go astray, and send us by another road to do your will. Hear us, O God.

Your mercy is great.

You are the guiding star of creation. We pray that our care for the land, seas, and skies will preserve the rich variety of all that you have made. Hear us, O God.

Your mercy is great.

You are the light of the nations. We pray that your abundant peace may reign in every land (*especially*). Uphold all who labor for human rights, shelter for the homeless, and protection of the vulnerable. Hear us, O God.
Your mercy is great.

You are the hope of those in need. We pray for all who face hardship, danger, loss, and illness (*especially*). In your compassion lift up their hearts and comfort them with your healing presence. Hear us, O God.
Your mercy is great.

You are the giver of all gifts. We pray that the ministries of this congregation will reflect your generosity in loving service. Lead us out of complacency to new ventures in faith. Hear us, O God.
Your mercy is great.

Here other intercessions may be offered.

You are the source and end of all our searching, and the faithful departed now rest in your light. Grant that we too may live with bold confidence in your grace, now and forever. Hear us, O God.
Your mercy is great.

Into the manger of your love, holy God, we lay our prayers, trusting in your promise made known to us in Jesus the Christ, our brother and Savior.
Amen.

Ideas and Images for the Day

The gifts of the magi, as delineated in today's gospel, direct us away from the cute, cuddly, cooing baby Jesus by pointing us to who Jesus really has come to be. The magi offer gold, a possession of kings; frankincense, used in ritual to indicate the presence of the deity; and myrrh, an oil used at the time of death as well as for anointing priests. By their gifts, the wise men reveal the identity of this child: the king before whom nations will bow, the anointed high priest of God, and the suffering servant who will die for the ones he has come to serve.

1. The readings also point to what God's kingdom will be like—all nations will serve God (Ps. 72:11), sons and daughters will be gathered from far away (Isa. 60:4), the poor will be delivered (Ps. 72:4), and outsiders will be heirs of God's promises (Eph. 3:6). In God's kingdom, relationships—between nations, within families, among people, between God and humanity—are healed. Around the table, healing occurs now as God gathers people from diverse places and reconciles them as one body.

2. Around the time of Epiphany homes and church buildings are often blessed. A blessing for a home recognizes all the ways people practice their faith in daily life. Consider using a ritual of blessing for your own church building, especially on January 6, the day of Epiphany. Carry symbols of the faith as you go—a cross, a light, and water for *asperses*. Invite children into holy play as they sprinkle people and spaces with remembrances of baptismal living. Resources for blessing can be found in *Evangelical Lutheran Worship Pastoral Care*.

3. In today's gospel, an encounter with Jesus changes the direction of the magi's lives: choosing not to return to Herod, they go home by another road (Matt. 2:12). Invite people from your congregation whose lives have been changed through an encounter with Christ to share their story as part of your worship time. Consider giving a short homily on the gospel, bringing out the theme of the magi's encounter with Jesus, and then invite others to share their own stories of how God has been made manifest in their lives.

4. T. S. Eliot's poem "Journey of the Magi" asks, in the voice of the magi, "were we led all that way for birth or for death?" (*Collected Poems 1909–1962* [San Diego: Harcourt Brace, 1970], p. 100). Were the magi led to Jesus for birth or for death or both? The poem illustrates how the birth of Jesus puts to death the comfort the magi felt with the ways of Herod's kingdom.

Hymns for Worship

Gathering
The first Noel   ELW 300, LBW 56
As with gladness men of old   ELW 302, LBW 82
Angels, from the realms of glory   ELW 275, LBW 50

Hymn of the Day
O Morning Star, how fair and bright   ELW 308, LBW 76
   WIE SCHÖN LEUCHTET
What child is this   ELW 296, LBW 40   *GREENSLEEVES*
Bright and glorious is the sky   ELW 301, LBW 75
   DEJLIG ER DEN HIMMEL BLÅ

Offering
Arise, your light has come!   ELW 314, WOV 652
In the bleak midwinter   ELW 294

Communion
Brightest and best of the stars   ELW 303, LBW 84
I want to walk as a child of the light   ELW 815, WOV 649
This little light of mine   ELW 677, TFF 65

Sending
Rise, shine, you people!   ELW 665, LBW 393
Songs of thankfulness and praise   ELW 310, LBW 90

Additional Hymns and Songs

We three kings of Orient are   WOV 646
Sister Mary   TFF 60
All hail King Jesus   W&P 3

Music for the Day
Psalmody and Acclamations

Ferguson, John. *Gospel Acclamations for Advent–Transfiguration.*
Hobby, Robert. "Psalm 72:1-7, 10-14" from PWA, Evangelical
    Lutheran Worship Edition.
Mummert, Mark. "Psalm 72," Refrain 1, from PSCY.

Choral

Carlson, J. Bert. "Epiphany Light." SATB, org, opt assembly.
    AFP 9780800664176.
Haugen, Marty. "Arise, Shine!" 2 pt mxd or SAB, opt assembly,
    kybd, gtr, opt insts. GIA G-3266.
Laster, James H. "We Three Kings." SATB, kybd, vln, fc.
    AFP 9780800664183.
o Weber, Paul. "Arise, Shine." SATB. AFP 9780800677367.

Children's Choir

Cool, Jayne Southwick. "Bright Morning Star." 2 pt, kybd.
    AFP 9780800664213.
Kemp, Helen. "Set the Sun Dancing!" UE, U, kybd, hb. CG CGA780.
Patterson, Mark. "Star of Wonder" from *Young ChildrenSing.*
    AFP 9780800676803.

Keyboard / Instrumental

o Albrecht, Mark. "Greensleeves" from *Augsburg Organ Library:
    Christmas.* Org. AFP 9780800659356.

o Busarow, Donald. "Wie schön leuchten" from *With Music Crowned.*
    Org, 2 inst. CPH 97-7324U1.
o Dahl, David P. "Dejlig er den himmel blå" from *A Scandinavian
    Suite for Organ.* Org. AFP 9780800678432.
o Henkelmann, Brian. "Dejlig er den himmel blå" from *Chorale Pre-
    ludes for the Liturgical Year,* vol. 1. Kybd, fl. CPH 97-7227U1.

Handbell

o Callahan, Frances. "O Morning Star, How Fair and Bright." 2 oct,
    L3. MSM 30-200.
Page, Anna Laura. "Behold the Star." 3-5 oct, L3. CG CGB607.
Raney, Joel. "We Three Kings." 3-6 oct hb, opt D5-A7 hc, perc,
    synth, L3+. HOP 2482 (HB). HOP 2482P (inst parts).

Praise Ensemble

• Baloche, Paul. "Offering" (with Christmas lyric). INT.
• Dix, William. "What Child Is This?" Praisecharts.com Publishing.
    ELW 296.
• Farrell, Bernadette. "Christ, Be Our Light." OCP. ELW 715.
• Howard, Adrian/Pat Turner. "Salvation Belongs to Our God." Resto-
    ration Music.
• Hughes, Tim. "Here I Am to Worship." Thankyou Music/INT.
• Kendrick, Graham. "Shine, Jesus, Shine." Make Way Music.
    ELW 671.

Global

African American spiritual. "Sister Mary." U. TFF 60.
Aguiar, Ernani. "Acalanto para o Menino Jesus/Carol for the Baby
    Jesus" from *World Carols for Choirs.* SATB. OXF 019353231X.

o denotes suggestions that relate to the hymn of the day.
• denotes songs that are available on iTunes®.

TIME AFTER EPIPHANY

PREPARING FOR THE TIME AFTER EPIPHANY

I Had an Epiphany

The people who walked in darkness have seen a great light;
those who lived in a land of deep darkness—
on them light has shined. (Isa. 9:2)

Some Christians call Epiphany "Little Christmas," and in the North American context it might be wise to celebrate this season as such. The greens and lights and tinsel of the Christmas holidays ward off the encroaching darkness of winter, but these are, by and large, tossed out on the curb by December 26, right at the time when winter gets genuinely cold and dismal. Robust celebration of the time after Epiphany might counteract this trend. In other words, leave the lights on and hanging.

In the Preparing for Christmas planning pages (pp. 45–47), we offered ideas and suggestions for the feast of Epiphany, January 6. Refer back to those notes if you are reading this section and still seek ideas to prepare for that feast day. The focus of these pages, however, will be on the Sundays after Epiphany, which, though officially "low" days in the church calendar, can also be celebrated in a way comparable to the twelve days of Christmas, as the continuing unfolding of the manifestation of the Son of God, the reality show to end all reality shows, a genuine theophany.

The word *epiphany* has gone into disuse in much of the English-speaking world, and so it might require new interpretation. The most common residual occurrence of it is in the phrase "I had an epiphany," by which speakers mean they had an insight, realization, or idea. This gets at one aspect of epiphany—that it is a time of greater light, a showing of the light. However, just as the incarnation cannot and should not be spoken of in general, as if incarnational theology can mean something on its own apart from Christ, so too the use of the word *epiphany* in this context leaves the term at a general level, applying to all insights or ideas, rather than keeping its christological content as the showing or manifestation of the revelation of God in human form in the person of Jesus Christ.

So be clear. Epiphany is a showing of the manifestation of the glory of God in Jesus Christ to the nations. It can take a whole season to unpack such a confession.

Reality Show

Viewership of reality television shows has increased dramatically since its inception in a decade or so ago. It is frustrating to note that attendance at the church's reality show par excellence (worship) has decreased during the same period. The audience for reality shows is likely attracted for a variety of reasons—drama, competition, voyeurism, escape. But it does beg the question: Is public worship in our assemblies so tepid and flat that a "reality" show on a flat-screen television feels more intimate, real, and enlivening?

Tertullian, Chrysostom, and other church fathers often argued that we should avoid all spectacles, like carnivals or gladiatorial combat. There is wisdom in such an approach. However, the intriguing approach is to re-present a spectacle in a way that draws eye and ears, not to entertain, but to manifest sin, show forth Jesus Christ, and make manifest the true spectacle of the gospel.

Consider the spectacle of these Epiphany days. It begins with Jesus Christ made manifest to the nations through the visitation of the magi. It continues with the spectacle of Jesus' baptism, drowned in those quick waters by that strange man, John, perched upon by that quirky bird the Holy Spirit. Later, Jesus initiates his ministry at the edge of the water, calling slimy fishermen to be his disciples. They quickly learn, when he goes up on the mount and preaches, that discipleship under this Lord is spectacular only in the lack of spectacularity. It's a show with good news for the poor, meek, hungry, thirsty, merciful, pure in heart, peacemakers, and persecuted. Finally, Jesus makes a spectacle even of the commandments of God, ramping them up to what seems an almost impossible level.

And if all that were not sufficient spectacle to overshadow anything that could possibly happen on a reality television show, the spectacle concludes with a vision of Jesus Christ, the Son of God, transformed and transfigured in a vision of glory. Be afraid—be very afraid!

The opening chapters of 1 Corinthians are read concurrently with these gospel readings, and Paul in that correspondence antes up, increasing the spectacle factor by proclaiming, maybe for the first time in the history of religion, the folly and weakness of God. It is as if Paul has admitted that God is at risk of being voted off the island! Frankly, we preachers and worship leaders are not worth our salt if we cannot take these texts, which virtually leap off the page and into our vision, and simply make them manifest and visible. All they need is to be taken out and shown, like diamonds, puppies, or newborn infants.

Congregations might also consider highlighting some of the ways various cultures celebrate this time after Epiphany. Because of the 2009 ELCA Youth Gathering and the volunteer work many congregations have done in the Gulf Coast region, parishioners may have a special place in their hearts for New Orleans. Epiphany is, in New Orleans, the beginning of the Mardi Gras season. Worship leaders could consider lifting various traditions from Mardi Gras, maybe especially the king cake tradition, since Epiphany is sometimes called "king cake season." Mardi Gras might also be an example of how to lift up and celebrate community, culture, and food, maybe even to go on parade and out in costume, prior to the more penitential and somber Lenten season.

Some European communities leave the greenery of Christmas up until February 2, the presentation of Jesus in the temple. This can help sustain the message of life during these cold days, maybe especially if the congregation selects greens that are sustainable, planted in pots and therefore still alive throughout the winter months.

Smell. Wash. Repeat.

Set stuff on fire. Light extra candles. Make generous use of incense. If there's a fireplace in the church, use it. If there are ovens in which bread can be baked, bake there. Not enough is made in our churches of the fragrance of Christ (Eph. 5:2) or, for that matter, the fragrance of our prayers rising up like incense (Ps. 141). In fact, in our context we have come to expect that we will smell very little anywhere. Yet, if we return to the gospel readings for this season, we can imagine the smells that attend each place. The magi bring frankincense and myrrh. Jesus calls fishermen who were, at that moment, bringing in fish. He is baptized by John, whose clothes, diet, and habits likely resulted in some peculiar odors. We might also remember that the poor, the hungry, and the thirsty often lack the means of controlling or covering their scent.

So allow the church to be filled with the faithful scent of the sacraments, the wonderful glorious smoke and haze of worship rising to God. Pray stinky prayers for smelly people that they might be anointed with the salve of the gospel.

Then wash. The visionary smells implicit in these texts are bookended by two stories that imply cleaning—the baptism of Jesus and his transfiguration. Let water and white have pride of place. Brighten and whiten albs, chasubles, robes, altar cloths, and other paraments that have grown grey or yellowed. Keep water out in the baptismal font, and keep it clean.

Theophany

The older name for this feast is *theophany*, which means the incarnation as the revelation of God. This term accentuates in a more striking way the connection between Epiphany and Christmas. The term is used in a wider context, sometimes referring to the appearance of deities in such literature as *The Iliad* or *The Epic of Gilgamesh*. In this sense, it is possible to consider the entire season of Christmas and Epiphany a theophany. At Christmas, the emphasis is on the appearance of the Son of God, born of Mary. Then Epiphany shines further light on—or "shows"—this appearance to the nations, first to the magi, and then by way of messengers to a wider and wider audience.

The repeated response to this "showing" of the Son of God is awe and wonder. The magi bow down in wonder. John is driven to wonderful proclamation by the sheer presence of Jesus. Or consider Isaiah 42:8-9, read on January 9, the Baptism of Our Lord:

I am the LORD, that is my name;
    my glory I give to no other,
    nor my praise to idols.
See, the former things have come to pass,
    and new things I now declare;
before they spring forth,
    I tell you of them.

Or consider the injunction from Leviticus for the seventh Sunday after Epiphany, "You shall be holy, for I the LORD your God am holy" (Lev. 19:2). This can and should be heard as a moral imperative. However, holiness is more than just being moral. It is an attribute of God. So Leviticus literally invites us into the mystery of being like God. Is this not awe-inducing?

Do you experience awe in worship? Does your congregation? Consider making the time after Epiphany the season that the assembly especially attends to that aspect of worship that is beyond rational—the holy, the awesome, the glorious, the sublime. In the recently conducted U.S. Congregational Life Study (http://www.elca.org/~/media/CEE9790CB5FA4DAE995EC51908991594.ashx), church members across the country were asked, "How often do you experience awe during worship services at this congregation?" Among the respondents, 4.4 percent said always, 16.1 percent said often, 51.6 percent said sometimes, and 28 percent said never. If 79.6 percent of our congregation members are experiencing awe during worship only sometimes or never, it may be time to up the "awe" factor.

How might this be accomplished? First, try to note the places where worship has become hyper-rational. Is the entire liturgy focused on practical outcomes, clear communication, getting an obvious (and often moralistic) message across? Certainly, there is room for clear communication in plain English. You don't need to bring back mass in Latin. However, a good portion of the liturgy of the church, and many of its greatest hymns, move beyond rational communication into the language of uninhibited praise. As Isaiah declares, "Shout out, do not hold back! Lift up your voice like a trumpet!" (Isa. 58:1).

Thanksgivings at the table are a prime example. Consider prayer III, designated for Advent through Epiphany of Our Lord. The presiding minister is invited to begin with these words, "Holy One, the beginning and the end" and then continue with an exalted list of "blesseds." The prayer concludes, "All praise and glory are yours, Holy One of Israel, Word of God incarnate, Power of the Most High, one God, now and forever" (*Evangelical Lutheran Worship*, p. 110). The language keeps piling on and on. At one level, it does not accomplish something, or introduce a new concept. It is language that is entering the sublime, and it almost calls to be shouted. It is the language to speak while on fire with the Spirit, having just prayed the epiclesis.

This awe and sublimity can also be made manifest in music. One of the most spectacular is Philipp Nicolai's "O Morning Star, how fair and bright!" (ELW 308). The stanzas of this hymn begin with narrative and full sentences. But the hymn is structured so that at the conclusion of each stanza, the rhythm drives toward the language of adoration and praise. Stanza 5, for example, concludes, "Sing out! Ring out! Jubilation! Exultation! Tell the story! Praise to Christ, who reigns in glory!"

In fact, the entire liturgy and many of our hymns are loaded with these beautiful redundancies. Rather than elide them, accentuate them. Do the poetry. Pause over them. Sing the hymn of praise with gusto. Roll the glorious words of the prayer of the day over the lips. Offer time for silence—often overlooked as the place where awe and glory sneak in.

Seasonal Checklist

- See pages 46–47 for helps related to celebrating the Epiphany of Our Lord on January 6.
- If the Baptism of Our Lord (Jan. 9) will be observed as a baptismal festival, publicize the festival for the congregation and arrange for baptismal preparation sessions with parents, sponsors, and candidates. When the day arrives, set out the following for each baptismal candidate:
  - Towel
  - Baptismal candle
  - Shell (if used)
  - Oil for anointing
  - Fresh water in font or ewer
- If a form of baptismal remembrance is used, evergreen branches for sprinkling may be desired.
- If the Alleluia will be symbolically buried or bid farewell on the festival of the Transfiguration, make the appropriate arrangements (for example, prepare for the burial of an Alleluia banner).
- Select a time to prepare king cakes or other festive items for the season.
- On the festivals of the Baptism of Our Lord and Transfiguration, consider using thanksgiving for baptism instead of confession and forgiveness during the gathering portion of the service.
- Use the Kyrie on the festivals of the Baptism of Our Lord and Transfiguration; omit it on the "green" Sundays after Epiphany.
- Use the hymn of praise ("Glory to God").
- Use the Nicene Creed for festival Sundays after Epiphany; use the Apostles' Creed for the "green" Sundays after Epiphany.
- The Presentation of Our Lord and many commemorations occur during this period. Consider highlighting some in the prayers and daily office.
- See the Blessing of Candles in the seasonal rites section (p. 76).
- The Week of Prayer for Christian Unity is January 18–25. Resources for observing this week of prayer may be obtained from the Graymoor Ecumenical and Interreligious Institute (http://www.geii.org/).

WORSHIP TEXTS FOR THE TIME AFTER EPIPHANY

Confession and Forgiveness

All may make the sign of the cross, the sign marked at baptism,
as the presiding minister begins.

Blessed be the holy Trinity, ☩ one God,
who spread out the heavens and the earth,
who gives light and breath to the nations,
who makes all things new.
Amen.

Let us confess our sin in the presence of God
and one another.

Silence is kept for reflection.

Holy and healing God,
we confess that we have fallen short
of the life you desire for us.
We choose our priorities over your commandments.
We divide the body of Christ.
The earth groans under our demands.
Have mercy, O God.
Restore us and all things to health,
that we may do justice,
love kindness,
and walk humbly with you. Amen.

Hear the voice from heaven:
"You are my own, my beloved."
You belong to Christ,
and through the power of the cross
☩ your sins are all forgiven.
God is faithful and will strengthen you,
that your light may shine before others,
that you may be God's holy people in the world.
Amen.

Greeting

The grace of God in Christ Jesus,
poured out in every gift of the Holy Spirit,
be with you all.
And also with you.

Offering Prayer

Merciful God, as grains of wheat scattered upon the hills
were gathered together to become one bread,
so let your church be gathered together
from the ends of the earth into your kingdom,
for yours is the glory through Jesus Christ, now and forever.
Amen.

Invitation to Communion

Come to the Lamb of God,
who takes away the sin of the world.

Prayer after Communion

Ever-faithful God, you have taken us again into your arms
and nourished us as your dear children.
Lead us and guide us,
that we may share our bread and your healing light
with those who hunger and thirst,
through Jesus Christ, our Savior and Lord.
Amen.

Sending of Communion

Compassionate God, as Jesus called disciples to follow him,
bless those who go forth to share your word and sacrament
with those who are *sick/homebound/imprisoned*.
May these gifts be signs of our love and prayers,
that through the sharing of the body and blood of Christ,
all may know your grace and healing revealed
in Jesus Christ our Lord.
Amen.

Blessing

God the Father, the Majestic Glory;
God the Son, the Morning Star;
and God the Holy Spirit, the Comforter,
bless you and + grant you peace.
Amen.

Dismissal

Go in peace. Share the good news.
Thanks be to God.

SEASONAL RITES FOR THE TIME AFTER EPIPHANY

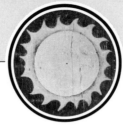

Week of Prayer for Christian Unity

The Week of Prayer for Christian Unity is January 18–25. Resources for observing this week of prayer may be obtained from the Graymoor Ecumenical and Interreligious Institute, 475 Riverside Dr., Room 1960, New York, NY 10115; email: lmnygeii.org@aol.com; phone: 212/870-2330; or at www.geii.org. Resources on the Web site include a brief history of the Week of Prayer for Christian Unity, an ecumenical celebration of the word of God, music suggestions, bulletin announcements, and more.

Blessing of the Candles

On the feast of the Presentation of Our Lord (Candlemas), February 2, some traditions dedicate the candles to be used in worship during the following year. The candles may be brought forward with the offering, or they may be placed on a table near the altar prior to the service.

The presiding minister may lead this prayer before the offering prayer.
Let us pray.
Blessed are you, O Lord our God, ruler of the universe.
You have enriched our lives
with every good and perfect gift;
you have commanded us
to show your splendor to our children
and to praise you with lives of love, justice, and joy.
Accept these candles which we offer in thanksgiving;
may they be to us a sign of Christ,
the Light of the world,
the light no darkness can overcome.
Bring us all at length to your perfect kingdom,
where you live and reign with the Son and the Holy Spirit,
now and forever.
Amen.

Recognition of Ministries in the Congregation

This order is intended for use when recognizing those who contribute their time, energy, and talents to various ministries of the congregation. Additional resources are provided for those who are being recognized upon completing a time of service.

When set within Holy Communion or the Service of the Word, this order may be used as part of the sending, before the blessing.

The assembly is seated. The presiding minister addresses the assembly.
Dear friends: United with all the baptized in the one body of Christ, anointed with the gift of the Holy Spirit, we are joined in God's mission for the life of the world. We are called to that mission in our daily lives and in the ministries we share as the church of God.

Recognition upon Completion of Service

When people are being recognized upon completing a time of service, the presiding minister may address the assembly with these or similar words.
Today it is our privilege to give thanks for those who are completing a time of service in the ministry of _____ within this congregation.

Those completing a time of service may stand. Their names may be read.

The presiding minister continues with prayer.
Let us pray.
Almighty God, your Holy Spirit equips the church
with a rich variety of gifts.
We give thanks for the ways these gifts
have been shown forth among us
through *your servants / [names].*
We praise you for shared joys and accomplishments,
and we commend our work to you.
Grant that we may continue to bear witness to Christ
in lives that are built on faith and love;
through Jesus Christ, our Savior and Lord.
Amen.

Recognition When Beginning or Continuing Service

When people are being recognized as they begin or continue their service, the presiding minister may address the assembly with these or similar words.

Today it is [also] our privilege to recognize and support those who are engaged in the work of this congregation, especially those in the ministry of _____.

Those who are beginning or continuing their service in the ministry being recognized may stand. Their names may be read.

The presiding minister addresses those who are beginning or continuing their service.

Sisters and brothers,
both your work and your rest are in God.
Will you endeavor to pattern your life
on the Lord Jesus Christ,
in gratitude to God and in service to others,
as you carry out the ministry of _____
in this congregation?
Response: I will, and I ask God to help me.

The assembly stands. The presiding minister addresses the assembly.
People of God, I ask you:
Will you support these your *sisters and brothers*
in their service,
and will you share in the mutual ministry
that Christ has given to all who are baptized?
We will, and we ask God to help us.

Prayer appropriate to the ministry being recognized is said, and prayers for other ministries may also be said, using one or more of the following, or in similar words.
Let us pray.

The ministry of worship

God of grace, you gather us into one and nourish us with
word and sacrament,
and we give you thanks in worship and with our lives.
Bless those who serve as _____,
that your word may be proclaimed with clarity,
that your banquet may be served with joy and reverence,
that your house may reflect your glory,
and that all who are gathered may know your welcome;
through Jesus Christ, our Savior and Lord.
Amen.

or

O God of majesty, saints and angels delight to worship you,
and by grace we join their unending hymn.
Bless those who serve among us as _____,
that in worship we may sound forth the joy of your presence
and make music to the glory of your name;
through Jesus Christ, our Savior and Lord.
Amen.

The ministry of education

O God of wisdom, in your goodness
you provide faithful teachers for your church.
Bless those who serve as _____.
Help us all to study your word and engage your world,
that together we may grow in knowledge and love,
pursue what is good, and seek to do your will;
through Jesus Christ, our Savior and Lord.
Amen.

The ministry of witness

O God of our salvation,
you sent your Son to gather the whole world into your embrace.
Bless those who serve as _____,
and send us all forth as witnesses to Christ in word and deed,
proclaiming boldly the power of his forgiveness
and the hope of his resurrection;
through the same Jesus Christ, our Savior and Lord.
Amen.

The ministry of service

O God of mercy, your Son washed the feet of his disciples
and commanded us to love one another as he loves us.
Bless those who carry out the ministry of _____
in word and deed.
Send us all forth with the will to serve others
as he was the servant of all,
Jesus Christ, our Savior and Lord.
Amen.

The ministry of stewardship

O God, creator of heaven and earth,
we thank you for the many gifts we receive from your bounty.
Bless those who serve among us as _____,
who call us to exercise care and stewardship for all your gifts.
Move us to respond in gratitude to your gracious goodness;
through Jesus Christ, our Savior and Lord.
Amen.

Prayers for other ministries may be said.

*The order may conclude with one of the following or another
suitable prayer.*

Let us pray.
We give you thanks, O God,
for all who respond to the call to serve in your name.
Give them joy and fulfillment,
care and guidance in their tasks.
Help us all to give willingly and to receive thankfully
the gifts of ministry,
that your name may be glorified,
your people live in peace,
and your will be done;
through Jesus Christ, our Savior and Lord.
Amen.

or

Almighty God,
your Holy Spirit equips the church with a rich variety of gifts.
Grant that we may use them to bear witness to Christ
in lives that are built on faith and love.
Make us ready to live the gospel and eager to do your will,
so that we may share with all your church
in the joys of eternal life;
through Jesus Christ, our Savior and Lord.
Amen.

The service concludes with the blessing and dismissal.

NOTES ON THE SERVICE

This order brings to the attention of the congregation the mission and ministry to which all the baptized are called. It specifically recognizes those who are or will be serving in particular ministries of the congregation, especially those serving as volunteers. Those completing a time of service such as a term of office may also be recognized, as well as those who may be celebrating an anniversary of service.

The entire order may be used on a day when the congregation chooses to celebrate and recognize all of those involved in ministries. Or, the appropriate part of the order may be used to recognize a particular ministry on a special day (such as when teaching and learning are central, when an outreach emphasis is planned, when attention is given to church music and the arts, or when committees are chosen and begin functioning).

The order is included in the sending section of the service in order to make the connection between the sending of the assembly into God's mission and those particular avenues of ministry through which that mission is carried out in the congregation's work. An alternative location for the order is before the prayers of intercession.

A recognition of worship ministry may include acolytes, ushers and ministers of hospitality, sacristans and altar guild members, assisting ministers, readers, communion ministers within the assembly or to the homebound, volunteer church musicians, singers and instrumentalists, and worship committee members.

A recognition of education ministry may include church school teachers, superintendents, catechists, mentors, youth advisers, nursery workers, and education committee members. Depending on the circumstances, either this order or Installation of Lay Professional Staff may be appropriate for day school teachers or early childhood center teachers who are not on one of the churchwide rosters.

A recognition of witness ministry may include evangelism visitors, ministers of hospitality, mission development team members, and evangelism committee members.

A recognition of service ministry may include pastoral care team members, visitors to the hospitalized and homebound, those engaged in community ministries of service and justice, and social ministry committee members.

A recognition of stewardship ministry may include stewardship callers, volunteer coordinators, those who care for finances and property, and stewardship committee members.

Certificates of service or other tokens of appreciation may be presented to those completing a time of service, either after that section of the rite or at another suitable time.

From *Evangelical Lutheran Worship Occasional Services for the Assembly* (Augsburg Fortress, 2009).

January 9, 2011
Baptism of Our Lord
Lectionary 1

In the waters of the Jordan, Jesus is revealed as the beloved Son of God. Through this great epiphany, Jesus fulfills all righteousness and becomes the servant of God who will bring forth justice and be a light to the nations. In the waters of baptism we too are washed by the Word, anointed by the Spirit, and named God's beloved children. Our baptismal mission is to proclaim good news to all who are oppressed or in need of God's healing.

Prayer of the Day

O God our Father, at the baptism of Jesus you proclaimed him your beloved Son and anointed him with the Holy Spirit. Make all who are baptized into Christ faithful to their calling to be your daughters and sons, and empower us all with your Spirit, through Jesus Christ, our Savior and Lord, who lives and reigns with you and the Holy Spirit, one God, now and forever.

Gospel Acclamation

Alleluia. A voice from heaven said, "This is my Son, [|] the Beloved,* with whom I [|] am well pleased." *Alleluia.* (Matt. 3:17)

Readings and Psalm
Isaiah 42:1-9

God's servant Israel is endowed with the Spirit in order to bring justice to the nations. The servant will not exercise authority boisterously or with violence, nor will weariness ever keep it from fulfilling its task. God's old promises have been fulfilled; the new assignment of the servant is to bring light to the nations.

Psalm 29

The voice of the Lord is upon the waters. (Ps. 29:3)

Acts 10:34-43

Peter crosses the sharp religious boundary separating Jews from Gentiles and proclaims the good news of God's inclusive forgiveness in Jesus' name to Cornelius, a Roman centurion. As a result of Peter's preaching, Cornelius and his family become the first Gentiles to be baptized in the name of Jesus Christ.

Matthew 3:13-17

Before Jesus begins his ministry, he is baptized by John, touched by the Spirit, and identified publicly as God's child.

Preface   Baptism of Our Lord

Color   White

Prayers of Intercession

The prayers are prepared locally for each occasion. The following examples may be adapted or used as appropriate.

As God's beloved children, let us pray that the light of Christ shine on the nations, the church, and all those in need.
A brief silence.

That you raise up prophets in the church to call us to faithful service on behalf of the oppressed and all who suffer, let us pray.
Have mercy, O God.

That we honor your creation and the gift of water by caring for oceans, lakes, rivers, and streams (*especially . . . a local body of water may be named*), let us pray.
Have mercy, O God.

That leaders of nations show no partiality as they work for the good of all, especially immigrants, refugees, prisoners, and those without a voice in our societies, let us pray.
Have mercy, O God.

That the light of your healing shine on those living with illness, addiction, loneliness, or anxiety (*especially*), let us pray.
Have mercy, O God.

That you strengthen this assembly to live out our baptismal promises as we witness to your grace in our homes, workplaces, and communities, let us pray.
Have mercy, O God.

Here other intercessions may be offered.

That with the faithful departed we may see the heavens opened and hear your voice declare us beloved daughters and sons, let us pray.
Have mercy, O God.
Receive our prayers and our hopes, God of mercy and justice, for we pray in the name of Christ, the light of the world.
Amen.

Ideas and Images for the Day

Frederick Dale Bruner, in *Matthew: A Commentary* (Grand Rapids: Eerdmans, 2004), says that he considers Jesus' first miracle to have occurred at his baptism. The miracle is that Jesus was humble. The divine Son of God humbles himself by allowing John to baptize him. This act of humility is an act of obedience to God and solidarity with all humankind. Jesus has no sins to be forgiven. However, for us, he goes down to the river of repentance with all the other sinners to be baptized. Jesus' baptism, his first adult act as recorded in Matthew's gospel, gives us a clear indication of how Jesus will act for his entire life. The Son of God will come down with us, on our level, identifying with our needs, all the way to the cross.

1. The song "Jesus loves me!" (ELW 595) reminds us that we know Jesus loves us because the Bible tells us so. In Matthew's gospel, Jesus first demonstrates this by being baptized. Jesus' decision to be baptized is a clear witness of Christ's love for us. Sing, "Jesus loves me! this I know, for his *baptism* tells me so." Invite the assembly to sing along. You could also use a pine bough dipped in the water of the font to sprinkle the assembly.

2. Imagine the scene in the wilderness around the Jordan River as Jesus approached. John, dressed in camel's hair, wading knee deep in the river, was shouting at the crowds who had come from all of Judea to confess their sins. The scene might have resembled a carnival, filled with chaotic activity and sinners of all kinds. It doesn't sound like the place you would find holiness or divine love, but that is exactly what happens. In the title song of her album *Carnival Love* (Capitol, 2000), Amy Correia sings about how the side-show workers in a carnival, cast out by the rest of the world, find love with one another because they are able to love each for exactly who they are. Jesus, in his baptism, says he loves us exactly for who we are. Find the song on iTunes or Amazon or see her Web site: http://amycorreia.com.

3. Why do those being baptized often wear special clothes? Because in baptism we are clothed with Christ.

Baptismal garments symbolize how, as Christ identified with us in his baptism, we are connected to Christ in our baptism. We put on his identity as God's beloved daughters and sons. A liturgical song that could be used to highlight this is "You have put on Christ" (ELW 211).

4. Jesus' baptism in the Jordan River symbolizes how in Christ the barriers between us are broken down. The ELCA's Peace Not Walls campaign (http://www.elca.org/peacenotwalls) invites us to learn, pray, and act for peace in a deeply divided present-day Holy Land.

Hymns for Worship
Gathering
I bind unto myself today   ELW 450, LBW 188
Crashing waters at creation   ELW 455
Hail to the Lord's anointed   ELW 311, LBW 87

Hymn of the Day
When Jesus came to Jordan   ELW 305, WOV 647
   KING'S LYNN
Christ, when for us you were baptized   ELW 304
   LOBT GOTT, IHR CHRISTEN
Waterlife   ELW 457, W&P 145   *WATERLIFE*

Offering
Songs of thankfulness and praise   ELW 310, LBW 90
Arise, your light has come!   ELW 314, WOV 652

Communion
Come, beloved of the Maker   ELW 306
Baptized and Set Free   ELW 453
Brightest and best of the stars   ELW 303, LBW 84

Sending
The only Son from heaven   ELW 309, LBW 86
I'm going on a journey   ELW 446

Additional Hymns and Songs
Song over the waters   W&P 127
Baptized into your name most holy   LBW 192
Mark how the Lamb of God's self-offering   HFG 141, NCH 167

Music for the Day
Psalmody and Acclamations
Ferguson, John. *Gospel Acclamations for Advent–Transfiguration.*
Mummert, Mark. "Psalm 29," Refrain 1, from PSCY.
Wetzler, Robert. "Psalm 29" from PWA, Evangelical Lutheran Worship Edition.

Choral

Foley, John. "Come to the Water." SATB, cong, pno, inst. OCP 9489.

Highben, Zebulon M. "I'm Going on a Journey." U, pno, DB, tenor sax, opt solo, opt assembly. AFP 9780800664022.

Pasch, William Allen. "Baptized in Jordan." SATB. AFP 9780800664169.

Pinkham, Daniel. "For the Gift of Water." SATB, opt org. ECS 5204.

Children's Choir

Cool, Jayne Southwick. "With the Help of the Spirit of the Lord." U/2 pt, kybd. CG CGA508

French Traditional. "I Was Baptized, Happy Day!" from *LifeSongs*. LE, U, kybd.

Weber, Paul. "When You Pass Through the Waters." U/2 pt, kybd. MSM 50-0501.

Keyboard / Instrumental

o Cherwien, David. "King's Lynn" from *Augsburg Organ Library: Baptism and Communion*. Org. AFP 9780800623555.

o Porter, Rachel Trelstad. "King's Lynn" from *Introductions and Alternate Accompaniments for Piano*, vol. 2. Pno. AFP 9780800639150.

o Sedio, Mark. "King's Lynn" from *How Blessed This Place*. Org. AFP 9780800658038.

o Walther, Johann Gottfried. "Lobt Gott, ihr Christen." Org. Various editions.

Handbell

Afdahl, Lee. "Danish Star Carol."2-3 oct, L2. ALF 00-23145.

Honoré, Jeffrey. "Go My Children, with My Blessing." 3 or 5 oct, L2. CPH 97-7344.

Larson, Katherine Jordahl. "Beautiful Savior." 3-4 oct, L2. AFP 9780800653965.

Praise Ensemble

Bell, John. "Will You Come and Follow Me?" GIA. ELW 798

● Carpenter, Kelly. "Draw Me Close." Mercy/VIN.

● Foote, Billy/Charles Horne. "Sing to the King." WT/Sixsteps Music.

● Haugen, Marty. "Awake, O Sleeper." GIA.

● Haugen, Marty. "Song over the Waters." GIA. W&P 127

● Smith, Henry. "Give Thanks." INT.

Global

Belihu, Almaz. "When Jesus Worked Here on Earth" from *Set Free: A Collection of African Hymns*. SATB. AFP 9780806600451.

Sedio, Mark, arr. "Nimemwona Bwana/We Have Seen the Lord" from *Global Choral Sounds*. SATB. CPH 98-3610. ELW 869.

Saturday, January 15

Martin Luther King Jr., renewer of society, martyr, died 1968

Martin Luther King Jr. is remembered as an American prophet of justice among races and nations, a Christian whose faith undergirded his advocacy of vigorous yet nonviolent action for racial equality. A pastor of churches in Montgomery, Alabama, and Atlanta, Georgia, his witness was taken to the streets in such other places as Birmingham, Alabama, where he was arrested and jailed while protesting against segregation. He preached nonviolence and demanded that love be returned for hate. Awarded the Nobel Peace Prize in 1964, he was killed by an assassin on April 4, 1968. Though most commemorations are held on the date of the person's death, many churches hold commemorations near Dr. King's birth date of January 15, in conjunction with the American civil holiday honoring him. An alternate date for the commemoration would be his death date, April 4.

o denotes suggestions that relate to the hymn of the day.
● denotes songs that are available on iTunes®.

82

January 16, 2011
Second Sunday after Epiphany
Lectionary 2

Today's gospel opens with further reflection on Jesus' baptism. He is the Lamb of God who takes away the sin of the world, and the one anointed by the Spirit. In the liturgy we come and see Christ revealed among us in word and meal. We go forth to invite others to come and worship the Holy One, and to receive the gifts of grace and peace made known among us.

Prayer of the Day

Holy God, our strength and our redeemer, by your Spirit hold us forever, that through your grace we may worship you and faithfully serve you, follow you and joyfully find you, through Jesus Christ, our Savior and Lord.

Gospel Acclamation

Alleluia. In the ˡ Word was life,* and the life was the light ˡ of all people. *Alleluia.* (John 1:4)

Readings and Psalm

Isaiah 49:1-7

Here the servant Israel speaks for herself and acknowledges herself as God's secret weapon. Called before her birth like Jeremiah and John the Baptist, the servant is not only to restore Israel itself. The servant's ultimate assignment is to bring news of God's victory to the ends of the earth. God in faithfulness has chosen Israel for this task.

Psalm 40:1-11

I love to do your will, O my God. (Ps. 40:8)

1 Corinthians 1:1-9

Though God's church in Corinth is a fractious congregation beset with many conflicts, Paul opens this letter by spotlighting the multiple ways God has enriched and sustained its life as part of the divine call into the fellowship of our Lord Jesus Christ.

John 1:29-42

John the Baptist's witness to Jesus initiates a chain of testimony as his disciples begin to share with others what they have found.

Preface   Sundays

Color   Green

Prayers of Intercession

The prayers are prepared locally for each occasion. The following examples may be adapted or used as appropriate.

As God's beloved children, let us pray that the light of Christ shine on the nations, the church, and all those in need.
A brief silence.

For leaders in the church and all the baptized, that we may invite others to come and see Christ revealed in water and word, bread and wine. Lord, in your mercy,
hear our prayer.

For our nation, for our president and the members of congress, that we labor together for the common good, raising up those overwhelmed by poverty or violence. Lord, in your mercy,
hear our prayer.

For coastlands and distant islands, for urban, suburban, and rural communities, that in using wisely the resources of the earth, we honor your creation. Lord, in your mercy,
hear our prayer.

For those unemployed or underemployed, for those living with oppression, poverty, hunger, illness, or anxiety (*especially*), that you strengthen them with grace and courage in the face of their need. Lord, in your mercy,
hear our prayer.

For our community of faith, for those living in care facilities and those absent from us, and for those seeking signs of your presence, that you nourish us all at your bountiful table. Lord, in your mercy,
hear our prayer.

Here other intercessions may be offered.

We give you thanks for all your holy ones who served you in life and now rest in your peace. Gather us, with them, until the day of your coming in glory. Lord, in your mercy,
hear our prayer.

Receive our prayers and hopes, God of mercy and justice, for we pray in the name of Christ, the light of the world.
Amen.

Ideas and Images for the Day

The time after Epiphany is the church's time to invite us to come and see who this one born in a manger will be, and to discover what this one born to a young woman might mean for us and for the world. Today's gospel tells us that Jesus is the "Lamb of God who takes away the sin of the world," "the Son of God," and "the Messiah." These appellations show us that the coming of Jesus has meaning not just for those who follow him, but for all people and all the world. As we are invited to "come and see" who Jesus is, we are reminded that God's forgiveness and love proclaimed in Jesus Christ is meant to be good news for all people. Like John and Andrew in today's gospel, we are called to share with others who we have seen Jesus to be.

1. *National Geographic* published an astonishing photograph by James Snyder of a frog that swallowed a Christmas light (September 2009, p. 6). You can see the light glowing through the body of the frog. What do we do with the light of Christ that was revealed to us at Christmas? Do we swallow it up and keep it to ourselves, or do we let it shine for all to come and see? See the image at http://ngm.nationalgeographic.com/your-shot/top-shots-2009.

2. That God came to earth in such an unlikely way, born in a stable to a teenage mother, shows us that there is no place so lowly or so unlikely that God cannot be seen there. Where are the desolate places in your life, in your community, in your world where God might be present in ways that you have not thought to look?

3. The membership of Lutheran churches is growing the fastest in Africa, and is in decline in Europe and North America. What might North American Lutherans learn from their sisters and brothers in Africa about how to invite others to "come and see" who Jesus is? Christians of the Mafa ethnic group of Cameroon commissioned a series of images depicting Jesus as an African in order to highlight the universal message of Christ's coming into the world and Christ's identification with all peoples. The image of Jesus calling his first two disciples, from today's gospel, can be seen at http://jesusmafa.com/anglais/pagetprod2.htm.

4. "Show and tell" is another way to say "come and see." Most children are familiar with bringing something they treasure from home to school and showing it to their classmates as they tell about what it is.

Perhaps children could be asked to bring something to show and tell at church, or the leader could show and tell about Jesus, or the children could be asked how they might show and tell about Jesus in their school or neighborhood or home.

Hymns for Worship
Gathering
O God of light   ELW 507, LBW 237
Christ, whose glory fills the skies   ELW 553, LBW 265
Rise, shine, you people!   ELW 665, LBW 393

Hymn of the Day
The only Son from heaven   ELW 309, LBW 86
   HERR CHRIST, DER EINIG GOTTS SOHN
Hail to the Lord's anointed   ELW 311, LBW 87
   FREUT EUCH, IHR LIEBEN
Come, beloved of the Maker   ELW 306   JILL

Offering
We have seen the Lord   ELW 869
Now the silence   ELW 460, LBW 205

Communion
Now behold the Lamb   ELW 341, TFF 128
He comes to us as one unknown   ELW 737, WOV 768
Christ, Be Our Light   ELW 715

Sending
We are marching in the light   ELW 866, WOV 650
This little light of mine   ELW 677, TFF 65

Additional Hymns and Songs
Listen! You nations of the world   LBW 14
You are my hiding place   W&P 160

Music for the Day
Psalmody and Acclamations
Ferguson, John. *Gospel Acclamations for Advent–Transfiguration.*
Folkening, John. "Psalm 40:1-11" from PWA, Evangelical Lutheran Worship Edition.
Wold, Wayne L. "Psalm 40" from PSCY.

Choral
Bell, John A. "The Summons (Will You Come and Follow Me)." 2 pt mxd or SA, pno, fl, opt gtr, opt assembly. GIA G-5410.
Keesecker, Thomas. "Around You, O Lord Jesus." SAB, pno, opt hb. AFP 9780800664336.
Simon, Julia. "Follow Me." U/opt 2 pt, pno. AFP 9780800664046.

Willan, Healey. "Behold the Lamb of God." SATB or 2 pt mxd, org. CPH 98-1509.

Children's Choir

Bouman, Paul. "Behold the Lamb of God." 2 pt, kybd. CPH 98-1088WEB.

Russian folksong. "Come into God's Presence" from *LifeSongs*. LE, U, kybd. AFP 9780806642703.

Wold, Wayne. "Lamb of God." U, org. MSM 80-830.

Keyboard / Instrumental

o Bach, J. C. "Herr Christ, der einig Gotts Sohn." Org. Various editions.

o Burkhardt, Michael. "Freut euch, ihr lieben" from *Five Christmas Hymn Improvisations*, set 1. Org. MSM 10-111.

o Busarow, Donald. "Herr Christ, der einig Gotts Sohn" from *With Music Crowned*. Org, 2 inst. CPH 97-7324U1.

o Schmidt, Thomas. "Freut euch, ihr lieben" from *All Glory Be to God on High*. Org. MSM 10-562.

Handbell

o Kinyon, Barbara. "Hail to the Lord's Anointed." 2-3 oct, L2+. JEF JHS9100.

Lamb, Linda. "Jesus Calls Us O'er the Tumult." 2-3 oct, L3+. GIA G-6591.

Tucker, Sondra. "I Want to Walk as a Child of the Light." 3-5 oct, L3. AFP 9780800658861.

Praise Ensemble

• Green, Melody. "There Is a Redeemer." Birdwing Music. W&P 140.

• Jernigan, Dennis. "You Are My All in All (Jesus, Lamb of God)." Shepherd's Heart Music. W&P 76.

• Ledner, Michael. "You Are My Hiding Place." MAR. W&P 160

• Millard, Bart/Pete Kipley. "Word of God, Speak." Simpleville Music.

• Paris, Twila. "Lamb of God." Straightway Music/Mountain Spring Music. ELW 336.

• Wimber, John. "Spirit Song." Mercy/VIN. W&P 130.

Global

African American spiritual, arr. Mark Sedio. "We Believe That This Is Jesus" from *Global Choral Sounds*. SATB. CPH 98-3610.

Rantatalo, Matti, arr. Mark Sedio. "Oi, Jumalan Karitsa/Agnus Dei/Lamb of God" from *Global Choral Sounds*. SATB. CPH 98-3610.

Monday, January 17

Antony of Egypt, renewer of the church, died around 356

Antony was born in Qemen-al-Arous, Upper Egypt, and was one of the earliest Egyptian desert fathers. Born to Christian parents from whom he inherited a large estate, he took personally Jesus' message to sell all that you have, give to the poor, and follow Christ. After making arrangements to provide for the care of his sister, he gave away his inheritance and became a hermit. Later, he became the head of a group of monks who lived in a cluster of huts and devoted themselves to communal prayer, worship, and manual labor under Antony's direction. The money they earned from their work was distributed as alms. Antony and his monks also preached and counseled those who sought them out. Antony and the desert fathers serve as a reminder that certain times and circumstances call Christians to stand apart from the surrounding culture and renounce the world in service to Christ.

Pachomius, renewer of the church, died 346

Another of the desert fathers, Pachomius (puh-KOME-ee-us) was born in Egypt about 290. He became a Christian during his service as a soldier. In 320 he went to live as a hermit in Upper Egypt, where other hermits lived nearby. Pachomius organized them into a religious community in which the members prayed together and held their goods in common. His rule for monasteries influenced both Eastern and Western monasticism through the Rule of Basil and the Rule of Benedict, respectively.

Tuesday, January 18

Confession of Peter
Week of Prayer for Christian Unity begins

The Week of Prayer for Christian Unity is framed by two commemorations, the Confession of Peter (a relatively recent addition to the calendar) and the older Conversion of Paul. Both apostles are remembered together on June 29, but these two days give us an opportunity to focus on key events in each of their lives. Today we remember that Peter was led by God's grace to acknowledge Jesus as "the Christ, the Son of the living God" (Matt. 16:16). This confession is the common confession that unites us with Peter and with all Christians of every time and place.

o denotes suggestions that relate to the hymn of the day.
• denotes songs that are available on iTunes®.

Wednesday, January 19

Henry, Bishop of Uppsala, martyr, died 1156

Henry, an Englishman, became bishop of Uppsala, Sweden, in 1152 and is regarded as the patron of Finland. He traveled to Finland with the king of Sweden on a mission trip and remained there to organize the church. He was murdered in Finland by a man he had rebuked and who was disciplined by the church. Henry's burial place became a center of pilgrimage. His popularity as a saint is strong in both Sweden and Finland.

Friday, January 21

Agnes, martyr, died around 304

Agnes was a girl of about thirteen living in Rome, who had chosen a life of service to Christ as a virgin, despite the Roman emperor Diocletian's ruling that had outlawed all Christian activity. The details of her martyrdom are not clear, but she gave witness to her faith and was put to death as a result, most likely by the sword. Since her death, the church has honored her as one of the chief martyrs of her time.

January 23, 2011
Third Sunday after Epiphany
Lectionary 3

Jesus begins his public ministry by calling fishers to leave their nets and follow him. In Jesus the kingdom of God has come near. We who have walked in darkness have seen a great light. We see this light most profoundly in the cross—as God suffers with us and all who are oppressed by sickness, sin, or evil. Light dawns for us as we gather around the word, the font, and the holy table. We are then sent to share the good news that others may be "caught" in the net of God's grace and mercy.

Prayer of the Day

Lord God, your lovingkindness always goes before us and follows after us. Summon us into your light, and direct our steps in the ways of goodness that come through the cross of your Son, Jesus Christ, our Savior and Lord.

Gospel Acclamation

Alleluia. Jesus preached the good news [1] of the kingdom* and cured every sickness a- [1] mong the people. *Alleluia.* (Matt. 4:23)

Readings and Psalm

Isaiah 9:1-4

The northern tribes of Zebulun and Naphtali experienced defeat, but they are assured that their condition will be reversed when God makes a light-filled appearance. The joy they will experience will resemble celebrations of great harvests, because God will deliver them from everything that diminishes or oppresses them. The people in the northern parts of Israel have experienced "gloom" and "darkness" because of the destruction wrought by Assyrian military forces. To these people, the prophet announces the shining of a great light of salvation.

Psalm 27:1, 4-9

The Lord is my light and my salvation. (Ps. 27:1)

1 Corinthians 1:10-18

Paul calls on the Corinthians to end their dissensions and share the unified outlook of the gospel. Discord arises when we forget that we belong not to human leaders or institutions but to Christ who was crucified for us. Indeed, the unifying word of the cross of Christ is the center of the gospel and the power of God's salvation.

Matthew 4:12-23

Jesus begins his public ministry shortly after John the Baptist is imprisoned by Herod. He proclaims the nearness of God's reign and calls four fishermen to be his first disciples.

Preface   Sundays

Color   Green

Prayers of Intercession

The prayers are prepared locally for each occasion. The following examples may be adapted or used as appropriate.

As God's beloved children, let us pray that the light of Christ shine on the nations, the church, and all those in need.

A brief silence.

For our communities of faith, that, turning from quarreling and division, we may find our unity in the cross of Christ. Lord, in your mercy,

hear our prayer.

For the nations of the world, and for an end to oppression, hunger, and violence. Lord, in your mercy,

hear our prayer.

For all who care for water, soil, plants, and animals, and that we may live with greater simplicity and love for creation. Lord, in your mercy,

hear our prayer.

For all living with disease, grief, conflict, poverty, depression, or despair (*especially*), that your healing may dawn on them. Lord, in your mercy,

hear our prayer.

For this congregation and its leaders, that our ministries of preaching, teaching, and healing may proclaim the good news of your kingdom. Lord, in your mercy,

hear our prayer.

Here other intercessions may be offered.

Gather us, with all the saints, into the wide net of your grace, that we may follow you with faith and courage. Lord, in your mercy,

hear our prayer.

Receive our prayers and hopes, God of mercy and justice, for we pray in the name of Christ, the light of the world.

Amen.

Ideas and Images for the Day

In today's gospel, Jesus, who first withdraws (Matt. 4:12), also invites others to follow him (4:19, 21). The word *anachoreo* (to withdraw) is used ten times in Matthew's gospel—each time as Jesus' response to violence or conflict. In Jesus, a new kingdom has drawn near, a kingdom of nonviolence and nonretaliation. Jesus' withdrawal is not simply passivity but points to a vision of an alternate way of reigning as sovereign. Into this new reign, Jesus calls the disciples to follow

him, a way that will eventually lead to the cross. The way appears foolish and weak to those who cannot discern it, but to those God calls, it is wisdom and strength, the light and power of God.

1. In the film *Hotel Rwanda* (United Artists, 2004), the main character, Paul Rusesabagina, a hotel manager, faces the violence of the Rwandan genocide by providing refuge for those fleeing their homes. His action is not without risk, as those in power threaten the lives of Paul and his family. However, by retaliating not with violent force but with compassion, generosity, and courage, Paul shines as a light in the darkness of war. Baptized into Christ's death and resurrection, disciples are called to shine as lights in a dark world. How is this call risky at times?

2. Martin Luther writes, "The chief article and foundation of the gospel is that before you take Christ as an example, you . . . recognize him as a gift, as a present that God has given you that is your own ("A Brief Introduction on What to Look for and Expect in the Gospels [1521]," *Martin Luther's Basic Theological Writings*, Timothy F. Lull, ed. [Minneapolis: Fortress Press, 1989], p. 106). In other words, before the doing of the law, Christ comes as gift and blessing. Today's gospel holds two commands from Jesus: repent (Matt. 4:17) and follow me (4:19). First, God's kingdom draws near in the gift of Jesus; afterwards, repentance and discipleship follow.

3. The hymn "We are marching in the light" (ELW 866) has its roots in resistance to apartheid as people claimed God's reign of justice and peace as their own in the midst of oppression. If the congregational context is appropriate, use this resistance hymn. Another hymn appropriate for the day is "Christ, Be Our Light" (ELW 715), which sings of longing for light, peace, food, and shelter, and also suggests ways that disciples participate in God's reign by being light, peace, food, and shelter for others.

4. Invite children to play follow the leader during a children's time. When we follow the leader, what do we do? We imitate the leader's actions. Tell the story of Jesus calling the disciples to follow him. What kind of leader was Jesus? Encourage children to think about how they follow Jesus and what actions of Jesus we might try to embody as disciples. Consider passing out shoeprints for children to draw or write ideas on once they return to their seats.

Hymns for Worship

Gathering

Thy strong word   ELW 511, LBW 233
I want to walk as a child of the light   ELW 815, WOV 649
Come, follow me, the Savior spake   ELW 799, LBW 455

Hymn of the Day

O Christ, our light, O Radiance true   ELW 675, LBW 380
O JESUS CHRISTE, WAHRES LICHT
Thy strong word   ELW 511, LBW 233   *EBENEZER*
Christ, Be Our Light   ELW 715   *CHRIST, BE OUR LIGHT*

Offering

Drawn to the Light   ELW 593
Listen, God is calling   ELW 513, WOV 712, TFF 130

Communion

Come, beloved of the Maker   ELW 306
You have come down to the lakeshore   ELW 817, WOV 784
The Son of God, our Christ   ELW 584, LBW 434

Sending

Lift every voice and sing   ELW 841, LBW 562, TFF 296
I love to tell the story   ELW 661, LBW 390, TFF 228

Additional Hymns and Songs

Now we offer   WOV 761, TFF 129
They cast their nets   LBW 449
Christ calls us now, as long ago   ASF 29

Music for the Day

Psalmody and Acclamations

Ferguson, John. *Gospel Acclamations for Advent–Transfiguration.*
Nelson, Ronald A. "Psalm 27:1, 4-9" from PWA, Evangelical Lutheran Worship Edition.
Organ, Anne Krentz. "Psalm 27:1, 4-9" from PSCY.
"The Lord Is My Light." TFF 61.

Choral

○ Busarow, Donald. "Thy Strong Word." SAB, assembly, org, 2 tpts. MSM 60-9000.
○ Hobby, Robert A. "O Christ Our Light, O Radiance True." 2 pt mxd, ob, kybd. CPH 98-2891U50.
Martinson, Joel. "We All Are One in Mission" from *Augsburg Easy Choirbook*, vol. 2. 2 pt mxd, org. AFP 9780800677510.
○ Thomas, Andre. "Walk in the Light." SATB, pno. CG CGA-1063.

Children's Choir

Fischer-Armstrong, June. "I Am the Light of the World" from *Life-Songs*. U, kybd.
Paradowski, John. "Arise and Shine." U/2 pt, kybd, opt hb. CG CGA1039.

Zorzin, Alejandro. "Jesus Brings a Message" from *LifeSongs*. U, kybd.

Keyboard / Instrumental

○ Hobby, Robert A. "Ebenezer" from *Three Epiphany Preludes*, set 2. Org. MSM 10-209.
○ Miller, Aaron David. "O Jesu Christe, wahres Licht" from *Introductions and Alternate Accompaniments for Piano*, vol. 7. Pno. AFP 9780800623654.
○ Schmoltze, Ron. "Ebenezer" from *A Song in the Journey*. Org. AFP 9780800679026.
○ Trapp, Lynn. "Christ, Be Our Light" from *Jubilee*, vol. III. Org. CPH 97-7245U1.

Handbell

○ Behnke, John. "Thy Strong Word." 3-5 oct, L2. CPH 97-7113.
Waldrop, Tammy. "How Deep the Father's Love for Us." 3-5 oct hb, opt 7 hc, opt narr, L2+. ALF 00-31749.
Wissinger, Kathleen. "Light and Shine." 3-5 oct hb, opt 3 oct hc, L3. HOP 2467.

Praise Ensemble

● Brown, Brenton. "Lord, Reign in Me." VIN.
● Farrell, Bernadette. "Christ, Be Our Light." OCP. ELW 715.
● Tomlin, Chris. "We Fall Down." WT.
● Tomlin, Chris/Daniel Carson/Ed Cash/Jesse Reeves. "Jesus Messiah." WT/Sixsteps Music.
● Walker, Tommy. "He Knows My Name." Doulos Publishing.
● Zschech, Darlene. "The Potter's Hand." Hillsong/INT.

Global

Bouknight, Lillian, arr. Paul Gainer. "The Lord Is My Light." SATB. TFF 61.
Czech hymn tune. "The Lord Is My Light" from *Many and Great: Songs of the World Church*. SSATB. GIA G-3649.

Tuesday, January 25

Conversion of Paul

Week of Prayer for Christian Unity ends

Today the Week of Prayer for Christian Unity comes to an end. The church remembers how a man of Tarsus named Saul, a former persecutor of the early Christian church, was turned around by God's grace to become one of its chief preachers. The risen Christ appeared to Paul on the road to Damascus and called him to proclaim the gospel. The narratives describing Paul's conversion in the Acts of the Apostles, Galatians, and 1 Corinthians inspire this commemoration, which was first celebrated among the Christians of Gaul.

○ denotes suggestions that relate to the hymn of the day.
● denotes songs that are available on iTunes®.

Wednesday, January 26

Timothy, Titus, and Silas, missionaries

On the two days following the celebration of the Conversion of Paul, his companions are remembered. Timothy, Titus, and Silas were missionary coworkers with Paul. Timothy accompanied Paul on his second missionary journey and was commissioned by Paul to go to Ephesus, where he served as bishop and overseer of the church. Titus was a traveling companion of Paul, accompanied him on the trip to the council of Jerusalem, and became the first bishop of Crete. Silas traveled with Paul through Asia Minor and Greece and was imprisoned with him at Philippi, where they were delivered by an earthquake.

Thursday, January 27

Lydia, Dorcas, and Phoebe, witnesses to the faith

On this day the church remembers three women who were companions in Paul's ministry. Lydia was Paul's first convert at Philippi in Macedonia. She was a merchant of purple-dyed goods, and because purple dye was extremely expensive, it is likely that Lydia was a woman of some wealth. Lydia and her household were baptized by Paul, and for a time her home was a base for Paul's missionary work. Dorcas is remembered for her charitable works, particularly making clothing for needy widows. Phoebe was a *diakonos*, a deaconess in the church at Cenchreae, near Corinth. Paul praises her as one who, through her service, looked after many people.

Friday, January 28

Thomas Aquinas, teacher, died 1274

Thomas Aquinas (uh-KWY-nus) was a brilliant and creative theologian of the thirteenth century. He was first and foremost a student of the Bible and profoundly concerned with the theological formation of the church's ordained ministers. As a member of the Order of Preachers (Dominicans), he worked to correlate scripture with the philosophy of Aristotle, which was having a renaissance in Aquinas's day. Some students of Aristotle's philosophy found in it an alternative to Christianity. But Aquinas immersed himself in the thought of Aristotle and worked to explain Christian beliefs in the philosophical culture of the day.

January 30, 2011
Fourth Sunday after Epiphany
Lectionary 4

Who are the blessed ones of God? For Micah, they are those who do justice, love kindness, and walk humbly with God. For Paul, they are the ones who find wisdom in the weakness of the cross. For Jesus, they are the poor, mourners, the meek, those who hunger for righteousness, the merciful, the pure in heart, the peacemakers. In baptism we find our blessed identity and calling in this countercultural way of living and serving.

Prayer of the Day

Holy God, you confound the world's wisdom in giving your kingdom to the lowly and the pure in heart. Give us such a hunger and thirst for justice, and perseverance in striving for peace, that in our words and deeds the world may see the life of your Son, Jesus Christ, our Savior and Lord.

Gospel Acclamation

Alleluia. Rejoice | and be glad,* for your reward is | great in heaven. *Alleluia.* (Matt. 5:12)

Readings and Psalm

Micah 6:1-8

With the mountains and the foundations of the earth as the jury, God brings a lawsuit against Israel. God has "wearied" Israel with a long history of saving acts. God does not want or expect lavish sacrifices to attempt to earn divine favor. Rather God empowers the people to do justice, to love loyalty to God, and to walk shrewdly in God's service.

Psalm 15

Lord, who may abide upon your holy hill? (Ps. 15:1)

I Corinthians 1:18-31

According to the world's standards of power and might, the message of the cross seems stupid and offensive. Yet this word reveals the paradoxical way God has chosen to work power and salvation through weakness, rejection, and suffering. Hence the message of the cross becomes true wisdom and power for believers.

Matthew 5:1-12

Jesus opens the Sermon on the Mount by naming those who are blessed in the reign of God.

Preface   Sundays

Color   Green

Prayers of Intercession

The prayers are prepared locally for each occasion. The following examples may be adapted or used as appropriate.

As God's beloved children, let us pray that the light of Christ shine on the nations, the church, and all those in need.
A brief silence.

That the church may proclaim Christ crucified and announce your blessing on the poor in spirit, and those who hunger and thirst for righteousness. Hear us, O God.
Your mercy is great.

That all government and civic leaders turn from self-interest and seek justice, kindness, and humility. Hear us, O God.
Your mercy is great.

That we treat the earth with reverence, honor its diverse nations and peoples, and share of its bountiful resources. Hear us, O God.
Your mercy is great.

That you comfort those who mourn, those who are persecuted for their beliefs or convictions, and those who face anxiety or illness (*especially*). Hear us, O God.
Your mercy is great.

That you nourish us at your table, so that we may extend mercy to others and be makers of peace in our communities, families, and workplaces. Hear us, O God.
Your mercy is great.

Here other intercessions may be offered.

In thanksgiving for all your blessed ones, especially those who gave their lives for the sake of the gospel, who now rejoice in heaven. Hear us, O God.
Your mercy is great.

Receive our prayers and hopes, God of mercy and justice, for we pray in the name of Christ, the light of the world.
Amen.

Ideas and Images for the Day

In today's first reading, God cries, "O my people, what have I done to you? In what have I wearied you? Answer me!" (Micah 6:3). The people of God have forgotten God's deliverance and who God has called them to be. They seem to be awaiting further instructions, and so they are reminded that this is how you shall live: do justice, love kindness, walk humbly. In the Sunday assembly, God surrounds the gathered people with reminders of who and whose they are: we splash in the waters of baptism, are brought to new life in the word, are forgiven around bread and wine, and sent as blessed ones to do justice and mercy as, together, we await the fulfillment of the kingdom.

1. Place images of places and people awaiting justice or mercy in the gathering space of your church. As the prophet Micah reminds, the church is public about its faith—doing, living, and walking in these places. Jesus not only calls these people and places blessed but also calls the people of God to serve and embody them.

2. Christians are people of the story. Around the table and in the gathered assembly the story of salvation is recalled. The eucharistic prayer offers opportunity to remember God's salvation throughout history. Around the table, we thank God who is the source of all food, daringly implore God to feed those who are hungry, and are ourselves formed into bread for the hungry. Consider using thanksgiving at the table IV, VI, VIII, or X in *Evangelical Lutheran Worship*.

3. The beatitudes appear at the very beginning of Jesus' Sermon on the Mount. Before any obedience or disobedience can occur, Jesus pronounces blessing and offers a view of the kingdom coming near in his presence. Instructions will follow, but here, God's blessing is the foundation from which the community lives.

4. Invite children to lead a "noisy offering" this Sunday, either during the children's time (if your congregation has one) or during the offering. Gather metal buckets and invite those in the gathered assembly to drop change into the buckets as they are passed by the children. Designate a social ministry in your area or within the wider church to receive the offering. Explain how one of the ways we do justice, love mercy, and walk humbly is by providing for the needs of others and explain how the supporting ministry does this through its work.

Hymns for Worship
Gathering
Let streams of living justice   ELW 710
Oh, praise the gracious power   ELW 651, WOV 750
Rise up, O saints of God!   ELW 669, LBW 383

Hymn of the Day
We Are Called   ELW 720, W&P 147   *WE ARE CALLED*
O God of mercy, God of light   ELW 714, LBW 425
   JUST AS I AM
Oh, praise the gracious power   ELW 651, WOV 750
   CHRISTPRAISE RAY

Offering
When the poor ones   ELW 725
Let justice flow like streams   ELW 717, WOV 763

Communion
Blest are they   ELW 728, WOV 764
Jesus the very thought of you   ELW 754, LBW 316
Thee we adore, O Savior   ELW 476, LBW 199

Sending
To be your presence   ELW 546
The Spirit sends us forth to serve   ELW 551, WOV 723

Additional Hymns and Songs
Hope of the world   LBW 493
Blessed are you   DH 86
What does the Lord require   HS91 811

Music for the Day
Psalmody and Acclamations
Ferguson, John. *Gospel Acclamations for Advent–Transfiguration.*
Jennings, Carolyn. "Psalm 15" from PSCY.
Nelson, Ronald A. "Psalm 15" from PWA, Evangelical Lutheran Worship Edition.

Choral
Beck, John Ness. "Offertory." SATB, kybd, str. BP 1280.
Carter, John. "Blessed Are They Who Walk in the Pathways of Peace." SAB, pno. AFP 9780800675103.
o Hopson, Hal, arr. "Canticle of Love." SATB, org. AFP 9780800657796.
Jennings, Carolyn. "Blessed Are They." SATB, org, opt fl. CG CGA-896.

o denotes suggestions that relate to the hymn of the day.
● denotes songs that are available on iTunes®.

Children's Choir

Bedford, Michael. "Blessed Are They." U/2 pt, kybd, fl. CG CGA1025.

Vivaldi, Antonio. "Laudamus Te" from *Gloria*. UE, U, kybd. B&H M-051-46582-8.

Wold, Wayne. "Build New Bridges." U/2 pt, kybd. AFP 9780800657437.

Keyboard / Instrumental

o Culli, Benjamin. "Just as I Am" from *Saints with Christ*. Org. CPH 97-7226U1.

o Miller, Aaron David. "Christpraise Ray" from *Introductions and Alternate Accompaniments for Piano*, vol. 7. Pno. AFP 9780800623654.

o Sedio, Mark. "Just as I Am" from *Organ Tapestries*, vol. 1. Org. CPH 97-6812U1.

o Wold, Wayne L. "Christpraise Ray" from *Child of the Light*. Org. AFP 9780800657994.

Handbell

Burroughs, Bob. "Fanfare on Joyful, Joyful We Adore Thee." 5 oct, L3. From the Top Music 20155.

Dobrinski, Cynthia. "Be Thou My Vision." 3-6 oct, L3+. HOP 2263.

Manz, Paul/arr. Martha Lynn Thompson. "God of Grace and God of Glory." 4-5 oct, L3. MSM 30-810.

Praise Ensemble

• Foote, Billy. "You Are My King (Amazing Love)." WT/Sixsteps Music.

• Kendrick, Graham. "Amazing Love." Make Way Music.

• Moody, Dave. "All Hail King Jesus." WRD. W&P 3. Various editions.

• Redman, Matt. "Blessed Be Your Name." Thankyou Music.

• Tomlin, Chris/Jesse Reeves/Ed Cash. "How Great Is Our God." WT/Sixsteps Music.

• Tomlin, Chris/Jesse Reeves/Isaac Watts/JD Walt. "The Wonderful Cross." WT/Sixsteps Music.

Global

Bell, John, arr. "Hey, My Love" from *Heaven Shall Not Wait*. SATB. GIA G-3646.

Falam Chin traditional melody. "Lord of Region and of World" from *Sound the Bamboo*. STB. GIA G-6830.

Wednesday, February 2

Presentation of Our Lord

Forty days after the birth of Christ we mark the day Mary and Joseph presented him in the temple in accordance with Jewish law. There a prophetess named Anna began to speak of the redemption of Israel when she saw the young child. Simeon also greeted Mary and Joseph. He responded to the presence of the consolation of Israel in this child with the words of the Nunc dimittis. His song described Jesus as a "light for the nations."

Because of the link between Jesus as the light for the nations, and because an old reading for this festival contains a line from the prophet Zephaniah, "I will search Jerusalem with candles," the day is also known as Candlemas, a day when candles are blessed for the coming year.

Thursday, February 3

Ansgar, Bishop of Hamburg, missionary to Denmark and Sweden, died 865

Ansgar was a monk who led a mission to Denmark and later to Sweden, where he built the first church. His work ran into difficulties with the rulers of the day, and he was forced to withdraw into Germany, where he served as a bishop in Hamburg. Despite his difficulties in Sweden, he persisted in his mission work and later helped consecrate Gothbert as the first bishop of Sweden. Ansgar had a deep love for the poor. He would wash their feet and serve them food provided by the parish.

Saturday, February 5

The Martyrs of Japan, died 1597

In the sixteenth century, Jesuit missionaries, followed by Franciscans, introduced the Christian faith in Japan. But a promising beginning to those missions—perhaps as many as 300,000 Christians by the end of the sixteenth century—met complications from competition between the missionary groups, political difficulty between Spain and Portugal, and factions within the government of Japan. Christianity was suppressed. By 1630, Christianity was driven underground.

Today we commemorate the first martyrs of Japan, twenty-six missionaries and converts who were killed by crucifixion. Two hundred and fifty years later, when Christian missionaries returned to Japan, they found a community of Japanese Christians that had survived underground.

o denotes suggestions that relate to the hymn of the day.
• denotes songs that are available on iTunes®.

February 6, 2011
Fifth Sunday after Epiphany
Lectionary 5

Light shines in the darkness for the upright, the psalmist sings. Isaiah declares that when we loose the bonds of injustice and share our bread with the hungry, the light breaks forth like the dawn. In another passage from the Sermon on the Mount, Jesus, the light of the world, calls his followers to let the light of their good works shine before others. Through baptism we are sent into the world to shine with the light of Christ.

Prayer of the Day

Lord God, with endless mercy you receive the prayers of all who call upon you. By your Spirit show us the things we ought to do, and give us the grace and power to do them, through Jesus Christ, our Savior and Lord.

Gospel Acclamation

Alleluia. Jesus says, I am the light | of the world;* whoever follows me will have the | light of life. *Alleluia.* (John 8:12)

Readings and Psalm
Isaiah 58:1-9a [9b-12]

Shortly after the return of Israel from exile in Babylon, the people were troubled by the ineffectiveness of their fasts. God reminds them that outward observance is no substitute for genuine fasting that results in acts of justice, such as feeding the hungry, sheltering the homeless, and clothing the naked.

Psalm 112:1-9 [10]

Light shines in the darkness for the upright. (Ps. 112:4)

1 Corinthians 2:1-12 [13-16]

Though people such as the Corinthians are enamored with human philosophy and wisdom, Paul continuously presents God's hidden wisdom which is Jesus Christ crucified. True spiritual maturity involves judging ourselves and others in light of God's revelation in the cross.

Matthew 5:13-20

In the Sermon on the Mount, Jesus encourages his followers to be the salt of the earth and the light of the world, doing good works and keeping God's commandments.

Preface   Sundays

Color   Green

Prayers of Intercession

The prayers are prepared locally for each occasion. The following examples may be adapted or used as appropriate.

As God's beloved children, let us pray that the light of Christ shine on the nations, the church, and all those in need.
A brief silence.

Form your church to be the salt of the earth and the light of the world, that our good works may give you glory. Let us pray.
Have mercy, O God.

Use the collective work of government agencies, relief organizations, and advocacy groups to bring an end to injustice, oppression, hunger, and homelessness. Let us pray.
Have mercy, O God.

Bring healing to lands and waters that are polluted or neglected, and teach us restraint, that the resources of the earth may be distributed justly and fairly. Let us pray.
Have mercy, O God.

Tend to the needs of all who cry out to you, especially those facing economic uncertainty, those without hope, and those living with fear, grief, or illness (*especially*). Let us pray.
Have mercy, O God.

Gather this community of faith around the mystery of Christ crucified, that our lives be poured out for one another and for the sake of the world. Let us pray.
Have mercy, O God.

Here other intercessions may be offered.

Gather us, with all your holy ones, to receive what no eye has seen, no ear heard, and no heart conceived: the blessing of unending life in your presence. Let us pray.
Have mercy, O God.

Receive our prayers and hopes, God of mercy and justice, for we pray in the name of Christ, the light of the world.
Amen.

Ideas and Images for the Day

The missional emphasis of the Epiphany season continues and is expanded today. In Isaiah, God lays forth a mission for God's people—feed the hungry, care for the homeless, clothe the naked. When this mission is accomplished God says, "Your light shall break forth like the dawn." Paul details his Spirit-led mission to share the wonders of God's love. Jesus teaches his disciples, "You are the light of the world. . . . Let your light shine before others" (Matt. 5:14, 16). Created in God's image, the spark of the divine is alive in all of us. The light shines through us as we live out God's mission for our lives each day.

1. As we live the mission God has given us, we become reflectors of God's light. Robert Fulghum writes a compelling story about how the true meaning of our life can be discerned as we reflect light into troubled places of the world, and in doing so, teach others to do likewise. You can read this brief illustration at http://groups.gaia.com/gaia_books/12401/it-was-on-fire-when-i-lay-down-on-it/by_robert-fulghum.

2. Marianne Williamson wrote: "We were born to make manifest the glory of God that is within us. It's not just in some of us; it's in everyone. And as we let our own light shine, we unconsciously give other people permission to do the same. As we are liberated from our own fear, our presence automatically liberates others." For the full quote see http://skdesigns.com/internet/articles/quotes/williamson/our_deepest_fear/.

3. Follow the star to . . . Arlington, Texas? Today is the "high holy day" Super Bowl Sunday, where two teams battle it out at Cowboys Stadium! Often there are players and coaches who use the platform of the Super Bowl to share their faith and publicize their charitable foundations as they let their light shine. Check the players and coaches of this year's teams and share some of the inspiring stories of these athletes who shine beyond the field of play.

4. Too often we have over-sentimentalized the "salt and light" sayings of Jesus. There is a hard truth to letting our light shine and being salt for the earth. Martin Niemöller, in the face of Nazi persecution, arrest, and death during World War II, called for his fellow Christians to be the "light of the world." You can read this historic sermon at http://www.abcog.org/niemoll.htm. Being salt and light can be a very difficult calling.

5. Together with the children of the congregation, gather around the paschal candle and light a taper while having a conversation about how it is common to light a candle at baptism to symbolize "letting our light shine." Each child could receive a small flashlight to remind them to let their light shine throughout the week.

Hymns for Worship

Gathering

Lord of light   ELW 688, LBW 405
We are marching in the light   ELW 866, WOV 650, TFF 63
God, whose almighty word   ELW 673, LBW 400

Hymn of the Day

Rise, shine, you people!   ELW 665, LBW 393   WOJTKIEWIECZ
Gather Us In   ELW 532, WOV 718   GATHER US IN
O God of light   ELW 507, LBW 237   ATKINSON

Offering

Light shone in darkness   ELW 307
Lord, whose love in humble service   ELW 712, LBW 423

Communion

Christ, Be Our Light   ELW 715
I want to walk as a child of the light   ELW 815, WOV 649
We Are Called   ELW 720, W&P 147

Sending

Go, make disciples   ELW 540, W&P 47
Let justice flow like streams   ELW 717, WOV 763

Additional Hymns and Songs

Jesus, the Light of the world   TFF 59
You are the seed   WOV 753
Bring Forth the Kingdom   HS91 821

Music for the Day

Psalmody and Acclamations

Ferguson, John. *Gospel Acclamations for Advent–Transfiguration.*
Nelson, Ronald A. "Psalm 112:1-9 [10]" from PWA, Evangelical Lutheran Worship Edition.
Pavlechko, Thomas. "Psalm 112," Refrain 3, from PSCY.

Choral

Routley, Erik. "Light and Salt." SATB, org. GIA G-2300.
Sedio, Mark. "Light Shone in Darkness." SATB, pno. AFP 9780800678302.
Thomas, Andre. "Walk in the Light." U or 2 pt, pno. CG CGA-1062.
○ Wood, Dale. "Rise, Shine!" SATB, org. AFP 9780800655921.
   The Augsburg Choirbook. AFP 9780800656782.

○ denotes suggestions that relate to the hymn of the day.
● denotes songs that are available on iTunes®.

Children's Choir

Haugen, Marty. "Bring Forth the Kingdom," from *LifeSongs*. U, kybd.

Mahnke, Allan. "We Praise You for the Sun." U, kybd, opt perc, rec, vln. CG CGA153.

Makeever, Ray. "Brighter Than the Sun" from *Dancing at the Harvest*. U, kybd.

Keyboard / Instrumental

○ Albrecht, Mark. "Gather Us In" from *Timeless Tunes*, vol. 1. Pno, inst. MSM 10-111.

○ Behnke, John A. "Gather Us In." Org. CPH 97-6455U1.

○ Cherwien, David. "Wojtkiewiecz" from *Augsburg Organ Library: Epiphany*. Org. AFP 9780800659349.

○ Hobby, Robert A. "Atkinson" from *O God of Light*. Org. MSM 60-8002A.

Handbell

○ Helman, Michael. "Variations on 'Gather Us In.'" 3-5 oct hb, opt 3 oct hc, L4. AFP 9780800674922.

McChesney, Kevin. "Arise, Shine, Thy Light Has Come." 3-5 oct hb, L4. JEF JHS9108.

○ Roberts, Philip. "Gather Us In" from *Hymns for Handbells,* vol 1." 2-5 oct. GIA G-5770.

Praise Ensemble

• Farrell, Bernadette. "Christ, Be Our Light." OCP. ELW 715.

• Haugen, Marty. "Awake, O Sleeper." GIA.

• Hughes, Tim. "Here I Am to Worship." Thankyou Music/INT.

• Kendrick, Graham. "Shine, Jesus, Shine." Make Way Music. ELW 671.

• Redman, Matt. "Shine." Thankyou Music.

• Tomlin, Chris/Daniel Carson/Ed Cash/Jesse Reeves. "Jesus Messiah." WT/Sixsteps Music.

Global

Loh, I-to, arr. "Light of the World, Salt of the Earth" from *Sound the Bamboo*. U. GIA G-6830.

Vas, Charles. "Give Us Light/Jyothi dho Prabhu" from *Love and Anger: Songs of Lively Faith and Social Justice*. U. GIA G-4947.

February 13, 2011
Sixth Sunday after Epiphany
Lectionary 6

In today's reading from Deuteronomy we are called to choose life by loving and obeying God. Much of today's gospel reading echoes portions of the Ten Commandments. Jesus' instructions to the crowd reveal a pattern of behavior that honors both God and the neighbor, resulting in life and health for the whole community. We, too, are invited to embrace these commandments, not out of fear of retribution, but because God has promised that to do so means life for us.

Prayer of the Day

O God, the strength of all who hope in you, because we are weak mortals we accomplish nothing good without you. Help us to see and understand the things we ought to do, and give us grace and power to do them, through Jesus Christ, our Savior and Lord.

Gospel Acclamation

Alleluia. You are the light ' of the world.* A city set upon a hill can- ' not be hid. *Alleluia.* (Matt. 4:14)

Readings and Psalm
Deuteronomy 30:15-20

The Lord sets before the people of God a clear choice. Life and prosperity will come to the faithful; loss of the land will be the consequence of disobedience. Choosing life entails loving and holding fast to the Lord. Life in God's presence presupposes the promise made to the ancestors.

or Sirach 15:15-20

Wisdom literature has a high estimation of human possibilities. We are God's trusted creatures. Wisdom invites people to choose to keep God's commandments. Contrariwise, God does not command people to be wicked or give them permission to sin.

Psalm 119:1-8

Happy are they who follow the teaching of the LORD. (Ps. 119:1)

1 Corinthians 3:1-9

Human leaders in the church are not the ones who control ministry. Rather they are fellow workers who belong to God, the one who truly controls and continuously empowers the ministry of the church.

Matthew 5:21-37

In the Sermon on the Mount, Jesus exhorts his followers to embrace standards of righteousness that exceed legal requirements and traditional expectations.

Preface Sundays

Color Green

Prayers of Intercession

The prayers are prepared locally for each occasion. The following examples may be adapted or used as appropriate.
As God's beloved children, let us pray that the light of Christ shine on the nations, the church, and all those in need.
A brief silence.
For the people of God, that they may walk in your ways and observe your commandments. Lord, in your mercy,
hear our prayer.
For nations, communities, and families that are estranged by conflict or violence, and for the gift of reconciliation and mutual forgiveness. Lord, in your mercy,
hear our prayer.
For the earth and its resources, that by choosing life our decisions will honor the welfare of generations to come. Lord, in your mercy,
hear our prayer.
For victims of sexual violence; for those affected by divorce; for those living with addiction, anger, fear, or illness (*especially*), that they may know your healing love. Lord, in your mercy,
hear our prayer.

For this community of faith, that it may be a place of safety, support, integrity, and encouragement. Lord, in your mercy,
hear our prayer.
Here other intercessions may be offered.
For all your saints who served you in life and now rest from their labors, that you bring us all to the joy of everlasting life. Lord, in your mercy,
hear our prayer.
Receive our prayers and hopes, God of mercy and justice, for we pray in the name of Christ, the light of the world.
Amen.

Ideas and Images for the Day

A preacher looking for a "safe bet" is going to struggle this week! The gospel seems to be filled with tough teachings by Jesus in the Sermon on the Mount. The first and second readings also are difficult to dwell upon. But peel back the seemingly harsh exterior and we hear Moses speaking of true life dwelling in God's promise. We hear Paul teaching that God continually uses a variety of tools to re-create and nourish his people. Finally, we encounter Jesus interpreting the law as grace-filled teachings for a new kind of community. So take a deep breath and don't be afraid, crack open the "tough exterior" and experience the love and grace of these texts.

1. What an interesting gospel passage to reflect upon as we prepare for Valentine's Day! Jesus teaches us about how to care for one another when there are disagreements; he teaches us what love is and what it is not. He paints a picture of what a loving community ought to be if we live into the commandments. In what concrete ways do we live according to these teachings of Jesus? In what ways do we not live up to these teachings?

2. From the beginning to the end of the Sermon on the Mount, Jesus' teachings mark a movement from the scriptures to Jesus as the ultimate authority. Richard Jensen writes that the teachings of Jesus are "divided into five great discourses reminiscent of the five books of Moses. He teaches with authority, an authority that goes beyond Moses. Time and again in his teaching in the Sermon on the Mount Jesus cites the Law of Moses and adds, 'But I say to you . . . '" (Jensen, *Preaching Matthew's Gospel: A Narrative Approach* [Lima, OH: CSS, 1998], p. 75). Through the Sermon on the Mount, Jesus places himself as the authority over and above Moses and the scriptures. This teaching sets the stage for the public ministry of Jesus.

3. Monty Python's *The Life of Brian* (Starz/Anchor Bay, 1979) has a classic scene depicting the Sermon on the Mount. In this scene followers who are listening to

Jesus are behaving in a way that is the opposite of what Jesus is teaching. The irony of this scene is an opportunity to laugh at a caricature of ourselves as followers and then to ask, "How can we adhere more closely to these teachings of Jesus?"

4. With Valentine's Day coming, talk with the children about love. Ask the children for ways they know God loves them and how they show others their care and love. Jesus teaches us about how to love our neighbors by respecting others and by keeping our promises. Give each child two hearts cut from construction paper. Explain that they each get one to enjoy as they remember God's love. The other is to share with someone else and to remind that person that God loves her or him.

Hymns for Worship
Gathering
O God, my faithful God   ELW 806, LBW 504
Holy Spirit, ever dwelling   ELW 582, LBW 523
Joyful, joyful we adore thee   ELW 836, LBW 551

Hymn of the Day
O Christ, our hope   ELW 604, LBW 300
  LOBT GOTT, IHR CHRISTEN
Oh, that the Lord would guide my ways   ELW 772, LBW 480
  EVAN
In all our grief   ELW 615, WOV 739   FREDERICKTOWN

Offering
Where charity and love prevail   ELW 359, LBW 126
Eternal Spirit of the living Christ   ELW 402, LBW 441

Communion
Let us ever walk with Jesus   ELW 802, LBW 487
Healer of our every ill   ELW 612, WOV 738
God, when human bonds are broken   ELW 603, WOV 735

Sending
Songs of thankfulness and praise   ELW 310, LBW 90
Praise the Lord, rise up rejoicing   ELW 544, LBW 196

Additional Hymns and Songs
Eternal ruler of the ceaseless round   LBW 373
Open our lives to the Word   DH 8

Music for the Day
Psalmody and Acclamations
Ferguson, John. *Gospel Acclamations for Advent–Transfiguration.*
Mummert, Mark. "Psalm 119:1-8," Refrain 1, from PSCY.
Nelson, Ronald A. "Psalm 119:1-8" from PWA, Evangelical Lutheran Worship Edition.

Choral
Buxtehude, Dietrich. "Everything You Do" from *Chantry Choirbook.* SATB, org. AFP 9780800657772.
Hampton, Keith. "True Light." SATB, pno. EAR.
Hobby, Robert A. "Strengthen for Service." 2 pt mxd, opt assembly, org. AFP 9780800678265.
Proulx, Richard. "Strengthen for Service" from *Augsburg Choirbook.* SATB. AFP 9780800656782.

Children's Choir
Anonymous. "This Is My Commandment" from *LifeSongs.* LE, U, kybd.
Marshall, Jane. "God Speaks: The Twin Commandments." U, kybd. CG CGA535.
Meek, Pauline. "The Great Commandments" from *LifeSongs.* U, kybd.

Keyboard / Instrumental
○ Bender, Jan. "Evan" from *Twenty-Four Hymn Introductions*, vol. 2. Org. CPH 97-5303U1.
○ Cherwien, David. "Fredericktown" from *Organ Plus One.* Org, inst. AFP 9780800656188.
○ Eggert, John. "Lobt Gott, ihr Christen" from *Creative Hymn Accompaniments for Organ*, vol. 2. Org. CPH 97-6851U1.
○ Organ, Anne Krentz. "Fredericktown" from *Woven Together*, vol. 1. Pno. AFP 9780800658168.

Handbell
○ Afdahl, Lee. "The Lord's My Shepherd (Evan)." 3 or 5 oct hb, opt 2 oct hc, opt chimetree, L3. AFP 9780800659905.
McMichael, Catherine. "Fantasy on 'Trust and Obey.'" 3-5 oct, L3. AGEHR AG35282.
Page, Anna Laura. "Day by Day." 3-5 oct hb, opt 2 oct hc, L3. CG CGB314.

Praise Ensemble
● Grant, Amy/Michael W. Smith. "Thy Word." Meadowgreen Music/WRD. W&P 144.
● Green, Melody. "There Is a Redeemer." Birdwing Music. W&P 140.
● Millard, Bart/Pete Kipley. "Word of God, Speak." Simpleville Music.
● Redman, Matt. "The Heart of Worship." Thankyou Music.
● Tomlin, Chris. "Forever." WT/Sixsteps Music.
● Tomlin, Chris/Cary Pierce/Jesse Reeves/Jon Able. "Awesome Is the Lord Most High." WT.

Global
Sosa, Pablo. "Allí Está Jesús" from *Éste es el Día.* U. GIA G-7021.
Swahili, trad. "Bwana awabariki/May God Grant You a Blessing" from *Agape: Songs of Hope and Reconciliation.* SATB. Lutheran World Federation. AFP 9780191000133. TFF 162.

○ denotes suggestions that relate to the hymn of the day.
● denotes songs that are available on iTunes®.

Monday, February 14

Cyril, monk, died 869; Methodius, bishop, died 885; missionaries to the Slavs

These two brothers from a noble family in Thessalonika in northeastern Greece were priests and missionaries. After some early initial missionary work by Cyril among the Arabs, the brothers retired to a monastery. They were later sent to work among the Slavs, the missionary work for which they are most known. Since Slavonic had no written form at the time, the brothers established a written language with the Greek alphabet as its basis. They translated the scriptures and the liturgy using this Cyrillic alphabet. The Czechs, Serbs, Croats, Slovaks, and Bulgars regard the brothers as the founders of Slavic literature. The brothers' work in preaching and worshiping in the language of the people are honored by Christians in both East and West.

Friday, February 18

Martin Luther, renewer of the church, died 1546

On this day in 1546, Martin Luther died at the age of sixty-two. For a time, he was an Augustinian monk, but it is his work as a biblical scholar, translator of the Bible, public confessor of the faith, reformer of the liturgy, theologian, educator, and father of German vernacular literature that holds him in our remembrance. In Luther's own judgment, the greatest of all of his works was his catechism, written to instruct people in the basics of faith. And it was his baptism that sustained him in his trials as a reformer.

February 20, 2011
Seventh Sunday after Epiphany
Lectionary 7

In today's first reading we hear, "You shall be holy, for I the LORD your God am holy." Yet we know we cannot achieve perfection. Our attempts to love neighbors and even our enemies fall short of what God desires for us. Yet in Jesus we see one who loved even those who persecuted and killed him. We are made holy in baptism, and forgiven at the table of God's mercy. As a people made holy by God, we go in peace to love as we have been loved.

Prayer of the Day

Holy God of compassion, you invite us into your way of forgiveness and peace. Lead us to love our enemies, and transform our words and deeds to be like his through whom we pray, Jesus Christ, our Savior and Lord.

Gospel Acclamation

Alleluia. In those who obey the ˈ word of Christ,* the love of God has ˈ reached perfection. *Alleluia.* (1 John 2:5)

Readings and Psalm
Leviticus 19:1-2, 9-18

The Holiness Code in Leviticus urges people to be holy since God is holy. Holiness is lived out in partiality for and consideration of the poor and the weak. We are to love our neighbors as ourselves.

Psalm 119:33-40

Teach me, O LORD, the way of your statutes. (Ps. 119:33)

I Corinthians 3:10-11, 16-23

Jesus Christ is the foundation of the church and its ministry. We are God's temple because God's Spirit dwells in us, and we belong to Christ. Hence we are called to build wisely upon this sure foundation not for our own benefit but for others to experience Christ's benefits.

Matthew 5:38-48

In the Sermon on the Mount, Jesus declares an end to the law of vengeance. God's people will respond to evil with love and forgiveness.

Preface   Sundays

Color   Green

Prayers of Intercession

The prayers are prepared locally for each occasion. The following examples may be adapted or used as appropriate.

As God's beloved children, let us pray that the light of Christ shine on the nations, the church, and all those in need.
A brief silence.

That the church may be a temple of God's presence, built upon the foundation of Christ and united in our one baptism, let us pray.

Have mercy, O God.

That the leaders of nations serve with honesty and justice, honoring our neighbors in all circumstances of life, let us pray.

Have mercy, O God.

That in our call to holy living we treat your gifts of land and natural resources with dignity and concern for the health of all creation, let us pray.

Have mercy, O God.

That you teach us to love and forgive even our enemies, and that you open our hearts to the needs of those seeking food, shelter, or health (*especially*), let us pray.

Have mercy, O God.

That you bless the ministries of this congregation (*especially*), that your welcome and hospitality may lead us to love our neighbors as ourselves, let us pray.

Have mercy, O God.

Here other intercessions may be offered.

Unite us, with all your saints, in life and death, in the present and future, until we worship with them in your eternal temple. Let us pray.

Have mercy, O God.

Receive our prayers and hopes, God of mercy and justice, for we pray in the name of Christ, the light of the world.

Amen.

Ideas and Images for the Day

Both the Leviticus and Matthew readings give us directions for living a holy life. But they remain only laws, with the potential to drain life instead of give it, if they are not rooted in Jesus' life and the holiness Jesus gives us. Leviticus sets forth the totality of the holiness God expects in our lives, from finances to purchasing decisions to familial relationships, and Matthew expands this holiness further by including the love of enemies. Each Levitical law ends with "I am the Lord," and, interestingly, Jesus ends with almost the same formula in invoking God's perfection. This repetition of God's holiness and perfection is important and highlights our own lack of holiness. But it's even more important that it is Jesus who delivers this message, since he not only embodies that holiness but offers it to us as well, and enables us to live out God's laws.

1. There has been lots of news and discussion in recent years concerning the United States' treatment of enemies, especially alleged terrorists and prisoners of war. It is debatable whether Jesus' words are applicable to national public policy, and Christians come down on different sides of this question. For recent commentary on this from a Christian perspective, check http://www.sojo.com and search the archives for "torture," "love of enemies," or "prisoners."

2. *Dead Man Walking* (MGM, 1995), in which a nun visits a prisoner on Death Row, is a classic movie (and book) example of loving our enemies in a tangible, practical way. See http://www.spiritualityandpractice.com for a synopsis, review, and discussion guide.

3. There are many ways we profit from the blood of neighbors, from the infamous "blood diamonds" to sweatshop labor. We therefore have many opportunities, both as communities and individuals, to make changes in our purchasing and investment decisions. http://www.coopamerica.org is a great resource for fair-trade and sweat-free purchasing, socially responsible investing, and green living.

4. The command in Leviticus not to harvest everything is the law that Boaz followed in the famous story of Ruth and Naomi, who survived because they were able to collect the gleanings of the field. Think about what we do with our leftovers—do we dump what we don't need, or do we find ways to share with those less fortunate? Consider assembling a bag of "trash" and letting kids examine what's in it, what could have been reused or shared, and how we can have less trash in the first

place. Some suggestions for inclusion: blank or minimally used paper, old clothing with usable buttons or zippers, plastic yogurt containers, cast-off toys.

Hymns for Worship
Gathering
Awake, O sleeper, rise from death   ELW 452, WOV 745
O day of peace   ELW 711, WOV 762
All my hope on God is founded   ELW 757, WOV 782

Hymn of the Day
The church of Christ, in every age   ELW 729, LBW 433
WAREHAM
Bring Peace to Earth Again   ELW 700   PACE MIO DIO
Lord of glory, you have bought us   ELW 707, LBW 424
HYFYRDOL

Offering
Goodness is stronger than evil   ELW 721
Jesu, Jesu, fill us with your love   ELW 708, WOV 765, TFF 83

Communion
Lord of all nations, grant me grace   ELW 716, LBW 419
O Jesus, joy of loving hearts   ELW 658, LBW 356
Creating God, your fingers trace   ELW 684, WOV 757

Sending
Love divine, all loves excelling   ELW 631, LBW 315
Hallelujah! We sing your praises   ELW 535, WOV 722,
   TFF 158

Additional Hymns and Songs
Now in this banquet   W&P 104
O God, empower us   LBW 422

Music for the Day
Psalmody and Acclamations
Ferguson, John. *Gospel Acclamations for Advent–Transfiguration.*
Mummert, Mark. "Psalm 119: 33-40," Refrain 1, from PSCY.
Nelson, Ronald A. "Psalm 119:33-40" from PWA, Evangelical Lutheran Worship Edition.

Choral
Bisbee, B. Wayne. "O Splendor of God's Glory Bright." 2 pt trbl or mxd, pno. AFP 9780800659257.
Ellingboe, Bradley. "In the Beauty of Holiness." SATB, kybd, fl. AFP 9780800664251.
Farrant, Richard. "Lord, For Thy Tender Mercy's Sake." SATB. Various editions.
Fleming, Larry L. "Humble Service." SATB. AFP 9780800646226.

Organ, Anne Krentz, arr. "Around You, O Lord Jesus." SAB, pno, opt assembly. AFP 9780800679248.

Children's Choir
Cool, Jayne Southwick. "Walk an Extra Mile." U, kybd, drm. CG CGA519.
Gifford, Nancy. "Light of Light." U, kybd. CG CGA1162.
Traditional. "Love God and Your Neighbor" from *LifeSongs.* U, kybd.

Keyboard / Instrumental
o Blair, Dallas. "Hyfrydol" from *Hymn Introductions and Descants for Trumpet and Organ,* set 3. Org, tpt. MSM 20-141.
o Diemer, Emma Lou. "Wareham" from *Augsburg Organ Library: Summer.* Org. AFP 9780800676871.
o Johnson, David M. "Hyfrydol" from *Wedding Music,* book 5. Org. AFP 9780800648961.
o Miller, Aaron David. "Wareham" from *Chorale Preludes for Piano in Traditional Styles.* Pno. AFP 9780800679033.

Handbell
o Geschke, Susan. "Lord of Glory." 2-3 oct, L1. ALF 00-19640.
Morris, Hart. "Beyond All Praising." 3-5 oct hb, opt 3 oct hc, L2+. CPH 97-7117.
Sherman, Arnold. "Song of Peace." 3-5 oct, opt U or 3 pt choir, L3+. RR HB0046.

Praise Ensemble
● Angrisano, Steve/Tom Tomaszek. "Go, Make a Difference." Spiritandsong.com.
● Anonymous. "Create in Me a Clean Heart." W&P 34. Various editions.
● Carpenter, Kelly. "Draw Me Close." Mercy/VIN.
● Egan, Jon. "I Am Free." Vertical Worship Songs/INT.
● Hughes, Tim. "Beautiful One." Thankyou Music.
● Peterson, Hans/Larry Olson. "All Are Welcome" from *Work of the People,* vol. 1. Dakota Road Music.

Global
Harling, Per. "Du är helig/You Are Holy" from *Pave the Way: Global Songs 3.* U. AFP 9780800676896. ELW 525.
Kijugo, Joas, arr. "The Love of God Almighty" from *Set Free: A Collection of African Hymns.* SATB, cant. AFP 9780806600451.

Wednesday, February 23

Polycarp, Bishop of Smyrna, martyr, died 156
Polycarp was bishop of Smyrna (in present-day western Turkey) and a link between the apostolic age and the church at the end of the second century. He is said to have been

o denotes suggestions that relate to the hymn of the day.
● denotes songs that are available on iTunes®.

known by John, the author of Revelation. In turn he was known by Iranaeus, bishop of Lyon in France, and Ignatius of Antioch. At the age of eighty-six he was martyred for his faith. When urged to save his life and renounce his faith, Polycarp replied, "Eighty-six years I have served him, and he never did me any wrong. How can I blaspheme my king who saved me?" The magistrate who made the offer was reluctant to kill a gentle old man, but he had no choice. Polycarp was burned at the stake, his death a testimony to the cost of renouncing temptation.

Friday, February 25
Elizabeth Fedde, deaconess, died 1921

Fedde was born in Norway and trained as a deaconess. In 1882, at the age of thirty-two, she was asked to come to New York to minister to the poor and to Norwegian seafarers. Her influence was wide-ranging, and she established the Deaconess House in Brooklyn and the Deaconess House and Hospital of the Lutheran Free Church in Minneapolis. She returned home to Norway in 1895 and died there.

February 27, 2011
Eighth Sunday after Epiphany
Lectionary 8

Christians recognize that the source of all good things is the God who feeds the birds and clothes the grass of the field. We rejoice that we are held in the palm of God's hand. God cannot forget us any more than a woman could forget her nursing child. Nourished at the Lord's table, we share these gifts with those who are anxious, hungry, poor, or in any kind of need.

Prayer of the Day

God of tender care, like a mother, like a father, you never forget your children, and you know already what we need. In all our anxiety give us trusting and faithful hearts, that in confidence we may embody the peace and justice of your Son, Jesus Christ, our Savior and Lord.

Gospel Acclamation

Alleluia. The steadfast love of the LORD ˡ never ceases,*
God's mercies never come ˡ to an end. *Alleluia.* (Lam. 3:22)

Readings and Psalm
Isaiah 49:8-16a

The Lord shows motherly compassion for God's suffering people. Even if a nursing mother could under rare circumstances forget her child, God will never forget us.

Psalm 131

Like a child upon its mother's breast, my soul is quieted within me. (Ps. 131:2)

1 Corinthians 4:1-5

We are servants and stewards of Christ whose primary responsibility is to be trustworthy. We do not stand over others as their judge, but we stand under Christ to whom we will be held accountable.

Matthew 6:24-34

In the Sermon on the Mount, Jesus encourages his followers to trust in God rather than material wealth.

Preface Sundays

Color Green

Prayers of Intercession

The prayers are prepared locally for each occasion. The following examples may be adapted or used as appropriate.

As God's beloved children, let us pray that the light of Christ shine on the nations, the church, and all those in need.

A brief silence.

That the baptized may be servants of Christ and stewards of the mysteries we celebrate in this assembly. Lord, in your mercy,

hear our prayer.

That the leaders of nations, states, cities, and towns extend compassionate care to those without food, clothing, or shelter. Lord, in your mercy,

hear our prayer.

That our gratitude for the birds of the air and the flowers of the field lead us to treasure each day, care for the earth, and seek the welfare of generations to come. Lord, in your mercy,

hear our prayer.

That like a patient mother you comfort all those who suffer with illness, grief, worry, or anxiety (*especially*). Lord, in your mercy,

hear our prayer.

That as we strive first for your kingdom, you feed us at your bountiful table and deepen our faith in your provident care. Lord, in your mercy,

hear our prayer.

Here other intercessions may be offered.

That you gather us with all your holy ones, who treasured the riches of your grace and whose names are inscribed on the palms of your hands. Lord, in your mercy,

hear our prayer.

Receive our prayers and hopes, God of mercy and justice, for we pray in the name of Christ, the light of the world.

Amen.

Ideas and Images for the Day

One of the hardest, if not the hardest, teachings of Jesus for us twenty-first–century folks is in today's gospel: Don't worry. Don't worry about food, don't worry about clothes, don't worry about tomorrow. It's a modern obsession to worry, regardless of how much we make or how careful we are. We even worry about the fact that we worry so much! Jesus makes it clear that our security is not in bank accounts, retirement funds, or relaxation techniques. Our security and peace—financial, emotional and spiritual—is rooted in God's promise of provision. When we focus our energy on seeking God, there will be enough. This is the confidence of a weaned child with its mother: because the babe experienced the complete fulfillment of its hunger, the child has the assurance that future needs will be filled as well.

1. Most people know the Bob Marley song "Three Little Birds" by its refrain, "Every little thing is gonna be all right," and think of it strictly as an ode to the island lifestyle. Of course we know that everything is all right not because we're on vacation, but because God promises to take care of us. This truth is alluded to in the song, as three birds sing their song of assurance to the singer. There are many recordings and covers of this song, including one by Elizabeth Mitchell (*You Are My Little Bird*, Smithsonian Folkways, 2006) and another by child star Connie Talbot (*Over the Rainbow*, Rainbow Recording Company, 2007).

2. Gather pictures of models, fashion icons, and royalty and compare these with a vase of fresh flowers. Which is better dressed? If possible, give each child a flower and invite the congregation to reflect on how much time they spend worrying about their looks versus seeking God's kingdom. Find pictures in *People* magazine and by searching online for images of, for example, Mary Queen of Scots, King Louis XIII, or Tsarina Alexandra.

3. People rarely talk about their personal finances, since it so easily invites judgment or implies self-righteousness. But hearing the stories of fellow Christians who have given generously without concern for their own future or have experienced God's provision is inspiring and important. Invite congregants to share their stories with worship leaders in advance of the service. These stories can then be shared anonymously, perhaps with the congregation singing "Seek ye first the kingdom of God" (WOV 783, W&P 122) between testimonies.

4. John Wesley, whose death we commemorate this week, (along with his brother Charles) was famous for his dictum: Gain all you can, save all you can, give all you can. He himself lived frugally, increasing the amount that he gave away as his earnings increased. Read more in this 1872 sermon on "The Use of Money": http://gbgm-umc.org/umw/Wesley/serm-050.stm.

Hymns for Worship
Gathering

Sing praise to God, the highest good   ELW 871, LBW 542
Great is thy faithfulness   ELW 733, WOV 771, TFF 283
Praise to the Lord, the Almighty   ELW 858/859, LBW 543

Hymn of the Day

All depends on our possessing   ELW 589, LBW 447
ALLES IST AN GOTTES SEGEN

The numberless gifts of God's mercies   ELW 683
JAG KAN ICKE RÄKNE DEM ALLA

O Christ the same   ELW 760   *RED HILL ROAD*
WOV 778   *LONDONDERRY AIR*

Offering

Lord of all hopefulness   ELW 765, LBW 469
The numberless gifts of God's mercies   ELW 683

Communion

Children of the heavenly Father   ELW 781, LBW 474
Mothering God, you gave me birth   ELW 735, WOV 769
How Great Thou Art   ELW 856, LBW 532

Sending

In thee is gladness   ELW 867, LBW 552
Now thank we all our God   ELW 839/840, LBW 533/534

Additional Hymns and Songs

Seek ye first the kingdom of God   WOV 783, TFF 149
The thirsty fields drink in the rain   WOV 714
His eye is on the sparrow   TFF 252

Music for the Day
Psalmody and Acclamations

Ferguson, John. *Gospel Acclamations for Advent–Transfiguration.*
Miller, Aaron David. "Psalm 131" from PSCY.
Pelz, Walter L. "Psalm 131" from PWA, Evangelical Lutheran Worship Edition.

Choral

Bach, J. S. "Jesus, My Sweet Pleasure/Jesu, meine Freude" from *Bach for All Seasons.* AFP 9780800658540.
DeLalande, Michel-Richard. "My Soul Trusted in God." U, kybd, C inst, opt bass inst. AFP 9780800679132.
Handel, G. F. "Ev'ry Valley" from *Messiah.* Tenor solo, kybd or orch. Various editions.
○ Schalk, Carl. "O Christ the Same." SATB, org. AFP 9780800678272.

Children's Choir

Baker, Henry. "I Am Trusting You, Lord Jesus" from *LifeSongs.* LE, U, kybd.
Schubert, Franz. "In Our Work and In Our Play" from *LifeSongs.* LE, U, kybd.
Sleeth, Natalie. "Fear Not for Tomorrow" from *LifeSongs.* UE, U, kybd.

Keyboard / Instrumental

○ Behnke, John A. "Alles ist an Gottes Segen" from *Five Preludes of Praise,* set 6. Org. CPH 97-7301U1.

○ Mahnke, Allan. "Alles ist an Gottes Segen" from *Thirteen Pieces for Treble Instrument and Organ.* Org, inst. CPH 97-6765U1.
○ Organ, Anne Krentz. "Red Hill Road" from *Reflections on Hymn Tunes for Fall Festivals.* Pno. AFP 9780800663834.
○ Wold, Wayne L. "Alles ist an Gottes Segen" from *Water, Word, Meal.* Org. AFP 9780800677558.

Handbell

Hollander, Lynne. "Seek Ye First." 2 oct, L1. ALF 00-31746.
○ McFadden, Jane. "O Christ the Same." 2-3 oct hb, opt C or Bb inst, opt hc, L2. AFP 9780800656294.
Moklebust, Cathy. "Children of the Heavenly Father." 3-5 oct hb, opt 3 oct hc, L2. CG CGB139.

Praise Ensemble

● Byrd, Marc/Steve Hindalong. "God of Wonders." New Spring Music/INT.
● Foote, Billy/Cindy Foote. "You Are God Alone (Not a God)." Billy Foote Music/INT.
● Kendrick, Graham. "Here Is Bread." Make Way Music. ELW 483. Various editions.
● LeBlanc, Lenny. "There Is None Like You." INT.
● Ledner, Michael. "You Are My Hiding Place." MAR. W&P 160
● Mullins, Rich. "Awesome God." BMG Songs, Inc.

Global

Bell, John, arr. "Don't Be Afraid" from *Come, All You People: Shorter Songs for Worship.* SAB. GIA G-4391.
Young-Soo, Nah. "Look and Learn" from *Sent by the Lord: Songs of the World Church,* vol 2. U. GIA G-3740.

Tuesday, March 1
George Herbert, hymnwriter, died 1633

As a student at Trinity College, Cambridge, England, George Herbert excelled in languages and music. He went to college with the intention of becoming a priest, but his scholarship attracted the attention of King James I. Herbert served in parliament for two years. After the death of King James and at the urging of a friend, Herbert's interest in ordained ministry was renewed. He was ordained a priest in 1630 and served the little parish of St. Andrew Bremerton until his death. He was noted for unfailing care for his parishioners, bringing the sacraments to them when they were ill, and providing food and clothing for those in need. Herbert is best remembered, however, as a writer of poems and hymns such as "Come, My Way, My Truth, My Life" (ELW 816).

○ denotes suggestions that relate to the hymn of the day.
● denotes songs that are available on iTunes®.

Wednesday, March 2

John Wesley, died 1791; Charles Wesley, died 1788; renewers of the church

The Wesleys were leaders of a revival in the Church of England. Their spiritual discipline (or method) of frequent communion, fasting, and advocacy for the poor earned them the name "Methodists." The Wesleys were missionaries in the American colony of Georgia for a time, but returned to England discouraged. Following a conversion experience while reading Luther's *Preface to the Epistle to the Romans*, John was perhaps the greatest force in eighteenth-century revival. The brothers' desire was that the Methodist Societies would be a movement for renewal in the Church of England, but after their deaths the societies developed a separate status.

Charles wrote more than six hundred hymns, including "Hark! The Herald Angels Sing" (ELW 270), "Christ, Whose Glory Fills the Skies" (ELW 553), and "Love Divine, All Loves Excelling" (ELW 631).

March 6, 2011

Transfiguration of Our Lord
Last Sunday after Epiphany

Today's festival is a bridge between the Advent-Christmas-Epiphany cycle that comes to a close today and the Lent-Easter cycle that begins in several days. On the mount of transfiguration Jesus is revealed as God's beloved Son, echoing the words at his baptism. This vision of glory sustains us as Jesus faces his impending death in Jerusalem.

We turn this week to Ash Wednesday and our yearly baptismal journey from Lent to Easter. Some churches put aside the alleluia at the conclusion of today's liturgy. This word of joy will be omitted during the penitential season of Lent and will be sung again at Easter.

Prayer of the Day

O God, in the transfiguration of your Son you confirmed the mysteries of the faith by the witness of Moses and Elijah, and in the voice from the bright cloud declaring Jesus your beloved Son, you foreshadowed our adoption as your children. Make us heirs with Christ of your glory, and bring us to enjoy its fullness, through Jesus Christ, our Savior and Lord, who lives and reigns with you and the Holy Spirit, one God, now and forever.

Gospel Acclamation

Alleluia. This is my [|] Son, my Chosen,* lis- [|] ten to him! *Alleluia.* (Luke 9:35)

Readings and Psalm
Exodus 24:12-18

At Mount Sinai, Moses experienced the presence of God for forty days and forty nights. The "glory of the Lord" settled on the mountain, and on the seventh day God called out to Moses. On the mountain God gave Moses the stone tablets inscribed with the ten commandments.

Psalm 2

You are my son; this day have I begotten you. (Ps. 2:7)

or Psalm 99

Proclaim the greatness of the Lord; worship upon God's holy hill. (Ps. 99:9)

2 Peter 1:16-21

At the transfiguration, God's voice was heard, declaring Jesus to be the beloved Son. By the activity of the Holy Spirit, God's voice continues to be heard through the word of scripture.

Matthew 17:1-9

Shortly before he enters Jerusalem, where he will be crucified, Jesus is revealed to his disciples in a mountaintop experience of divine glory called the transfiguration.

Preface   Transfiguration

Color White

Prayers of Intercession

The prayers are prepared locally for each occasion. The following examples may be adapted or used as appropriate.

As God's beloved children, let us pray that the light of Christ shine on the nations, the church, and all those in need.
A brief silence.

Grant to those who worship on this holy day a glimpse of your glory, that we might see your presence in all the gifts of daily life. Hear us, O God.
Your mercy is great.

Reveal yourself to us in the splendor of mountains and clouds, sunshine and rain, that our praise may lead us to care tenderly for your creation. Hear us, O God.
Your mercy is great.

Give to the leaders of nations a vision of the world at peace, that they work together for the good of all the people of the earth. Hear us, O God.
Your mercy is great.

Draw near to all those living with fear or anxiety, grief or illness (*especially*), that your morning star may dawn in their hearts. Hear us, O God.
Your mercy is great.

Feed this assembly with your word and holy meal, that we may be transfigured to be the body of Christ for the world. Hear us, O God.
Your mercy is great.

Here other intercessions may be offered.

Unite our prayers with those of all your saints until, with them, we behold your majesty and praise your unending glory. Hear us, O God.
Your mercy is great.

Receive our prayers and hopes, God of mercy and justice, for we pray in the name of Christ, the light of the world.
Amen.

Ideas and Images for the Day

We often speak of mountaintop experiences as those joyous times we look forward to with excitement and look back upon fondly, such as summer camp or an annual hiking trip. The mountaintop moments in today's readings were different: awe-inspiring, yes, but also full of devouring fires, clouds, and fear. The truth is, we can no more plan our mountaintop times with God than we can summon God's fire. God's place is to invite, ours to respond, faces bowed to the ground. But that doesn't mean there is nothing to do in the meantime. On the contrary, the traditional disciplines of Lent—fasting, prayer, and gifts to the poor—all help us maintain the eyes, ears, and heart to see and hear God whenever and wherever God appears.

1. The transfiguration is a popular image for icons, as well as classical and contemporary art. Use images as bulletin covers, set up at prayer stations, or projected onto a screen. Find images at http://diglib.library.vanderbilt.edu/act-processquery.pl?code=ACT&SortOrder=Title&LectionaryLink=ATran and http://www.servicioskoinonia.org/cerezo/dibujosA/60TransfiguracionA.jpg.

2. The fact that God comes in clouds throughout today's readings makes sense when we consider the otherworldly feeling we get when enveloped in mist or fog. The limited vision sharpens our perception of whatever we do see, and other senses are heightened as well. Consider ways to recreate this atmosphere in your worship space: lighting incense, renting a fog machine, or draping the walls and ceiling with billowy, gauzy cloth.

3. Those guiding mountain climbs or hikes can tell you that the descent requires more care than the ascent and is when most accidents happen. Bring in some hiking and climbing equipment (boots, backpack, hiking stick, carabiner, rope) and talk about the mountain journeys in today's stories. Focus on why Moses, Jesus, and his disciples didn't stay on the mountain and why they need to take care when coming down.

4. Even though they didn't fully understand it, it was still good for Peter, James, and John to get a visual and auditory affirmation of Jesus' identity to sustain them through the coming hard days. What personal experiences do we have of encounters with Jesus that we can hold onto and look forward to when days get tough?

5. At the moment of his transfiguration, God proclaims Jesus to be the "beloved son." Understanding how deeply we are loved by God transfigures us too, and this love gives us the strength to go down the mountain and work to transform the world. *The Velveteen Rabbit* by Margery Williams (New York: Doubleday, 1922) shares this theme of transformation through love. The text and illustrations are available at http://digital.library.upenn.edu/women/williams/rabbit/rabbit.html.

Hymns for Worship
Gathering

O Morning Star, how fair and bright! ELW 308, LBW 76
Christ, whose glory fills the skies ELW 553, LBW 265
Shine, Jesus, shine ELW 671, WOV 651, TFF 64

Hymn of the Day

Jesus on the mountain peak   ELW 317   BETHOLD
WOV 653   ST. ALBINUS
Oh, wondrous image, vision fair   ELW 316, LBW 80
DEO GRACIAS
Come, beloved of the Maker   ELW 306   JILL

Offering

The only Son from heaven   ELW 309, LBW 86
How good, Lord, to be here!   ELW 315, LBW 89

Communion

Beautiful Savior   ELW 838, LBW 518
Love divine, all loves excelling   ELW 631, LBW 315
Let all mortal flesh keep silence   ELW 490, LBW 198

Sending

Alleluia, song of gladness   ELW 318
We are marching in the light   ELW 866, WOV 650, TFF 63

Additional Hymns and Songs

Majesty   W&P 94
Awake, O sleeper!   DH 63
And have the bright immensities   LBW 391

Music for the Day
Psalmody and Acclamations

Ferguson, John. *Gospel Acclamations for Advent–Transfiguration.*
Jennings, Carolyn. "Psalm 2" from PSCY.
Roberts, Leon C. "Bow Down before the Holy Mountain of God (Psalm 99)." TFF 11.
Roberts, William Bradley. "Psalm 99," Refrain 2, from PSCY.
Seltz, Martin A. "Psalm 99" from PWA, Evangelical Lutheran Worship Edition.
Wetzler, Robert. "Psalm 2" from PWA, Evangelical Lutheran Worship Edition.

Choral

Cherwien, David/M. A. Balakireff. "Send Out Thy Light." SATB. MSM 50-6035.
○ Hofreiter, Paul W. "Anthem for Transfiguration." SATB, org. AFP 9780800664190.
Pooler, Marie, arr. "Be Thou My Vision" from *Augsburg Easy Choirbook*, vol. 1. U, desc, kybd. AFP 9780800676025.
○ Scholz, Robert, arr. "Oh, Wondrous Type! O Vision Fair." SATB, hb, opt perc. MSM 50-2600.

Children's Choir

Hughes, Pamela. "Come to the Mountain" from *LifeSongs.* LE, U, kybd.
Makeever, Ray. "Bright and Morning Star" from *Dancing at the Harvest.* U, kybd.

○ denotes suggestions that relate to the hymn of the day.
● denotes songs that are available on iTunes®.

Tunseth, Kathy. "Come to the Mountain" from *Worship & Praise.* U, kybd. AFP 9780806638508.

Keyboard / Instrumental

○ Eggert, John. "Deo gracias" from *Six Hymn Preludes*, vol. 2. Org. CPH 97-5912U1.
○ Helman, Michael. "Deo gracias" from *Five for Autumn.* Org. AFP 9780800676711.
○ Miller, Aaron David. "Bethold" from *Introductions and Alternate Accompaniments for Piano*, vol. 2. Pno. AFP 9780800623609.
Shepperd, Mark. "Trumpet Tune in C" from *Trumpet Tunes for Organ.* Org, tpt. MSM 10-977.

Handbell

Behnke, John. "When Morning Gilds the Skies." 3-5 oct, L4. AFP 9780800674861.
Kinyon, Barbara. "When Morning Gilds the Skies." 2-3 oct, L3-. HOP 2223.
○ Tucker, Sondra. "Festival Prelude on Deo Gracias." 3-6 oct hb, opt 3-6 oct hc, L4. BP HB325.

Praise Ensemble

● Brown, Brenton. "Lord, Reign in Me." VIN.
● Kendrick, Graham. "Shine, Jesus, Shine." Make Way Music. ELW 671.
● Redman, Matt. "Better Is One Day." Thankyou Music.
● Smith, Michael W. "Agnus Dei." Sony/ATV Music.
● Story, Laura. "Indescribable." WT/Sixsteps Music.
● Tomlin, Chris/Daniel Carson/Ed Cash/Jesse Reeves. "Jesus Messiah." WT/Sixsteps Music.

Global

Kortekangas, Olli. "Iloitse, maa!/Halleluja-laulu" from *Agape: Songs of Hope and Reconciliation.* U. Lutheran World Federation. AFP 9780191000133.
Syria, traditional. "Halle, Hallelujah" from *Pave the Way: Global Songs 3.* U. AFP 9780800676896.

Monday, March 7

Perpetua and Felicity and companions, martyrs at Carthage, died 202

In the year 202 the emperor Septimius Severus forbade conversions to Christianity. Perpetua, a noblewoman, Felicity, a slave, and other companions were all catechumens at Carthage in North Africa. They were imprisoned and sentenced to death. Perpetua's father, who was not a Christian, visited her in prison and begged her to lay aside her Christian convictions in order to spare her life and spare the family from scorn. Perpetua responded and told her father, "We know that we are not placed in our own power but in that of God."

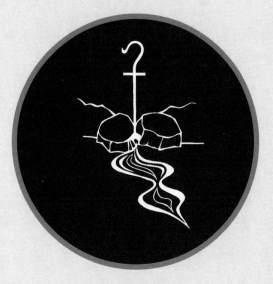

LENT

PREPARING FOR LENT

Hermeneutics of Suspicion

Before we seek to score points against the genetic fallacies and ad hominem arguments of modern atheists, before we "turn suspicion against the suspicious," perhaps we ought to adopt self-suspicion "as the hermeneutics of Lent." We ought to consider the possibility that in our own religion, "what presents itself as an altruistic virtue may be, in terms of motive and function, only an egoistic vice dressed up in its Sunday-go-to-meetin' clothes."[1]

In the summer of 2009, Rob Bell hosted Poets, Prophets, Preachers, a conference on reclaiming the art of the sermon. One presenter at the event, Peter Rollins, convenes an "iconic" collective that offers experiments in transformance art, sometimes also called theodramatic events. The collective, called Ikon, defies easy or simple definition. However, it is fair to say that what they are up to, at least in part, is to offer a radical, postmodern form of worship for those on the margins of faith and the church. To learn more about Ikon, visit http://www.ikon.org.uk or http://faithasawayoflife.typepad.com/blog/2009/02/atheism-for-lent-practicing-music-video-divina.html.

For our purposes, we consider one exercise Ikon engages in that can inform our Lenten worship preparations. They call it "Atheism for Lent." Each year, they read a book influenced by, or about, the prominent hermeneuts of suspicion: Feuerbach, Marx, Freud, and Nietzsche. This practice, though radical, resonates with Cornelius Plantinga's idea in *Not the Way It's Supposed to Be*, quoted above, and may be a fruitful approach to Lent in 2011.

Why? Because our own religion can easily become an egoistic vice dressed up in Sunday-go-to-meetin' clothes, and our own people, and especially our neighbors, know this. Pastors and church leaders are not unfamiliar with the critique that the church is full of hypocrites who act one way on Sunday and another way the rest of the week. And truthfully, even the leaders of the churches—maybe especially the leaders of the churches—are guilty of this. So Lent, the season of repentance, begins with a reminder of our profound sin and mortality (Ash Wednesday), and walks us all the way to a cross which, if we are honest, we

recognize as the place where we crucified the Son of God. It is not at all out of place, during this time, to listen to those suspicious of religion, and suspicious of the church, precisely in order to encourage and develop our own self-suspicion.

There are other ways to exercise self-suspicion during Lent. One is to recommit to the practice of confession. Encourage regular corporate confession in the assembly, but also exercise the rite of individual confession and forgiveness. Begin with yourself and the leadership. Do not encourage the members of the congregation to schedule a time for individual confession and forgiveness if you have not first confessed yourself. Remember also to take small steps in this, because individual confession and forgiveness is a rite that has fallen into disuse in most of our churches, and so can be intimidating in even small doses. Teach it and discuss it in small groups and with key leaders. Ask a neighboring pastor to hear your confession if you are the sole pastor in a congregation. Find a monastic community or religious order that practices individual confession and find out whether opportunity is available to learn about and make use of the confessional. Seek out a neighboring pastor also if you feel uncomfortable confessing to your own pastor. And remember that all the baptized are welcome to hear confession and speak words of forgiveness.

Ash Wednesday

Each of the sections in *Evangelical Lutheran Worship* begins with an introduction that includes one or more "patterns" for worship. It is worthwhile to review these patterns at the beginning of a new church season in order to step back and examine the overall shape of the rite. This is especially useful when planning worship for Lent and the Three Days, because "on several key days at the center of the church year . . . worship takes a particular shape" (*Evangelical Lutheran Worship*, p. 247).

Ash Wednesday is an especially solemn day, and focuses on repentance. This much is generally known. But the overall shape of the service for Ash Wednesday is penitential, not just the individual elements of it. The assembly is called to gather in silence. This is often difficult to accomplish in reality, and may require special planning. Signs can

---

[1] Cornelius Plantinga Jr., *Not the Way It's Supposed to Be: A Breviary of Sin*, referencing Westphal, "Taking Suspicion Seriously" (Eerdmans, 1995), p. 111.

help, or special instructions to the greeters, but lighting and environment also play a role. It may even help to announce on the Sunday prior to Ash Wednesday that when people arrive, they remember the solemn and penitential nature of the service, prepare themselves for silence, shut off their phones, pray as they drive or ride a bus or walk to the service, and in every way enter into the season with solemnity.

The service then continues with a reading (or better, a chanted version) of Psalm 51. Consider inviting a solo voice to sing some verses and a small ensemble to sing antiphonally with the single voice. This can accentuate the psalm as a prayer on the lips of David *and* of the gathered community.

The readings and sermon are followed by a special invitation to Lent and an opportunity for confession of sin. Prepare a way for the assembly to make confession not only with their mouths but also with their bodies. Provide kneelers if possible. If not, suggest a prayer posture. In some settings, this might be as simple as inviting worshipers to open their hands and turn them slightly upwards as they pray, in this way showing their empty hands desirous of mercy.

Following the confession, the assembly moves, kneels, hears that they are dust, and receives ashes on their foreheads. Near the end of the service, a prayer asks that God "accompany our journey through these forty days" and "renew us in the gift of baptism." The assembly has embarked on a journey, a fast, hungry for a liberating word they know is on the way—hungry with and for Jesus for forty days.

Lenten Lectionary

The lectionary for Lent encourages and trains readers in self-suspicion. This begins on Ash Wednesday, which is a service of the church that trains us in the ministry of irony. We hear Joel declare, "Rend your hearts and not your clothing" (Joel 2:13), and Jesus say, "Whenever you fast, do not look dismal, like the hypocrites, for they disfigure their faces so as to show others that they are fasting" (Matt. 6:16). But then the assembly wears ash and oil on their foreheads in a visible symbol of piety. The preacher, who may later in the service pray long prayers, reads Jesus' words, "Whenever you pray, do not be like the hypocrites; for they love to stand and pray in the synagogues and at the street corners, so that they may be seen by others" (Matt. 6:5). Hypocrisy indeed!

However, do not let the readings dissuade from the practices. Let the tensions stand. The tensions preach, for they cut to the heart if we listen with the heart. These tensions run throughout the Lenten season, and they are worth noting, even drawing out as a theme. The devil is the first instigator, tempting Jesus in the wilderness by quoting the very word of God (Matt. 4:5). Nicodemus, seemingly so faithful and curious, is not brave enough, let alone faithful enough, to travel by day, and instead visits Jesus at night. Self-protection? Symbolism? In any event, worship leaders and preachers beware, and attend to Jesus' question, "Are you a teacher of [the church], and yet you do not understand these things?" (John 3:10).

As the gospel readings for Lent continue, it is the Gospel of John that takes center stage, and the self-suspicion continues. However, there is a new literary strategy at work. Repeatedly, characters in the readings fail to understand something. The Samaritan woman does not understand, at least at first, Jesus' meaning concerning living water. Next, a blind man sees (literally and figuratively), while the Pharisees, so convinced of their ability to see, are found uttering (ironically), "Surely we are not blind, are we?" (John 9:40). Finally, even Jesus' closest friends, Mary and Martha, in their brush with the death of their brother, Lazarus, are catechized in true faithfulness. As we read through each of these misunderstandings and further developments, something becomes clear. Our own vision is clarified. We see with new eyes. John's gospel teaches the reader by learning from the mistakes of others.

These texts so clearly focus on self-suspicion and "seeing" that it is almost imperative that worship leaders find ways to show forth the gospel readings in their worship space. Consider lifting out and rephrasing key questions in the gospels, then printing them on posters or banners to place throughout the church building. "We are not blind, are we?" "Where can I find this living water?" "Why, Jesus, did you let my loved one die?" "Are you really the Son of God?"

Each of these stories can also be readily portrayed in art, glass, mosaic, or 3-D. Consider soliciting the artistic talents of the members of the congregation, and create a "Stations of Lent." The series would be: temptation of Jesus, Nicodemus at night, Samaritan woman at the well, blind man receives sight and puzzles Pharisees, and Lazarus being raised from the dead.

Lent Midweek

Some congregations are so busy with programs, small groups, choir rehearsals, meetings, and events that Lenten midweek services simply add to the mix and crowd it. In these congregations, the discipline of midweek Lenten devotional services may be an invitation to simplify. Martha Grace Reese, in her resource *Unbinding the Gospel* (Chalice Press, 2008), an evangelism and prayer resource designed to be used over a forty-day period like Lent, suggests that churches cancel all other events while studying the book, in order to fast, pray, and simplify. Congregations don't necessarily need to study such a book during Lent, but they may do well to simplify during this season in order to make space for the "disciplines" of Lent.

Other congregations, however, are so weak in their small-group ministries, so enervated in general, that Lenten midweek services may be exactly the discipline needed to spark renewed passion for the gospel of Jesus Christ and the patterns of church life that can sustain and flame that passion. In congregations like this, make use of Lenten midweek services not to simplify but instead to offer opportunities for deepening and development. Prepare meals together with a prayer service built into the meal. Review the abundant resources that are available to renew Lent as a season of baptismal spirituality. The midweek service can provide context and pattern for small-group meetings, communal meals, and an emphasis on spiritual journey, fasting, and prayer.

Seasonal Checklist

- Review the liturgies for Ash Wednesday and the Sunday of the Passion provided in *Evangelical Lutheran Worship* (Assembly Edition, pp. 247–257; Leaders Edition, pp. 611–627).
- Purchase new resources for Lent and the Three Days that contain insights, images, ideas, commentary, practical tips, songs, and responses to help your congregation deepen its worship life during the days from Ash Wednesday to Easter: *Worship Guidebook for Lent and the Three Days* and *Music Sourcebook for Lent and the Three Days*, both from Augsburg Fortress.
- Arrange to simplify the worship environment during Lent. Center environment on the font and table.

- Order worship participation leaflets if used for the Ash Wednesday and/or Passion Sunday liturgies.
- Burn palms from the previous Passion Sunday or obtain ashes from a church supplier for use on Ash Wednesday (March 9).
- If midweek services will be held during Lent, determine the style, content, and leadership. See the seasonal rites section for possibilities (pp. 114–121). Order bulletin covers if needed.
- If a healing service will be held during Lent, consider using the order provided in *Evangelical Lutheran Worship Occasional Services for the Assembly*.
- If corporate and individual confession and forgiveness will be offered during Lent, consider using the orders provided in *Evangelical Lutheran Worship*, pp. 238–244.
- Consider ordering eco-palms for Passion Sunday (http://www.lwr.org/palms/). Additional palm branches or plants might be used as part of the worship environment that day. If long, individual palm fronds are used, they will need to be separated ahead of time. Reserve leftover palm branches to be burned for ashes the following year.
- Determine how and where the procession with palms will take place on Passion Sunday. Prepare signs or recruit volunteers to help direct people. Determine how those with physical disabilities will participate in the process or be seated ahead of time.
- Schedule a rehearsal of readers in preparation for the passion reading on Passion Sunday.

WORSHIP TEXTS FOR LENT

Confession and Forgiveness

All may make the sign of the cross, the sign marked at baptism,
as the presiding minister begins.
Blessed be the holy Trinity, ✝ one God,
the well of eternal life,
the light of the world,
the breath giving life to dry bones.
Amen.

Let us confess our sin
in the presence of God and of one another.

Silence is kept for reflection.

Gracious God,
we confess that we have sinned
in thought, word, and deed,
by what we have done
and by what we have left undone.
Forgive us and give us strength
to turn from sin
and to serve you in newness of life. Amen.

By water and the Holy Spirit,
God gives us new birth,
and through the death and resurrection of Jesus Christ,
God forgives us all our sins.
Almighty God strengthen us in all goodness
and keep us in eternal life.
Amen.

OR

Let us confess our sin
in the presence of God and of one another.

Silence is kept for reflection.

Holy God, holy and mighty, holy and immortal,
have mercy on us.

For self-centered living,
and for failing to walk with humility and gentleness:
Holy God, holy and mighty, holy and immortal,
have mercy on us.

For longing to have what is not ours,
and for hearts that are not at rest with ourselves:
Holy God, holy and mighty, holy and immortal,
have mercy on us.

For misuse of human relationships,
and for unwillingness to see the image of God in others:
Holy God, holy and mighty, holy and immortal,
have mercy on us.

For jealousies that divide families and nations,
and for rivalries that create strife and warfare:
Holy God, holy and mighty, holy and immortal,
have mercy on us.

For reluctance in sharing the gifts of God,
and for carelessness with the fruits of creation:
Holy God, holy and mighty, holy and immortal,
have mercy on us.

For hurtful words that condemn,
and for angry deeds that harm:
Holy God, holy and mighty, holy and immortal,
have mercy on us.

For idleness in witnessing to Jesus Christ,
and for squandering the gifts of love and grace:
**Holy God, holy and mighty, holy and immortal,
have mercy on us.**

In the mercy of almighty God,
Jesus Christ was given to die for us,
and for his sake God forgives us all our sins.
Through the Holy Spirit God cleanses us
and gives us the power to proclaim
the mighty acts of the one who called us
out of darkness into his marvelous light.
As a called and ordained minister of the church of Christ,
and by his authority,
I therefore declare to you
the entire forgiveness of all your sins,
in the name of the Father, and of the + Son,
and of the Holy Spirit.
Amen.

Greeting

The free gift of grace in Jesus Christ,
the reconciling love of God,
and the life and peace of the Holy Spirit
be with you all.
And also with you.

Offering Prayer

God our provider,
you have not fed us with bread alone,
but with words of grace and life.
Bless us and these your gifts,
which we receive from your bounty,
through Jesus Christ our Lord.
Amen.

Invitation to Communion

Come to Christ, broken and poured out for you.

Prayer after Communion

Merciful God,
accompany our journey through these forty days.
Renew us in the gift of baptism,
that we may provide for those who are poor,
pray for those in need,
fast from self-indulgence,
and above all that we may find our treasure
in the life of your Son,
Jesus Christ, our Savior and Lord.
Amen.

Sending of Communion

Eternal God,
whose glory is revealed in the crucified and risen Lord,
bless those who go forth to share your word and sacrament
with our sisters and brothers
who are *sick/homebound/imprisoned*.
In your love and care, nourish and strengthen
those to whom we bring this communion
in the body and blood of your Son,
that we may all feast upon your abundant love
made known in Jesus Christ our Lord.
Amen.

Blessing

The blessed, holy Trinity
keep you in grace,
lead you in light,
and + give you peace.
Amen.

Dismissal

Go in peace. Remember the poor.
Thanks be to God.

Midweek Lenten Series: By Faith

What is faith? The text from Hebrews 11:1 defines it in this way: "Now faith is the assurance of things hoped for, the conviction of things not seen." This series focuses on the book of Hebrews, especially the eleventh chapter. The first four weeks provide a journey through the faith of the Old Testament figures, especially Noah, Abraham, Moses, and the Israelites. The fifth week brings us to Jesus, "the perfecter of our faith," and his path to the cross.

The opening dialogue, response following the reflection, and blessing are based on passages from Hebrews. The responsive prayer incorporates themes from Hebrews 12–13.

Overview

Week of Lent 1: The Faith of Noah
By faith, Noah built the ark, gathered the animals, watched the waters rise, and received the rainbow promise. How do we have faith in things not yet seen?

Week of Lent 2: The Faith of Abraham
By faith, Abraham journeyed to an unknown land, trusted in God's promise of a son, and offered up that son as a sacrifice. When faith means taking a risk, how do we respond?

Week of Lent 3: The Faith of Moses
By faith, Moses chose the hard path to follow God's call. How does our faith affect the choices we must make?

Week of Lent 4: The Faith of the Israelites
By faith, generations of Israelites wandered the wilderness, entered the promised land, heard the words of the prophets, and suffered persecution. Amid life's joys and difficulties, how do we persevere in our faith?

Week of Lent 5: Jesus, the Perfecter of Our Faith
Enduring the cross, Jesus became "the pioneer and perfecter of our faith." How does the way of the cross define our faith?

Opening Dialogue

Long ago God spoke to our ancestors
in many and various ways, by the prophets,
but in these last days God has spoken to us by the Son.
He is the reflection of God's glory
and the exact imprint of God's very being,
and he sustains all things by his powerful word.
Since we have confidence by the new and living way
opened for us by Jesus,
**let us approach with a true heart
in full assurance of faith.**

Gathering Song

Week of Lent 1: Chief of sinners though I be   ELW 609
Week of Lent 2: Will you come and follow me   ELW 798
Week of Lent 3: For by grace you have been saved   ELW 598
Week of Lent 4: Faith of our fathers   ELW 812/813
Week of Lent 5: Let us ever walk with Jesus   ELW 802

Reading

Week of Lent 1: Hebrews 11:1-7
Week of Lent 2: Hebrews 11:1, 8-22
Week of Lent 3: Hebrews 11:1, 23-28
Week of Lent 4: Hebrews 11:1, 29-40
Week of Lent 5: Hebrews 12:1-2

Reflection

The reflection may conclude:
Now faith is the assurance of things hoped for,
the conviction of things not seen.

Hymn of the Day

Week of Lent 1: When peace like a river   ELW 785
Week of Lent 2: Bless now, O God, the journey   ELW 326
Week of Lent 3: Guide me ever, great Redeemer   ELW 618
Week of Lent 4: We've come this far by faith   ELW 633
Week of Lent 5: He comes to us as one unknown   ELW 737

Prayers

Surrounded by a great cloud of witnesses, let us pray for the church, those in need, and all of God's creation.

A brief silence.

Faithful God, shower the world with your lovingkindness,
that all may know your peace.
Open our eyes to the needs of our neighbors,
that all may know your love.
Comfort the sick and dying,
that all may know your mercy.
Guide our leaders in the way of truth,
that all may know your justice.
Focus our hearts on the way of the cross,
that all may have faith in you.

Let us pray in the words of Martin Luther:
Behold, Lord, an empty vessel that needs to be filled. My Lord, fill it. I am weak in the faith; strengthen me. I am cold in love; warm me and make me fervent, that my love may go out to my neighbor. I do not have a strong and firm faith; at times I doubt and am unable to trust you altogether. O Lord, help me. Strengthen my faith and trust in you. In you I have sealed the treasure of all I have. I am poor; you are rich and came to be merciful to the poor. I am a sinner; you are upright. With me, there is an abundance of sin; in you is the fullness of righteousness. Therefore I will remain with you, of whom I can receive, but to whom I may not give. Amen. (*Evangelical Lutheran Worship*, p. 87)

Lord's Prayer

Finally, let us pray with the words our Savior gave us:
Our Father . . .

Blessing

The God of peace,
who brought back from the dead our Lord Jesus,
the great shepherd of the sheep,
make you complete in everything good
so that you may do God's will,
through Jesus Christ, to whom be the glory forever and ever.
Amen.

Sending Hymn

Week of Lent 1: Great is thy faithfulness   ELW 733
Week of Lent 2: That priceless grace   ELW 591
Week of Lent 3: As the deer runs to the river   ELW 331
Week of Lent 4: We walk by faith   ELW 635
Week of Lent 5: My faith looks up to thee   ELW 759

The Way of the Cross

The Way of the Cross may be used for individual prayer or as a public liturgy, particularly on the Fridays in Lent. The congregation may assemble in the church, or at another appointed place (especially if outdoor stations are to be made).

In the name of the Father, and of the + Son,
and of the Holy Spirit.
Amen.

Lord, have mercy.
Christ, have mercy.
Lord, have mercy.

Lord's Prayer

We will glory in the cross of our Lord Jesus Christ,
in whom is our salvation, our life, and resurrection.

Let us pray.
Mercifully assist us, O Lord God of our salvation,
that we may remember with joy the mighty acts
whereby you have given us life everlasting;
through Jesus Christ our Lord.
Amen.

The procession moves to the first station.

First Station
Jesus Is Condemned to Death

We adore you, O Christ, and we bless you.
By your holy cross you have redeemed the world.

As soon as it was morning, the chief priests held a consultation with the elders and scribes and the whole council. They bound Jesus, led him away, and handed him over to Pilate. Pilate spoke to the crowd: "What do you wish me to do with the man you call the king of the Jews?" They shouted back, "Crucify him!" Pilate said to them, "Why, what evil has he done?" But they shouted all the more, "Crucify him!" So, after flogging Jesus, Pilate handed him over to be crucified.

God did not spare his own Son,
but delivered him up for us all.

Hymns
They crucified my Lord   ELW 350, TFF 80
Precious Lord, take my hand   ELW 773, WOV 731, TFF 193

Let us pray.
Almighty God, your Son our Savior suffered at the hands of sinners and endured the shame of the cross. Grant that we may walk in the way of his cross and find it the way of life and peace; through your Son, Jesus Christ our Lord.
Amen.

Holy God, holy and mighty, holy and immortal,
have mercy on us.

The procession moves to the second station.

Second Station
Jesus Takes Up His Cross

We adore you, O Christ, and we bless you.
By your holy cross you have redeemed the world.

Carrying the cross by himself, Jesus went out to the place called The Place of the Skull, which in Hebrew is called Golgotha. Although he was a Son, he learned obedience through what he suffered. Like a lamb that is led to the slaughter and like a sheep that before its shearers is silent, so he did not open his mouth. Worthy is the Lamb who was slain to receive power and riches, and wisdom and strength, and honor and glory and blessing.

The Lord has laid on him the iniquity of us all:
for the transgression of my people was he stricken.

Hymns
Jesus, keep me near the cross   ELW 335, TFF 73
Let all that is within me cry, "Holy!" TFF 282

Let us pray.
Almighty God, whose beloved Son willingly endured the agony and shame of the cross for our redemption: Give us courage to take up our cross and follow him; who lives and reigns forever and ever.
Amen.

Holy God, holy and mighty, holy and immortal,
have mercy on us.

The procession moves to the third station.

Third Station
The Cross Is Laid on Simon of Cyrene

We adore you, O Christ, and we bless you.
By your holy cross you have redeemed the world.

As they led Jesus away, they seized a man, Simon of Cyrene, who was coming from the country, and they laid the cross on him, and made him carry it behind Jesus. "If any want to become my followers, let them deny themselves and take up their cross and follow me. Take my yoke upon you, and learn from me; for my yoke is easy, and my burden is light."

Whoever does not carry the cross and follow me
cannot be my disciple.

Hymns
Lead me, guide me   ELW 768, TFF 70, W&P 84
All to Jesus I surrender   TFF 235

Let us pray.
Heavenly Father, whose blessed Son came not to be served but to serve: Bless all who, following in his steps, give themselves to the service of others; that with wisdom, patience, and courage, they may minister in his name to the suffering, the friendless, and the needy; for the love of him who laid down his life for us, your Son our Savior Jesus Christ.
Amen.

Holy God, holy and mighty, holy and immortal,
have mercy on us.

The procession moves to the fourth station.

Fourth Station
Jesus Meets the Women of Jerusalem

We adore you, O Christ, and we bless you.
By your holy cross you have redeemed the world.

A great number of the people followed Jesus, and among them were women who were wailing for him. But Jesus turned to them and said, "Daughters of Jerusalem, do not weep for me, but weep for yourselves and for your children."

Those who sowed with tears
will reap with songs of joy.

Hymns
I want Jesus to walk with me   ELW 325, WOV 660, TFF 66
By the waters of Babylon   TFF 67

Let us pray.
Teach your church, O Lord, to mourn the sins of which it is guilty, and to repent and forsake them; that, by your pardoning grace, the results of our iniquities may not be visited upon our children and our children's children; through Jesus Christ our Lord.
Amen.

Holy God, holy and mighty, holy and immortal,
have mercy on us.

The procession moves to the fifth station.

Fifth Station
Jesus Is Stripped of His Garments

We adore you, O Christ, and we bless you.
By your holy cross you have redeemed the world.

When they came to a place called Golgotha, they offered him wine to drink, mixed with gall; but when he tasted it, he would not drink it. The soldiers divided his garments among them by casting lots. This was to fulfill what the scripture says, "They divided my clothes among themselves, and for my clothing they cast lots."

They gave me gall to eat,
and when I was thirsty they gave me vinegar to drink.

Hymns
Now behold the Lamb   ELW 341, TFF 128
When the storms of life are raging   TFF 198
Oh, freedom   TFF 208

Let us pray.
O God, your Son chose the path which led to pain before joy and the cross before glory. Plant his cross in our hearts, so that in its power and love we may come at last to joy and glory; through your Son, Jesus Christ our Lord.
Amen.

Holy God, holy and mighty, holy and immortal,
have mercy on us.

The procession moves to the sixth station.

Sixth Station
Jesus Is Nailed to the Cross

We adore you, O Christ, and we bless you.
By your holy cross you have redeemed the world.

When they came to the place that is called The Skull, there they crucified Jesus; and with him they crucified two criminals, one on the right, and one on the left. He poured out himself to death, and yet he bore the sin of many.

They pierce my hands and my feet;
they stare and gloat over me.

Hymns
On a hill far away   TFF 77
Were you there   ELW 353 (sts. 1-3), TFF 81 (sts. 1-3)

Let us pray.
Lord Jesus Christ, you stretched out your arms of love on the hard wood of the cross that everyone might come within the reach of your saving embrace. So clothe us in your Spirit that we, reaching forth our hands in love, may bring those who do not know you to the knowledge and love of you; for the honor of your name.
Amen.

Holy God, holy and mighty, holy and immortal,
have mercy on us.

The procession moves to the seventh station.

Seventh Station
Jesus Dies on the Cross

We adore you, O Christ, and we bless you.
By your holy cross you have redeemed the world.

When Jesus saw his mother and the disciple whom he loved standing beside her, he said to his mother, "Woman, behold your son." Then he said to the disciple, "Behold your mother." And when Jesus had received the vinegar he said, "It is finished!" Then he bowed his head and gave up his spirit.

Christ for us became obedient unto death,
even death on a cross.

Hymns
That priceless grace   ELW 591, TFF 68
Calvary   ELW 354, TFF 85

Let us pray.
O God, you gave your only Son to suffer death on the cross for our redemption, and by his glorious resurrection you delivered us from the power of death. Make us die every day to sin, so that we may live with him forever in the joy of the resurrection; who lives and reigns now and forever.
Amen.

Holy God, holy and mighty, holy and immortal,
have mercy on us.

The procession moves to the eighth station.

Eighth Station
Jesus Is Laid in the Tomb

We adore you, O Christ, and we bless you.
By your holy cross you have redeemed the world.

When it was evening, there came a rich man from Arimathea, named Joseph, who was also a disciple of Jesus. He went to Pilate and asked for the body of Jesus. Then Pilate ordered it to be given to him. So Joseph took the body and wrapped it in a clean linen cloth and laid it in his own new tomb, which he had hewn in the rock. He then rolled a great stone to the door of the tomb.

You will not abandon me to the grave,
nor let your holy one see corruption.

Hymns

Were you there   ELW 353 (sts. 4-5), TFF 81 (sts. 4-5)
King of my life   TFF 86

Let us pray.
O God, your blessed Son was laid in a tomb in a garden, and rested on the Sabbath day. Grant that we who have been buried with him in the waters of baptism may find our perfect rest in his eternal and glorious kingdom; where he lives and reigns forever and ever.
Amen.

Holy God, holy and mighty, holy and immortal,
have mercy on us.

The procession may move to the chancel or the place of gathering.

Conclusion

Savior of the world, by your cross and precious blood you have redeemed us.
Save us and help us, we humbly beseech you, O Lord.

Let us pray.
We thank you, heavenly Father, that you have delivered us from the dominion of sin and death and brought us into the kingdom of your Son; and we pray that, as by his death he has recalled us to life, so by his love he may raise us to eternal joys; who lives and reigns with you, in the unity of the Holy Spirit, one God, now and forever.
Amen.

To Christ our Lord who loves us, washed us in his own blood, and made us a kingdom of priests to serve his God and Father, to him be glory and dominion forever and ever.
Amen.

NOTES ON THE SERVICE

The Way of the Cross is a devotion adapted from a custom observed by Christian pilgrims who said prayers in Jerusalem at a series of places in that city associated with the passion of Jesus.

Traditionally, there have been as many as fourteen stations. Of these, eight are based directly on events of scripture and are included in this rite. Each station includes sentences and responses, scripture verses, a prayer, and a hymn.

Although the rite is especially appropriate on the Fridays in Lent, it does not displace the proper liturgy for Good Friday.

The Way of the Cross resonates with several aspects of African and African American Christian traditions: an association with struggle and suffering; the concepts of pilgrimage and marching for justice; and a hymnic tradition that proclaims the saving blood and cross of Christ.

Traditionally, the procession moves to stations at a series of plain wooden crosses placed along the walls of the church. With each cross there may also be a pictorial representation of the event being remembered.

Stations may also be made outside the church walls as a public witness. Outdoor stations may be made at significant locations in the immediate neighborhood where healing is needed and where associations between the contemporary struggles of life and the events of Christ's suffering can be made (for example, sites where crimes have occurred, abandoned buildings, or other places of human struggle).

Visual depictions for the stations may include sculpture, paintings, murals, photographs, or modern images, possibly created by people from the community.

The hymns listed are suggestions. Other appropriate hymns and songs may be sung, and individual stanzas may be selected as needed. The opening and closing sentences at each station, "We adore you, O Christ" and "Holy God," may be sung to a variety of musical settings.

The one who presides may lead sentences and prayers; the prayer provided for each station or an appropriate free prayer may be used. One or more readers may proclaim the scripture verses. An assisting minister may carry a large, rough-hewn wooden cross in procession.

From This Far by Faith: An African American Resource for Worship *(Augsburg Fortress, 1999), adapted.*

March 9, 2011
Ash Wednesday

Lent begins with a solemn call to fasting and repentance as we begin our journey to the baptismal waters of Easter. As we hear in today's readings, now is the acceptable time to return to the Lord. During Lent the people of God will reflect on the meaning of their baptism into Christ's death and resurrection. The sign of ashes suggests our human mortality and frailty. What seems like an ending is really an invitation to make each day a new beginning, in which we are washed in God's mercy and forgiveness. With the cross on our brow, we long for the spiritual renewal that flows from the springtime Easter feast to come.

Prayer of the Day

Almighty and ever-living God, you hate nothing you have made, and you forgive the sins of all who are penitent. Create in us new and honest hearts, so that, truly repenting of our sins, we may receive from you, the God of all mercy, full pardon and forgiveness through your Son, Jesus Christ, our Savior and Lord, who lives and reigns with you and the Holy Spirit, one God, now and forever.
or
Gracious God, out of your love and mercy you breathed into dust the breath of life, creating us to serve you and our neighbors. Call forth our prayers and acts of kindness, and strengthen us to face our mortality with confidence in the mercy of your Son, Jesus Christ, our Savior and Lord, who lives and reigns with you and the Holy Spirit, one God, now and forever.

Gospel Acclamation

Return to the ¹ LORD, your God,* who is gracious and merciful, slow to anger, and abounding in ¹ steadfast love. (Joel 2:13)

Readings and Psalm
Joel 2:1-2, 12-17

Because of the coming Day of the Lord, the prophet Joel calls the people to a community lament. The repentant community reminds God of his gracious character and asks God to spare the people, lest the nations doubt God's power to save.

or Isaiah 58:1-12

Shortly after the return of Israel from exile in Babylon, the people were troubled by the ineffectiveness of their fasts.

God reminds them that outward observance is no substitute for genuine fasting that results in acts of justice, such as feeding the hungry, sheltering the homeless, and clothing the naked. Sincere repentance will lead to a dramatic improvement of their condition.

Psalm 51:1-17

Have mercy on me, O God, according to your steadfast love. (Ps. 51:1)

2 Corinthians 5:20b—6:10

The ministry of the gospel endures many challenges and hardships. Through this ministry, God's reconciling activity in the death of Christ reaches into the depths of our lives to bring us into a right relationship with God. In this way, God accepts us into the reality of divine salvation.

Matthew 6:1-6, 16-21

In the Sermon on the Mount, Jesus commends almsgiving, prayer, and fasting, but emphasizes that spiritual devotion must not be done for show.

Preface Lent

Color Purple

Prayers of Intercession

The prayers are prepared locally for each occasion. The following examples may be adapted or used as appropriate.
As we return to the waters of baptism during this season of Lent, let us pray for the church, those in need, and all of God's creation.
A brief silence.

Help us return to you with all our hearts. Give us the will and the words to pray, in the assembly of believers and in the privacy of our rooms. God of mercy,
hear our prayer.

Teach us to treasure the earth you have made. Bring new life to rivers, oceans, and trees, and to all the animal species that are dying. God of mercy,
hear our prayer.

Now is the acceptable time for us to learn your way of peace. Plant peace in our hearts, in our homes, and in every nation, that it might sprout and flourish. God of mercy,
hear our prayer.

Grant comfort and endurance to all those who suffer from hardships, calamities, beatings, imprisonments, riots, sleepless nights, or hunger. Bring healing to the sick, and rest to the weary (*especially*). God of mercy,
hear our prayer.

Center our congregation in the cross of Christ, the cross of ashes and rebirth. Take away any obstacles standing in the way of serving our neighbor. God of mercy,
hear our prayer.

Here other intercessions may be offered.

As we remember the saints who have gone before us, fill us with hope for the day of salvation, when the ruins will be rebuilt, the streets restored, and the waters will never fail. God of mercy,
hear our prayer.

Into your hands, God of abundant grace, we commend all for whom we pray, trusting in your mercy, through Jesus Christ, our Savior.
Amen.

Ideas and Images for the Day

With ash and soot we begin this Lenten season with confession; we begin with Psalm 51; we begin on our knees. Today this ancient prayer placed on our lips becomes new again: "Have mercy on me, O God, according to your steadfast love; according to your abundant mercy blot out my transgressions." As we confess our unfaithfulness to God, our lackluster love for our neighbors, our neglect of suffering and injustice in the world, we ask God to wash us, to purge us, to create in us clean hearts. This Lent, amid our confession, we listen for the call to return to the LORD our God who is gracious and merciful, abounding in steadfast love (Joel 2:13).

1.   In the preface to his commentary on the psalms, Martin Luther said they "radiate such a sweet and lovely fragrance" that Psalms "could well be called a 'little

Bible' since it contains, set out in the briefest and most beautiful form, all that is to be found in the whole Bible." The psalms capture the fullness of the human experience—the "stormy seas of life" as well as its "lovely pleasure-gardens." Luther concludes by observing that the book of Psalms tastes "good and sweet to those who read it" (*Martin Luther: Selections from His Writings*, John Dillenberger, ed. [New York: Anchor Books, Doubleday, 1962], pp. 38–39). Such glorious descriptions attest to Luther's fondness for the psalms. He knew the power that these prayers evoke when sung and read. How might Psalm 51 kindle in us its power on this holy day?

2.   Consider ways in which the beautiful form and sweet fragrance of Psalm 51 might be accented in worship:

   •   Use different voices to highlight the back-and-forth action between God and the psalm's author in the verses. Careful attention to the text reveals the following pattern: verses 1-2, God's action; verses 3-5, author's action; verses 6-12, God's action; verses 13-15, author's action; verses 16-17, God's action. What does this dialogue say about our relationship with God?

   •   Select an arrangement of this psalm to be sung antiphonally between choir and assembly at the outset of worship.

   •   How might a lone instrument (cello, for example) played during the reading of the psalm highlight the rich tones embedded in the text?

   •   If the imposition of ashes is offered, have a solo voice read Psalm 51 during this time. How will these words be heard during this penitential ritual?

3.   Giving of alms, prayer, and fasting are highlighted in today's appointed gospel, an excerpt from Jesus' Sermon on the Mount. Avoid making these traditional disciplines of Lent a personal goal to be accomplished in forty days; rather, as a community seek to live into these disciplines together. Offer teaching sessions on prayer; invite the children to determine what social services the assembly's offerings will support throughout Lent; hold congregational fasts each Wednesday in Lent, as opposed to the traditional soup-and-salad suppers prevalent in many worship settings. Live out the Lenten disciplines together!

Hymns for Worship and Music for the Day

Because of the nature of this day, music suggestions are listed by place in the service and not categorized by type of leadership. Most suggestions require assembly participation.

Gathering

Psalm 51 (see Psalmody)

Campbell, Jonathan Strommen. "Canticle of Joel." *Music Sourcebook for Lent and the Three Days* S404. AFP 9780806670409.

Jennings, Carolyn. "Litany for Lent." *Music Sourcebook* S417.

Kyrie ELW 151–158 or from communion settings.

Psalmody

Cherwien, David. "Psalm 51" from PSCY.

Mummert, Mark. "Psalm 103:8-14" from PSCY. (Alternate psalm.)

Raabe, Nancy. "Have Mercy on Me, O God (Psalm 51:1-17)." *Music Sourcebook* S402.

Schalk, Carl, or May Schwarz. "Psalm 51:1-17" from PWA, Evangelical Lutheran Worship Edition.

Gospel Acclamation

Fluellen, Jay. "Return to the Lord." *Music Sourcebook* S407.

Miller, Aaron David. *Gospel Acclamations for Lent—Holy Trinity.*

Organ, Anne Krentz. "Return to the Lord." *Music Sourcebook* S419.

Hymn of the Day

Eternal Lord of love, behold your church   ELW 321
OLD 124TH

Out of the depths I cry to you   ELW 600, LBW 295
AUS TIEFER NOT

Our Father, we have wandered   ELW 606, WOV 733
HERZLICH TUT MICH VERLANGEN

Confession of Sin

Music Sourcebook for Lent and the Three Days includes four musical settings of texts for corporate confession of sin, one using the text in the Ash Wednesday service (S408), and others using the text from Corporate Confession and Forgiveness, ELW Leaders Edition, p. 603 (S409–S411).

Imposition of Ashes

Haskel, Marilyn. "Return to the Lord." *Music Sourcebook* S414.

Mummert, Mark. "Remember That You Are Dust." *Music Sourcebook* S413.

Psalm 51 (if not used earlier in the service—see Psalmody)

Savior, when in dust to you   ELW 601, LBW 91

Setting the Table

Music Sourcebook for Lent and the Three Days includes an appendix with hymn stanzas appropriate for use during the setting of the table on this and other days. These stanzas are also included on the CD-ROM that accompanies the volume.

Communion

Restore in us, O God   ELW 328, WOV 662

Softly and tenderly Jesus is calling   ELW 608

Once we sang and danced   ELW 701

Sending

On my heart imprint your image   ELW 811, LBW 102

Be thou my vision   ELW 793, WOV 776

Thursday, March 10

Harriet Tubman, died 1913; Sojourner Truth, died 1883; renewers of society

Harriet Tubman was born into slavery in Maryland and remained a slave until about age thirty when, fearing she would be sold and moved farther south, she escaped with the help of the Underground Railroad. After that, she helped about three hundred others to escape until slavery was abolished. After the Civil War, her home in Auburn, New York, became a center for women's rights and served the aged and poor.

Sojourner Truth, too, was born a slave, in New York state. Her birth name was Isabella. After slavery was abolished in New York in 1827, she was freed and, while working as a housekeeper, became deeply involved in Christianity. A number of years later, she discerned a call to become a preacher. Taking the name Sojourner Truth, she set out on an evangelistic journey, where people found her testimony to be deeply moving. In later life, she also became a popular speaker against slavery and for women's rights.

Saturday, March 12

Gregory the Great, Bishop of Rome, died 604

Gregory was born into a politically influential family. At one time he held political office and at another time he lived as a monk, all before he was elected to the papacy. Gregory's work was extensive. He influenced public worship through the establishment of a lectionary and prayers to correlate with the readings. He established a school to train church musicians. Gregorian chant is named in his honor. He wrote a treatise underscoring what is required of a pastor serving a congregation. He sent missionaries to preach to the Anglo-Saxons who had invaded England. And at one time he organized distribution of grain during a shortage of food in Rome.

March 13, 2011
First Sunday in Lent

Today's gospel tells of Jesus' temptation in the desert. His forty-day fast becomes the basis of our Lenten pilgrimage. In the early church Lent was a time of intense preparation for those to be baptized at the Easter Vigil. This catechetical focus on the meaning of faith is at the heart of our Lenten journey to the baptismal waters of Easter. Hungry for God's mercy, we receive the bread of life to nourish us for the days ahead.

Prayer of the Day

Lord God, our strength, the struggle between good and evil rages within and around us, and the devil and all the forces that defy you tempt us with empty promises. Keep us steadfast in your word, and when we fall, raise us again and restore us through your Son, Jesus Christ, our Savior and Lord, who lives and reigns with you and the Holy Spirit, one God, now and forever.

Gospel Acclamation

One does not live by ¹ bread alone,* but by every word that comes from the ¹ mouth of God. (Matt. 4:4)

Readings and Psalm
Genesis 2:15-17; 3:1-7

Human beings were formed with great care, to be in relationship with the creator, creation, and one another. The serpent's promise to the first couple that their eyes would be opened led, ironically, to the discovery only that they were naked.

Psalm 32

You forgave me the guilt of my sin. (Ps. 32:6)

Romans 5:12-19

Through Adam's disobedience, humanity came under bondage to sin and death, from which we cannot free ourselves. In Christ's obedient death, God graciously showers on us the free gift of liberation and life.

Matthew 4:1-11

Jesus experiences anew the temptations that Israel faced in the wilderness. As the Son of God, he endures the testing of the evil one.

Preface Lent

Color Purple

Prayers of Intercession

The prayers are prepared locally for each occasion. The following examples may be adapted or used as appropriate.

As we return to the waters of baptism during this season of Lent, let us pray for the church, those in need, and all of God's creation.

A brief silence.

Let us pray for the one, holy, catholic church; for all preparing for baptism; for all hungering for grace. Give us your Word of Life, for we cannot live on bread alone. God of mercy,

hear our prayer.

Let us pray for the earth and all the fruits of your creation; for rain forests and deserts; for polar ice caps and wetlands; for wilderness lands and wild animals. God of mercy,

hear our prayer.

Let us pray for the nations, plagued by war and famine (*especially*); for those who govern and those who work for justice; for the most vulnerable, especially children. God of mercy,

hear our prayer.

Let us pray for those in need of angels to wait on them; for the sick and those in prison (*especially*); for the homeless and destitute; for all for whom we forget to pray. God of mercy,

hear our prayer.

Let us pray for this assembly; for those who make music in our worship and those who serve on the altar guild; for church school teachers and those who care for our grounds. God of mercy,

hear our prayer.

Here other intercessions may be offered.

Let us give thanks for the faithful witnesses who have gone before us, that together with them, we might seek to serve you alone. God of mercy,
hear our prayer.
Into your hands, God of abundant grace, we commend all for whom we pray, trusting in your mercy, through Jesus Christ, our Savior.
Amen.

Ideas and Images for the Day

"Satan," "tempter," "serpent," and "devil" are some of the many names and images ascribed to evil in scripture. But are not these names and images neglected and forgotten in our modern era? After all, speech of devils and serpents is often met with incredulous looks and disbelieving hearts. Yet, Matthew reorientates us to the truth of the devil's power. In the wilderness Jesus encounters an evil as real as its opposite, resurrection. The great tempter seeks to undermine Jesus' mission before he even begins; testimony that evil has much to fear of our Jesus! Nonetheless, Jesus will not be dissuaded. "Away with you, Satan!" proclaims the redeemer of the cosmos. Thus, the Lenten journey begins— a journey that takes us to the cross, where evil is cast away and crushed underfoot.

1. Sadly, teaching about the devil is a challenge often avoided in the church. Ponder the following words of Martin Luther in the *Large Catechism*: "Let Christians constantly read and teach, learn and meditate and ponder. Let them never stop until they have proved by experience and are certain that they have taught the devil to death and have become more learned than God himself and all God's saints." Our Christian vocation moves us to contemplate the necessity of traveling to Golgotha and beyond.

2. Prior to this Sunday, implement a simple survey asking congregation members whether or not they believe in the devil. Take this same survey into the surrounding community. Use this data to inform the sermon for the Sunday, and publish your findings in the bulletin or on the overhead screens. What does this say about the perception of evil or the devil in the world?

3. Plan a thanksgiving for baptism at the outset of worship. During the thanksgiving, include the "Profession of Faith" from the baptismal liturgy (*Evangelical Lutheran Worship*, p. 229). As in the ancient church, highlight the renunciation of sin, evil, and the devil by inviting the assembly to face west, the place where the sun sets. In a similar way, face east—where the sun rises—as the assembly professes their faith in the triune God.

4. "Save us from the time of trial and deliver us from evil." On this Sunday, the sixth and seventh petitions of the Lord's Prayer are embodied in Jesus' wilderness wrestling with the devil. How do we understand the significance of our own temptations and encounters with evil even as we pray the prayer of Jesus?

Hymns for Worship
Gathering

Great Litany   ELW 238, LBW page 168
Bless now, O God, the journey, ELW 326
The glory of these forty days   ELW 320, WOV 657

Music Sourcebook for Lent and the Three Days includes three litanies (S416-S418) suitable for gathering music on the Sundays in Lent.

Hymn of the Day

A mighty fortress is our God   ELW 503–505, LBW 228/229
   EIN FESTE BURG
God, my Lord, my strength   ELW 795, LBW 484   *PÁN BŮH*
Jesus, still lead on   ELW 624, LBW 341   *SEELENBRÄUTIGAM*

Offering

As the sun with longer journey   ELW 329, WOV 655
Lord, keep us steadfast in your word   ELW 517, LBW 230

Communion

Lord Jesus, you shall be my song   ELW 808
I want Jesus to walk with me   ELW 325, WOV 660, TFF 66
If God my Lord be for me   ELW 788, LBW 454

Sending

Guide me ever, great Redeemer   ELW 618, LBW 343
Lord, keep us steadfast in your word   ELW 517, LBW 230

Additional Hymns and Songs

Lord, my strength   W&P 93
Jesus, tempted in the desert   RS 548, HFG 65
Now let us all with one accord   HS91 738

Music for the Day
Psalmody and Acclamations

Anderson, Mark. "Psalm 32," Refrain 2, from PSCY.
Bruxvoort-Colligan, Richard. "Unfailing Love (Psalm 32:3, 5)"
   from *Sharing the Road*. AFP 9780800678630.
Miller, Aaron David. *Gospel Acclamations for Lent–Holy Trinity*.
Schwarz, May. "Psalm 32" from PWA, Evangelical Lutheran Worship Edition.

Choral

Bach, J. S. "Lord Jesus Christ, God's Only Son" from *Bach for All Seasons*. U, kybd. AFP 9780800658540.

○ Cherwien, David. "Concertato on 'A Mighty Fortress.'" SATB, org, br, assembly. AMSI 2010S.

○ Ferguson, John. "A Mighty Fortress." SATB, org, tpt. AFP 9780800676421.

○ Pelz, Walter. "O Lord, throughout These Forty Days." SA(T)B, kybd, opt C inst. AFP 9780800637538.

Children's Choir

Helgen, John. "Psalm 32" from *ChildrenSing Psalms*. U, kybd. AFP 9780800663872.

Powell, Robert. "A Lenten Prayer." U, kybd, fl. CG CGA159

Price, Ann. "We Love Because God First Loved Us" from *LifeSongs*. LE, U, kybd.

Keyboard / Instrumental

○ Blair, Dallas. "Ein feste Burg" from *Hymn Introductions and Descants for Trumpet and Organ*, set 2. Org, tpt. MSM 20-702.

○ Farlee, Robert Buckley. "Pán Bůh" from *Gaudeamus!* Org. AFP 9780800655389.

○ Manz, Paul O. "Seelenbräutigam" from *Augsburg Organ Library: Lent*. Org. AFP 9780800658977.

○ Raabe, Nancy M. "Ein feste Burg" from *Day of Arising: A Tapestry of Musical Traditions*. Pno. AFP 9780800637460.

Handbell

Childers, Brian. "I Want Jesus to Walk with Me." 3-5 oct, opt C inst, perc, L3+. HOP 2463 (HB). HOP 2463P (C inst and perc).

Lamb, Linda. "Guide Me, O Thou Great Jehovah." 2 oct, L2-. BP HB272.

○ Page, Anna Laura. "A Mighty Fortress Is Our God." 3-5 oct hb, opt 3 oct hc, L3. AFP 9780800658847.

Praise Ensemble

Beech, Jay. "Out in the Wilderness." W&P 115. Various editions.

● Klein, Laurie. "I Love You, Lord." House of Mercy Music/MAR. W&P 67

● Ledner, Michael. "You Are My Hiding Place." MAR. W&P 160

● Paris, Twila. "Lamb of God." Straightway Music/Mountain Spring Music. ELW 336

● Redman, Matt. "The Heart of Worship." Thankyou Music.

● Tomlin, Chris/Louie Giglio. "Take My Life." WT/Sixsteps Music.

Global

Bell, John. Arr. "The Courage to Say No" from *The Courage to Say No: 23 Songs for Lent and Easter*. U. GIA G-4244.

Bell, John, arr. "The Temptations" from *Heaven Shall Not Wait*, vol. 1. U. GIA G-3646.

Thursday, March 17

Patrick, bishop, missionary to Ireland, died 461

At sixteen, Patrick was kidnapped by Irish pirates and sold into slavery in Ireland. He himself admitted that up to this point he cared little for God. He escaped after six years, returned to his family in southwest Britain, and began to prepare for ordained ministry. He later returned to Ireland, this time to serve as a bishop and missionary. He made his base in the north of Ireland and from there made many missionary journeys, with much success. In his autobiography he denounced the slave trade, perhaps from his own experience as a slave. Patrick's famous baptismal hymn to the Trinity, "I Bind unto Myself Today" (ELW 450), can be used as a meditation on Lent's call to return to our baptism.

Saturday, March 19

Joseph, Guardian of Jesus

The gospels are silent about much of Joseph's life. We know that he was a carpenter or builder by trade. The Gospel of Luke shows him acting in accordance with both civil and religious law by returning to Bethlehem for the census and by presenting the child Jesus in the temple on the fortieth day after his birth. The Gospel of Matthew tells of Joseph's trust in God, who led him through visionary dreams. Because Joseph is not mentioned after the story of a young Jesus teaching in the temple, it is assumed that he died before Jesus reached adulthood.

○ denotes suggestions that relate to the hymn of the day.
● denotes songs that are available on iTunes®.

March 20, 2011
Second Sunday in Lent

During Lent we journey with all those around the world who will be baptized at the Easter Vigil. In today's gospel Jesus tells Nicodemus that he must be born of water and Spirit. At the font we are given a new birth as daughters and sons of God. As God made a covenant with Abraham, in baptism God promises to raise us up with Christ to new life. From worship we are sent forth to proclaim God's love for all the world.

Prayer of the Day

O God, our leader and guide, in the waters of baptism you bring us to new birth to live as your children. Strengthen our faith in your promises, that by your Spirit we may lift up your life to all the world through your Son, Jesus Christ, our Savior and Lord, who lives and reigns with you and the Holy Spirit, one God, now and forever.

Gospel Acclamation

The Son of Man must be | lifted up,* that whoever believes in him may have e- | ternal life. (John 3:14-15)

Readings and Psalm

Genesis 12:1-4a

God's call of Abram and Sarai has a clear purpose—that through them all the families of the earth would gain a blessing. As they set out on their journey they are accompanied by promises of land, nation, and a great reputation.

Psalm 121

I lift up my eyes to the hills; my help comes from the LORD. (Ps. 121:1, 2)

Romans 4:1-5, 13-17

In the person and example of Abraham we discover that a right relationship with God does not involve earning a reward from God but entails trusting God's promises. Abraham is the forebear and model for both Jews and Gentiles, because we too trust that ours is a God who gives life to the dead.

John 3:1-17

A curious Pharisee visits Jesus by night to learn from the teacher his friends reject. Jesus speaks to him about life in the Spirit and the kingdom of God.

Preface   Lent

Color   Purple

Prayers of Intercession

The prayers are prepared locally for each occasion. The following examples may be adapted or used as appropriate.

As we return to the waters of baptism during this season of Lent, let us pray for the church, those in need, and all of God's creation.

A brief silence.

You call us to faith again and again. Bind together all those born of water and the Spirit, that your church might be one in Jesus' name. God of mercy,

hear our prayer.

You gave your only-begotten Son so that the world might be saved through him. Save the polluted waters, the devastated forests, and the species in danger of extinction. God of mercy,

hear our prayer.

You promised, in Abraham, to bless all the nations of the world. Bestow wisdom on world leaders; bring an end to international conflicts; and grant safety to all who live in fear. God of mercy,

hear our prayer.

You are a light to those who live in darkness. Be present with all who work or watch or worry through the night, especially hospice volunteers, night nurses, and security guards. God of mercy,

hear our prayer.

You give strength to the weary. Breathe new life into the ministries of this congregation, that we might share your word of hope with the strangers outside our doors. God of mercy,

hear our prayer.

Here other intercessions may be offered.

You inspire us with the stories of our ancestors in the faith. Keep us in communion with all the saints, until at last we find our rest in you. God of mercy,
hear our prayer.
Into your hands, God of abundant grace, we commend all for whom we pray, trusting in your mercy, through Jesus Christ, our Savior.
Amen.

Ideas and Images for the Day

When did Nicodemus come to Jesus? By night! So subtle, so easily missed, yet so very, very important! Under the cover of darkness, with shadows dancing in the torchlight, Nicodemus made his way to Jesus, beset by questions he can ask only under cover of darkness. Like a moth fluttering in the night sky, Nicodemus was irresistibly drawn to the light, Jesus the Christ, the light of the world. Following in the furtive footsteps of Nicodemus, we engage Jesus with our own questions. But the Spirit, through the light of Christ, calls us out from the shadows, and in fact, exposes us to the brilliance of God's love—a love that meets our questioning hearts with nothing less than life eternal!

1. How do we translate Jesus' words regarding rebirth in the opening verses of this gospel text: "born from above" (NRSV) or "born again" (NIV)? Perhaps it is best if we do not choose between the two but rather hold them in a creative tension as Jesus' words shape our understanding of the sacrament of baptism. As an exercise for a Bible study, Sunday school class, or forum, walk through the liturgy of Holy Baptism (*Evangelical Lutheran Worship*, pp. 227–231) highlighting birth/rebirth/creation language used throughout the rite. How does this rich imagery guide us into deeper reflection on the gift of baptism?

2. In worship today replace the confession with a responsive reading from Martin Luther's *Small Catechism*. Invite the assembly to turn to pages 1164–1165 in *Evangelical Lutheran Worship* and read Luther's teaching on the sacrament of holy baptism. The leader ought to ask the questions, and the assembly responds accordingly. Punctuate the action by leading from the baptismal font.

3. As part of the children's message encourage the children to be like Nicodemus and ask faithful questions. After all, our Christian journeys are shaped and marked by our questions. Hand out note cards and invite the children to go home and compose a list of two or three questions with their families. Encourage them to bring them back sometime in Lent to be put on display in the narthex. Important: do not promise to answer the questions! Rather, we lift up our questions to God, trusting in the light of Christ to guide us, even and especially when we do not have answers.

4. The seashell has been a symbol of baptism since the conception of the Christian church. Hand out seashells to each person as they enter the sanctuary for worship. Use the symbol as reminder—in song, sermon, and sending—that we are born of Spirit and dripping in the gifts of grace.

Hymns for Worship
Gathering
Restore in us, O God   ELW 328, WOV 662
If you but trust in God to guide you   ELW 769, LBW 453
Lift high the cross   ELW 660, LBW 377

Hymn of the Day
God loved the world   ELW 323   *ROCKINGHAM OLD*
   LBW 292   *DIE HELLE SONN LEUCHT*
This is the Spirit's entry now   ELW 448   *LAND OF REST*
   LBW 195   *PERRY*
Lord, thee I love with all my heart   ELW 750, LBW 325
   HERZLICH LIEB

Offering
Mothering God, you gave me birth   ELW 735, WOV 769
O living breath of God   ELW 407, LCC 368

Communion
My faith looks up to thee   ELW 759, LBW 479
We are baptized in Christ Jesus   ELW 451, WOV 698
For by grace you have been saved   ELW 598, W&P 38

Sending
All who believe and are baptized   ELW 442, LBW 194
Eternal Lord of love, behold your church   ELW 321

Additional Hymns and Songs
As Moses raised the serpent up   NCH 605
I shall not be moved   TFF 147
Lord, as a pilgrim   LBW 485

Music for the Day
Psalmody and Acclamations
Bruxvoort-Colligan, Richard. "God Is Holding Your Life (Psalm 121)" from *Sharing the Road*. AFP 9780800678630.
Erickson, Rick. "Psalm 121," Refrain 1, from PSCY.

Miller, Aaron David. *Gospel Acclamations for Lent–Holy Trinity.*

Roberts, Leon C. "My Help Shall Come from the Lord (Psalm 121)." TFF 16.

Shepperd, Mark. "Psalm 121" from PWA, Evangelical Lutheran Worship Edition.

Choral

Bach, J. S. "Lord, Thee I Love With All My Heart" from *Bach for All Seasons.* SATB. AFP 9780800658540.

Chilcott, Bob. "God So Loved the World." SATB, sop solo. OXF 9780193432765.

Courtney, Vicki Tucker. "How Great Is This Love!" SATB, pno. AFP 9780806697369.

Distler, Hugo. "For God So Loved the World/Also hat Gott die Welt geliebet" from *Chantry Choirbook.* SAB. AFP 9780800657772.

Keesecker, Thomas. "God So Loved the World." SA(T)B, kybd, fl, opt gtr, assembly. AFP 9780806697635.

Kemp, Helen. "A Mountain Psalm." 2 pt mxd or SA, pno, opt assembly. CG CGA-1061.

Children's Choir

Bedford, Michael. "Psalm 121" from *ChildrenSing Psalms.* U, kybd. AFP 9780800663872.

Johnson, Ralph. "As Moses Lifted Up." U, kybd, fl. CG CGA550.

Patterson, Mark. "Witness." U/2 pt, kybd. CG CGA1138.

Keyboard / Instrumental

o Hassell, Michael. "Land of Rest" from *Folkways,* vol. 1. Pno, inst. AFP 9780800656904.

o Kimball, James D. "Rockingham Old" from *Five Hymn Preludes.* Org. MSM 10-862.

o Manz, Paul O. "Herzlich lieb" from *Nine Hymn Improvisations.* Org. MSM 10-875.

o Organ, Anne Krentz. "Land of Rest" from *Eight for Eighty-Eight,* vol. 3. Pno, inst. AFP 9780800623494.

Handbell

Dobrinski, Cynthia. "Lift High the Cross." 3-5 oct, L3. HOP 1491.

Linker, Janet/Jane McFadden. "Morning Has Broken." 3 or 5 oct, L2. AFP 9780800654320.

o Rogers, Sharon Elery. "Two Songs of Hope and Rest." 2-3 oct, L1. FLA HP5465.

Praise Ensemble

● Bullock, Geoff. "The Power of Your Love." WRD/MAR.

● Foote, Billy. "You Are My King (Amazing Love)." WT/Sixsteps Music.

● Green, Melody. "There Is a Redeemer." Birdwing Music. W&P 140. Hanson, Handt. "Broken in Love." Prince of Peace Publishing. W&P 24. Various editions.

● Herms, Bernie/Mark Hall. "Praise You in this Storm." WRD.

● Kendrick, Graham. "Amazing Love." Make Way Music.

Global

Guarani, trad. "Oré poriajú verekó/Lord, Have Mercy" from *Agape: Songs of Hope and Reconciliation.* U, gtr. Lutheran World Federation. AFP 9780191000133.

Li, Peo-chen. "May the Lord, Mighty God" from *Sound the Bamboo.* 2 pt. GIA G-6830.

Monday, March 21

Thomas Cranmer, Bishop of Canterbury, martyr, died 1556

Cranmer was serving as bishop of Taunton in England when he was chosen by King Henry VIII to become archbishop of Canterbury, largely because Cranmer would agree to the king's divorce from Catherine of Aragon. Cranmer's lasting achievement is contributing to and overseeing the creation of the Book of Common Prayer, which in revised form remains the worship book of the Anglican Communion. He was burned at the stake under Queen Mary for his support of the Protestant Reformation.

Tuesday, March 22

Jonathan Edwards, teacher, missionary to American Indians, died 1758

Edwards was a minister in Connecticut and described as the greatest of the New England Puritan preachers. One of Edwards's most notable sermons found its way into contemporary anthologies of literature. In this sermon, "Sinners in the Hands of an Angry God," he spoke at length about hell. However, throughout the rest of his works and his preaching he had more to say about God's love than God's wrath. His personal experience of conversion came when he felt overwhelmed with a sense of God's majesty and grandeur, rather than a fear of hell. Edwards served a Puritan congregation, where he believed that only those who had been fully converted ought to receive communion; his congregation thought otherwise. Edwards left that congregation and carried out mission work among the Housatonic Indians of Massachusetts. He became president of the College of New Jersey, later to be known as Princeton University.

o denotes suggestions that relate to the hymn of the day.
● denotes songs that are available on iTunes®.

130

Thursday, March 24

Oscar Arnulfo Romero, Bishop of El Salvador, martyr, died 1980

Romero is remembered for his advocacy on behalf of the poor in El Salvador, though it was not a characteristic of his early priesthood. After being appointed as archbishop of San Salvador, he preached against the political repression in his country. He and other priests and church workers were considered traitors for their bold stand for justice, especially defending the rights of the poor. After several years of threats to his life, Romero was assassinated while presiding at the eucharist. During the 1980s thousands died in El Salvador during political unrest.

Friday, March 25

Annunciation of Our Lord

Nine months before Christmas the church celebrates the annunciation. In Luke the angel Gabriel announces to Mary that she will give birth to the Son of God, and she responds, "Here am I, the servant of the Lord." Ancient scholars believed that March 25 was also the day on which creation began and was the date of Jesus' death on the cross. Thus, from the sixth to eighth centuries, March 25 was observed as New Year's Day in much of Christian Europe.

March 27, 2011
Third Sunday in Lent

In today's gospel the Samaritan woman asks Jesus for water, an image of our thirst for God. Jesus offers living water, a sign of God's grace flowing from the waters of baptism. The early church used this gospel and those of the next two Sundays to deepen baptismal reflection during the final days of preparation before baptism at Easter. As we journey to the resurrection feast, Christ comes among us in word, bath, and meal—offering us the life-giving water of God's mercy and forgiveness.

Prayer of the Day

Merciful God, the fountain of living water, you quench our thirst and wash away our sin. Give us this water always. Bring us to drink from the well that flows with the beauty of your truth through Jesus Christ, our Savior and Lord, who lives and reigns with you and the Holy Spirit, one God, now and forever.

Gospel Acclamation

Lord, you are truly the Savior | of the world;* give me this living water that I may never | thirst again. (John 4:42, 15)

Readings and Psalm
Exodus 17:1-7

Because the thirsty Israelites quarreled with Moses and put the Lord to the test, Moses cried out in desperation to the Lord. The Lord commanded Moses to strike the rock to provide water for the people. The doubt-filled question—"Is the Lord among us or not?"—received a very positive answer.

Psalm 95

Let us shout for joy to the rock of our salvation. (Ps. 95:1)

Romans 5:1-11

Though we often hear that God helps those who help themselves, here Paul tells us that through Jesus' death God helps utterly helpless sinners. Since we who had been enemies are reconciled to God in the cross, we now live in hope for our final salvation.

John 4:5-42

Jesus defies convention to engage a Samaritan woman in conversation. Her testimony, in turn, leads many others to faith.

Preface Lent

Color Purple

Prayers of Intercession

The prayers are prepared locally for each occasion. The following examples may be adapted or used as appropriate.

As we return to the waters of baptism during this season of Lent, let us pray for the church, those in need, and all of God's creation.

A brief silence.

We pray for the church around the globe; for denominations with which we are in full communion; for pastors, other rostered leaders, musicians, and lay ministers; for all thirsty for your word. God of mercy,

hear our prayer.

We pray for living water; for deep wells and safe sewer systems; for acid-free rain and oil-free oceans; for clean and abundant drinking water for every human being. God of mercy,

hear our prayer.

We pray for those nations who are now at war (*especially*); for refugees and all who suffer from post-traumatic stress; for international peacemakers and relief workers. God of mercy,

hear our prayer.

We pray for those who are homeless and outcast; for those suffering from malaria or HIV/AIDS; for those with mental or physical disabilities. God of mercy,

hear our prayer.

We pray for all those preparing for baptism; for divorced and single persons in our assembly; for members who cannot be here today; for all who are quarreling with one another. God of mercy,

hear our prayer.

Here other intercessions may be offered.

You know everything we have ever done, and still you love us. We thank you for giving us hope in the communion of saints, who drink from the rock that is Christ. God of mercy,

hear our prayer.

Into your hands, God of abundant grace, we commend all for whom we pray, trusting in your mercy, through Jesus Christ, our Savior.

Amen.

Ideas and Images for the Day

The woman at the well is a familiar text for many people. Some may easily assume this gospel simply urges us to stand with the marginalized, especially women, and then congratulate themselves for being just like Jesus. But a more critical and searching look at this text calls us to the reality that Jesus doesn't just stand with *the other*, Jesus stands with *your* other; *your church's* other. Your church's "Samaritans" may be homosexuals, evangelicals, urban people, rural people, conservatives, liberals, the poor, the rich, the dying, or single parents. Your church's Samaritans could very well be the key to this text. Because, like it or not, when we draw lines between ourselves and other people, Jesus is always on the *other* side of that line. So communities and individuals who thirst for the living water might look to who of their own Samaritans might be at the well chatting it up with who we thought was exclusively *our* Jesus; but who, in reality, is the living water who comes to us in the strange and the stranger.

1. The pastoral leadership at St. Gregory of Nyssa Episcopal Church in San Francisco http://www.saintgregorys. org/ say this prayer before each liturgy: "Blessed be God the Word, who came to his own and his own received him not, for in this way God glorifies the stranger. O God, show us your image in all who come here today, that we may welcome them, and you."

2. *Take This Bread: A Radical Conversion,* by Sara Miles (Ballantine Books, 2008), is the unforgettable telling of one woman's conversion to the faith from atheism. She literally walked into a church from off the street, took the eucharist, and her life changed in complete, messy, and glorious ways. Her response to the gospel is a hilarious tale of starting a food pantry out of her church's sanctuary and how the strange and stranger continue to convert her to this beautiful faith.

3. This image of the woman at the well could be used as a bulletin cover or as a projected image in the sanctuary: http://home.fuse.net/claver/livingwater.html.

4. The animated children's film *Up* (Disney/Pixar, 2009) could be used as a great example of how the neighbor we do not choose is the way in which God sometimes chooses to change us.

Hymns for Worship
Gathering

What wondrous love is this   ELW 666, LBW 385
O Jesus, joy of loving hearts   ELW 658, LBW 356
As the sun with longer journey   ELW 329, WOV 655

Hymn of the Day

As the deer runs to the river   ELW 331   *JULION*
Come to me, all pilgrims thirsty   ELW 777   *BEACH SPRING*
I heard the voice of Jesus say   ELW 332, LBW 497
   THIRD MODE MELODY   ELW 611   *KINGSFOLD*

Offering

Take, oh, take me as I am   ELW 814
O Bread of life from heaven   ELW 480, sts. 1, 2;
   LBW 222, sts. 1, 2

Communion

Jesus, keep me near the cross   ELW 335, TFF 73
Rock of Ages, cleft for me   ELW 623, LBW 327
For all the faithful women   ELW 419, st. 8

Sending

Crashing waters at creation   ELW 455
Guide me ever, great Redeemer   ELW 618, LBW 343

Additional Hymns and Songs

We have been told   HS91 817
Surely it is God who saves me   WOV 635
Christ, you give us living water   SIC 31

Music for the Day
Psalmody and Acclamations

Bruxvoort-Colligan, Richard. "Let Us Shout for Joy! (Psalm 95:1-7)"
   from *Sharing the Road*. AFP 9780800678630.
Harbor, Rawn. "Come, Ring Out Your Joy to the Lord (Psalm 95)."
   TFF 9.
Miller, Aaron David. *Gospel Acclamations for Lent–Holy Trinity.*
Schwarz, May. "Psalm 95" from PWA, Evangelical Lutheran Worship Edition.
Sedio, Mark. "Psalm 95," Refrain 1, from PSCY.

Choral

Farlee, Robert Buckley. "O Blessed Spring." SATB, ob (vln or cl), org,
   opt assembly. AFP 9780800654245. *Augsburg Choirbook.*
   AFP 9780800656782.
○ Highben, Zebulon M. "Come to Me, All Pilgrims Thirsty." SATB,
   org, solo inst (ob or cl), assembly. AFP 9780800621414.

○ Horn, Richard. "I Heard The Voice of Jesus Say." SAB, org or hp.
   MSM 50-6203.
Parker, Alice/Robert Shaw. "My God Is a Rock." SATB, div, solo.
   LG 51107.

Children's Choir

Bruxvoort-Colligan, Richard. "Let Us Shout for Joy! (Psalm 95:1-7)"
   from *Sharing the Road*. AFP 9780800678630.
Hopson, Hal. "Lord, We Come to Praise You." U/2 pt, kybd, opt hb.
   CG CGA774.
Makeever, Ray. "All Was Not Well" from *Dancing at the Harvest*. U,
   kybd. AFP 9780800655945.
Wold, Wayne. "Song at the Well." U, kybd. AFP 9780800674656.

Keyboard / Instrumental

○ Callahan, Charles. "Third Mode Melody" from *A Lenten Meditation*.
   Org. MSM 20-300.
○ Linker, Janet. "Beach Spring" from *Augsburg Organ Library: Baptism
   and Communion*. Org. AFP 9780800623555.
○ Organ, Anne Krentz. "Beach Spring" from *Woven Together*, vol. 1.
   Pno, inst. AFP 9780800658168.
○ Raabe, Nancy M. "Julion" from *Grace and Peace*, vol. 1. Pno.
   AFP 9780800677602.

Handbell

○ Geschke, Susan. "As the Deer." 3-5 oct hb, opt 3 oct hc, L2+.
   HOP 2464.
○ Helman, Michael. "Lord, Whose Love in Humble Service (Beach
   Spring)." 3-5 oct hb, opt 3 oct hc, L3. CG CGB586.
Raney, Joel/Arnold Sherman. "What Wondrous Love Is This?" 3-5
   oct, L3-. HOP 2392.

Praise Ensemble

Bell, John. "Will You Come and Follow Me?" GIA. ELW 798
● Doerksen, Brian. "Come, Now Is the Time to Worship." VIN.
● Evans, Darrell. "Let the River Flow." VIN/INT.
● Nystrom, Martin. "As the Deer." House of Mercy Music. W&P 9.
Peterson, Hans/Larry Olson/David Lee Brown. "Child of the
   Water." Dakota Road Music.
● Redman, Matt. "The Heart of Worship." Thankyou Music.

Global

Lim, Swee Hong. "Lord, Have Mercy" from *Sound the Bamboo*. U.
   GIA G-6830. ELW 158.
Loh, I-to. Lord, Have Mercy/Ch'iu Chu lienim women" from *Sent by
   the Lord: Songs of the World Church, Vol 2*. U. GIA G-3740.

○ denotes suggestions that relate to the hymn of the day.
● denotes songs that are available on iTunes®.

Tuesday, March 29

Hans Nielsen Hauge, renewer of the church, died 1824

Hans Nielsen Hauge was a layperson who began preaching about "the living faith" in Norway and Denmark after a mystical experience that he believed called him to share the assurance of salvation with others. At the time, itinerant preaching and religious gatherings held without the supervision of a pastor were illegal, and Hauge was arrested several times. He also faced great personal suffering: his first wife died, and three of his four children died in infancy.

Thursday, March 31

John Donne, poet, died 1631

This priest of the Church of England is commemorated for his poetry and spiritual writing. Most of his poetry was written before his ordination and is sacred and secular, intellectual and sensuous. He saw in his wife, Anne, glimpses of the glory of God and a human revelation of divine love. In 1615 he was ordained and seven years later he was named dean of St. Paul's Cathedral in London. By that time his reputation as a preacher was firmly in place. In his poem "Good Friday, 1613. Riding westward," he speaks of Jesus' death on the cross: "Who sees God's face, that is self life, must die; What a death were it then to see God die?"

April 3, 2011
Fourth Sunday in Lent

Baptism is sometimes called enlightenment. The gospel for this Sunday is the story of the man born blind healed by Christ. I was blind, but now I see, declares the man. In baptism God opens our eyes to see the truth of who we are: God's beloved sons and daughters. As David was anointed king of Israel, in baptism God anoints our head with oil, and calls us to bear witness to the light of Christ in our daily lives.

Prayer of the Day

Bend your ear to our prayers, Lord Christ, and come among us. By your gracious life and death for us, bring light into the darkness of our hearts, and anoint us with your Spirit, for you live and reign with the Father and the Holy Spirit, one God, now and forever.

Gospel Acclamation

Jesus says, I am the light | of the world;* whoever follows me will have the | light of life. (John 8:12)

Readings and Psalm

1 Samuel 16:1-13

Samuel anointed David even though he was the eighth-oldest son of Jesse and did not match his brothers in height or other physical characteristics. With the anointing came endowment with the Spirit of the Lord, designating David as the Lord's chosen successor to Saul.

Psalm 23

You anoint my head with oil. (Ps. 23:5)

Ephesians 5:8-14

Because we now live in the divine light that is Jesus Christ, we conduct our lives in ways that reflect the light of Christ, so that our activity is truly pleasing to God.

John 9:1-41

Jesus heals a man born blind, provoking a hostile reaction that he regards as spiritual blindness to the things of God.

Preface Lent

Color Purple

Prayers of Intercession

The prayers are prepared locally for each occasion. The following examples may be adapted or used as appropriate.

As we return to the waters of baptism during this season of Lent, let us pray for the church, those in need, and all of God's creation.

A brief silence.

Let us pray for Christians around the world, made one in baptism; for ecumenical partnerships; and for our sisters and brothers in other faith communities. God of mercy, **hear our prayer.**

Let us pray for the receding polar ice caps, and the disappearing glaciers; for polluted waterways and garbage-filled oceans; for the shrinking rain forests and the many creatures that call them home. God of mercy, **hear our prayer.**

Let us pray for kings and queens; for presidents and prime ministers; for legislatures and court systems; and for local governments, that all these may serve their peoples with justice. God of mercy, **hear our prayer.**

Let us pray for day-care providers and librarians; for business owners and artists; for social workers and custodians; for farmers and scientists; for the sick and for all who cannot find work (*especially*). God of mercy, **hear our prayer.**

Let us pray for the members of this assembly, and for any visitors among us, that we all might see and proclaim you as the light of the world. God of mercy, **hear our prayer.**

Here other intercessions may be offered.

Let us give thanks for the many witnesses, living and dead, who have served you in astonishing ways; and let us pray for all those who grieve for the dead. God of mercy, **hear our prayer.**

Into your hands, God of abundant grace, we commend all for whom we pray, trusting in your mercy, through Jesus Christ, our Savior. **Amen.**

Ideas and Images for the Day

One heresy in the early church was called Donatism. The Donatists held that the sacraments were only efficacious if presided over by priests who were sinless. It didn't take the church long to realize that if it held to this policy there would be no sacraments for anyone. So if the gospel can be proclaimed through the preaching of a sinner, then we must allow for the possibility that God's healing may be accomplished through extraordinary means. God chooses a boy too young to be taken seriously to anoint as one chosen to lead Israel. God chooses to heal a blind man on the sabbath with dirt and saliva, much to the dismay of the good religious people who were certain they knew better. Lent is a time to reevaluate. Let it also be a time to see the ways in which we are blind to what God is doing around us because we too think we know better. Bottom line: God often uses the unexpected to accomplish salvation.

1. Use a Magic Eye picture (http://www.magiceye.com/) or some other optical illusion as an illustration for a children's sermon. Point to how our perceptions are not always accurate. There are indeed times when the way we see things can get in the way of us seeing how God is present and at work in our own lives and in the world around us.

2. Based on a real life story, the film *Erin Brockovich* (Universal Studios, 2000) tells the story of a woman who was instrumental in bringing a class-action environmental suit against one the country's largest power companies, despite the fact that she had no legal training whatsoever, was a poor single mother, and dressed "inappropriately."

3. Church of the Apostles (http://www.apostleschurch. org/home.php), a Lutheran/Episcopal emerging church in Seattle, is a community comprised largely of single young adults, several of whom in 2006 worked at a Goth nightclub. Rather than holding all their Holy Week services in the church building, they decided to celebrate the Easter Vigil at the Goth nightclub as a rave (techno-dance party) called "Rise." They lit a fire outside, read the scriptures, had several adult baptisms, and celebrated the eucharist. What some would judge as a secular space was made sacred!

4. Make a prayer station at which people can write down situations/dynamics/relationships in their lives they are willing to have God redeem/transform/heal in surprising ways. Invite the community to include petitions in the prayers of the people that address the possibility of transformation and resurrection in areas of the church, the world, and all those in need we perceive to be beyond help or health.

Hymns for Worship
Gathering

Christ, the life of all the living   ELW 339, LBW 97
God, whose almighty word   ELW 673, LBW 400
O Christ, your heart, compassionate   ELW 722

Hymn of the Day

Lead me, guide me   ELW 768, TFF 70   LEAD ME, GUIDE ME
What God ordains is good indeed   ELW 776, LBW 446
WAS GOTT TUT
Drawn to the Light   ELW 593   LA CROSSE

Offering

You, dear Lord   ELW 702, LLC 429
Be thou my vision   ELW 793, WOV 776

Communion

Amazing grace, how sweet the sound   ELW 779, LBW 448
In the cross of Christ I glory   ELW 324, LBW 104
You Are Mine   ELW 581, W&P 158

Sending

Awake, O sleeper, rise from death   ELW 452, WOV 745
O God of mercy, God of light   ELW 714, LBW 425

Additional Hymns and Songs

Open our eyes, Lord   W&P 113, TFF 98
O Sun of justice   WOV 659
Your hand, O Lord, in days of old   LBW 431

Music for the Day
Psalmody and Acclamations

Bruxvoort-Colligan, Richard. "My Love Is My Shepherd (Psalm 23)" from *Sharing the Road*. AFP 9780800678630.
Farlee, Robert Buckley. "Psalm 23," Refrain 3, from PSCY.
Haugen, Marty. "Shepherd Me, O God." ELW 780.
Miller, Aaron David. *Gospel Acclamations for Lent–Holy Trinity.*
Schwarz, May. "Psalm 23" from PWA, Evangelical Lutheran Worship Edition.

Choral

Haugen, Marty. "Shepherd Me, O God." SATB or 2 pt mxd, assembly, kybd, gtr, opt insts. GIA G-2950.
Schütz, Heinrich. "O Lord, I Trust Your Shepherd Care" from *Chantry Choirbook*. SATB, opt org. AFP 9780800657772.
Scott, K. Lee. "Open My Eyes." SATB, org. CPH 98-2904.
Zimmermann, Heinz Werner. "Psalm 23." SATB, org, DB. AFP 9780800645380. *Augsburg Choirbook*. AFP 9780800656782.

Children's Choir

Comer, Marilyn. "Psalm 23" from *ChildrenSing Psalms*. U, kybd. AFP 9780800663872.
Hopson, Hal. "Savior, Like a Shepherd Lead Us." U/2 pt, kybd, opt fl. CG CGA978.
Kemp, Helen. "The Good Shepherd." 2 pt, kybd. CG CGA1079.

Keyboard / Instrumental

○ Busarow, Donald. "Was Gott tut" from *With Music Crowned*. Org, 2 inst. CPH 97-7324U1.
Manz, Paul O. "Aria." Org. MSM 10-906.
○ Marpurg, Friedrich Wilhelm. "Was Gott tut." Org. Various editions.
○ Walther, Johann Gottfried. "Was Gott tut." Org. Various editions.

Handbell

Afdahl, Lee. "The Lord's My Shepherd." 3 or 5 oct hb, opt 3 oct hc and chime tree, L3. AFP 9780800659905.
McAninch, Diane. "Healer of Our Every Ill." 2-3 oct hb, opt 2 oct hc, L2. GIA G-7286.
Moklebust, Cathy. "The Lord Is My Shepherd." 3-6 oct, opt vln, L2+. CG CGB628.

Praise Ensemble

● Akers, Doris. "Lead Me, Guide Me." ELW 768.
● Cull, Bob. "Open Our Eyes." MAR/WRD. W&P 113.
● Farrell, Bernadette. "Christ, Be Our Light." OCP. ELW 715.
● Park, Andy. "Only You." Mercy/VIN. Various editions.
● Redman, Matt. "You Never Let Go." Thankyou Music.
● Tomlin, Chris/John Newton/John Rees/Edwin Excell/Louie Giglio. "Amazing Grace (My Chains Are Gone)." WT.

Global

Brazilian, trad. "Ouve, Senhor, eu estour clamando/Hear Me, O Lord" from *Agape: Songs of Hope and Reconciliation*. U, gtr. Lutheran World Federation. AFP 9780191000133.
Watts, Trisha. "I Will Live for You Alone" from *Agape: Songs of Hope and Reconciliation*. U, gtr. Lutheran World Federation. AFP 9780191000133.

Monday, April 4

Benedict the African, confessor, died 1589

Born a slave on the island of Sicily, Benedict first lived as a hermit and labored as a plowman after he was freed. When the bishop of Rome ordered all hermits to attach themselves to a religious community, Benedict joined the Franciscans, where he served as a cook. Although he was illiterate, his fame as a confessor brought many visitors to the humble and holy cook, and he was eventually named superior of the community. A patron saint of African Americans, Benedict is remembered for his patience and understanding when confronted with racial prejudice and taunts.

○ denotes suggestions that relate to the hymn of the day.
● denotes songs that are available on iTunes®.

Wednesday, April 6

Albrecht Dürer, died 1528; Matthias Grünewald, died 1529; Lucas Cranach, died 1553; artists

These great German artists revealed through their work the mystery of salvation and the wonder of creation. Dürer's work reflected the apocalyptic spirit of his time. Though he remained a Roman Catholic, he was sympathetic to Martin Luther's reforming work. Grünewald's paintings are known for their dramatic forms, vivid colors, and depiction of light. Cranach's work includes many fine religious examples and several portraits of Martin Luther. Cranach was also widely known for his woodcuts.

Saturday, April 9

Dietrich Bonhoeffer, theologian, died 1945

Bonhoeffer (BON-heh-fer) was a German theologian who, at the age of twenty-five, became a lecturer in systematic theology at the University of Berlin. In 1933, and with Hitler's rise to power, Bonhoeffer became a leading spokesman for the Confessing Church, a resistance movement against the Nazis. He was arrested in 1943. He was linked to a failed attempt on Hitler's life and sent to Buchenwald, then to Schönberg prison. After leading a worship service on April 8, 1945, at Schönberg prison, he was taken away to be hanged the next day. His last words as he left were, "This is the end, but for me the beginning of life." *Evangelical Lutheran Worship* includes a hymn (626) by Bonhoeffer, "By Gracious Powers."

April 10, 2011

Fifth Sunday in Lent

In today's gospel Jesus reveals his power over death by raising Lazarus from the dead. The prophet Ezekiel prophesies God breathing new life into dry bones. To those in exile or living in the shadows of death, these stories proclaim God's promise of resurrection. In baptism we die with Christ that we might also be raised with him to new life. At the Easter Vigil we will welcome new sisters and brothers at the baptismal font, as we renew our baptismal promises.

Today is the commemoration of Mikael Agricola, Bishop of Turku, who died in 1557.

Prayer of the Day

Almighty God, your Son came into the world to free us all from sin and death. Breathe upon us the power of your Spirit, that we may be raised to new life in Christ and serve you in righteousness all our days, through Jesus Christ, our Savior and Lord, who lives and reigns with you and the Holy Spirit, one God, now and forever.

Gospel Acclamation

I am the resurrection ⁱ and the life;* whoever believes in me will ⁱ never die. (John 11:25, 26)

Readings and Psalm

Ezekiel 37:1-14

Ezekiel's vision of the valley of dry bones is a promise that Israel as a nation, though dead in exile, will live again in their land through God's life-giving spirit. Three times Israel is assured that through this vision they will know that "I am the Lord."

Psalm 130

I wait for you, O LORD; in your word is my hope. (Ps. 130:5)

Romans 8:6-11

For Paul, Christian spirituality entails living in the reality of the Holy Spirit. The driving force behind our actions and values is not our sinful desire for self-satisfaction but the very Spirit by which God raised Jesus from the dead and will also raise us from the dead.

John 11:1-45

Jesus is moved to sorrow when his friend Lazarus falls ill and dies. Then, in a dramatic scene, he calls his friend out of the tomb and restores him to life.

Preface Lent

Color Purple

Prayers of Intercession

The prayers are prepared locally for each occasion. The following examples may be adapted or used as appropriate.

As we return to the waters of baptism during this season of Lent, let us pray for the church, those in need, and all of God's creation.

A brief silence.

You are the Lord: You have spoken, and you will act. Give your church confidence that in this life, you feed us with your word, and answer our every prayer. God of mercy,
hear our prayer.

You breathe into our dry bones, and we live. We pray for the universe, the solar system, and our fragile planet; for all creatures that creep or swim or fly or run. God of mercy,
hear our prayer.

You open our graves and bring us up from death. We pray for those who are afraid; for those who live in hiding; for those who have buried too many loved ones. God of mercy,
hear our prayer.

You wept at Lazarus's tomb and weep with us when we mourn. We pray for widows and orphans; for those who are depressed; for those who are sick (*especially*); and for those who have lost hope. God of mercy,
hear our prayer.

You are the resurrection and the life. We pray for our congregation; for the very old and very young among us; for singers, readers, ushers, acolytes, and those who help serve communion. God of mercy,
hear our prayer.

Here other intercessions may be offered.

You are our Messiah and teacher. We thank you for giving us examples of faithful living in the saints who have gone before us (*especially Mikael Agricola, bishop*). God of mercy,
hear our prayer.

Into your hands, God of abundant grace, we commend all for whom we pray, trusting in your mercy, through Jesus Christ, our Savior.
Amen.

Ideas and Images for the Day

Hope overcomes despair for God's people: this is the message of the readings for today. The hope of new life is evident in the story of "dry bones" from Ezekiel; Psalm 130 sings of hope in God; the work of God's Spirit gives hope of new life in Paul's letter to the church at Rome; and the Gospel of John tells the hope-filled story of the raising of Lazarus from the dead. The gospel gives us encouraging words to sustain us through the despair of Christ's passion and brings us to the fulfillment of hope on Easter. Martha's wistful words to Jesus, "Lord, if you had been here. . . . But even now I know that God will give you whatever you ask of him" (John 11:21-22), reflect the hope of God's people in the face of despair, even in the face of death.

1. The story of Lazarus is well known and beloved among Christians. People who may not know all the details of the story are, at least, aware that Jesus raises Lazarus from the dead. Ask members of the congregation to volunteer telling a piece of the story as they remember it. Fill in the details with the help of others. At the conclusion of this oral review, invite the congregation to listen carefully to a reading of the story. We listen well when we seek to clarify our memories.

2. *Esperar* is a Spanish verb that means both "to wait" and "to hope." There is no hope without waiting, no wait without hoping. Today's readings provide opportunity to reflect on the promise of God that provides hope in our Lenten wait for new life.

3. *The Lazarus Project* (Sony, 2008) borrows the theme of new life from the gospel. Rated PG-13, the movie offers a dramatic and disturbing plot that ends, well, happily. The film is often criticized by viewers for its ending. Why do people resist this story of hope? Do we, as Christians, resist the happy ending of our Lenten story? Do we, at times, choose to live with the despair of the passion of Christ instead of the hope of the resurrection?

4. The character of Thomas in the Lazarus story is short on hope. Jesus' disciples remind him of the attempt to stone him the last time they were in Judea. Thomas remarks, "Let us also go, that we may die with him." The character Eeyore from A. A. Milne's *Winnie the Pooh* (Disney Enterprises, 1997) comes to mind. The story of Eeyore's birthday from *Winnie the Pooh and a Day for Eeyore* illustrates lack of hope. Parts of the story can be alternately told or read for a children's sermon. A good place to begin is with the line from the story: "Eeyore followed the stream back to his Gloomy Spot."

Hymns for Worship
Gathering

Through the night of doubt and sorrow   ELW 327, LBW 355
Jesus is a rock in a weary land   ELW 333
Restore in us, O God   ELW 328, WOV 662

Hymn of the Day

The Word of God is source and seed   ELW 506, WOV 658
　　GAUDEAMUS DOMINO
Jesus lives, my sure defense   ELW 621, LBW 340
　　JESUS, MEINE ZUVERSICHT
Abide with me   ELW 629, LBW 272   EVENTIDE

Offering

Seed that in earth is dying   ELW 330
The Word of God is source and seed   ELW 506, WOV 658

Communion

I am the Bread of life   ELW 485, WOV 702
Lord, thee I love with all my heart   ELW 750, LBW 325
My faith looks up to thee   ELW 759, LBW 479

Sending

You are the way   ELW 758, LBW 464
What wondrous love is this   ELW 666, LBW 385

Additional Hymns and Songs

We shall rise again   RS 872
Weary of all trumpeting   WOV 785
O Christ, who shared our mortal life   LSB 552

Music for the Day
Psalmody and Acclamations

Bruxvoort-Colligan, Richard. "We Wait in Hope for Your Word (Psalm 130)" from *Sharing the Road*. AFP 9780800678630.
Farlee, Robert Buckley. "Psalm 130," Refrain 2, from PSCY.
Kallman, Daniel. "Psalm 130" from PWA, Evangelical Lutheran Worship Edition.
Miller, Aaron David. *Gospel Acclamations for Lent–Holy Trinity.*
"Out of the Depths I Cry to You." ELW 600.

Choral

Ferguson, John. "Psalm 130: Out of the Depths." SATB, org. AFP 9780800656072.
○ Hirt, Lucy. "Abide With Me." SATB, div. HAL 08738051.
Schalk, Carl. "Out of the Depths." SAB, org. MSM 50-3410.
Sedio, Mark. "Rich in Promise." 2 pt mxd, pno. AFP 9780800657925.

Children's Choir

Mayo, Becki Slagle/Lynn Shaw Bailey. "Dry Bones." U, kybd. CG CGA1112.

Pelz, Walter. "Psalm 130." U, kybd, opt assembly. CG CGA980.
Weber, Paul. "When You Pass Through the Waters." U/2 pt, kybd. MSM 50-0501.

Keyboard / Instrumental

○ Hobby, Robert A. "Eventide" from *For All the Saints, Hymn Preludes for Funerals*, vol. 1. Org. AFP 9780800675371.
○ Organ, Anne Krentz. "Eventide" from *Woven Together*, vol. 1. Pno, inst. AFP 9780800658168.
○ Osterland, Karl. "Gaudeamus Domino" from *Lift One Voice*. Org. AFP 9780800659004.
○ Shehi, Christina. "Eventide" from *Piano Plus*, vol. 2. Pno, inst. AFP 978080063728.

Handbell

○ Geschke, Susan. "Abide with Me." 3-5 oct hb, opt 3-4 oct hc, L2. HOP 2423.
Mathis, William. "Beneath the Cross of Jesus." 3-5 oct, L2. SMP 20/1172S (3 oct), 20/1173S (4-5 oct).
○ Smith, Vicki. "Abide with Me." 3-5 oct, L2. CPH 97-6962.

Praise Ensemble

● Anonymous. "Create in Me a Clean Heart." W&P 34. Various editions.
● Bullock, Geoff. "The Power of Your Love." WRD/MAR.
● Egan, Jon. "I Am Free." Vertical Worship Songs/INT.
● Mark, Robin. "Days of Elijah." Daybreak Music/INT.
● Scott, Kathryn. "Hungry." VIN.
● Tomlin, Chris/Louie Giglio. "Take My Life." WT/Sixsteps Music.

Global

Bell, John. "Behold the Lamb of God" from *Come, All You People: Shorter Songs for Worship*. SAB. GIA G-4391.
Liberius, R. F. "Khudaya, rahem kar" from *Agape: Songs of Hope and Reconciliation*. U, gtr. Lutheran World Federation. AFP 9780191000133.

Sunday, April 10

Mikael Agricola, Bishop of Turku, died 1557

Agricola was consecrated as the bishop of Turku in 1554, without papal approval. As a result, he began a reform of the Finnish church along Lutheran lines. He translated the New Testament, the prayerbook, hymns, and the mass into Finnish, and through this work set the rules of orthography that are the basis of modern Finnish spelling. His thoroughgoing work is particularly remarkable in that he accomplished it in only three years. He died suddenly on a return trip from negotiating a peace treaty with the Russians.

○ denotes suggestions that relate to the hymn of the day.
● denotes songs that are available on iTunes®.

April 17, 2011
Sunday of the Passion
Palm Sunday

Today's liturgy begins with a palm procession, commemorating Jesus' triumphal entry into Jerusalem. Quickly the tone of the service changes as we meditate upon Jesus' passion and death. Because this story is so central to our faith, we hear Matthew's account of the passion today and John's version on Good Friday. Though Jesus is obedient even unto death on the cross, he is exalted by God. We gather to remember his offering for the life of the world, and to be fed by his life-giving mercy. This holy week will culminate in the celebration of the Three Days of Jesus' suffering, death, and resurrection.

Prayer of the Day

Everlasting God, in your endless love for the human race you sent our Lord Jesus Christ to take on our nature and to suffer death on the cross. In your mercy enable us to share in his obedience to your will and in the glorious victory of his resurrection, who lives and reigns with you and the Holy Spirit, one God, now and forever.

or

Sovereign God, you have established your rule in the human heart through the servanthood of Jesus Christ. By your Spirit, keep us in the joyful procession of those who with their tongues confess Jesus as Lord and with their lives praise him as Savior, who lives and reigns with you and the Holy Spirit, one God, now and forever.

or

O God of mercy and might, in the mystery of the passion of your Son you offer your infinite life to the world. Gather us around the cross of Christ, and preserve us until the resurrection, through Jesus Christ, our Savior and Lord, who lives and reigns with you and the Holy Spirit, one God, now and forever.

Gospel Acclamation

Christ humbled himself and became obedient to the point of death—even death | on a cross.* Therefore God also highly exalted him and gave him the name that is above | every name. (Phil. 2:8-9)

Readings and Psalm

***Procession with Palms:* Matthew 21:1-11**

Isaiah 50:4-9a

The servant of the Lord expresses absolute confidence in his final vindication, despite the fact that he has been struck and spit upon. This characteristic of the servant played an

important role in the early church's understanding of the suffering, death, and resurrection of Jesus.

Psalm 31:9-16

Into your hands, O Lord, I commend my spirit. (Ps. 31:5)

Philippians 2:5-11

Paul uses an early Christian hymn to help us comprehend Jesus' obedient selflessness on the cross and how God has made Christ lord over all reality. The perspective of the cross becomes the way we rightly understand God, Christ, our own lives, and fellowship within the community of Christ.

Matthew 26:14—27:66 or Matthew 27:11-54

In fulfillment of scripture and obedience to God's will, Jesus goes to the cross so that a new covenant in his blood may bring forgiveness of sins. Even the soldiers who crucify him recognize him to be the Son of God.

Preface Sunday of the Passion

Color Scarlet *or* Purple

Prayers of Intercession

The prayers are prepared locally for each occasion. The following examples may be adapted or used as appropriate.

As we return to the waters of baptism during this season of Lent, let us pray for the church, those in need, and all of God's creation.

A brief silence.

We pray that the same mind be in your church as was in Christ Jesus; that we continue to bless the one who comes in the name of the Lord. God of mercy,

hear our prayer.

We pray that the earth, the seas, the stars, and every living creature bow before you; that all human beings be humble stewards of the world we call home. God of mercy,
hear our prayer.
We pray that those with authority show great mercy; that war-weary nations be sustained by your word; that innocent victims not be condemned. God of mercy,
hear our prayer.
We pray that you feed the hungry; free the captives; clothe the naked; heal the sick (*especially*); end torture; and turn our swords into plowshares. God of mercy,
hear our prayer.
We pray that all of us, who desert, deny, or betray you, be forgiven; that during this Holy Week ears are opened to the life-giving story of your death and resurrection. God of mercy,
hear our prayer.
Here other intercessions may be offered.
Hold us in communion with the faithful witnesses who have gone before us, until that day when we join them at the feast that is to come. God of mercy,
hear our prayer.
Into your hands, God of abundant grace, we commend all for whom we pray, trusting in your mercy, through Jesus Christ, our Savior.
Amen.

Ideas and Images for the Day

The servanthood of a teacher in Isaiah, the outcast in the psalm, those who bow down in Philippians: today's readings teach humility. On this day we move from Christ's "triumphant" ride on a humble donkey to the humiliation of the cross. The humility of the characters in the passion story is in question: Judas, Pilate, the Twelve, chief priests and elders, Barabbas, the crowd, the soldiers, two bandits. There is only one truly humble person in this story: Jesus the Christ. Matthew's humble Jesus cries out from the cross to ask God why he has been forsaken. Only in the stories of the resurrection do other humble characters appear: the centurion, the women, Joseph of Arimathea. Among other things, the lack of humility is what brings about the passion of Christ.

1. "Humility" seems a dated word in our time and place. We find it a hard word to define. Could it be that we struggle to describe that which we do not live? C. S. Lewis wrote: "Humility is not thinking less of yourself but thinking of yourself less." That is good news! A sermon helping listeners to reflect on humility—the kind of humility that leaves our self-esteem intact and so leads us to esteem others—may give new life to this neglected virtue.

2. It may be a good Sunday to avoid the spotlight. Preachers, worship leaders, readers, and musicians might consider leading worship out of sight, from the pew, from the rear of the worship space, from behind a visual barrier. The emphasis shifts, then, from self to honor the humble Christ, in short, from self to worship.

3. Suggest to young people an online exercise. Ask them to search for "donkey pictures cross." They will discover the legend of the donkey's cross. Discuss the differences between sacred text and legend. Is it possible to learn faith from sources other than sacred text?

4. In the reading from Philippians, at the conclusion of an early Christ hymn, Paul reminds us that true humility allows all people to bow at the name of Jesus and to confess, to esteem Jesus as Lord. Why do we "bow" when we pray? How does our physical position imply humility but not humiliation? How is it that "all people" will bow down? Will "all people" come to confess Jesus as Lord? What does this mean? These thoughts and questions, in an adult education setting, provide opportunity for important conversation regarding the universality of God's grace.

5. Notice the word "teacher" or "rabbi" in two of today's readings. The prophet Isaiah encourages those gifted with the "tongue of a teacher" to "listen as those who are taught." Jesus describes himself as "the teacher" (Matt. 26:18) in today's gospel. Recognition of teaching as vocation highlights the special humility of good teachers, teachers who allow themselves to learn from their students.

Hymns for Worship
Gathering
All glory, laud, and honor   ELW 344, LBW 108
Ride on, ride on in majesty!   ELW 346, LBW 121
Prepare the royal highway   ELW 264, LBW 26

Hymn of the Day
My song is love unknown   ELW 343, WOV 661
    LOVE UNKNOWN   LBW 94   *RHOSYMEDRE*
Jesus, I will ponder now   ELW 345, LBW 115
    JESU KREUZ, LEIDEN UND PEIN
Christ, the life of all the living   ELW 339, LBW 97
    JESU, MEINES LEBENS LEBEN

Offering
On my heart imprint your image   ELW 811, LBW 102
Come to the table   ELW 481

Communion

A lamb goes uncomplaining forth   ELW 340, LBW 105
Calvary   ELW 354, TFF 85
There in God's garden   ELW 342, WOV 668

Sending

Jesus, I will ponder now   ELW 345, LBW 115
Go to dark Gethsemane   ELW 347, LBW 109

Additional Hymns and Songs

At the name of Jesus   W&P 12
All glory, laud, and honor   NCH 217, H82 155

Music for the Day
Psalmody and Acclamations

Bruxvoort-Colligan, Richard. "Into Your Hands (Psalm 31:5, 15)" from *Sharing the Road*. AFP 9780800678630.

Miller, Aaron David. *Gospel Acclamations for Lent–Holy Trinity*.

Sedio, Mark. "Psalm 31," Refrain 1, from PSCY.

Sedio, Mark. "Psalm 31:9-16" from PWA, Evangelical Lutheran Worship Edition.

Choral

○ Cherwien, David. "My Song Is Love Unknown." SAB, opt assembly, org, fl. AFP 9780800655488.

Christiansen, F. Melius. "Lamb of God." SATB. AFP 9780800652593. *Augsburg Choirbook*. AFP 9780800656782.

Larkin, Michael. "O Sacred Head, Now Wounded." SATB, pno. AFP9780806697345.

Nelson, Ronald A. "Hosanna to the Son of David." SAB. Celebrations Unlimited CU-231.

Thompson, Randall. "Pueri Hebraeorum." SSAATTBB or SATB and insts. ECS 3082.

Young, Carlton R. "Hosanna." SATB. AFP 9780800697314.

Children's Choir

Anderson, Norma. "The Walk to Calvary." U, kybd. CG CGA739.

Patterson, Mark. "Sing Hosanna" from *Young ChildrenSing*. U, kybd. AFP 9780800676803.

Sleeth, Natalie. "Little Grey Donkey." U, kybd, opt ob, perc. CG CGA84.

Keyboard / Instrumental

○ Busarow, Donald. "Jesu Kreuz, Leiden und Pein" from *With Music Crowned*. Org, 2 inst. CPH 97-7324U1.

○ Callahan, Charles. "Love Unknown" from *A Lenten Prelude for Flute and Organ*. Org, fl. MSM 20-360.

○ Organ, Anne Krentz. "Jesu, meines Lebens Leben" from *Christ, Mighty Savior*. Pno. AFP 9780800656805.

○ Peeters, Flor. "Jesu, meines Lebens Leben" from *Augsburg Organ Library: Lent*. Org. AFP 9780800658973.

Handbell

Hall, Jefferey. "Crucifixion." 3-5 oct hb, opt 2-5 oct hc, L3-. JEF JHS9433.

○ Moklebust, Cathy. "My Song Is Love Unknown." 3-5 oct, L3. CG CGB203.

Stephenson, Valerie. "All Glory, Laud, and Honor." 3-5 hb, opt 3 oct hc, L2. LOR 20/1419L.

Praise Ensemble

● LeBlanc, Lenny/Paul Baloche. "Above All." INT.

● Morgan, Reuben. "I Give You My Heart." Hillsong/INT.

● Paris, Twila. "He Is Exalted." Straightway Music. W&P 55.

● Redman, Matt. "Once Again." Thankyou Music.

● Tomlin, Chris/Jesse Reeves/Isaac Watts/JD Walt. "The Wonderful Cross." WT/Sixsteps Music.

● Tuttle, Carl. "Hosanna." Shadow Spring Music.

Global

Chinula, Charles. "Behold the Holy Lamb of God" from *The Courage to Say No: 23 Songs for Lent and Easter*. SATB, cant. GIA G-4244.

Sato, Taihei. "Why Has God Forsaken Me?" from *Sound the Bamboo*. U. GIA G-6830.

○ denotes suggestions that relate to the hymn of the day.
● denotes songs that are available on iTunes®.
142

April 18, 2011
Monday in Holy Week

During Holy Week some communities gather each day to meditate on Jesus' final days before his death on the cross. Today's gospel commemorates the anointing of Jesus by Mary, a foreshadowing of his death and burial. Isaiah speaks of the suffering servant who is a light for the nations and who faithfully brings forth justice. For Christians, Jesus' suffering is the path to resurrection and new life. We eagerly await the celebration of the great Three Days later this week.

Prayer of the Day

O God, your Son chose the path that led to pain before joy and to the cross before glory. Plant his cross in our hearts, so that in its power and love we may come at last to joy and glory, through Jesus Christ, our Savior and Lord, who lives and reigns with you and the Holy Spirit, one God, now and forever.

Gospel Acclamation

May I never boast of | anything* except the cross of our Lord | Jesus Christ. (Gal. 6:14)

Readings and Psalm
Isaiah 42:1-9

God's servant Israel is endowed with the Spirit in order to bring justice to the nations. The servant will not exercise authority boisterously or with violence, nor will weariness ever keep it from fulfilling its task. God's old promises have been fulfilled; the new assignment of the servant is to bring light to the nations.

Psalm 36:5-11

All people take refuge under the shadow of your wings. (Ps. 36:7)

Hebrews 9:11-15

Prior to Christ, forgiveness was mediated through animal sacrifice. Christ came as the great high priest to establish a new covenant. Through his blood we are liberated from our sins and promised eternal life.

John 12:1-11

A few days after raising Lazarus from the dead, Jesus visits the man's home. Lazarus's sister Mary is criticized when she anoints the feet of Jesus with costly perfume.

Preface   Sunday of the Passion

Color   Scarlet *or* Purple

April 19, 2011
Tuesday in Holy Week

As the great Three Days draw near, some communities gather each day of Holy Week for worship. Paul proclaims Christ crucified as the wisdom and power of God. Jesus speaks of the grain of wheat that falls into the earth and dies in order that it may bear fruit. We die with Christ in baptism that we may be raised with him to new life. We will celebrate this great mystery of death and resurrection at the Easter Vigil later this week.

Prayer of the Day

Lord Jesus, you have called us to follow you. Grant that our love may not grow cold in your service, and that we may not fail or deny you in the time of trial, for you live and reign with the Father and the Holy Spirit, one God, now and forever.

Gospel Acclamation

May I never boast of | anything* except the cross of our Lord | Jesus Christ. (Gal. 6:14)

Readings and Psalm
Isaiah 49:1-7

Here the servant Israel speaks for herself and acknowledges herself as God's secret weapon. Called like Jeremiah and John the Baptist before her birth, the servant is not only to restore Israel itself, but the servant's ultimate assignment is to bring news of God's victory to the ends of the earth. God in faithfulness has chosen Israel for this task.

Psalm 71:1-14

From my mother's womb you have been my strength. (Ps. 71:6)

1 Corinthians 1:18-31

To the world, the word of the cross is silly, because it claims God's power is most fully revealed in complete, utter weakness. For those who are being saved, however, the word of the cross unveils God's true wisdom, power, and source of true life.

John 12:20-36

Knowing that his hour has come, Jesus announces that his death will be an exaltation. God's name will be glorified when his death draws people to new life.

Preface   Sunday of the Passion

Color   Scarlet *or* Purple

Tuesday, April 19

Olavus Petri, priest, died 1552; Laurentius Petri, Bishop of Uppsala, died 1573; renewers of the church

These two brothers are commemorated for their introduction of the Lutheran movement to the Church of Sweden after studying at the University of Wittenberg. They returned home and, through the support of King Gustavus Vasa, began their work. Olavus published a catechism, hymnal, and a Swedish version of the mass. He resisted attempts by the king to gain royal control of the church. Laurentius was a professor at the university in Uppsala. When the king wanted to abolish the ministry of bishops, Laurentius persuaded him otherwise. The historic episcopate continues in Sweden to this day. Together the brothers published a complete Bible in Swedish and a revised liturgy in 1541.

April 20, 2011
Wednesday in Holy Week

This day was formerly called "Spy Wednesday," an allusion to the gospel accounts in which Judas is identified as the betrayer of Jesus. As Jesus endured the suffering of the cross, we are called to run the race of life with perseverance, confident of the joy to come. In the Three Days, which begin tomorrow evening, we will journey with Christ from darkness to light, from captivity to freedom, from death to life.

Prayer of the Day

Almighty God, your Son our Savior suffered at human hands and endured the shame of the cross. Grant that we may walk in the way of his cross and find it the way of life and peace, through Jesus Christ, our Savior and Lord, who lives and reigns with you and the Holy Spirit, one God, now and forever.

Gospel Acclamation

May I never boast of¹ anything* except the cross of our Lord¹ Jesus Christ. (Gal. 6:14)

Readings and Psalm
Isaiah 50:4-9a

The servant of the Lord expresses absolute confidence in his final vindication, despite the fact that he has been struck and spit upon. This characteristic of the servant played an important role in the early church for understanding the suffering, death, and resurrection of Jesus.

Psalm 70

Be pleased, O God, to deliver me. (Ps. 70:1)

Hebrews 12:1-3

In the way of the cross, Jesus has blazed the trail for our salvation. With faithful perseverance, we follow in his footsteps.

John 13:21-32

At the last supper, Jesus identifies Judas Iscariot as the one who will betray him, and sends him on his way.

Preface   Sunday of the Passion

Color   Scarlet *or* Purple

THE THREE DAYS

PREPARING FOR THE THREE DAYS

For something as ancient and as central to the Christian faith as the days of Maundy Thursday, Good Friday, and Easter are, these days generate a surprising amount of questions and misunderstanding, and the services for them have gone through a lot of changes in recent years. Why is this? A number of possible reasons could be considered. First, recent decades have brought us out of a period when churches pretty much did the same things every year in a prescribed way, and we are still adjusting to what it means to have flexibility and to use it in an informed and responsible way. What is the place of carefully constructed liturgical patterns these days? Second, the tide of post-Christianity still seems to be surging in, at least in the Northern Hemisphere, and the church is struggling to cope with that reality. If the events of Holy Week are unknown to many, how is the church to commemorate them in a way that makes sense? Third, and probably of most importance as we prepare for these days, is that the observance of these days, above all others, requires a high level of assent that belief in Christ as redeemer of the world is true, reliable, and takes precedence over every other allegiance we may have. While we know that making that confession brings with it life and joy, it is one with which many people these days, in our society, have a great deal of difficulty. Yet without that prerequisite, the rites of these days, already unfamiliar even to church-goers because of their once-a-year character, make no sense at all.

And so the questions come. How do we make these days more accessible? How do we invite the unchurched into them? What rituals can and should we jettison? How can we make these days easy for people? Perhaps we can replace the liturgies with a grand pageant, a harmonized version of the passion stories in the gospels, complete with all the special effects we can muster. Perhaps we can simply reduce the amount of scripture involved, lessen the demands for a less-attentive age.

Perhaps. But before adopting such a strategy, we do well to reexamine why we observe these days at all. Are they really primarily for evangelism, for bringing newcomers into the church? Yes, we are charged to be welcoming at all times, and true, Easter Sunday will bring the usual press of strangers in the door. But remember: these days are at the very core of Christianity. That's true not only of the stories they tell, but of the ways we come to grips with those events in our worship. That is to say, while we could put on a drama that would portray Jesus at table, and on trial, and being crucified, and risen, the church's worship has always involved much more than telling the biblical story. Through our worship, we actually become involved in—a part of—those events. No longer are they just something that happened thousands of years ago; now they are living, active, urgent events. And we are no mere passive bystanders; we are part of the story.

How does this happen? Begin with Maundy Thursday (called Holy Thursday in many denominations). The gospel tells of Jesus interrupting the meal with his disciples to wash their feet as a sign of service. A dramatization could reenact this, complete with Peter's initial indignant refusal. If that's as far as it went, though, we would still be left as spectators. The liturgy draws us in by proposing that the entire assembly (or as many as will do so) be included in the footwashing. As Gail Ramshaw writes in the helpful resource *Worship Guidebook for Lent and the Three Days* (Augsburg Fortress, 2009):

> In this ritual . . . we are invited to do what Christ did: to demonstrate the reality of the body of Christ, first by being served by another, and then by serving the next. And this service is not only an attitude in one's head: it is an action that extends all the way to our hands and our feet. Our entire body is pulled into and expresses our covenant within the body of Christ. [p. 102]

That's how liturgy is different from reenactment: we become part of the story. Incidentally, see that same *Worship Guidebook* for extensive background on these liturgies as well as a wealth of suggestions on how to put them into practice.

The meal of Maundy Thursday can provide another example for how liturgy can serve us. Some churches substitute or supplement the service for this day with a "seder" meal modeled after both the medieval Jewish passover meal and Jesus' last meal with his followers. While well intentioned, is this practice missing the point? We are not Jewish, nor are we living in the first century. To pretend that we are may lift up the play-acting aspects to the point that we miss where the real power is located. The prayer after communion appointed for the day brings the focus back where it belongs:

> Lord Jesus, in a wonderful sacrament you strengthen us with the saving power of your suffering, death, and resurrection. May this sacrament of your body and blood so work in us that the fruits of your redemption will show forth in the way we live. (ELW LE, p. 633)

That is, in the way we live *today*, in 2011. It is now, not thousands of years ago; and it is we, not only those first disciples, who through this meal receive the benefits of Christ's suffering, death, and resurrection. Again, the liturgy brings us into the presence of Christ not in a pretend way but in reality.

Before moving on to the other days of the Three Days service, it would be worthwhile to return to that question of including the outsider, because it is an important one. If an unchurched person came to a Maundy Thursday worship done as outlined in *Evangelical Lutheran Worship*, what might his or her reaction be? Certainly the patterns and language are not those of the general society. At the very beginning, we hear about a "struggle against sin, death, and the devil," categories that don't come up much in secular life. As the service moves along, there are extensive Bible readings from Old and New Testaments, a sermon (itself an extended sort of speech that is rarely encountered by many non-churchgoers), that odd footwashing ritual, people coming forward to receive bits of bread and wine that—they may be informed—are really the body and blood of Christ. It can hardly be disputed that such words and actions would seem strange.

And yet, is that reason for tossing them out or even radically altering them? Remember, the church makes the claim that it *is*, indeed, something quite different from the rest of the world. It is in the church that true life and salvation are offered to all. So if people get the sense that they have stepped into a foreign environment and that what's going on here is something very different from their normal life, isn't that appropriate?

Of course, it can be argued with justification that if visitors are so confused they just walk back out the door, then we have failed in our mission to make disciples of them. And that's where hospitality comes in. The church has a treasury of these rich services developed over the

centuries, services that work on many different layers at once. Christians have found that they can use them for a lifetime and still not fully plumb their depths. So of course they will be hard to take in immediately. So the welcoming church keeps the rich services that offer so much, but helps introduce the newcomer (and the regular churchgoer!) to them. Some of this can be done through print, by providing explanatory notes in the service folder or a separate pamphlet that explains in simple terms why we do what we do. Probably even more effective, though, is the personal touch. Ask those members who are more familiar with these services to be on the lookout for newcomers who may need help. Without being pushy or intimidating, offer to be a companion on the journey through the Three Days, giving entry-level support for why and how we do this wonderful three-day service.

Now, back to that liturgy, and the ways it helps the death and resurrection of Jesus come alive for the worshipers. When we reconvene on Good Friday, we may face a stark visual environment if, as suggested, all the nonessential furnishings have been removed at the end of the Maundy Thursday portion. Just as the church is stripped down, so we find that we have reduced the "clutter" in what we are about in our worship: now we are down to considering the core, the death and resurrection of Christ. And yet it is noteworthy what is still present in the service, including a Christ who is both suffering servant and the reigning king, and the church's concern for those outside its circle. Other ways of marking Jesus' death in worship often miss both of those emphases.

The readings for the day include the familiar Isaiah passage that speaks of the servant of God who was despised and rejected, who was wounded for our transgressions, and by whose bruises we are healed. Understandably, this chapter has long been used by the church to speak of Christ. But note that both in this and in the passion from John that is the centerpiece of the Good Friday service, Christ is in control. In Isaiah, "he poured out *himself* to death." In John, from the betrayal in the garden through the appearance before Pilate, and even on the cross, Jesus is setting the tone. At the end, he bows his head and gives up his spirit. Christ voluntarily gives up his life for us and in so doing conquers death once and for all—that is the truth the liturgy, the church, wants us to catch. A drama that is based on a mishmash of all four gospels and focuses, say, on the wounds of Christ, is liable to miss that crucial focus. But we need to know on this central day of the year that even the powers of evil and death had to submit themselves to Christ as he reigned from the cross.

And there's more. The church, being a largely human institution, often has a tendency to look inward, to care primarily for itself and its own. This comes out in many ways: how the money is spent, how the sermon texts are chosen, who gets prayed for. But the liturgy for Good Friday that has been handed down to us resists that tendency, especially in the prayers. The service includes one of the oldest forms of prayer in the church, the bidding prayer (LE pp. 636–638). Not only the form, but much of the content is centuries old. And while we do, of course, pray for ourselves—the church—in it, what is noteworthy is how much of it is focused outward: to the Jewish people, to those who do not share our faith, to those who do not believe in God, for creation, those who serve in public office, for those in need. Once again, the liturgy helps us in that we don't just see the body of Christ hanging on the cross; we *become* the body of Christ, and Christ's concerns are our concerns.

Finally, we move to the great festival of Christ's resurrection, as it begins with the Vigil of Easter and continues on Easter Sunday. There is no way for humans to comprehend what happened then, when Christ smashed completely the dominion of death. Yet again, though, the historic services help us become part of that reality as nothing else could. Because while we need to use words in our worship, they are insufficient to even come close to expressing the fullness of Easter. So we include dramatic movement, fire, water, exultant song, spellbinding stories, and much more—all tested over centuries until they have become finely crafted entrances into aspects of the resurrection. To take one example, if we were to try to come up with an announcement of Christ's resurrection, could we do any better than the Easter Proclamation (LE pp. 646–647), which practically trips over itself in piling up images of jubilation, even including the bees who made the wax for the paschal candle! And the readings—left to our own devices, we probably would have thought of including Romans and John, but it is sheer genius to go all the way back to the beginning, to creation, and then tracing through up to twelve readings how the resurrection is the culmination of all that God has done for us. As the readings continue, as we respond to them, the reality of God's triumphant love for us begins to sink in.

And so it continues—through baptism, through "the feast of victory for our God," through the joyful celebrations of Easter Sunday and beyond. The church's liturgical heritage, especially in these Three Days, is something very different from a museum piece. It is nothing less than a pathway to God's living presence among us.

Seasonal Checklist

- Review the liturgies for Maundy Thursday, Good Friday, and the Vigil of Easter in *Evangelical Lutheran Worship* (Assembly Edition, pp. 258–270; Leaders Edition, pp. 628–653).
- See extensive backgrounds and practical helps for these days in *Worship Guidebook for Lent and the Three Days* (AFP 9780806670416), as well as additional music for the services in the companion *Music Sourcebook for Lent and the Three Days* (9780806670409).
- Arrange rehearsals for all the liturgies of the Three Days. These services are unique, so all worship leaders, even those who have been involved in previous years, need to prepare for their roles.
- Be sure that altar guild members are well equipped and informed about their tasks for these busy days.
- Order worship participation leaflets if used for the Good Friday service.
- Order bulletin covers for Holy Week services.
- It is helpful to prepare printed materials for worship leaders for the Three Days. Consider placing all the texts and musical resources needed into three-ring binders (ceremonial binders in liturgical colors are available from Augsburg Fortress). Highlight speaking parts and instructions for each worship leader in individual copies.
- Publicize Holy Week and Easter services in local newspapers and other media.
- Arrange for a thorough cleaning of the worship space sometime between the Maundy Thursday liturgy and the Easter Vigil.
- Consider silencing bells or chimes from the beginning of the Maundy Thursday service until the hymn of praise at the Easter Vigil (or the first celebration of Easter).
- Determine whether additional handheld candles are needed for the Easter Vigil.
- Purchase a new paschal candle.
- Prepare extra communion elements and communionware needed for large numbers of communicants during Holy Week and Easter.
- If the Easter Vigil (or Easter Sunday) is to be observed as a baptismal festival, see the suggestions for the Baptism of Our Lord in the Time after Epiphany checklist, p. 73.
- Look ahead to the checklist on page 169 as you plan for the Easter season.

WORSHIP TEXTS FOR THE THREE DAYS

MAUNDY THURSDAY

Confession and Forgiveness

Friends in Christ,
in this Lenten season we have heard our Lord's call
to struggle against sin, death, and the devil—
all that keeps us from loving God and each other.
This is the struggle to which we were called at baptism.
[We have shared this discipline of Lent with new brothers
and sisters in Christ who will be baptized at the Easter Vigil.]

Within the community of the church,
God never wearies of forgiving sin
and giving the peace of reconciliation.
On this night let us confess our sin against God
and our neighbor,
and enter the celebration of the great Three Days
reconciled with God and with one another.

Silence is kept for reflection.

Most merciful God,
**we confess that we are captive to sin
and cannot free ourselves.
We have sinned against you in thought, word, and deed,
by what we have done and by what we have left undone.
We have not loved you with our whole heart;
we have not loved our neighbors as ourselves.
For the sake of your Son, Jesus Christ,
have mercy on us.
Forgive us, renew us, and lead us,
so that we may delight in your will
and walk in your ways,
to the glory of your holy name. Amen.**

In the mercy of almighty God,
Jesus Christ was given to die for us,
and for his sake God forgives us all our sins.
As a called and ordained minister of the church of Christ
and by his authority, I therefore declare to you
the entire forgiveness of all your sins,
in the name of the Father, and of the ☩ Son,
and of the Holy Spirit.
Amen.

Greeting

The grace of our Lord Jesus Christ, the love of God,
and the communion of the Holy Spirit be with you all.
And also with you.

Offering Prayer

God of glory,
receive these gifts and the offering of our lives.
As Jesus was lifted up from the earth,
draw us to your heart in the midst of this world,
that all creation may be brought from bondage to freedom,
from darkness to light, and from death to life;
through Jesus Christ, our Savior and Lord.
Amen.

Invitation to Communion

Where charity and love abide, there is God.
Rejoice in this holy communion.

Prayer after Communion

Lord Jesus, in a wonderful sacrament
you strengthen us with the saving power
of your suffering, death, and resurrection.
May this sacrament of your body and blood
so work in us that the fruits of your redemption
will show forth in the way we live,
for you live and reign with the Father and the Holy Spirit,
one God, now and forever.
Amen.

VIGIL OF EASTER

Greeting

The grace of our Lord Jesus Christ, the love of God,
and the communion of the Holy Spirit be with you all.
And also with you.

Sisters and brothers in Christ, on this most holy night
when our Savior Jesus Christ passed from death to life,
we gather with the church throughout the world
in vigil and prayer. This is the passover of Jesus Christ.
Through light and the word,
through water and oil, bread and wine,
we proclaim Christ's death and resurrection,
share Christ's triumph over sin and death,
and await Christ's coming again in glory.

Offering Prayer

Blessed are you, O God, ruler of heaven and earth.
Day by day you shower us with blessings.
As you have raised us to new life in Christ,
give us glad and generous hearts,
ready to praise you and to respond to those in need,
through Jesus Christ, our Savior and Lord.
Amen.

Invitation to Communion

In Christ we are one body,
for though many, we share one bread and cup. Alleluia.

Prayer after Communion

Mighty and compassionate God,
you have brought us over from death to life
through your Son, our risen Savior,
and you have fed us with spiritual food
in the sacrament of his body and blood.
Send us now into the world in peace,
and grant us strength and courage
to love and serve you
with gladness and singleness of heart;
through Jesus Christ our Lord.
Amen.

Blessing

The God of peace,
who brought again from the dead our Lord Jesus,
the great shepherd of the sheep,
by the blood of the eternal covenant,
make you complete in everything good
so that you may do God's will,
working in you that which is pleasing in God's sight;
through ✛ Jesus Christ,
to whom be the glory forever and ever.
Amen.

Dismissal

Go in peace. Share the good news. Alleluia.
Thanks be to God. Alleluia.

April 21, 2011
Maundy Thursday

With nightfall our Lenten observance comes to an end, and we gather with Christians around the world to celebrate the Three Days of Jesus' death and resurrection. At the heart of the Maundy Thursday liturgy is Jesus' commandment to love one another. As Jesus washed the feet of his disciples, we are called to follow his example as we humbly care for one another, especially the poor and the unloved. At the Lord's table we remember Jesus' sacrifice of his life, even as we are called to offer ourselves in love for the life of the world.

Prayer of the Day

Holy God, source of all love, on the night of his betrayal, Jesus gave us a new commandment, to love one another as he loves us. Write this commandment in our hearts, and give us the will to serve others as he was the servant of all, your Son, Jesus Christ, our Savior and Lord, who lives and reigns with you and the Holy Spirit, one God, now and forever.

or

Eternal God, in the sharing of a meal your Son established a new covenant for all people, and in the washing of feet he showed us the dignity of service. Grant that by the power of your Holy Spirit these signs of our life in faith may speak again to our hearts, feed our spirits, and refresh our bodies, through Jesus Christ, our Savior and Lord, who lives and reigns with you and the Holy Spirit, one God, now and forever.

Gospel Acclamation

I give you a ¹ new commandment,* that you love one another just as I ¹ have loved you. (John 13:34)

Readings and Psalm
Exodus 12:1-4 [5-10] 11-14

Israel remembered its deliverance from slavery in Egypt by celebrating the festival of Passover. This festival featured the Passover lamb, whose blood was used as a sign to protect God's people from the threat of death. The early church described the Lord's supper using imagery from the Passover, especially in portraying Jesus as the lamb who delivers God's people from sin and death.

Psalm 116:1-2, 12-19

I will lift the cup of salvation and call on the name of the Lord. (Ps. 116:13)

I Corinthians 11:23-26

In the bread and cup of the Lord's supper, we experience intimate fellowship with Christ and with one another, because it involves his body given for us and the new covenant in his blood. Faithful participation in this meal is a living proclamation of Christ's death until he comes in the future.

John 13:1-17, 31b-35

The story of the last supper in John's gospel recalls a remarkable event not mentioned elsewhere: Jesus performs the duty of a slave, washing the feet of his disciples and urging them to do the same for one another.

Preface   Maundy Thursday

Color   Scarlet *or* White

Prayers of Intercession

The prayers are prepared locally for each occasion. The following examples may be adapted or used as appropriate.

Let us pray for renewed life in the church, abundant hope in the world, and holy compassion for all those in need.
A brief silence.

Holy and merciful God, gather your people around one heavenly food, the body and blood of Christ. Unite us with him, so that we may show his love to all the world. Hear us, O God.
Your mercy is great.

Draw forth from the earth grain and fruit that nourishes the body. In our eating and drinking remind us of your goodness and of Christ's sacrifice for our sake. Hear us, O God.
Your mercy is great.

Free all who are in bondage, as you did for Israel, the first chosen of your covenant. Free us all from the bondage of sin through the new covenant in Christ's blood. Hear us, O God.
Your mercy is great.

Kneel at the feet of all who are in great need (*especially*). Show them your compassion, and surround them with people who will lovingly serve them. Hear us, O God.
Your mercy is great.
Accompany the sisters and brothers of Christ through this great celebration of his death and resurrection. Encourage us to bear Christ for a world in need. Hear us, O God.
Your mercy is great.
Here other intercessions may be offered.
Teach us by the witness of all who faithfully confessed Christ crucified and risen for the salvation of the world. Call us to follow you as they did. Hear us, O God.
Your mercy is great.
Into your hands, O God, we commend all for whom we pray, in the name of the One who endured the cross, forgives our sins, and feeds us at his table, Jesus Christ our Lord.
Amen.

Ideas and Images for the Day

John's is the only gospel in which Jesus does not institute the Lord's supper at his last Passover with the disciples. Rather, at John's last supper Jesus gives his followers a way to live out the grace they receive through every encounter with God's grace: to love and serve one another. The church teaches that this "one another" means all of humanity and, in fact, all of God's creation.

1. A regular Thursday night inner-city youth basketball game was cancelled for a special Maundy Thursday service in the church's gym/dining hall. Some of the youth forgot the change in schedule and noisily burst in at their usual time, dressed for the game, during the service. After a moment of startled silence, the kids were invited to join in worship, which many of them did. The solemn celebration continued, another surprise development resulting from Jesus' command to the church to love one another.

2. A footwashing at the Maundy Thursday service is one ritualized response to Jesus' command to love and serve. Every Sunday morning service has its own ritual version of Jesus' command, and our response, in the dismissal of the assembly. *Evangelical Lutheran Worship* (p. 115) offers four options, but some congregations use their own variations based on the day's theme (for example, "feed the hungry, love your neighbor").

3. As you plan for the Three Days, consider Maundy Thursday as the date for welcoming children to regular participation in holy communion. Use Lent as a time of instruction for the children. Have the children bake the bread for the eucharist. The welcoming of the children to the table for the first time can deepen the experience of the meal and the day for the first communicants and the whole assembly. *Fed and Forgiven* resources (Augsburg Fortress, 2009) provide helps for communion preparation for various ages.

4. The 30 Hour Famine is a youth program that helps church groups raise money to alleviate hunger among the world's most at-risk populations. Through community service and a thirty-hour fast by participants, the program also raises awareness in the community, and among the youth themselves, of the prevalence of hunger in the world and the real possibility of its eradication. For information go to http://www.30hourfamine.org/.

5. The film *Hotel Rwanda* (United Artists, 2004) tells the story of the 1994 Rwandan genocide from the point of view of Paul Rusesabagina, the manager of a luxury hotel in the capital city of Kigali. Risking his own life and the lives of his family, Rusesabagina is credited with saving the lives of 1,200 Rwandans by hiding them in his hotel and bribing the military to spare them. The film, a true story, portrays Rusesabagina as a practical man driven to extraordinary heroism by love for his neighbor.

Hymns for Worship and Music for the Day

Because of the nature of this day, music suggestions are listed by place in the service and not categorized by type of leadership. All suggestions require assembly participation.

Laying On of Hands

Mummert, Mark. "Come, Let Us Return." *Music Sourcebook for Lent and the Three Days* S435. AFP 9780806670409.
"Forgive Your People / Perdona a tu pueblo." *Music Sourcebook* S437, LLC 339.
Healer of our every ill   ELW 612

Psalmody

Mummert, Mark. "Psalm 116," Refrain 1, from PSCY.
Farlee, Robert Buckley. "Psalm 116:1-2, 12-19" from PWA, Evangelical Lutheran Worship Edition.

Gospel Acclamation

Miller, Aaron David. *Gospel Acclamations for Lent—Holy Trinity.*
Schwandt, Daniel. "I Give You a New Commandment." *Music Sourcebook* S440.
A new commandment   WOV 664

Hymn of the Day

Jesu, Jesu, fill us with your love   ELW 708   *CHEREPONI*

Where charity and love prevail   ELW 359, LBW 126
   TWENTY-FOURTH

O Lord, we praise you   ELW 499, LBW 215
   GOTT SEI GELOBET UND GEBENEDEIET

Footwashing

Farlee, Robert Buckley. "Forgive As You Have Been Forgiven." *Music Sourcebook* S445.

Raabe, Nancy. "Love of Christ Poured Out for Us." *Music Sourcebook* S443.

Ubi caritas et amor / Where true charity and love abide   ELW 642, WOV 665

Love consecrates the humblest act   ELW 360, LBW 122

Setting the Table

Music Sourcebook for Lent and the Three Days includes an *appendix with hymn stanzas appropriate for use during the setting of the table on this and other days. These stanzas are also included on the CD-ROM that accompanies the volume.*

Communion

Now we join in celebration   ELW 462, LBW 203

Jesus is a rock in a weary land   ELW 333

Lord, who the night you were betrayed   ELW 463, LBW 206

Stripping of the Altar

Highben, Zebulon M. "Lord, I Cry to You (Psalm 88)." *Music Sourcebook* S446.

Raabe, Nancy. "Psalm 88" from PSCY.

Sending

None

Thursday, April 21

Anselm, Bishop of Canterbury, died 1109

This eleventh- and twelfth-century Benedictine monk stands out as one of the greatest theologians between Augustine and Thomas Aquinas. He is counted among the medieval mystics who emphasized the maternal aspects of God. Of Jesus Anselm says, "In sickness you nurse us and with pure milk you feed us." Anselm is perhaps best known for his "satisfaction" theory of atonement. He argued that human rebellion against God demands a payment, but because humanity is fallen it is incapable of making that satisfaction. But God takes on human nature in Jesus Christ, Anselm proposed, in order to make the perfect payment for sin.

April 22, 2011
Good Friday

At the heart of the Good Friday liturgy is the passion according to John, which proclaims Jesus as a triumphant king who reigns from the cross. The ancient title for this day—the triumph of the cross—reminds us that the church gathers not to mourn this day but to celebrate Christ's life-giving passion and to find strength and hope in the tree of life. In the ancient bidding prayer we offer petitions for all the world for whom Christ died. Today's liturgy culminates in the Easter Vigil tomorrow evening.

Prayer of the Day

Almighty God, look with loving mercy on your family, for whom our Lord Jesus Christ was willing to be betrayed, to be given over to the hands of sinners, and to suffer death on the cross; who now lives and reigns with you and the Holy Spirit, one God, forever and ever.

or

Merciful God, your Son was lifted up on the cross to draw all people to himself. Grant that we who have been born out of his wounded side may at all times find mercy in him, Jesus Christ, our Savior and Lord, who lives and reigns with you and the Holy Spirit, one God, now and forever.

Gospel Acclamation

Look to Jesus, who for the sake of the joy that was set before him endured the cross, disregard- ¹ ing its shame,* and has taken his seat at the right hand of the ¹ throne of God. (Heb. 12:2)

Readings and Psalm

Isaiah 52:13—53:12

The fourth servant poem promises ultimate vindication for the servant, who made his life an offering for sin. The early church saw in the servant's pouring himself out to death and being numbered with the transgressors important keys for understanding the death of Jesus.

Psalm 22

My God, my God, why have you forsaken me? (Ps. 22:1)

Hebrews 10:16-25

In the death of Jesus, forgiveness of sins is worked and access to God is established. Hence, when we gather together for worship and when we love others we experience anew the benefits of Jesus' death.

or Hebrews 4:14-16; 5:7-9

In his death Jesus functions as great high priest who experiences temptation and suffering in order that we would receive mercy and find grace, because he is the source of true salvation.

John 18:1—19:42

On Good Friday, the story of Jesus' passion—from his arrest to his burial—is read in its entirety from the Gospel of John.

Holy communion is normally not celebrated on Good Friday; accordingly, no preface is provided. The worship space having been stripped on the preceding evening, no paraments are used today.

Prayers of Intercession

On Good Friday, the church's ancient Bidding Prayer is said or sung. See Evangelical Lutheran Worship Leaders Edition, pp. 636–638.

Ideas and Images for the Day

With the words "It is finished," Jesus' mission is complete. By the power of the cross our redemption is accomplished. As we meditate on the consequences of God's sacrifice on this day, the church proclaims the good news that the cross of Christ is both necessary and sufficient for our salvation. With the command of Maundy Thursday lingering in our ears and hearts, Good Friday reminds us that the freedom to obey comes only as a gift from God.

1. We meet the crucified Christ in the suffering of those who are least able to defend themselves from the forces of violence and death in the world. Doctors Without Borders (http://doctorswithoutborders.org/) is an organization through which medical personnel work for minimal pay, offering their services to victims of human-made catastrophes in the most abject and

dangerous settings. Through the support of this and similar organizations, with prayer and offerings, we lift up the cross and share its message of salvation with the world.

2. Theodore Dubois' oratorio "Seven Last Words of Christ" takes as its text a traditional compilation, from all four gospels, of Jesus' words from the cross. The seventh word, "It is finished," is the briefest and most meditative of the sections, reflecting the somber finality of the moment. The piece ends with a choral expression of adoration, thanksgiving, and, ultimately, joy. Hear it in its entirety at http://www.archive.org/details/TheodoreDuboisTheSevenLastWords.

3. Worship during the Three Days, and Good Friday in particular, is inherently dramatic. The reading of St. John's Passion in today's service benefits from the use of several voices and the participation of the assembly. If you have not used booklets presenting the Passion in dialogue form on the Sunday of the Passion, consider it for today. Otherwise, simply alternating male and female readers of various ages creates a simpler, but effective, form of the dramatization. Booklets are available for purchase at http://www.augsburgfortress.org.

4. Many elements of today's service lend themselves to the participation of all but the youngest children. If a form of a Service of Light and Darkness is planned, youngsters can extinguish candles; with rehearsal older children can be recruited to read portions of the gospel and offer the bids for the bidding prayer; and the procession with the cross, again with rehearsal, can be accomplished by several children and youth working together.

Hymns for Worship and Music for the Day

Because of the nature of this day, music suggestions are listed by place in the service and not categorized by type of leadership. All suggestions require assembly participation.

Gathering

None

Psalmody

Farlee, Robert Buckley. "Psalm 22" from PWA, Evangelical Lutheran Worship Edition.

Mummert, Mark. "Psalm 22" from PSCY.
Witte, Marilyn. "My God, My God (Psalm 22)." *Music Sourcebook for Lent and the Three Days* S448. AFP 9780806670409.

Gospel Acclamation

Miller, Aaron David. *Gospel Acclamations for Lent—Holy Trinity.*
Organ, Anne Krentz. "Return to the Lord." *Music Sourcebook* S419.
Sturm, Ike. "Look to Jesus (Gospel Acclamation)." *Music Sourcebook* S449.

Passion Reading

Music Sourcebook for Lent and the Three Days includes an appendix with hymn stanzas appropriate for interspersing with sections of the reading.

Bach, J. S., ed. Thomas Pavlechko. *Chorales from the St. John Passion.* SATB. AFP 9780800663704.

Hymn of the Day

Holy God, holy and glorious   ELW 637   NELSON
Tree of Life and awesome mystery   ELW 334   THOMAS
Lift high the cross   ELW 660, LBW 377   CRUCIFER

Procession of the Cross

Organ, Anne Krentz. "Behold, the Life-Giving Cross" and "We Adore You, O Christ." *Music Sourcebook* S459.
Pavlechko, Thomas. "Behold, the Life-Giving Cross" and "We Adore You, O Christ." *Music Sourcebook* S458.

Solemn Reproaches

Anderson, Kevin, and Russian Orthodox traditional. "Solemn Reproaches." *Music Sourcebook* S460.
Farlee, Robert Buckley. "Solemn Reproaches of the Cross." SATB, solo, pno. AFP 9780800674724.

We Glory in Your Cross

Haugen, Marty. "Adoramus te Christe / We adore you, O Christ." *Music Sourcebook* S469.
Organ, Anne Krentz. "We Glory in Your Cross." *Music Sourcebook* S466.

Hymn of Triumph

Sing, my tongue   ELW 355/356, LBW 118
There in God's garden   ELW 342, WOV 668

April 23, 2011
Resurrection of Our Lord
Vigil of Easter

This is the night! This is our Passover with Christ from darkness to light, from bondage to freedom, from death to life. Tonight is the heart of our celebration of the Three Days and the pinnacle of the church's year. The resurrection of Christ is proclaimed in word and sign, and we gather around a pillar of fire, hear ancient stories of our faith, welcome new sisters and brothers at the font, and share the food and drink of the promised land. Raised with Christ, we go forth into the world, aflame with the good news of the resurrection.

Prayer of the Day

Eternal giver of life and light, this holy night shines with the radiance of the risen Christ. Renew your church with the Spirit given us in baptism, that we may worship you in sincerity and truth and may shine as a light in the world, through your Son, Jesus Christ our Lord, who lives and reigns with you and the Holy Spirit, one God, now and forever.

or

O God, you are the creator of the world, the liberator of your people, and the wisdom of the earth. By the resurrection of your Son free us from our fears, restore us in your image, and ignite us with your light, through Jesus Christ, our Savior and Lord, who lives and reigns with you and the Holy Spirit, one God, now and forever.

Gospel Acclamation

Alleluia. Let us sing to the Lord, who has ¹ triumphed gloriously;* our strength and our might, who has become ¹ our salvation. *Alleluia.* (Exod. 15:1-2)

Vigil Readings and Responses

Readings marked with an asterisk are not omitted.

*1 Genesis 1:1—2:4a

Creation

Response: Psalm 136:1-9, 23-26

God's mercy endures forever. (Ps. 136:1)

2 Genesis 7:1-5, 11-18; 8:6-18; 9:8-13

Flood

Response: Psalm 46

The Lord of hosts is with us; the God of Jacob is our stronghold. (Ps. 46:7)

3 Genesis 22:1-18

Testing of Abraham

Response: Psalm 16

You will show me the path of life. (Ps. 16:11)

*4 Exodus 14:10-31; 15:20-21

Deliverance at the Red Sea

Response: Exodus 15:1b-13, 17-18

I will sing to the Lord, who has triumphed gloriously. (Exod. 15:1)

*5 Isaiah 55:1-11

Salvation freely offered to all

Response: Isaiah 12:2-6

With joy you will draw water from the wells of salvation. (Isa. 12:3)

6 Proverbs 8:1-8, 19-21; 9:4b-6
or Baruch 3:9-15, 32—4:4

The wisdom of God

Response: Psalm 19

The statutes of the Lord are just and rejoice the heart. (Ps. 19:8)

7 Ezekiel 36:24-28

A new heart and a new spirit

Response: Psalms 42 and 43

I thirst for God, for the living God. (Ps. 42:2)

8 Ezekiel 37:1-14

Valley of the dry bones

Response: Psalm 143

Revive me, O Lord, for your name's sake. (Ps. 143:11)

9 Zephaniah 3:14-20

The gathering of God's people
Response: Psalm 98
Lift up your voice, rejoice, and sing. (Ps. 98:4)

10 Jonah 1:1—2:1

The deliverance of Jonah
Response: Jonah 2:2-3 [4-6] 7-9
Deliverance belongs to the Lord. (Jonah 2:9)

11 Isaiah 61:1-4, 9-11

Clothed in the garments of salvation
Response: Deuteronomy 32:1-4, 7, 36a, 43a
Great is our God, the Rock, whose ways are just.
(Deut. 32:3-4)

*12 Daniel 3:1-29

Deliverance from the fiery furnace
Response: Song of the Three 35–65
Praise and magnify the Lord forever. (Song of Thr. 35)

New Testament Reading and Gospel
Romans 6:3-11

We were incorporated into the death of Jesus Christ in baptism and so were liberated from the dominion of sin. We also anticipate that we will be incorporated into the resurrection of Christ and so will be liberated from the hold death has over our mortal bodies.

John 20:1-18

John's gospel describes the confusion and excitement of the first Easter: the stone is moved, disciples race back and forth, and angels speak to a weeping woman. Then, Jesus himself appears.

Preface Easter

Color White *or* Gold

Prayers of Intercession

The prayers are prepared locally for each occasion. The following examples may be adapted or used as appropriate.
Trusting in the renewal of all things through Christ's death and resurrection, we pray for the church, those in need, and all of God's creation.
A brief silence.
Holy and life-giving God, you pierce the darkness of this world with the light of Christ. Dispel the darkness of our hearts with his light of new life. Hear us, O God.
Your mercy is great.

You cleanse your people with living waters, washing away their sins and joining them to Christ's death and resurrection. Fill the newly baptized with your abundant life. Hear us, O God.
Your mercy is great.
You destroy the bonds of death and grant newness of life. Break the chains of all who are oppressed, and give them the freedom of new life in Christ. Hear us, O God.
Your mercy is great.
You deliver your people in time of crisis and trial. Attend to all who suffer from illness, despair, and grief (*especially*). Call them by name, as they cry out to you. Hear us, O God.
Your mercy is great.
You reveal your redeeming power in the empty tomb. When we are lost and empty, fill us with your redemption, and make us into bearers of salvation for a world in need. Hear us, O God.
Your mercy is great.
Here other intercessions may be offered.
You have joined all the saints to Christ's death and resurrection. As we give thanks for their lives, keep us alive in faith that the darkest hour is followed by brightest dawn. Hear us, O God.
Your mercy is great.
Into your wide embrace, O God, we commend all for whom we pray, trusting in the mercy you have shown us through Christ our Savior.
Amen.

Ideas and Images for the Day

God brings us through fire and water, out of death and night, welcoming us into the light of life. Tonight we light a new Christ candle from a new fire. By the light of that flame we share stories of God's work among us—creation and deliverance through fire and water. We gather at the baptismal font, giving thanks for water that is a sign of death to sin and rebirth into eternal life and for the fire of the Spirit, animating ashes and dry bones. Tonight, as we welcome new brothers and sisters in Christ through baptism, we remember how on the first Easter Christ welcomed Mary: calling her by name, bringing her out of weeping into the joyous light of Easter morning.

1. *Selaginella lepidophylla* (also known as resurrection plant, dinosaur plant, or the rose of Jericho) is a 400 million-year-old example of God's creation persisting through fire, flood, ice, and drought. How can the image of the reviving plant—unexpectedly unfurling leaves from a dried out, dead-looking ball—relate to the astonishing rebirths we celebrate

tonight? See http://faculty.ucc.edu/biology-ombrello/ pow/resurrection_plant.htm or search "Selaginella lepidophylla" for more information. Videos of the plant reviving are available on YouTube; search for "resurrection plant."

2. Plan ahead during Lent to involve children and youth in the readings and ritual actions of the Easter Vigil. Different Sunday school classes can perform different readings, for example, or mixed-age groups can be formed. Plan to present at least one reading in a way that actively involves the entire congregation (all ages): for example, prompt the congregation to provide sound effects for the creation story.

3. In some Roman Catholic traditions, salt is added to baptismal water. The biblical basis for this is 2 Kings 2:19-22: Elisha makes the land fruitful by purifying the water with salt; likewise, salt is used in these traditions to purify the baptismal water. How is the water in your font connected to the waters of creation (Gen. 1), the flood waters (Gen. 7), the Red Sea (Exod. 14), the wells of salvation (Isa. 12:3; 55:1), the stormy sea (Jonah 1:4-17), and to Mary Magdalene's tears (John 20:11)? How does water connect us with other people of faith?

4. While we welcome the resurrected Jesus with "Alleluia!" tonight, John's gospel makes it clear that above all it is Jesus who welcomes *us* and calls us by name. We are called to extend this welcome. *Radical Welcome: Embracing God, the Other, and the Spirit of Transformation*, by Stephanie Spellers (Harrisburg, PA: Church Publishing, 2006), is a resource for congregations. A January/February 2009 *Lutheran Woman Today* article by Spellers is available online: http://www.elca.org/ Growing-In-Faith/Ministry/Women-of-the-ELCA/ Lutheran-Woman-Today/Articles/2009/Jan_Feb/Radical-Welcome.aspx.

Hymns for Worship and Music for the Day

Because of the nature of this day, music suggestions are listed by place in the service and not categorized by type of leadership. All suggestions require assembly participation.

Fire and Procession

Abbey of Gethsemani. "Song for the Lighting of the Fire." *Music Sourcebook for Lent and the Three Days* S470. AFP 9780806670409.

Haugen, Marty. "Light of Christ (Easter Vigil Procession)." *Music Sourcebook* S472.

Easter Proclamation

Haugen, Marty. "Easter Proclamation (Exsultet)." *Music Sourcebook* S474.

Traditional chant. "Easter Proclamation (Exsultet)." *Music Sourcebook* S473.

Vigil Readings and Responses

1   Creation

Friesen-Carper, Paul. "God's Mercy Endures Forever (Psalm 136)." *Music Sourcebook* S476.

Many and great, O God / Wakantanka taku nitawa   ELW 837, WOV 794

2   Flood

Harbor, Rawn, and Daniel Schwandt. "The Lord of Hosts Is with Us (Psalm 46)." *Music Sourcebook* S478.

Erickson, Rick. "Psalm 46" from PSCY.

3   Testing of Abraham

I want Jesus to walk with me   ELW 325, WOV 660

Schwarz, May. "Psalm 16" from PWA, Evangelical Lutheran Worship Edition.

4   Deliverance at the Red Sea

Friesen-Carper, Paul. "The Lord Is My Strength (Exodus 15)." *Music Sourcebook* S481.

Sedio, Mark. "Exodus 15:1b-13, 17-18" from PWA, Evangelical Lutheran Worship Edition.

5   Salvation freely offered to all

Highben, Zebulon M. "With Joy You Will Draw Water (Isaiah 12)." *Music Sourcebook* S484.

Mummert, Mark. "Isaiah 12:2-6" from PSCY.

6   The wisdom of God

Farlee, Robert Buckley. "The Teaching of the Lord (Psalm 19)." *Music Sourcebook* S485.

We eat the bread of teaching   ELW 518

7   A new heart and a new spirit

As the deer runs to the river   ELW 331

Weidler, Scott. "As the Deer Longs (Psalms 42 and 43)." *Music Sourcebook* S486.

8   Valley of the dry bones

O living breath of God / Soplo de Dios viviente   ELW 407

Schwandt, Daniel, and John Weaver. "Revive Me, O God (Psalm 143)." *Music Sourcebook* S487.

9 The gathering of God's people

Sedio, Mark. "Psalm 98" from PWA, Evangelical Lutheran Worship Edition.

Vaughan Williams, Ralph. "Unto God, Our Savior (Psalm 98)" KING'S WESTON. *Music Sourcebook* S488.

10 The deliverance of Jonah

Jennings, Carolyn. "Jonah Prayed (Jonah 2)." *Music Sourcebook* S489.

Pavlechko, Thomas. "Jonah 2:2-3 [4-6] 7-9" from PSCY.

11 Clothed in the garments of salvation

Mummert, Mark. "Deuteronomy 32:1-4, 7, 36a, 43a" from PSCY.

Warren, George W., arr. May Schwarz. "Deuteronomy 32:1-4, 7, 36a, 43a" from PWA, Evangelical Lutheran Worship Edition.

12 Deliverance from the fiery furnace

Berthier, Jacques. "Surrexit Christus: The Lord Is Risen (Song of the Three)." *Music Sourcebook* S493.

Potter, Doreen. "All You Works of God (Song of the Three)." LINSTEAD. *Music Sourcebook* S494.

Procession to the Font

Highben, Zebulon M. "Processional Refrains." *Music Sourcebook* S471.

Springs of water, bless the Lord   ELW 214

We know that Christ is raised   ELW 449, LBW 189

Setting the Table

Music Sourcebook for Lent and the Three Days includes an appendix with hymn stanzas appropriate for use during the setting of the table on this and other days. These stanzas are also included on the CD-ROM that accompanies the volume.

Communion

At the Lamb's high feast we sing   ELW 362, LBW 210

Pelz, Walter L. "Our Paschal Lamb, That Sets Us Free." REGION THREE. *Music Sourcebook* S499.

Signs and wonders   ELW 672

Sending

Christ is risen! Alleluia!   ELW 382

Come, you faithful, raise the strain   ELW 363, LBW 132

Christ the Lord is risen today; Alleluia!   ELW 369, LBW 128

Saturday, April 23

Toyohiko Kagawa, renewer of society, died 1960

Toyohiko Kagawa (toy-oh-hee-koh ka-ga-wah) was born in 1888 in Kobe, Japan. Orphaned early, he was disowned by his remaining extended family when he became a Christian. Kagawa wrote, spoke, and worked at length on ways to employ Christian principles in the ordering of society. His vocation to help the poor led him to live among them. He established schools, hospitals, and churches. He also worked for peace and established the Anti-War League. He was arrested for his efforts to reconcile Japan and China after the Japanese attack of 1940.

April 24, 2011
Resurrection of Our Lord
Easter Day

On this day the Lord has acted! On the first day of the week God began creation, transforming darkness into light. On this, the "eighth day" of the week, Jesus Christ was raised from the dead. We celebrate this new creation in the waters of baptism and in the feast of victory. With great joy we celebrate this day of days, even as we begin the great fifty days of Easter. Filled with hope, we go forth to share the news that Christ is risen!

Prayer of the Day

O God, you gave your only Son to suffer death on the cross for our redemption, and by his glorious resurrection you delivered us from the power of death. Make us die every day to sin, that we may live with him forever in the joy of the resurrection, through your Son, Jesus Christ our Lord, who lives and reigns with you and the Holy Spirit, one God, now and forever.

or

God of mercy, we no longer look for Jesus among the dead, for he is alive and has become the Lord of life. Increase in our minds and hearts the risen life we share with Christ, and help us to grow as your people toward the fullness of eternal life with you, through Jesus Christ, our Savior and Lord, who lives and reigns with you and the Holy Spirit, one God, now and forever.

Gospel Acclamation

Alleluia. Christ, our paschal lamb, ¹ has been sacrificed.* Therefore, let us ¹ keep the feast. *Alleluia.* (1 Cor. 5:7, 8)

Readings and Psalm

Acts 10:34-43

Peter's sermon, delivered at the home of Cornelius, a Roman army officer, is a summary of the essential message of Christianity: Everyone who believes in Jesus, whose life, death, and resurrection fulfilled the words of the prophets, "receives forgiveness of sins through his name."

or Jeremiah 31:1-6

This passage makes clear that God's final word is always "Yes." Because God's love is everlasting, God always remains faithful. Ancient Israel is assured that it will be rebuilt and have plentiful crops. The people of God too will ultimately be reunited.

Psalm 118:1-2, 14-24

This is the day that the LORD has made; let us rejoice and be glad in it. (Ps. 118:24)

Colossians 3:1-4

Easter means new life for us as it first meant new life for Christ. His resurrection reshapes the entire focus and motivation for our lives, since we are now hidden with the risen Christ in God.

or Acts 10:34-43

See above.

Matthew 28:1-10

Sorrow gives way to "fear and great joy" when two women are sent by an angel to proclaim the good news: Jesus is risen!

or John 20:1-18

John's gospel describes the confusion and excitement of the first Easter: the stone is moved, disciples race back and forth, and angels speak to a weeping woman. Then, Jesus himself appears.

Preface Easter

Color White *or* Gold

Prayers of Intercession

The prayers are prepared locally for each occasion. The following examples may be adapted or used as appropriate.

Trusting in the renewal of all things through Christ's death and resurrection, we pray for the church, those in need, and all of God's creation.

A brief silence.

God of life, awaken us to the celebration of new life in Christ. Open our hearts in this gathering around word and sacrament to your action for the life of the world. Hear us, O God.

Your mercy is great.

Awaken us to the movement of your life-giving Spirit throughout all creation. Bless plants and animals blossoming into new life. Hear us, O God.

Your mercy is great.

Awaken us to your justice and righteousness for all nations. Stir up in us longing for your mercy and eagerness to seek your will in all we do. Hear us, O God.

Your mercy is great.

Awaken us to the care and compassion you show people in greatest need. Encourage us to extend compassionate, caring hands to those who are ill, lonely, and fearful (*especially*). Hear us, O God.

Your mercy is great.

Awaken us to your mission of gathering all nations through the saving act of Christ. As we celebrate our new life in him, lead us to boldly proclaim his new life for all people. Hear us, O God.

Your mercy is great.

Here other intercessions may be offered.

Awaken us to the resurrection of Christ revealed in the lives of the saints. Sustain us in the hope of his coming to fulfill the work of redemption and to make all things new. Hear us, O God.

Your mercy is great.

Into your wide embrace, O God, we commend all for whom we pray, trusting in the mercy you have shown us through Christ our Savior.

Amen.

Ideas and Images for the Day

Easter turns the world upside down. It defies our expectations: Mary does not recognize the resurrected Jesus (John 20:14), the good news is heralded by an earthquake and terrifying angels and is brought to the women of the church first, rather than to the Twelve (Matt. 28:1-10). The radical reversals prophesied in scripture and revealed in Christ's life and ministry culminate in the good news we proclaim today: Christ, through death, has triumphed over death.

"The stone that the builders rejected has become the chief cornerstone" (Ps. 118:22). Only God could do this—so while Easter can (and should) be unsettling, we also celebrate it with great joy (Matt. 28:8). This is the day that the Lord has made!

1. Leymah Gbowee's story is about radical reversals: God at work to turn the world upside down through peaceful, powerful prayer. *Pray the Devil Back to Hell* (Fork Films, 2008) is a documentary film about her work with the Christian/Muslim women's group Liberian Mass Action for Peace. An audio interview and transcript with background information about Gbowee is available at http://www.spotlightradio.net/listen/women-in-white/. Gbowee's Profile in Courage Award acceptance speech and other resources are at http://www.jfklibrary.org/Education+and+Public+Programs/Profile+in+Courage+Award/Award+Recipients/Leymah+Gbowee+and+the+Women+of+Liberia/.

2. For something potentially unsettling and definitely joyful, get the whole congregation involved in the children's message: involve all ages in singing an "Alleluia!" song. Do "Praise Ye the Lord (Alleluia!)": one side of the congregation sings the "Alleluia," the other side sings "Praise Ye the Lord," and the children join in for the last verse. For lyrics and instructions, see http://dragon.sleepdeprived.ca/songbook/songs8/S8_14.htm.

3. Our comfort with the logic of this world is deep-seated. One needs only look at the literary tradition of horror—from vampires to zombies to Frankenstein's monster—to see that humans find something "unnatural" in life after death. Death seems so final, so certain. So, it makes sense that, along with great joy, the disciples might experience fear, doubt, and confusion when they meet the risen Christ. Rather than subverting the natural order, Christ's resurrection *restores* it—overcoming the "logic" of the finality of death and replacing it with glorious, everlasting life in abundance.

4. The poem "i thank You God for most this amazing," by e. e. cummings (*100 Selected Poems*, New York: Grove Press, 1950), can be read as an expression of daily Easter: the death and resurrection that isn't once a liturgical year but an integral part of human experience and God's creation. Poet e. e. cummings presents God as "everything which is yes": how is that a reversal of our expectations?

Hymns for Worship

Gathering

Jesus Christ is risen today   ELW 365, LBW 151
We know that Christ is raised   ELW 449, LBW 189
Now all the vault of heaven resounds   ELW 367, LBW 143

Hymn of the Day

Christ Jesus lay in death's strong bands   ELW 370, LBW 134
CHRIST LAG IN TODESBANDEN

Now all the vault of heaven resounds   ELW 367, LBW 143
LASST UNS ERFREUEN

Christ has arisen, alleluia   ELW 364, WOV 678
MFURAHINI, HALELUYA

Offering

Christ is arisen   ELW 372, LBW 136
Be not afraid   ELW 388

Communion

At the Lamb's high feast we sing   ELW 362, LBW 210
Now the green blade rises   ELW 379, LBW 148
Christ the Lord is risen today!   ELW 373, LBW 130

Sending

Thine is the glory   ELW 376, LBW 145
The strife is o'er, the battle done   ELW 366, LBW 135

Additional Hymns and Songs

Awake, arise, lift up your voice   HS91 743
Alleluia, alleluia, give thanks   WOV 671
Up from the grave he arose   TFF 94

Music for the Day

Psalmody and Acclamations

Ellingboe, Bradley. "Psalm 118:1-2, 14-24" from PWA, Evangelical Lutheran Worship Edition.
Miller, Aaron David. *Gospel Acclamations for Lent–Holy Trinity.*
Mummert, Mark. "Psalm 118," Refrain 1, from PSCY.
"This Is the Day." TFF 262.

Choral

o Bach, J. S. "Christ Jesus Lay in Death's Strong Bands" from *Bach for All Seasons*. SATB. AFP 9780800658540.
Breedlove, Jennifer Kerr. "Early Easter Morning." 2 pt mxd or SA, kybd, opt hb. GIA G-5894.
Frahm, Frederick. "Now Christ Is Risen from the Dead." 2 pt mxd, kybd. AFP 9780800678920.

o Hobby, Robert A. "Now All the Vault of Heaven Resounds." SAB, org, 2 tpts, opt hb, assembly. AFP 9780800658656.
Jennings, Carolyn. "Awake, My Heart." SATB, pno or org, opt hb. AFP 9780806697321.
Wicks, Christopher. "Come Away to the Skies." SAB, kybd. AFP 9780806697222.

Children's Choir

Patterson, Mark. "Alleluia, Christ Is Risen" from *ChildrenSing*. U, kybd. AFP 9780800677695.
Sleeth, Natalie. "This Is the Day" from *LifeSongs*. UE, U, kybd.
Wold, Wayne. "The Whole World Sings Alleluia." U, kybd. CG CGA708.

Keyboard / Instrumental

o Eggert, John. "Christ lag in Todesbanden" from *Six Hymn Preludes*, vol. 1. Org. CPH 97-5893U1.
o Held, Wilbur. "Christ lag in Todesbanden" from *Six Preludes on Easter Hymns*. Org. CPH 97-5330U1.
o Nelhybel, Vaclav. "Lasst uns erfreuen" from *Festival Hymns and Processionals*. Br. Conductor score HOP 750.
o Raabe, Nancy M. "Mfurahini, haleluya" from *Grace and Peace*, vol. 2. Pno. AFP 9780800679016.

Handbell

Benton, Douglas. "Christ the Lord Is Risen Today." 3-5 hb, br, org, opt SATB, L2. HOP 5573HB (hb). 5573B (Full Score). 5573 (SATB).
o Lamb, Linda. "Bell Peal on Lasst Uns Erfreuen." 3-5 oct, L1. SHW HP5453.
Organ, Anne Krentz. "Earth and All Stars and Alleluia! Jesus Is Risen." 3 oct hb, opt 2 oct hc, L2. AFP 9780800658083.

Praise Ensemble

● Egan, Jon. "I Am Free." Vertical Worship Songs/INT.
● Founds, Rick. "Lord, I Lift Your Name on High." MAR. ELW 857
● LeBlanc, Lenny/Paul Baloche. "Above All." INT.
● Morgan, Reuben. "My Redeemer Lives." Hillsong/INT.
● Smith, Henry. "Give Thanks." INT.
● Walker, Tommy. "That's Why We Praise Him." Doulos Music.

Global

Sosa, Pablo. "Éste es el Día/This Is the Day" from *Éste es el Día*. U. GIA G-7021.
Toppenberg, Edouard. "Hallelu, Let the People All Sing" from *Let the Peoples Sing*. SATB. AFP 9780800675394.

o denotes suggestions that relate to the hymn of the day.
● denotes songs that are available on iTunes®.

April 24, 2011
Resurrection of Our Lord
Easter Evening

Isaiah proclaims the great feast to come, when God will swallow up death forever. Paul invites us to celebrate the paschal feast with the unleavened bread of sincerity and truth. The Easter evening gospel tells of the risen Christ being made known to the disciples in the breaking of the bread. Our hearts burn within us as the hope of the resurrection is proclaimed in our midst, and as Jesus appears to us at the holy table.

Prayer of the Day

O God, whose blessed Son made himself known to his disciples in the breaking of bread, open the eyes of our faith, that we may behold him in all his redeeming work, Jesus Christ, our Savior and Lord, who lives and reigns with you and the Holy Spirit, one God, now and forever.

Gospel Acclamation

Alleluia. Our hearts ¹ burn within us* while you open to ¹ us the scriptures. *Alleluia.* (Luke 24:32)

Readings and Psalm

Isaiah 25:6-9

The prophet portrays a wonderful victory banquet at which death, which in ancient Canaan was depicted as a monster swallowing everyone up, will be swallowed up forever. The prophet urges celebration of this victory, which is salvation.

Psalm 114

Tremble, O earth, at the presence of the LORD. (Ps. 114:7)

1 Corinthians 5:6b-8

In preparation to celebrate Passover, God's people cleaned out all the old leaven from their homes. Paul draws on this practice to portray Christ as our Passover lamb whose sacrifice means that we now clean out the old leaven of malice and wickedness from our lives and replace it with sincerity and truth.

Luke 24:13-49

On the day of his resurrection, Jesus joins two disciples on the road to Emmaus and makes himself known to them in the breaking of bread.

Preface Easter

Color White *or* Gold

Monday, April 25

Mark, Evangelist

Though Mark himself was not an apostle, it is likely that he was a member of one of the early Christian communities. It is possible that he is the John Mark of Acts 12 whose mother owned the house where the apostles gathered. The gospel attributed to him is brief and direct. It is considered by many to be the earliest gospel. Tradition has it that Mark went to preach in Alexandria, Egypt, became the first bishop there, and was martyred.

Friday, April 29

Catherine of Siena, theologian, died 1380

Catherine of Siena was a member of the Order of Preachers (Dominicans), and among Roman Catholics she was the first woman to receive the title Doctor of the Church. She was a contemplative and is known for her mystical visions of Jesus. This gift of mysticism apparently extended back into her childhood, much to the dismay of her parents, who wanted her to be like other children. Catherine was a humanitarian who worked to alleviate the suffering of the poor and imprisoned. She was also a renewer of church and society and advised both popes and any persons who told her their problems. Catherine's contemplative life was linked to her concern for the poor and suffering. She is a reminder that prayer and activism belong together.

EASTER

PREPARING FOR EASTER

The chanted proper preface is an often overlooked resource for funding the liturgical imagination. Depending on the season, it typically performs a dual task. First, it situates the communion liturgy within the narrative, offering a creedal formulation appropriate to the season. Second, and important for our purposes here, it proclaims the broad eschatological vision to all those who are gathered in praise before they sing the unending hymn:

> *Holy, holy, holy Lord, God of power and might,*
> *heaven and earth are full of your glory.*
> *Hosanna in the highest.*
> *Blessed is he who comes in the name of the Lord.*
> *Hosanna in the highest.*

The season of Easter is an especially fallow season to reconsider this vision. In this chant and song, the assembly is invited to imagine that they are not alone when singing the holy, holy, holy. Not only are there churches throughout the world singing this song on the same day. This song is also sung throughout time, and the entire heavenly host is singing along—angels and archangels, cherubim and seraphim, the saints in light, and, in fact, all of creation.

Try this experiment. Stand at the altar/table in your worship space. Take a moment to read through or chant the proper preface. Then imagine that the holy, holy, holy is sung not by you alone, but by heaven and earth. The very stones under foot. The air. The fields. Birds and plants. Snow and water. Angels and the heavenly host. A creational chorus encompassing heaven and earth. Certainly this is a rich enough vision to enrich all of your worship preparations for the Easter season. All art, music, texts, and environment is called to evoke its depth and multiplicity of vision. Consider re-viewing famous evocations of the vision, such as Dante's beatific vision in the *Paradiso* or the visions of Hildegard of Bingen.

The hymn that follows the proper preface, the "Holy, holy, holy" (or *Sanctus*), has a long tradition in the life of the church, and it is an assembly of biblical texts, including Isaiah 6:3 and Matthew 21:9. Worshipers are therefore singing a hymn that has a long tradition in the musical heritage of the church and that also forms them in the first language of faith, the language of scripture. Congregations might consider reviewing this portion of the liturgy in small snippets each Sunday, during the children's sermon or another time, and comparing the original biblical text to its translation for use in worship. Since scripture is the primary language of the liturgy, and many worshipers have the liturgy memorized, congregations may be pleasantly surprised to learn how much of the Bible they have memorized without realizing it. See "Scripture and Worship" in *Evangelical Lutheran Worship* (pp. 1154–1159). Congregations might also consider using alternative settings of "Holy, holy, holy," such as hymns 189–193 in *Evangelical Lutheran Worship*.

New Creation

Fundamental to both individual and corporate Christian formation is a growing awareness of the church's standing as the new creation in Christ (2 Cor. 5:17). The church is called to a revolution in its understanding of the relationship between creation and new creation because of Easter. The Easter proclamation is that God loves God's creation, and especially the firstborn of God's new creation (Col. 1:18; Rev. 1:5), enough to redeem it, all of it, rather than lifting his Son out of it and setting him above it. Jesus Christ in his resurrection brings all of creation along with him into the resurrection, for what he has assumed, he has redeemed.

Jesus Christ assumed human flesh. As we now know, human flesh is composed of many different elements. All elements heavier than oxygen (like heavy metals) can only be formed in supernovae. Elements lighter than oxygen are found in stars like our sun, which means we are composed of elements found in local stars, but the heavier elements could only have come from stellar explosions. No wonder all of creation sings "Holy, holy, holy" at the eucharist. In Jesus Christ, not only humanity, but all of creation, is redeemed and caught up into divinity (Rom. 8:23).

The witness of the resurrection is that the tomb was empty. Resurrection is therefore not simply a spiritual reality, the guarantee that after Christ died he lived on in some ethereal form. Resurrection means the raising of the dead.

God did not simply take on the semblance of human form at the incarnation. Through Christ's death and resurrection, God overcame and transcended death *in the body* and extends the promise of participation in that resurrection to all those who call on God's name. As the creed declares, "I believe in the resurrection of the body."

Although every season of the church year provides opportunity for celebrating the goodness of God's good creation, worship leaders may consider a creation and environment focus during the Easter season. Easter is an especially good time to *sing* about creation. Many churches put on Christmas pageants and rehearse music to perform especially for that season. Has your church ever considered celebrating an Easter pageant? Might a special musical performance during April be just the thing to offer special emphasis and energy in what are sometimes waning days of the Sunday school season?

The musical *All Nature Sings*, with music by Aaron David Miller and text by Herbert Brokering (Augsburg Fortress, 2009), would be an excellent choice to enhance creation-themed worship. The 25-minute running time can work well as the message of the day, framed within the liturgical elements of the service. The story is led by a minstrel who moves across the earth gathering the gifts of creation: wind and air, trees and plants, water, birds—all are gathered and presented in a final hymn of praise to God. The musical can be performed by kids ages 8–13 or a choir of young women. There are many options for performance, from a simple staging to costumes, props, and sets.

In addition to the children's musical *All Nature Sings*, churches might consider performing or listening to special music for the Easter season. Much has been done for Holy Week in classical music, like the Passions of Johann Sebastian Bach and Osvaldo Golijov, among many others.

One musician especially attuned to the profundity of the resurrection is Olivier Messiaen. His *Et Exspecto Resurrectionem Mortuorum* is the most explicit of his compositions on the theme of resurrection. Resurrection, and especially the sense of new creation implicit in resurrection, is a theme that runs throughout his oeuvre. One piece in particular unites the themes we have been discussing here. "The Resurrected and the Song of the Star Aldebaran" is the eighth movement in his ninety-minute piece *From the Canyons to the Stars*. Messiaen was famous for visiting national parks (in this case, Bryce Canyon, in Utah), then writing compositions in response to what he saw. He also famously spent hours sitting in woods transcribing the songs of birds for use in his works. Messiaen was a devout Catholic, and was the organist for Trinity Cathedral in Paris for decades. He had ears for the worship of the church, but also the worship of all of creation.

Why mention a famous (but still for many obscure) composer in seasonal planning pages for Easter? First of all, if we're honest, resurrection is not an easy theme to evoke adequately either in preaching or worship. Although it is central to the faith we confess, it also extends beyond words, beyond thought. It is part of the mystery of faith. One reviewer of Messiaen's "The Resurrected and the Song of the Star Aldebaran" writes, "It strikes a meditative mood, with strings chanting a gently shifting melody while stars twinkle and birds twitter in the glockenspiel, piccolo, and piano. Messiaen adds slithery harmonics to end phrases, as if a silken thread of light carries the song that connects the earthborn boulders and birds to a celestial afterworld" (http://www.npr.org/templates/story/story.php?storyId=98077930). Is this not one of the vocations of the church's song, to be a silken thread of light that carries the song that connects earthborn peoples and all of creation to the celestial afterworld? Maybe the music of the church during Easter can carry on this silken, slithery tenor, with special instrumentation, musical experimentation, great pageantry, and time for the mysterious and ethereal.

Acts of the Apostles

The Easter season offers two opportunities for *lectio continua*. Preachers might consider preaching through one of the two series offered during this time, the readings from 1 Peter or from Acts. First Peter is powerful, but it is more paranesis and proclamation than story or history, and some assemblies may benefit from the direct retelling of the Acts of the Apostles during these fifty days. Acts begins as Luke ends, with an account of Jesus ascending into heaven. This is helpful to keep in mind, as the feast of the Ascension is celebrated during the Easter season (June 2). The Ascension text is read twice during Easter, once at the feast of the Ascension, and again on the seventh Sunday of Easter. Worship planners and preachers may want to familiarize themselves with a good theological work on the Ascension, like Douglas Farrow's *Ascension and Ecclesia* (T&T Clark, 1999).

The first three Sundays *after* Easter are devoted to readings from Acts 2. These are the heady, spirit-filled first days of the church. The next two Sundays leap to famous events in the lives of the first martyr, Stephen, and the great missionary to the Gentiles, Paul. The Day of Pentecost returns worshipers once again to Acts 2. This redundancy of readings is helpful and can allow for a special focus on three crucial themes in the Acts of the Apostles: the power of the Spirit in the mission of the church (pneumatology); the centrality of witness to Jesus in the mission of the church (christology); and the powerful role of the apostles themselves in proclaiming and living out their lives in that Spirit and under the lordship of Jesus (missiology).

On the Road with Jesus

Some preachers and worship leaders will prefer to preach specifically from the gospel readings for this season. If this is the case, it may help Easter season proclamation to consider environment and hymnody as resources for preaching the account of the resurrection. It might be useful to divide the gospel readings into two distinct units. Easter 2 and 3 are accounts of Jesus' appearance to the disciples, in the upper room, and on the road to Emmaus. Easter 4–7 are sermons and prayers of Jesus, including his "good shepherd" sermon (John 10:1-10), his "I am the way, and the truth, and the life" sermon (John 14:1-14), his Advocate sermon (John 14:15-21), and Jesus' prayer that "they may be one, as we are one" (John 17:1-11).

For the first two Sundays of the Easter season, then, congregations can focus on the "gospel of the fifty days," specifically Jesus' preaching and teaching while he was with the disciples after his resurrection and before his ascension. However, those who prepared the lectionary were wise to include readings during these days from Christ's preaching and praying *prior* to his crucifixion, because the church does not rely only on what Jesus had to say (and what he did) after his resurrection. Instead, the resurrection brought new light and understanding to the community of those who had been with him during his earthly ministry. So during the Easter season we return to sermons and prayers already heard before his crucifixion, but now heard with new knowledge and in the power of the Spirit.

How can the church environment include an emphasis on Jesus' resurrection appearances? Consider living out examples of the paradox of Jesus' resurrected life. He eats fish (broil fish outside church and hand it out to anyone who will eat it), but also passes through walls (find art illustrating Christ's resurrected transcendence). He seems both out of touch and unrecognizable, and yet very sensitive and more than real. Review Paul's creedal declaration of the resurrection appearances in 1 Corinthians 15:3-7.

Hymns that focus on Christ's resurrection appearances include "O sons and daughters, let us sing" (ELW 386), recounting various resurrection appearances; and "Be not afraid" (ELW 388), a Taizé setting of Jesus' words to the disciples. Finally, "With high delight let us unite" (ELW 368) weaves together many of these themes nicely and might be learned as a special hymn sung Easter 4–7. Additionally, these four Sundays are a chance to pick up one song each week in praise of Jesus Christ, but from these perspectives: good shepherd, the way, sending the Holy Spirit, and prayer for unity. Consider these four hymns as appropriate to each day, respectively: "The Lord's my shepherd" (ELW 778), "O Word of God incarnate" (ELW 514), "O Spirit of life" (ELW 405), and "You Are Mine" (ELW 581).

Seasonal Checklist

- Use the Kyrie, hymn of praise ("This is the feast"), and Nicene Creed.
- Thanksgiving at the table; see options in *Evangelical Lutheran Worship*, especially Prayer IV.
- Publicize Ascension and Pentecost services, helping the congregation understand the importance of these festivals.
- Determine ways to emphasize the Day of Pentecost, such as using red flowers or balloons, inviting people to wear red, or using a diversity of languages in scripture readings, prayers, or music for the day.
- On Pentecost, seven votive candles in red glass holders may be lighted on or near the altar/table to recall the gifts of the Spirit identified in the rites of Holy Baptism and Affirmation of Baptism.
- If your congregation celebrates affirmation of baptism (confirmation) during this season, review the rite in *Evangelical Lutheran Worship*.

WORSHIP TEXTS FOR EASTER

Confession and Forgiveness

Thanksgiving for baptism (ELW pp. 97, 119) is especially appropriate for use during the Easter season instead of confession and forgiveness. The following is provided for occasions during the Easter season when an order for confession and forgiveness is desired.

All may make the sign of the cross, the sign marked at baptism, as the presiding minister begins.
Blessed be the holy Trinity, ✛ one God,
who gives us a new birth into a living hope,
who raises us with Christ from death,
who fills us with the Holy Spirit.
Amen.

Let us repent of our sin and claim the promise of God.

Silence is kept for reflection.

Living God,
we confess before you and one another
our futile ways,
our pursuit of perishable things,
our own part in crucifying the Lord Jesus.
Forgive us, O God;
renew the face of the earth;
and give us the assurance
that you have rescued us from the power of sin
and made us alive in the Spirit forever.
Amen.

Christ suffered for sins once for all
in order to bring you to God.
Now you are God's people;
now you have received mercy.
In the name of the risen ✛ Lord Jesus,
I declare to you that your sins are forgiven.
Lay aside guilt, put away shame,
for you are chosen and precious in God's sight.
Live in the marvelous light of Christ.
Amen.

Greeting

Alleluia! Christ is risen!
Christ is risen indeed! Alleluia!

The grace of our Lord Jesus Christ, the love of God,
and the communion of the Holy Spirit be with you all.
And also with you.

Offering Prayer

Blessed are you, O God, ruler of heaven and earth.
Day by day you shower us with blessings.
As you have raised us to new life in Christ,
give us glad and generous hearts,
ready to praise you and to respond to those in need,
through Jesus Christ, our Savior and Lord.
Amen.

Invitation to Communion

The disciples knew the Lord Jesus in the breaking of the bread.
Come to the table of the risen Christ.

Prayer after Communion

Mighty and compassionate God,
you have brought us over from death to life
through your Son, our risen Savior,
and you have fed us with spiritual food
in the sacrament of his body and blood.
Send us now into the world in peace,
and grant us strength and courage
to love and serve you
with gladness and singleness of heart;
through Jesus Christ our Lord.
Amen.

Sending of Communion

Eternal God,
whose glory is revealed in the crucified and risen Lord,
bless those who go forth to share your word and sacrament
with our sisters and brothers
who are *sick/homebound/imprisoned*.
In your love and care, nourish and strengthen
those to whom we bring this communion
in the body and blood of your Son,
that we may all feast upon your abundant love
made known in Jesus Christ our Lord.
Amen.

Blessing

The God of peace,
who brought again from the dead our Lord Jesus,
the great shepherd of the sheep,
by the blood of the eternal covenant,
make you complete in everything good
so that you may do God's will,
working in you that which is pleasing in God's sight;
through + Jesus Christ,
to whom be the glory forever and ever.
Amen.

Dismissal

Go in peace. Share the good news. Alleluia.
Thanks be to God. Alleluia.

Thanksgiving for Baptism

This order may be used in various circumstances outside the weekly assembly to give thanks for the gift of baptism. Examples of settings in which this order might be used include a conference or retreat, a small group meeting for study or mutual support, or an outdoor camp or recreation area. The gathering may be near a body of water, or a bowl of water may be placed in the midst of those who are gathered. A candle may be lighted and placed near the water.

Those present may make the sign of the cross, the sign marked at baptism, as the leader begins.
In the name of the Father,
and of the ✛ Son,
and of the Holy Spirit.
Amen.

or
Blessed be the holy Trinity, ✛ one God,
the fountain of living water,
the rock who gave us birth,
our light and our salvation.
Amen.

One of the following or another appropriate scripture passage is read.
Psalm 29:3, 11
Psalm 98:7-8
Romans 6:3-5
2 Corinthians 5:17
Revelation 22:1-2

The leader addresses those who are gathered.
Joined to Christ in the waters of baptism,
we are clothed with God's mercy and forgiveness.
Let us give thanks for the gift of baptism.

The leader gives thanks, using one of the following prayers or similar words.
Holy God, holy and merciful, holy and mighty,
you are the river of life,
you are the everlasting wellspring,
you are the fire of rebirth.

Glory to you for oceans and lakes, for rivers and streams.
Here particular bodies or sources of water may be named.
Honor to you for cloud and rain, for dew and snow.
Your waters are below us, around us, above us:
our life is born in you.
You are the fountain of resurrection.

Praise to you for your saving waters:
Noah and the animals survive the flood,
Hagar discovers your well.
The Israelites escape through the sea,
and they drink from your gushing rock.
Naaman washes his leprosy away,
and the Samaritan woman will never be thirsty again.

Praise to you for the water of baptism
and for your Word that saves us in this sacrament.
Breathe your Spirit into all who are gathered here
and into all creation.
Illumine our days. Enliven our bones. Dry our tears.
Wash away the sin within us, and drown the evil around us.

Satisfy all our thirst with your living water,
Jesus Christ, our Savior,
who lives and reigns with you and the Holy Spirit,
one God, now and forever.
Amen.

or
We give you thanks, O God,
for in the beginning your Spirit moved over the waters
and by your Word you created the world,
calling forth life in which you took delight.

Through the waters of the flood
you delivered Noah and his family.
Through the sea you led your people Israel
from slavery into freedom.
At the river your Son was baptized by John
and anointed with the Holy Spirit.
By water and your Word you claim us as daughters and sons,
making us heirs of your promise and servants of all.

We praise you for the gift of water that sustains life,
and above all we praise you for the gift of new life
in Jesus Christ.
Shower us with your Spirit,
and renew our lives with your forgiveness, grace, and love.

To you be given honor and praise
through Jesus Christ our Lord
in the unity of the Holy Spirit, now and forever.
Amen.

or

We give you thanks, holy and gracious God,
for you created the waters of the earth:
wide oceans, rushing streams, clear lakes, mighty rivers.
Here particular bodies or sources of water may be named.

You led your people through the sea
and called them to life in covenant with you.
Your Son was baptized in the river Jordan
to begin his mission among us.
You pour out your Holy Spirit to renew the face of the earth.

Through this water remind us of the gift of baptism.
Renew us in your promise
so that we may serve this world in all its need;
through Jesus Christ, our Savior and Lord,
who lives and reigns with you and the Holy Spirit,
one God, now and forever.
Amen.

*Assembly singing may follow, especially song related to baptism. As
a reminder of the gift of baptism, those present may be sprinkled
with water during this time.*

The order concludes with this or another suitable blessing.
Almighty God,
who gives us a new birth by water and the Holy Spirit
and forgives us all our sins,
strengthen us in all goodness
and by the power of the Holy Spirit
keep us in eternal life through Jesus Christ our Lord.
Amen.

NOTES ON THE SERVICE

*This brief order is an adaptation of the thanksgiving for baptism
from the Evangelical Lutheran Worship service of Holy Communion.*

*Sprinkling with water is one of several ways in which a visible
and tangible reminder of baptism may be employed. Another
option, especially when a small group is gathered with a bowl
of water in their midst, is to have each person make the sign of
the cross upon herself/himself or upon her/his neighbor, using
water from the bowl.*

Suggested service music and hymns:

214	Springs of Water, Bless the Lord
447	O Blessed Spring
449	We Know That Christ Is Raised
450	I Bind unto Myself Today
453	Baptized and Set Free
454	Remember and Rejoice
455	Crashing Waters at Creation
459	Wade in the Water
835	All Creatures, Worship God Most High!
836	Joyful, Joyful We Adore Thee
837	Many and Great, O God
881	Let All Things Now Living

From *Evangelical Lutheran Worship Occasional Services for the Assembly* (Augsburg
Fortress, 2009).

Welcoming People to Communion

At a service in which individuals or a group of people who have been baptized on another occasion mark the beginning of their regular participation in holy communion, the presiding minister may acknowledge the event with an announcement (for example, before the service or before the readings) that is baptismal in orientation. The prayers of intercession may include a suitable petition for the occasion.

Example of a welcome

Today this community of faith rejoices with the following *people* who *join* in sharing the meal of holy communion: *name/s.*

In the sacrament of holy baptism, we are welcomed into the body of Christ and sent to share in the mission of God. In the sacrament of holy communion, God unites us in Jesus Christ and nourishes us for that mission. Living among God's faithful people, we are strengthened by God's word and this holy supper to proclaim the good news of God in Christ through word and deed, to serve all people, following the example of Jesus, and to strive for justice and peace in all the earth.

Let us welcome *these sisters and brothers* in Christ to holy communion.
Welcome to the Lord's table. We thank God for you. We pray that you will find joy and strength in this meal, until we feast forever at God's heavenly banquet.

Examples of petitions for the prayers of intercession

For *those* who *join* in sharing the meal of holy communion this day [*name/s*], we thank you. As you made *them* your own in baptism, feed and nourish *them* always with your forgiveness, grace, and love.

or

For *those* who *join* in sharing the meal of holy communion this day [*name/s*], we thank you. May *they* know you are near. Make *them* one with all your people. Help *them* share with others the new life you give *them* in baptism, in your word, and at your table.

It may be most natural for those being welcomed to come to the table on this day with those who are accompanying them on their journey of faith—such as parents, families, and sponsors.

Blessing at the Table

Some congregations have the practice of offering a blessing at the table to those who are not yet communing, whether children or adults. The sign of the cross may be traced on the person's forehead, with or without accompanying words. This sign is both a reminder of baptism for the baptized and a symbol of the love of Christ that extends to all people.

A baptismal reminder is also appropriate for words that may be spoken by a communion minister. If words are used, they may vary significantly depending on the age and circumstances of the one coming for a blessing. Suggestions for such a blessing—when the minister knows that the person is baptized—include the following or similar words.

Remember your baptism, and be joyful.

You belong to Christ, in whom you have been baptized.

Blessed be God, who chose you in Christ.

Remember your baptism. Jesus loves you.

Words that may be appropriate whether or not a person is baptized include the following.

(from Welcome to Baptism:)
Receive the sign of the cross, a sign of God's endless love and mercy for you.

(from Luther's Small Catechism:)
God the Father, Son, and Holy Spirit watch over you.

Jesus loves you and cares for you.

God be with you and bless you.

From *Evangelical Lutheran Worship Occasional Services for the Assembly* (Augsburg Fortress, 2009).

Blessing of Graduates

In the gathering rite or following the hymn of the day, the presiding minister addresses the assembly.

We are delighted to recognize high school graduates of *name of congregation* today. It is our privilege to affirm these members of our congregation who have completed one phase of their lives and move with great expectations to another.

The presiding minister addresses the graduates.

Graduates, please stand as your names are read.

An assisting minister reads the graduates' names.

The presiding minister addresses the graduates.

Graduates, as you celebrate your achievements and prepare to begin new endeavors, be mindful of your grounding in faith, and of your vocation to serve God in all your life's work and accomplishments.

Let us pray.

Gracious God, you bless your servants with many achievements. We give thanks especially for the milestones that *name/s* have attained. As they begin new phases of their lives, may they also know your love and experience your peace in all the experiences they encounter. Bless also the parents of these students, who have raised their children and nourished them in the Christian faith. Give them strength in your continuing presence and give them many joyful reunions with their sons and daughters, who may be leaving home soon to begin new and varied ventures, through Jesus Christ our Lord.
Amen.

The service continues with gathering song or the prayers of intercession.

At the sending, before the blessing, graduates and their parents may gather with the ministers at the font. Parents may place a hand on the shoulders of their children. The assembly may be invited to extend a hand in blessing as the presiding minister prays for God's blessing in these or similar words.

Go out into the world in peace;
be of good courage;
hold to what is good;
return no one evil for evil;
strengthen the faint-hearted;
support the weak;
help the suffering;
honor all people;
love and serve our God,
rejoicing in the power of the Holy Spirit.[1]
Amen.

The service concludes with the blessing and the dismissal.

[1]From "Affirmation of the Vocation of the Baptized in the World" in *Welcome to Christ: Lutheran Rites for the Catechumenate* (Augsburg Fortress, 1997), p. 60.

Blessing of Mothers

God of all creation,
pour out your blessing on all mothers
and those who provide motherly care.
You have made them in your image
and given them children to love and care for in your name.
Bless them with a heart like your heart:
loving and kind, comforting and strong,
nurturing and grace-filled.
As they participate in your ongoing creativity,
give them discernment
to help their children discover their unique gifts.
As they teach their children,
grant them wisdom to know what is truly valuable.
As they strive to share your unconditional love,
give them long-suffering patience and a lively sense of humor.
As they model your mercy,
help them extend the forgiveness
they themselves freely receive from you.
In all circumstances fortify their faith,
that they may love you above all.
We ask this in Jesus' name.
Amen.

Rogation Days

Stewardship of creation is an ongoing ministry in the church. The creation that God declared good is entrusted to the care of humankind. Exercising that care is one dimension of daily Christian discipleship. Rogation Days are a way for the church to honor God for the gift of creation and to pray for the land, the gift of labor, and the needs of all people.

Rogation Days were traditionally celebrated during the fifty days of Easter on the Monday, Tuesday, and Wednesday before Ascension Day. The word Rogation has its roots in the Latin word that means to ask or petition, and it comes from the ancient introit for the Sunday preceding the Ascension. In some places the celebrations of Rogation Days were quite elaborate and included processions from the church to and around fields while asking for God's blessing.

Churches that have maintained the practice of celebrating Rogation Days no longer mark these days specifically before Ascension. Instead, Rogation Days are celebrated at times and places that meet local needs. With an increased awareness of the need for the stewardship of creation both within the church and within contemporary culture, the themes of thanksgiving for the land and petitions for a fruitful earth may be adapted around broader cultural celebrations of Earth Day.

Although Rogation Days are agricultural celebrations, they are not solely for rural congregations. These days underscore the dependence of all people, urban and rural, on the fruitfulness of the earth and human labor. The themes of Rogation Days may be highlighted in a special worship service or in prayers of intercession in the Sunday assembly during the spring.

A set of propers appropriate to the Stewardship of Creation from Evangelical Lutheran Worship *(page 63) is provided below. These propers include prayers traditionally used for Rogation Days: a prayer for fruitful seasons and a prayer for the stewardship of creation. If a service is scheduled in a rural area at a representative farm or field, the "General Order of Blessing" from* Evangelical Lutheran Worship Occasional Services for the Assembly *may be used or adapted (pages 155–158; see also Autumn seasonal rites on pages 258–259 of this volume).*

Hymns to mark Rogation Days might include any of the hymns under the topics of Creation, Preservation, or Stewardship listed in various hymn indexes. "We plow the fields and scatter" (ELW 680/681) or an adaptation of St Francis's Canticle of the Sun such as "All creatures, worship God most high!" (ELW 835) would be particularly appropriate to highlight our dependence on, and our stewardship of, God's gift of creation.

Stewardship of Creation

Preface of the season, or Sundays

Color of the season

Prayer of the Day

Almighty God, Lord of heaven and earth,
we humbly pray that your gracious providence
may give and preserve to our use
the fruitfulness of the land and the seas;
and may prosper all who labor therein,
that we, who are constantly receiving good things
from your hand, may always give you thanks,
through Jesus Christ, our Savior and Lord. **Amen.**

or

Merciful Creator, your hand is open wide
to satisfy the needs of every living creature.
Make us always thankful for your loving providence;
and grant that we,
remembering the account that we must one day give,
may be faithful stewards of your good gifts,
through Jesus Christ, our Savior and Lord. **Amen.**

Gospel Acclamation

Alleluia. Let the sea roar, and all that fills it; let the rivers
| clap their hands;* let the hills ring out with joy be- | fore
the LORD. *Alleluia.* (Ps. 98:7, 8)

Readings and Psalm

Job 38:1-11, 16-18
Psalm 104:1, 13-23 *or* Psalm 104:24-35
O LORD, how manifold are your works! (Ps. 104:24)
1 Timothy 6:6-10, 17-19
Luke 12:13-21

May 1, 2011
Second Sunday of Easter

In today's gospel the risen Christ appears to the disciples and offers them the gift of peace. Even amid doubts and questions, we experience the resurrection in our Sunday gathering around word and meal, and in our everyday lives. Throughout the coming Sundays of Easter the first two readings will be from the Acts of the Apostles and the first letter of Peter. Even as the early Christians proclaimed the resurrection, we rejoice in the new birth and living hope we receive in baptism.

On May 1 the church remembers Philip and James, apostles. The lesser festival of St. Philip and St. James' day may be observed this year on May 2.

Prayer of the Day

Almighty and eternal God, the strength of those who believe and the hope of those who doubt, may we, who have not seen, have faith in you and receive the fullness of Christ's blessing, who lives and reigns with you and the Holy Spirit, one God, now and forever.

Gospel Acclamation

Alleluia. Blessed are those who ' have not seen* and yet have come ' to believe. *Alleluia.* (John 20:29)

Readings and Psalm

Acts 2:14a, 22-32

After the Holy Spirit came to the apostles on Pentecost, Peter preaches the gospel to the gathered crowd. He tells them that Jesus, who obediently went to his death according to God's plan, was raised from the dead by God. Finally, he appeals to scripture, quoting Psalm 16:8-11, to show that Jesus is the Messiah: though crucified, the risen Jesus is now enthroned.

Psalm 16

In your presence there is fullness of joy. (Ps. 16:11)

1 Peter 1:3-9

This epistle was written to encourage Christians experiencing hardships and suffering because of their faith in Christ. The letter opens by blessing God for the living hope we have through Christ's resurrection even in the midst of difficult circumstances and surroundings.

John 20:19-31

The risen Jesus appears to his disciples, offering them a benediction, a commission, and the gift of the Holy Spirit. But one of their number is missing, and his unbelief prompts another visit from the Lord.

Preface   Easter

Color   White

Prayers of Intercession

The prayers are prepared locally for each occasion. The following examples may be adapted or used as appropriate.

In this season of resurrection, we lift up to God all those in need in the church and throughout the world.
A brief silence.

Alleluia! We thank you for your church and its mission. Give us courage to take good news into a world that does not know you. Hear us, O God.
Your mercy is great.

Alleluia! We thank you for your creation. Challenge us to use its resources wisely, generously, and respectfully. Hear us, O God.
Your mercy is great.

Alleluia! We thank you for leaders throughout our world. Equip them to do justice and love mercy. Hear us, O God.
Your mercy is great.

Alleluia! We thank you for all the good things you have given us. Transform our thanks into compassion for those who are poor in body, mind, or spirit (*especially*). Hear us, O God.
Your mercy is great.

Alleluia! We thank you for this congregation, its pastor/s and lay leaders. Equip us with a sense of purpose in this place to serve our neighbors (*especially*). Hear us, O God.
Your mercy is great.

Here other intercessions may be offered.

Alleluia! We thank you for the resurrection we have been promised through Jesus' death and resurrection. Bring us together again one day with all the saints (*especially Phillip*

and James, apostles). Hear us, O God.
Your mercy is great.
Into your care, O God, we place ourselves and all our prayers, trusting your promise of new life in Jesus Christ, our risen Savior.
Amen.

Ideas and Images for the Day

In his preaching about the Jesus God raised up, Peter points to what people know from their own experience and what God makes known—that it is impossible for Jesus to be held by the power of death. So we sing today with the psalmist in gratitude to God, who shows the path of life and who makes it possible for us to live in hope. We might pray fervently with Thomas, "show me," but these stories of Jesus appearing are so that we might know deep in our bodies and souls that Jesus is alive and gives us life.

1. Anatoly Kushch, Ukrainian sculptor, created *The Great Famine* sculpture depicting today's gospel. It shows the hand of Jesus with each finger representing a person looking into the wound in the middle of the hand. One could be the disciple Thomas who did not believe until he saw and felt. Kushch writes that it is difficult to believe "without seeing it with one's own eyes and touching it with one's hands" (http://www.brama.com/news/press/010822kushch_monument.html).

2. Before the peace, remind children that whenever the risen Jesus appeared to disciples, he said, "Peace be with you." These are Jesus' words we share with one another. Look into the eyes of the person. Take their hands in yours—can you see and feel the risen Christ? Jesus promises to be with us in holy communion, which begins with sharing Jesus' words and greeting each other with a touch, reminding us that Jesus is present among the people gathered.

3. What is happening in the world today? Are there news items that stick out because they are unbelievable—the reality doesn't sink in either because it seems too horrible or too wonderful to be true? Are there news items that are easier to believe because you have seen with your own eyes? How might we respond in Jesus' name to current events? We are a church tied together through "God's work, our hands." For specific examples, see the "Our Faith in Action" section of the ELCA's Web site, http://www.elca.org/OFIA.

4. *Up*, Disney/Pixar's animated film of 2009, is a story of life after death. Carl is a seventy-eight-year-old man who has lost his inspiration for living, his now-deceased wife, Ellie. Russell is a lonely kid who shows up one day on Carl's doorstep, trying to earn a merit badge. The two come together by chance but have an adventure of a lifetime as they grow in friendship and hope and learn not to be afraid of the future because they have one another. Watch for these threads of the story: Carl's guilt over letting Ellie down but her setting him free; Carl's throwing out the dusty furniture once he senses that freedom; Carl's standing in like a father for Russell. "Through believing, you may have life in his name."

Hymns for Worship
Gathering
Christ the Lord is risen today; Alleluia!   ELW 369, LBW 128
O sons and daughters, let us sing   ELW 386, LBW 139
That Easter day with joy was bright   ELW 384, LBW 154

Hymn of the Day
We walk by faith   ELW 635   *SHANTI*   WOV 675
   DUNLAP'S CREEK
Alleluia! Christ is arisen   ELW 375, LLC 361
   SANTO DOMINGO
Thine is the glory   ELW 376, LBW 145   *JUDAS MACCABAEUS*

Offering
We have seen the Lord   ELW 869
This joyful Eastertide   ELW 391, st. 1; LBW 149;
   WOV 676, st. 1

Communion
Alleluia! Christ is arisen   ELW 375, LLC 361
The peace of the Lord   ELW 646
Come, you faithful, raise the strain   ELW 363, LBW 132

Sending
Hallelujah! We sing your praises   ELW 535, WOV 722,
   TFF 158
Christ is risen! Alleluia!   ELW 382, LBW 131

Additional Hymns and Songs
These things did Thomas count as real   LSB 472, NCH 254
Make songs of joy   LBW 150
Without seeing you   GC 844

Music for the Day
Psalmody and Acclamations
Miller, Aaron David. *Gospel Acclamations for Lent–Holy Trinity.*
Miller, Aaron David. "Psalm 16," Refrain 3, from PSCY.
Sedio, Mark. "Psalm 16" from PWA, Evangelical Lutheran Worship Edition.

Choral

- Burkhardt, Michael. "Thine Is The Glory." SATB, br, org, assembly. MSM 60-4009.
- Costello, Michael D. "We Walk by Faith and Not by Sight." 2 pt mxd, pno, C inst (or cl). MSM 50-5109.
- Helman, Michael. "We Walk by Faith." SATB, pno, opt hb, fl. AFP 9780800659752.

    Kellermeyer, David M. "Morning Has Broken." SATB, kybd, cl, opt bass, dr. set. AFP9780806697215.

    Nystedt, Knut. "Peace I Leave with You." SATB. AFP 9780800652678.

Children's Choir

Ferguson, John. "Jesus, My Lord and God." U, kybd. AFP 9780800646196.

Luecke, O. William. "Do You Know Who Died for Me" from *LifeSongs*. LE, U, kybd.

Spiritual. "Come and See" from *LifeSongs*. LE, U, kybd.

Keyboard / Instrumental

- Blair, Dallas. "Judas Maccabaeus" from *Hymn Introductions and Descants for Trumpet and Organ*, set 1. Org, tpt. MSM 20-400.
- Cherwien, David. "Shanti" from *Six Organ Preludes*. Org. GIA G-4291.
- Potter, Emily Maxson. "Judas Maccabaeus" from *Augsburg Organ Library: Easter*. Org. AFP 9780800659363.
- Sadowski, Kevin J. "Judas Maccabaeus" from *Twelve Hymn Preludes*. Org. CPH 97-6830U1.

Handbell

Buckwalter, Karen. "In Thee Is Gladness." 3 oct hb, 3 oct hc, L1+. CG CGB573.

- Dobrinski, Cynthia. "Thine Is the Glory." 3-6 oct, L2+. HOP 2354.

    Young, Philip. "Good Christian Friends, Rejoice and Sing! and This Joyful Eastertide." 2-3 oct, L2+. AFP 9780800656270.

Praise Ensemble

- Barnett, Marie. "Breathe." Mercy/VIN.
- Iverson, Daniel. "Spirit of the Living God." Birdwing Music. W&P 129.
- Jernigan, Dennis. "You Are My All in All (Jesus, Lamb of God)." Shepherd's Heart Music. W&P 76.
- Kendrick, Graham. "Here Is Bread." Make Way Music. ELW 483. Various editions.
- Tomlin, Chris/John Newton/John Rees/Edwin Excell/Louie Giglio. "Amazing Grace (My Chains Are Gone)." WT.
- Wimber, John. "Spirit Song." Mercy/VIN. W&P 130.

Global

Savall, Teresita. "Tú eres amor/You, Source of All Love" from *Agape: Songs of Hope and Reconciliation*. U, gtr. Lutheran World Federation. AFP 9780191000133.

Yoruba, trad. "Aleluya Y'in Louwa/Alleluia, Praise the Lord" from *Agape: Songs of Hope and Reconciliation*. SATB. Lutheran World Federation. AFP 9780191000133.

Monday, May 2

Philip and James, Apostles (transferred)

Philip was one of the first disciples of Jesus, who after following Jesus invited Nathanael to "come and see." According to tradition, Philip preached in Asia Minor and died as a martyr in Phrygia. James, the son of Alphaeus, is called "the Less" (meaning "short" or "younger") to distinguish him from another apostle named James who is commemorated July 25. Philip and James are commemorated together because the remains of these two saints were placed in the Church of the Apostles in Rome on this day in 561.

Athanasius, Bishop of Alexandria, died 373

Athanasius (ath-an-AY-shus) attended the Council of Nicaea in 325 as a deacon and secretary to the bishop of Alexandria. At the council, and when he himself served as bishop of Alexandria, he defended the full divinity of Christ against the Arian position held by emperors, magistrates, and theologians. Because of his defense of the divinity of Christ, he was considered a troublemaker and was banished from Alexandria on five occasions. As bishop, one of his paschal letters to surrounding bishops gives a list for books that should be considered canonical scripture. He lists the twenty-seven New Testament books that are recognized today.

Wednesday, May 4

Monica, mother of Augustine, died 387

Monica was married to a pagan husband who was ill-tempered and unfaithful. She rejoiced greatly when both her husband and his mother became Christian. But it is because she is the mother of Augustine that she is best known. Monica had been a disciple of Ambrose, and eventually Augustine came under his influence. Almost everything we know about Monica comes from Augustine's *Confessions*, his autobiography. She died far from her home but said to her son, "Do not fret because I am buried far from our home in Africa. Nothing is far from God, and I have no fear that God will not know where to find me, when Christ comes to raise me to life at the end of the world." Her dying wish was that her son remember her at the altar of the Lord, wherever he was.

○ denotes suggestions that relate to the hymn of the day.
● denotes songs that are available on iTunes®.

May 8, 2011
Third Sunday of Easter

Today's gospel begins with two disciples walking to Emmaus, overcome with sadness, loss, and disappointment. They had hoped Jesus, who was crucified, would be the one to redeem Israel! Yet the risen Christ walks with them, and then opens their eyes in the breaking of the bread. Each Sunday our hearts burn within us as the scriptures are proclaimed and Christ appears to us as bread is broken and wine is poured. The story of Emmaus becomes the pattern of our worship each Lord's day.

Today is the commemoration of Julian of Norwich, renewer of the church, who died around 1416.

Prayer of the Day

O God, your Son makes himself known to all his disciples in the breaking of bread. Open the eyes of our faith, that we may see him in his redeeming work, who lives and reigns with you and the Holy Spirit, one God, now and forever.

Gospel Acclamation

Alleluia. Our hearts ' burn within us* while you open to ' us the scriptures. *Alleluia.* (Luke 24:32)

Readings and Psalm

Acts 2:14a, 36-41

Today's reading is the conclusion of Peter's sermon preached following the giving of the Holy Spirit to the apostles on the day of Pentecost. The center of his preaching is the bold declaration that God has made the crucified Jesus both Lord and Christ.

Psalm 116:1-4, 12-19

I will call on the name of the Lord. (Ps. 116:13)

1 Peter 1:17-23

The imagery of exile is used to help the readers of this letter understand that they are strangers in a strange land. Christians no longer belong to this age. Through the death of Christ we belong to God, so that our focus, faith, and hope are no longer on such things as silver or gold.

Luke 24:13-35

The colorful story of Jesus' appearance to two disciples on the road to Emmaus answers the question of how Jesus is to be recognized among us. Here, he is revealed through the scriptures and in the breaking of bread.

Preface Easter

Color White

Prayers of Intercession

The prayers are prepared locally for each occasion. The following examples may be adapted or used as appropriate.

In this season of resurrection, we lift up to God all those in need in the church and throughout the world.

A brief silence.

Reveal yourself in your church, O Lord. Make us into physical and spiritual bread for the whole world. Hear us, O God. **Your mercy is great.**

Reveal yourself in the beauty of creation, O Lord. Bless the nature around us. Help us honor the message of new life we see in it. Hear us, O God. **Your mercy is great.**

Reveal yourself through the work of this world's leaders, O Lord. Inundate them with your wisdom and compassion so the nations are showered with peace. Hear us, O God. **Your mercy is great.**

Reveal yourself to those in need, O Lord. Send your angels to comfort, strengthen, and heal all those we remember before you now (*especially*). Hear us, O God. **Your mercy is great.**

Reveal yourself in this congregation, O Lord. Smile on us with the joy of a mother who loves her children. Hear us, O God. **Your mercy is great.**

Here other intercessions may be offered.

Reveal yourself to us in the breaking of the bread, O Lord. Show us your grace through the lives of all the saints (*especially Julian of Norwich, renewer of the church*) and all those we remember before you now. Hear us, O God. **Your mercy is great.**

Into your care, O God, we place ourselves and all our prayers, trusting your promise of new life in Jesus Christ, our risen Savior.
Amen.

Ideas and Images for the Day

The people who hear Peter's testimony and preaching are cut to the heart. The writer of 1 Peter instructs believers to love deeply from the heart. The disciples who encounter the risen Christ notice afterward that their hearts were "burning" within them as Jesus reveals the scriptures and then himself to them in the breaking of the bread. Whether a call to repentance, hope, recognition, or love, people are deeply affected by encounters with the one raised from death to become followers of Jesus' way. They not only turn from their sin and doubt but literally change direction, going back from Emmaus to Jerusalem with renewed courage, faith, and hope. These heart-changing encounters with Jesus fulfill a promise from God for the whole community, from those who have lived a long life to those who are children.

1. "To live in this world you must be able to do three things: to love what is mortal; / to hold it against your bones knowing your own life depends on it; / and, when the time comes to let it go, to let it go." From "In Blackwater Woods" by Mary Oliver, in *Cries of the Spirit* (Boston, Beacon Press: 1991), p. 129 (http://www.panhala.net/Archive/In_Blackwater_Woods.html).

2. Cleopas and the unnamed disciple walked for a long while with Jesus, talking and listening, until it was evening. If it can be done in your community, consider a traveling worship experience, beginning outside with a long walk—with scriptures, conversation, and listening—and ending at small tables with a meal in which you break bread together. Create an experience and atmosphere for encountering the risen Christ in one another, so that as worshipers go back to their homes, they can say with the early disciples, "Were not our hearts burning within us?"

3. Arguably, children can understand what it is to be walking down the road, discussing things that worry them even more clearly than adults. Ask kids what they've been talking about at the playground or after school this week. What is worrying them? What are they wondering about? Jesus listens to a whole description of how Cleopas and the other disciple are thinking and feeling before engaging them in conversation, and clearly that works. They are anxious for him to stay with them awhile longer. How might you provide opportunities/resources to nurture these kinds of important conversations within families this week?

4. "On the Road to Emmaus" is a liturgical opera by Susan Hulsman Bingham based on Luke 24. Because Cleopas is walking with an unnamed disciple, one setting of the opera is set for tenor, soprano, and baritone. Sound clip, reviews, synopsis and ordering information are at http://www.chancelopera.com/aaCHAN%20OPS/6%20Emm2.html.

Hymns for Worship
Gathering

Christ is risen! Shout Hosanna!   ELW 383, WOV 672
Awake, my heart, with gladness   ELW 378, LBW 129
Alleluia! Jesus is risen!   ELW 377, WOV 674, TFF 91

Hymn of the Day

Day of arising   ELW 374   *RAABE*
We who once were dead   ELW 495, LBW 207
    MIDDEN IN DE DOOD
That Easter day with joy was bright   ELW 384   *PUER NOBIS*
    LBW 154   *ERSCHIENEN IST DER HERRLICH TAG*

Offering

Let us talents and tongues employ   ELW 674, WOV 754
Be not afraid   ELW 388

Communion

Bread of life, our host and meal   ELW 464
You satisfy the hungry heart   ELW 484, WOV 711
Draw us in the Spirit's tether   ELW 470, WOV 703

Sending

The risen Christ   ELW 390
Abide, O dearest Jesus   ELW 539, LBW 263

Additional Hymns and Songs

Open our eyes, Lord   TFF 98
Christ has been raised   DH 66
I danced in the morning   HS91 798

Music for the Day
Psalmody and Acclamations

Miller, Aaron David. *Gospel Acclamations for Lent–Holy Trinity.*
Mummert, Mark. "Psalm 116," Refrain 1, from PSCY.
Roberts, Leon C. "I Will Call Upon the Name of the Lord (Psalm 116)." TFF 14.
Sedio, Mark. "Psalm 116:1-4, 12-19" from PWA, Evangelical Lutheran Worship Edition.

Choral

Hovland, Egil. "Stay With Us." SATB, org or pno. AFP 9780800658823.

Kosche, Kenneth T. "We Walk by Faith and Not by Sight." SATB. MSM 50-6031.

Pelz, Walter. "Stay With Us." SATB, fl, org. CPH 98-2920.

o Schalk, Carl. "Day of Arising." SATB, org. AFP 9780800658670.

Children's Choir

Helgen, John. "Come, Let Us Eat." U/2 pt, kybd, perc. AFP 9780800679354.

McRae, Shirley. "Psalm 116" from *ChildrenSing Psalms*. U, kybd. AFP 9780800663872.

McRae, Shirley. "Your Trusting Child." U, kybd, opt sop glock, fl, fc. CG CGA614.

Keyboard / Instrumental

o Harbach, Barbara. "Puer nobis" from *Gloria!* Org. AFP 9780800677534.

o Manz, Paul O. "Midden in de dood" from *Nine Hymn Improvisations*. Org. MSM 10-875.

o Maynard, Lynette. "Puer nobis" from *Songs for All Seasons*, vol. 2. Pno. AFP 9780800677862.

o Miller, Aaron David. "Raabe" from *Chorale Preludes for Piano in Traditional Styles*. Pno. AFP 9780800679033.

Handbell

Lamb, Linda. "This Joyful Eastertide." 3-5 oct, L3. AGEHR AG35281.

o Moklebust, Cathy. "That Easter Day with Joy Was Bright." 2-3 oct, L1. CG CGB281.

Stults, Tyleen. "Haleluya." 3-5 oct hb, opt perc, L3-. RR SM7007.

Praise Ensemble

• Baloche, Paul. "Open the Eyes of My Heart." INT.

• Baloche, Rita. "I Will Celebrate." MAR.

• Cull, Bob. "Open Our Eyes." MAR/WRD. W&P 113.

• Green, Melody. "There Is a Redeemer." Birdwing Music. W&P 140.

• O'Shields, Michael. "I Will Call Upon the Lord." Sound III and All Nations Music/LOR. W&P 70.

• Paris, Twila. "He Is Exalted." Straightway Music. W&P 55.

Global

Farlee, Robert Buckley, arr. "Cristo vive/Christ Is Risen." SATB, perc. AFP 9780800658830.

Nyberg, Anders, arr. "Hamba Nathi/Come, Walk With Us" from *Global Songs 2*. SATB, cant. AFP 9780800656744.

Sunday, May 8

Julian of Norwich, renewer of the church, died around 1416

Julian (or Juliana) was most likely a Benedictine nun living in an isolated cell attached to the Carrow Priory in Norwich (NOR-rich), England. Definite facts about her life are sparse. However, when she was about thirty years old, she reported visions that she later compiled into a book, *Sixteen Revelations of Divine Love*, a classic of medieval mysticism. The visions declared that love was the meaning of religious experience, provided by Christ who is love, for the purpose of love. A prayer and a hymn attributed to Julian are included in *Evangelical Lutheran Worship* (p. 87, #735).

Monday, May 9

Nicolaus Ludwig von Zinzendorf, renewer of the church, hymnwriter, died 1760

Count Zinzendorf was born into an aristocratic family and after the death of his father was raised by his Pietistic grandmother. This influence was a lasting one, and he moved away from what he felt was an overly intellectual Lutheranism. When he was twenty-two, a group of Moravians asked permission to live on his lands. He agreed, and they established a settlement they called Herrnhut, or "the Lord's watch." Eventually worldwide Moravian missions emanated from this community. Zinzendorf participated in these missions and is also remembered for writing hymns characteristic of his Pietistic faith, including "Jesus, Still Lead On" (ELW 624).

Saturday, May 14

Matthias, Apostle

After Christ's ascension, the apostles met in Jerusalem to choose a replacement for Judas. Matthias was chosen over Joseph Justus by the casting of lots. Little is known about Matthias, and little is reported about him in the account of his election in Acts 1:15-26. Matthias traveled among the disciples from the beginning of Jesus' ministry until his ascension. His task, after he was enrolled among the eleven remaining disciples, was to bear witness to the resurrection.

Matthias was formerly commemorated on February 24, though the reason for that date is not known. More recently the Roman Catholic Church moved the celebration to May 14, so that it falls after the celebration of Jesus' resurrection, when Matthias was chosen as an apostle.

o denotes suggestions that relate to the hymn of the day.
● denotes songs that are available on iTunes®.

182

May 15, 2011
Fourth Sunday of Easter

Today is sometimes called "Good Shepherd Sunday." Jesus is called the "gate" of the sheep in today's gospel. The risen Christ opens the way to abundant life. He anoints our heads with oil and guides us beside the still waters of our baptism. Each Sunday he spreads a feast before us in the midst of the world's violence and war. We go forth to be signs of the resurrection and extend God's tender care to all creation.

Prayer of the Day

O God our shepherd, you know your sheep by name and lead us to safety through the valleys of death. Guide us by your voice, that we may walk in certainty and security to the joyous feast prepared in your house, through Jesus Christ, our Savior and Lord, who lives and reigns with you and the Holy Spirit, one God, now and forever.

Gospel Acclamation

Alleluia. Jesus says, I am ⎹ the good shepherd.* I know my own and my ⎹ own know me. *Alleluia.* (John 10:14)

Readings and Psalm

Acts 2:42-47

Today's reading is a description of life in the community following Peter's sermon on the day of Pentecost, when the Spirit was outpoured on God's people. This new community is founded on the teachings of the apostles and sustained in the breaking of the bread.

Psalm 23

The Lᴏʀᴅ is my shepherd; I shall not be in want. (Ps. 23:1)

1 Peter 2:19-25

Doing the right things does not guarantee that one will not experience difficulties, hardships, rejection, or even suffering. Here Christ is presented as the model for our path of endurance and loyalty to God, particularly in the midst of adversity.

John 10:1-10

Jesus uses an image familiar to the people of his day to make a point about spiritual leadership. Good shepherds bring people to life through Jesus, but those who avoid Jesus are dangerous to the flock.

Preface Easter

Color White

Prayers of Intercession

The prayers are prepared locally for each occasion. The following examples may be adapted or used as appropriate.

In this season of resurrection, we lift up to God all those in need in the church and throughout the world.

A brief silence.

Shepherd us, O God. Gather your people around the table you have prepared for us. In your mercy,

hear our prayer.

Shepherd us, O God. Gather your people beside clean water and green pastures so that creation is a gift for all. In your mercy,

hear our prayer.

Shepherd us, O God. Gather your people into the ways of peace and into lives where no one lives in fear. In your mercy,

hear our prayer.

Shepherd us, O God. Gather your people with your goodness and mercy. Bring healing and wholeness to all those who suffer (*especially*). In your mercy,

hear our prayer.

Shepherd us, O God. Gather your people in this place. Lead us beyond our wants into works of mission and ministry. In your mercy,

hear our prayer.

Here other intercessions may be offered.

Shepherd us, O God. Gather your people of every generation. Anoint us with grace and fill our cups to overflowing with the salvation you have promised to all your saints. In your mercy,

hear our prayer.

Into your care, O God, we place ourselves and all our prayers, trusting your promise of new life in Jesus Christ, our risen Savior.
Amen.

Ideas and Images for the Day

Abundant life is promised to those who follow Jesus. But what is meant by abundant life? Some Christians, and much of contemporary American culture, interpret an abundant life to mean the "good life" of many fine things, an opulent lifestyle. But Psalm 23 imagines an abundant life not in material terms but in relational terms. An abundant life is one lived in the presence of God, in the company of the Lord. Whether one is in green pastures or the darkest valley, there is nothing to want, because God is present. The image of Jesus as our shepherd reminds us that he is with us at all times, providing through his presence all we need.

1. Jesus says his sheep will know his voice and follow him. Whose voices do the children recognize, even without seeing them? You could invite the children to close their eyes and have various people, parents, Sunday school teachers, pastors, and other speak and see if the children can recognize their voices. To know someone's voice means that you have been with that person a lot, that you have a relationship with them. How do we learn to recognize the voice of Jesus? Who speaks in Jesus' voice to us?

2. What does it mean to not be in want? In his explanation of the fourth petition of the Lord's Prayer, Martin Luther asserts that what we need is our daily bread and that we are invited to receive it with gratitude (Small Catechism, *Evangelical Lutheran Worship*, pp. 1163–1164). We easily turn our desires into wants or needs. We can get used to extravagances and think we cannot live without them. But Christ's presence in our lives helps us focus on what we truly need. How does our perception of what is and is not a need change our attitude about whether we have an abundant life?

3. Is it possible to have an abundant life while others want for their daily bread? In his book *Hunger and Happiness: Feeding the Hungry, Nourishing Our Souls* (Minneapolis: Augsburg Fortress, 2009), L. Shannon Jung insists that the plight of hungry people is related to the spiritual want of those who have enough. He offers ideas for how to nourish both physical and spiritual hunger.

4. Icons are meant to be contemplated slowly, so the viewer is opened up to the truth about who is being viewed. An icon of Jesus the Good Shepherd can be used to focus our thoughts on what it means to be in relationship with the Lord who is the shepherd of our souls. One beautiful example is available on the Web site of St. John the Baptist Icon Studio and Workshop in Blue River, Wisconsin; http://www.stjohnsiconstudio.com/Home/the-icon-studio/icon-gallery.

Hymns for Worship
Gathering

Good Christian friends, rejoice and sing! ELW 385, LBW 144
I know that my Redeemer lives! ELW 619, LBW 352
Christ the Lord is risen today; Alleluia! ELW 369, LBW 128

Hymn of the Day

The King of love my shepherd is ELW 502, LBW 456
    ST. COLUMBA
Rise, O Sun of righteousness ELW 657
    SONNE DER GERECHTIGKEIT
Savior, like a shepherd lead us ELW 789 BRADBURY
    LBW 481 HER VIL TIES

Offering

My Shepherd, you supply my need ELW 782
Christ Jesus lay in death's strong bands ELW 370, sts. 1, 3, 4; LBW 134, sts. 1, 3, 4

Communion

You satisfy the hungry heart ELW 484, WOV 711
At the Lamb's high feast we sing ELW 362, LBW 210
Shepherd me, O God ELW 780

Sending

Praise the Lord, rise up rejoicing ELW 544, LBW 196
God be with you till we meet again ELW 536, TFF 157

Additional Hymns and Songs

Our Paschal Lamb, that sets us free WOV 679
With a shepherd's care GC 654, RS 738

Music for the Day
Psalmody and Acclamations

Bruxvoort-Colligan, Richard. "My Love Is My Shepherd (Psalm 23)" from *Sharing the Road*. AFP 9780800678630.
Farlee, Robert Buckley. "Psalm 23," Refrain 1, from PSCY.
Miller, Aaron David. *Gospel Acclamations for Lent–Holy Trinity.*
My Shepherd, You Supply My Need. ELW 782.

Roberts, Leon C. "The Lord Is My Shepherd (Psalm 23)." TFF 3.

Shepperd, Mark. "Psalm 23" from PWA, Evangelical Lutheran Worship Edition.

The Lord's My Shepherd. ELW 778.

Choral

Cool, Jayne Southwick. "I Am Jesus' Little Lamb." 2 pt mxd or SA, kybd, fl, narr. AFP 9780800676216.

Ferguson, John. "The King of Love My Shepherd Is." SATB, org, opt assembly. GIA G-4011.

Roberts, William Bradley, arr. "Savior, Like a Shepherd Lead." U, kybd, opt C inst. AFP 9780800646981. *The Augsburg Easy Choirbook,* vol. 1. AFP 9780800676025.

Wetzler, Robert. "Shepherd, Lead Us." SATB, piano. AFP 9780800697178.

Zimmermann, Heinz Werner. "Psalm 23." SATB, org, DB. AFP 9780800645380. *Augsburg Choirbook.* AFP 9780800656782.

Children's Choir

Comer, Marilyn. "Psalm 23" from *ChildrenSing Psalms.* U, kybd. AFP 9780800663872.

Cool, Jayne Southwick. "I Am Jesus' Little Lamb." U/2 pt, kybd, fl. AFP 9780800676216.

Horman, John. "Jesus Christ Is Risen." U/2 pt, kybd. CG CGA129.

Keyboard / Instrumental

Cherwien, David. "St. Columba" from *Organ Plus One.* Org, inst. AFP 9780800656188.

Ferguson, John. "Partita on At the Lamb's High Feast (Sonne der Gerechtigkeit)." Org. MSM 10-400.

Kallman, Daniel. "Bradbury" from *Three Hymns for Two Violins and Piano.* Pno, 2 vln. MSM 20-971.

Organ, Anne Krentz. "Sonne der Gerechtigkeit" from *Reflections on Hymn Tunes for Holy Communion,* vol. 1. Pno. AFP 9780800679095.

Handbell

Geschke, Susan. "Savior, Like a Shepherd Lead Us." 2 oct, L2-. HOP 2449.

Roberts, Philip. "Shepherd Me, O God." 3-6 oct hb, opt 3-6 oct hc, L3. GIA G-7255.

Wagner, Douglas. "The King of Love My Shepherd Is." 2-5 oct, L3-. BP HB50.

Praise Ensemble

- Evans, Darrell/Chris Springer. "Redeemer, Savior, Friend." INT.
- Kendrick, Graham. "Here Is Bread." Make Way Music. ELW 483. Various editions.
- Morgan, Reuben. "I Give You My Heart." Hillsong/INT.
- Redman, Matt. "Blessed Be Your Name." Thankyou Music.
- Redman, Matt. "Once Again." Thankyou Music.
- Redman, Matt. "You Never Let Go." Thankyou Music.

Global

Dexter, Noel. "The Lord Is My Shepherd" from *Let the Peoples Sing.* SATB. AFP 9780800675394.

Mahamba, Deogratias. "Heri Ni Jina/Blessed Is the Name of Jesus" from *Global Choral Sounds.* SATB, cant, perc. CPH 98-3610.

Wednesday, May 18

Erik, King of Sweden, martyr, died 1160

Erik, long considered the patron saint of Sweden, ruled from 1150 to 1160. He is honored for efforts to bring peace to the nearby pagan kingdoms and for his crusades to spread the Christian faith in Nordic lands. He established a protected Christian mission in Finland that was led by Henry of Uppsala. As king, Erik was noted for his desire to establish fair laws and courts and for his concern for the poor and sick. Erik was killed by a Danish army that approached him at worship on the day after the Ascension. He is reported to have said, "Let us at least finish the sacrifice. The rest of the feast I shall keep elsewhere." As he left worship he was killed.

Saturday, May 21

Helena, mother of Constantine, died around 330

Wife of the co-regent of the West, Helena (or Helen) was mother of Constantine, who later became Roman emperor. After he was converted to Christianity, he influenced her also to become Christian. From that point she lived an exemplary life of faith, particularly through acts of generosity toward the poor. She is also remembered for traveling through Palestine and building churches on the sites she believed to be where Jesus was born, where he was buried, and from which he ascended.

o denotes suggestions that relate to the hymn of the day.
● denotes songs that are available on iTunes®.

May 22, 2011
Fifth Sunday of Easter

As we continue to celebrate the fifty days of Easter, today's gospel includes Jesus' promise that he goes to prepare a place for his followers in his Father's house. Our baptism commissions us to share Jesus' mission in the world. As First Peter reminds us, we are a holy people, called to proclaim the one who called us out of darkness into light. In words and deeds we bear witness to the risen Christ—our way, our truth, our life.

Prayer of the Day

Almighty God, your Son Jesus Christ is the way, the truth, and the life. Give us grace to love one another, to follow in the way of his commandments, and to share his risen life with all the world, for he lives and reigns with you and the Holy Spirit, one God, now and forever.

Gospel Acclamation

Alleluia. I am the way, the truth, | and the life.* No one comes to the Father ex- | cept through me. *Alleluia.* (John 14:6)

Readings and Psalm
Acts 7:55-60

Stephen was one of the seven men chosen by the apostles to serve tables so that the apostles could be free to serve the word (Acts 6:1-6). Stephen does more than distribute food, however. For his preaching of God's word, he becomes the first martyr of the faith.

Psalm 31:1-5, 15-16

Into your hands, O Lord, I commend my spirit. (Ps. 31:5)

I Peter 2:2-10

Christ is the cornerstone of God's saving work and the foundation of our lives. We are God's chosen, holy people who continuously celebrate and declare the mercy of God we experience through Jesus Christ.

John 14:1-14

On the night that he is to be arrested, Jesus shares final words with his disciples. As the one through whom God is known, he promises to go before them and act on their behalf.

Preface   Easter

Color   White

Prayers of Intercession

The prayers are prepared locally for each occasion. The following examples may be adapted or used as appropriate.

In this season of resurrection, we lift up to God all those in need in the church and throughout the world.

A brief silence.

O God, who calls us out of darkness, illumine your church and all who serve it. Let your light shine in its mission. Hear us, O God.

Your mercy is great.

Illumine the gift of your creation. Let your light shine in its beauty and our care of it. Hear us, O God.

Your mercy is great.

Illumine the nations of the world with peace and prosperity. Let your light shine in the work of our world's leaders. Hear us, O God.

Your mercy is great.

Illumine the needs of the poor, the sick, the oppressed, and the dying (*especially*). Let your light shine through those who care for them. Hear us, O God.

Your mercy is great.

Illumine the needs of the people of this congregation. Let your light shine in our joys and heal our sorrows. Hear us, O God.

Your mercy is great.

Here other intercessions may be offered.

Illumine the lives of all the baptized (*especially those who have died in faith*). Let your light shine through the promise of salvation. Hear us, O God.

Your mercy is great.

Into your care, O God, we place ourselves and all our prayers, trusting your promise of new life in Jesus Christ, our risen Savior.

Amen.

Ideas and Images for the Day

The words of today's gospel are most often heard during a funeral service, providing wonderful assurance that the one who has died in Christ has now taken up residence in their heavenly home. But these words are less about a place than a relationship: our relationship with Jesus and God the Father. They tell us that in Jesus we know all we need to know about God and that the hope of one day being with Christ fully and forever is as real as the works we are called to do in his name today.

1. Consider using the Thanksgiving for Baptism from the funeral service in *Evangelical Lutheran Worship* (p. 280) during the gathering. This liturgical text reinforces the implication of the gospel, that Christ passed from death to resurrected life, so that in baptism we too, who one day will die, can receive the gift of resurrected life with Christ.

2. In ABC's show *Extreme Makeover: Home Edition*, a family in need is given a new dwelling place. One important aspect of the show is that in the new home, each family member's room is given special design elements reflecting that person's personality. The room is prepared especially for them.

3. In his poem "Heaven," Gerhard Frost witnesses a young girl in an airport who sees her destination not as a place but as a person: "Grandma's." The poem concludes "Perhaps heaven isn't a place but a Face" (*Seasons of a Lifetime: A Treasury of Meditations*, Minneapolis: Augsburg, 1989, p. 28).

4. *What's Heaven?* (New York: St. Martin's Press, 2007), by Maria Shriver, addresses children's questions about death and heaven through a conversation between a mother and her daughter.

5. In the ancient world, the Straits of Gibraltar, between Spain and North Africa, were considered the end of the world. Mythology suggested that pillars were erected there by Hercules with the inscription *non plus ultra*—"no more beyond." After Christopher Columbus returned from his exploration of the Americas, Spain's motto became *Plus ultra*—"more beyond." A monument to Columbus in Valladolid, Spain, depicts a lion breaking off the *Non* of Hercules' pillars, leaving only *plus ultra*. You can see the monument, by Antonio Susillo, at http://www.vanderkrogt.net/statues/object.php?webpage=CO&record=es099. Jesus has given us a witness that there is more beyond this world as well.

Hymns for Worship

Gathering

Here, O Lord, our servants gather   ELW 530
Alleluia! Jesus is risen!   ELW 377, WOV 674, TFF 91
Evening and morning   ELW 761, LBW 465

Hymn of the Day

You are the way   ELW 758, LBW 464   DUNDEE
With high delight let us unite   ELW 368, LBW 140
     MIT FREUDEN ZART
Christ is alive! Let Christians sing   ELW 389, LBW 363
     TRURO

Offering

Come, my way, my truth, my life   ELW 816, LBW 513
Blessing, Honor, and Glory   ELW 433, W&P 21

Communion

Sing with all the saints in glory   ELW 426, WOV 691
I received the living God   ELW 477, WOV 700
Now We Remain   ELW 500, W&P 106

Sending

Hallelujah! Jesus lives!   ELW 380, LBW 147
Send me, Jesus   ELW 549, TFF 245

Additional Hymns and Songs

We come, O Christ, to you   HFG 6
Go in peace and serve the Lord   W&P 46
To go to heaven   TFF 181

Music for the Day

Psalmody and Acclamations

Bruxvoort-Colligan, Richard. "Into Your Hands (Psalm 31:5, 15)" from *Sharing the Road*. AFP 9780800678630.
Miller, Aaron David. *Gospel Acclamations for Lent–Holy Trinity*.
Sedio, Mark. "Psalm 31," Refrain 1, from PSCY.
Sedio, Mark. "Psalm 31:1-5, 15-16" from PWA, Evangelical Lutheran Worship Edition.

Choral

Ashdown, Franklin D. "As the Branch Is to the Vine." SATB, org, opt assembly. SMP 10/3071S.
Desprez, Josquin. "O Mighty Word of God Come Down" from *Chantry Choirbook*. SATB. AFP 9780800657772.
Ferguson, John. "Christ the Lord Is Risen Today!" SATB, drm, picc. AFP 9780800646363.
Schelat, David. "I Received the Living God." 2 pt mixed, org. AFP 9780806697109.
Stroope, Z. Randall. "The Call." SATB, org. MSM 50-6515.

Children's Choir

Bouman, Paul. "Thanks Be to God." 2 pt, kybd. CPH 98-2342.

Cool, Jayne Southwick. "The Way, the Truth, the Life." U, kybd. AFP 9780800674670.

Costello, Michael. "In Thee Is Gladness." U, kybd, C inst. MSM 50-4300.

Keyboard / Instrumental

o Busarow, Donald. "Mit Freuden zart" from *With Music Crowned*. Org, 2 inst. CPH 97-7324U1.

o Ferguson, John. "Dundee" from *Three Psalm Preludes*. Org. AFP 9780800656843.

o Miller, Aaron David. "Truro" from *Improvisations for Organ and Instrument*. Org, inst. AFP 9780800621599.

o Wold, Wayne L. "Truro" from *Intonations*, vol. 14. Org. SEL 160-734.

Handbell

o Linker, Janet/Jane McFadden. "Christ Is Alive! All Christians Sing." 3-5 oct hb, org, br ensemble, opt tpt, opt 3-5 oct hc, L3+. BP HB208 (hb org/full score). HB208B (tpt). HB208C (2 tpt, tbn, hrn, tba, timp).

o McChesney, Kevin. "Sing Praise to God, Who Reigns Above." 2-3 oct, L3. AGEHR AG23006 (2-3 oct). AG35181 (3-5 oct). Stephenson, Valerie. "From Death to Life Eternal." 3-5 oct hb, opt 3 oct hc, L3. LOR 20/1289L.

Praise Ensemble

• Carpenter, Kelly. "Draw Me Close." Mercy/VIN.

• Crouch, Andraé. "Soon and Very Soon." Bud John Songs, Inc./ Crouch Music. ELW 439.

Hanson, Handt/Paul Murakami. "Be My Home." Prince of Peace Publishing. W&P 16.

• Houghton, Israel/Michael Gungor. "Friend of God." INT.

• Tomlin, Chris/Daniel Carson/Ed Cash/Jesse Reeves. "Jesus Messiah." WT/Sixsteps Music.

• Walker, Tommy. "He Knows My Name." Doulos Publishing.

Global

Bell, John. "Who Am I?" from *Heaven Shall Not Wait*. U. GIA G-3646.

Hehe tune, arr. Austin Lovelace. "Christ Is the Way" from *Set Free: A Collection of African Hymns*. SATB, cant. AFP 9780806600451.

Tuesday, May 24

Nicolaus Copernicus, died 1543; Leonhard Euler, died 1783; scientists

Remembering scientists such as Copernicus and Euler offers an opportunity to ponder the mysteries of the universe and the grandeur of God's creation. Copernicus is an example of a renaissance person. He formally studied astronomy, mathematics, Greek, Plato, law, medicine, and canon law. He also had interests in theology, poetry, and the natural and social sciences. Copernicus is chiefly remembered for his work as an astronomer and his idea that the sun, not the earth, is the center of the solar system.

Euler (oy-ler) is regarded as one of the founders of the science of pure mathematics and made important contributions to mechanics, hydrodynamics, astronomy, optics, and acoustics.

Friday, May 27

John Calvin, renewer of the church, died 1564

John Calvin began his studies in theology at the University of Paris when he was fourteen. In his mid-twenties he experienced a conversion that led him to embrace the views of the Reformation. His theological ideas are systematically laid out in his *Institutes of the Christian Religion*. He is also well known for his commentaries on scripture. He was a preacher in Geneva, was banished once, and then later returned to reform the city under a theocratic constitution.

o denotes suggestions that relate to the hymn of the day.
• denotes songs that are available on iTunes®.

May 29, 2011
Sixth Sunday of Easter

Jesus does not leave his followers orphaned. Through the Holy Spirit Jesus comes to abide with his disciples of every generation. As Pentecost draws near, we are reminded that the risen Christ dwells in us as the Spirit of truth. We receive this Spirit in baptism and pray that in our gathering around the Lord's table the Spirit will transform us to be the body of the risen Christ in the world.

Today is the commemoration of Jiří Tranovský, hymnwriter, who died in 1637.

Prayer of the Day

Almighty and ever-living God, you hold together all things in heaven and on earth. In your great mercy receive the prayers of all your children, and give to all the world the Spirit of your truth and peace, through Jesus Christ, our Savior and Lord, who lives and reigns with you and the Holy Spirit, one God, now and forever.

Gospel Acclamation

Alleluia. Those who love me will keep my word, and my Fa- ¹ ther will love them,* and we will come to them and make our ¹ home with them. *Alleluia.* (John 14:23)

Readings and Psalm

Acts 17:22-31

In Athens, Paul faces the challenge of proclaiming the gospel to Greeks who know nothing of either Jewish or Christian tradition. He proclaims that the "unknown god" whom they worship is the true Lord of heaven and earth who will judge the world with justice through Jesus, whom God has raised from the dead.

Psalm 66:8-20

Bless our God, you peoples; let the sound of praise be heard. (Ps. 66:8)

I Peter 3:13-22

Christians have a zeal for doing what is right in God's eyes no matter what the circumstances because in baptism we are saved and made alive. Thus our Christian beliefs and behavior are to be a matter of public record just as our baptism is.

John 14:15-21

In final words to his disciples on the night of his arrest, Jesus encourages obedience to his commandments and speaks of the Spirit, who will be with them forever.

Preface Easter

Color White

Prayers of Intercession

The prayers are prepared locally for each occasion. The following examples may be adapted or used as appropriate.

In this season of resurrection, we lift up to God all those in need in the church and throughout the world.

A brief silence.

You join us as one in baptism, but we often bicker and cause schisms. Transform your church into a faithful witness to the living Christ. Hear us, O God.

Your mercy is great.

You gave us the gift of creation, but we often misuse its resources. Transform us into good stewards. Hear us, O God.

Your mercy is great.

You bless the nations of the world, but we curse one another and cause war. Transform us into peacemakers and reconcilers. Hear us, O God.

Your mercy is great.

You stand beside us in our sorrows and pains, but we forget those most in need. Transform us into healers and caregivers. Hear us, O God.

Your mercy is great.

You built a church for us, but we focus on things inside these walls instead of what is beyond our doors. Transform us into missionaries. Hear us, O God.

Your mercy is great.

Here other intercessions may be offered.

You sent your advocate, but we still fear death. Transform our fears into a proclamation of resurrection, assisted by the witness of the saints (*especially Jiří Tranovský, hymnwriter, whom we commemorate today*). Hear us, O God.

Your mercy is great.

Into your care, O God, we place ourselves and all our prayers, trusting your promise of new life in Jesus Christ, our risen Savior.
Amen.

Ideas and Images for the Day

"I will not leave you orphaned," Jesus promises us in today's gospel. God is not some ruthless heavenly spectator judging us as on reality television, relishing our failures, wishing to exchange us for a better or more attractive child, no curmudgeonly "Daddy Warbucks" in the sky. Rather, God comes to love us in Jesus, singularly loving and accepting, seeking our trust, promising to be ever-present with us in the Holy Spirit. This Holy Advocate moves us even when we don't recognize its power, even when it seems "an unknown God" (Acts 17:23). Though we might battle an elemental loneliness, we have not been abandoned.

1. The musical *Annie* (Columbia Pictures, 1982), is named for its central character, an orphan. Her story often contains caricatures, but it may be helpful for contrasting God's unconditional love with human brokenness as evidenced in troubled parents who cannot care for their children or demonstrating a kind of conditional love as orphans grow older and worry they are not "cute" enough for adoption. For Christians, tomorrow ("I love ya, tomorrow") holds hope for us as eschatological people, but we live through the "hard knocks" of the present with the help of the Spirit.

2. The premise behind *The Lion, the Witch, and the Wardrobe,* by C. S. Lewis, is that Lucy, Susan, Edmund, and Peter are children temporarily orphaned during World War II. Their parents send them to stay with a distant uncle to remain safe. The Narnia fantasy world Lucy discovers through the wardrobe challenges them, changing them into royalty, recognizing their gifts: hope in time of great despair and loneliness.

3. James 1:27 calls us to justice and compassion for the orphan and the widow. Compassion International (http://www.compassion.com/) and other like-minded charitable organizations provide care for children living in poverty (some orphans, some not). Supporting and connecting with one child is a tangible way for a youth group or other small group within the congregation to sponsor and care for a particular individual, exchange letters or photos, and remember the orphaned in prayer.

4. The feeling of being orphaned is not limited to children. Bangor (Maine) International Airport is the U.S. gateway for soldiers' departures and arrivals to and from Iraq and Afghanistan. Citizens of Bangor have surprised tired soldiers with applause, handshakes, and cell phones to call their loved ones. *The Way We Get By* (http://www.thewaywegetbymovie.com/) is a documentary telling the story of three seniors involved in this effort, and the video or its trailer could be used for sermon illustration or adult education. From the synopsis: "the film carefully builds stories of heartbreak and redemption, reminding us how our culture casts our elders, and too often our soldiers, aside." This film highlights the Spirit in action: ordinary folk sharing grace with strangers.

Hymns for Worship
Gathering
Oh, sing to the Lord   ELW 822, WOV 795, TFF 274
We know that Christ is raised   ELW 449, LBW 189
Come, thou almighty King   ELW 408, LBW 522

Hymn of the Day
Dear Christians, one and all, rejoice   ELW 594, LBW 299
   NUN FREUT EUCH
Come down, O love divine   ELW 804, LBW 508
   DOWN AMPNEY
Come, gracious Spirit, heavenly dove   ELW 404
   HERR JESU CHRIST, MEINS   LBW 475   *WAREHAM*

Offering
Like the murmur of the dove's song   ELW 403, WOV 685
Many and great, O God   ELW 837, WOV 794

Communion
Loving Spirit   ELW 397, WOV 683
Children of the heavenly Father   ELW 781, LBW 474
Jesus loves me!   ELW 595, TFF 249

Sending
Alleluia! Sing to Jesus   ELW 392, LBW 158
The risen Christ   ELW 390

Additional Hymns and Songs
We have been told   HS91 817
Shout for joy, loud and long   WOV 793
No Greater Love   HS91 804

Music for the Day
Psalmody and Acclamations
Farlee, Robert Buckley. "Psalm 66," Refrain 3, from PSCY.
Miller, Aaron David. *Gospel Acclamations for Lent–Holy Trinity.*
Organ, Anne Krentz. "Psalm 66:8-20" from PWA, Evangelical Lutheran Worship Edition.

Choral

Costello, Michael D. "Children of the Heavenly Father." SATB, opt U, pno, fl. AFP 9780806697093

Gumpeltzhaimer, Adam. "O Praise the Lord." SAB. GIA G-2294.

○ Livingston, Donald D./William H. Mathis. "Come Down, O Love Divine." SSATB, org. AFP 9780800675356.

Nelson, Ronald A. "If You Love One Another." U/SA, kybd. SEL 422-841.

Tallis, Thomas. "If Ye Love Me." SATB. Various editions.

Children's Choir

Bedford, Michael. "Oh, Come, With Body and Mind." U/2 pt, kybd. CG CGA1142.

Organ, Anne Krentz. "Fe y Esperanza." U/2 pt, kybd, opt perc, opt C inst. CG CGA1129.

Sleeth, Natalie. "If You Love Me" from *LifeSongs*. U, kybd.

Keyboard / Instrumental

○ Bender, Jan. "Herr Jesu Christ, meins" from *Master Organ Works of Jan Bender*, vol. 1. Org. CPH 97-7098U1.

○ Carter, John. "Nun freut euch" from *Introductions and Alternate Accompaniments*, vol. 6. Pno. AFP 9780800623647.

○ Leavitt, John. "Nun freut euch" from *Three Hymn Settings*. Org. MSM 10-932.

○ Sedio, Mark. "Down Ampney" from *Augsburg Organ Library: Easter*. Org. AFP 9780800659363.

Handbell

Lamb, Linda. "Holy Spirit, Breath of God." 3-5 oct hb, opt 2 oct hc, L2. LOR 20/1470L.

Stephenson, Valerie. "I've Got the Joy (Down in My Heart)." 3-5 oct, opt bng, cym, L2. CG CGB579.

○ Wissinger, Kathleen. "Sketches on 'Down Ampney.'" 3-6 oct hb, opt 3-5 oct hc, L3+. LOR 20/1428L.

Praise Ensemble

● Kendrick, Graham. "God of the Poor." INT/Make Way Music. W&P 17. Various editions.

● Morgan, Reuben. "My Redeemer Lives." Hillsong/INT.

● Mullins, Rich. "Awesome God." BMG Songs.

● Story, Laura. "Indescribable." WT/Sixsteps Music.

● Tomlin, Chris/Jesse Reeves/Ed Cash. "How Great Is Our God." WT/Sixsteps Music.

● Wimber, John. "Spirit Song." Mercy/VIN. W&P 130.

Global

Haya tune, arr. Joas Kijugo. "The Love of God Almighty" from *Set Free: A Collection of African Hymns*. SATB, cant. AFP 9780806600451.

Sedio, Mark. "Alleluia Verse in African Style" from *Global Choral Sounds*. SATB, cant, perc. CPH 98-3610.

○ denotes suggestions that relate to the hymn of the day.
● denotes songs that are available on iTunes®.

Sunday, May 29
Jiří Tranovský, hymnwriter, died 1637

Jiří Tranovský (YEAR-zhee truh-NOF-skee) is considered the "Luther of the Slavs" and the father of Slovak hymnody. Trained at the University of Wittenberg in the early seventeenth century, Tranovský was ordained in 1616 and spent his life preaching and teaching in Prague, Silesia, and finally Slovakia. He produced a translation of the Augsburg Confession and published his hymn collection *Cithara Sanctorum* (Lyre of the Saints), the foundation of Slovak Lutheran hymnody.

Tuesday, May 31
Visit of Mary to Elizabeth

Sometime after the Annunciation, Mary visited her cousin Elizabeth. This occasion is sometimes referred to simply as "The Visitation." Elizabeth greeted Mary with the words "Blessed are you among women," and Mary responded with her famous song, the Magnificat. Luke's gospel tells that even John the Baptist rejoiced and leapt in his mother's womb when Elizabeth heard Mary's greeting. On this festival two women are seen: one, seemingly too old to have a child, bears the last prophet of the old covenant, and the other, quite young, bears the incarnate Word and the new covenant.

Wednesday, June 1
Justin, martyr at Rome, died around 165

Justin was born of pagan parents. At Ephesus he was moved by stories of early Christian martyrs and came under the influence of an elderly Christian man he met there. Justin described his conversion by saying, "Straightway a flame was kindled in my soul and a love of the prophets and those who are friends of Christ possessed me." Justin was a teacher of philosophy and engaged in debates about the truth of Christian faith. He was arrested and jailed for practicing an unauthorized religion. He refused to renounce his faith, and he and six of his students, one a woman, were beheaded.

Justin's description of early Christian worship around the year 150 is one of the foundations of the church's pattern of worship, East and West.

June 2, 2011
Ascension of Our Lord

In today's gospel the risen Christ ascends into heaven and his followers are assured that the Spirit will empower them to be witnesses throughout the earth. The disciples were told to not gaze up into heaven to look for Jesus; we find his presence among us as we proclaim the word and share the Easter feast. We too long for the Spirit to enliven our faith and invigorate our mission.

Prayer of the Day

Almighty God, your only Son was taken into the heavens and in your presence intercedes for us. Receive us and our prayers for all the world, and in the end bring everything into your glory, through Jesus Christ, our Sovereign and Lord, who lives and reigns with you and the Holy Spirit, one God, now and forever.

or

Almighty God, your blessed Son, our Savior Jesus Christ, ascended far above all heavens that he might fill all things. Mercifully give us faith to trust that, as he promised, he abides with us on earth to the end of time, who lives and reigns with you and the Holy Spirit, one God, now and forever.

Gospel Acclamation

Alleluia. Go and make disciples of all nations, ˡ says the Lord;* I am with you always, to the end ˡ of the age. *Alleluia.* (Matt. 28:19, 20)

Readings and Psalm

Acts 1:1-11

Before he is lifted into heaven, Jesus promises that the missionary work of the disciples will spread out from Jerusalem to all the world. His words provide an outline of the book of Acts.

Psalm 47

God has gone up with a shout. (Ps. 47:5)

or Psalm 93

Ever since the world began, your throne has been established. (Ps. 93:2)

Ephesians 1:15-23

The risen and exalted Christ reigns over the entire universe. The author of Ephesians prays that we would be given the wisdom to comprehend this and display it through love toward others.

Luke 24:44-53

On the day of his ascension, Jesus leaves his disciples with a commission, a blessing, and a promise of the Holy Spirit.

Preface   Ascension

Color   White

Prayers of Intercession

The prayers are prepared locally for each occasion. The following examples may be adapted or used as appropriate.

In this season of resurrection, we lift up to God all those in need in the church and throughout the world.

A brief silence.

For your church, that we speak your message in tongues that are comprehensible to all. Hear us, O God.

Your mercy is great.

For your creation, that we respect and value its beauty and worth. Hear us, O God.

Your mercy is great.

For those who live in danger throughout the world: soldiers serving abroad, missionaries, and those who endure religious persecution, that they experience peace and hospitality. Hear us, O God.

Your mercy is great.

For the poor, the sick, the lonely, the abused, the outcast, and the dying (*especially*), that they receive healing and joy. Hear us, O God.

Your mercy is great.

For those we love and for those who love us, for the people of this congregation, that we be set afire with the gifts of the Spirit. Hear us, O God.

Your mercy is great.

Here other intercessions may be offered.

For all those who have died in faith, that we meet them at the unending feast you have prepared for all your people. Hear us, O God.

Your mercy is great.

Into your care, O God, we place ourselves and all our prayers, trusting your promise of new life in Jesus Christ, our risen Savior.

Amen.

Ideas and Images for the Day

We often cast our eyes upward to look for God. When we are feeling lonely or misunderstood, we raise our hands to ask why, or shake our fists in gestures of prayer, anguish, or praise. While the scriptures promise that God is king of all the earth, sitting on his holy throne (Psalm 47), we need not only look up for God's action in our lives. Our ascended Lord lives in the heavens, but Jesus does not leave his disciples—or us—to fumble while he naps in the clouds. Before he ascends, Jesus promises that we are clothed with the Holy Spirit's power, witnesses "to the ends of the earth" (Acts 1:8).

1. *Braveheart* (Icon, 1995) is a movie portrayal of Scotsman William Wallace, who fought for freedom. His ally Stephen the Irishman is portrayed as mad with his frequent conversation heavenward, comic relief in a violent movie. The movie's profanity will turn some off, but mentioning this colorful character in a men's Bible study, Alpha study, or even a sermon highlights the question of how our ascended Lord interacts with us. Since people who talk to God out loud are "weird," how do we seek God—and how does God seek us—when conversation with the heavens is for madmen and fools?

2. Some churches have early morning Ascension Day services. Try making an adventure or trek to enjoy an outdoor worship location (with snacks/coffee to share afterward). Especially for a group of active youth or adults, a setting outside in a "high place," whatever that means in your locale—a tall building's roof, a mountain hike, even the top of a sturdy children's playground set—gives us both a new heavenly view and a sense of the Spirit clothing us to be witnesses as we return to our everyday activities.

3. Exploring our physical gestures for prayer is a way to invite worshipers into a larger sense of God's presence among us. Have children demonstrate prayer postures and examine how the gestures show our relationship and trust with God—reverence, friendship, frustration, love, and more: kneeling at a communion rail, hands cupped; bowed head, interlaced fingers; holding hands with neighbors; fists in anguish at bad news/lament; hands uplifted in formal prayer or informally singing; eyes closed or open.

4. Presenting a slide show of paintings of the Ascension with the help of a visual arts teacher would make good discussion for adult education time. You could develop a brief slide show yourself, or ask a web-savvy youth to do so to accompany a hymn on a screen simply by doing an online image search using the keyword "ascension."

Hymns for Worship
Gathering
Hail thee, festival day! (Ascension)   ELW 394, LBW 142
The head that once was crowned   ELW 432, LBW 173
Crown him with many crowns   ELW 855, LBW 170

Hymn of the Day
A hymn of glory let us sing!   ELW 393, LBW 157
    LASST UNS ERFREUEN
Lord, you give the great commission   ELW 579, WOV 756
    ABBOT'S LEIGH
Alleluia! Sing to Jesus   ELW 392, LBW 158   HYFRYDOL

Offering
My Lord of light   ELW 832, WOV 796
Lord, enthroned in heavenly splendor   ELW 475, LBW 172

Communion
Beautiful Savior   ELW 838, LBW 518
At the name of Jesus   ELW 416, LBW 179
Praise, praise! You are my rock   ELW 862

Sending
Rejoice, for Christ is king!   ELW 430, LBW 171
Go, make disciples   ELW 540, W&P 47

Additional Hymns and Songs
Up through endless ranks of angels   LBW 159
And have the bright immensities   LBW 391
O Love of God, how strong and true   HS91 800

Music for the Day
Psalmody and Acclamations

Anderson, Mark. "Psalm 93" from PSCY.

Bruxvoort-Colligan, Richard. "Psalm 47" from PSCY.

Miller, Aaron David. *Gospel Acclamations for Lent–Holy Trinity.*

Pelz, Walter L. "Psalm 47" from PWA, Evangelical Lutheran Worship Edition.

Schalk, Carl. "Psalm 93" from PWA, Evangelical Lutheran Worship Edition.

Choral

Cherwien, David. "Up Through Endless Ranks of Angels." SAB, opt assembly, org, opt tpt. AFP 9780800658816.

Finzi, Gerald. "God Is Gone Up." SATB, TTBB, div, org. B&H M-060-03028-4.

Fleming, Larry L. "Lord of the Dance." SATB. AFP 9780800655358.

Forsberg, Charles. "Fairest Lord Jesus." SSAA, kybd. AFP 9780800664367.

Roberts, William Bradley. "In All These You Welcomed Me." U, org, opt ob or other inst. AFP 9786000001209. *Augsburg Easy Choirbook,* vol. 2. AFP 9780800677510.

Children's Choir

Albrecht, Tamara. "Ascension Anthem" from *Singing through the Church Year.* U/2 pt canon, hb/hc, Orff. MSM 90-37.

Patterson, Mark. "Sing, Rejoice, Clap Your Hands" from *Young ChildrenSing.* U, kybd. AFP 9780800676803.

Sleeth, Natalie. "Go Now In Peace" from *LifeSongs.* U, kybd.

Keyboard / Instrumental

○ Cherwien, David. "Abbot's Leigh" from *Two Hymntune Preludes.* Org. GIA G-4477.

○ Mitchell-Wallace, Sue and John H. Head. "Hyfrydol" from *Timeless Music for Weddings and Special Occasions.* Org, tpt. HOP 8160.

○ Organ, Anne Krentz. "Lasst uns erfreuen" from *Be Thou My Vision.* Pno. AFP 9780800678524.

○ Vaughan Williams, Ralph. "Hyfrydol" from *Augsburg Organ Library: Epiphany.* Org. AFP 9780800659349.

Handbell

○ Afdahl, Lee. "Abbot's Leigh." 3-5 oct, L2+. HOP 2103.

Gramann, Fred. "A Glorious Everlasting Hallelujah Raise." 3-5 oct hb, opt 2 oct hc, L4. AGEHR AG35186.

○ McChesney, Kevin. "Symphonia on Hyfrydol." 3-5 oct, opt orch, L4. JEF JHS9300.

Praise Ensemble

● Baloche, Paul. "Open the Eyes of My Heart, Lord" INT.

● Founds, Rick. "Lord, I Lift Your Name on High." ELW 857. MAR.

● Moody, Dave. "All Hail King Jesus." WRD. W&P 3. Various editions.

● Ruis, David. "You're Worthy of My Praise." MAR.

● Tomlin, Chris/Daniel Carson/Ed Cash/Jesse Reeves. "Jesus Messiah." WT/Sixsteps Music.

● Tomlin, Chris/Louie Giglio. "Holy Is the Lord." WT/Sixsteps Music.

Global

Ghanian tune, arr. John Bell. "When Our Master Jesus Went Away" from *The Courage To Say No: 23 Songs for Lent and Easter.* SATB, cant. GIA G-4244.

Olson, Howard S., arr. "He's Ascended into Heaven" from *Set Free: A Collection of African Hymns.* SATB, cant. AFP 9780806600451.

Friday, June 3

John XXIII, Bishop of Rome, died 1963

In his ministry as a bishop of Venice, John (then Archbishop Roncalli) was loved by his people. He visited parishes and established new ones. He had warm affection for the working class—he himself was the child of Italian peasants—and he worked at developing social-action ministries. At age seventy-seven he was elected bishop of Rome. Despite the expectation that he would be a transitional pope, he had great energy and spirit. He convened the Second Vatican Council to open the windows of the church and "let in the fresh air of the modern world." The council brought about great changes in Roman Catholic worship, changes that have influenced Lutherans and many other Protestant churches as well.

The Martyrs of Uganda, died 1886

Christianity had been introduced to Uganda after 1877, but was made available primarily to those in the court of King Mutesa. His successor, King Mwanga, was angered by these Christian members of the court whose first allegiance was not to him but to Christ. On June 3, 1886, thirty-two young men were burned to death for refusing to renounce Christianity. Other martyrs followed. But many were impressed by the confident manner in which these Christians went to their deaths, and the persecution led to a much stronger Christian presence in the country.

○ denotes suggestions that relate to the hymn of the day.
● denotes songs that are available on iTunes®.

June 5, 2011
Seventh Sunday of Easter

In these days between Ascension and Pentecost, we gather with the disciples in the upper room, waiting for the Spirit to transform the church around the world. In today's gospel Jesus prays for his followers and for their mission in his name. Amid religious, social, and economic divisions, we seek the unity that Jesus had with his Father. Made one in baptism, we go forth to live our faith in the world, eager for the unity that God intends for the whole human family.

Today is the commemoration of Boniface, Bishop of Mainz, missionary to Germany, and martyr, who died in 754.

Prayer of the Day

O God of glory, your Son Jesus Christ suffered for us and ascended to your right hand. Unite us with Christ and each other in suffering and in joy, that all the world may be drawn into your bountiful presence, through Jesus Christ, our Savior and Lord, who lives and reigns with you and the Holy Spirit, one God, now and forever.

Gospel Acclamation

Alleluia. I will not leave you orphaned, ¹ says the Lord.*
I am com- ¹ ing to you. *Alleluia.* (John 14:18)

Readings and Psalm

Acts 1:6-14

Today's reading is part of the introduction to the narrative of the outpouring of the Spirit on Pentecost. These verses tell of the risen Lord's conversation with his disciples on the eve of his ascension.

Psalm 68:1-10, 32-35

Sing to God, who rides upon the clouds. (Ps. 68:4)

1 Peter 4:12-14; 5:6-11

Our faith in Christ does not make us immune from the scorn of others. Nevertheless, we are to resist the designs of evil when we experience disparagement from others, because we trust God's grace will strengthen and guide us.

John 17:1-11

On the night before his crucifixion, Jesus prays to his heavenly Father, asking that those who continue his work in this world will live in unity.

Preface   Ascension

Color   White

Prayers of Intercession

The prayers are prepared locally for each occasion. The following examples may be adapted or used as appropriate.

In this season of resurrection, we lift up to God all those in need in the church and throughout the world.
A brief silence.

We want to know you, O God. Let your church be a sign of your wisdom and understanding. Make us one with Christ. Hear us, O God.

Your mercy is great.

Let your creation be a sign of your power and might. Make us one with Christ. Hear us, O God.

Your mercy is great.

Let the nations of the world be a sign of your peace and counsel. Make us one with Christ. Hear us, O God.

Your mercy is great.

Let your healing word be a sign of your knowledge in the lives of those in need (*especially*). Make us one with Christ. Hear us, O God.

Your mercy is great.

Let this congregation be a sign of your gracious power and our service to you. Make us one with Christ. Hear us, O God.

Your mercy is great.

Here other intercessions may be offered.

Let our lives, together with all those who have died (*especially Boniface, bishop, missionary, and martyr*), be a sign of joy in your presence. Make us one with Christ. Hear us, O God.

Your mercy is great.

Into your care, O God, we place ourselves and all our prayers, trusting your promise of new life in Jesus Christ, our risen Savior.

Amen.

Ideas and Images for the Day

At the ascension we, like the disciples in today's reading in Acts, are left looking at the sky. Jesus brings us back to earth. The Jesus of the High Priestly Prayer speaks not only from the perspective of the risen and ascended one, but as the Word of God, now made flesh. Jesus' prayer frequently also mentions the "world"—the world at once hostile to God and God's anointed, and yet also beloved of God. With Jesus' commissioning today we have our work to do, because the one who gives meaning to all creation now imparts the necessary word for our work in the world. The Living One works through us as "words within the world." The church becomes the imperfect vessel through whom Christ works, for the sake of the world.

1. Gil Bailie, in *Violence Unveiled*, offers a unique description of the church's role in history: "In every instance, the institution in closest proximity to the Gospel's explosive charge is the institution we call the church . . . the church, like Peter, is both a stumbling block and a cornerstone. It is the latter only when it is consciously contrite for being and having been the former" (New York: Crossroad, 1995, pp. 274–275). How does this quotation help us wrestle with the contradiction of being "in the world but not of the world"?

2. The Chapel of the Ascension in Jerusalem is famous for containing the "last footprints of Jesus" on a stone slab within the chapel. How might Jesus' footsteps be seen and celebrated in the life of the church? In your congregation? Where are the footsteps leading you? For a picture of the footprints visit: http://www.sacred-destinations.com/israel/jerusalem-chapel-of-ascension.htm.

3. Writer Kathleen Norris experimented with silence when she worked as a teacher at an elementary school. After periods of silence, the children's images "often had a depth and maturity that was unlike anything else they wrote. . . . One third grader's poem turned into a prayer: 'Silence is spiders spinning their webs, it's like a silkworm making its silk. Lord, help me to know when to be silent.'" Read the whole story in *Amazing Grace* (New York: Riverhead, 1998), pp. 16–17.

4. Dr. Seuss's *Oh, the Places You'll Go!* (New York: Random House, 1993) is a humorous relating of life's adventures and misadventures. It is also a parable of the church's life in the world and the places our journey of discipleship may take us. Children may enjoy the clever pictures and story, which can be used as an illustration of the challenges and thrills of a church in mission.

Hymns for Worship
Gathering

The head that once was crowned   ELW 432, LBW 173
Christ is the king!   ELW 662, LBW 386
Christ is alive! Let Christians sing   ELW 389, LBW 363

Hymn of the Day

Oh, love, how deep   ELW 322, LBW 88   DEO GRACIAS
Lord, who the night you were betrayed   ELW 463, LBW 206   SONG 1
The church's one foundation   ELW 654, LBW 369   AURELIA

Offering

As the grains of wheat   ELW 465, WOV 705
We are all one in Christ   ELW 643, LCC 470

Communion

I come with joy   ELW 482
Lord, who the night you were betrayed   ELW 463, LBW 206
Father, we thank you   ELW 478, WOV 704

Sending

Thine the amen   ELW 826, WOV 801
Lord, you give the great commission   ELW 579, WOV 756

Additional Hymns and Songs

You are the seed   TFF 226, WOV 753
God, you spin the whirling planets   PH 285
Catch the Vision! Share the Glory   HS91 814

Music for the Day
Psalmody and Acclamations

Messner, Sally. "Psalm 68:1-10, 32-35" from PWA, Evangelical Lutheran Worship Edition.
Miller, Aaron David. *Gospel Acclamations for Lent–Holy Trinity.*
Pavlechko, Thomas. "Psalm 68:1-10, 32-35" from PSCY.

Choral

Cherwien, David. "Up Through Endless Ranks of Angels." SAB, opt assembly, org, opt tpt. AFP 9780800658816.

o Ferguson, John. "The Church's One Foundation." SATB, org, br. AFP 9780800658311.

Fleming, Larry L. "Lord of the Dance." SATB. AFP 9780800655358.
Helgen, John. "I Come with Joy." 2 pt mxd, SATB, pno, org. AFP 9780800677145.
Leavitt, John. "A Celtic Prayer." SATB, kybd. AFP 9780800664329.

Children's Choir

Hopson, Hal. "Love One Another." U/2 pt, kybd. CG, CGA741
Vasile, Paul. "Let All the World in Every Corner Sing." UE, U, kybd. MSM 50-6405.
Widestrand, Olle. "Many Are the Lightbeams" from *LifeSongs*. U, kybd.

o denotes suggestions that relate to the hymn of the day.
● denotes songs that are available on iTunes®.

Keyboard / Instrumental

- Blair, Dallas. "Aurelia" from *Hymn Introductions and Descants for Trumpet and Organ*, set 4. Org, tpt. MSM 20-703.
- Miller, Aaron David. "Deo gracias" from *Augsburg Organ Library: Epiphany*. Org. AFP 9780800659349.
- Organ, Anne Krentz. "Aurelia" from *Piano Reflections for the Church Year*. Pno. AFP 9780800674748.
- Schaffner, John Hebden. "Song 1" from *Organ Music for the Seasons*, vol. 1. Org. AFP 9780800657239.

Handbell

Hakes, Derek. "Sing and Rejoice." 3-5 oct, L3-. LOR 20/1363L.
- McChesney, Kevin. "The Church's One Foundation." 3-5 oct, L2. Jeffers JHS9454. Will be available at handbellworld.com in summer 2010.
- Tucker, Sondra. "The Church's One Foundation." 2-3 oct, L2. CPH 97-6903.

Praise Ensemble

- Adkins, Donna. "Glorify Thy Name." MAR. W&P 42.
- Agnew, Todd/Chris Collins/Edwin Excell/John Newton. "Grace Like Rain." Ardent/Koala Music.
- Foote, Billy/Cindy Foote. "You Are God Alone (Not a God)." Billy Foote Music/INT.
- Morgan, Reuben. "I Give You My Heart." Hillsong/INT.
- Scott, Kathryn. "Hungry." VIN.
- Tomlin, Chris/John Newton/John Rees/Edwin Excell/Louie Giglio. "Amazing Grace (My Chains Are Gone)." WT.

Global

Dexter, Noel, arr. "Peace and Love" from *Let the Peoples Sing*. SATB. AFP 9780800675394.

Sosa, Pablo. "Heaven Is Singing for Joy/El cielo canta alegria" from *Éste es el Día*. U. GIA G-7021. ELW 664.

Sunday, June 5

Boniface, Bishop of Mainz, missionary to Germany, martyr, died 754

Boniface (his name means "good deeds") was born Wynfrith in Devonshire, England. He was a Benedictine monk who at the age of thirty was called to missionary work among the Vandal tribes in Germany. His first missionary attempt was unsuccessful, but he returned two years later and was able to plant the gospel in an area filled with superstitious and violent practices. He led large numbers of Benedictine monks and nuns in establishing churches, schools, and seminaries. Boniface was also a reformer. He persuaded two rulers to call synods to put an end to the practice of selling church offices to the highest bidder. Boniface was

preparing a group for confirmation on the eve of Pentecost when he and they were killed by a band of pagans.

Tuesday, June 7

Seattle, chief of the Duwamish Confederacy, died 1866

Noah Seattle was chief of the Suquamish tribe and later became chief of the Duwamish Confederacy, a tribal alliance. When the tribes were faced with an increasing number of white settlers, Seattle chose to live and work peacefully with them rather than engage in wars. After Seattle became a Roman Catholic, he began the practice of morning and evening prayer in the tribe, a practice that continued after his death. On the centennial of his birth, the city of Seattle—named for him against his wishes—erected a monument over his grave.

Thursday, June 9

Columba, died 597; Aidan, died 651; Bede, died 735; renewers of the church

These three monks from the British Isles were pillars among those who kept alive the light of learning and devotion during the Middle Ages. Columba founded three monasteries, including one on the island of Iona, off the coast of Scotland. That monastery was left in ruins after the Reformation but today is home to an ecumenical religious community. Aidan, who helped bring Christianity to the Northumbria area of England, was known for his pastoral style and ability to stir people to charity and good works. Bede was a Bible translator and scripture scholar. He wrote a history of the English church and was the first historian to date events *anno Domini* (A.D.), "year of our Lord." Bede is also known for his hymns, including "A Hymn of Glory Let Us Sing!" (ELW 393).

Saturday, June 11

Barnabas, Apostle

The Eastern church commemorates Barnabas as one of the Seventy commissioned by Jesus. Though he was not among the Twelve mentioned in the gospels, the book of Acts gives him the title of apostle. His name means "son of encouragement." When Paul came to Jerusalem after his conversion, Barnabas took him in over the fears of the other apostles, who doubted Paul's discipleship. Later, Paul and Barnabas traveled together on missions. At the Council of Jerusalem, Barnabas defended the claims of Gentile Christians in relation to the Mosaic law.

○ denotes suggestions that relate to the hymn of the day.
● denotes songs that are available on iTunes®.

June 11, 2011
Vigil of Pentecost

At this liturgy we gather in vigilant prayer as the disciples did in the days preceding Pentecost. Our world waits for an end to war and violence. The whole creation waits for an end to suffering. With undying hope we pray for the crowning gift of Easter—the Spirit of the risen Christ among us.

Prayer of the Day

Almighty and ever-living God, you fulfilled the promise of Easter by sending the gift of your Holy Spirit. Look upon your people gathered in prayer, open to receive the Spirit's flame. May it come to rest in our hearts and heal the divisions of word and tongue, that with one voice and one song we may praise your name in joy and thanksgiving; through Jesus Christ, our Savior and Lord, who lives and reigns with you and the Holy Spirit, one God, now and forever.

Gospel Acclamation

Alleluia. Come, Holy Spirit, fill the hearts¹ of your faithful,* and kindle in us the fire¹ of your love. *Alleluia.*

Readings and Psalm
Exodus 19:1-9

At Sinai God assured Israel that they were God's prized possession and commissioned them to serve as mediating priests for the nations. God's word spoken to Moses is the basis of the people's trust.

or Acts 2:1-11

Believers are filled with the Spirit to tell God's deeds.

Psalm 33:12-22

The Lord is our helper and our shield. (Ps. 33:20)

or Psalm 130

There is forgiveness with you. (Ps. 130:4)

Romans 8:14-17, 22-27

The Holy Spirit has made us God's children who eagerly await the glorious future God has prepared for all of creation. While we cannot fully see what God has in store for us and creation, we eagerly anticipate it in hope. Even when we are unable to pray, the same Spirit prays for us.

John 7:37-39

Jesus describes the Holy Spirit as living water, quenching the thirst of all who come to him and filling the hearts of believers till they overflow.

Preface Vigil and Day of Pentecost

Color Red

June 12, 2011
Day of Pentecost

Today's festival derives its name from the Jewish festival of Pentecost, observed fifty days after Passover. On the fiftieth day of Easter we celebrate the Holy Spirit as the power of God among us that heals, forgives, inspires, and unites. In the reading from Acts, images of wind and fire describe the Spirit poured out on disciples of all nations. In John's gospel the risen Christ breathes the Spirit on his followers on Easter evening. In the one Spirit we are baptized into one body, and at the Lord's table the Spirit unites us for witness in the world.

Prayer of the Day

O God, on this day you open the hearts of your faithful people by sending into us your Holy Spirit. Direct us by the light of that Spirit, that we may have a right judgment in all things and rejoice at all times in your peace, through Jesus Christ, your Son and our Lord, who lives and reigns with you and the Holy Spirit, one God, now and forever.

Gospel Acclamation

Alleluia. Come, Holy Spirit, fill the hearts ˡ of your faithful,* and kindle in us the fire ˡ of your love. *Alleluia.*

Readings and Psalm

Acts 2:1-21

Pentecost was a Jewish harvest festival that marked the fiftieth day after Passover. Luke portrays the Holy Spirit being poured out upon the disciples before the gathered and astonished people assembled in Jerusalem for the festival. Filled with the Spirit, the disciples were able to witness to the power of Christ's resurrection.

or Numbers 11:24-30

The Spirit of God rested upon seventy elders in Israel who had been chosen to share the burden of leadership with Moses. When some became jealous that two others also had the spirit and could prophesy, Moses said that he hoped that all of God's people would be prophets.

Psalm 104:24-34, 35b

Send forth your Spirit and renew the face of the earth. (Ps. 104:30)

1 Corinthians 12:3b-13

Paul is helping the Corinthians understand the relationship between our God-given unity and Spirit-created diversity. The Spirit creates the unity of faith and gives all Christians diverse gifts for the common benefit of all. We need one another's diverse spiritual gifts, because the same Spirit has given them to each person for the common good.

or Acts 2:1-21

See above.

John 20:19-23

The risen Jesus appears to his disciples, offering them a benediction, a commission, and the gift of the Holy Spirit.

or John 7:37-39

Jesus describes the Holy Spirit as living water, quenching the thirst of all who come to him and filling the hearts of believers till they overflow.

Preface   Vigil and Day of Pentecost

Color   Red

Prayers of Intercession

The prayers are prepared locally for each occasion. The following examples may be adapted or used as appropriate.

In this season of resurrection, we lift up to God all those in need in the church and throughout the world.

A brief silence.

Come, Holy Spirit, into your church and its people. Fill us with the power and purpose of the gospel. Hear us, O God.

Your mercy is great.

Come, Holy Spirit, into the world around us. Infuse us with the sights, smells, and sounds of the richness of creation. Hear us, O God.

Your mercy is great.

Come, Holy Spirit, into the nations of the world. Rain down your peace onto nations at war or in crisis (*especially*). Hear us, O God.

Your mercy is great.

Come, Holy Spirit, into the lives of those in need (*especially*). Blanket them with hope and healing. Hear us, O God.
Your mercy is great.
Come, Holy Spirit, into our community of faith. Support us in our mission, our celebrations, and our woes. Hear us, O God.
Your mercy is great.
Here other intercessions may be offered.
Come, Holy Spirit, into our thanksgiving for the lives of all the faithful departed (*especially*). Remind us of the joy that is to come. Hear us, O God.
Your mercy is great.
Into your care, O God, we place ourselves and all our prayers, trusting your promise of new life in Jesus Christ, our risen Savior.
Amen.

Ideas and Images for the Day

Pentecost is the crowning achievement of the Jesus story. Now, more than ever, the disciples in the upper room would have just cause to sing the "Dayenu" ("It would have been enough") verses from the Passover seder meal, but revised: It would have been enough for the Word and wisdom of God to have been born in the flesh . . . Dayenu! It would have been enough for the Word to grow to adulthood and share his stunning parables about God's gracious activity in the world . . . Dayenu! It would have been enough for this Word to say to his enemies, "Father, forgive them" . . . Dayenu! It would have been enough for this Word to have died on a cross for us . . . Dayenu! It would have been enough that he rose again in blessing, not vengeance . . . Dayenu! But now, beyond what we would even expect—the Word becomes our word and it is written on our hearts at Pentecost . . . Dayenu! It is enough, and more than enough to enflame our ministry of reconciliation in a world in need of a healing word.

1. At Pentecost there is no going back to old ways. Astronauts who have viewed the earth from outer space speak from a new perspective about the beauty and fragility of the earth (http://www.space.com/missionlaunches/090422-astronauts-earth-day.html). So it is with us at Pentecost. We are no longer captive to the old myths of ego and power, and the breath of new life forever changes our perspective on history and our stories.

2. Pablo Picasso once said that every act of creation is predicated on an act of destruction. When God created heaven and earth chaos was destroyed. While wind and fire are known for their destructive force, in the Bible they are also creative: wind from heaven blew over the waters, and with heaven's fire God called Moses into mission. How else can wind and fire conjure images of healing and renewal?

3. In *To Dance with God* (New York: Paulist Press, 1986), Gertrude Mueller Nelson provides insightful reflections and family celebrations for the day of Pentecost. Among her helpful illustrations is a comparison of the inflation of our egos as opposed to the spirited infusion of our whole being. "When the wind blows, it shakes the dead wood out of the trees. . . .When there isn't even a breath of wind, we languish in the doldrums of its absence." At Pentecost, Nelson says, we catch our breath: "*Suddenly there came a sound from heaven as of a rushing wind. The nature of an awakening, or of an inspiration is like that. Suddenly, it hits us. We say, 'Aha!'*" (p. 189).

4. Blow up a red balloon as full as possible without popping it. Between breaths, describe how the Holy Spirit is like wind inflating the balloon. Ask the children where they think the balloon will land once you release it. Now let it go! Comment on how the direction the Spirit offers us can be surprising, just as it was with the disciples.

Hymns for Worship
Gathering
O day full of grace   ELW 627, LBW 161
Hail thee, festival day! (Pentecost)   ELW 394, LBW 142
Creator Spirit, heavenly dove   ELW 578, LBW 284

Hymn of the Day
Come, Holy Ghost, God and Lord   ELW 395, LBW 163
   KOMM, HEILIGER GEIST, HERRE GOTT
O living Breath of God/*Soplo de Dios viviente*   ELW 407, LLC 368   *VÅRVINDAR FRISKA*
Gracious Spirit, heed our pleading   ELW 401, WOV 687
   NJOO KWETU, ROHO MWEMA

Offering
Lord, listen to your children praying   ELW 752, WOV 775, TFF 247
Draw us in the Spirit's tether   ELW 470, WOV 703

Communion
Spirit of Gentleness   ELW 396, WOV 684
Loving Spirit   ELW 397, WOV 683
Now to the Holy Spirit let us pray   ELW 743, LBW 317

Sending
God of tempest, God of whirlwind   ELW 400
Holy Spirit, ever dwelling   ELW 582, LBW 523

Additional Hymns and Songs
Spirit Song   W&P 130
There's a sweet, sweet Spirit in this place   TFF 102
Praise the Spirit in creation   WOV 682

Music for the Day
Psalmody and Acclamations

Harbor, Rawn. "Lord, Send Out Your Spirit! (Psalm 104)." TFF 13.

Makeever, Ray. "When You Send Forth Your Spirit (Psalm 104)" from *Dancing at the Harvest.*

Miller, Aaron David. *Gospel Acclamations for Lent–Holy Trinity.*

Mummert, Mark. "Psalm 104," Refrain 2, from PSCY.

Pelz, Walter L. "Psalm 104:24-34, 35b" from PWA, Evangelical Lutheran Worship Edition.

Choral

Adams, Jonathan. "The Lone, Wild Bird." SATB, pno. AFP 9780800697185.

Busarow, Donald. "Come, Holy Spirit." SAB, org, opt assembly. AFP 9780806697086.

Ferguson, John. "Hymn to the Spirit." SATB, div, vla or cl. MSM 50-5003.

o Helgen, John. "O Living Breath of God." SAB, pno. AFP 9780800621506.

Scott, K. Lee. "Gracious Spirit, Dwell with Me" (Adore te devote). 2 pt mxd, org. AFP 9780800646134. *The Augsburg Choirbook.* AFP 9780800656782. *Augsburg Easy Choirbook, Vol. 1.* AFP 9780800676025.

Wetzler, Robert. "O Spirit." SATB, kybd, opt vln or C inst. SMP 10/3077S.

Children's Choir

Colvin, Tom. "Spirit Friend" from *LifeSongs.* U, kybd.

Cool, Jayne Southwick. "Pentecost Fire." U, kybd. CG CGA502.

Makeever, Ray. "When You Send Forth Your Spirit (Psalm 104)" from *Dancing at the Harvest.* U, kybd.

Keyboard / Instrumental

o Kolander, Keith. "Njoo kwetu, Roho mwema" from *When Our Song Says Peace.* Pno. AFP 9780800623456.

o Pachelbel, Johann. "Komm, Heiliger Geist, Herre Gott" from *Organ Literature for the Church Year.* Org. Belwin Mills DM 00254.

o Pelz, Walter. "Komm, Heiliger Geist, Herre Gott" from *Pentecost Suite.* Org, inst. CPH 97-6712U1.

o Raabe, Nancy M. "Njoo kwetu, Roho mwema" from *Grace and Peace,* vol. 2. Pno. AFP 9780800679016.

Handbell

Afdahl, Lee. "Spirit in the Wind." 3-5 oct, L3. AFP 9780800655440.

Eithun, Sandra. "Spirit of God, Descend Upon My Heart." 3-5 oct hb, opt 3 oct hc, opt fl, L3-. Soundforth Productions 259333.

McChesney, Kevin. "Holy Spirit, Gift of God." 2-3 oct, L2. CPH 97-6881.

Praise Ensemble

● Barnett, Marie. "Breathe." Mercy/VIN.

● Doerksen, Brian. "Come, Now Is the Time to Worship." VIN.

● Doerksen, Brian. "Refiner's Fire." VIN.

● Evans, Darrell. "Let the River Flow." VIN/INT.

● Park, Andy. "The River Is Here." Mercy/VIN.

● Wimber, John. "Spirit Song." Mercy/VIN. W&P 130.

Global

Lim, Swee Hong. "May the Love of the Lord" from *Agape: Songs of Hope and Reconciliation.* U, gtr. Lutheran World Federation. AFP 9780191000133.

Rockson, Caroline. "Nyame ne Sunsum, sian brao!/O Holy Spirit, Come Down" from *Agape: Songs of Hope and Reconciliation.* U, gtr. Lutheran World Federation. AFP 9780191000133.

Tuesday, June 14

Basil the Great, Bishop of Caesarea, died 379; Gregory, Bishop of Nyssa, died around 385; Gregory of Nazianzus, Bishop of Constantinople, died around 389; Macrina, teacher, died around 379

The three men in this group are known as the Cappadocian fathers; all three explored the mystery of the Holy Trinity. Basil was influenced by his sister Macrina to live a monastic life, and he settled near the family estate in Caesarea. Basil's Longer Rule and Shorter Rule for monastic life are the basis for Eastern monasticism to this day, and express a preference for communal monastic life over that of hermits. Gregory of Nazianzus (nah-zee-AN-zus) was sent to preach on behalf of the Orthodox faith against the Arians in Constantinople, though the Orthodox did not have a church there at the time. He defended Orthodox trinitarian and Christological doctrine, and his preaching won over the city. Gregory of Nyssa (NISS-uh) was the younger brother of Basil the Great. He is remembered as a writer on spiritual life and the contemplation of God in worship and sacraments.

Macrina (muh-CREE-nuh) was the older sister of Basil and Gregory of Nyssa. She received an excellent education centered on the Bible, and when her fiancé died she devoted herself to the pursuit of Christian perfection. She was a leader of a community, based at the family estate, dedicated to asceticism, meditation, and prayer. Macrina's teaching was influential within the early church.

o denotes suggestions that relate to the hymn of the day.
● denotes songs that are available on iTunes®.

TIME AFTER PENTECOST

SUMMER

SUMMER   AUTUMN   NOVEMBER

PREPARING FOR SUMMER

Plain Old Lectionary

The Revised Common Lectionary for the Time after Pentecost includes a complementary lectionary series and a semicontinuous lectionary series. The complementary series provides Old Testament readings and psalms chosen for their relationship to the gospels. The semicontinuous series provides Old Testament readings and psalms that, while not as explicitly connected to the gospels, explore many of the books and stories not covered by the complementary series. *Evangelical Lutheran Worship* indicates in its introduction to the two series that "the goals of the lectionary are best realized when one series or the other is used consistently throughout the Time after Pentecost" (p. 37).

If worship leaders intend to follow this advice, they will need to decide relatively early whether to make use of the semicontinuous or complementary series. Some congregations may find that a preaching series on the semicontinuous series will attract worshipers, especially if sermons and worship are designed to draw out the dominant theme of the series.

That being said, the shared text for both series is the gospel reading for the day. For these summer months, the gospel readings offer a leisurely stroll through Matthew 10–16. This is an amazing series of texts. This summer gospel series offers in miniature a close summary of Jesus' earthly ministry. This includes comforting, prophetic words and instructions on how to receive the prophets (Matt. 10:40-42; 11:16-19, 25-30), a cluster of parables (chap. 13), three miracles (feeding the five thousand, walking on water, and the healing of a Canaanite woman), and finally, a doctrinal statement of who Christ is, first on the lips of Peter (Matt. 16:13-20), and then from Christ himself (Matt. 16:21-28).

These gospel readings offer a clear arc for preaching through the summer. Begin by preaching on the overall reception of the prophets and the reception of Jesus' ministry. Continue with the most enigmatic, and yet crystal clear, visions of that prophetic ministry, his parables. Third, proclaim Christ in his miracles. Finally, like Peter, confess Jesus as Lord, and then confess what it means that Jesus is Lord: "He must go to Jerusalem and undergo great suffering at the hands of the elders and chief priests and scribes, and be killed, and on the third day be raised" (Matt. 16:21).

Finally, congregations that do not currently encourage a daily Bible reading schedule may consider drawing attention to the daily lectionary published in *Evangelical Lutheran Worship*, pp. 1121–1153. This daily lectionary is closely related to the Sunday lectionary. "The readings are chosen so that the days leading up to Sunday (Thursday through Saturday) prepare for the Sunday readings. The days flowing out from Sunday (Monday through Wednesday) reflect upon the Sunday readings" (p. 1121). Another excellent resource for encouraging Bible reading during the summer is the ninety-day Bible reading challenge, http://www.biblein90days.com.

Summer Splendor

Let the gospel readings from Matthew 10–16 guide decisions regarding worship space and environment during these summer months. Specifically, find ways to illustrate through art, space, lighting, and décor these themes:

1. Jesus as prophet
2. Giving a cup of cold water to little ones
3. Christ's yoke is light, and easy to bear
4. Sowing seed
5. Harvesting weeds and wheat
6. Tree–yeast–pearl
7. Feeding the five thousand
8. Jesus silencing the storm
9. Healing of the Canaanite woman
10. Peter confessing Jesus as Lord
11. Jesus proclaiming his message of sacrificial love

Ambitious worship planners might consider creating a triptych or diorama of these events and parables, or even a series of stations, banners, or paintings illustrating these luminous moments in Christ's earthly ministry. Other congregations hoping to illustrate these moments, but without resources to create major displays, might utilize found objects and spread them around the worship space—move a painting of Jesus from the Sunday school to the sanctuary, fill the baptismal bowl and then place a full cup of clear water in a clear cup next to it, place bags of seed on tables, or stalks of wheat in the narthex. As an alternative, choose one simple object to illustrate the reading each Sunday, and place it stark and alone on a table in the center of the worship space or near the pulpit or reading desk.

Finally, does your worship space already illustrate any of these parables or stories in its art and architecture? If so, consider drawing attention to that in the bulletin and in preaching. Often the static worship space, like background music, fades from our attention. If specific gospel readings are illustrated in a stained glass window or wall painting, now is the chance to draw attention to, and celebrate, those artistic creations.

A sometimes more difficult task is to consider the actual reordering of the worship space itself to match the season. If congregations do indeed experience reduced attendance in the summer months, for example, are there ways to bracket off some pews or chairs to encourage the assembly to be seated more closely together? Might the summer Sundays also be a chance to worship out of doors, in a park, on the church grounds, or even at a community center, fair, or farm? Have you ever gathered a group spontaneously to worship in the middle of a storm? Summer is a tremendous opportunity to take the church (the people of God) out of the building and into the community as public sign and witness to God's in-breaking kingdom, manifested in free worship and praise.

The Fourth of What?

Many congregations wrestle with the issue of national flags and what to do with them, where to place them. This has become a contentious issue in some congregations, and we are called to walk carefully with those who might be offended either by the removal of flags from the worship space or too prominent display of them.

Nevertheless, as the summer flows into the Fourth of July season, congregations are remiss not to recognize a moment in civic life when the church has an opportunity to preach the gospel in relation to culture, and specifically in relation to patriotism. How are Christians appropriately patriotic? *Evangelical Lutheran Worship* includes a section of National Songs. Clearly the church has a long history of needing to find ways to celebrate God's gift of ordering our common life together as a nation, while not elevating the nation to an inappropriate level over against the other nations of the world, nations also called and blessed by God.

An especially appropriate and theologically rich hymn to sing on or around national holidays is "This is my song" (ELW 887). This hymn celebrates the appropriate joy worshipers have in living in a nation they cherish and give thanks for, while recognizing that God blesses other nations

as well. The hymn concludes with a stanza situating all of these national sentiments within the more lofty view of God's coming kingdom: "This is my prayer, O God of all earth's kingdoms, your kingdom come; on earth your will be done."

In the United States, if your congregation offers special Independence Day observances, take the opportunity as worship leader and preacher to situate the spirit of that holiday within the larger purview of God's salvific work and ordering of all the nations. Take the time, for example, to do a simple study of Romans 13, where Paul proclaims that "those authorities that exist have been instituted by God" (13:1). It would also be appropriate to celebrate other commemorations and feast days during the summer months, maybe especially the Presentation of the Augsburg Confession (June 25), an event many consider the independence day for Lutherans; Bartolomé de Las Casas, missionary to the Indies (July 17), who was the first to expose the oppression of the native peoples of the West Indies and Central America by the Europeans; or Augustine, Bishop of Hippo (Aug. 28), whose *City of God* is one of the earliest and most powerful expressions of a political vision for the ideal Christian society.

Assembly Song

Using a cantor to sing the psalm with the assembly joining in on the refrain can be a wonderful way to employ "special music" during the summer when choirs are generally on hiatus. Singing the psalm in its fullness (rather than eliminating it or speaking it) can be a way to keep music going during summer worship, especially if singing the psalm is not the assembly's usual practice. And it's a great way to involve singers in leading the assembly as cantor (honing worship leadership skills) while working around vacation schedules and decreased attendance. *Psalm Settings for the Church Year* (2 volumes, Augsburg Fortress, 2008) has tons of material for assembly singing of the psalms with cantor and assembly. Many different composers and musical styles are represented in this resource.

How accessible are your congregational song habits? Who selects hymns? Do they take into account issues of familiarity, singability, and appropriateness for the setting and instrumentation? How is the sound system working? Anything need to be fixed, updated, or improved? If summer is a time when worship leaders have a bit more time (fewer rehearsals), maybe it is a good time to practice portions of hymns and liturgy that introduce the music, and conclude it. How well does the organist or pianist *support* the assembly in their singing? Two books by church musician Paul Westermeyer are excellent resources for reviewing these practices: *The Church Musician* and *Te Deum: The Church and Music* (both available from Augsburg Fortress).

Summer Travels

Have you heard this humorous dialogue? Congregation member: "We take summer off from worship to get away to the cabin." Pastor: "That's okay; God doesn't care about you during the summer either." One unfortunate habit in many of our churches is reduction in worship participation. This lower attendance is often attributed to vacations. Is lower summer attendance really something we simply want to accommodate ourselves to?

When our members are on vacation, they could be worshiping at churches in the places where they vacation. Conversely, families and individuals visiting the area in which your church is situated may be able to worship with you for a week, if they can find you and easily discover worship times and feel welcome. No matter what time of year it is, Christians are called to honor the sabbath, and the sabbath happens weekly. Dispel the myth that lighter summer attendance is acceptable. Consider some of the following ideas to encourage worship attendance by your members while they travel, or to attract visitors to your church in the summer months.

- Design a "_____ was here" poster with the name of your church in the blank. Publish this poster in your church newsletter, and encourage members to take the poster on vacation, and take a photo of themselves in front of churches they visit while on vacation. Publish these photos in a church newsletter.
- Publicize the ELCA or ELCIC Web site (as appropriate) and the "Find a Congregation" tool there, so members can locate churches at which to worship during their travels.
- Advertise your congregation in the appropriate locations for your geographical area. Stop in and visit with directors of camping sites, hotels, and other travel destinations. Set up a special banner outside the church that reads: "Travelers Welcome" or "Visitors Welcome." Review all signs directing visitors into the sanctuary and through your building. Organize a summer accessibility committee to make sure your church is accessible for those with special needs.

Seasonal Checklist

- If the summer worship schedule changes, notify local newspapers, update your Web site, and change listings on exterior signs and church answering machines.
- If your space is not air conditioned, consider ways to help worshipers stay cool during warm weather.
- Respectfully review how and where a national flag is displayed in the worship space or on church property. For guidance, read http://www.elca.org/Growing-In-Faith/Worship/Learning-Center/FAQs/Flags.aspx.
- If outdoor services are held, make sure that the details for the service are covered thoroughly. Do a mental or actual walk-through or rehearsal of the whole service to confirm what needs to be brought to the outdoor site.
- Omit the Kyrie (except on the festival of Holy Trinity).
- Use the Nicene Creed for Holy Trinity; use the Apostles' Creed for remaining Sundays in this season.
- Use the blessing and sending for mission in the seasonal rites section (p. 210) for groups participating in congregational mission trips, youth gatherings, etc.
- Use the farewell and godspeed in the seasonal rites section (p. 211) when people are transferring out of the congregation or moving to a new community, or to bid farewell to graduates leaving for college, other study, or other opportunities.
- Use the Father's Day blessing in the seasonal rites section (p. 213).

WORSHIP TEXTS FOR SUMMER

Confession and Forgiveness

All may make the sign of the cross, the sign marked at baptism, as the presiding minister begins.

Blessed be the holy Trinity, ✚ one God,
the sower, the seed, the fruit;
our lifeboat, our treasure, our leaven.
Blessed be God forever.
Amen.

Let us confess our sin
in the presence of God and of one another.

Silence is kept for reflection.

God of heaven and earth,
we name before you the sin that enslaves us,
the sin that wounds us and others,
the sin that scars our world.
Forgive us and heal us.
Guard us from all evil.
Give to us and the whole creation
the freedom of the glory of the children of God.
Amen.

Come, all who are weary,
all who carry heavy burdens.
As tender as parent to child,
so gentle is God to us.
As high as heaven is above earth,
so vast is God's love for us.
As far as east is from west,
so far God removes our sin,
renewing our lives in ✚ Jesus Christ.
Amen.

Greeting

The grace of our Lord Jesus Christ,
the love of God from which nothing can separate us,
and the life-giving Holy Spirit be with you all.
And also with you.

Offering Prayer

God of mercy and grace,
the eyes of all wait upon you,
and you open your hand in blessing.
Fill us with good things at your table,
that we may come to the help of all in need,
through Jesus Christ, our redeemer and Lord.
Amen.

Invitation to Communion

Come to the table prepared before you.
Taste of God's goodness and mercy.

Prayer after Communion

Generous God,
we give you thanks that again this day
you have opened wide your hand
and satisfied us with the food of life,
the body and blood of Christ.
Sharing your compassionate heart,
may we be blessed and given
to all who hunger and thirst;
through Jesus Christ, our Savior and Lord.
Amen.

Sending of Communion

O God of tender compassion,
as you healed the sick and welcomed the stranger,
bless those who leave this assembly
to share the gifts of this table
with our sisters and brothers
who are *sick/homebound/imprisoned.*
May they be sustained by the love and prayers
of this community,
and by the Bread of life that satisfies all hunger,
Jesus Christ our Lord.
Amen.

Blessing

God all mighty,
God most merciful
bless us, keep us, and ☩ grant us peace.
Amen.

Dismissal

Go in peace. Serve the Lord.
Thanks be to God.

Blessing and Sending for Mission

This order is intended for use when material resources or people are being sent forth from the assembly as a tangible expression of the baptismal call to share in Christ's mission to all the world.

This order may precede the blessing and the dismissal in a congregation's primary service, or it may be adapted to be used independently.

The leader addresses the assembly, adapting these words to the occasion.

Friends in Christ: Today we give thanks to God and seek God's blessing as we send *these* _____ to *description of destination and purpose*.

Let us pray.
Blessed are you, O Lord our God, ruler of the universe.
You made the whole earth for your glory;
all creation praises you.
We lift our voices to join the songs of heaven and earth
in thanksgiving for the many blessings you have given us.

Renew in us the commitment
to use our gifts in the service of others,
and especially of those in need.
Let us be your hands to feed the hungry,
shelter the homeless,
clothe the naked, comfort the weary and outcast,
welcome the stranger, care for creation,
and be loving neighbors to all people.

The leader continues with one or more of the following petitions, adapting as appropriate.

Sending of people

Bless those who go out from here to labor *in/at* _____.
Prosper the work of their hands.
Bless those who receive [them and] the fruits of their labor,
and may those who are sent receive blessing in return.
May the gifts they use and share
be signs of your love to all people.

Food, sustenance

Bless these _____.
May those who receive them be nourished and strengthened,
and may these gifts be a sign of your love to all people.

Medical and personal-care supplies

Bless these _____.
May those who receive them be cared for and healed,
and may these gifts be a sign of your love to all people.

Clothing, quilts

Bless these _____.
May those who receive them find dignity in their use and comfort in their warmth,
and may these gifts be a sign of your love to all people.

The prayer concludes:
To you, O God,
be glory and honor through your Son, Jesus Christ,
in the unity of the Holy Spirit,
in your church and in the world, now and forever.
Amen.

The service concludes with the blessing and the dismissal.

From *Evangelical Lutheran Worship Occasional Services for the Assembly* (Augsburg Fortress, 2009).

Farewell and Godspeed

Farewell and Godspeed is an affirmation of the corporate nature of the baptismal faith, for use when people leave a congregation. It may be adapted for use when people leave a field of service in another organization or institution. When set within Holy Communion or the Service of the Word, this order is used following the prayers of intercession or before the blessing.

A representative of the congregation comes forward with those who are leaving the congregation and addresses the assembly.
Name/s, as you leave our *congregation,* we wish to bid you farewell.

One of the following or another appropriate scripture passage may be read.
Exodus 23:20
Isaiah 43:1-3
John 8:12

Brief comments about those who are leaving and their life in the congregation may follow.

The presiding minister continues with these words, or with similar words appropriate to the person/s and the circumstances.
[In holy baptism our Lord Jesus Christ received you and made you *members* of his church.] When you came to *this congregation* we rejoiced to welcome you into the mission we share as the people of God. In this community you have come to know and to share in God's loving purpose for you and for all creation. God has blessed you in this community, and God has blessed us through you.

The presiding minister may continue, as appropriate.
We encourage you to continue to receive and share God's gifts in *name of new congregation or location,* united with us in the body of Christ and the mission we share.

One of the following or another appropriate prayer is said.
Let us pray.
Eternal God, we thank you for *name/s*
and for the time we have shared with *them.*
As *they have* been a blessing to us,
so now send *them* forth to be a blessing to others;
through Jesus Christ, our Savior and Lord.
Amen.

or
Gracious God,
we thank you for the work and witness
of your *servant/s name/s,*
who *have* enriched this *congregation*
and shared *their* gifts with *their colleagues/friends/family.*
Now bless and preserve *them* at this time of transition.
Day by day, guide *them* and give *them* what is needed,
friends to cheer *their* way,
and a clear vision of that to which you are now calling *them.*
By your Holy Spirit be present in *their* pilgrimage,
that *they* may travel with the one who is the way, the truth, and the life, Jesus Christ our Lord.
Amen.

The service continues with the greeting of peace or with the blessing.

NOTES ON THE SERVICE

The first sentence in the address to those departing may be omitted if one or more persons among those departing are not baptized.

Departure from a community may occur in difficult circumstances, such as in connection with broken relationships. Pastoral assessment of the situation may suggest the use of other prayers or rites, such as individual or corporate confession and forgiveness, instead of or in addition to Farewell and Godspeed.

From Evangelical Lutheran Worship Occasional Services for the Assembly (Augsburg Fortress, 2009).

Blessing of Bicycles

A reading from the prophet Ezekiel: When the living creatures moved, the wheels moved beside them; and when the living creatures rose from the earth, the wheels rose. Wherever the spirit would go, they went, and the wheels rose along with them; for the spirit of the living creatures was in the wheels. When they moved, the others moved; when they stopped, the others stopped; and when they rose from the earth, the wheels rose along with them; for the spirit of the living creatures was in the wheels. *(Ezek. 1:19-21)*

Holy wisdom, holy word.
Thanks be to God.

Let us pray.
Present in a world groaning under the excesses of consumption, we acknowledge the inherent goodness of nonmotorized, human-powered transportation and give thanks for the simple beauty of the bicycle. God of life,
hear our prayer.
Present in a community filled with children, we pray for those learning to ride. Keep them smart, safe, and visible on their neighborhood roads. God of life,
hear our prayer.
Present in a community filled with strife, we pray for the victims of road rage and bike theft. We ask for the strength to forgive people who behave in unkind ways. God of life,
hear our prayer.
Present in a world of work, we pray for those who build, repair, and clean our bikes and those who rely on bicycles to earn their living. Bless those who choose not drive to work and those for whom driving isn't even an option. God of life,
hear our prayer.
Present in a community of beautiful diversity, we ask your protection and blessing on all who ride: recreational riders, athletes, homeless folks, students, children, eco-warriors, bike messengers, and all the others who take to the streets, bike paths, parks, and mountains. Keep us safe as we ride. God of life,
hear our prayer.

Let us remember all those who have died while riding *(especially).*
A brief silence.
God of life,
Hear our prayer.

May the road rise to meet you.
May the wind be ever at your back.
May all your journeying be joyous.
And until we meet again, may God hold you and your bicycles in the palm of God's hand.

Go in peace and safety.
Amen.

Blessing of Bicycles and Other Wheeled Things

This seasonal blessing may be used at the sending, before the dismissal, if you will be gathering around bicycles/scooters/rollerblades outdoors or someplace other than the worship space. Another option would be to use it during the children's sermon, with equipment that people have brought that relates to biking or other wheeled activities: water bottles, toe clips, helmets, bike locks, reflective clothing, knee or elbow pads, etc.

The presiding minister, assisting minister, members of the youth group, or active cyclists in the congregation could lead different components of the litany and the prayer.

We give you thanks for warm weather
and time to play in your delightful creation.
**You are with us on our way to work, to the pool,
around the neighborhood, and across town.**
We give you thanks for wheels that are fast
and helmets that protect.
**You are with us in the whoosh of the wind
and the pop of the wheel.**
We give you thanks for friends and companions as we ride.
**You are with us in our laughter,
in our races, and in our friendships.**

God of play and transport,
We are thrilled to be able to experience your world
from the seat of our motorcycles and bicycles,
from our skateboards and scooters and rollerblades.

Keep those who ride mindful of cars and animals,
rocks on the trails, and rounding corners.
Keep those who drive aware of speedy bicycles,
new riders wavering in their steadiness,
and the tenderness of training wheels.

Bless these wheels
that they would move us from place to place safely.
Bless the helmets that we wear
that they would protect us if we fall
and be a sign to those around us that we value the life you
have given us.

Be the wind at our back and the strength to push up a hill.
Grant us safe travel throughout our days
and guide us safely home each night.
In Jesus' name we pray.
Amen.

Blessing of Fathers

God of all creation,
pour out your blessing on all fathers
and those who provide fatherly care.
You have made them in your image
and given them children to love and care for in your name.
Bless them with a heart like your heart:
discerning and thoughtful, bold and decisive,
compassionate and loving.
As they model for their children
the life that is lived by faith and not by sight,
grant them courage under pressure
and confidence in your power.
When troubles threaten to overwhelm them,
grant them your coping calm.
When doubts give rise to anxiety,
shore up their trust in your promises.
When joy fills their days,
grant them a keen gratitude for your abundant supply of grace.
Season them with a lively sense of humor, Lord,
for it will make life richer for us all.
In all circumstances preserve them as your own.
We ask this in Jesus' name.
Amen.

June 19, 2011
The Holy Trinity
First Sunday after Pentecost

Though the word trinity is not found in the scriptures, today's second reading includes the apostolic greeting that begins the liturgy: The grace of our Lord Jesus Christ, the love of God, and the communion of the Holy Spirit be with you all. In the gospel Jesus sends his disciples forth to baptize in the name of the Father, and the Son, and the Holy Spirit. More than a doctrine, the Trinity expresses the heart of our faith: we have experienced the God of creation made known in Jesus Christ and with us always through the Holy Spirit. We celebrate the mystery of the Holy Trinity in word and sacrament, as we profess the creed, and as we are sent into the world to bear witness to our faith.

Prayer of the Day

Almighty Creator and ever-living God: we worship your glory, eternal Three-in-One, and we praise your power, majestic One-in-Three. Keep us steadfast in this faith, defend us in all adversity, and bring us at last into your presence, where you live in endless joy and love, Father, Son, and Holy Spirit, one God, now and forever.

or

God of heaven and earth, before the foundation of the universe and the beginning of time you are the triune God: Author of creation, eternal Word of salvation, life-giving Spirit of wisdom. Guide us to all truth by your Spirit, that we may proclaim all that Christ has revealed and rejoice in the glory he shares with us. Glory and praise to you, Father, Son, and Holy Spirit, now and forever.

Gospel Acclamation

Alleluia. Holy, holy, holy is the | Lᴏʀᴅ of hosts;* God's glory fills | the whole earth. *Alleluia.* (Isa. 6:3)

Readings and Psalm

Genesis 1:1—2:4a

This first creation story reached its current form during the crisis of the Babylonian exile of the people of Israel. God, not their captors' god Marduk, was responsible for their existence. God created women and men as rulers over creation, to preserve and protect it. God also rested on the seventh day, hallowing that day forever as the Sabbath.

Psalm 8

How majestic is your name in all the earth! (Ps. 8:1)

2 Corinthians 13:11-13

Paul closes a challenging letter to the Corinthians with an appeal to Christian fellowship grounded in the triune harmony of Christ's grace, God's love, the Spirit's partnership.

Matthew 28:16-20

After his resurrection, Jesus summons his remaining disciples and commissions them to baptize and teach all nations in the name of Father, Son, and Holy Spirit.

Preface   Holy Trinity

Color   White

Prayers of Intercession

The prayers are prepared locally for each occasion. The following examples may be adapted or used as appropriate.

Led by the Holy Spirit, and with the whole people of God in Christ Jesus, let us pray for the church, those in need, and all of God's creation.

A brief silence.

Embolden your church to reach out to the ends of the earth that all may become your disciples. Bless the ministry of all the baptized, that they may speak boldly of your love. Hear us, O God.

Your mercy is great.

Enrich your creation and bless all who tend the land. Teach us to be good stewards of all you have given us so that your abundance can be shared with others. Hear us, O God.

Your mercy is great.

Empower the leaders of all nations to lead with an authority guided by your wisdom and mercy. Bring peace to areas of the world where there is conflict (*especially*), that there may be harmony. Hear us, O God.

Your mercy is great.

Embrace all who are suffering: those who are hungry, poor, homeless, oppressed, or ill (*especially*). In every situation help them to know you are with them always. Hear us, O God.

Your mercy is great.

Enable this congregation to support all families. Strengthen fathers and all who nurture, that they may guide with wisdom, gentleness, and grace. Hear us, O God.

Your mercy is great.

Here other intercessions may be offered.

Encourage us in our faith until that day when we will join all the saints in your eternal presence and glory. Hear us, O God.

Your mercy is great.

Into your hands, O God, we commend ourselves and all for whom we pray, trusting in your abundant mercy, through Jesus Christ, our Savior and Lord.

Amen.

Ideas and Images for the Day

The festival of the Holy Trinity celebrates the wonder of relationship with God while leaving us distinct dissatisfaction with our limited understanding of what God is. While guarding against the idolatry of language, we survey our scripture, doctrine, creeds, and symbols of our heritage. Equally important, we pray for God to inspire fresh, innovative ideas of God in the present moment. Today's gospel contains one of the few biblical references to the trinitarian formula. As the eleven are commissioned to make disciples, baptize, and teach, we are invited to consider our calling to influence the world with the good news of God's love.

1. Language is the primary way many adults both understand and limit God. Abandoning the dependence on the spoken word is a great gift of our children. Allow them to lead the way this Sunday. With large pieces of paper on the walls of the worship space, welcome the crayon pictures of your youngest faithful. This can be done either prior to the service, as part of education time, or during worship in the offering, prayers, even the sermon time.

2. For the prayer of the day, make naming God the central prayer, allowing the scriptural diversity of images to challenge and inspire the assembly. Create a script for a variety of voices. Suggestions: rock, judge, shepherd, bread, warrior, home, and song. Images for the presence of God include wind, water, fire, foreigner, mother, father, child, and community. Biblical settings to acknowledge the presence of God include: the wilderness and in the city, in the desert and the thriving garden, in seasons of both doubt and trust, grief and celebration.

3. In the Old Testament, the Holy One of Israel is referred to as *YHWH*, the Tetragrammaton. As the Ten Commandments forbid God's name to be spoken in vain, Yahwists, and later the people of Israel, held God's sacred name unspeakable. Though most Christian Bibles render the name "Lord," many Jewish people today do not pronounce the name of God. What would it be like to so revere the holy presence of God that we chose to never speak God's name?

4. Sandy Eisenberg Sasso's book *In God's Name* is designed for children and unfolds a story exploring how people come to image God (Woodstock, VT: Jewish Lights Publishing, 1994).

5. Setting aside for a time Luther's explanation of the articles of the Creed, we can express the doctrine of the Holy Trinity in a narrative fashion. Consider that most people experience the divine in at least three dimensions: God transcendent beyond our ken, that part of the divine which is eternally a great mystery (the first person); God enfleshed in our neighbor in the fellowship of Jesus Christ (the second person); and God mystically within us, the gift of enlightenment by the Holy Spirit (the third person).

Hymns for Worship
Gathering

Holy, holy, holy, Lord God Almighty!   ELW 413, LBW 165
Rise, shine, you people!   ELW 665, LBW 393
Come, thou almighty King   ELW 408, LBW 522

Hymn of the Day

Lord, you give the great commission   ELW 579, WOV 756
   ABBOT'S LEIGH
Come, join the dance of Trinity   ELW 412   KINGSFOLD
Creator Spirit, heavenly dove   ELW 577   VENI CREATOR SPIRITUS
   ELW 578, LBW 284   KOMM, GOTT SCHÖPFER

Offering

Come, all you people   ELW 819, WOV 717
Now the silence   ELW 460, LBW 205

Communion

Creating God, your fingers trace   ELW 684, WOV 757
Mothering God, you gave me birth   ELW 735, WOV 769
When long before time   ELW 861, WOV 799

Sending

Holy God, we praise your name   ELW 414, LBW 535
Father most holy   ELW 415, LBW 169

Additional Hymns and Songs

O threefold God of tender unity   WLP 743
God is One, unique and holy   HS91 753
Holy, holy   W&P 60

Music for the Day
Psalmody and Acclamations

Makeever, Ray. "Who Are We (Psalm 8)" from *Dancing at the Harvest*.
Miller, Aaron David. *Gospel Acclamations for Lent–Holy Trinity*.
Mummert, Mark. "Psalm 8," Refrain 1, from PSCY.
Shute, Linda Cable. "Psalm 8" from PWA, Evangelical Lutheran Worship Edition.

Choral

Burkhardt, Michael. "Creating God, Your Fingers Trace." 2 pt, org. opt C inst, hb, cello. AFP 9780800664206.
○ Hopp, Roy. "Come, Join the Dance of Trinity." SATB, kybd. AFP 9780800678296.
Ives, Grayston. "Listen, Sweet Dove." SATB, org. GIA G-4209.
Powell, Rosephayne. "The Word Was God." SATB, div. Gentry Publications (HAL) JG2323.
Sleeth, Natalie. "Go Into The World." 3 pt (trbl or mxd), kybd. CG CGA-209.

Children's Choir

Cool, Jayne Southwick. "I'm a Disciple, Too!" U/2 pt, kybd. AFP 9780800674571.
Helgen, John. "Psalm 8" from *ChildrenSing Psalms*. U, kybd. AFP 9780800663872.
Kemp, Helen. "God's Great Lights." U, kybd, opt assembly. CPH

Keyboard / Instrumental

○ Cherwien, David. "Kingsfold" from *Organ Plus,* vol. 2. Org, inst. AFP 9780800678548.
○ Larsen, Libby. "Veni Creator Spiritus" from *A New Liturgical Year*. Org. AFP 9780800656712.
○ Organ, Anne Krentz. "Kingsfold" from *Woven Together*, vol. 2. Pno, inst. AFP 9780800677664.
○ Peeters, Flor. "Veni Creator Spiritus" from *Augsburg Organ Library: Easter*. Org. AFP 9780800659363.

Handbell

○ Moklebust, Cathy, "God Is Here!" from *Hymn Stanzas for Handbells*." 2-3 oct, L3. AFP 9780800657338.
○ Wagner, Dean. "Fantasy on Kingsfold." 3-5 oct, L2+. HOP 2134.
Watanabe, Kiyo. "Holy, Holy, Holy." 3-5 oct, L2. GIA G-7449.

Praise Ensemble

- Adkins, Donna. "Glorify Thy Name." MAR. W&P 42.
- Coelho, Terry. "Father, I Adore You." MAR. W&P 37.
- Crowder, David. "O Praise Him." WT/Sixsteps Music.
- Howard, Adrian/Pat Turner. "Salvation Belongs to Our God." Restoration Music.
- Smith, Michael W. "Great Is the Lord." Meadowgreen Music. W&P 53.
- Tomlin, Chris/Jesse Reeves/Ed Cash. "How Great Is Our God." WT/Sixsteps Music.

Global

Bayiga, Bayiga. "O Saint Esprit, viens sur nous/Spirit of God, Visit Us" from *Agape: Songs of Hope and Reconciliation*. U, gtr. Lutheran World Federation. AFP 9780191000133.
Loh, I-to, arr. "For the Beauty of the Earth" from *Sound the Bamboo*. U. GIA G-6830.

Tuesday, June 21
Onesimos Nesib, translator, evangelist, died 1931

Onesimos (oh-NESS-ee-mus neh-SEEB) was born into the Oromo people of Ethiopia. He was captured by slave traders and taken from his homeland to Eritrea, where he was bought, freed, and educated by Swedish missionaries. He translated the Bible into Oromo and returned to his homeland to preach the gospel. His tombstone includes a verse from Jeremiah 22:29, "O land, land, land, hear the word of the Lord!"

Friday, June 24
John the Baptist

The birth and life of John the Baptist is celebrated exactly six months before Christmas Eve. For Christians in the Northern Hemisphere, these two dates are deeply symbolic. John said that he must decrease as Jesus increased. According to tradition, John was born as the days are longest and then steadily decrease, while Jesus was born as the days are shortest and then steadily increase. In many countries this day is celebrated with customs associated with the summer solstice.

○ denotes suggestions that relate to the hymn of the day.
● denotes songs that are available on iTunes®.

216

Saturday, June 25

Philipp Melanchthon, renewer of the church, died 1560

Though he died on April 19, Philipp Melanchthon (meh-LAHNK-ton) is commemorated today because of his connection with the Augsburg Confession. Colleague and co-reformer with Martin Luther, Melanchthon was a brilliant scholar, known as "the teacher of Germany." The University of Wittenberg hired him as its first professor of Greek, and there he became a friend of Luther. Melanchthon was a popular professor—even his classes at six in the morning had as many as six hundred students. As a reformer he was known for his conciliatory spirit and for finding areas of agreement with fellow Christians. He was never ordained.

Presentation of the Augsburg Confession, 1530

On this day in 1530 the German and Latin editions of the Augsburg Confession were presented to Emperor Charles of the Holy Roman Empire. The Augsburg Confession was written by Philipp Melanchthon and endorsed by Martin Luther and consists of a brief summary of points in which the reformers saw their teaching as either agreeing with or differing from that of the Roman Catholic Church of the time. In 1580 when the *Book of Concord* was drawn up, the unaltered Augsburg Confession was included as the principal Lutheran confession.

June 26, 2011
Time after Pentecost — Lectionary 13

The welcome of baptism is for all God's children. This baptismal gift sets us free from the power of sin and death. In today's gospel, Christ promises that the disciple who gives a cup of cold water to the little ones serves Christ himself. From worship we are sent on our baptismal mission: to serve the little ones of this world and to be a sign of God's merciful welcome.

Prayer of the Day

O God, you direct our lives by your grace, and your words of justice and mercy reshape the world. Mold us into a people who welcome your word and serve one another, through Jesus Christ, our Savior and Lord.

Gospel Acclamation

Alleluia. You are a chosen race, a royal priesthood, a ᴵ holy nation,* in order that you may proclaim the mighty acts of the one who called you out of darkness into his ᴵ marvelous light. *Alleluia.* (1 Peter 2:9)

Readings and Psalm

Jeremiah 28:5-9

Through a symbolic action, Jeremiah insisted that Judah and all the surrounding nations should submit to the king of Babylon. Hananiah contradicted Jeremiah, who in reply insisted that Hananiah's rosy prediction should not be believed until it came true. God confirmed the word of Jeremiah and sentenced the false prophet Hananiah to death (vv. 16-17).

Psalm 89:1-4, 15-18

Your love, O Lᴏʀᴅ, forever will I sing. (Ps. 89:1)

Romans 6:12-23

Sin is an enslaving power that motivates us to live self-serving, disobedient lives. Sin's final payoff is death. We, however, have been set free from sin's slavery to live obediently under God's grace, whose end is the free gift of eternal life.

Matthew 10:40-42

When Jesus sends his disciples out as missionaries, he warns them of persecution and hardships they will face. He also promises to reward any who aid his followers and support their ministry.

Semicontinuous reading and psalm

Genesis 22:1-14

Abraham was prepared to obey God's command in the midst of extreme contradiction: the child to be sacrificed is the very child through whom Abraham is to receive descendants. God acknowledged Abraham's obedient faith, and Abraham offered a ram in the place of his son Isaac.

Psalm 13

I trust in your unfailing love, O Lord. (Ps. 13:5)

Preface   Sundays

Color   Green

Prayers of Intercession

The prayers are prepared locally for each occasion. The following examples may be adapted or used as appropriate.

Led by the Holy Spirit, and with the whole people of God in Christ Jesus, let us pray for the church, those in need, and all of God's creation.

A brief silence.

Let us pray for the church, that, having been freed from the bonds of sin and made holy in the waters of baptism, it may offer the gospel freely to all people. Hear us, O God.

Your mercy is great.

Let us pray for the world, that the earth and its creatures may be tended with care and bear fruit for all to share. Hear us, O God.

Your mercy is great.

Let us pray for the leaders of all nations, that they may be instruments of righteousness and peace in the face of injustice and conflict (*especially*). Hear us, O God.

Your mercy is great.

Let us pray for all who are held captive: to human trafficking, sweatshops, prostitution, drugs and alcohol, or any illness (*especially*), that they may know true freedom in Christ. Hear us, O God.

Your mercy is great.

Let us pray for this congregation, that all who enter our doors may experience welcome in the name of Jesus. Hear us, O God.

Your mercy is great.

Here other intercessions may be offered.

Let us give thanks for all the faithful who have been brought from death to eternal life by the grace of Christ (*especially*). Keep us in hope until the day we join them in glory. Hear us, O God.

Your mercy is great.

Into your hands, O God, we commend ourselves and all for whom we pray, trusting in your abundant mercy, through Jesus Christ, our Savior and Lord.

Amen.

Ideas and Images for the Day

The faithful life has a natural reward of embodying the gospel of Jesus Christ. Living in new life means disciples name their joys and sorrows as dimensions of the breadth and depth of Christ's story and their purpose as Christ's purpose. Following his challenging words about what it takes to be a disciple, in Matthew 10:34-39, Jesus speaks a startling word of grace—that he intends his followers to consider themselves radically identified with both himself and God (Matt. 10:40). In this way, our lives of faith have natural consequences, including a kind of reward vastly different than the world knows in paychecks and punishments.

1. Invite children to imagine they are Jesus. How would they expect to be treated? (Perhaps with royal dignity and awe, respect and devotion.) Next invite them to the mindset that when they come across any person (teacher, parent, fellow student) they are meeting Jesus. When they encounter Jesus, how do they treat him? What would the world be like if everyone treated everyone else as Jesus, and if everyone saw themselves as Christ's love embodied?

2. Jesus' words of identification in the gospel connect us to Genesis 1:27—that we are created in the image of God's holiness. There is an ancient story in Midrash that says each person has a band of angels going before him or her proclaiming, "Make way! Make way! Here comes an image of God!" (Dennis G. Shulman, *The Genius of Genesis* [Lincoln, NE: iUniverse Books, 2003], pp. 28–29). The song "Make Way," by The River's Voice (*Pilgrims to a New World*, 2009), may be used as a meditation as part of the sermon. Listen at http://www.riversvoice.com/index.php?page=cds.

3. A few weeks prior, poll the congregation with this written query in a bulletin insert: "What's the point of being a Christian?" In the sermon, affirm the wide range of responses people gave, with an emphasis on the words in today's gospel, that we are invited into a life connected with Christ's purpose.

4. Bob Dylan's song "Gotta Serve Somebody" (from the album *Slow Train Coming*, Columbia Records, 1979) points to the natural law of life that Paul refers to as he addresses the church in Rome (Romans 6). "It may be the devil, or it may be the Lord, but you're gonna have to serve somebody." Listen at http://www.bobdylan.com/#/songs/gotta-serve-somebody.

5. Is it surprising that one of the marks of faithfulness would be simple hospitality? Beyond an external sign of discipleship, offering a cup of cold water (Matt. 10:42) or visiting a prisoner (Matt. 25:36) is directly serving the Holy One of creation. Matters of faith are often best met not with intellect but imagination. In worship, the Holy Spirit shapes our imaginations, opening them to Christ's presence in every moment. The result is a community of people who are prepared to see Christ in their neighborhood and ready to respond *as* Christ to the cries of need they hear.

Hymns for Worship
Gathering
Oh, praise the gracious power   ELW 651, WOV 750
God is here!   ELW 526, WOV 719
Let us go now to the banquet   ELW 523, LCC 410

Hymn of the Day
Let us ever walk with Jesus   ELW 802, LBW 487
LASSET UNS MIT JESU ZIEHEN
All Are Welcome   ELW 641   TWO OAKS
Lord, speak to us, that we may speak   ELW 676, LBW 403
CANONBURY

Offering
As we gather at your table   ELW 522
We give thee but thine own   ELW 686, LBW 410

Communion
Lord, whose love in humble service   ELW 712, LBW 423
Strengthen for service, Lord   ELW 497, LBW 218
All who love and serve your city   ELW 724, LBW 436

Sending
The church of Christ, in every age   ELW 729, LBW 433
To be your presence   ELW 546

Additional Hymns and Songs
God without and within   SCR 70
What have we to offer?   W&P 156

Music for the Day
Psalmody and Acclamations
Haugen, Marty. "Psalm 13" from PSCY.
Krentz, Michael. "Psalm 89:1-4, 15-18" and "Psalm 13" from PWA, Evangelical Lutheran Worship Edition.
Pavlechko, Thomas. "Psalm 89:1-4, 15-18" from PSCY.
Wold, Wayne L. *Gospel Acclamations for Summer.*

Choral
Beethoven, Ludwig van/ed. K. Lee Scott. "Prayer" from *Rejoice Now My Spirit.* MH solo, kybd. AFP 9780800651084.
Handel, G. F. "Oh Death, Where Is Thy Sting?" from *Messiah.* AT duet, kybd. Various editions.
o Manz, Paul. "Let Us Ever Walk With Jesus." U, org. MSM 50-9405.
Scott, K. Lee. "Gracious Spirit, Dwell with Me" (Adore te devote). 2 pt mxd, org. AFP 9780800646134. *The Augsburg Choirbook.* AFP 9780800656782. *Augsburg Easy Choirbook,* vol. 1. AFP 9780800676025.

Children's Choir
Powell, Robert J. "O Praise the Lord, Ye Children." 3 pt canon, kybd. CG CGA163.
Schultz, Larry E. "Whoever Welcomes You, Welcomes Me." U/2 pt, kybd, fl. CG CGA1067.
Sleeth, Natalie. "Come! Come! Everybody Worship" from *LifeSongs.* U, kybd.

Keyboard / Instrumental
o Cherwien, David. "Lasset uns mit Jesu ziehen" from *Organ Plus,* vol. 2. Org, inst. AFP 9780800678548.
o Kerr, J. Wayne. "Lasset uns mit Jesu ziehen" from *Let Us Walk with Jesus.* Org. AFP 9780800677831.
o Schmoltze, Ron. "Two Oaks" from *A Song in the Journey.* Org. AFP 9780800679026.
o Travis, Albert L. "Canonbury" from *Join to Sing!* Org. MSM 10-791.

Handbell
o Behnke, John. "Let Us Ever Walk with Jesus." 3 oct, L2. CPH 97-7106.
o Haugen, Marty/arr. Diane McAninch. "Prelude on All Are Welcome." 3-5 oct hb, opt 3 oct hc, fl, L3. GIA G-7083.
Helman, Michael. "Aria." 3-6 oct hb, opt 3-5 oct hc, L2. CG CGB582.

Praise Ensemble
Bell, John. "Will You Come and Follow Me?" GIA. ELW 798.
Dyer, Max. "I Will Sing, I Will Sing." Celebration. W&P 73. Various editions.
• Hine, Stuart. "How Great Thou Art." Stuart Hine Music. ELW 856.
• Maher, Matt/Chris Tomlin. "Your Grace Is Enough." Spiritandsong.com.
• Tomlin, Chris. "Forever." WT/Sixsteps Music.
• Tomlin, Chris/John Newton/John Rees/Edwin Excell/Louie Giglio. "Amazing Grace (My Chains Are Gone)." WT.

Global
Bell, John, arr. "The Love of God Comes Close" from *Love and Anger: Songs of Lively Faith and Social Justice.* U. GIA G-4947.
Martinez, Salvador T. "Let Heaven Your Wonders Proclaim" from *Sent by the Lord: Songs of the World Church,* vol 2. U. GIA G-3740.

o denotes suggestions that relate to the hymn of the day.
• denotes songs that are available on iTunes®.

Monday, June 27

Cyril, Bishop of Alexandria, died 444

Remembered as an outstanding theologian as well as a contentious personality, Cyril defended the orthodox teachings about the person of Christ against Nestorius, bishop of Constantinople. Nestorius taught that the divine and human natures of Christ were entirely distinct, and therefore Mary could not be referred to as the *theotokos*, or bearer of God. This conflict, which also had roots in a rivalry for preeminence between Alexandria and Constantinople, involved all of the major Christian leaders of the time, including the patriarchs of Rome, Antioch, and Jerusalem, and finally also the emperor. In the end it was decided that Cyril's interpretation, that Christ's person included both divine and human natures, was correct.

Tuesday, June 28

Irenaeus, Bishop of Lyons, died around 202

Irenaeus (ee-ren-AY-us) believed that the way to remain steadfast to the truth was to hold fast to the faith handed down from the apostles. He believed that only Matthew, Mark, Luke, and John were trustworthy gospels. Irenaeus was an opponent of gnosticism and its emphasis on dualism. As a result of his battles with the gnostics, he was one of the first to speak of the church as "catholic." By catholic he meant that local congregations did not exist by themselves but were linked to one another in the whole church. He also maintained that this church was not contained within any national boundaries. He argued that the church's message was for all people, in contrast to the gnostics and their emphasis on "secret knowledge."

Wednesday, June 29

Peter and Paul, Apostles

These two are an odd couple of biblical witnesses to be brought together in one commemoration. It appears that Peter would have gladly served as the editor of Paul's letters: in a letter attributed to him, Peter says that some things in Paul's letters are hard to understand. Paul's criticism of Peter is more blunt. In Galatians he points out ways that Peter was wrong. One of the things that unites Peter and Paul is the tradition that says they were martyred together on this date in 67 or 68. What unites them more closely is their common confession of Jesus Christ. In the gospel reading appointed for this day, Peter declares that Jesus is the Christ through whom the foundation of the church is established. In the second reading, we hear of Paul's faithfulness to the end, by God's help. Together Peter and Paul lay a foundation and build the framework for our lives of faith through their proclamation of Jesus Christ.

Friday, July 1

Catherine Winkworth, died 1878;
John Mason Neale, died 1866; hymn translators

Neale was an English priest associated with the movement for church renewal at Cambridge. Winkworth lived most of her life in Manchester, where she was involved in promoting women's rights. These two hymn writers translated many hymn texts into English. Catherine Winkworth devoted herself to the translation of German hymns, nineteen of which are included in *Evangelical Lutheran Worship*; the fourteen hymn translations of John Mason Neale in the collection represent his specialization in ancient Latin and Greek hymns.

July 3, 2011
Time after Pentecost — Lectionary 14

The mystery of God's ways is sometimes hidden from the wise and intelligent. Jesus associates with the lowly and outcast. Like Paul, we struggle with our own selfish desires and seek God's mercy and forgiveness. We gather to be refreshed by Christ's invitation: "Come to me, all you that are weary." Gathered around word, water, and meal, we find rest for our souls.

On July 3 the church remembers Thomas, apostle. The lesser festival of St. Thomas' day may be observed this year on July 4.

Prayer of the Day

You are great, O God, and greatly to be praised. You have made us for yourself, and our hearts are restless until they rest in you. Grant that we may believe in you, call upon you, know you, and serve you, through your Son, Jesus Christ, our Savior and Lord.

Gospel Acclamation

Alleluia. Blessed are you, Lord of ˡ heav'n and earth;*
you have revealed these ˡ things to infants. *Alleluia.*
(Matt. 11:25)

Readings and Psalm
Zechariah 9:9-12

The coming messianic king will inaugurate an era of disarmament and prosperity. Because of God's covenant with Israel, they are designated as "prisoners of hope."

Psalm 145:8-14

The Lᴏʀᴅ is gracious and full of compassion. (Ps. 145:8)

Romans 7:15-25a

Life enslaved under sin is a catch-22 existence in which we know good but do not do it and do things we know to be bad. Through Jesus Christ, God has set us free from such a futile existence.

Matthew 11:16-19, 25-30

Jesus chides people who find fault with both his ministry and that of John the Baptist. He thanks God that wisdom and intelligence are not needed to receive what God has to offer.

Semicontinuous reading and psalm
Genesis 24:34-38, 42-49, 58-67

The marriage of Isaac and Rebekah helped to fulfill God's promise that Abraham and Sarah would become the ancestors of many nations. While her family urged delay, Rebekah eagerly set out to meet Isaac.

Psalm 45:10-17

God has anointed you with the oil of gladness. (Ps. 45:7)

or Song of Solomon 2:8-13

Arise, my love, my fair one, and come away.
(Song of Sol. 2:10)

Preface   Sundays

Color   Green

Prayers of Intercession

The prayers are prepared locally for each occasion. The following examples may be adapted or used as appropriate.

Led by the Holy Spirit, and with the whole people of God in Christ Jesus, let us pray for the church, those in need, and all of God's creation.

A brief silence.

Guide your church, that, freed from the law of sin, it may delight in serving you and your gospel for the sake of all people. Hear us, O God.

Your mercy is great.

Bless our efforts to care for the earth and its resources so that it may flourish from generation to generation. Hear us, O God.

Your mercy is great.

Reveal your wisdom to the leaders of all nations, that they may lead with humility and justice. Grateful for our country's freedoms, help us work for peace around the globe (*especially*). Hear us, O God.

Your mercy is great.

Give rest to all who are weary or burdened: those who are poor, hungry, oppressed, ill, or grieving (*especially*), that they may know your peace. Hear us, O God.
Your mercy is great.

Empower this congregation to take on Christ's yoke, serving one another with gentle and humble hearts, that this community may witness the strength of your love. Hear us, O God.
Your mercy is great.

Here other intercessions may be offered.

Reinvigorate our confession of the faith until that day we join the saints who have received their eternal rest in glory (*especially the apostle Thomas, whom we remember today*). Hear us, O God.
Your mercy is great.

Into your hands, O God, we commend ourselves and all for whom we pray, trusting in your abundant mercy, through Jesus Christ, our Savior and Lord.
Amen.

Ideas and Images for the Day

Jesus offers a yoke as a model of growing as disciples. A yoke is an image of surrendering, giving way, and accepting. At first glance, though, a yoke is a burden, and a means of doing work. The first ancient readers or hearers of Matthew viewed it as a symbol of obedience to God's law and wisdom. Generally, our instinct is to resist yokes and laws. Jesus invites us to think of God's law and wisdom as a means to surrender, give way, and accept something graceful and positive—rest, ease, lightness. The gospel links humility to freedom.

1. In her sermon "The Open Yoke," Barbara Brown Taylor reflects on the yoke she habitually places on herself and the way it exhausts her soul (*The Seeds of Heaven: Sermons on the Gospel of Matthew*, Louisville: Westminster John Knox, 2004, pp. 15–22). Then she reflects on the way in which God appears, and she accepts the lighter yoke God has made for her, a yoke for two— Jesus and us.

2. The Web site for Alcoholics Anonymous, http://www.aa.org/, is a gateway to many stories of recovering addicts and their stories about how God helped them in ways they could not help themselves. It will also lead one to meetings—one does not have to be in recovery to go to an "open" meeting. Many times, meetings will advertise that they have a speaker, a recovering addict telling his or her story. As you listen, reflect on this question: How does the experience of sharing one's story of addiction free the person telling—and receiving—it?

3. Prayer and meditation can serve as vital ways of throwing off our self-made yokes for a lighter yoke. The poem "Walking Meditation with Thich Nhat Hanh" by Tess Gallagher is part of a larger reflection on meditation and its power. Read the poem at http://speakingoffaith.publicradio.org/programs/thichnhathanh/poem-walkingmeditation.shtml.

4. Plant seeds and watch them grow to model the process of surrendering to God's law and wisdom and the fruits of such a discipline. A seed represents God's law and wisdom, and the yoke of which Jesus speaks. The dirt represents discipleship. The growth process represents surrender, giving way, acceptance, and humility. You can watch time-lapse videos of germinating seeds at YouTube.com; search "seed germination." You can also watch this process in a slower way by planting seeds in a glass container. You might place these germinating and growing seeds in a variety of places in your building.

Hymns for Worship
Gathering
Give Me Jesus   ELW 770, WOV 777, TFF 165
Arise, my soul, arise!   ELW 827, LBW 516
Before you, Lord, we bow   ELW 893, LBW 401

Hymn of the Day
Come to me, all pilgrims thirsty   ELW 777   BEACH SPRING
I heard the voice of Jesus Say   ELW 332, LBW 497
    THIRD MODE MELODY   ELW 611   KINGSFOLD
Softly and tenderly Jesus is calling   ELW 608, WOV 734
    THOMPSON

Offering
Light dawns on a weary world   ELW 726
Lord of all hopefulness   ELW 765, LBW 469

Communion
Day by day   ELW 790, WOV 746
If you but trust in God to guide you   ELW 769, LBW 453
What a friend we have in Jesus   ELW 742, LBW 439

Sending
We've come this far by faith   ELW 633, TFF 197
Just a closer walk with thee   ELW 697, TFF 253

Additional Hymns and Songs
Come unto me   DH 27
As the lyre to the singer   HS91 791
Come to me, O weary traveler   NSR 66, HFG 53

Music for the Day
Psalmody and Acclamations

Brugh, Lorraine. "Psalm 45," Refrain 2, from PSCY.

Makeever, Ray. "Psalm 145:8-14" from PWA, Evangelical Lutheran Worship Edition.

Mummert, Mark. "Psalm 145," Refrain 3, from PSCY.

Pelz, Walter L. "Psalm 45:10-17" and "Song of Solomon 2:8-13" from PWA, Evangelical Lutheran Worship Edition.

Sedio, Mark. "Song of Solomon 2:8-13" from PSCY.

Wold, Wayne L. *Gospel Acclamations for Summer.*

Choral

o Cherwien, David. "Softly and Tenderly Jesus Is Calling." SATB, solo. MSM 50-6304.

o Highben, Zebulon M. "Come to Me, All Pilgrims Thirsty." SATB, org, solo inst (ob or cl), assembly. AFP 9780800621414.

Leaf, Robert. "Come With Rejoicing." U, kybd. AFP 9780800645755.

Scott, K. Lee. "A Song of Trust" from *Sing a Song of Joy.* ML solo, kybd. AFP 9780800652821.

Children's Choir

Bisbee, B. Wayne. "The Eyes of All Wait Upon Thee." U, kybd. CG CGA874.

Makeever, Ray. "God Is Compassionate" from *Dancing at the Harvest.*

Patterson, Mark. "My God Is With Me" from *Young ChildrenSing.* U, kybd. AFP 9780800676803.

Keyboard / Instrumental

o Albrecht, Mark. "Thompson" from *Timeless Tunes for Piano and Solo Instrument*, vol. 3. Pno, inst. AFP 9780800675035.

o Hobby, Robert A. "Thompson" from *For All the Saints: Hymn Preludes for Funerals*, vol. 2. Org. AFP 9780800679105.

o Porter, Rachel Trelstad. "Beach Spring" from *Day by Day.* Pno. AFP 9780800656324.

o Wold, Wayne L. "Beach Spring" from *Augsburg Organ Library: Lent.* Org. AFP 9780800658977.

Handbell

o Endean, Judy. "Come, Ye Sinners, Poor and Needy." 2 oct, L2. Soundforth Productions 215988.

o Honoré, Jeffrey. "Beach Spring Stomp." 3-5 oct hb, opt 3 oct hc, L3+. CPH 97-7133.

o Waldrop, Tammy. "Raymond Brown's 'Softly and Tenderly.'" 3-5 oct, opt solo, L2. ALF 00-31744.

Praise Ensemble

• Byrd, Marc/Steve Hindalong. "God of Wonders." New Spring Music/INT.

• Lafferty, Karen. "Seek Ye First." MAR. WOV 783.

• Ledner, Michael. "You Are My Hiding Place." MAR. W&P 160

• Redman, Matt. "Blessed Be Your Name." Thankyou Music.

• Smith, Michael W./Deborah Smith. "Great Is the Lord." Meadowgreen Music. W&P 53.

• St. James, Rebecca/Matt Bronleewe. "Quiet You with My Love." Up in the Mix Music.

Global

Hassell, Michael, arr. "Mayenziwe/Your Will Be Done." SATB, kybd. AFP World Song 9780800676254.

Pantou, Rudolf R. "Soft the Master's Love Song" from *Sound the Bamboo.* U. GIA G-6830.

Monday, July 4
Thomas, Apostle (transferred)

Thomas is perhaps best remembered as "Doubting Thomas." But alongside this doubt, the Gospel of John shows Thomas as fiercely loyal: "Let us also go, that we may die with him" (John 11:16). And John's gospel shows Thomas moving from doubt to deep faith. Thomas makes one of the strongest confessions of faith in the New Testament, "My Lord and my God!" (John 20:28). From this confession of faith, ancient stories tell of Thomas's missionary work to India, where Christian communities were flourishing a thousand years before the arrival of sixteenth-century missionaries.

The feast of St. Thomas is observed on various dates, and a long tradition in the West placed it on December 21. In 1969, however, the Roman Catholic calendar moved it to July 3 in agreement with the Syrian Church. *Evangelical Lutheran Worship* follows this ecumenical trend.

Wednesday, July 6
Jan Hus, martyr, died 1415

Jan Hus was a Bohemian priest who spoke against abuses in the church of his day in many of the same ways Luther would a century later. He spoke against the withholding of the cup at the eucharist and because of this stance was excommunicated, not for heresy but for insubordination toward his archbishop. He preached against the selling of indulgences and was particularly mortified by the indulgence trade of two rival claimants to the papacy who were raising money for war against each other. He was found guilty of heresy by the Council of Constance and burned at the stake. The followers of Jan Hus became known as the Czech Brethren and eventually continued as the Moravian Church.

o denotes suggestions that relate to the hymn of the day.
• denotes songs that are available on iTunes®.

July 10, 2011
Time after Pentecost — Lectionary 15

God's word is like the rain that waters the earth and brings forth vegetation. It is also like the sower who scatters seed indiscriminately. Our lives are like seeds sown in the earth. Even from what appears to be little, dormant, or dead, God promises a harvest. At the Lord's table we are fed with the bread of life, that we may bear fruit in the world.

Prayer of the Day

Almighty God, we thank you for planting in us the seed of your word. By your Holy Spirit help us to receive it with joy, live according to it, and grow in faith and hope and love, through Jesus Christ, our Savior and Lord.

Gospel Acclamation

Alleluia. The word is very ' near to you;* it is in your mouth and ' in your heart. *Alleluia.* (Deut. 30:14)

Readings and Psalm

Isaiah 55:10-13

God's word to Israel's exiles is as sure and effective as never-failing precipitation. Their return to the Holy Land in a new exodus is cheered on by singing mountains and by trees that clap their hands.

Psalm 65:[1-8] 9-13

Your paths overflow with plenty. (Ps. 65:11)

Romans 8:1-11

There is no condemnation for those who live in Christ. God sent Christ to accomplish what the law was unable to do: condemn sin and free us from its slavery. The Spirit now empowers proper actions and values in our lives and gives us the promise of resurrected life.

Matthew 13:1-9, 18-23

In Matthew's gospel, both Jesus and his disciples "sow the seed" of God's word by proclaiming the good news that "the kingdom of heaven is near." Now, in a memorable parable, Jesus explains why this good news produces different results in those who hear.

Semicontinuous reading and psalm
Genesis 25:19-34

Although Jacob was younger than his twin, Esau, he eventually gets the birthright away from his brother. Jacob is portrayed in the Bible as deceptive, gripping his brother when he came out of the womb and driving a hard bargain by buying the birthright for a bowl of lentils.

Psalm 119:105-112

Your word is a lamp to my feet and a light upon my path. (Ps. 119:105)

Preface   Sundays

Color   Green

Prayers of Intercession

The prayers are prepared locally for each occasion. The following examples may be adapted or used as appropriate.

Led by the Holy Spirit, and with the whole people of God in Christ Jesus, let us pray for the church, those in need, and all of God's creation.

A brief silence.

Let us pray for the people of God, that as they sow seeds of love and mercy, the gospel may be received with joy and take root and grow. Hear us, O God.

Your mercy is great.

Let us pray for the oceans and the beaches of the earth, that pollution may be reversed and life again flourish underwater and on the shores. Hear us, O God.

Your mercy is great.

Let us pray for the leaders of all nations, that the seeds of justice may be planted where there is inequality and seeds of peace where there is disharmony (*especially*). Hear us, O God.

Your mercy is great.

Let us pray for all who suffer condemnation at the hands of others and for all who are sick or suffering in any way (*especially*), that they may know freedom in Jesus Christ. Hear us, O God.

Your mercy is great.

Let us pray for this congregation, that we may be good soil, bearing the fruits of the spirit a hundredfold in service to Christ. Hear us, O God.

Your mercy is great.

Here other intercessions may be offered.

Let us give thanks for the faithful departed, that they, having set their mind on the Spirit and having received their reward, may be models of faithfulness for us. Hear us, O God.

Your mercy is great.

Into your hands, O God, we commend ourselves and all for whom we pray, trusting in your abundant mercy, through Jesus Christ, our Savior and Lord.

Amen.

Ideas and Images for the Day

God brings forth life in places where people see only death. The children of Israel surely saw death in every direction. Paul looks at his own life and, at first, sees nothing beyond spiritual death. Then, in the parable of the sower, three-fourths of the seeds die and three-fourths of the sections of the field are inhospitable to flourishing life. Similarly, we might look at the world and ourselves and only see the places that are absent and inhospitable to God's love. All the readings go a step further, however, to articulate or reveal God bringing forth life—God renews the covenant with the children of Israel, and Paul reflects on God bringing forth life from the death of Jesus. The parable of the sower elicits reflection, repentance, and, ultimately, new life from its readers and hearers in considering the sort of spiritual life they practice. Are we hospitable or inhospitable to God's word? This parable is a vivid reminder of all God has overcome—rocks, scorching sun, thorns, and snatching—to bring life to the world.

1. The poem "Picnic, Lightening" (from *Picnic, Lightening*, Pittsburgh: University of Pittsburgh Press, p. 24) by Billy Collins gives words to the image of fragile life shining forth through and in the midst of death. He describes filling his flower boxes with compost, made of dying things, and then planting fragile flowers into the compost. The flowers eventually thrive and show that life happens even in the midst of death.

2. Zion Lutheran Church in Ferndale, Michigan, makes liturgical art by recycling trash that members collect in their neighborhood. They find items like bike reflectors, aluminum pie tins, and swimming noodles and make them into large musical instruments, which they display in their worship space. Watch their video, "People's Trash, God's Treasure," at http://www.godsworkourhands.org/v/354,peoples-trash,-god. Look for trash in your neighborhood and then create images that appear in the readings during this season.

3. In the book *Farmer Boy*, by Laura Ingalls Wilder (New York: HarperCollins Children's Books: 2004, p. 191), Almanzo raises a pumpkin with great care. He carefully prunes a vine, removes yellow pumpkin blossoms, and sets up his pumpkin to drink from a bowl of milk. The fragile "wee" pumpkin grows to an enormous size and wins first prize at the fair. Death and careful attention are necessary steps toward Almanzo's goal of growing an enormous pumpkin.

4. People in cities are growing gardens on plots of land that were once vacant lots. They bring forth life from something that one might consider dead. Use your Internet search engine to locate stories and images of urban community gardens. Advent Lutheran Church in Madison, Wisconsin, made a video (http://www.godsworkourhands.org/v/351,nurturing-soul-and-soil.html) about their garden. The video also contains a song children can learn quickly.

Hymns for Worship

Gathering

What is this place   ELW 524
Open now thy gates of beauty   ELW 533, LBW 250
Lord, let my heart be good soil   ELW 512, WOV 713

Hymn of the Day

As rain from the clouds   ELW 508   *AFTON WATER*
The Word of God is source and seed   ELW 506, WOV 658
GAUDEAMUS DOMINO
For the fruit of all creation   ELW 679, WOV 760
AR HYD Y NOS   LBW 563   *SANTA BARBARA*

Offering

We plow the fields and scatter   ELW 680/681, LBW 362
Accept, O Lord, the gifts we bring   ELW 691, WOV 759

Communion

Lord, your hands have formed   ELW 554, WOV 727
Build us up, Lord   ELW 670
As the grains of wheat   ELW 465, WOV 705

Sending

Almighty God, your word is cast   ELW 516, LBW 234
Sent forth by God's blessing   ELW 547, LBW 221

Additional Hymns and Songs

When seed falls on good soil   LBW 236
Open our lives to your word   DH 8
Bring Forth the Kingdom   W&P 22, HS91 821

Music for the Day
Psalmody and Acclamations

Long, Larry J. "Psalm 65," Refrain 1, from PSCY.

Makeever, Ray. "Psalm 65:[1-8] 9-13" from PWA, Evangelical Lutheran Worship Edition.

Mummert, Mark. "Psalm 119:105-112" from PSCY.

Shepperd, Mark. "Psalm 119:105-112" from PWA, Evangelical Lutheran Worship Edition.

Weber, Paul D. *Gospel Acclamations for Summer.*

Choral

Ferguson, John. "Word of God Come Down on Earth." SATB, org. GIA G-3764.

Greene, Maurice/ed. K. Lee Scott. "You Visit the Earth" from *Sing Forth God's Praise.* MH solo, kybd. AFP 9780800675264.

Jennings, Carolyn. "Blessed Are They." SATB, org, opt fl. CG CGA-896.

Mendelssohn, Felix/arr. K. Lee Scott. "I Will Sing of Thy Great Mercies" from *Sing a Song of Joy.* Solo, kybd. AFP 9780800652821.

Children's Choir

Haugen, Marty. "Bring Forth the Kingdom" from *LifeSongs.* U, kybd.

Makeever, Ray. "Thanksgiving to the Living God" from *Dancing at the Harvest.* U, kybd.

Wold, Wayne. "Jesus, Be Our Bread." U/2 pt, kybd. GIA G5439.

Keyboard / Instrumental

○ Hassell, Michael. "Ar hyd y nos" from *Folkways,* vol. 1. Pno, inst. AFP 9780800656904.

○ Manz, Paul O. "Ar hyd y nos" from *Three Hymn Improvisations.* Org. MSM 10-867.

○ Miller, Aaron David. "Afton Water" from *Augsburg Organ Library: Baptism and Communion.* Org. AFP 9780800623555.

○ Wold, Wayne L. "Afton Water" from *Water, Word, Meal.* Org. AFP 9780800677558.

Handbell

Afdahl, Lee. "For As the Rain Comes Down." 3-5 oct hb, opt 4 oct hc, fc and rain sticks, L4. AFP 9780800658151.

○ Moklebust, Cathy. "God, Who Made the Earth and Heaven (Ar hyd y nos)" from *Hymn Stanzas for Handbells.* 4-5 oct, L3. AFP 9780800655761.

Thomson, Patricia. "Dancing Raindrops." 3-5 oct, L3. AGEHR AG35274.

Praise Ensemble

● Brown, Brenton. "Lord, Reign in Me." VIN.

● Hanson, Handt. "Lord, Let My Heart Be Good Soil." Prince of Peace Publishing. ELW 512. Various editions.

● Haugen, Marty. "As the Grains of Wheat." GIA G-3601. ELW 465.

Huerta, Leila/Joe Huerta. "Go Out with Joy." MAR. W&P 48. Various editions.

● Park, Andy. "Only You." Mercy/VIN. Various editions.

● Scott, Kathryn. "Hungry." VIN.

Global

Ikalahan (Philippines) trad. "Lord, Your Hands Have Formed." U. ELW 554.

Young-Soo, Nah. "Look and Learn" from *Sent by the Lord: Songs of the World Church,* vol 2. U. GIA G-3740.

Monday, July 11
Benedict of Nursia, Abbot of Monte Cassino, died around 540

Benedict is known as the father of Western monasticism. He was educated in Rome but was appalled by the decline of life around him. He went to live as a hermit, and a community of monks came to gather around him. In the prologue of his rule for monasteries he wrote that his intent in drawing up his regulations was "to set down nothing harsh, nothing burdensome." It is that moderate spirit that characterizes his rule and the monastic communities that are formed by it. Benedict encourages a generous spirit of hospitality, saying that visitors to Benedictine communities are to be welcomed as Christ himself.

Tuesday, July 12
Nathan Söderblom, Bishop of Uppsala, died 1931

In 1930, this Swedish theologian, ecumenist, and social activist received the Nobel Prize for peace. Söderblom (ZAY-der-blom) saw the value of the ancient worship of the church catholic and encouraged the liturgical movement. He also valued the work of liberal Protestant scholars and believed social action was a first step on the path toward a united Christianity. He organized the Universal Christian Council on Life and Work, one of the organizations that in 1948 came together to form the World Council of Churches.

○ denotes suggestions that relate to the hymn of the day.
● denotes songs that are available on iTunes®.

July 17, 2011

Time after Pentecost — Lectionary 16

It is an age-old question: why is there evil in the world? In the parable of the wheat and the weeds Jesus suggests that both grow together until the harvest. With Paul, we long for the day that all creation will be set free from bondage and suffering. Having both weeds and wheat within us, we humbly place our hope in the promises of God, and from the Lord's table we go forth to bear the fruit of justice and mercy.

Today is the commemoration of Bartolomé de Las Casas, missionary to the Indies, who died in 1566.

Prayer of the Day

Faithful God, most merciful judge, you care for your children with firmness and compassion. By your Spirit nurture us who live in your kingdom, that we may be rooted in the way of your Son, Jesus Christ, our Savior and Lord.

Gospel Acclamation

Alleluia. My word shall accomplish that | which I purpose,* and succeed in the thing for | which I sent it. *Alleluia.* (Isa. 55:11)

Readings and Psalm

Isaiah 44:6-8

God claims the right to sole rule, because God announces things that actually do happen, while supposed divine opponents remain silent. God is Israel's redeemer, that is, the best brother or sister they ever had.

***or* Wisdom 12:13, 16-19**

God's deeds of forgiveness and gift of hope indicate that God's faithful people must also show kindness. No other god cares for all people.

Psalm 86:11-17

Teach me your way, O Lord, and I will walk in your truth. (Ps. 86:11)

Romans 8:12-25

For Paul, true spirituality means that we experience the reality of the Spirit, which enables us to pray as God's children, keeps us in solidarity with creation, and gives us unseen hope that God will liberate us and creation from bondage to death and decay.

Matthew 13:24-30, 36-43

Jesus tells a parable about the co-existence of good and evil in this world. God's judgment will remove all evildoers and causes of sin, but not until the end of human history.

Semicontinuous reading and psalm

Genesis 28:10-19a

God's graciousness to Jacob is shown in God's revelation of the divine self to the patriarch, who is running for his life after cheating his brother Esau out of the family inheritance. Jacob promises that if God brings him back to the land, he will be loyal to God and give God a tenth of everything.

Psalm 139:1-12, 23-24

You have searched me out and known me. (Ps. 139:1)

Preface Sundays

Color Green

Prayers of Intercession

The prayers are prepared locally for each occasion. The following examples may be adapted or used as appropriate.

Led by the Holy Spirit, and with the whole people of God in Christ Jesus, let us pray for the church, those in need, and all of God's creation.

A brief silence.

We pray for all the children of God, that as joint heirs with Christ, they may witness to the hope that is within them. Hear us, O God.

Your mercy is great.

We pray for all of creation that groans with longing to be set free from decay and misuse and to be restored to wholeness. Hear us, O God.

Your mercy is great.

We pray for the nations of the world, that even though good and evil may exist side by side, justice and mercy prevail. Bring peace to war-torn areas (*especially*). Hear us, O God.
Your mercy is great.
We pray for all who need hope: the orphaned, lost, ill, or dying (*especially*), that they may have patience even as they wait upon you. Hear us, O God.
Your mercy is great.
We pray for this congregation, that, having received the spirit of adoption into God's family, we support foster and adoptive families. Hear us, O God.
Your mercy is great.
Here other intercessions may be offered.
We give thanks for the example of brothers and sisters in Christ, who, having lived righteous lives, now shine like the sun in the kingdom of God (*especially Bartolomé de Las Casas, missionary to the Indies, whom we commemorate today*). Hear us, O God.
Your mercy is great.
Into your hands, O God, we commend ourselves and all for whom we pray, trusting in your abundant mercy, through Jesus Christ, our Savior and Lord.
Amen.

Ideas and Images for the Day

In today's gospel, Jesus interprets a parable for the disciples; he announces that all evildoers will be thrown into the furnace of fire, while the righteous will shine like the sun. The "Son of Man" will judge the world. St. Paul, however, in his letter to the church at Rome, focuses on God as *merciful* judge. He proclaims that all creation will be freed from decay and receive redemption. Paul reminds us our hope lies with God, our parent through a spirit of adoption. This dichotomous picture of God as judge and giver of mercy began with last Sunday's texts and evidences itself in readings from Romans and Matthew across the next four Sundays. In some cases the God of mercy is highlighted in Paul's letter, at other times in the gospel. This good news, however, is always present!

1. Bible study with adults or teenagers might use a concordance, in book form or online, to locate Matthew's disturbing phrase "weeping and gnashing of teeth," used several times in this gospel, but rarely elsewhere in the Bible. What does this usage tell us about the writer of this gospel? Does this writer also proclaim good news? What passages reflecting God's mercy are located in this gospel?

2. The Truth and Reconciliation Commission established in South Africa following the abolition of apartheid sought justice with mercy for victims and perpetrators alike. Search the Internet for information regarding the actions taken by this court. Contrast the findings with the Nuremberg Trials following World War II. These are real life examples of humans, according to their own understanding, seeking to extend justice and mercy. The complexities of the task readily become apparent.

3. A farmer in the congregation or a visit to a local craft store may provide a bundle of dried wheat. Weeds are generally readily available from gardens or roadsides. Children will appreciate the opportunity to see the contrasts and similarities between weeds and wheat. A discussion of how the wheat becomes bread for our table will be helpful, particularly to those who live in the city. Be mindful of children's allergies. Some may need to avoid touching the plants.

4. Marty Haugen's hymn "As the grains of wheat" (ELW 465) connects table to text for this Sunday. The words are from a second-century Christian document called the *Didache*. These words are written in chapter 9: "Even as this broken bread was scattered over the hills, and was gathered together and became one, so let Thy Church be gathered together from the ends of the earth into Thy kingdom." The full document is at http://www.earlychristianwritings.com. Our use of wheat for the table reflects nearly two thousand years of history!

Hymns for Worship
Gathering
O Holy Spirit, enter in   ELW 786, LBW 459
We plow the fields and scatter   ELW 680/681, LBW 362, LCC 492
Oh, worship the King   ELW 842, LBW 548

Hymn of the Day
Come, ye thankful people, come   ELW 693, LBW 407
ST. GEORGE'S, WINDSOR
Almighty God, your word is cast   ELW 516, LBW 234
ST. FLAVIAN
On what has now been sown   ELW 550, LBW 261
DARWALL'S 148TH

Offering
Praise and thanksgiving   ELW 689, LBW 409
As the grains of wheat   ELW 465, WOV 705

Communion
Neither death nor life   ELW 622
Great is thy faithfulness   ELW 733, WOV 771
Lord our God, with praise we come   ELW 730, LBW 244

Sending

Father, we thank you   ELW 478, WOV 704
Spread, oh, spread, almighty Word   ELW 663, LBW 379

Additional Hymns and Songs

Beauty for brokenness   W&P 17
Ancient of days   HCW 11
Don't be worried   TFF 212

Music for the Day
Psalmody and Acclamations

Haugen, Marty. "Psalm 139" from PSCY.
Mummert, Mark. "Psalm 86," Refrain 2, from PSCY.
Sedio, Mark. "Psalm 86:11-17" and "Psalm 139:1-12, 23-24" from PWA, Evangelical Lutheran Worship Edition.
Weber, Paul D. *Gospel Acclamations for Summer.*

Choral

Bach, J. C. F. "In the Resurrection Glorious" from *Chantry Choirbook*. SATB, org. AFP 9780800657772.
Bisbee, B. Wayne. "Teach Me Your Way, O Lord." 2 pt mxd, kybd. AFP 9780800654795.
Marcello, Benedetto/arr. Dale Grotenhuis. "Teach Me Now, O Lord." 2 pt mxd, kybd. MSM 50-9418.
Scott, K. Lee. "The Call" from *Sing a Song of Joy*. ML solo, kybd. AFP 9780800652821.

Children's Choir

Curry, Craig. "Joyful, Joyful, We Adore Thee." U/2 pt, kybd. CG CGA1170.
Sedio, Mark. "Teach Me Your Way." U/2 pt, kybd. AMSI 711.
Shaw, Timothy. "Teach Me Your Way, O Lord." U/2 pt, kybd. CG CGA1081.

Keyboard / Instrumental

○ Nelhybel, Vaclav. "Darwall's 148th" from *Festival Hymns and Processionals*. Br. Conductor score HOP 750.
○ Powell, Robert J. "St George's Windsor" from *Three for Thanksgiving*. Inst. CPH 97-5976U1.
○ Wold, Wayne L. "Prelude, Meditation and Finale on Darwall's 148th." Org. AFP 9780800656706.
○ Young, Jeremy. "St Flavian" from *At the Foot of the Cross*. Pno. AFP 9780800655396.

Handbell

○ Bisbee, B. Wayne. "Prelude on St. George's Windsor." 2 oct hb, fl or cl, L3. National Music NMHB505.
○ Evanovich, Joshua. "Rejoice, Give Thanks and Sing." 3-5 oct, L3. GIA G-7288.

○ Tucker, Sondra. "Come, Ye Thankful People, Come." 3-5 oct hb, opt org, opt br, opt assembly, L3. SHW HP5419 (hb). HP 5420 (org). LB 5752 (full score/br).

Praise Ensemble

• Adkins, Donna. "Glorify Thy Name." MAR. W&P 42.
• Anonymous. "Create in Me a Clean Heart." W&P 34. Various editions.
• Doerksen, Brian. "Refiner's Fire." VIN.
• Evans, Darrell. "Let the River Flow." VIN/INT.
• Hall, Charlie. "Give Us Clean Hands." WT/Sixsteps Music.
• Zschech, Darlene. "The Potter's Hand." Hillsong/INT.

Global

Courtney, Roger. "O Let Us Spread the Pollen of Peace" from *Agape: Songs of Hope and Reconciliation*. U, gtr. Lutheran World Federation. AFP 9780191000133.
Olson, Howard S./arr. A. Louise Anderson. "Praised Be the Rock" from *Set Free: A Collection of African Hymns*. SATB. AFP 9780806600451.

Sunday, July 17
Bartolomé de Las Casas, missionary to the Indies, died 1566

Bartolomé de Las Casas was a Spanish priest and a missionary in the Western Hemisphere. He first came to the West while serving in the military, and he was granted a large estate that included a number of indigenous slaves. When he was ordained in 1513, he granted freedom to his servants. This act characterized much of the rest of Las Casas's ministry. Throughout the Caribbean and Central America, he worked to stop the enslavement of native people, to halt the brutal treatment of women by military forces, and to promote laws that humanized the process of colonization.

Friday, July 22
Mary Magdalene, Apostle

The gospels report Mary Magdalene was one of the women of Galilee who followed Jesus. She was present at Jesus' crucifixion and his burial. When she went to the tomb on the first day of the week to anoint Jesus' body, she was the first person to whom the risen Lord appeared. She returned to the disciples with the news and has been called "the apostle to the apostles" for her proclamation of the resurrection. Because John's gospel describes Mary as weeping at the tomb, she is often portrayed in art with red eyes. Icons depict her standing by the tomb and holding a bright red egg, symbol of the resurrection.

○ denotes suggestions that relate to the hymn of the day.
• denotes songs that are available on iTunes®.

Saturday, July 23

Birgitta of Sweden, renewer of the church, died 1373

Birgitta (beer-GEE-tuh) was married at age thirteen and had four daughters with her husband. She was a woman of some standing who, in her early thirties, served as the chief lady-in-waiting to the queen of Sweden. She was widowed at the age of thirty-eight, shortly after she and her husband had made a religious pilgrimage. Following the death of her husband the religious dreams and visions that had begun in her youth occurred more regularly. Her devotional commitments led her to give to the poor and needy all that she owned, and she began to live a more ascetic life. She founded an order of monks and nuns, the Order of the Holy Savior (Brigittines), whose superior was a woman. Today the Society of St. Birgitta is a laypersons' society that continues her work of prayer and charity.

July 24, 2011

Time after Pentecost — Lectionary 17

As Solomon prays for wisdom, we seek to more deeply know the treasures of faith. In today's gospel Jesus offers everyday images that reveal to us the reign of God: a tree that becomes a sheltering home, yeast that penetrates and expands, a treasured pearl, a net that gains a great catch. Even as we seek the riches of God's reign, the great surprise is that God's grace finds us first!

Prayer of the Day

Beloved and sovereign God, through the death and resurrection of your Son you bring us into your kingdom of justice and mercy. By your Spirit, give us your wisdom, that we may treasure the life that comes from Jesus Christ, our Savior and Lord.

Gospel Acclamation

Alleluia. Many will come from | east and west* and will eat in the king- | dom of heaven. *Alleluia.* (Matt. 8:11)

Readings and Psalm

1 Kings 3:5-12

Because Solomon did not ask for long life, riches, or the defeat of his enemies, God gave him what he asked for: wisdom to govern the people well. In verse 13 God gives him additional honor and riches beyond compare.

Psalm 119:129-136

When your word is opened, it gives light and understanding. (Ps. 119:130)

Romans 8:26-39

These words celebrate the depth of God's actions for us. Through Christ's death for us and the activity of the Spirit praying for us, we are fused to God's love poured out in Jesus Christ. Nothing, not even death itself, is able to separate us from such incredible divine love.

Matthew 13:31-33, 44-52

Throughout Matthew's gospel, Jesus and his disciples proclaim the good news that "the kingdom of heaven is near!" Here, Jesus offers several brief parables that explore the implications of this announcement for people's lives.

Semicontinuous reading and psalm

Genesis 29:15-28

The young shepherd Jacob met his match in the old shepherd, Laban, his father-in-law. Laban gave Jacob his older daughter, Leah, when he had promised to give him Rachel. Jacob worked fourteen years to earn his favorite wife, Rachel, but the years seemed like a few days because of his love for her.

Psalm 105:1-11, 45b

Make known the deeds of the Lord among the peoples. Hallelujah! (Ps. 105:1, 45)

or **Psalm 128**

Happy are they who follow in the ways of God. (Ps. 128:1)

Preface   Sundays

Color   Green

Prayers of Intercession

The prayers are prepared locally for each occasion. The following examples may be adapted or used as appropriate.
Led by the Holy Spirit, and with the whole people of God in Christ Jesus, let us pray for the church, those in need, and all of God's creation.
A brief silence.
Let us pray for Christians everywhere, that they may work together for good. Help them always to act in accord with God's good purposes. Hear us, O God.
Your mercy is great.
Let us pray for the restoration of forests, fields, and prairies that provide homes for birds, wild animals, and livestock. Teach us to respect all land and creatures. Hear us, O God.
Your mercy is great.
Let us pray for rulers and people in power, that they act responsibly for the good of all people. Search their hearts, O God, and lead them to work for justice (*especially*). Hear us, O God.
Your mercy is great.
Let us pray for all who are suffering hardship: those who are hungry, unemployed, persecuted, naked, or ill (*especially*). Give them the assurance that nothing can separate them from your love. Hear us, O God.
Your mercy is great.
Let us pray for this assembly that we may diligently seek the treasure of God's kingdom. Make us rise up like leaven to serve. Hear us, O God.
Your mercy is great.
Here other intercessions may be offered.
Let us give thanks for the saints before us, who are more than conquerors through Christ and now live in glory. Let their witness teach us how to serve. Hear us, O God.
Your mercy is great.
Into your hands, O God, we commend ourselves and all for whom we pray, trusting in your abundant mercy, through Jesus Christ, our Savior and Lord.
Amen.

Ideas and Images for the Day

A string of parables describe the kingdom of heaven, and then we hear Jesus' question: "Have you understood all this?" The mustard seed, yeast, hidden treasure, pearls—these bring good news of growth and joy and riches. Then come the fish, the furnace of fire, and the weeping and gnashing of teeth. Once again this week we hear of a God of mercy and justice. Once again there is good news to be heard in Paul's letter to the church at Rome—nothing will ever separate us from God's love in Christ Jesus. How will we reconcile these two images of God? Solomon asks God for the wisdom to discern between good and evil, for the understanding to live out both justice and mercy as a ruler of God's people. God was pleased with Solomon's request.

1. The gospel parables are salted with words implying that the kingdom of heaven is not readily visible. Greek roots emphasize that the kingdom must be carefully sought out. The mustard seed is "smaller than" (*mikroteron*, as in our word microscopic) all other seeds. The man "having found" (*euron*, as in eureka) a treasure buys the field in which it is hidden. A merchant "seeking" a pearl, also "having found" it, buys it. How and where do we find the small signs of the kingdom of heaven?

2. Just as parables help us access the meaning of the gospel, so objects help children access the parables. A mustard seed and an imitation pearl attached with clear tape to an index card provide a tactile resource for children. Both are objects from nature, one that grows into a great bush, one that is mysteriously grown inside an oyster. How the bush and the pearl grow is miraculous, as is God's miraculous love for all creation.

3. The parable of good fish and bad fish is simple to understand; the lines between God's justice and God's mercy are difficult to grasp. The movie *The Burning Plain* (Magnolia Pictures, 2009), while a bit graphic at times, illustrates our confusion. A teenager unintentionally but thoughtlessly commits a horrible crime for which she is never called to account. The victims of her crime are by no means innocent. Justice is not served, and yet, by the end of the film, she finds mercy. Which characters in this film are "good fish"? Which are "bad fish"? Is it our responsibility to sort the fish? Or God's?

4. Marty Haugen's hymn "Bring Forth the Kingdom" (W&P 22) calls us to bring forth God's kingdom with the planting of seeds of justice and mercy in our world. A leader and the assembly may sing the stanzas antiphonally, line by line, with all singing the refrain.

Hymns for Worship
Gathering
Open now thy gates of beauty   ELW 533, LBW 250
Gather Us In   ELW 532, WOV 718
Jesus, priceless treasure   ELW 775, LBW 457/458

Hymn of the Day
God of grace and God of glory   ELW 705, LBW 415
  CWM RHONDDA
All my hope on God is founded   ELW 757, WOV 782
  MICHAEL
We Are Called   ELW 720, W&P 147   *WE ARE CALLED*

Offering
Accept, O Lord, the gifts we bring   ELW 691, WOV 759
Let the vineyards be fruitful   ELW 181

Communion
Neither death nor life   ELW 622
Soul, adorn yourself with gladness   ELW 488/489, LBW 224
Be thou my vision   ELW 793

Sending
Sent forth by God's blessing   ELW 547, LBW 221
Build us up, Lord   ELW 670

Additional Hymns and Songs
You are the seed   WOV 753, TFF 226
Seek ye first   WOV 783, W&P 122

Music for the Day
Psalmody and Acclamations
Bruxvoort-Colligan, Richard. "Psalm 128" from PSCY.
Kallman, Daniel. "Psalm 119:129-136" from PWA, Evangelical Lutheran Worship Edition.
Keesecker, Thomas. "Psalm 128" from PWA, Evangelical Lutheran Worship Edition.
Mummert, Mark. "Psalm 119:129-136" from PSCY.
Pelz, Walter L. "Psalm 105:1-11, 45b" from PWA, Evangelical Lutheran Worship Edition.
Weber, Paul D. *Gospel Acclamations for Summer.*
Woehr, Roland. "Psalm 105" from PSCY.

Choral
Bach, J. S. "Jesus, My Sweet Pleasure/Jesu, meine Freude" from *Bach for All Seasons.* AFP 9780800658540.
Berger, Jean. "The Eyes of All Wait Upon Thee." SATB. AFP 9780800645595. *The Augsburg Choirbook.* AFP 9780800656782.

Handel, G. F. "If God Is for Us, Who Is Against Us?" from *Messiah.* Sop solo, kybd. Various editions.
Scott, K. Lee. "So Art Thou to Me" from *Rejoice Now, My Spirit.* ML solo, kybd. AFP 9780800651091.

Children's Choir
Arabic Folksong. "The Tiny Seed" from *LifeSongs.* U, kybd.
Bolt, Conway A. Jr. "The Kingdom of God." U/2 pt, kybd. CG CGA677.
Gabarain, Cesareo. "You Are the Seed" from *LifeSongs.* U, kybd.

Keyboard / Instrumental
o Clarke, Andrew. "Michael" from *Three English Hymn Tunes for Organ.* Org. MSM 10-854.
  Dahl, David P. "An English Suite for Organ." Org. AFP 9780800674953.
o Eggert, John. "Michael" from *Six Hymn Preludes*, vol. 2. Org. CPH 97-5912U1.
o Organ, Anne Krentz. "Cwm Rhondda" from *Piano Reflections for the Church Year.* Pno. AFP 9780800674748.

Handbell
o Edwards, Dan. "God of Grace and God of Glory" 3 oct, L3. SHW 5450.
o McChesney, Kevin. "God of Grace and God of Glory" 3-5 oct, L3. CPH 97-6584.
o Page, Anna Laura. "Cwm Rhondda Festal." 3-5 oct, L3. Ring Out Press 3239.

Praise Ensemble
• Bullock, Geoff. "The Power of Your Love." WRD/MAR.
• Carpenter, Kelly. "Draw Me Close." Mercy/VIN.
• Doerksen, Brian/Brenton Brown. "Hallelujah (Your Love Is Amazing)." VIN.
• Grul, Daniel/John Ezzy/Steve McPherson. "Jesus, Lover of My Soul." Hillsong/INT.
• Houghton, Israel/Michael Gungor. "Friend of God." INT.
• Smith, Martin. "I Could Sing of Your Love Forever." Curious? Music.

Global
Mahamba, DeoGratias. "Heri Ni Jina" from *Global Choral Sounds.* SATB, cant, perc. CPH 98-3610. ELW 797.
Sosa, Pablo. "Tuyo es el Reino/Yours in the Kingdom" from *Éste es el Día.* U. GIA G-7021.

o denotes suggestions that relate to the hymn of the day.
• denotes songs that are available on iTunes®.

Monday, July 25

James, Apostle

James is one of the sons of Zebedee and is counted as one of the twelve disciples. Together with his brother John they had the nickname "sons of thunder." One of the stories in the New Testament tells of their request for Jesus to grant them places of honor in the kingdom. They are also reported to have asked Jesus for permission to send down fire on a Samaritan village that had not welcomed them. James was the first of the Twelve to suffer martyrdom and is the only apostle whose martyrdom is recorded in scripture. He is sometimes called James the Elder to distinguish him from James the Less, commemorated with Philip on May 1, and James of Jerusalem, commemorated on October 23.

Thursday, July 28

Johann Sebastian Bach, died 1750; Heinrich Schütz, died 1672; George Frederick Handel, died 1759; musicians

These three composers have done much to enrich the worship life of the church. Johann Sebastian Bach drew on the Lutheran tradition of hymnody and wrote about two hundred cantatas, including at least two for each Sunday and festival day in the Lutheran calendar of his day. He has been called "the fifth evangelist" for the ways he proclaimed the gospel through his music. George Frederick Handel was not primarily a church musician, but his great work *Messiah* is a musical proclamation of the scriptures. Heinrich Schütz wrote choral settings of biblical texts and paid special attention to ways his composition would underscore the meaning of the words.

Friday, July 29

Mary, Martha, and Lazarus of Bethany

Mary and Martha are remembered for the hospitality and refreshment they offered Jesus in their home. Following the characterization drawn by Luke, Martha represents the active life, Mary the contemplative. Mary is identified in the fourth gospel as the one who anointed Jesus before his passion and who was criticized for her act of devotion. Lazarus, Mary's and Martha's brother, was raised from the dead by Jesus as a sign of the eternal life offered to all believers. It was over Lazarus's tomb that Jesus wept for love of his friend.

Olaf, King of Norway, martyr, died 1030

Olaf is considered the patron saint of Norway. In his early career he engaged in war and piracy in the Baltic and in Normandy. In Rouen, though, he was baptized and became a Christian. He returned to Norway, succeeded his father as king, and from then on Christianity was the dominant religion of the realm. He revised the laws of the nation and enforced them with strict impartiality, eliminating the possibility of bribes. He thereby alienated much of the aristocracy. The harshness that he sometimes resorted to in order to establish Christianity and his own law led to a rebellion. After being driven from the country and into exile, he enlisted support from Sweden to try to regain his kingdom, but he died in battle.

July 31, 2011
Time after Pentecost — Lectionary 18

In today's first reading God invites all who are hungry or thirsty to receive food and drink without cost. Jesus feeds the hungry multitude and reveals the abundance of God. At the eucharistic table we remember all who are hungry or poor in our world today. As we share the bread of life, we are sent forth to give ourselves away as bread for the hungry.

Prayer of the Day

Glorious God, your generosity waters the world with goodness, and you cover creation with abundance. Awaken in us a hunger for the food that satisfies both body and spirit, and with this food fill all the starving world; through your Son, Jesus Christ, our Savior and Lord.

Gospel Acclamation

Alleluia. One does not live by ¹ bread alone,* but by every word that comes from the ¹ mouth of God. *Alleluia.* (Matt. 4:4)

Readings and Psalm
Isaiah 55:1-5

God invites Israel to a great feast at which both food and drink are free. God also promises to make an everlasting covenant with all the people, with promises that previously had been limited to the line of kings. As David was a witness to the nations, these nations shall now acknowledge the ways in which God has glorified Israel.

Psalm 145:8-9, 14-21

You open wide your hand and satisfy the desire of every living thing. (Ps. 145:16)

Romans 9:1-5

This begins a new section in Paul's letter in which he will deal with the place of Israel in God's saving plan. He opens by highlighting how Israel's heritage and legacy include being God's children, having God's covenants, being given God's law, participating in worship of God, and receiving divine promises.

Matthew 14:13-21

After John the Baptist is murdered, Jesus desires a time of solitude. Still, his compassion for others will not allow him to dismiss those who need him, and he is moved to perform one of his greatest miracles.

Semicontinuous reading and psalm
Genesis 32:22-31

Jacob wrestled all night with God, and when God wanted to get away as dawn was breaking, Jacob would not let God go until God had blessed him. Jacob's name is changed to Israel to mark his new relationship with God as he enters the land. Jacob is astonished that he remains alive after seeing God face to face.

Psalm 17:1-7, 15

I shall see your face; when I awake, I shall be satisfied. (Ps. 17:15)

Preface   Sundays

Color   Green

Prayers of Intercession

The prayers are prepared locally for each occasion. The following examples may be adapted or used as appropriate.

Led by the Holy Spirit, and with the whole people of God in Christ Jesus, let us pray for the church, those in need, and all of God's creation.

A brief silence.

You desire that all people come to you. Give your church a passion to reach out to others with the good news of your love for all humankind. Hear us, O God.

Your mercy is great.

You created a world in which all life is sustainable. Open wide our hearts and minds, that those who are blessed with abundance live simply so that others may simply live. Hear us, O God.

Your mercy is great.

You are the Lord of all nations and all peoples. Create understanding among all people of faith so that we may together work for global peace (*especially*). Hear us, O God. **Your mercy is great.**

You turn no one away. In your compassion feed the hungry, cure the sick, and calm the fearful (*especially*). Grant them the peace only you can give. Hear us, O God. **Your mercy is great.**

You provide the bread of life for your people. Nourish this congregation on the body and blood of your Son, that we may be strengthened to serve. Hear us, O God. **Your mercy is great.**

Here other intercessions may be offered.

You sustain us in our faith. We give you thanks for the witnesses who have gone before us. May their example guide us until we are joined with them in glory. Hear us, O God. **Your mercy is great.**

Into your hands, O God, we commend ourselves and all for whom we pray, trusting in your abundant mercy, through Jesus Christ, our Savior and Lord. **Amen.**

Ideas and Images for the Day

Jesus is able to feed us abundantly, even with scraps. He meets earthly needs by feeding the crowds and continues now to offer himself as holy meal, freely given to all, no matter their income or rank in society. Advertisers have trained us that what's proclaimed as FREE usually isn't. More often, it's a ploy to get our money for some other, larger, purchase. Today we are invited to trust and receive Jesus' free gift of love without mistrusting that he's got up his sleeve some scheme to swindle our money.

1. "No such thing as a free lunch" says the old cliché, in contrast to the hungry and thirsty receiving food and drink without cost (Isa. 55:1). When we invite newcomers to worship, saying God's grace is free in one breath but then passing the offering plate in the next can send a confusing message. See if you have the resources to host a true free lunch, giving cold drinks for strollers at a local park, hand out $5 bills to purchase lunches at a local drive-through window—share *without* asking for anything in return or leaving a basket out to collect a "freewill offering."

2. While we know Jesus' gifts are free, free can be synonymous with worthless. Showing examples of cheap toys from the kids' value meal or the gleanings from a day at the state fair often shows "free" to mean clutter but no substance. If possible, show examples of "free stuff" from a summertime fair—ads, papers, plastic toys, pens, stickers. Contrast it by having children name free things that have great value (libraries, hugs, friendship, love), with the reminder that love from Jesus is freely given, and that it's the good kind of free.

3. CROP Walk, an event sponsored by Church World Services, crosses many communities and denominational lines bringing congregations together to raise money for world hunger. Many in the world are forced to walk long distances just for fresh water, a privilege we North Americans enjoy so much more easily than much of the world. The CROP logo is a familiar red stop sign, saying "Help CROP Stop Hunger." See http://www.churchworldservice.org/site/PageServer?pagename=crop_main for resources about CROP Walk.

4. When job-hunting is hard, people hunger not only for literal food but for the satisfaction that comes with productive work. Isaiah 55:2 highlights that we "spend . . . money for that which is not bread, and labor for that which does not satisfy." "Come, the banquet hall is ready," from El Salvador (*Global Songs 2*), names this challenge, pleading in its refrain: "God, we're hungry for an honest wage, for housing, and for bread. Strengthen us with this communion for the struggle still ahead."

Hymns for Worship

Gathering

All who hunger, gather gladly   ELW 461
We come to the hungry feast   ELW479, WOV 766
United at the table   ELW 498, LCC 408

Hymn of the Day

Break now the bread of life   ELW 515, LBW 235
   BREAD OF LIFE
When the poor ones/*Cuando el pobre*   ELW 725, LLC 508
   EL CAMINO
Lord, whose love in humble service   ELW 712, LBW 423
   BEACH SPRING

Offering

Come, let us eat   ELW 491, LBW 214, TFF 119
Let us talents and tongues employ   ELW 674, WOV 754, TFF 232

Communion

God extends an invitation   ELW 486, LCC 397
You satisfy the hungry heart   ELW 484, WOV 711
The church of Christ, in every age   ELW 729, LBW 433

Sending

Hallelujah! We sing your praises   ELW 535, WOV 722, TFF 158

I love to tell the story   ELW 661, LBW 390, TFF 228

Additional Hymns and Songs

Hope of the world   LBW 493

Come to the feast   RS 642, GC 503

My God, your table now is spread   HS91 769, H82 321

Music for the Day
Psalmody and Acclamations

Busarow, Donald. "Psalm 17:1-7, 15" from PSCY.

Krentz, Michael. "Psalm 17:1-7, 15" from PWA, Evangelical Lutheran Worship Edition.

Makeever, Ray. "Psalm 145:8-9, 14-21" from PWA, Evangelical Lutheran Worship Edition.

Mummert, Mark. "Psalm 145," Refrain 1, from PSCY.

Weber, Paul D. *Gospel Acclamations for Summer.*

Choral

Berger, Jean. "The Eyes of All Wait Upon Thee." SATB. AFP 9780800645595. *The Augsburg Choirbook.* AFP 9780800656782.

◦ Fleming, Larry L. "Humble Service." SATB. AFP 9780800646226.

Franck, Cesár/ed. Susan Palo Cherwien. "O Bread of Life/Panis Angelicus" from *To God Will I Sing.* ML solo, kybd. AFP 9780800674342.

Hayes, Mark. "Give Me Jesus" from *10 Spirituals for Solo Voice.* MH solo, pno. ALF 17954 Book.

Children's Choir

Anonymous. "What a Mighty Word God Gives" from *Worship & Praise.* U, kybd. AFP 9780806638508.

Folkening, John. "Feed Us, Jesus" from *LifeSongs.* U, kybd.

Hopson, Hal. "Jesus Fed the Hungry Thousands." U, kybd. HOP JR221.

Keyboard / Instrumental

◦ Henkelmann, Brian. "Beach Spring" from *Chorale Preludes for the Liturgical Year,* vol. 1. Kybd, fl. CPH 97-7227U1.

◦ Kosnik, James. "Bread of Life" from *Musica Sacra,* vol. 6. Org. CPH 97-7208U1.

◦ Roberts, Al. "El Camino" from *Piano Plus,* vol. 2. Pno, inst. AFP 978080063728.

◦ Sedio, Mark. "Beach Spring" from *Dancing in the Light.* Pno. AFP 9780800656546.

Handbell

◦ Helman, Michael. "Lord, Whose Love Through Humble Service." 3-5 oct hb, opt 3 oct hc, L3. CG CGB586.

◦ McChesney, Kevin. "Beach Spring." 3-5 oct, L2. BP HB238.

Stephenson, Valerie. "O Jesus, I Have Promised." 3-6 oct hb, opt 2-4 oct hc, L2+. CGA CGB404.

Praise Ensemble

● Chisholm, Thomas/William Runyan. "Great Is Thy Faithfulness." HOP.

● Grant, Amy/Michael W. Smith. "Thy Word." Meadowgreen Music/WRD. W&P 144.

● Park, Andy. "Only You." Mercy/VIN. Various editions.

● Redman, Matt. "Blessed Be Your Name." Thankyou Music.

● Scott, Kathryn. "Hungry." VIN.

● Zschech, Darlene. "Shout to the Lord." Hillsong/INT. ELW 821.

Global

Kolling, Miria T. "God Extends an Invitation/Nuestro Padres nos invita." ELW 486.

Prescod, Patrick, arr. "Communion Hymn" from *Let the Peoples Sing,* vol. 1. SATB. AFP 9780800675394.

◦ denotes suggestions that relate to the hymn of the day.
● denotes songs that are available on iTunes®.

236

August 7, 2011
Time after Pentecost — Lectionary 19

Elijah finds the presence of God not in earthquake, wind, or fire, but in the sound of sheer silence. When the disciples face a great storm on the sea, they cry out with fear. Jesus says: "Take heart, it is I; do not be afraid." Amid the storms of life, we gather to seek the calm presence of Christ that soothes our fears. In comforting words of scripture and in the refreshing bread and cup of the eucharist, God grants us peace and sends us forth to be a sign of God's presence to others.

Prayer of the Day

O God our defender, storms rage around and within us and cause us to be afraid. Rescue your people from despair, deliver your sons and daughters from fear, and preserve us in the faith of your Son, Jesus Christ, our Savior and Lord.

Gospel Acclamation

Alleluia. I wait for ˈ you, O Lᴏʀᴅ;* in your word ˈ is my hope. *Alleluia.* (Ps. 130:5)

Readings and Psalm
1 Kings 19:9-18

On Mount Horeb, where God had appeared to Moses with typical signs of God's presence—earthquake, wind, and fire—Elijah now experienced God in "sheer silence." God assured Elijah that he is not the only faithful believer. Seven thousand Israelites are still loyal. God instructed Elijah to anoint two men as kings and to anoint Elisha as his own successor.

Psalm 85:8-13

I will listen to what the Lᴏʀᴅ God is saying. (Ps. 85:8)

Romans 10:5-15

A right relationship with God is not something we achieve by heroic efforts. It is a gift received in the proclamation whose content is Jesus Christ. This proclaimed word creates our faith in the Lord Jesus Christ. Hence Christian proclamation is an indispensable component of God's saving actions.

Matthew 14:22-33

Matthew's gospel typically portrays Jesus' disciples as people of "little faith" who fail despite their best intentions. In this story, Matthew shows how Jesus comes to the disciples when they are in trouble and sustains them in their time of fear and doubt.

Semicontinuous reading and psalm
Genesis 37:1-4, 12-28

Though Joseph was Jacob's favorite son, his jealous brothers sold him into slavery. Judah, who protected Joseph's life, later gives a moving speech before Joseph in Egypt, indicating that the brothers had changed their ways (44:18-34).

Psalm 105:1-6, 16-22, 45b

Make known the deeds of the Lᴏʀᴅ among the peoples. Hallelujah! (Ps. 105:1, 45)

Preface   Sundays

Color   Green

Prayers of Intercession

The prayers are prepared locally for each occasion. The following examples may be adapted or used as appropriate.

With the whole people of God in Christ Jesus, let us pray for the church, those in need, and all of God's creation.
A brief silence.
O God: We pray for all who gather today in your name in every land. Increase their faith and service. Lord, in your mercy,
hear our prayer.

From the tiniest ladybug to the grandest ocean—your entire creation is a masterpiece, full of power and beauty. Help us treat this gift with respect and care. Lord, in your mercy,
hear our prayer.

For all nations in conflict and for those in need (*especially*), we ask for your presence, O God. We pray for peace and for all who fight for the rights of others. Lord, in your mercy,
hear our prayer.

We pray for all who are suffering (*especially*) that relief might come and grief be quieted. For those who are afraid, give them courage and strength. Lord, in your mercy,
hear our prayer.

Look with mercy on this congregation, O God. Be present in this place to guide our steps and light our path. Lord, in your mercy,
hear our prayer.
Here other intercessions may be offered.
We give thanks, O God, for the faithful service of all who abide with you in heaven. May their examples of faith give us insight for own pilgrimage on earth. Lord, in your mercy,
hear our prayer.
Into your hands, gracious God, we commend all for whom we pray, trusting in your mercy; through Jesus Christ, our Savior.
Amen.

Ideas and Images for the Day

In a world filled with noise and empty words, God comes to us as stillness and silence, even to the point that wind ceases (Matt. 14:32). Jesus walks over stormy waters to his disciples, entering their boat and being present with them despite their fears and doubts. Today's readings encourage us to keep our words spare and meaningful, lay aside our little faith with its wordy worries, and listen for God, who comes to us as quieting comfort.

1. Ask small children questions such as, "When you are scared by a thunderstorm, what do you do?" You could prepare a "storm kit" for examples (favorite blanket, flashlight, a teddy bear or doll, snacks, storm radio, toilet paper). Explain that Jesus' disciples were frightened by a storm, but Jesus came to sit in the boat with them when they were afraid. Jesus is not simply a security blanket or flashlight, but a friend with us in our fear.

2. In Depeche Mode's "Enjoy the Silence" (*Violator*, Mute Records, 1990) composer Martin Gore expresses his frustration with words: "Vows are spoken / To be broken . . . / Words are meaningless / And forgettable." Gore's lyrics proclaim truth about the world: we disappoint each other with empty promises, leading to little faith in others or God. By contrast, Jesus grasps our hands, pulls us from the water, and stills the wind. Enjoy the silence. http://www.youtube.com/watch?v=dAN9sKlOZxE&feature=related or http://en.wikipedia.org/wiki/Enjoy_the_Silence.

3. Yoga is a Hindu religious practice, though it could benefit the Christian seeking to silence everyday stress and be open to the insight of the Holy Spirit. Try watching a video such as PM Yoga (Gaiam, 2000): http://www.gaiam.com/product/yoga-studio/yoga-media/yoga-for-beginners/am+pm+yoga+for+beginners+dvd.do.

Most stretches are challenging for beginners, but playing "Introduction" or "Centering" for a women's group or Bible study could provide interreligious discussion on learning from yoga to calm our racing minds and give deliberation to our bodily prayer and meditation.

4. As we gather to worship, the confession and forgiveness encourages silence (*Evangelical Lutheran Worship*, p. 95). This week's readings lend themselves to intentional silence. Warn worshipers first about your intentions so they don't grow uncomfortable at an assumed mistake—but then add silence into a few more places in worship, perhaps between petitions of prayers, following the readings or before the Lord's Prayer.

5. Silence can be stillness in the soothing or awesome presence of God, or it can be a reaction of fear and little faith to remain silent or retreat at injustice. German Lutheran pastor Dietrich Bonhoeffer resisted the Nazi regime in World War II. Denise Giardina's novel *Saints and Villains* (Fawcett Books, 1987) contrasts Bonhoeffer's personal faith challenges with government attempts to silence his teaching. His 1945 execution did not silence his legacy of courage and ethical challenge.

Hymns for Worship
Gathering
Evening and morning   ELW 761, LBW 465
How firm a foundation   ELW 796, LBW 507
Shout to the Lord   ELW 821, W&P 124

Hymn of the Day
God, my Lord, my strength   ELW 795, LBW 484   *PÁN BŮH*
Praise, praise! You are my rock   ELW 862
   ZACHARY WOODS ROCK
Jesus, Savior, pilot me   ELW 755, LBW 334   *PILOT*

Offering
Calm to the waves   ELW 794
Now the silence   ELW 460, LBW 205

Communion
Eternal Father, strong to save   ELW 756, LBW 467
My life flows on in endless song   ELW 763, WOV 781
When peace like a river   ELW 785, LBW 346, TFF 194

Sending
What a fellowship, what a joy divine   ELW 774, WOV 780,
   TFF 220
O God, our help in ages past   ELW 632, LBW 320

Additional Hymns and Songs

Walk across the water   DH 69
You are my hiding place   W&P 160

Music for the Day
Psalmody and Acclamations

Harbor, Rawn. "O Lord, Let Us See Your Kindness (Psalm 85)." TFF 8.

Makeever, Ray. "Dancing at the Harvest (Psalm 85)" from *Dancing at the Harvest.*

Makeever, Ray. "Psalm 85:8-13" from PWA, Evangelical Lutheran Worship Edition.

Mummert, Mark. "Psalm 85," Refrain 1, from PSCY.

Pelz, Walter L. "Psalm 105:1-6, 16-22, 45b" from PWA, Evangelical Lutheran Worship Edition.

Weber, Paul D. *Gospel Acclamations for Summer.*

Woehr, Roland. "Psalm 105" from PSCY.

Choral

Biery, James. "The Waters of Life." SATB, org. AFP 9780800657683. *The Augsburg Choirbook.* AFP 9780800656782.

Davis, Katherine K. "Who Was the Man?" U, kybd. CG CGA-110.

Manz, Paul. "Let Us Ever Walk With Jesus." U, org. MSM 50-9405.

Ray, Robert. "He Never Failed Me Yet." SATB, kybd, solo. HAL 44708014.

Children's Choir

Makeever, Ray. "Dancing at the Harvest (Psalm 85)" from *Dancing at the Harvest.* U, kybd.

Makeever, Ray. "Walk Across the Water" from *Dancing at the Harvest.* U, kybd.

Scarlatti, Domenico. "We Will Sing for Joy." U, kybd. CG CGA 202.

Keyboard / Instrumental

○ Cherwien, David. "Pilot" from *Let It Rip! at the Piano,* vol. 1. Pno. AFP 9780800659066.

○ Cool, Jayne Southwick. "Pilot" from *Piano Plus,* vol. 2. Pno, inst. AFP 978080063728.

○ Eggert, John. "Pán Bůh" from *Six Hymn Preludes,* vol. 2. Org. CPH 97-5912U1.

○ Gehring, Philip. "Pán Bůh" from *Four Hymn Preludes.* Org. CPH 97-6501U1.

Handbell

○ Groth, Robert. "Jesus, Savior, Pilot Me." 4 oct. Robert Groth Productions MGR8301.

McFadden, Jane. "How Can I Keep from Singing." 3-5 oct, L3. AFP 9780800658120.

Stephenson, Valerie. "Eternal Father Strong to Save." 3-6 oct hb, opt 3-6 oct hc, L4. CG CGB515.

Praise Ensemble

• Foote, Billy/Charles Horne. "Sing to the King." WT/Sixsteps Music.

• Hughes, Tim. "Beautiful One." Thankyou Music.

• Hughes, Tim. "Here I Am to Worship." Thankyou Music/INT.

• Mark, Robin. "Days of Elijah." Daybreak Music/INT.

• Redman, Matt. "Better Is One Day." Thankyou Music.

• Tomlin, Chris/Jesse Reeves/Isaac Watts/JD Walt. "The Wonderful Cross." WT/Sixsteps Music.

Global

Lee, Dong Hoon. "Lonely the Boat" from *Sound the Bamboo.* U. GIA G-6830.

Thangaraj, M. Thomas. "Ocean of Love" from *Pave the Way: Global Songs 3.* U. AFP 9780800676896.

Monday, August 8
Dominic, founder of the Order of Preachers (Dominicans), died 1221

Dominic was a Spanish priest who preached against the Albigensians, a heretical sect that held gnostic and dualistic beliefs. Dominic believed that a stumbling block to restoring heretics to the church was the wealth of clergy, so he formed an itinerant religious order, the Order of Preachers (Dominicans), who lived in poverty, studied philosophy and theology, and preached against heresy. The method of this order was to use kindness and gentle argument, rather than harsh judgment, to bring unorthodox Christians back to the fold. Dominic was opposed to burning Christians at the stake. Three times Dominic was offered the office of bishop, which he refused so that he could continue in his work of preaching.

Wednesday, August 10
Lawrence, deacon, martyr, died 258

Lawrence was one of seven deacons of the congregation at Rome and, like the deacons appointed in Acts, was responsible for financial matters in the church and for the care of the poor. Lawrence lived during a time of persecution under the emperor Valerian. The emperor demanded that Lawrence surrender the treasures of the church. Lawrence gathered lepers, orphans, the blind and lame. He brought them to the emperor and said, "Here is the treasure of the church." This act enraged the emperor, and Lawrence was sentenced to death. Lawrence's martyrdom was one of the first to be observed by the church.

○ denotes suggestions that relate to the hymn of the day.
• denotes songs that are available on iTunes®.

Thursday, August 11

Clare, Abbess of San Damiano, died 1253

At age eighteen, Clare of Assisi heard Francis preach a sermon in a church in town. From that time, she determined to follow in his example of Christian living. With Francis's help (and against the wishes of her father) she and a growing number of companions established a women's Franciscan community, called the Order of Poor Ladies, or Poor Clares. She became a confidante and advisor to Francis, and in standing up against the wishes of popes for the sake of maintaining complete poverty, she helped inspire other women to pursue spiritual goals.

Saturday, August 13

Florence Nightingale, died 1910; Clara Maass, died 1901; renewers of society

When Florence Nightingale decided she would be a nurse, her family was horrified. In the early 1800s nursing was done by people with no training and no other way to earn a living. Florence trained at Kaiserswerth, Germany, with a Lutheran order of deaconesses. She returned home and worked to reform hospitals in England. Nightingale led a group of thirty-eight nurses to serve in the Crimean War, where they worked in appalling conditions. She returned to London as a hero and resumed her work there for hospital reform.

Clara Maass was born in New Jersey and served as a nurse in the Spanish-American War, where she encountered the horrors of yellow fever. She later responded to a call for subjects in research on yellow fever. During the experiments, which included receiving bites from mosquitoes, she contracted the disease and died. The commemoration of these women invites the church to give thanks for all who practice the arts of healing.

August 14, 2011
Time after Pentecost — Lectionary 20

In Isaiah we hear that God's house shall be a house of prayer for all people and that God will gather the outcasts of Israel. The Canaanite woman in today's gospel is a Gentile, an outsider, who is unflinching in her request that Jesus heal her daughter. As Jesus commends her bold faith, how might our church extend its mission to those on the margins of society? In our gathering around word and meal we receive strength to be signs of comfort, healing, and justice for those in need.

Today is the commemoration of the martyrs Maximilian Kolbe, who died in 1941, and Kaj Munk, who died in 1944.

Prayer of the Day

God of all peoples, your arms reach out to embrace all those who call upon you. Teach us as disciples of your Son to love the world with compassion and constancy, that your name may be known throughout the earth, through Jesus Christ, our Savior and Lord.

Gospel Acclamation

Alleluia. Jesus preached the good news | of the kingdom*
and cured every sickness a- | mong the people. *Alleluia.*
(Matt. 4:23)

Order Now
for 2012—Year B

sundays and seasons

Sundays and Seasons 2012—Year B
Save time with this comprehensive worship planning guide based on the Revised Common Lectionary. Provides all you need to prepare worship for the whole church year.

978-1-4514-0000-7 .... $39.00
(2 or more $32.00 ea.)

Worship Planning Calendar 2012—Year B
The perfect complement to *Sundays and Seasons*. Spiral-bound, this is both an appointment calendar and a workbook for preparing worship. Contains daily lectionary reading citations.

978-1-4514-0001-4 .... $22.00

SAVE 15%—2012 Combo Pack
Sundays and Seasons & Worship Planning Calendar
Sundays and Seasons and the Worship Planning Calendar work together to save you time and provide all you need to prepare engaging worship.

ED014867 .... $52.00
($61.00 if purchased separately)

SundaysandSeasons.com
SundaysandSeasons.com saves you time and effort by providing content and tools to plan worship flexibly and easily for your weekly bulletin or projection. Includes content from all ELCA worship volumes, clip-art, NRSV Bible, children's bulletins, and more!

Visit **sundaysandseasons.com** for more information.

Words for Worship 2012—Year B
This CD-ROM contains texts and graphical files with content from *Evangelical Lutheran Worship*. Also includes week-to-week elements from *Lectionary for Worship, Year B*; *Sundays and Seasons 2012*; and *Psalter for Worship Year B*, Evangelical Lutheran Worship edition.

978-1-4514-0002-1 .... $199.00

Shipping and Handling
Prices and Product Availability are subject to change without notice.

Sales Tax: Exempt customers must provide Augsburg Fortress with a copy of their state-issued exemption certificate. Customers without tax-exempt status must add applicable state/province and local sales tax for their area. Canadian customers will be charged GST.

Shipping Charges are additional on all orders. U.S. and Canadian orders (except U.S. cash orders) are assessed actual shipping charges based on standard group rates. Additional shipping charges are accessed for expedited service requests and international shipments.

Return Policy: With proof of purchase, non-dated, in print product in saleable condition may be returned for credit. Please call customer service at 1-800-328-4648 (U.S.) or 1-800-265-6397 (Canada) for assistance if you receive items that are damaged, defective, or were shipped in error. Specific return restrictions apply to some product lines. Please contact us prior to returning a special order item or item shipped directly from the manufacturer. Send U.S. order returns by a secure, prepaid, traceable method to the Augsburg Fortress Distribution Center, 4001 Gantz Road, Suite E., Grove City, Ohio 43123-1891. Canadian orders may be returned to Augsburg Fortress Canadian Distribution Center, 500 Trillium Drive, Box 9940, Kitchener, Ontario N2G 4Y4

AUGSBURG FORTRESS   PRJ014684-0210

Worship Planning Resources 2012
Year B Order Form

To order by mail, detach, fold, and seal your completed card. Please be sure to attach postage. You can also order by calling 1-800-328-4648, faxing 1-800-722-7766, or visiting our online store at augsburgfortress.org.

SHIP TO _____

Address _____

City _____

State _____ Zip _____

Phone _____

E-mail _____

BILL TO _____

Address _____

City _____

State _____ Zip _____

Phone _____

METHOD OF PAYMENT *(select one)*

AF Account # _____

Credit Card # _____

Exp. Date _____   *Card must be valid through Sept. 2011. Products ship Aug. 2011.*

Signature _____
Signature required on all credit card orders.

Sundays and Seasons 2012
QTY: _____ 978-1-4514-0000-7 .... $39.00*
QTY: _____ 978-6-0001-7434-7 .... Standing Order

Worship Planning Calendar 2012
QTY: _____ 978-1-4514-0001-4 .... $22.00*
QTY: _____ 978-6-0001-7435-4 .... Standing Order

Combo Pack 2012
QTY: _____ ED014867 .... $52.00*
QTY: _____ 978-6-0001-7436-1 .... Standing Order

Words for Worship 2012
QTY: _____ 978-1-4514-0002-1 .... $199.00*

New Proclamation 2012: Advent–Holy Week
QTY: _____ 978-0-8006-9771-6 .... $27.00*

New Proclamation 2012: Easter–Christ the King
QTY: _____ 978-0-8006-9772-3 .... $27.00*

Calendar of Word and Season 2012 *(without imprinting)*
QTY: _____ 978-1-4514-0004-5 .... $10.95*
QTY: _____ 978-6-0001-7439-2 .... Standing Order

Church Year Calendar 2012
QTY: _____ 978-1-4514-0003-8 .... $1.95*

Bread for the Day 2012
QTY: _____ 978-1-4514-0006-9 .... $8.95*

Ritual Lectionary, Year B
QTY: _____ 978-0-8066-5611-3 .... $115.00*

Study Edition Lectionary, Year B
QTY: _____ 978-0-8066-5612-0 .... $27.50*

Prices do not include shipping. Prices valid through April 1, 2011.

Place Stamp Here

Detach this card, fold it in half here, and seal the edges.

Order Now
for 2012—Year B

sundays and seasons

Great gifts and useful resources for living the church's year!

New Proclamation 2012

New Proclamation is your essential companion to Lectionary preaching, offering the best in creative, searching, and responsible interpretation of the biblical lectionary texts, presented by scholars of exegesis and preaching.

Advent–Holy Week, *978-0-8006-9771-6* $27.00
Easter–Christ the King, *978-0-8006-9772-3* $27.00

Bread for the Day 2012

Bible readings and prayers for the full year. Follows the daily lectionary. Quantity discounts available.

978-1-4514-0006-9 .... $8.95

Calendar of Word and Season 2012—Year B

Full-color wall calendar with room for adding family and church activities. Features beautiful art each month and identifies church festivals, national holidays, the color of the day, and Revised Common Lectionary citations. 8³/₈" x 10⁷/₈". Spiral-bound and punched for hanging.

978-1-4514-0004-5

Quantity	1–11	12–49	50–99	100–499	500+
Price	$10.95	$4.50	$3.50	$3.00	$2.50

Church Year Calendar 2012—Year B

Provides dates, lectionary readings, hymn of the day, and the liturgical color for each Sunday and festival. The ideal time-saver for pastors, worship and music directors, choir members, altar guilds, and all who live by the liturgical year. Two-sided. 11" x 8½".

978-1-4514-0003-8

Quantity	1–11	12–99	100+
Price	$1.95	$0.85	$0.75

Ritual Lectionary—Year B
978-0-8066-5611-3 .... $115.00

Study Lectionary with Reader Helps—Year B
978-0-8066-5612-0 .... $27.50

Thank you for your order!

Readings and Psalm

Isaiah 56:1, 6-8

The prophet calls upon Israel to do justice in view of God's imminent intervention to save. Righteousness and obedience define who belongs to the Israelite community—not race, nationality, or any other category.

Psalm 67

Let all the peoples praise you, O God. (Ps. 67:3)

Romans 11:1-2a, 29-32

God has not rejected Israel. Rather, the call and gifts of God are irrevocable, so that while all have been disobedient, God has mercy upon all.

Matthew 15:[10-20] 21-28

Jesus teaches his disciples that true purity is a matter of the heart rather than outward religious observances. Almost immediately, this teaching is tested when a woman considered to be pagan and unclean approaches him for help.

Semicontinuous reading and psalm

Genesis 45:1-15

Moved to tears by Judah's plea on behalf of Benjamin, Joseph declares, "I am Joseph!" and asks, "Is my father still alive?" The evil intent of the brothers had been trumped by God's using Joseph to preserve many lives at a time of famine.

Psalm 133

How good and pleasant it is to live together in unity. (Ps. 133:1)

Preface   Sundays

Color   Green

Prayers of Intercession

The prayers are prepared locally for each occasion. The following examples may be adapted or used as appropriate.
With the whole people of God in Christ Jesus, let us pray for the church, those in need, and all of God's creation.
A brief silence.
O God: We pray for all who gather today to lift songs of praise to you from choir lofts or cathedrals or hilltops. Lord, in your mercy,
hear our prayer.
We pray for your creation. Show mercy to every injured and suffering creature, and to every species losing its habitat. Lord, in your mercy,
hear our prayer.

For all nations in conflict (*especially*), we ask for your presence, O God. We pray for your grace to settle in the hearts of all who govern, that justice and peace be established for all. Lord, in your mercy,
hear our prayer.
We pray for all who are suffering (*especially*). We pray for hungry children, fearful parents, grieving loved ones, abused spouses, and those we now name in our hearts, that they may know your peace. Lord, in your mercy,
hear our prayer.
We pray for this congregation, especially those among us preparing to return to school: students and teachers, librarians and custodians, bus drivers and principals. Lord, in your mercy,
hear our prayer.
Here other intercessions may be offered.
With thanksgiving, O God, we remember all who abide with you in heaven (*especially the martyrs Maximilian Kolbe and Kaj Munk*). Lord, in your mercy,
hear our prayer.
Into your hands, gracious God, we commend all for whom we pray, trusting in your mercy; through Jesus Christ, our Savior.
Amen.

Ideas and Images for the Day

"We are beggars; this is true," are reported to be Martin Luther's last written words. Christians are "beggars" for God's grace, undeserving but graced nonetheless. In today's gospel, the Canaanite woman might be seen as a "beggar" for Jesus' healing for her daughter. Encountering resistance and insult, she persists with both humility and audacity. She is denied a place at the table at first, but she will accept even "crumbs" in the faith that Jesus' healing power and love are intended even for her. This story reminds us that even though crumbs from God's table would be enough, we are offered instead the abundance of Jesus' own self in bread and wine.

1. As disciples of Jesus and "beggars" for God's grace, we live the same paradox of humility and audacity, *boldly* coming to Jesus and *humbly* acknowledging our need. We demonstrate both as worshipers, which could be highlighted in elements of worship: saying or singing "Kyrie eleison" (echoing the woman's "Have mercy on me, Lord") and noting the way one approaches communion with hands outstretched, literally seeking a handout, trusting that it is for us.

2. By transforming Jesus' metaphor of dogs into a bold point about "crumbs" falling from the table, the Canaanite woman calls our attention to people who often get the "crumbs" that trickle down from more affluent or mainstream society. For example, an article by Therese Quinn uses these terms to talk about race and class in relation to public education: "Biscuits and Crumbs: Art Education after Brown v. Board of Education." The article is available at http://www.saic.edu/gallery/albums/userpics/10758/08_Biscuits.pdf.

3. Many stories challenging notions of insiders and outsiders could be connected to this story about God's love, which embraces not only Jews but also Gentiles. For example, in Mark Twain's classic book for young people, *The Prince and the Pauper* (BiblioLife, 2009), the two main characters trade places. Now the outsider, the prince struggles with the realities of poverty and need, and the pauper encounters the responsibilities and abundance of a royal insider.

4. The film *Radio* (Revolution Studios, 2003) tells the story of a developmentally challenged man on the margins of society whose life is transformed when Coach Jones welcomes him into the high school football team. No longer receiving just crumbs, Radio experiences the abundant love of the team, then the school, then the whole town. The movie was based on a *Sports Illustrated* article by Gary Smith ("Someone to Lean On," December 16, 1996), which contains this grace-filled line: "If there was room in the program for Radio, then who *couldn't* be included, who *wasn't* welcome to join the community at its largest weekly gatherings?" The article is at http://sportsillustrated.cnn.com/vault/article/magazine/MAG1009232/5/index.htm.

Hymns for Worship
Gathering
Rise, shine, you people! ELW 665, LBW 393
Oh, praise the gracious power ELW 651, WOV 750
Oh, for a thousand tongues to sing ELW 886, LBW 559

Hymn of the Day
O Christ the healer, we have come ELW 610, LBW 360 DISTRESS
There's a wideness in God's mercy ELW 587 ST. HELENA
ELW 588, LBW 290 LORD, REVIVE US
My faith looks up to thee ELW 759, LBW 479 OLIVET

Offering
In Christ there is no east or west ELW 650, LBW 359, TFF 214
Creating God, your fingers trace ELW 684, WOV 757

Communion
Healer of our every ill ELW 612, WOV 738
All Are Welcome ELW 641
Lord, whose love in humble service ELW 712, LBW 423

Sending
Soli Deo Gloria ELW 878
Lord of glory, you have bought us ELW 707, LBW 424

Additional Hymns and Songs
Let all the people praise DH 38
When in the hour of deepest need LBW 303
Here, master, in this quiet place HFG 72

Music for the Day
Psalmody and Acclamations
Bruxvoort-Colligan, Richard. "Sharing the Road (Psalm 133)" from *Sharing the Road.* AFP 9780800678630.
Harbor, Rawn. "Let the Peoples Praise You, O God (Psalm 67). TFF 7.
Makeever, Ray. "Let All the People Praise (Psalm 67)" from *Dancing at the Harvest.*
Makeever, Ray. "Psalm 67" from PWA, Evangelical Lutheran Worship Edition.
Messner, Sally. "Psalm 133" from PWA, Evangelical Lutheran Worship Edition.
Mummert, Mark. "Psalm 67," Refrain 1, from PSCY.
Organ, Anne Krentz. "Psalm 133" from PSCY.
Sosa, Pablo. "Behold, How Pleasant/Miren qué bueno." ELW 649.
Weber, Paul D. *Gospel Acclamations for Summer.*

Choral
Distler, Hugo. "Praise to the Lord, the Almighty" from *Chantry Choirbook.* SATB. AFP 9780800657772.
o Ellingboe, Bradley. "There's a Wideness in God's Mercy." SATB, kybd. AFP 9780800676544.
Hellerman, Fred/Fran Minkoff/arr. David Cherwien. "O Healing River" from *To God Will I Sing.* MH solo, kybd. AFP 9780800674342.
Keith, Paul Randall. "God, Be Merciful unto Us." SATB, org. AFP9780806697239.
Rutter, John. "For the Beauty of the Earth." SA, pno. HIN HMC-469.

o denotes suggestions that relate to the hymn of the day.
● denotes songs that are available on iTunes®.

Children's Choir

Bedford, Michael. "Let All the People Praise You, O God." U/2 pt, fl, kybd. CG CGA933.

Makeever, Ray. "Let All the People Praise (Psalm 67)" from *Dancing at the Harvest*. U, kybd.

Page, Sue Ellen. "Jesus' Hands Were Kind Hands." U, kybd, fl. CG CGA485.

Keyboard / Instrumental

○ Carter, John. "Olivet" from *Hymns for Piano*, vol. 2. Pno. HOP 8197.

Peek, Richard. "Sonatina for Organ Manuals" from *Organ Music for the Seasons*, vol. 3. Org. AFP 9780800675646.

○ Raabe, Nancy M. "Olivet" from *Grace and Peace*, vol. 3. Pno. AFP 9780806696959.

○ Sedio, Mark. "Olivet" from *Organ Tapestries*, vol. 2. Org. CPH 97-6861U1.

Handbell

Eithun, Sandra. "I Love to Tell the Story." 3-5 oct hb, opt 3 oct hc, L3. AGHER AG35242.

○ Helman, Michael. "My Faith Looks Up to Thee." 3-5 oct hb, opt 3-5 oct hc, L2. CPH 97-7240.

○ McChesney, Kevin/Gordon E. Young. "My Faith Looks Up to Thee." 3-5 oct hb, opt 3 oct hc, L2+. HOP 2386.

Praise Ensemble

● Doerksen, Brian. "Refiner's Fire." VIN.

● Egan, Jon. "I Am Free." Vertical Worship Songs/INT.

● Morgan, Reuben. "I Give You My Heart." Hillsong/INT.

● Redman, Matt. "You Never Let Go." Thankyou Music.

● Tomlin, Chris/Ed Cash/Stephan Sharp. "Made to Worship." WT/Sixsteps Music.

● Zschech, Darlene. "Worthy Is the Lamb." Hillsong/INT.

Global

Prescod, Patrick, arr. "Let All the Peoples Praise You/Todos los pueblos canten" from *Let the Peoples Sing*. SATB. AFP 9780800675394.

Trad. Greek melody. "Kyrie Eleison" from *Sent by the Lord: Songs of the World Church*, vol 2. U. GIA G-3740.

Sunday, August 14

Maximilian Kolbe, died 1941; Kaj Munk, died 1944; martyrs

Father Kolbe was a Franciscan priest, born Raymond Kolbe. After spending some time working in Asia, he returned in 1936 to his native Poland, where he supervised a friary that came to house thousands of Polish war refugees, mostly Jews. The Nazis were watching, however, and he was arrested. Confined in Auschwitz, Kolbe gave generously of his meager resources and finally volunteered to be starved to death in place of another man who was a husband and father. After two weeks, he was executed by a lethal injection.

Kaj (pronounced KYE) Munk, a Danish Lutheran pastor and playwright, was an outspoken critic of the Nazis, who occupied Denmark during the Second World War. His plays frequently highlighted the eventual victory of the Christian faith despite the church's weak and ineffective witness. The Nazis feared Munk because his sermons and articles helped to strengthen the Danish resistance movement. He was executed by the Gestapo on January 5, 1944.

Monday, August 15

Mary, Mother of Our Lord

The church honors Mary with the Greek title *theotokos*, meaning God-bearer. Origen first used this title in the early church, and the councils of Ephesus and Chalcedon upheld it. Luther upheld this same title in his writings. The honor paid to Mary as *theotokos* and mother of our Lord goes back to biblical times, when Mary herself sang, "from now on all generations will call me blessed" (Luke 1:48). Mary's life revealed the presence of God incarnate, and it revealed God's presence among the humble and poor. Mary's song, the Magnificat, speaks of reversals in the reign of God: the mighty are cast down, the lowly are lifted up, the hungry are fed, and the rich are sent away empty-handed.

Saturday, August 20

Bernard, Abbot of Clairvaux, died 1153

Bernard was a Cistercian monk who became an abbot of great spiritual depth. He was a mystical writer deeply devoted to the humanity of Christ who emphasized the inner human experience of prayer and contemplation. He was critical of one of the foremost theologians of the day, Peter Abelard, because he believed Abelard's approach to faith was too rational and did not provide sufficient room for mystery. Bernard's devotional writings are still read today. His sermon on the Song of Solomon treats that Old Testament book as an allegory of Christ's love for humanity. Bernard wrote several hymns that are still sung today in translation, including "Jesus, the Very Thought of You" (ELW 754).

August 21, 2011
Time after Pentecost — Lectionary 21

In Isaiah the people are bid to look to their spiritual ancestors as the rock from which they were hewn. Jesus declares that the church will be built on the rock of Peter's bold confession of faith. God's word of reconciliation and mercy are keys to the church's mission. Paul urges us to not be conformed to this world, but to offer our bodies as a living sacrifice, using our individual gifts to build up the body of Christ. From the table we go forth to offer our spiritual worship through word and deed.

Prayer of the Day

O God, with all your faithful followers of every age, we praise you, the rock of our life. Be our strong foundation and form us into the body of your Son, that we may gladly minister to all the world, through Jesus Christ, our Savior and Lord.

Gospel Acclamation

Alleluia. You are ¹ the Messiah,* the Son of the ¹ living God. *Alleluia.* (Matt. 16:16)

Readings and Psalm
Isaiah 51:1-6

Just as God had called Abraham and Sarah and given them many descendants, so now God offers comfort to Zion. God's deliverance will come soon and will never end.

Psalm 138

O Lord, your steadfast love endures forever. (Ps. 138:8)

Romans 12:1-8

In response to God's merciful activity, we are to worship by living holistic, God-pleasing lives. Our values and viewpoints are not molded by this age, but are transformed by the Spirit's renewing work. God's grace empowers different forms of service among Christians, but all forms of ministry function to build up the body of Christ.

Matthew 16:13-20

At a climactic point in Jesus' ministry, God reveals to Peter that Jesus is "the Messiah, the Son of the living God," and Jesus responds with the promise of a church that will overcome the very gates of Hades.

Semicontinuous reading and psalm
Exodus 1:8—2:10

The brave Hebrew midwives defied Pharaoh to save many infants from death. When the mother of Moses placed him in a basket in the Nile, the daughter of Pharaoh found him, adopted him, and brought him up. But the sister of Moses and his mother played crucial roles in this drama.

Psalm 124

We have escaped like a bird from the snare of the fowler. (Ps. 124:7)

Preface   Sundays

Color   Green

Prayers of Intercession

The prayers are prepared locally for each occasion. The following examples may be adapted or used as appropriate.

With the whole people of God in Christ Jesus, let us pray for the church, those in need, and all of God's creation.
A brief silence.
O God: We pray for your church and for the proclamation of your gospel. Give energy and confidence to all who work to make your love a reality on earth. Lord, in your mercy,
hear our prayer.
We give thanks for crops nearing harvest. We give thanks for water and sunlight. We give thanks for the nourishment we receive from your creation. Lord, in your mercy,
hear our prayer.
For all nations in poverty or under persecution (*especially*), we ask for your presence, O God. We pray for peace and reconciliation among all people. Lord, in your mercy,
hear our prayer.

Be present with all who are suffering: those who are ill, grieving, angry, addicted, or afraid (*especially*), that they may be comforted. Lord, in your mercy,
hear our prayer.
We lift up your church in this place, O God. Bless our pastor/s, our Sunday school teachers, our youth and elderly, our communion servers, funeral-lunch preparers, and those who maintain our building. Lord, in your mercy,
hear our prayer.
Here other intercessions may be offered.
We give thanks, O God, for those who have gone before us. For lives of service and examples of faith, we are grateful. Lord, in your mercy,
hear our prayer.
Into your hands, gracious God, we commend all for whom we pray, trusting in your mercy; through Jesus Christ, our Savior.
Amen.

Ideas and Images for the Day

In late August, students are preparing to go back to school, and many churches gear up for a new year of Sunday school. It is a good time to be reminded of the heart of Christian formation: conformation and transformation (Rom. 12:2). As it was for Peter, part of formation is learning to confess Jesus as the Messiah. But then Peter discovers what that confession means for him: Jesus calls him by name and tells him who he is. There is a connection for us too, between learning to confess Jesus and hearing him say to us, "You are . . . ." As we explore our own formation as Christian disciples, Isaiah invites us to consider whether we are truly a "chip off the old block" of our forebears in the faith.

1. In traditional Lutheran worship, we make two confessions on many Sundays: a confession of sin and a confession of faith. In the first, we acknowledge who we are as sinner and saint, and in the second, we acknowledge who God is in the mystery of the Trinity.

2. The song "You Are Mine" (ELW 581) can help us imagine ourselves in Peter's place—having a similar conversation with Jesus and asking him to reveal our identity as we follow him. In the song, we sing the words and hear them coming from Jesus: "I have called you each by name."

3. Discovering our identity as Jesus' disciples is a lifelong process, but it starts early—as early as baptism. Invite children to put on name tags with their own names and wonder with them how Jesus might complete the sentence "You are . . ." (special, unique, loved, talented). Older children might name gifts of talents, experiences, or personality that Jesus could point out to them. Since the process continues throughout life, children could also hand out name tags to the whole congregation (if practical) and invite teens and adults to consider the same questions for themselves.

4. For some helpful language on the connection between faith formation and teaching ministries, review the ELCA's social statement "Our Calling in Education" (http://www.elca.org/What-We-Believe/Social-Issues/Social-Statements/Education.aspx). At this time of year, many campus ministries also are preparing for students to return to class. Plentiful resources to celebrate campus ministry and its important work in forming identity are available at http://archive.elca.org/campusministry/celebrate100/presources.html.

Hymns for Worship
Gathering
Christ is made the sure foundation   ELW 645, LBW 367, WOV 747
O Holy Spirit, enter in   ELW 786, LBW 459
Christ is the king!   ELW 662, LBW 386

Hymn of the Day
Built on a rock   ELW 652, LBW 365
KIRKEN DEN ER ET GAMMELT HUS
The church's one foundation   ELW 654, LBW 369   *AURELIA*
My hope is built on nothing less   ELW 596/597, LBW 293/294
THE SOLID ROCK/MELITA

Offering
Yours, Lord, is the glory   ELW 849, LCC 605
We Are an Offering   ELW 692, W&P 146

Communion
O Savior, precious Savior   ELW 820, LBW 514
Faith of our Fathers   ELW 812, 813, LBW 500
Holy God, holy and glorious   ELW 637

Sending
We all are one in mission   ELW 576, WOV 755
Take my life, that I may be   ELW 583, 685, LBW 406

Additional Hymns and Songs
Seek ye first   WOV 783, TFF 149
Let kings and prophets yield their name   HFG 99

Music for the Day
Psalmody and Acclamations

Keesecker, Thomas. "Psalm 138" from PWA, Evangelical Lutheran Worship Edition.

Pavlechko, Thomas. "Psalm 124" from PWA, Evangelical Lutheran Worship Edition.

Pavlechko, Thomas. "Psalm 138," Refrain 2, from PSCY.

Weber, Paul D. *Gospel Acclamations for Summer.*

Weber, Paul D. "Psalm 124," Refrain 1, from PSCY.

Choral

○ Burkhardt, Michael. "Built on a Rock." SATB, assembly, hb, tpt, org. MSM 60-9014A.

Hillert, Richard. "The Lord Is My Light and My Salvation." U, kybd, B-flat or C inst. GIA G-4951.

Mendelssohn, Felix. "On God Alone My Hope I Build" from *Chantry Choirbook.* SATB. AFP 9780800657772.

Scott, K. Lee. "King of Glory, King of Peace" from *Rejoice Now My Spirit.* MH solo, kybd. AFP 9780800651084.

Children's Choir

Lindh, Jody. "I Give You Thanks." U, kybd, perc, opt bass, synth. CG CGA561.

Lord, Suzanne. "Faith That's Sure" from *LifeSongs.* U, kybd.

Makeever, Ray. "Holy One, In You Alone" from *Dancing at the Harvest.* U, kybd.

Keyboard / Instrumental

○ Held, Wilbur. "The Solid Rock" from *Six Gospel Hymn Preludes.* Org. MSM 10-523.

○ Manz, Paul O. "Aurelia" from *Three Hymn Settings for Organ,* set 2. Org. MSM 10-525.

○ Miller, Aaron David. "Kirken den er et gammelt hus" from *Chorale Preludes for Piano in Traditional Styles.* Pno. AFP 9780800679033.

○ Peeters, Flor. "Kirken den er et gammelt hus" from *Augsburg Organ Library: November.* Org. AFP 9780800658960.

Handbell

○ Helman, Michael. "Built on A Rock." 3-5 oct, L3. ALF 00-19006.

○ Lamb, Linda. "The Solid Rock." 3-5 oct, L2. ALF 00-25336.

○ Tucker, Sondra. "The Church's One Foundation." 2-3 oct, L2. CPH 97-6903.

Praise Ensemble

● Coomes, Tommy/Mike Fay. "As We Gather." MAR.

● Haugen, Marty. "As the Grains of Wheat." GIA. ELW 465.

● Kendrick, Graham. "God of the Poor." INT/Make Way Music. W&P 17. Various editions.

Liles, Dwight. "We Are an Offering." Bug and Bear Music/WRD. ELW 692, W&P 146. Various editions.

● Peterson, Hans/Larry Olson. "All Are Welcome" from *Work of the People,* vol. 1. Dakota Road Music.

● Wimber, John. "Spirit Song." Mercy/VIN. W&P 130.

Global

African American spiritual. "Jesus Is a Rock in a Weary Land." ELW 333.

Trad. Nyanga, Zambia. "Chimwemwe mwa Yesu/Rejoice in Jesus" from *Agape: Songs of Hope and Reconciliation.* U, gtr. Lutheran World Federation. AFP 9780191000133.

Wednesday, August 24
Bartholomew, Apostle

Bartholomew is mentioned as one of Jesus' disciples in Matthew, Mark, and Luke. The list in John does not include him but rather Nathanael. These two are therefore often assumed to be the same person. Except for his name on these lists of the Twelve, little is known. Some traditions say Bartholomew preached in India or Armenia following the resurrection. In art, Bartholomew is pictured holding a flaying knife to indicate the manner in which he was killed.

○ denotes suggestions that relate to the hymn of the day.
● denotes songs that are available on iTunes®.

August 28, 2011
Time after Pentecost — Lectionary 22

The prophet Jeremiah speaks of the incurable wound of his suffering, yet finds in God's words the delight of his heart. When Peter doesn't grasp Jesus' words about suffering, Jesus tells the disciples they will find their lives in losing them. Such sacrificial love is described by Paul when he urges us to associate with the lowly and not repay evil with evil. In worship we gather as a community that we might offer ourselves for the sake of our suffering world.

Today is the commemoration of Augustine, Bishop of Hippo, who died in 430, and Moses the Black, monk and martyr, who died around 400.

Prayer of the Day

O God, we thank you for your Son, who chose the path of suffering for the sake of the world. Humble us by his example, point us to the path of obedience, and give us strength to follow your commands, through Jesus Christ, our Savior and Lord.

Gospel Acclamation

Alleluia. May the God of our Lord Jesus Christ enlighten the eyes ˡ of our hearts,* so that we may know the hope to which ˡ God has called us. *Alleluia.* (Eph. 1:17, 18)

Readings and Psalm
Jeremiah 15:15-21

Jeremiah's delight in the word of the Lord is contradicted by the heaviness of God's hand upon him and God's seeming unfaithfulness. God's tough love to Jeremiah says that if he repents, he will be allowed to continue in his strenuous ministry. Jeremiah is strengthened by the simple words: "I am with you."

Psalm 26:1-8

Your love is before my eyes; I have walked faithfully with you. (Ps. 26:3)

Romans 12:9-21

Paul presents benchmarks for faithful relationships with Christians and non-Christians. Love is the unflagging standard of our behavior. When we encounter evil, we do not resort to its tactics but seek to overcome it with good. While Christians cannot control the actions and attitudes of others, we seek to live at peace with all people.

Matthew 16:21-28

After Peter confesses that Jesus is "the Messiah, the Son of the living God" (16:16), Jesus reveals the ultimate purpose of his ministry. These words prove hard to accept, even for a disciple whom Jesus has called a "rock."

Semicontinuous reading and psalm
Exodus 3:1-15

Moses experienced the call of God when God appeared to him in a bush that burned but was not consumed. When Moses expressed his unworthiness, God promised to be with him. When Moses objected that people would demand to know God's name, God revealed his personal name, Yahweh (I AM WHO I AM), or the LORD. Israel discovered God's true identity when God took them out of Egypt.

Psalm 105:1-6, 23-26, 45b

Make known the deeds of the LORD among the peoples. Hallelujah! (Ps. 105:1, 45)

Preface   Sundays

Color   Green

Prayers of Intercession

The prayers are prepared locally for each occasion. The following examples may be adapted or used as appropriate.

With the whole people of God in Christ Jesus, let us pray for the church, those in need, and all of God's creation.
A brief silence.

O God: We pray for all who work today to share the good news of your Son, Jesus Christ. We especially remember those who gather under the threat of persecution, that they might be sustained. Lord, in your mercy,
hear our prayer.

From the smallest ant to the tallest tree—your entire creation is a masterpiece and a gift. Help us treat your creation with respect and care. Lord, in your mercy,
hear our prayer.

For all nations at war or facing disease and poverty (*especially*), we ask for your life-giving presence and peace, O God. We pray for clean water and an end to hunger. Lord, in your mercy,
hear our prayer.

Look with compassion on all who are suffering: the unemployed, abused and neglected children, people who are depressed and lonely, and those facing challenges to their health (*especially*). Lord, in your mercy,
hear our prayer.

Look with kindness on this community, O God. Weave us into a net that provides comfort and support, refuge and friendship. Lord, in your mercy,
hear our prayer.

Here other intercessions may be offered.

With thanksgiving, O God, we remember all who abide with you in heaven (*especially Augustine, Bishop of Hippo, and Moses the Black, monk and martyr*). Lord, in your mercy,
hear our prayer.

Into your hands, gracious God, we commend all for whom we pray, trusting in your mercy; through Jesus Christ, our Savior.
Amen.

Ideas and Images for the Day

Peter may be the "rock" on which Christ will build the church (Matt. 16:18), but when Jesus reveals the suffering that will come first, Peter becomes a tempter and "stumbling block." Assuming God must have a *different* way to save the world, Peter protests Jesus' suffering and death. Jesus explains to Peter and all his disciples that, in fact, this *is* the way to life—losing one's life in order to find it. In times when we too are tempted by a worldly way of comfort and success, convinced that surely God must have an easier way than the way of the cross, this gospel reminds us that resurrection and life await on the other side of suffering and death.

1. The crucifixion isn't the only time when disciples might wonder if God has a different, more comfortable way to save the world. Martin Luther made this observation about Jesus' birth: "Our God begins with angels and ends with shepherds. Why does he do such preposterous things? . . . Our common sense revolts and says, 'Could not God have saved the world some other way?'" (*Martin Luther's Christmas Book*, ed. Roland H. Bainton [Minneapolis: Augsburg Fortress, 1997], p. 40).

2. The season of Lent often raises awareness of the call to "lose our lives" and follow the way of the cross. However, this awareness in our own discipleship does not *always* follow the liturgical calendar; liturgical seasons teach us attitudes and practices we need any time of year. So how about observing Holy Week in August? Following the way or "stations" of the cross is a Holy Week tradition in many congregations. See pages 116–121 in this volume for an example. Many online resources are available; http://www.newadvent.org/cathen/15569a.htm details the history of the practice.

3. The controversial film *The Last Temptation of Christ* (Cineplex-Odeon Films, 1988) imagines Jesus' temptation at his death in a way reminiscent of Peter's protest: surely God has another way, and surely Jesus doesn't *really* have to suffer. Tempted by a vision of a normal life as a human man with a family, Jesus ultimately resists even this last temptation in order to die on the cross and accomplish God's salvation.

4. Construct or draw two doors or paths, one marked by a cross and the other with a symbol of comfort and success (crown, dollar sign, etc.). Invite children to imagine what might be behind each door or on each path. Why might one choose each one? The way of comfort and success may look easier in the short term, but Jesus promises that the way of the cross leads to new life. (If you use a path, Robert Frost's famous poem "The Road Not Taken" might also provide some inspiration.)

Hymns for Worship
Gathering

Son of God, eternal Savior   ELW 655, LBW 364
For the beauty of the earth   ELW 879, LBW 561
Come, follow me, the savior spake   ELW 799, LBW 455

Hymn of the Day

Will you come and follow me   ELW 798   *KELVINGROVE*
Take up your cross, the Savior said   ELW 667   *BOURBON*
   LBW 398   *NUN LASST UNS DEN LEIB BEGRABEN*
Lift high the cross   ELW 660, LBW 377   *CRUCIFER*

Offering

Lord Jesus, you shall be my song   ELW 808
By gracious powers   ELW 626, WOV 736

Communion

Day by day   ELW 790, WOV 746
Let us ever walk with Jesus   ELW 802, LBW 487
Jesus, still lead on   ELW 624, LBW 341

Sending

Rise, O church, like Christ arisen   ELW 548
Lift high the cross   ELW 660, LBW 377

Additional Hymns and Songs

We will glorify   W&P 154, TFF 281
Step by step   W&P 132
If you believe and I believe   WLP 806, GC 722

Music for the Day
Psalmody and Acclamations

Messner, Sally. "Psalm 26:1-8" from PWA, Evangelical Lutheran
Worship Edition.

Pelz, Walter L. "Psalm 105:1-6, 23-26, 45b" from PWA, Evangelical
Lutheran Worship Edition.

Weber, Paul D. *Gospel Acclamations for Summer.*

Woehr, Roland. "Psalm 105" from PSCY.

Wold, Wayne L. "Psalm 26" from PSCY.

Choral

○ Bell, John A. "The Summons (Will You Come and Follow Me)". 2 pt
mxd or SA, pno, fl, opt gtr, opt assembly. GIA G-5410.

Bouman, Paul. "'Take Up Your Cross,' the Savior Said." SATB.
SEL 420-617.

○ Hobby, Robert A. "Lift High the Cross." SATB, org, br, cym, timp,
opt assembly. MSM 60-7020.

Schelat, David. "Praise the Lord, God's Glories Show." SAB, conga
drms. OXF 9780193865518.

Children's Choir

Brokering, Lois. "What Does It Mean to Follow Jesus?" from *Life-
Songs.* U, kybd.

Cool, Jayne Southwick. "A Prayer for Peace." U, kybd.
AFP 9780800664114.

Makeever, Ray. "Thanksgiving to the Living God" from *Dancing at
the Harvest.* U, kybd.

Keyboard / Instrumental

○ Arnatt, Ronald. "Crucifer" from *Augsburg Organ Library: November.*
Org. AFP 9780800658960.

○ Frahm, Frederick. "Crucifer" from *Faith Alive*, vol. 1. Org.
AFP 9780800675738.

○ Manz, Paul O. "Bourbon" from *Two Lenten Hymns for Flute, Oboe
and Organ.* Org, fl, ob. MSM 20-370.

○ Organ, Anne Krentz. "Kelvingrove" from *Come to Us, Creative
Spirit.* Pno. AFP 9780800659042.

Handbell

Frizzell, J. D. "For the Beauty of the Earth." 3-5 oct hb, opt 3 oct hc,
L2+. AGEHR AG35286.

○ McAninch, Diane. "Lift High the Cross." 2-3 oct, L2-. HOP 2357.

Stitt, Julie. "I Want Jesus to Walk with Me." 3-6 oct, L4.
AGEHR AG36031.

Praise Ensemble

● Baloche, Paul. "Open the Eyes of My Heart." INT.
Bell, John. "Will You Come and Follow Me?" GIA G-5410. ELW 798.

● LeBlanc, Lenny/Paul Baloche. "Above All." INT.

● Redman, Matt. "The Heart of Worship." Thankyou Music.

● Tomlin, Chris/Jesse Reeves/Isaac Watts/JD Walt. "The Wonderful
Cross." WT/Sixsteps Music.

● Zschech, Darlene. "Worthy Is the Lamb." Hillsong/INT.

Global

Dexter, Noel. "I Come to the Cross" from *Let the Peoples Sing*. SATB.
AFP 9780800675394.

Loh, I-to. "Christ Is Our Peace" from *Sound the Bamboo*. U.
GIA G-6830.

Sunday, August 28
Augustine, Bishop of Hippo, died 430

Augustine was one of the greatest theologians of the Western church. Born in North Africa, he was a philosophy student in Carthage, where he later became a teacher of rhetoric. Much of his young life was a debauched one. As an adult he came under the influence of Ambrose, the bishop of Milan, and through him came to see Christianity as a religion appropriate for a philosopher. Augustine was baptized by Ambrose at the Easter Vigil in 387. He was ordained four years later and made bishop of Hippo in 396. Augustine was a defender of the Christian faith and argued, against the Donatists, that the holiness of the church did not depend on the holiness of its members, particularly the clergy, but that holiness comes from Christ, the head of the church. Augustine's autobiography, *Confessions*, tells of his slow movement toward faith and includes the line "Late have I loved thee."

Moses the Black, monk, martyr, died around 400

A man of great strength and rough character, Moses the Black was converted to Christian faith toward the close of the fourth century. Prior to his conversion he had been a thief and a leader of a gang of robbers. The story of his conversion is unknown, but eventually he became a desert monk at Skete. The habit of his monastic community was white, though Moses is reported to have said, "God knows I am black within." The change in his heart and life had a profound impact on his native Ethiopia. He was murdered when Berber bandits attacked his monastery.

○ denotes suggestions that relate to the hymn of the day.
● denotes songs that are available on iTunes®.

Friday, September 2

Nikolai Frederik Severin Grundtvig, bishop, renewer of the church, died 1872

Grundtvig was one of two principal Danish theologians of the nineteenth century; the other was Søren Kierkegaard. Grundtvig's ministry as a parish pastor had a difficult start. He was officially censured after his first sermon, though he did receive approval a year later to be ordained. He served with his father for two years but was unable to receive a call for seven years after that. In 1826 he was forced to resign after he attacked the notion that Christianity was merely a philosophical idea rather than God's revelation made known to us in Christ and through word and sacrament. This belief would be a hallmark of Grundtvig's writing. He spent his last thirty-three years as a chaplain at a home for elderly women. From his university days he was convinced that poetry spoke to the human spirit better than prose. He wrote more than a thousand hymns, including "God's Word Is Our Great Heritage" (ELW 509).

TIME AFTER PENTECOST

AUTUMN

SUMMER   AUTUMN   NOVEMBER

Preparing for Autumn

Reconciliation Rally

September is a conflicted month in the life of many churches. On the one hand, it is simply the continuation of the lengthy Time after Pentecost. On the other hand, it is the season for Rally Day, Labor Day, Comeback Sunday, school-year blessings, harvest festivals, and stewardship drives. How to balance these competing forces? It is likely that many congregations simply repurpose the lectionary texts so that they preach the preselected message. As in, "Well, this gospel is really about the extravagance of forgiveness, but this is Rally Sunday, so let's find a way to have it address the beginning of another Sunday school year." This is not always a bad approach. Certainly, preachers and worship leaders always need to find creative ways to connect the lectionary to the local context. Life happens, and it is part of the creativity of reading scripture to connect what happens daily to what we read in scripture daily.

Consider encouraging making connections between scripture and life in your congregation this fall. Faith Inkubators has developed a model for five-minute at-home devotions that they call the Faith Five (http://www.faithink.com/Inkubators/faith5.asp):

1. SHARE highs and lows of the day
2. READ and highlight a verse of scripture in your Bible
3. TALK about how the verse relates to your highs and lows
4. PRAY for your highs and lows, for your family, and for the world
5. BLESS one another

If we ask our parishioners to do this daily, it only makes sense that even the Sunday lectionary is read via this hermeneutical strategy. What are we up to this week? What are our highs and lows? Let's talk about how the gospel relates to our highs and lows.

However, a danger in this approach is eisegesis, "the process of misinterpreting a text in such a way that it introduces one's own ideas, reading into the text" (http://en.wikipedia.org/wiki/Eisegesis). One reason congregations use the lectionary is to avoid eisegesis. By adopting a three-year schedule for reading, ostensibly the goal is to be read by the scriptures, allowing them to imbue and shape our ideas, and inspire in us greater faithfulness and Christlikeness.

This might be accomplished by giving Rally Day completely over to proclamation on the actual central theme of the gospel readings for the first few Sundays of autumn—forgiveness and reconciliation. What if the rally cry of the church is not "Let's get enthusiastic! Let's kick off another amazing, successful year"—but rather "Lord have mercy! Let us learn to forgive one another from the heart!" If the congregation is engaged in a stewardship appeal, imagine stewarding not only material gifts and spiritual gifts, but the gift the reformers called the Office of the Keys, based on Matthew 18:18, "Whatever you bind on earth will be bound in heaven, and whatever you loose on earth will be loosed in heaven." What if the congregation devoted itself to reviewing and reciting the section of the Small Catechism devoted to the Office of the Keys? What kind of rally might that be?

Re-Formation

Christians learn to be Christian in Sunday school and confirmation, right? A pervasive myth in our churches is that Christian education is where faith is formed. This is why so many parents drop their children off for Sunday school but do not attend worship with them. However, most experts in pedagogy will tell you that children learn by what they do, and what they see done, more than what they are told to do but seldom see. This pertains to worship in a profound way.

One of the most prevalent misconceptions in the church around worship practices, for example, is that to receive the Lord's supper rightly, one must understand it cognitively. So some churches require children at some grade level to attend classes before they receive their first communion. In the meantime, Sunday after Sunday, if the children are in worship with their parents, they see the host elevated, the words of promise spoken in relation to the meal, and an invitation extended to receive it, but then they are excluded. They are crossed over and crossed out from receiving the meal, sometimes very literally, when they have the sign of the cross marked on their foreheads.

These congregations have listened to Paul's instructions, "For all who eat and drink without discerning the body, eat and drink judgment against themselves" (1 Cor. 11:29), but have misunderstood its implications. They have misunderstood, first, how individuals come to discern the body rightly. Discernment is not ensured by attending a class and completing a workbook—discernment is learned through the order of worship itself, where the pastor declares what the meal is, and how to be prepared to receive it. Training in discernment is liturgical. Second, discernment of the body refers not necessarily (or only) to the body that is present in, with, and under the bread (real presence), but the body as the gathered community (ecclesiology, body of Christ). In this sense, it means discerning that all those who are in worship together, together with all those in every time and place who gather around this meal, are themselves the body of Christ, gathered in worship and praise of God the Father.

What if we rethought this practice from a "re-formation" perspective, and realized that children are formed by worship practices themselves, and that this applies at every level. If they receive the meal weekly and hear the words "This is for you for the forgiveness of sins," they will learn through the actual worship practice *what* the meal is (the body and blood of Jesus in, with, and under the bread and the wine), *why* they are receiving it (for the forgiveness of sins), and what the *outcome* of receiving it is (incorporation into the body of Christ, strengthening and keeping us in God's grace). Participation in worship and the sacraments is itself, then, in this sense, re-formation.

This applies not only to what is admittedly a matter of some dispute in our churches, but to our worship practices more widely taken. Children learn to worship God by worshiping God, not by being told about the importance of worshiping. Children learn to pray by praying, not by being taught models and methods of prayer. Actually, all of us, not just children, learn this way, but it is in this autumn season that many congregations especially focus on children's ministries like Sunday school and confirmation. So it is a good time to remind ourselves that worship is itself training in Christian discipleship and formation in faith.

So seek out and employ as many methods as you know how to encourage families to worship together, and to train (re-form) their children in faith through right worship. Offer ideas weekly on how children can be full participants in the liturgy of the church. Use hands, face, and body posture in ways that help the whole body pray. Practice singing and teach singing. Teach parents to guide their children along in the hymnal. If churches use projected words for the songs, give instructions to parents on how to direct their children's attention to the proper resources in the sanctuary. Teach children to splash themselves with water from the font and make the sign of the cross in remembrance of their baptism. Regularly offer ideas on how families can take these practices into their own homes. Extend the invitation to communion to all the baptized.

The Autumn Leaves

The falling leaves drift by the window
The autumn leaves of red and gold. . . .

This jazz standard, originally a French song, "Les feuilles mortes" (the dead leaves), is a touching evocation of the spiritual and relational longing of this season. There are many beautiful ways to weave the autumn leaves into worship art and space. Gardens and yards have come to the end of their cornucopia-like productivity, and many gardeners may be looking for ways to make use of this abundance. Consider constructing a large harvest display of produce, flowers, and plants that can then be donated to a local soup kitchen or pantry. Set up a bulb exchange in the narthex or church parking lot. Many resources are available for designing plant displays or wreaths with which to grace walls, doors, and windows. And although green is still the liturgical color for the season, many stoles, altar frontals, and banner patterns appropriately mix the darker hues of fall into patterns and weaves with green to match the deepening (and fading) colors of the season.

Avoid treating autumn like a second spring, as if all these colors, or even all of this abundance, is full of new life comparable to the spring of the year. The abundance of fall is the richness of the end of life. Many people find their latter years abundant indeed, rich in convergences, sometimes in wealth, relationships, and time. But this wealth comes at the end, and in complete knowledge that the end is near. The end of the liturgical year is approaching. Most plants harvested in the fall give up their life in the process of bringing the fruits to fullness.

So sing songs in this autumn season that accentuate the loamy wealth of death, such as "As saints of old" (ELW 695), "For the fruit of all creation" (ELW 679), "We give thee but thine own" (ELW 686), or "Sing to the Lord of harvest" (ELW 694). In fact, many of the hymns located in the "Stewardship" section of *Evangelical Lutheran Worship* are appropriate and worthy of consideration during this season, as are hymns recommended under "Growth" in the topical index of hymns, such as "God, whose farm is all creation" (ELW 734).

The Churchbook

Frederick Dale Bruner divides his commentary on Matthew into two volumes. The first, on chapters 1–12, is subtitled *The Christbook*, and the second, on chapters 13–28, is subtitled *The Churchbook* (*Matthew: A Commentary,*

Eerdmans, 2004). During the summer months, the gospel readings for each Sunday introduced worshipers to the "churchbook" half of Matthew, but now in these autumn months the theme of church truly comes to the fore. In September and October, the gospel readings for each Sunday continue to be from chapters 18–23. Since this is such a coherent series, congregations may wish to stay with the series and use the readings for Lectionary 31 (Oct. 30) rather than the readings for Reformation Sunday.

Here's the internal coherence. Chapters 18–20 of Matthew can be considered sermons on community, what Bruner terms "the little sermon on the mount" (p. ix). Chapter 18, read the first two Sundays of September, focuses on the doctrine of Christian community, and especially issues of confrontation and forgiveness. Chapter 20, read the third Sunday, is clear proclamation on vocation. All three function as a unit, proclaiming how to reprove sin, how to forgive, and how to work and earn without envying others. Underlying it all are expressions of God's grace.

The readings from chapters 21 and 22, read September 25, October 2, and October 9, offer parables on true faith. The emphasis here, a topic often neglected in church proclamation, is that what has been given can also be taken away and given to others. Many of those who are convinced that they have the gift and are secure in it, but then neglect it, can lose it. Here are the significant "red letter" quotes from each reading: "Truly I tell you, the tax collectors and the prostitutes are going into the kingdom of God ahead of you" (Matt. 21:31); "Therefore I tell you, the kingdom of God will be taken away from you and given to a people that produces the fruits of the kingdom" (Matt. 21:43); "The wedding is ready, but those invited were not worthy. Go therefore into the main streets, and invite everyone you find to the wedding banquet" (Matt. 22:8-9).

Finally, the readings for October 16 and 23 (most of Matt. 22:15-46, split into two sections) emerge out of a conversation on how to be thoughtful and faithful people. First, a political question: What should we do about taxes? Second, a hermeneutical question: What is the greatest commandment? Third, an eschatological question: How can we identify the lordship of the Christ?

Furthermore, if worship leaders and preachers choose to read the Matthew text for October 30 rather than the Reformation Sunday text, they will still have a gospel reading well-suited to the theme of reformation, precisely because in this section of Matthew, Jesus teaches about false and true religious leadership, a Reformation theme if ever there was one.

Seasonal Checklist

- For ideas for celebrating Canada's October 10 Day of Thanksgiving, see Preparing for November (pp. 298–299).
- If the worship schedule changes, notify local newspapers, update your Web site, and change listings on exterior signs and church answering machines.
- If a blessing of backpacks or Sunday school teachers will be held, see possible orders in the seasonal rites section.
- Begin planning for Advent 2011.
- Retain the Kyrie, and reintroduce confession and forgiveness if this had been omitted during the summer months.
- Use the hymn of praise ("Glory to God") or a hymn equivalent.
- Use the Nicene Creed for Reformation Sunday; use the Apostles' Creed for other Sundays in these months.
- If Affirmation of Baptism for confirmation youth will be on Reformation Sunday, begin making preparations.
- Consider using the Affirmation of Christian Vocation in *Evangelical Lutheran Worship* near Labor Day/ Labour Day as a way to recognize the various kinds of daily work in which the assembly is engaged. See also the brief essay on page 13 of this volume.
- If Bibles will be distributed to young readers, consider having their parents or baptismal sponsors involved in physically handing over the Bibles as a way to honor promises made at baptism. Words to accompany this action are provided in the seasonal rites section.

WORSHIP TEXTS FOR AUTUMN

Confession and Forgiveness

All may make the sign of the cross, the sign marked at baptism,
as the presiding minister begins.

Blessed be the holy Trinity, ✝ one God,
who forgives our sin, heals every illness,
saves us from death, enfolds us with tender care,
and crowns us with steadfast love.
Amen.

Let us confess our sin
in the presence of God and of one another.

Silence is kept for reflection.

God of abundant mercy,
we confess that we are more ready
to be forgiven than to forgive others.
We hold too closely your gifts to us.
We trample your vineyard, our good earth.
Have mercy, O God;
turn us again to you and toward others;
and grant that we may live for you and die in you,
for the sake of Jesus Christ, our redeemer and Lord.
Amen.

God is generous and faithful,
forgiving sins without number,
welcoming all to the feast,
giving us a place among the saints.
Through the humble obedience of ✝ Christ Jesus,
who went to the cross for our sake,
you are forgiven and made whole.
The Spirit of God is at work in you,
enabling you to live for one another.
Amen.

Greeting

Grace and peace from our God and Father,
hope in our Lord Jesus Christ,
and the consolation of the Holy Spirit
be with you all.
And also with you.

Offering Prayer

Merciful God, as grains of wheat scattered upon the hills
were gathered together to become one bread,
so let your church be gathered together
from the ends of the earth into your kingdom,
for yours is the glory through Jesus Christ, now and forever.
Amen.

Invitation to Communion

Come, you that are blessed by God.
Come to the banquet.

Prayer after Communion

God our shepherd,
you have gathered us again from scattered places
and nourished us with rich food in word and sacrament.
Go with us now, that we may seek the lost,
bind up the injured, and strengthen the weak,
until you gather us and all the saints into your eternal feast
with Jesus Christ, our Savior and Lord.
Amen.

Sending of Communion

Gracious God, you took the form of a servant,
offering yourself as food, comfort, and strength
to a sick and hurting world.
Anoint with a servant heart
those who take your word and sacrament
to our sisters and brothers
in their homes/in prisons/in hospitals.
Grant grace, mercy, healing, and hope to those
who feast on your body and blood
and receive your words of new life.
May we all recognize that we have a place and a home
in the body of our Lord Jesus Christ.
Amen.

Blessing

The peace of God,
which surpasses all understanding,
✛ guard your hearts and your minds in Christ Jesus.
Amen.

Dismissal

Go in peace. The Lord is near.
Thanks be to God.

General Order of Blessing

God's goodness is revealed in creation: "And God saw that it was good" (Gen. 1:10). God's goodness may also be evident in the way material things of creation are put to use by human beings, and in many of the activities that are part of human life and labor.

While acknowledging that the power of sin affects God's creation and the ways we use or misuse God's gifts, the church provides orders of blessing so that we may give thanks to God for every gift, recognize God's claim in every sphere of life, bear witness to God's promise that "the creation itself will be set free from its bondage to decay" (Rom. 8:21), and join the whole creation in praising God.

When people are gathered at the place of blessing, the leader begins.
Friends in Christ: Today we give thanks to God and we seek God's blessing as we gather to *bless/dedicate* this _____ to the praise and glory of God.

A psalm or canticle may follow.

One or more scripture passages may be read.

A hymn may be sung.

The leader begins the prayers.
The Lord be with you.
And also with you.

Let us pray.
Blessed are you, O Lord our God, ruler of the universe.
You made the whole earth for your glory;
all creation praises you.
We lift our voices to join the songs of heaven and earth,
of things seen and unseen.
You stretched out the heavens like a tent;
you divided the day from the night;
you appointed times and seasons for work and rest,
for tearing down and building up.
You blessed your people through all generations
and guided them in life and death:

Abraham and Sarah; Moses and Miriam;
Isaiah and all the prophets;
Mary, mother of our Lord;
Peter, James, John, and all the apostles;
and all the saints and witnesses in your church of ages past,
in whom your Spirit spoke and moved.

The leader continues with one of the following or another appropriate conclusion to the prayer.
We give you thanks, O God,
as we *set apart/dedicate* this _____
to your glory and praise.
Grant us faith to know your gracious purpose in all things,
give us joy in them,
and lead us to the building up of your kingdom;
through your Son, Jesus Christ, our Savior and Lord,
who lives and reigns with you and the Holy Spirit,
one God, now and forever.
Amen.

or
We give you thanks, O God,
for those who labor *in/at* _____,
and we ask you to bless the fruits of their work.
Grant us faith to know your gracious purpose in all things,
and continue your blessings to us
through the bounty of your creation;
through your Son, Jesus Christ, our Savior and Lord,
who lives and reigns with you and the Holy Spirit,
one God, now and forever.
Amen.

The service concludes:
Let us bless the Lord.
Thanks be to God.

The blessing of almighty God,
the Father, the ✚ Son, and the Holy Spirit,
be with us all.
Amen.

NOTES ON THE SERVICE

This general order of blessing is for use and adaptation in various circumstances besides those for which other, more specific orders are provided. It requires care and pastoral judgment on the part of the leader, first of all in discerning whether the use of an order of blessing is appropriate. The order also requires preparation—especially in the selection of scripture readings, hymns, and prayers—so that the order is suitable to the place, activity, or object under consideration.

Two general concluding prayers are provided. The first is an example of a prayer related to elements of creation, material things that have been crafted from them, or a place—especially one where something new is beginning. The second is an example of a prayer related to an occupation or activity carried out for the good of the human family and the whole creation. In developing the concluding prayer for a particular occasion, the leader may draw on suitable images from the scripture that is selected and from the circumstances for which the order of blessing is designed.

The order may be augmented with psalms, hymns, and canticles, the Lord's Prayer and other prayers, and a procession to the place where the blessing will be conducted.

Psalms and canticles may include the following.

Psalm 8   *How majestic is your name in all the earth! (Ps. 8:1)*

Psalm 65   *Your paths overflow with plenty. (Ps 65:11)*

Psalm 66   *Come and see the works of God, how awesome are God's deeds. (Ps. 66:5)*

Psalm 104   *Send forth your Spirit and renew the face of the earth. (Ps. 104:30)*

Psalm 136   *God's mercy endures forever. (Ps. 136:1)*

Psalm 145   *You open wide your hand and satisfy the desire of every living thing. (Ps. 145:16)*

ELW 227, 228   *We Praise You, O God*

Scripture readings may include the following.

Deuteronomy 26:1-11   *Offering the first fruits*

Job 38:1-11, 16-18   *God the creator of land, sea, and sky*

Matthew 13:3-9   *Parable of the sower*

Luke 5:1-9   *Jesus calls the fishermen*

Acts 16:13-15   *A businesswoman supports Paul's work*

Romans 12:1-5   *Offering ourselves according to various gifts*

2 Corinthians 9:6-15   *Sowing, reaping, and sharing*

1 Timothy 6:7-10, 17-19   *Take hold of the life that really is life*

Hymns may include the following.

678	God, Whose Giving Knows No Ending
679	For the Fruit of All Creation
680, 681	We Plow the Fields and Scatter
684	Creating God, Your Fingers Trace
689	Praise and Thanksgiving
724	All Who Love and Serve Your City
726	Light Dawns on a Weary World
731	Earth and All Stars!
733	Great Is Thy Faithfulness
734	God, Whose Farm Is All Creation
736	God the Sculptor of the Mountains
738	God Created Heaven and Earth
739	Touch the Earth Lightly
740	God of the Sparrow
756	Eternal Father, Strong to Save
817	You Have Come Down to the Lakeshore
828	Alleluia! Voices Raise
835	All Creatures, Worship God Most High!
836	Joyful, Joyful We Adore Thee
837	Many and Great, O God
839, 840	Now Thank We All Our God
845	Voices Raised to You
858, 859	Praise to the Lord, the Almighty
878	Soli Deo Gloria
879	For the Beauty of the Earth
881	Let All Things Now Living

Commissioning and Blessing of Teachers

The following order may be used within the congregation's primary service as a way to recognize those responsible for ministry to and with children and youth. It may be used with as much flexibility as necessary or desired. The leader role may be shared among several people, as suggested.

Those being commissioned for ministry with children and youth gather with the leaders. The first leader addresses the assembly.
A reading from First Corinthians. Now there are varieties of gifts, but the same Spirit; and there are varieties of services, but the same Lord; and there are varieties of activities, but it is the same God who activates all of them in everyone. To each is given the manifestation of the Spirit for the common good. (1 Cor. 12:4-7)

The first leader addresses those being commissioned.
Brothers and sisters, you have volunteered your time, your energy, and your gifts to the children, youth, and family ministries of this congregation. Will you offer your giftedness to this ministry in the confidence that it comes from God?
Response: I will, and I ask God to help me.

The second leader addresses the assembly.
A reading from Proverbs. Trust in the LORD with all your heart, and do not rely on your own insight. In all your ways acknowledge him, and he will make straight your paths. (Prov. 3:5-6)

The second leader addresses those being commissioned.
Will you carry out this ministry centered in Christ's call, striving to trust God as your guide and inspiration?
Response: I will, and I ask God to help me.

The third leader addresses the assembly.
A reading from Ephesians. I pray that you may be strengthened in your inner being with power through God's Spirit, and that Christ may dwell in your hearts through faith, as you are being rooted and grounded in love. I pray that you may have the power to comprehend, with all the saints, what is the breadth and length and height and depth, and to know the love of Christ that surpasses knowledge, so that you may be filled with all the fullness of God. (Eph. 3:16-19)

The third leader addresses those being commissioned.
Will you trust in God's care, seek to grow in love for those you serve, strive for excellence in your skills, and honor the gospel with a faithful life?
Response: I will, and I ask God to help me.

The assembly stands. The first leader addresses the assembly.
I now ask you, people of *name of congregation*: Will you today renew your commitment to our youngest brothers and sisters, our children and youth who look to you for guidance, support, and examples of righteous living?
We will, and we ask God to help us.

Those being commissioned face the assembly. The second leader addresses the assembly.
People of *name of congregation*, will you claim these gifted people as those called by God to help carry out our congregation's ministry to children, youth, and families? Will you support them and enthusiastically celebrate the work they do?
We will, and we ask God to help us.

The third leader addresses the assembly.

Will you pray for these leaders and the young people they serve, celebrating our children and youth as the ones Jesus blessed and welcomed?

We will, and we ask God to help us.

The presiding minister continues.

Let us pray. Gracious God, for Jesus' sake, empower these ministers to care for the young ones in our family of faith. Help them to teach faithfully, lead patiently, and guide confidently. Stir up in these servants the gift of your Holy Spirit: the spirit of wisdom and understanding, the spirit of counsel and might, the spirit of knowledge and fear of the Lord, the spirit of joy in your presence, both now and forever.

Amen.

People in the assembly may raise their hands in blessing as the presiding minister continues.

Almighty God, who has given you the gifts and the will to do these things, graciously give you the strength and compassion to perform them.

Amen.

The first leader concludes with these or similar words.

On behalf of *name of congregation*, we now commission you for ministry, grateful for your gifts and your willingness to serve.

The assembly may offer acclamation with applause.

Blessing of Backpacks

This blessing is suitable for a Sunday before school begins, and may be publicized for several Sundays beforehand. The ritual may be modified to include adults, who could be encouraged in advance to bring their laptops, PDAs, work boots, cell phones, or other tools of their trade. This blessing, however, focuses upon children starting the school year.

Have the children come forward at the appointed time, wearing their backpacks. Mark 10:13-16, Romans 12:4-8, or another appropriate scripture passage may be read once the children have gathered.

Dear God,
as we get ready to start another year in school,
we ask your blessing on these backpacks,
and especially on these children who will wear them.
As they do the very important work of being students,
bless them with:
eagerness to learn, that their world may grow large;
respect for teachers and students,
that they may form healthy relationships;
love for nature,
that they may become caretakers of your creation;
happiness when learning is easy
and stick-to-it-iveness when it is hard;
faith in Jesus as their best teacher and closest friend.
We ask that you would protect these, your own children.
Watch over them and keep them safe
as they travel to and from school.
As they learn, help them also to discover
the different gifts that you have given each one of them
to be used in your work in the world.
As they hear the many voices that will fill their days,
help them to listen most carefully for your voice,
the one that tells them you will love them always,
no matter what.
We ask this in Jesus' name.
Amen.

Blessings for Teachers and Students

For the marvels of your creation,
we praise you, O God.
For the opportunity to explore and study,
we praise you, O God.
For those who guide us, teachers and mentors,
we praise you, O God.
Teach us your ways and guide us in your path,
for you are the creator of all that is seen and unseen.
Amen.

or

Let us pray for all who are beginning a new school year,
that both students and teachers
will be blessed in their academic endeavors.

Almighty God, you give wisdom and knowledge.
Grant teachers the gift of joy and insight,
and students the gift of diligence and openness,
that all may grow in what is good and honest and true.
Support all who teach and all who learn,
that together we may know and follow your ways;
through Jesus Christ our Lord.
Amen.

Presentation of the Bible

A representative of the congregation may present a Bible to each person. These or similar words may be spoken:
Receive this Bible.
Hear God's word with us.
Learn and tell its stories.
Discover its mysteries.
Honor its commandments.
Rejoice in its good news.
May God's life-giving word
inspire you and make you wise.

September 4, 2011
Time after Pentecost — Lectionary 23

Conflict is a part of relationships and life in community. Jesus' words in today's gospel are often used in situations having to do with church discipline. The prophet Ezekiel tells of warning the wicked to turn from their ways, and Paul reminds us that love is the fulfilling of the law. We gather in the name of Christ, assured that he is present among us with gifts of peace and reconciliation.

Prayer of the Day

O Lord God, enliven and preserve your church with your perpetual mercy. Without your help, we mortals will fail; remove far from us everything that is harmful, and lead us toward all that gives life and salvation, through Jesus Christ, our Savior and Lord.

Gospel Acclamation

Alleluia. In Christ God was reconciling the world ' to himself,* entrusting the message of reconcilia- ' tion to us. *Alleluia.* (2 Cor. 5:19)

Readings and Psalm
Ezekiel 33:7-11

God appointed Ezekiel as a sentinel for the house of Israel. Ezekiel must faithfully convey God's warnings to the people. Remarkably, God—who is about to attack Jerusalem—gives a warning with the hope that repentance will make the attack unnecessary.

Psalm 119:33-40

I desire the path of your commandments. (Ps. 119:35)

Romans 13:8-14

The obligation of Christians is to love one another and so fulfill the heart and goal of the law. Clothes make the person as we "put on the Lord Jesus Christ" and live today in light of the future God has in store for us.

Matthew 18:15-20

Jesus offers practical advice to his disciples on how individuals—and the church as a whole—should show wrongdoers their need for repentance.

Semicontinuous reading and psalm
Exodus 12:1-14

Israel remembered its deliverance from slavery in Egypt by celebrating the festival of Passover. This festival featured the Passover lamb, whose blood was used as a sign to protect God's people from the threat of death. The early church described the Lord's supper using imagery from the Passover, especially in portraying Jesus as the lamb who delivers God's people from sin and death.

Psalm 149

Sing the Lord's praise in the assembly of the faithful. (Ps. 149:1)

Preface   Sundays

Color   Green

Prayers of Intercession

The prayers are prepared locally for each occasion. The following examples may be adapted or used as appropriate.

Seeking the renewal of the Holy Spirit in our communities and in our world, we pray for the church, those in need, and all of God's creation.

A brief silence.

Holy and life-giving God, unite your people in a life of righteousness and loving-kindness. Form us as your witnesses, so that when people seek compassion, they may find it in Christ-centered community. Lord, in your mercy,
hear our prayer.

Bless the labors of farmers, herders, packagers, and all who work for the harvest and distribution of food. Make them a strong link between your abundant creation and all hungry people. Lord, in your mercy,
hear our prayer.

Guide the work of all elected officials. Create and encourage accountability in governments. Use these servants of the people to uphold justice in our world. Lord, in your mercy,
hear our prayer.

Make the presence of Christ known among those who are ill, grieving, and broken-hearted. Bring your gifts of healing and wholeness to all who are sick and suffering (*especially*). Lord, in your mercy,
hear our prayer.

Grant a spirit of thankfulness to all whose daily needs are met. Give hope to those who are unemployed or underemployed. Bind us together in service to one another. Lord, in your mercy,
hear our prayer.

Here other intercessions may be offered.

As we recall the lives of the saints who have revealed Christ to us, open our eyes to see his face in those gathered with us. Strengthen our faith in his ongoing work of redemption. Lord, in your mercy,
hear our prayer.

Into your hands, holy God, we commend all for whom we pray, trusting in your abundant mercy; through Jesus Christ our Savior.
Amen.

Ideas and Images for the Day

Jesus says, "For where two or three are gathered in my name, I am there among them," (Matt. 18:20). In these Sundays after Pentecost, we are repeatedly reminded that God has not abandoned us and that Christ's resurrection and ascension are a beginning for us, not an end. The readings this week focus on the practical work of the gathered Christian community: turning from sin to repentance, from conflict to reconciliation. The question is as relevant today as it was for the disciples and the first Christians: how do we live together, work together, as the body of Christ? We have been saved by grace, liberated by God's love to love one another. What does it mean for us and for our community to "put on the Lord Jesus Christ" (Rom. 13:14) and to clothe ourselves in love?

1. In an episode of *The Simpsons*, Homer has a run-in with a bear and is humiliated; he swears revenge and builds a bear-fighting suit. The suit is ridiculous, and he's not even wearing it when he meets the bear again. At their second meeting, Homer and the bear begin to understand each other, and Homer realizes the bear needs his help to safely make it into Springfield's wildlife refuge. The bear gets past the hunters by wearing Homer's bear-fighting suit. The episode deals with themes of reconciliation, and Homer's homemade armor becomes an opportunity for selfless, loving action (Rom. 13:12) (Fox, November 30, 2003, Season 15, Episode 5, "The Fat and the Furriest." A synopsis is available at http://www.thesimpsons.com/recaps/season15/#episode5).

2. The Forgiveness Project (http://www.theforgiveness project.com/) is a British-based charitable organization that gathers and shares real-life stories of forgiveness, reconciliation, and conflict resolution. In addition to their work in prisons, schools, and faith communities, the Forgiveness Project shares true stories of reconciliation on its Web site, showing positive alternatives to sustained conflict and revenge.

3. Get children involved in leading the sharing of the peace. Most people, adults included, may not realize that this part of weekly worship is one of the oldest Christian liturgical traditions and one of its purposes is to be a time of reconciliation before holy communion. For one Presbyterian pastor's reflections on the importance of this part of worship, go to http://www.faithcommunity-novi.org/sermon/ser03266.htm.

4. What does it mean to "put on the armor of light" and "put on the Lord Jesus Christ" (Rom. 13:12, 14)? If your church has costumes for children—or if you have some T-shirts with logos or brand names on them—use these to demonstrate that Paul is not telling us to dress a certain way, but to show we are Christians by our loving actions and "wearing" that love wherever we go.

Hymns for Worship
Gathering
Joyful, joyful we adore thee   ELW 836, LBW 551
O Christ, your heart, compassionate   ELW 722
As we gather at your table   ELW 522

Hymn of the Day
Beloved, God's chosen   ELW 648   *ANDREW'S SONG*
God, when human bonds are broken   ELW 603, WOV 735   *MERTON*
Lord of all nations, grant me grace   ELW 716, LBW 419   *BEATUS VIR*

Offering
Blessed be the name   ELW 797
God, whose giving knows no ending   ELW 678, LBW 408

Communion
Draw us in the Spirit's tether   ELW 470, WOV 703
I come with joy   ELW 482
In all our grief   ELW 615, WOV 739

Sending

Praise, my soul, the King of heaven   ELW 865/864,
 LBW 549
Where charity and love prevail   ELW 359, LBW 126, TFF 84

Additional Hymns and Songs

Awake, O sleeper   GC 803, HS91 813
Bind us together   TFF 217, WOV 748
A story for all people   W&P 2

Music for the Day
Psalmody and Acclamations

Becker, John W. "Psalm 119:33-40" from PWA, Evangelical Lutheran Worship Edition.

Mummert, Mark. "Psalm 119:33-40," Refrain 2, from PSCY.

Pelz, Walter L. "Psalm 149" from PWA, Evangelical Lutheran Worship Edition.

Schalk, Carl F. *Gospel Acclamations for Autumn.*

Schwandt, Daniel E. "Psalm 149" from PSCY.

Choral

Bisbee, B. Wayne. "Teach Me Your Way, O Lord." 2 pt mxd, kybd. AFP 9780800654795.

Marcello, Benedetto/arr. Dale Grotenhuis. "Teach Me Now, O Lord." 2 pt mxd, kybd. MSM 50-9418.

Hurd, David. "Teach Me, O Lord." SATB. GIA G-2715.

White, David Ashley. "O Bread of Life from Heaven." 2 pt mxd, org. AFP 9780800650919. *The Augsburg Choirbook.* AFP 9780800656782.

Children's Choir

Butler-Moore, Nylea. "I Can Picture Jesus Toiling." U, fl, kybd. GIA G3820.

Kemp, Helen. "Prayer Litany." UE, 2 pt, kybd, ob. CG CGA747.

Litz, Helen. "Prayer of St. Francis." U, kybd/hp. CG CGA242.

Keyboard / Instrumental

o Benson, Robert A. "Merton" from *A Lovely Rose.* Org. AFP 9780800675714.

o Organ, Anne Krentz. "Andrew's Song" from *Introductions and Alternate Accompaniments*, vol. 7. Pno. AFP 9780800623654.

o Sadowski, Kevin J. "Beatus vir" from *Eleven Hymn Preludes.* Org. CPH 97-6883U1.

o Sedio, Mark. "Beatus vir" from *Six Slovak Hymn Improvisations.* Org. MSM 10-833.

Handbell

Burroughs, Bob. "Let All Things Now Living." 3-5 oct, L3+. GIA G-6632.

Organ, Anne Krentz. "Earth and All Stars and Alleluia! Jesus Is Risen." 3 oct, L2. AFP 9780800658083.

Tucker, Sondra. "How Firm a Foundation." 3-5 oct hb, opt 7 hc, L2+. HOP 2435.

Praise Ensemble

• Baloche, Paul. "Open the Eyes of My Heart." INT.

• Haugen, Marty. "Awake, O Sleeper." GIA G-3290.

• Haugen, Marty. "Gather Us In." GIA G-2651. ELW 532.

• Nelson, Marc. "I Believe in Jesus." Mercy/VIN.

• Redman, Matt. "Better Is One Day." Thankyou Music.

• Tomlin, Chris/Ed Cash/Stephan Sharp. "Made to Worship." WT/Sixsteps Music.

Global

Hesla, Bret. "Let Us Put on the Clothes of Christ" from *Global Songs 2.* SATB. AFP 9780800656744. ELW 247.

Mxadana, George. "Alleluia" from *Sent by the Lord: Songs of the World Church*, vol 2. U. GIA G-3740.

Friday, September 9

Peter Claver, priest, missionary to Colombia, died 1654

Peter Claver was born into Spanish nobility and was persuaded to become a Jesuit missionary. He served in Cartagena (in what is now Colombia) by teaching and caring for the slaves. The slaves arrived in ships, where they had been confined in dehumanizing conditions. Claver met and supplied them with medicine, food, clothing, and brandy. He learned their dialects and taught them Christianity. He called himself "the slave of the slaves forever." Claver also ministered to the locals of Cartagena who were in prison and facing death.

o denotes suggestions that relate to the hymn of the day.
• denotes songs that are available on iTunes®.

September 11, 2011
Time after Pentecost — Lectionary 24

In today's second reading Paul questions why we judge one another, since we all stand before the judgment of God. Yet we do sin against one another, and Jesus' challenge that we forgive seventy-seven times reveals God's boundless mercy. When we hear the words of forgiveness in worship and sign ourselves with the cross, we are renewed in baptism to be signs of reconciliation in the world.

Prayer of the Day

O Lord God, merciful judge, you are the inexhaustible fountain of forgiveness. Replace our hearts of stone with hearts that love and adore you, that we may delight in doing your will, through Jesus Christ, our Savior and Lord.

Gospel Acclamation

Alleluia. We have an advocate, Jesus | Christ the righteous;* your sins are forgiven on account | of his name. *Alleluia.* (1 John 2:1, 12)

Readings and Psalm
Genesis 50:15-21

After Jacob's death, the brothers of Joseph begged for forgiveness for the crime they had done against him. You intended to do me harm, Joseph said, but God used this as an opportunity to do good and save many lives.

Psalm 103:[1-7] 8-13

Lord, you are full of compassion and mercy. (Ps. 103:8)

Romans 14:1-12

This Christian community has significant struggles with diversity. Here Paul helps us understand that despite different practices in worship and personal piety, we do not judge one another. All Christians belong to the Lord Jesus Christ, who died for all of us and will judge each of us.

Matthew 18:21-35

When Peter asks about the limits of forgiveness, Jesus responds with a parable that suggests human forgiveness should mirror the unlimited mercy of God.

Semicontinuous reading and psalm
Exodus 14:19-31

Having decided to let the Israelites go from Egypt, Pharaoh had second thoughts and sent his army after them (14:5-8).

Though the passage through the Red Sea became a sign of salvation for the people of Israel, Pharaoh's forces drowned in the waters. As a result the Israelites believed in the Lord and in the Lord's servant Moses.

Psalm 114

Tremble, O earth, at the presence of the Lord. (Ps. 114:7)

or Exodus 15:1b-11, 20-21

I will sing to the Lord, who has triumphed gloriously. (Exod. 15:1)

Preface Sundays

Color Green

Prayers of Intercession

The prayers are prepared locally for each occasion. The following examples may be adapted or used as appropriate.

Seeking the renewal of the Holy Spirit in our communities and in our world, we pray for the church, those in need, and all of God's creation.

A brief silence.

Merciful God, bind the body of Christ with the Spirit of forgiveness. Shape us to be bearers of mercy and justice in this world, and teach us to forgive as we have been forgiven. Lord, in your mercy,
hear our prayer.

Lead us to exercise justice for your creation. Move us to be good stewards of all you have made, and make us examples of how to care for every living thing. Lord, in your mercy,
hear our prayer.

Deepen our commitment to economic justice among all peoples. Sustain all who live in poverty, and grant the gift of compassion to those who regulate banks, property, and economic systems. Lord, in your mercy,
hear our prayer.

Send your healing presence to the lonely, afflicted, and anxious. Surround those who suffer with caring people, and give peace to all who are troubled (*especially*). Lord, in your mercy,
hear our prayer.

Reveal your mercy in times of crisis through the work of police officers, firefighters, emergency medical technicians, and all first responders. Give hope to those who have lost loved ones in emergencies. Lord, in your mercy,
hear our prayer.

Here other intercessions may be offered.

As we give thanks for all the saints, whose lives point to Christ crucified, turn our own eyes to the cross, where we find holy justice, mercy, compassion, and hope. Lord, in your mercy,
hear our prayer.

Into your hands, holy God, we commend all for whom we pray, trusting in your abundant mercy; through Jesus Christ our Savior.
Amen.

Ideas and Images for the Day

Being a disciple requires an expansive perspective on forgiveness. Today our perspective is broadened by the good news that God's forgiveness is not based on our idea of fairness, but rather on abundant, unimaginable grace. God "does not deal with us according to our sins, nor repay us according to our iniquities" (Ps. 103:10). The king forgives our entire debt, no matter how enormous it is (Matt. 18:23-27). We also are challenged to stretch our perspective and forgive each other. With Peter, we learn to stop keeping score (Matt. 18:21-22).

1. Use the order for confession and forgiveness you have chosen for this Sunday to shape the rest of the service. What words or phrases in this part of the liturgy expand your perspective on God's forgiveness?

2. For an exercise in perspective, see the 1968 educational film *Powers of 10*, on YouTube (http://www.youtube.com/watch?v=A2cmlhfdxuY). The nine-minute film takes a fixed point—picnickers in Chicago—and first zooms out to the farthest reaches of the galaxy, then in again to the subatomic level. This archetypal, perspective-altering, image sequence has been retooled many times for television and movies, including the final scene of *Men in Black* (Amblin Entertainment, 1997). What makes these images so enduringly powerful? Can this be both a celebration of the more expansive view God gives us and also a reminder of our limits?

3. Ten thousand talents is an unimaginably large debt: 150 thousand years' wages. In contrast, 100 denarii would be equivalent to 100 days' wages. To expand perspectives, explore ways to make these numbers tangible for all ages. One possibility is to fill a container with small objects representing one talent. Fifteen years' wages = 5,475 days' wages or 5,475 denarii, so fill a jar with (about) 5,475 of something you can let the children distribute to the congregation (small individual packages of fruit snacks, for example, and count the pieces, not the packages.) Use the weight of the container to help children imagine one talent, ten talents, 100 talents . . . 10,000 talents! God gives to and forgives us abundantly and freely, and God wants us to do the same with one another. Note that there may be leftovers in the container. Are there others, outside this congregation, with whom God's love can be shared?

4. Collect stories from local, national, and international news marking the tenth anniversary of the September 11 terrorist attacks. Note different perspectives based on audience, region, and the passage of time. What stories of forgiveness and reconciliation do you discern, and how do they relate to today's readings?

Hymns for Worship
Gathering

Let streams of living justice   ELW 710
How small our span of life   ELW 636
Earth and all stars!   ELW 731, LBW 558

Hymn of the Day

Forgive our sins as we forgive   ELW 605, LBW 307   DETROIT
In all our grief   ELW 615, WOV 739   FREDERICKTOWN
O God of every nation   ELW 713   LLANGLOFFAN
   LBW 416   TUOLUMNE

Offering

Goodness is stronger than evil   ELW 721
Now the silence   ELW 460, LBW 205

Communion

All who love and serve your city   ELW 724, LBW 436
When we are living   ELW 639, LCC 462
Our Father, we have wandered   ELW 606, WOV 733

Sending

We Are Called   ELW 720, W&P 147
Awake, O sleeper, rise from death   ELW 452, WOV 745

Additional Hymns and Songs

God of love, have mercy   DH 10
I trust, O Christ, in you alone   LBW 395
Stay with us   WOV 743

Music for the Day
Psalmody and Acclamations

Cherwien, David. "Psalm 103," Refrain 1, from PSCY.
Kallman, Daniel. "Psalm 103:[1-7] 8-13" from PWA, Evangelical Lutheran Worship Edition.
Makeever, Ray. "Bless the Lord (Psalm 103)" from *Dancing at the Harvest.*
Raabe, Nancy. "Exodus 15" from PSCY.
Sedio, Mark. "Exodus 15:1b-11, 20-21" from PWA, Evangelical Lutheran Worship Edition.
Schalk, Carl F. *Gospel Acclamations for Autumn.*
Schwandt, Daniel E. "Psalm 114" from PSCY.
Shute, Linda Cable. "Psalm 114" from PWA, Evangelical Lutheran Worship Edition.

Choral

Berthier, Jacques. "Ubi Caritas." SATB, kybd, opt insts. GIA G-2586.
Cherubini, Luigi/arr. Austin Lovelace. "Like As a Father." U/2 pt or SAB, pno. CG CGA156.
Mayernik, Luke. "Ubi Caritas." SATB, tenor solo. GIA G-7194.
Miller, Aaron David. "Sanctus." SAB, kybd. AFP9780806697154.
Organ, Anne Krentz. "Love One Another." SATB. AFP 9780800659646.

Children's Choir

Cherubini, Luigi. "Like As a Father." U/2 pt, kybd. CG CGA156.
Kosche, Kenneth. "Bless God's Holy Name." 2 pt, kybd, opt hb. CG CGA766.
Makeever, Ray. "For to This End" from *Dancing at the Harvest.* U, kybd.

Keyboard / Instrumental

○ Cherwien, David. "Llangloffan" from *Eight for Eighty-Eight,* vol. 2. Pno, inst. AFP 9780800659059.
○ Harbach, Barbara. "Llangloffan" from *Come Join the Dance: Folk Tunes and Spirituals for Organ.* Org. AFP 9780800678760.
○ Powell, Robert J. "Fredericktown" from *Sent Forth: Short Postludes for the Day.* Org. AFP 9780800654887.
○ Raabe, Nancy M. "Detroit" from *Day of Arising: A Tapestry of Musical Traditions.* Pno. AFP 9780800637460.

Handbell

Eithun, Sandra. "Tranquil Chimings." 2-3 oct hc or hb, L1-. CG CGB600.

McMichael, Catherine. "Contemplation on Ubi Caritas." 3-6 oct hb, opt 3 oct hc, L3+. AGEHR AG36036.
○ Roberts, Philip. "Sacred Harp Suite." 5 oct, L2. GIA G-6448.

Praise Ensemble

● Agnew, Todd/Chris Collins/Edwin Excell/John Newton. "Grace Like Rain." Ardent/Koala Music.
● Foote, Billy. "You Are My King (Amazing Love)." WT/Sixsteps Music.
● Founds, Rick. "Lord, I Lift Your Name on High." MAR. ELW 857.
Haas, David. "Now We Remain." GIA G-2709. ELW 500.
● Tomlin, Chris/John Newton/John Rees/Edwin Excell/Louie Giglio. "Amazing Grace (My Chains Are Gone)." WT.
● Tomlin, Chris/Jesse Reeves/Isaac Watts/JD Walt. "The Wonderful Cross." WT/Sixsteps Music.

Global

Shaha, Bart. "Lord, We Did Not Live Up to Your Teachings" from *Sound the Bamboo.* U. GIA G-6830.
Trad. South African. "Sanna, sannanina" from *Global Songs 2.* SATB. AFP 9780800656744.

Tuesday, September 13

John Chrysostom, Bishop of Constantinople, died 407

John was a priest in Antioch and an outstanding preacher. His eloquence earned him the nickname "Chrysostom" ("golden mouth"), but it also got him into trouble. As bishop of Constantinople he preached against corruption among the royal court. The empress, who had been his supporter, sent him into exile. His preaching style emphasized the literal meaning of scripture and its practical application. This interpretation stood in contrast to the common style at the time, which emphasized the allegorical meaning of the text.

Wednesday, September 14

Holy Cross Day

Helena, the mother of Constantine, made a pilgrimage to Israel to look for Christian holy sites. She found what she believed were the sites of the crucifixion and burial of Jesus, sites that modern archaeologists believe may be correct. Here Constantine built two churches. The celebration of Holy Cross Day originated with the dedication of the Church of the Resurrection in 335. Today the festival provides the church an opportunity to lift up the victory of the cross with a spirit of celebration that might be less suitable on Good Friday.

○ denotes suggestions that relate to the hymn of the day.
● denotes songs that are available on iTunes®.

Friday, September 16

Cyprian, Bishop of Carthage, martyr, died around 258

Cyprian worked for the unity of the church and cared for his flock in North Africa during a time of great persecution. During Cyprian's time as bishop many people had denied the faith under duress. In contrast to some who held the belief that the church should not receive these people back, Cyprian believed they should be welcomed into full communion after a period of penance. He insisted on the need for compassion in order to preserve the unity of the church. His essay *On the Unity of the Catholic Church* stressed the role of bishops in guaranteeing the visible, concrete unity of the church. Cyprian was also concerned for the physical well-being of the people under his care. He organized a program of medical care for the sick during a severe epidemic in Carthage.

Saturday, September 17

Hildegard, Abbess of Bingen, died 1179

Hildegard lived virtually her entire life in convents, yet was widely influential within the church. After an uneventful time as a nun, she was chosen as abbess of her community. She reformed her community as well as other convents. Around the same time, she began having visions and compiled them, as instructed, in a book she called *Scivias*. Hildegard's importance went beyond mysticism. She advised and reproved kings and popes, wrote poems and hymns, and produced treatises in medicine, theology, and natural history. She was also a musician and an artist.

September 18, 2011
Time after Pentecost — Lectionary 25

Matthew narrates one of Jesus' controversial parables, in which Jesus says the reign of God is like workers who get paid the same no matter when they start. When God changes his mind about punishing Nineveh for their evil ways, Jonah is angry. Yet God is gracious and merciful, abounding in steadfast love. In baptism we receive the grace of God that is freely given to all. As Luther wrote, in the presence of God's mercy we are all beggars.

Today is the commemoration of Dag Hammarskjöld, renewer of society, who died in 1961.

Prayer of the Day

Almighty and eternal God, you show perpetual lovingkindness to us your servants. Because we cannot rely on our own abilities, grant us your merciful judgment, and train us to embody the generosity of your Son, Jesus Christ, our Savior and Lord.

Gospel Acclamation

Alleluia. Open our ¹ hearts, O Lord,* to give heed to what is said ¹ by your Son. *Alleluia.*

Readings and Psalm
Jonah 3:10—4:11

After Jonah's short sermon in 3:4, the Ninevites all repented and God decided to spare the city. Jonah objected to this and became even more angry when God ordered a worm to destroy a plant that was providing shade. The book ends with a question that challenges any who are not ready to forgive: You, Jonah, are all worked up about a bush, but should not I be concerned about a hundred and twenty thousand Ninevites who do not know the difference between their right and left hands?

Psalm 145:1-8

The Lord is slow to anger and abounding in steadfast love. (Ps. 145:8)

Philippians 1:21-30

Paul writes to the Philippians from prison. Though he is uncertain about the outcome of his imprisonment, he is committed to the ministry of the gospel and calls on the Philippians to live lives that reflect and enhance the gospel mission.

Matthew 20:1-16

Jesus tells a parable about God's generosity, challenging the common assumption that God rewards people according to what they have earned or deserve.

Semicontinuous reading and psalm
Exodus 16:2-15

Faced with hunger in the wilderness, the Israelites longed for life back in Egypt and said they wished the exodus had never happened. Then God miraculously and graciously gave them quails and manna to eat.

Psalm 105:1-6, 37-45

Make known the deeds of the Lord among the peoples. Hallelujah! (Ps. 105:1, 45)

Preface Sundays

Color Green

Prayers of Intercession

The prayers are prepared locally for each occasion. The following examples may be adapted or used as appropriate.

Seeking the renewal of the Holy Spirit in our communities and in our world, we pray for the church, those in need, and all of God's creation.

A brief silence.

Generous and merciful God, pour out your grace upon your people, especially when we are suffering. Support us to persist joyfully in our lives, so that others may see your goodness. Lord, in your mercy,

hear our prayer.

Send your Spirit to move across lands and waters in this change of seasons. Grant the promise of life to all living things that prepare to be dormant in winter and to reawaken in spring. Lord, in your mercy,

hear our prayer.

Be present in the ongoing work of peacemakers (*like Dag Hammarskjöld, renewer of society, whom we commemorate today*). Use them to establish your peace among nations and your hope among peoples. Lord, in your mercy,

hear our prayer.

Guide those who are confused, are losing memory, or are failing in health (*especially*). Give them security in your abundant goodness and hope in your promises. Lord, in your mercy,

hear our prayer.

Transform our communities into places of welcome for those who have been shunned or marginalized. Send us forth with greetings of grace and peace on our lips. Lord, in your mercy,

hear our prayer.

Here other intercessions may be offered.

Gather us into the communion of saints, where we may always dwell in the love of Christ. Strengthen our mission of faithful living, as we bring others with us to this gathering. Lord, in your mercy,

hear our prayer.

Into your hands, holy God, we commend all for whom we pray, trusting in your abundant mercy; through Jesus Christ our Savior.

Amen.

Ideas and Images for the Day

Today we hear the conclusion of the book of Jonah, telling how God's grace saves Nineveh from destruction. Despite its salvation, Nineveh is still described by God as a city that does not know its right hand from its left (4:11). In the end, the people of Nineveh by and large do not have a clue. Sound familiar? Are we not clueless in how to treat one another; clueless in how to welcome the stranger; clueless in how to care for the outcast, the poor, and the uninsured; clueless, not knowing right from left? Nonetheless, God gives the only clue, the only promise that matters—Jesus Christ. We, like Nineveh, might confuse right and left from time to time, but we know the mercy and love God! Here is our clue!

1. The story of reluctant Jonah is one bursting with homiletical potential. It is a challenge to preach on a portion of the story without retelling it in its entirety. As such, it may be beneficial to read all four chapters of Jonah today. Even better, enlist a drama troupe from the congregation to perform the story, whale and all! This is a wonderful way to involve youth and children.

2. How does Jesus challenge our assumptions of economic justice? In today's gospel, Jesus' parable points us to an economy where the "last will be first, and the first will be last" (20:16). These are challenging words for an affluent society. Still, the challenge is before us. Engage the community in discussion on sustainable living and equitable distribution of wealth. A great resource for such conversations is the Evangelical Lutheran Church in America's social statement "Economic Life: Sufficient, Sustainable Livelihood for All," available at http://www.elca.org.

3. Is it possible to be obedient to Jesus' words in Matthew? Or obedient to God's call for mercy in the story of Jonah? When it comes to engaging scripture, Eugene Peterson asserts that obedience is precisely our call and charge. He writes, "Obedience is the thing, living in active response to the living God. The important question we ask of this text is not 'What does this mean?' but 'What can I obey?' A simple act of obedience will open up our lives to this text far more quickly than any number of Bible studies and dictionaries and concordances" (*Eat This Book: A Conversation in the Art of Spiritual Reading*, Grand Rapids, MI: Eerdmans, 2006, p. 71).

Hymns for Worship
Gathering
Lord of light ELW 688, LBW 405
Rise up, O saints of God! ELW 669, LBW 383
Great God, your love has called us ELW 358, WOV 666

Hymn of the Day
Salvation unto us has come ELW 590, LBW 297
   ES IST DAS HEIL
All who love and serve your city ELW 724 NEW ORLEANS
   LBW 436 BIRABUS
Lord of all hopefulness ELW 765, LBW 469 SLANE

Offering
Accept, O Lord, the gifts we bring ELW 691, WOV 759
As saints of old ELW 695, LBW 404

Communion
Take my life, that I may be ELW 583/685, LBW 406
There's a wideness in God's mercy ELW 587/588, LBW 290
All who love and serve your city ELW 724, LBW 436

Sending
O Zion, haste ELW 668, LBW 397
Voices raised to you ELW 845

Additional Hymns and Songs

Come, labor on   H82 541
Amid the world's bleak wilderness   LBW 378
What shall I render   TFF 239

Music for the Day
Psalmody and Acclamations

Keesecker, Thomas. "Psalm 145:1-8" and "Psalm 105:1-6, 37-45" from PWA, Evangelical Lutheran Worship Edition.
Mummert, Mark. "Psalm 145," Refrain 3, from PSCY.
Schalk, Carl F. *Gospel Acclamations for Autumn.*
Woehr, Roland. "Psalm 105" from PSCY.

Choral

○ Bach, J. S. "Salvation unto Us Has Come" from *Bach for All Seasons.* SATB. AFP 9780800658540.
○ Distler, Hugo. "Salvation unto Us Has Come" from *Chantry Choirbook.* SATB. AFP 9780800657772.
Ellingboe, Bradley. "There's a Wideness in God's Mercy." SATB, kybd. AFP 9780800676544.
Nelson, Ronald A. "Whoever Would Be Great Among You." SAB, gtr or kybd. AFP 9780800645809. *The Augsburg Choirbook.* AFP 9780800656782.

Children's Choir

Haas, David. "We Are Called" from *LifeSongs.* U, kybd.
Hancock, Vicki. "I Will Praise God." U, kybd, opt hb. CG CGA822.
Pote, Allen. "Praise the Goodness of God." U, kybd. CG CGA733.

Keyboard / Instrumental

○ Blair, Dallas. "Slane" from *Hymn Introductions and Descants for Trumpet and Organ*, set 4. Org, tpt. MSM 20-703.
○ Chapin, Rachel. "Slane" from *Lamb of God.* Pno. CPH 97-7093.
○ Hobby, Robert A. "Es ist das Heil" from *Three Hymn Embellishments.* Org. MSM 10-602.
○ Reuss, Jonathan. "Slane" from *Organ Festivity: Joyous Hymn Settings.* Org. AFP 9780800677848.

Handbell

○ Glasgow, Michael. "Prayer for Guidance." 3-6 oct hb, opt 3 oct hc, L3+. JEF JHS9431.
○ Larson, Katherine Jordahl. "Be Thou My Vision." 3-4 oct, L2. AFP 9780800653668.
○ Leavitt, John. "Be Thou My Vision." 3-4 oct, L3. CPH 97-7210.

Praise Ensemble

● Barnett, Marie. "Breathe." Mercy/VIN.
● Doerksen, Brian. "Hallelujah (Your Love Is Amazing)." VIN.
● Kilpatrick, Bob. "In My Life, Lord, Be Glorified." LOR.
● Schutte, Daniel L. "Here I Am, Lord." ELW 574.
● Smith, Martin. "The Happy Song." Curious? Music.
● Smith, Michael W. "Great Is the Lord." Meadowgreen Music. W&P 53.

Global

Gibson, Colin A. "For the Man and for the Woman" from *Sound the Bamboo.* U. GIA G-6830.
South African trad. "Hamba Nathi/Come, Walk with Us" from *Global Songs 2.* SATB. AFP 9780800656744.

Sunday, September 18
Dag Hammarskjöld, renewer of society, died 1961

Dag Hammarskjöld (HAH-mar-sheld) was a Swedish diplomat and humanitarian who served as secretary general of the United Nations. He was killed in a plane crash on this day in 1961, in what is now Zambia, while he was on his way to negotiate a cease-fire between the United Nations and the Katanga forces. For years Hammarskjöld had kept a private journal, and it was not until that journal was published as *Markings* that the depth of his Christian faith was known. The book revealed that his life was a combination of diplomatic service and personal spirituality, and of contemplation on the meaning of Christ in his life and action in the world.

Wednesday, September 21
Matthew, Apostle and Evangelist

Matthew ("Levi" in the gospels of Mark and Luke) was a tax collector for the Roman government in Capernaum. Tax collectors were distrusted because they were dishonest and worked as agents for a foreign ruler, the occupying Romans. In the gospels, tax collectors are mentioned as sinful and despised outcasts, but it was these outcasts to whom Jesus showed his love. Matthew's name means "gift of the Lord." Since the second century, tradition has attributed the first gospel to him.

○ denotes suggestions that relate to the hymn of the day.
● denotes songs that are available on iTunes®.

September 25, 2011
Time after Pentecost — Lectionary 26

Jesus' parable about two sons who don't do what they say reveals surprises in the reign of God, such as prostitutes and tax collectors going before others into God's kingdom. In the reading from Ezekiel the people question whether the ways of the Lord are unfair; instead they are to repent and turn to the Lord. Paul urges us to look to Christ as a model of humility, looking to the interests of others above our own. Nourished by the broken bread and shared cup, we offer our lives for the sake of our needy world.

Prayer of the Day

God of love, giver of life, you know our frailties and failings. Give us your grace to overcome them, keep us from those things that harm us, and guide us in the way of salvation, through Jesus Christ, our Savior and Lord.

Gospel Acclamation

Alleluia. My sheep hear my voice, | says the Lord;* I know them and they | follow me. *Alleluia.* (John 10:27)

Readings and Psalm
Ezekiel 18:1-4, 25-32

Ezekiel challenges those who think they cannot change because of what their parents were and did, or who think they cannot turn from their wicked ways. God insistently invites people to turn and live.

Psalm 25:1-9

Remember, O Lord, your compassion and love. (Ps. 25:6)

Philippians 2:1-13

As part of a call for harmony rather than self-seeking, Paul uses a very early Christian hymn that extols the selflessness of Christ in his obedient death on the cross. Christ's selfless perspective is to be the essential perspective we share as the foundation for Christian accord.

Matthew 21:23-32

After driving the moneychangers out of the temple (21:12), Jesus begins teaching there. His authority is questioned by the religious leaders, who are supposed to be in charge of the temple.

Semicontinuous reading and psalm
Exodus 17:1-7

Because the thirsty Israelites quarreled with Moses and put the Lord to the test, Moses cried out in desperation to the Lord. Nevertheless, the Lord commanded Moses to strike the rock to provide water for the people. The doubt-filled question—"Is the Lord among us or not?"—received a dramatic and positive answer.

Psalm 78:1-4, 12-16

We will recount to generations to come the power of the Lord. (Ps. 78:4)

Preface   Sundays

Color   Green

Prayers of Intercession

The prayers are prepared locally for each occasion. The following examples may be adapted or used as appropriate.
Seeking the renewal of the Holy Spirit in our communities and in our world, we pray for the church, those in need, and all of God's creation.
A brief silence.
Holy and righteous God, humble your people, and turn us back to you. Give us new hearts and new spirits, so that your will may be accomplished through the work of your servants. Lord, in your mercy,
hear our prayer.
Send rain and sunshine for the renewal of the earth. Inspire people with innovative ways to reduce and reverse pollution, so that plentiful nourishment may come forth from the earth. Lord, in your mercy,
hear our prayer.

Place words of truth on the tongues of political, religious, and cultural leaders. May they be agents of cooperation, justice, and peace for all peoples. Lord, in your mercy,
hear our prayer.

By your divine and compassionate power deliver those in the depths of human sorrow (*especially*). Assure them that Christ walks with them in their suffering. Lord, in your mercy,
hear our prayer.

Encourage us to make a joyful noise throughout all the earth, as we sing your praise. Loose our tongues to proclaim with gladness your righteousness and your care for humankind. Lord, in your mercy,
hear our prayer.

Here other intercessions may be offered.

In the lives of the saints, you reveal the abundant life that you intend for us. Open our lives to greater joy in Christ-like humility and in service to others. Lord, in your mercy,
hear our prayer.

Into your hands, holy God, we commend all for whom we pray, trusting in your abundant mercy; through Jesus Christ our Savior.
Amen.

Ideas and Images for the Day

In the parable of the two sons, Jesus makes the point that we are all equally in need of God's grace. Ezekiel tells us of the invitation God extends to everyone, "Turn, then, and live" (Ezek. 18:32). In Philippians, we read a vision of the day in which all creation speaks with a unified voice that Jesus Christ is Lord. All humans are in need of God's grace; God extends grace to all, and one day, we will confess that salvation as one people. All of the readings reveal the way in which all humans are equal in the eyes of God.

1. In the book and film *The Wizard of Oz* (L. Frank Baum, New York: Tor Publishing, 1993, pp. 117–120; MGM, 1939), Dorothy and her companions discover that the man they once thought was a magical Wizard is really a man using a lot of smoke and mirrors to convince people he has magical gifts he really does not possess. The narrative in the book is easily adaptable into a drama or skit. What/whom do we give power and elevate to a place of undue importance? How might we feel if we discovered this untruth?

2. Norman Rockwell's painting *Golden Rule* (1961) contains the faces of people from all over the world along with the statement "Do unto others as you would have them do unto you." This painting illustrates the way in which people are worthy of equal treatment. As a way

of experiencing this revelation, create your own piece of art by drawing or clipping pictures from magazines. Choose images of people you don't like or whom some might consider enemies.

3. Hans Christian Andersen's tale *The Emperor's New Clothes* tells the story of a ruler who is able to convince everyone around him to admire his "new clothes." At the end of the story, a child speaks up and tells the truth—the emperor is naked. Reflect on the way in which we convince ourselves or other people that someone is special for a false reason. What voices in our culture tell us that beneath superficial differences we are all equal in the eyes of God?

4. As a children's message, or for your own reflection, take two different containers and fill them with an equal amount of liquid. If you were to guess, would you say each container contained the same amount of liquid? Could others guess? What does this tell us about our perceptions about equality? How do we put people in "containers" that disguise their equality or skew our own perception of things?

Hymns for Worship
Gathering

God is here!   ELW 526, WOV 719
O God, my faithful God   ELW 806, LBW 504
The trumpets sound, the angels sing   ELW 531, W&P 139

Hymn of the Day

Lord, keep us steadfast in your word   ELW 517, LBW 230
ERHALT UNS, HERR
Oh, that the Lord would guide my ways   ELW 772, LBW 480   EVAN
Our Father, we have wandered   ELW 606, WOV 733
HERZLICH TUT MICH VERLANGEN

Offering

As the grains of wheat   ELW 465, WOV 705, W&P 10
Blessed be the name   ELW 797

Communion

Strengthen for service, Lord   ELW 497, LBW 218
O blessed spring   ELW 447, WOV 695
O Master, let me walk with you   ELW 818, LBW 492

Sending

The Lord now sends us forth   ELW 538, LCC 415
What God ordains is good indeed   ELW 776, LBW 446

Additional Hymns and Songs

Now we offer   WOV 761, TFF 129
Jesus, name above all names   W&P 77
Go and do   SCR 123

Music for the Day
Psalmody and Acclamations

Becker, John W. "Psalm 25:1-9" from PWA, Evangelical Lutheran Worship Edition.

Nicholson, Paul. "Psalm 78," Refrain 1, from PSCY.

Schalk, Carl F. *Gospel Acclamations for Autumn.*

Shepperd, Mark. "Psalm 78:1-4, 12-16" from PWA, Evangelical Lutheran Worship Edition.

Shute, Linda Cable. "Psalm 25," Refrain 4, from PSCY.

Choral

Anerio, Felice/ed. Walter Ehret. "Christ Became Obedient Even Unto Death." SATB. GIA G-1967.

○ Busarow, Donald. "Lord, Keep Us Steadfast in Your Word." 2 pt trbl, org, C inst. CPH 98-2602.

Keesecker, Thomas. "To You, O Lord." SATB, kybd. AFP 9780800664138.

Patterson, Mark. "Show Me Thy Ways." U, kybd. AFP 9780800676230.

Pelz, Walter L. "Show Me Thy Ways." SATB, gtr, ob or fl. AFP 9780800645427. *The Augsburg Choirbook.* AFP 9780800656782.

Children's Choir

Cool, Jayne Southwick. "Psalm 25" from *ChildrenSing Psalms.* U, kybd. AFP 9780800663872.

Cox, Joe. "Show Me Your Ways." UE, U/2 pt, kybd. ABP 9780687345816.

Patterson, Mark. "Show Me Thy Ways" from *ChildrenSing.* U, kybd. AFP 9780800677695.

Keyboard / Instrumental

○ Brahms, Johannes. "Herzlich tut mich verlangen." Org. Various editions.

○ Keesecker, Thomas. "Erhalt uns, Herr" from *Come Away to the Skies.* Pno. AFP 9780800656553.

○ Leupold, Anton Wilhelm. "Erhalt uns, Herr" from *Augsburg Organ Library: November.* Org. AFP 9780800658960.

○ Raabe, Nancy M. "Herzlich tut mich verlangen" from *Grace and Peace,* vol. 2. Pno. AFP 9780800679016.

Handbell

Gramann, Fred. "Fantasy on King's Weston." 3-6 oct, L5. HOP 1671.

Kinyon, Barbara. "All Hail the Power of Jesus' Name." 2-3 oct, L3. HOP 1658.

Moklebust, Cathy. "Immortal, Invisible, God Only Wise." 3-5 oct hb, opt 3-5 oct hc, L3+. CG CGB583.

Praise Ensemble

- Cain, Patricia. "Jesus Name Above All Names." INT. W&P 77.
- Doerksen, Brian. "Come, Now Is the Time to Worship." VIN.
- Espinosa, Eddie. "Change My Heart, O God." VIN. ELW 801.
- Hall, Charlie. "Give Us Clean Hands." WT/Sixsteps Music.
- Morgan, Reuben. "I Give You My Heart." Hillsong/INT.
- Redman, Matt. "Blessed Be Your Name." Thankyou Music.

Global

African American trad. "Guide My Feet" from *Pave the Way: Global Songs 3.* U. AFP 9780800676896.

South African trad. "Sizohamba naye/We Will Go with God" from *Global Songs 2.* SATB. AFP 9780800656744.

Thursday, September 29
Michael and All Angels

On this festival day the church ponders the richness and variety of God's created order and the limits of human knowledge of it. The scriptures speak of angels (the word means "messengers") who worship God in heaven, and in both testaments angels speak for God on earth. They are remembered most vividly as they appear to the shepherds and announce the birth of the Savior. Michael is an angel whose name appears in Daniel as the heavenly being who leads the faithful dead to God's throne on the day of resurrection. In Revelation, Michael fights in a cosmic battle against Satan.

Friday, September 30
Jerome, translator, teacher, died 420

Jerome is remembered as a biblical scholar and translator. Rather than choosing classical Latin as the basis of his work, he translated the scriptures into the Latin that was spoken and written by the majority of the persons in his day. His translation is known as the Vulgate, from the Latin word for *common.* While Jerome is remembered as a saint, he could be anything but saintly. He was well known for his short temper and his arrogance, although he was also quick to admit to his personal faults. Thanks to the work of Jerome, many people received the word in their own language and lived lives of faith and service to those in need.

○ denotes suggestions that relate to the hymn of the day.
● denotes songs that are available on iTunes®.

October 2, 2011
Time after Pentecost — Lectionary 27

In today's gospel reading, Jesus tells a parable of the vineyard, an image of Israel, the prophets' mission, and Christ's death. For Christians, the vineyard also speaks of God's love poured out in the blood of Christ, given to us for the forgiveness of sin. Grafted onto Christ the vine at baptism, we are nourished with wine and bread, that we may share Christ's sufferings and know the power of his resurrection.

Prayer of the Day

Beloved God, from you come all things that are good. Lead us by the inspiration of your Spirit to know those things that are right, and by your merciful guidance, help us to do them, through Jesus Christ, our Savior and Lord.

Gospel Acclamation

Alleluia. Jesus says, I chose you and ap- ¹ pointed you* to go and bear fruit ¹ that will last. *Alleluia.* (John 15:16)

Readings and Psalm
Isaiah 5:1-7

The prophet sings a sad, parable-like love song about the relationship between God and Israel. In this song Israel is compared to a promising vineyard. Despite God's loving care, the vineyard that is Israel has brought forth "wild grapes" of injustice and distress, when fine grapes of justice and righteousness were expected.

Psalm 80:7-15

Look down from heaven, O God; behold and tend this vine. (Ps. 80:14, 15)

Philippians 3:4b-14

Paul reviews some of his supposed credentials, which no longer have any bearing in comparison to the right relationship he has been given through the death of Christ. The power of Christ's resurrection motivates him to press on toward the ultimate goal, eternal life with Christ.

Matthew 21:33-46

Jesus tells a parable to the religious leaders who are plotting his death, revealing that their plans will, ironically, bring about the fulfillment of scripture.

Semicontinuous reading and psalm
Exodus 20:1-4, 7-9, 12-20

The God of the Exodus graciously gave Israel the Ten Commandments. Primarily stated as negative imperatives, the Ten Commandments forbid gross sins such as murder, adultery, theft, and perjury. In most of life they grant Israel freedom to live righteously, with maximum love for God and neighbor.

Psalm 19

The statutes of the Lord are just and rejoice the heart. (Ps. 19:8)

Preface   Sundays

Color   Green

Prayers of Intercession

The prayers are prepared locally for each occasion. The following examples may be adapted or used as appropriate.

In grateful response to God's endless bounty of grace, let us pray for the church, the world, and all those in need.
A brief silence.

Tend your vineyard, O God, with love and mercy, so that all who follow you might bear fruit. Lord, in your mercy,
hear our prayer.

Replenish the earth, O God, with the new soil of your grace. Grant that fields produce plentiful harvests, and that all your creation continue to provide fruit to sustain and nurture life. Lord, in your mercy,
hear our prayer.

Plant the seeds of justice, O God, by the movement of your Spirit in the nations of this world. Grant that world leaders (*especially*) would seek peace and prosperity for all. Lord, in your mercy,
hear our prayer.

Sustain all who suffer, O God, with your promise of new life. Strengthen those who are unemployed, marginalized, or persecuted. Renew those who struggle with mental and physical ailments (*especially*). Lord, in your mercy,
hear our prayer.

Shine your grace, O God, on the ministries of this congregation. Make your love known through the people in this place. Lord, in your mercy,
hear our prayer.

Here other intercessions may be offered.

Nurture your people, O God, with the blessed memory of those who have died (*especially*). Grant comfort to those who mourn by the promise of new life in Jesus Christ. Lord, in your mercy,
hear our prayer.

Into your hands, holy God, we commend all for whom we pray, trusting in your abundant mercy; through Jesus Christ our Savior.
Amen.

Ideas and Images for the Day

The Ten Commandments were given to God's children as guidelines for how to live with others and love one another. The act of one person can affect a whole community. The parable of the wicked tenants demonstrates how God used the small, disrespected person of Jesus Christ (the cornerstone) to sow peace between creation and God. The small deeds one does can grow larger in a negative sense, and these readings also show that God sometimes turns those small acts into something constructive and great. God also helps us perform good and loving deeds and nurtures those deeds so they bring goodness to a whole community.

1. Find the Tears for Fears music video "Sowing the Seeds of Love" on YouTube (Mercury/Universal, 1989). Toward the end of the video, one of the singers plants seeds that grow into large plants as they sing "I believe in love power." Reflect on what they might be planting and on God's power to take something small and make it huge.

2. Reflect with Jan Richardson on the way tiny spiritual seeds within us are parts of a larger web of violence in the world. Tell the story of Etty Hillesum, a Jewish woman who died in the Holocaust, to show how someone could focus on building a spiritual peace within oneself in the midst of great violence, and how that peace could grow. Read the reflection at http://paintedprayerbook.com/2008/10/02/violence-in-the-vineyard/.

3. Read the book *Sadako and the Thousand Paper Cranes,* by Eleanor Coerr (New York: Puffin Modern Classics, 1977), and retell it as a children's message in worship. Focus on the message of one girl's story becoming a much larger movement in the world. What does one paper crane look like? What does a whole flock of paper cranes look like? As you make the cranes, pray for peace or other constructive endeavors of God's commonwealth, and display them in your gathering or worship space.

4. Listen to the song "Must Be," by Lost and Found (from the album *This*, Lost and Found and Limb Records, 1998). "Must Be" articulates, in a simple way, how we are broken and saved at the same time. Here is the idea: even God can redeem the most wicked of tenants, or the consequences of wicked tenants.

Hymns for Worship
Gathering
Lord Christ, when first you came to earth ELW 727, LBW 421
How firm a foundation ELW 796, LBW 507
All creatures, worship God most high! ELW 835, LBW 527

Hymn of the Day
The church of Christ, in every age ELW 729, LBW 433
    WAREHAM
Thine the amen ELW 826, WOV 801 THINE
All who love and serve your city ELW 724 NEW ORLEANS
    LBW 436 BIRABUS

Offering
You are holy ELW 525
Accept, O Lord, the gifts we bring ELW 691, WOV 759

Communion
How clear is our vocation, Lord ELW 580
When I survey the wondrous cross ELW 803, LBW 482, TFF 79
There in God's garden ELW 342, WOV 668

Sending
Thine the amen ELW 826, WOV 801
Lord, dismiss us with your blessing ELW 545, LBW 259

Additional Hymns and Songs
Make me a channel of your peace W&P 95
Behold and tend this vine DH 39
O Christ the great foundation HS91 822, NCH 387

Music for the Day
Psalmody and Acclamations

Becker, John W. "Psalm 80:7-15" from PWA, Evangelical Lutheran Worship Edition.

Haugen, Marty. "Psalm 19," Refrain 3, from PSCY.

Makeever, Ray. "Behold and Tend This Vine (Psalm 80)" from *Dancing at the Harvest*.

Schalk, Carl F. *Gospel Acclamations for Autumn.*

Schwarz, May. "Psalm 19" from PWA, Evangelical Lutheran Worship Edition.

Wold, Wayne L. "Psalm 80," Refrain 2, from PSCY.

Choral

Ashdown, Franklin D. "As the Branch Is to the Vine." SATB, org, opt assembly. SMP 10/3071S.

Isaac, Heinrich. "O Bread of Life from Heaven" from *Chantry Choirbook*. SATB. AFP 9780800657772.

○ Schalk, Carl. "Thine the Amen, Thine the Praise." SATB, org, opt assembly. AFP 9780800646127.

Scott, K. Lee. "A Vineyard Grows." SAB, org, insts. MSM 50-9106.

Children's Choir

Burkhardt, Michael. "How Can I Keep from Singing?" U/2 pt, kybd. CG CGA852.

Makeever, Ray. "Behold and Tend This Vine (Psalm 80)" from *Dancing at the Harvest*. U, kybd.

Page, Sue Ellen. "Sing Alleluia!" U, kybd, opt perc. CG CGA415.

Keyboard / Instrumental

Bach, J. S. "Aria in C Minor" from *Preludes and Postludes for Manuals*, vol. 1. Org/pno. CPH 97-6553U1.

○ Miller, Aaron David. "Thine" from *Augsburg Organ Library: Autumn*. Org. AFP 9780800675790.

○ Organ, Anne Krentz. "Thine" from *Reflections on Hymn Tunes for Holy Communion*, vol. 1. Pno. AFP 9780800679095.

○ Webster, Richard. "Wareham" from *Triptych for Transfiguration*. Org. AFP 9780800677541.

Handbell

Behnke, John. "When Morning Gilds the Skies." 3-5 oct, L4. AFP 9780800674861.

Edwards, Dan. "Fantasy on When I Survey the Wondrous Cross." 3 oct, L2+. National Music HB593.

Helman, Michael. "Gift of Finest Wheat: You Satisfy the Hungry Heart." 3-5 oct hb, opt hc, L3. AFP 9780800657369.

Praise Ensemble

● Carpenter, Kelly. "Draw Me Close." Mercy/VIN.

● Crowder, David. "O Praise Him." WT/Sixsteps Music.

Glaeser, Mark/Donna Hanna. "Build Us Up, Lord." ELW 670.

● Hayford, Jack. "Majesty." Rocksmith Music.

● LeBlanc, Lenny/Paul Baloche. "Above All." INT.

● Tomlin, Chris/Jesse Reeves. "Famous One." WT/Sixsteps Music.

Global

Cambodian folk tune. "Cambodian Lord's Prayer" from *Global Choral Sounds*. SATB, cant, perc. CPH 98-3610.

Olson, Howard S. "I Truly Am the Vine" from *Set Free: A Collection of African Hymns*. SATB. AFP 9780806600451.

Tuesday, October 4
Francis of Assisi, renewer of the church, died 1226

Francis was the son of a wealthy cloth merchant. In a public confrontation with his father, he renounced his wealth and future inheritance and devoted himself to serving the poor. Francis described this act as being "wedded to Lady Poverty." Under his leadership the Order of Friars Minor (Franciscans) was formed, and they took literally Jesus' words to his disciples that they should take nothing on their journey and receive no payment for their work. Their task in preaching was to "use words if necessary." Francis had a spirit of gladness and gratitude for all of God's creation. This commemoration has been a traditional time to bless pets and animals, creatures Francis called his brothers and sisters. A prayer and a hymn attributed to St. Francis are included in *Evangelical Lutheran Worship* (p. 87, #835).

Theodor Fliedner, renewer of society, died 1864

Fliedner's (FLEED-ner) work was instrumental in the revival of the ministry of deaconesses among Lutherans. While a pastor in Kaiserswerth, Germany, he also ministered to prisoners in Düsseldorf. Through his ministry to prisoners, he came in contact with Moravian deaconesses, and it was through this Moravian influence that he was convinced that the ministry of deaconesses had a place among Lutherans. His work and writing encouraged women to care for those who were sick, poor, or imprisoned. Fliedner's deaconess motherhouse in Kaiserswerth inspired Lutherans all over the world to commission deaconesses to serve in parishes, schools, prisons, and hospitals.

○ denotes suggestions that relate to the hymn of the day.
● denotes songs that are available on iTunes®.
278

Thursday, October 6

William Tyndale, translator, martyr, died 1536

William Tyndale was ordained in 1521, and his life's desire was to translate the scriptures into English. When his plan met opposition from King Henry VIII, Tyndale fled to Germany, where he traveled from city to city, living in poverty and constant danger. He was able to produce a New Testament in 1525. Nine years later he revised it and began work on the Old Testament, which he was unable to complete. He was captured, tried for heresy, and burned at the stake. Miles Coverdale completed Tyndale's work, and the Tyndale-Coverdale version was published as the "Matthew Bible" in 1537. For nearly four centuries the style of this translation has influenced English versions of the Bible such as the King James (Authorized Version) and the New Revised Standard Version.

Friday, October 7

Henry Melchior Muhlenberg, pastor in North America, died 1787

Muhlenberg (MYOO-len-berg) was prominent in setting the course for Lutheranism in North America. He helped Lutheran churches make the transition from the state churches of Europe to a new identity on American soil. Among other things, he established the first Lutheran synod in America and developed an American Lutheran liturgy. His liturgical principles became the basis for the Common Service of 1888, used in many North American service books for a majority of the past century. That Muhlenberg and his work are remembered today was anticipated at his death. The inscription on his grave reads, in Latin, "Who and what he was, future ages will know without a stone." 2011 marks the three hundredth anniversary of his birth.

October 9, 2011
Time after Pentecost — Lectionary 28

In Isaiah we are given a vision of the great feast to come, when God will wipe away death forever. In Jesus' parable about a great banquet, those invited do not come, so the invitation is extended to others. In our liturgy God spreads a table before us. Even amid anxiety and hardship we rejoice in the peace of God that surpasses all understanding. With great joy we feast at the table of the Lord, and we go forth to share the wonderful invitation with others hungering and thirsting for the abundant life of God.

Prayer of the Day

Lord of the feast, you have prepared a table before all peoples and poured out your life with abundance. Call us again to your banquet. Strengthen us by what is honorable, just, and pure, and transform us into a people of righteousness and peace, through Jesus Christ, our Savior and Lord.

Gospel Acclamation

Alleluia. This is the LORD for whom [|] we have waited;*
let us be glad and rejoice in [|] God's salvation. *Alleluia.*
(Isa. 25:9)

Readings and Psalm
Isaiah 25:1-9

After a hymn of praise acknowledging God as a shelter for the poor, the prophet portrays a wonderful victory banquet at which death—which in ancient Canaan was depicted as a monster swallowing everyone up—will be swallowed up forever. The prophet urges celebration of this victory of salvation.

Psalm 23

You prepare a table before me, and my cup is running over. (Ps. 23:5)

Philippians 4:1-9

Though writing from prison and facing an uncertain future, Paul calls on the Philippians to rejoice and give thanks to God no matter what the circumstance. God's peace is with us and binds together our hearts and minds in Jesus Christ, especially when things around us do not seem peaceful.

Matthew 22:1-14

Jesus tells a parable indicating that the blessings of God's kingdom are available to all, but the invitation is not to be taken lightly.

Semicontinuous reading and psalm

Exodus 32:1-14

After Israel sinned by worshipping the golden calf, Moses interceded with God to spare Israel, lest the Egyptians conclude that God had evil intents in the Exodus. Moses reminds God of the promises God made to Israel's matriarchs and patriarchs.

Psalm 106:1-6, 19-23

Remember, O LORD, the favor you have for your people. (Ps. 106:4)

Preface Sundays

Color Green

Prayers of Intercession

The prayers are prepared locally for each occasion. The following examples may be adapted or used as appropriate.

In grateful response to God's endless bounty of grace, let us pray for the church, the world, and all those in need.
A brief silence.

Gracious God, unite the wills of your people. Empower us to be of the same mind in the Lord, so that through word and deed we might give faithful witness to you. Lord, in your mercy,
hear our prayer.

Creator of valleys and green pastures, of small towns and urban centers, give your care to this world. Inspire in us, your creatures, a love for all you have made, and grant us wisdom to care for it. Lord, in your mercy,
hear our prayer.

God of all people, establish your peace in the world. Give the leaders of the nations a desire for reconciliation and a yearning for justice. Lord, in your mercy,
hear our prayer.

Merciful God, lead all who are sick to the healing waters of your mercy. Bless the work of doctors, nurses, and caregivers, and through their efforts restore the sick to health (*especially*). Lord, in your mercy,
hear our prayer.

Holy God, by your power grant this congregation the faith to stand firm in Jesus Christ. Send your Spirit to this place, so that through all its ministries your wisdom and truth might be made known. Lord, in your mercy,
hear our prayer.

Here other intercessions may be offered.

God of blessed hope, comfort those who grieve with the promise of new life in Christ Jesus (*especially*). Give us the blessed assurance that you will swallow up death forever. Lord, in your mercy,
hear our prayer.

Into your hands, holy God, we commend all for whom we pray, trusting in your abundant mercy; through Jesus Christ our Savior.
Amen.

Ideas and Images for the Day

Today's gospel focuses on invitation and grace. Jesus tells the parable of the king who invites all people to a wedding banquet. At first this parable seems to portray a wide open and gracious invitation. However, by the end it is hard not to feel sorry for the poor guy who gets thrown out for not wearing the correct clothes! Through this story Jesus teaches that receiving God's grace changes us. We are called to bear fruit with our lives, sharing this grace with others. To live in the same way after receiving this gracious invitation is simply not an option.

1. In *The Cost of Discipleship*, Dietrich Bonhoeffer wrote, "Cheap grace means the justification of sin without the justification of the sinner. Grace alone does everything they say, and so everything can remain as it was before. . . . Cheap grace is the grace we bestow on ourselves. Cheap grace is the preaching of forgiveness without requiring repentance, baptism without church discipline, Communion without confession. . . . Cheap grace is grace without discipleship, grace without the cross, grace without Jesus Christ, living and incarnate" (http://www.crossroad.to/Persecution/Bonhoffer.html). Perhaps another way of putting it is that cheap grace is like showing up to the party without a robe! When we respond to the invitation of God's grace, it changes us forever. We are "clothed" in God's grace, bearing fruit with our lives as we share the invitation with others.

2. Dakota Road has a song based on today's gospel, called "All Are Welcome" (http://www.dakotaroad.com/indexlyrics.htm). This is a song of invitation, but the lyrics move toward a challenge in the end: "Go into the streets and cities to the farms and families, Tell about the splendid table, God's mercy." Responding to the invitation ultimately moves us to action and bearing fruit. Intersperse the verses of this song through your sermon teaching about God's invitation and our call to mission.

3. Invite everyone to worship this week. Create and send special invitations encouraging members to come, but also invite others for this week's service. Consider having a meal such as a barbecue or pot luck after worship. Use this culture of invitation to shape your sermon. What does it mean to invite? Who is invited to worship this week? Who might still be waiting to hear a word of invitation?

4. Invite all the children to come forward for a special message. Look around and say, "There are not enough kids here!" Instruct them to go and invite someone else from the congregation who is not a member of their family to join them. When everyone is settled, teach that God invites *everyone* to come and experience love and friendship. Distribute invitations for them to give to friends, inviting them to come to worship and Sunday school with the children next week.

Hymns for Worship
Gathering
As we gather at your table   ELW 522
Arise, my soul, arise!   ELW 827, LBW 516
Soul, adorn yourself with gladness   ELW 488/489, LBW 224, LCC 388

Hymn of the Day
Let us go now to the banquet   ELW 523, LLC 410
   VAMOS TODOS AL BANQUETE
We eat the bread of teaching   ELW 518   *WISDOM'S FEAST*
Now we join in celebration   ELW 462, LBW 203
   SCHMÜCKE DICH

Offering
The trumpets sound, the angels sing   ELW 531, W&P 139
Come, let us eat   ELW 491, LBW 214

Communion
At the Lamb's high feast we sing   ELW 362, LBW 210

God extends an invitation   ELW 486, LLC 397
Bread of life, our host and meal   ELW 464

Sending
O Lord, we praise you   ELW 499, LBW 215
Sent forth by God's blessing   ELW 547, LBW 221

Additional Hymns and Songs
A multitude comes from the east and the west   LBW 313
Grains of wheat   WOV 708, LLC 392
We come to your feast   GC 850

Music for the Day
Psalmody and Acclamations
Bruxvoort-Colligan, Richard. "My Love Is My Shepherd (Psalm 23)" from *Sharing the Road*. AFP 9780800678630.
Farlee, Robert Buckley. "Psalm 23," Refrain 2, from PSCY.
Mummert, Mark. "Psalm 106:1-6, 19-23" from PSCY.
Schalk, Carl F. *Gospel Acclamations for Autumn.*
Sedio, Mark. "Psalm 23" and "Psalm 106:1-6, 19-23" from PWA, Evangelical Lutheran Worship Edition.
"The King of Love My Shepherd Is." ELW 502.

Choral
Benson, Robert A. "Rejoice, the Lord Is King." U/2 pt trbl, kybd. AFP 9780800676698.
Ferguson, John. "Rejoice in the Lord." SATB, org. AFP 9780800679361.
Pote, Allen. "The Lord Is My Shepherd." SAB, SAT, or SATB, pno. CG CGA551.
Schalk, Carl. "The God of Love My Shepherd Is." SATB, 2 vln, org. MSM 50-8812.
Shaw, Timothy. "We're Marching to Zion." SATB, opt perc. AFP 9780800664275.

Children's Choir
Comer, Marilyn. "Psalm 23" from *ChildrenSing Psalms*. U, kybd. AFP 9780800663872.
Traditional. "Rejoice in the Lord Always" from *LifeSongs*. U, kybd.
Wold, Wayne. "To the Banquet Come" from *LifeSongs*. U, kybd.

Keyboard / Instrumental
○ Brahms, Johannes. "Schmücke dich." Org. Various editions.
○ Callahan, Charles. "Schmücke dich" from *Communion Music for Manuals*. Org. MSM 10-822.
○ Frahm, Frederick. "Schmücke dich" from *Faith Alive*, vol. 1. Org. AFP 9780800675738.
○ Organ, Anne Krentz. "Schmücke dich" from *Reflections on Hymn Tunes for Holy Communion*, vol. 2. Pno. AFP 9780800679091.

○ denotes suggestions that relate to the hymn of the day.
● denotes songs that are available on iTunes®.

Handbell

Buckwalter, Karen. "Songs for the Feast." 4-5 oct, L4-. BP HB192.

Dobrinski, Cynthia. "Joyful Reflections." 3-6 oct, L2+. HOP 2433.

Eithun, Sandra. "Break Thou the Bread of Life." 3-5 oct, L2+. Soundforth Productions 249029.

Praise Ensemble

- Jernigan, Dennis. "You Are My All in All (Jesus, Lamb of God)." Shepherd's Heart Music. W&P 76.
- Redman, Matt. "Better Is One Day." Thankyou Music.
- Redman, Matt. "You Never Let Go." Thankyou Music.
- Smith, Henry. "Give Thanks." INT.
- Tomlin, Chris/Jesse Reeves/Louie Giglio/Matt Maher. "I Will Rise." WT/Sixsteps Music.
- Tomlin, Chris/John Newton/John Rees/Edwin Excell/Louie Giglio. "Amazing Grace (My Chains Are Gone)." WT.

Global

Cuéllar, Guillermo. "Come, the Banquet Hall Is Ready" from *Global Songs 2*. SATB. AFP 9780800656744.

Feliciano, Francisco F. "The Lord Is My Shepherd" from *Sound the Bamboo*. SATB. GIA G-6830.

Monday, October 10

Day of Thanksgiving (Canada)

See Day of Thanksgiving (U.S.A.), pp. 317–319.

Saturday, October 15

Teresa of Ávila (Teresa de Jesús), teacher, renewer of the church, died 1582

Teresa of Ávila (AH-vee-la) is also known as Teresa de Jesús. She chose the life of a Carmelite nun after reading the letters of Jerome. Frequently sick during her early years as a nun, she found that when she was sick her prayer life flowered, but when she was well it withered. Steadily her life of faith and prayer deepened, and she grew to have a lively sense of God's presence with her. She worked to reform her monastic community in Ávila, which she believed had strayed from its original purpose. Her reforms asked nuns to maintain life in the monastic enclosure without leaving it and to identify with those who are poor by not wearing shoes. Teresa's writings on devotional life have enjoyed a wide readership.

October 16, 2011
Time after Pentecost — Lectionary 29

In today's first reading God uses the Gentile ruler Cyrus to accomplish divine purposes. When the Pharisees try to trap Jesus, he tells them to give the emperor what belongs to him and to God what belongs to God. To gather for worship reminds us that our ultimate allegiance is to God rather than to any earthly authority. Created in the image of God, we offer our entire selves in the service of God and for the sake of the world.

Prayer of the Day

Sovereign God, raise your throne in our hearts. Created by you, let us live in your image; created for you, let us act for your glory; redeemed by you, let us give you what is yours, through Jesus Christ, our Savior and Lord.

Gospel Acclamation

Alleluia. Shine like stars ¹ in the world;* holding fast to the ¹ word of life. *Alleluia.* (Phil. 2:15, 16)

Readings and Psalm

Isaiah 45:1-7

The prophet announces that Cyrus the Persian emperor is the one the Lord has anointed to end Israel's exile. The Lord makes this choice so that the whole world will recognize this Lord as the only God. Persia had a god of light and a god of darkness; the Lord claims sovereignty over both light and darkness.

Psalm 96:1-9 [10-13]

Ascribe to the Lᴏʀᴅ honor and power. (Ps. 96:7)

1 Thessalonians 1:1-10

Most likely this letter is the first written by Paul. Paul is giving pastoral encouragement and reassurances to new Christians living in an antagonistic pagan environment. Their commitment of faith, love, and hope makes them a model for other new Christian communities.

Matthew 22:15-22

After Jesus begins teaching in the temple, religious leaders try to trap him with questions. First they ask if God's people should pay taxes to an earthly tyrant like Caesar.

Semicontinuous reading and psalm
Exodus 33:12-23

Moses successfully interceded with God to accompany Israel to the holy land after their sin with the golden calf. In response to a request to display his glory, God recites a sentence that appears frequently in the Old Testament: "I will be gracious to whom I will be gracious." Moses is not allowed to see God's face, but only God's back.

Psalm 99

Proclaim the greatness of the Lᴏʀᴅ our God. (Ps. 99:5)

Preface   Sundays

Color   Green

Prayers of Intercession

The prayers are prepared locally for each occasion. The following examples may be adapted or used as appropriate.

In grateful response to God's endless bounty of grace, let us pray for the church, the world, and all those in need.
A brief silence.

God in heaven, send your Holy Spirit upon the church, that it might receive your word with joy and faithfully proclaim the gospel through word and deed. Lord, in your mercy,
hear our prayer.

Creating God, the heavens rejoice and the earth is glad, for you made them. Sustain all creation with your breath of life, and raise up from your people faithful stewards of creation. Lord, in your mercy,
hear our prayer.

God of all, the nations declare your glory, the people proclaim your wonders. Unite the people of this world in your love, and show them the way of peace. Lord, in your mercy,
hear our prayer.

Living God, grant your healing and mercy to all who are sick (*especially*). May the promise of the gospel come in word and in power to all who suffer. Lord, in your mercy, **hear our prayer.**

Lord, give this congregation the desire to sing to you a new song of your glory. Bless the work of volunteers and staff, of elected and rostered leaders, that through them you might be made known. Lord, in your mercy, **hear our prayer.**

Here other intercessions may be offered.

God the beginning and the end, you hold in your care those who have gone before us. Comfort those who mourn with the promise of the resurrection (*especially*), and at the last gather all the faithful in your holy kingdom. Lord, in your mercy, **hear our prayer.**

Into your hands, holy God, we commend all for whom we pray, trusting in your abundant mercy; through Jesus Christ our Savior. **Amen.**

Ideas and Images for the Day

For many congregations, autumn marks a time of prayer and conversation around stewardship and financial pledging for the year to come. Today's gospel provides an ideal time to reflect on stewardship of all sorts—time, talent and financial treasures. The Pharisees approach Jesus in a thinly veiled attempt to trap him on issues of financial obligations to the Roman government. In response, Jesus issues a challenge in return—give to Caesar what belongs to Caesar and give to God what belongs to God. This statement challenges us to ponder, if God created the world and everything in it, what doesn't belong to God?

1. The response by Jesus in this gospel is brilliant, as he teaches that everything belongs to God. At the beginning of the sermon, ask: "Is there anything that doesn't belong to God? If so, what?" Use people's responses to move into a deeper reflection on how we might be better stewards of the gifts God has given us.

2. By mid-October, both football season and stewardship campaigns are heating up. A scene that seems to repeat itself every year is the athlete who scores a winning touchdown and in the postgame interview says, "First I want to give all praise, honor, and glory to God." We often want to ask, "Will you include your multimillion dollar contract in that praise, honor, and glory?" Before laughing too hard at that, maybe we all need to ponder the question "What am I called to give?"

3. It has often been said that when we give of our time, talent, and treasure, paradoxically we receive in abundance. This point is vividly illustrated through a classic scene at the end of the movie *It's a Wonderful Life* (Republic Pictures, 1947). George has spent a lifetime caring for the people of his community and giving selflessly of his resources. Then, in his moment of dire need, the people of his town shower him with gifts and contributions beyond what he could possibly have imagined.

4. We can teach children about stewardship and illustrate today's gospel through sharing the Legend of Stone Soup. Background on this story is available at http://en.wikipedia.org/wiki/Stone_soup. This is the story of how two hungry travelers united a community when they empowered people to share their gifts. When a few people shared a little bit of food, many hungry and poor people were fed. Had the people hoarded their food, they would have gone hungry. When they shared their food there was more than enough.

Hymns for Worship
Gathering
Lift every voice and sing ELW 841, LBW 562, TFF 296
O God of every nation ELW 713, LBW 416
God is here! ELW 526, WOV 719

Hymn of the Day
All my hope on God is founded ELW 757, WOV 782
MICHAEL
Sing praise to God, the highest good ELW 871, LBW 542
LOBT GOTT DEN HERREN, IHR
How clear is our vocation, Lord ELW 580 REPTON

Offering
We raise our hands to you, O Lord ELW 690
We give thee but thine own ELW 686, LBW 410

Communion
Bread of life from heaven ELW 474
Your will be done ELW 741, TFF 243
Now the feast and celebration ELW 167, WOV 789

Sending
God of grace and God of glory ELW 705, LBW 415
Savior, again to your dear name ELW 534, LBW 262

Additional Hymns and Songs
You, Lord W&P 162
Give thanks TFF 292, W&P 41
Baited, the question rose HFG 113

Music for the Day
Psalmody and Acclamations

Becker, John W. "Psalm 96:1-9 [10-13]" from PWA, Evangelical Lutheran Worship Edition.

Messner, Sally. "Psalm 99" from PWA, Evangelical Lutheran Worship Edition.

Roberts, William Bradley. "Psalm 99," Refrain 1, from PSCY.

Schalk, Carl F. *Gospel Acclamations for Autumn.*

Shute, Linda Cable. "Psalm 96," Refrain 2, from PSCY.

Choral

Jennings, Kenneth. "Sing to the Lord a New Song." SATB, org, br, timp. AFP 9780800621551.

Lasky, David. "I Sing the Mighty Power of God." SATB, org. AFP 9780806697161.

Pavlechko, Thomas. "In Sacred Manner." SATB div, org, opt violin and/or br, timp. AFP 9780806697147.

Powell, Robert J. "Sing to the Lord with Joy and Gladness." U/2 pt, kybd. AFP 9780800676360.

Schein, Johann Hermann/ed. Ronald A. Nelson. "Sing to the Lord." SAB, kybd. MSM AE-14.

Scott, K. Lee. "Treasures in Heaven." 2-pt, kybd. AFP 9780800664282.

Sweelinck, Jan Pieterszoon. "Sing to the Lord, New Songs Be Raising" in *Chantry Choirbook.* SATB. AFP 9780800657772.

Children's Choir

Haydn, Joseph. "Sing to the Lord a New Song." U, kybd. CG CGA992.

Lindh, Jody. "Come, Let Us Sing." U, kybd, opt synth, glock, fl. CG CGA478.

Paradowski, John. "Forever We Shall Sing." U/2 pt, kybd, opt fl, perc. CG CGA1096.

Keyboard / Instrumental

o Burkhardt, Michael. "Michael" from *Eight Improvisations on 20th Century Hymn Tunes*, set 2. Org. MSM 10-533.

o Farlee, Robert Buckley. "Lobt Gott den Herren, ihr" from *Gaudeamus!* Org. AFP 9780800655389.

o Organ, Anne Krentz. "Repton" from *Come to Us, Creative Spirit.* Pno. AFP 9780800659042.

o Sedio, Mark. "Lobt Gott den Herren, ihr" from *Let Us Talents and Tongues Employ.* Org. AFP 9780800655723.

Handbell

McKlveen, Paul. "Take My Life and Let It Be." 3-5 oct hb, opt 3 oct hc, L3. CG CGB539.

Smith, Vicki. "Lift Every Voice and Sing." 3-5 oct, L3. CPH 97-6943.

o Stephenson, Valerie. "Sing Praise to God Who Reigns Above." 3-6 oct hb, opt 3-5 oct hc, opt tpt, L3. HOP 2494.

Praise Ensemble

● Chisholm, Thomas/William Runyan. "Great Is Thy Faithfulness." HOP.

● DeShazo, Lynn. "More Precious than Silver." INT.

● Scott, Kathryn. "Hungry." VIN.

● Smith, Henry. "Give Thanks." INT.

● Tomlin, Chris. "We Fall Down." WT.

● Tomlin, Chris/Louie Giglio. "Take My Life." WT/Sixsteps Music.

Global

Hesla, Bret. "Everything That We Have" from *Global Songs 2.* SATB. AFP 9780800656744. ELW 247.

Pangosban, Ben. "Sing a Song to the Lord" from *Sound the Bamboo.* U. GIA G-6830.

Monday, October 17
Ignatius, Bishop of Antioch, martyr, died around 115

Ignatius was the second bishop of Antioch, in Syria. It was there that the name "Christian" was first used to describe the followers of Jesus. Ignatius is known to us through his letters. In them he encouraged Christians to live in unity sustained with love while standing firm on sound doctrine. Ignatius believed Christian martyrdom was a privilege. When his own martyrdom approached, he wrote in one of his letters, "I prefer death in Christ Jesus to power over the farthest limits of the earth. . . . Do not stand in the way of my birth to real life." Ignatius and all martyrs are a reminder that even today Christians face death because of their faith in Jesus.

Tuesday, October 18
Luke, Evangelist

St. Luke is identified by tradition as the author of both Luke and Acts. Luke is careful to place the events of Jesus' life in both their social and religious contexts. Some of the most loved parables, including the good Samaritan and the prodigal son, are found only in this gospel. Luke's gospel has also given the church some of its most beautiful songs: the Benedictus sung at morning prayer, the Magnificat sung at evening prayer, and the Nunc dimittis sung at the close of the day. These songs are powerful witnesses to the message of Jesus Christ.

o denotes suggestions that relate to the hymn of the day.
● denotes songs that are available on iTunes®.

October 23, 2011
Time after Pentecost — Lectionary 30

Jesus' summary of the law in today's gospel echoes our first reading from Leviticus. We are called not only to love God with heart, soul, and mind, but also to love our neighbor as ourselves. It is out of such deep care that Paul shares the gospel with the Thessalonian community. In the confession of sins, we acknowledge that we have not loved God, neighbor, and self; yet we gather to hear the word of forgiveness and to be strengthened by word and meal to be signs of God's love and mercy in the world.

Today the church commemorates James of Jerusalem, martyr, who died around 62.

Prayer of the Day

O Lord God, you are the holy lawgiver, you are the salvation of your people. By your Spirit renew us in your covenant of love, and train us to care tenderly for all our neighbors, through Jesus Christ, our Savior and Lord.

Gospel Acclamation

Alleluia. Beloved, since God loved ' us so much,* we also ought to love ' one another. *Alleluia.* (1 John 4:11)

Readings and Psalm
Leviticus 19:1-2, 15-18

The holiness code in Leviticus urges people to be holy because God is holy. Holiness is lived out in partiality for and consideration of the poor and the weak. We are to love our neighbors as ourselves. God's people exercise justice and love in their dealings with one another.

Psalm 1

Their delight is in the law of the Lord. (Ps. 1:2)

1 Thessalonians 2:1-8

Paul uses maternal imagery to depict the caring and nurturing relationship he shares with the Thessalonian Christians. When he first came to their city it was not to benefit himself but to share the gospel with them, which was his responsibility as an apostle of Christ.

Matthew 22:34-46

Put on the spot by the Pharisees, Jesus displays wisdom by summarizing the law of God in just two commandments and by demonstrating the Messiah must be more than the son of David.

Semicontinuous reading and psalm
Deuteronomy 34:1-12

Before his death, Moses, who was not allowed to enter the holy land, was granted the right to see the land from Mount Nebo. The statement that no prophet has arisen in Israel like Moses (34:10) stands in tension with Deuteronomy 18:15 (God will "raise up for you a prophet like me") and led to the expectation that another Moses would still come. In several New Testament passages Jesus is identified as that prophet.

Psalm 90:1-6, 13-17

Show your servants your works, and your splendor to their children. (Ps. 90:16)

Preface   Sundays

Color   Green

Prayers of Intercession

The prayers are prepared locally for each occasion. The following examples may be adapted or used as appropriate.

In grateful response to God's endless bounty of grace, let us pray for the church, the world, and all those in need.

A brief silence.

Heavenly Father, you gave your people the law so that they might know how to live. Grant your church the faith and strength to live according to your law of love. Lord, in your mercy,

hear our prayer.

You created the fruit-bearing tree, a model for the godly life. Give your people the wisdom to tend to all of creation, so that in its beauty and life we might see a glimpse of your glory. Lord, in your mercy,

hear our prayer.

Divine ruler, you bid your people to live lives of justice and righteousness. Inspire the leaders of nations, states, provinces, and local communities to use their office not for personal gain but in humble service to their neighbor. Lord, in your mercy,
hear our prayer.

From generation to generation, you are the refuge of all who suffer. Hold in your care all who are poor, unemployed or underemployed, homeless, and who live without adequate medical care. Grant your healing mercies to all who are sick (*especially*). Lord, in your mercy,
hear our prayer.

Where two or three are gathered in your name, you promise to be present. Bless this congregation as it gathers around word and sacrament, in fellowship and prayer, in learning and service, in your holy name. Lord, in your mercy,
hear our prayer.

Here other intercessions may be offered.

In your love, gracious God, you hold (*James of Jerusalem, martyr, and*) all who have died in you. Comfort all who mourn with the promise of your never-ending embrace (*especially*), and give us the faith to look expectantly for your promised kingdom, where all will be given resurrection life. Lord, in your mercy,
hear our prayer.

Into your hands, holy God, we commend all for whom we pray, trusting in your abundant mercy; through Jesus Christ our Savior.
Amen.

Ideas and Images for the Day

Love God, love neighbor, and love self. Jesus is really into relationships! Oftentimes, even if unintentionally, we put loving self first, and because "we are bound to sin and cannot free ourselves" we usually do a poor job of actually loving ourselves. This means we have less love to give to neighbor and even less for God. Jesus puts relationship with God first. He doesn't do this to make us last but so that we can fully understand love and relationship the way God desires it for us.

1. The Bible is not a rule book but a love letter. God tells the people through Moses, "You shall be holy." The psalmist writes that we should take delight in the law. Jesus proclaims the two greatest commandments. When we perceive scripture as simply a list of dos and don'ts we miss the point. Rather than being rules, the commandments God has given help us relate to God and to our neighbor in loving ways.

2. Paul likens how he cared for the people in Thessalonica to being gentle as a nurse tenderly caring for her own children. Consider calling attention to the people in the assembly who are caretakers of others: parish nurses,

adults who care for elderly parents, parents of special-needs children, hospital workers. Use "Affirmation of Christian Vocation" or the prayer for caregivers and others who support the sick from *Evangelical Lutheran Worship* (pp. 84–85), or write an original prayer or ritual.

3. Children are concrete thinkers, but most understand the complex concept of love. While children need to hear the words "I love you," they also need to feel the concept of love tangibly and in concrete ways. Even in a congregation with few children, ask: How does your congregation show children tangible love? In what ways does it help children to show such love to others?

4. Tina Turner sang the words "What's love got to do with it? Who needs a heart when a heart can be broken?" The act of love requires vulnerability. Hearts can be broken, and good deeds can be punished, but God calls us to love, which means opening ourselves to being hurt. And yet there is real and powerful healing in loving God and loving others because it means fully experiencing the gospel.

5. Sarah Bernhardt wrote: "Your words are my food, your breath my wine. You are everything to me." Just as children need tangible examples of love in their lives, so do we all. The word and the meal we share in worship are tangible expressions of God's love for us. Word and meal send us out to care for and love our neighbor in tangible ways.

Hymns for Worship
Gathering

Love divine, all loves excelling   ELW 631, LBW 315
Joyful, joyful we adore thee   ELW 836, LBW 551
Great God, your love has called us   ELW 358, WOV 666

Hymn of the Day

To be your presence   ELW 546   ENGELBERG
Christ is the king!   ELW 662, LBW 386   BEVERLY
Jesu, Jesu, fill us with your love   ELW 708, WOV 765
   CHEREPONI

Offering

When the poor ones/*Cuando el pobre*   ELW 725, LCC 508
Come, my way, my truth, my life   ELW 816, LBW 513

Communion

Lord, thee I love with all my heart   ELW 750, LBW 325
Eternal Spirit of the living Christ   ELW 402, LBW 441
Goodness is stronger than evil   ELW 721

Sending

Let streams of living justice   ELW 710

Lord of all nations, grant me grace   ELW 716, LBW 419

Additional Hymns and Songs

Let me be yours forever   LBW 490

With all your heart   DH 95

Happy are they   TFF 1

Music for the Day
Psalmody and Acclamations

Cherwien, David. "Psalm 90," Refrain 1, from PSCY.

Harbor, Rawn. "Happy Are They (Psalm 1)" TFF 1.

Kallman, Daniel. "Psalm 90:1-6, 13-17" from PWA, Evangelical Lutheran Worship Edition.

"O God, Our Help in Ages Past." ELW 632.

Organ, Anne Krentz. "Psalm 1" from PWA, Evangelical Lutheran Worship Edition.

Schalk, Carl F. *Gospel Acclamations for Autumn.*

Wold, Wayne L. "Psalm 1," Refrain 2, from PSCY.

Choral

Clausen, René. "My God, How Wonderful Thou Art." SATB. AFP 9780800676995.

Hillert, Richard. "Happy Are Those Who Delight." U, org, fl, opt str. GIA G-4259.

Marshall, Jane M. "Blessed Is the Man." SATB, kybd. HIN HMC-627.

Proulx, Richard. "How Blest Are They." U, org, fl. AFP 9780800645434.

Children's Choir

Howard/Lyons. "Like a Tree" from *LifeSongs.* U, kybd.

Leaf, Robert. "To the Glory of Our King." U, kybd. CG CGA173.

Sleeth, Natalie. "If You Love Me" from *LifeSongs.* U, kybd.

Keyboard / Instrumental

○ Albrecht, Mark. "Engelberg" from *Timeless Tunes for Solo Instrument and Piano,* vol. 2. Pno, inst. AFP 9780800659851.

○ Cherwien, David. "Engelberg" from *Augsburg Organ Library: Easter.* Org. AFP 9780800659363.

○ Organ, Anne Krentz. "Jesu, Jesu, Fill Us With Your Love (Chereponi)." Pno, inst. CPH 97-6931.

○ Sedio, Mark. "Chereponi" from *Dancing in the Light.* Pno. AFP 9780800656546.

Handbell

○ Helman, Michael. "Jesu, Jesu, Fill Us with Your Love." 3-5 oct hb, opt 3 oct hc, L3. AFP 9780800658878.

○ McChesney, Kevin. "Festival Fanfare on Engelberg." 3-5 oct, L3. CPH 97-6843U50.

○ McChesney, Kevin. "Jesu, Jesu, Fill Us with Your Love." 2-3 oct, L2. AFP 11-10985. OP.

○ denotes suggestions that relate to the hymn of the day.
● denotes songs that are available on iTunes®.

Praise Ensemble

Harling, Per. "You Are Holy." ELW 525.

● Imboden, Marc/Tammi Rhoton. "You Are Holy (Prince of Peace)." Imboden Music.

● Kendrick, Graham. "Amazing Love." Make Way Music.

● Klein, Laurie. "I Love You, Lord." House of Mercy Music/MAR. W&P 67

● Morgan, Reuben. "I Give You My Heart." Hillsong/INT.

● Tomlin, Chris/Louie Giglio. "Holy Is the Lord." WT/sixsteps Music.

Global

Trad. Thai melody. "Happy Is He Who Walks in God's Wise Way" from *Sound the Bamboo.* U. GIA G-6830.

Zata, Mr. "Musande Mambo Mwari" from *Agape: Songs of Hope and Reconciliation.* SATB, perc. Lutheran World Federation. AFP 9780191000133.

Sunday, October 23

James of Jerusalem, martyr, died around 62

James became an early leader of the church in Jerusalem. He is described in the New Testament as the brother of Jesus, and secular historian Josephus calls James the brother of Jesus, "the so-called Christ." Little is known about James, but Josephus reported that the Pharisees respected James for his piety and observance of the law. His enemies had him put to death.

Wednesday, October 26

Philipp Nicolai, died 1608;
Johann Heermann, died 1647;
Paul Gerhardt, died 1676; hymnwriters

These three outstanding hymnwriters all worked in Germany during times of war and plague. When Philipp Nicolai was a pastor in Westphalia, the plague killed thirteen hundred of his parishioners. One hundred seventy people died in one week. His hymns "Wake, Awake, for Night Is Flying" (ELW 436) and "O Morning Star, How Fair and Bright!" (ELW 308) were included in a series of meditations he wrote to comfort his parishioners during the plague. The style of Johann Heermann's hymns moved away from the more objective style of Reformation hymnody toward expressing the emotions of faith. Among his hymns is the plaintive text "Ah, Holy Jesus" (ELW 349). Paul Gerhardt lost a preaching position at St. Nicholas Church in Berlin because he refused to sign a document stating he would not make theological arguments in his sermons. The author of beloved hymns such as "O Sacred Head, Now Wounded" (ELW 351), some have called Gerhardt the greatest of Lutheran hymnwriters.

Friday, October 28

Simon and Jude, Apostles

Little is known about Simon and Jude. In New Testament lists of the apostles, Simon the "zealot" or Cananaean is mentioned, but he is never mentioned apart from these lists.

Jude, sometimes called Thaddeus, is also mentioned in lists of the Twelve. At the last supper Jude asked Jesus why he had chosen to reveal himself to the disciples but not to the world. A traditional story about Simon and Jude says that they traveled together on a missionary journey to Persia and were both martyred there.

October 30, 2011
Reformation Sunday

On this day we celebrate the heart of our faith: the gospel of Christ—the good news—that makes us free! We pray that the Holy Spirit would continue to unite the church today in its proclamation and witness to the world. In the waters of baptism we are made one body; we pray for the day that all Christians will also be one at the Lord's table.

Prayer of the Day

Almighty God, gracious Lord, we thank you that your Holy Spirit renews the church in every age. Pour out your Holy Spirit on your faithful people. Keep them steadfast in your word, protect and comfort them in times of trial, defend them against all enemies of the gospel, and bestow on the church your saving peace, through Jesus Christ, our Savior and Lord, who lives and reigns with you and the Holy Spirit, one God, now and forever.

or

Gracious Father, we pray for your holy catholic church. Fill it with all truth and peace. Where it is corrupt, purify it; where it is in error, direct it; where in anything it is amiss, reform it; where it is right, strengthen it; where it is in need, provide for it; where it is divided, reunite it; for the sake of your Son, Jesus Christ, our Savior, who lives and reigns with you and the Holy Spirit, one God, now and forever.

Gospel Acclamation

Alleluia. If you continue in my word, you are truly | my disciples,* and you will know the truth, and the truth will | make you free. *Alleluia.* (John 8:31-32)

Readings and Psalm

Jeremiah 31:31-34

The renewed covenant will not be breakable, but like the old covenant it will expect the people to live upright lives. To know the Lord means that one will defend the cause of the poor and needy (Jer. 22:16). The renewed covenant is possible only because the Lord will forgive iniquity and not remember sin. Our hope lies in a God who forgets.

Psalm 46

The Lord of hosts is with us; the God of Jacob is our stronghold. (Ps. 46:7)

Romans 3:19-28

Paul's words stand at the heart of the preaching of Martin Luther and the other Reformation leaders. No human beings make themselves right with God through works of the law. We are brought into a right relationship with God through the divine activity centered in Christ's death. This act is a gift of grace that liberates us from sin and empowers our faith in Jesus Christ.

John 8:31-36

Jesus speaks of truth and freedom as spiritual realities known through his word. He reveals the truth that sets people free from sin.

Preface   Sundays

Color   Red

Prayers of Intercession

The prayers are prepared locally for each occasion. The following examples may be adapted or used as appropriate.

In grateful response to God's endless bounty of grace, let us pray for the church, the world, and all those in need.

A brief silence.

Wisdom of God, inspire your church to continue in your word. Where it is in error, purify it. Where it is true, sustain it. Pour out your Holy Spirit on your faithful people. Lord, in your mercy,

hear our prayer.

All of creation is a gift, O God, worthy of our wonder and deserving of our care. Inspire in us the desire to care for this gift, so that future generations might also revel in the beauty of this world. Lord, in your mercy,

hear our prayer.

God, you are in the midst of our cities and towns, our nations and our communities. Let your justice reign in all these places, so that through them we might catch a glimpse of the coming City of God. Lord, in your mercy,

hear our prayer.

Give strength and hope to those who are in bondage to oppression, poverty, or illness. Through your healing touch, free those who are sick (*especially*). Lord, in your mercy,

hear our prayer.

Pour out your Holy Spirit on this congregation. Renew its faith and mission that, following in the faithful footsteps of our ancestors, we might continue to bear witness to the one who frees us from sin and death for the promise of eternal life. Lord, in your mercy,

hear our prayer.

Here other intercessions may be offered.

Through your Son you have freed us from sin and death, giving us the hope and promise of eternal life. Comfort with this promise all who mourn (*especially*), and at the last draw us to your holy city. Lord, in your mercy,

hear our prayer.

Into your hands, holy God, we commend all for whom we pray, trusting in your abundant mercy; through Jesus Christ our Savior.

Amen.

Ideas and Images for the Day

This is a Sunday packed with beautiful images, deep-seeded ideas, and a rich history. For life-long Lutherans, these things can provoke a sense of pride in our denomination, but Reformation Sunday is not "Lutheran Pride Day." Instead it is a day focused on knowing God truthfully and in the process understanding who we are as people of faith and children of God in light of God's unbelievable grace.

1. "You will know the truth, and the truth will make you free." —John 8:32
   "You shall know the truth, and the truth will make you odd." —Flannery O'Connor
   "You shall know the truth, and the truth will make you mad." —Aldous Huxley
   "You shall know the truth, and the truth shall make you free." —Epigram on the CIA building, Washington, D.C.

2. Luther based his powerful Reformation hymn "A mighty fortress" on Psalm 46. Both the hymn and psalm proclaim the message of God who is our help even in the worst and scariest times. When disaster or tragedy strikes, panic can overwhelm us, but God tells us, "Be still, then, and know that I am God." Ask the congregation to be still for one minute during worship. Chances are they will find it difficult to do so.

3. Children often confuse Martin Luther with Martin Luther King Jr. Consider having Martin Luther or his wife, Katie, visit the children today to talk about some of the things that happened during the Reformation. Include props like a copy of the Ninety-five Theses or pictures of Luther's rose for them to color. A free copy of *A Bold Life of Faith*, a biography about Katie von Bora Luther, is available at http://www.elca.org/Growing-In-Faith/Ministry/Women-of-the-ELCA/All-our-resources/Affirming-Our-Gifts.aspx, and resources on Martin Luther are available at http://www.elca.org/ELCA/Search.aspx?q=martin+luther.

4. Having a permanent place of residency in the Father's house can give us the courage to be free. The place where we take up residency, says Jesus, is his word. The truth that sets us free will include law as well as gospel. It will remind us of our shortcomings as well as point us toward God's grace. Our place of residency may be more of a tent than a mansion. "Always dying, always rising" points us toward a church that is always evolving.

Hymns for Worship

Gathering

A mighty fortress is our God   ELW 503–505, LBW 228/229
Built on a rock   ELW 652, LBW 365
Listen, God is calling   ELW 513, WOV 712, TFF 130

Hymn of the Day

Lord, keep us steadfast in your word   ELW 517, LBW 230
    ERHALT UNS, HERR
Salvation unto us has come   ELW 590, LBW 297
    ES IST DAS HEIL
Oh, praise the gracious power   ELW 651, WOV 750
    CHRISTPRAISE RAY

Offering

That priceless grace   ELW 591, TFF 68
God, my Lord, my strength   ELW 795, LBW 484

Communion

For by grace you have been saved   ELW 598, W&P 38
The church of Christ, in every age   ELW 729, LBW 433
O Lord, we praise you   ELW 499, LBW 215

Sending

The church's one foundation   ELW 654, LBW 369
Thy strong word   ELW 511, LBW 233

Additional Hymns and Songs

O God, O Lord of heav'n and earth   LBW 396
I will sing, I will sing   W&P 73
The Lord of hosts is with us   TFF 6

Music for the Day

Psalmody and Acclamations

"A Mighty Fortress Is Our God." ELW 503–505.
Bruxvoort-Colligan, Richard. "God Is Our Shelter and Strength
    (Psalm 46)" from *Sharing the Road*. AFP 9780800678630.
Erickson, Rick. "Psalm 46," Refrain 1, from PSCY.
Harbor, Rawn. "The Lord of Hosts Is with Us (Psalm 46)." TFF 6.
Helgen, John. *Gospel Acclamations for Autumn*.
Miller, Aaron David. "Psalm 46" from PWA, Evangelical Lutheran
    Worship Edition.

Choral

o Busarow, Donald. "Lord, Keep Us Steadfast in Your Word."
    2 pt trbl, org, C inst. CPH 98-2602.
Ferguson, John. "A Mighty Fortress." SATB, org.
    AFP 9780800676421.

Mendelssohn, Felix. "Verleih uns Frieden/Grant Peace, We Pray"
    from *Chantry Choirbook*. SATB, org. AFP 9780800657772.
Walter, Johann. "I Build on God's Strong Word" from *Chantry
    Choirbook*. SATB. AFP 9780800657772.
Weber, Paul D. "I Will Sing the Story of Your Love." U/SATB, opt
    assembly, kybd. AFP 9780800657000.

Children's Choir

Bedford, Michael. "Two Psalms for Young Singers." U, kybd, opt hb.
    CG CGA1140.
Makeever, Ray. "Write Your Law upon Our Hearts" from *Dancing at
    the Harvest*. U, kybd.
Patterson, Mark. "Psalm 46" from *ChildrenSing Psalms*. U, kybd.
    AFP 9780800663872.

Keyboard / Instrumental

o Nelson, Ronald A., Robert J. Powell. "Erhalt uns, Herr" from *Song of
    the Gospel*, vol. 1. Org. CPH 97-7202.
o Proulx, Richard. "Es ist das Heil" from *Augsburg Organ Library:
    Epiphany*. Org. AFP 9780800659349.
o Sedio, Mark. "Erhalt uns, Herr" from *Music for the Paschal Season*.
    Org. AFP 9780800656232.
o Shaw, Timothy. "Es ist das Heil" from *Introductions and Alternate
    Accompaniments*, vol. 6. Pno. AFP 9780800623647.

Handbell

o Eithun, Sandra. "Lord, Keep Us Steadfast in Thy Word." 3-5 oct,
    L2+. CPH 97-7116.
McChesney, Kevin. "A Mighty Fortress Is Our God." 3-5 oct, L3. Jef-
    fers JHS9439.
Page, Anna Laura. "The Solid Rock." 3-5 oct, L3. CG CGB269.

Praise Ensemble

• Brown, Brenton. "Lord, Reign in Me." VIN.
• Grant, Amy/Michael W. Smith. "Thy Word." Meadowgreen Music/
    WRD. W&P 144.
• Millard, Bart/Pete Kipley. "Word of God, Speak." Simpleville Music.
• Morgan, Reuben. "I Give You My Heart." Hillsong/INT.
• Redman, Matt. "Once Again." Thankyou Music.
• Tomlin, Chris/Jesse Reeves/Ed Cash. "How Great Is Our God."
    WT/Sixsteps Music.

Global

Harbor, Rawn. "The Lord of Hosts Is with Us (Psalm 46)" from *This
    Far by Faith*. U.
Trad. Cambodian melody. "Now I Know" from *Pave the Way: Global
    Songs 3*. U. AFP 9780800676896.

o denotes suggestions that relate to the hymn of the day.
• denotes songs that are available on iTunes®.

291

October 30, 2011
Time after Pentecost — Lectionary 31

Micah declares God's condemnation of those who abhor justice. Jesus warns against hypocrisy. Paul urges the Thessalonians to lead a life worthy of God. Called to be humble servants, we gather for worship, seeking justice and welcoming all people to share the banquet of life. Today the Lutheran church gives thanks for events of the sixteenth-century Reformation that brought renewal and prays that the Holy Spirit continue to unite the church in its proclamation and witness.

Prayer of the Day

O God, generous and supreme, your loving Son lived among us, instructing us in the ways of humility and justice. Continue to ease our burdens, and lead us to serve alongside of him, Jesus Christ, our Savior and Lord.

Gospel Acclamation

Alleluia. You have one instructor, | the Messiah;* the greatest among you will | be your servant. *Alleluia.* (Matt. 23:10, 11)

Readings and Psalm
Micah 3:5-12

The Lord announces judgment against prophets who can be bribed to give favorable oracles. Because rulers too can be bribed to practice injustice, Micah announces the coming destruction of Jerusalem. Later, Jeremiah escaped execution because of Micah's daring precedent (Jer. 26:18-19).

Psalm 43

Send out your light and truth, that they may lead me. (Ps. 43:3)

I Thessalonians 2:9-13

Paul uses paternal imagery to depict the guidance and encouragement he provided to the Thessalonians. They received from Paul the word of God, which energizes their faith.

Matthew 23:1-12

Jesus encourages his disciples to obey the words of Moses they hear from their teachers, but to shun the hypocrisy and pretension of those who do not practice what they teach.

Semicontinuous reading and psalm
Joshua 3:7-17

The Lord promises to be with Joshua as the Lord was with Moses. The entry into the promised land was a liturgical procession in which the priests carried the ark of the covenant, the sign of the Lord's presence.

Psalm 107:1-7, 33-37

We give thanks to you, Lord, for your wonderful works. (Ps. 107:8)

Preface Sundays

Color Green

Prayers of Intercession

The prayers are prepared locally for each occasion. The following examples may be adapted or used as appropriate.

In grateful response to God's endless bounty of grace, let us pray for the church, the world, and all those in need.
A brief silence.

Send your light and truth to lead your church, O God, that it might faithfully proclaim the gospel through humble service and life-giving words. Lord, in your mercy,
hear our prayer.

God of all seasons, give rest to newly harvested land, protection to animals that migrate, and joy to your people who witness the marvels of the season. Lord, in your mercy,
hear our prayer.

Give wisdom and understanding to the world's leaders, O God, and a passion for peace to all people. Bless the work of local, state, and national governments, especially when they endeavor to support the lowly. Lord, in your mercy,
hear our prayer.

Healing God, bestow your grace and mercy upon all who are sick in body, mind, or spirit (*especially*). May they sense your comfort in this time of pain, and grant them your restoration. Lord, in your mercy,

hear our prayer.

You call this congregation to be a witness to the gospel. Nurturing us with word and sacrament, lead us into lives worthy of you. Lord, in your mercy,

hear our prayer.

Here other intercessions may be offered.

The dead rest in you, O God. Wipe the tears from the eyes of all who mourn. Fill them with the hope of resurrection and the promise of the life to come. Lord, in your mercy,

hear our prayer.

Into your hands, holy God, we commend all for whom we pray, trusting in your abundant mercy; through Jesus Christ our Savior.

Amen.

Ideas and Images for the Day

In October 1517 Martin Luther's Ninety-five Theses became public. It was a protest against the injustices he saw being committed by the church and its authorities. In today's readings we learn injustices were committed by the people in charge during biblical times as well, and times haven't changed. But while hypocrisy, bribery, and injustice seem a constant throughout our history, God's saving word is an even greater constant and a reason to thank God.

1. "But Dad, Billy's parents let him see R-rated movies." The job of a parent is not an easy one. Setting limitations and teaching responsible behavior requires steadfastness and determination, as well as love, in a world where doing whatever makes you feel good, even if it is to the detriment of others, often seems the norm. God the Father has the same problems as a parent. The good news is that God is indeed a steadfast, determined, and loving parent.

2. Little did Lenore Skenazy know, when she armed her nine-year-old son with a subway map, MetroCard, $20 in cash and several quarters in case he needed to make a phone call, then waved goodbye to him in Bloomingdale's, that she would be crowned America's Worst Mom. Her Web site, http://www.Freerangekids.com, explores how parents give their children freedom.

3. People often feel powerless to right the wrongs in the world. But as Christians we have the power of God's word, we have prayer, and we also have the gifts of our time, talent, and treasures. What causes does your congregation support? Invite a representative from such a group to talk about ways they have made a difference in people's lives, and collect a special offering and a list of volunteers to support their work.

4. Write burdens people experience—mortgage payments, housework, poverty, for example—on letter-sized pieces of paper. Have a volunteer stand in a visible location and tape the burdens to them until they are covered with paper burdens. Talk about ways in which God lifts those burdens from us as you remove the papers. Invite the congregation to write down their own burdens on pieces of paper, then drop them in a basket near the altar.

5. One of the Prophet Mohammed's companions, Anas b. Mâlik, tells a story of an elderly man who wanted an audience with the Prophet, but the people were slow to make room for him, so the Prophet said: "Whoever fails to show mercy to our children and honor to our elders is not one of us" (*Sunan al-Tirmidhî*, 1919). Help the children in the congregation understand how our actions define who we are as Christians.

Hymns for Worship

Gathering

Oh, praise the gracious power   ELW 651, WOV 750
All my hope on God is founded   ELW 757, WOV 782
Gather Us In   ELW 532, WOV 718

Hymn of the Day

Praise the Almighty!   ELW 877, LBW 539
   LOBE DEN HERREN, O MEINE SEELE
Canticle of the Turning   ELW 723   STAR OF COUNTY DOWN
Will you let me be your servant   ELW 659
   THE SERVANT SONG

Offering

Come to the table   ELW 481, W&P 33
Praise to the Lord, all of you   ELW 844

Communion

Love consecrates the humblest act   ELW 360, LBW 122
Come down, O Love divine   ELW 804, LBW 508
Lord, whose love in humble service   ELW 712, LBW 423

Sending

Soli Deo Gloria   ELW 878
Praise to you, O God of mercy   ELW 208, WOV 790

Additional Hymns and Songs

Father, I adore you   W&P 37
We are your people   NCH 309
The virtue of humility   HFG 132

Music for the Day
Psalmody and Acclamations

Farlee, Robert Buckley. "Psalm 107:1-7, 33-37" from PWA, Evangelical Lutheran Worship Edition.

Hobby, Robert A. "Psalm 43" from PWA, Evangelical Lutheran Worship Edition.

Schalk, Carl F. *Gospel Acclamations for Autumn.*

Woehr, Roland. "Psalm 43," Refrain 1, from PSCY.

Wold, Wayne L. "Psalm 107," Refrain 2, from PSCY.

Choral

Bankson, Jeremy. "Soli Deo Gloria." SATB, org, br, opt assembly. AFP 9780800678852.

Cherwien, David/M. A. Balakireff, M. A. "Send Out Thy Light." SATB. MSM 50-6035.

○ Cooney, Rory. "Canticle of the Turning." SAB, assembly, pno, insts, opt gtr. GIA G-3407.

Handel, G. F. "Ev'ry Valley" from *Messiah.* Tenor solo, kybd. Various editions.

Fleming, Larry L. "Humble Service." SATB. AFP 9780800646226.

Children's Choir

○ Helms, Judith. "Let Me Be Your Servant, Jesus" from *LifeSongs.* U, kybd.

Niederman, Peter. "Praise the Lord, His Glories Show." U, kybd. GIA G4743.

Patterson, Mark. "This Little Light of Mine." U/2 pt, kybd, opt tamb. CG CGA1108.

Keyboard / Instrumental

○ Behnke, John A. "Lobe den Herren, O meine Seele" from *Five Preludes of Praise*, set 4. Org. CPH 97-7039U1.

Corelli, Arcangelo. "Adagio" from *Baroque Music for Manuals*, vol. 1. Org. CPH 97-5341U1.

Greene, Maurice. "Trumpet Voluntary in C" from *The Classical Wedding for Solo Trumpet and Organ.* Org, tpt. HOP 181.

○ Schmoltze, Ron. "Star of County Down" from *A Song in the Journey.* Org. AFP 9780800679026.

Handbell

○ Buckwalter, Karen. "Praise to the Lord." 3-6 oct hb, opt hc, L3. BP HB290.

○ Edwards, Dan. "Our Great Redeemer's Praise." 3 oct, L2. CPH 97-7219.

○ Moklebust, Cathy/David Moklebust. "Praise to the Lord, the Almighty." 4-5 oct, org, opt assembly, L3. AFP 9780800658908 (HB). 9780800659332 (Full Score).

Praise Ensemble

● Anonymous. "Create in Me a Clean Heart." W&P 34. Various editions.

● Farrell, Bernadette. "Christ, Be Our Light." ELW 715.

● Furler, Peter. "It Is You." Ariose Music.

● Millard, Bart/Pete Kipley. "Word of God, Speak." Simpleville Music.

● Nystrom, Martin. "As the Deer." House of Mercy Music. W&P 9.

● Park, Andy. "Only You." Mercy/VIN. Various editions.

Global

Trad. Botswanan. "Reamo leboga/To God Our Thanks We Give" from *Global Songs 2.* SATB. AFP 9780800656744. ELW 682.

Trad. Mozambique. "Nzamuranza" from *Pave the Way: Global Songs 3.* SATB, cant. AFP 9780800676896.

Monday, October 31
Reformation Day

By the end of the seventeenth century, many Lutheran churches celebrated a festival commemorating Martin Luther's posting of the Ninety-five Theses, a summary of the abuses in the church of his time. At the heart of the reform movement was the gospel, the good news that it is by grace through faith that we are justified and set free.

Tuesday, November 1
All Saints Day

The custom of commemorating all of the saints of the church on a single day goes back at least to the third century. All Saints celebrates the baptized people of God, living and dead, who make up the body of Christ. We remember all who have died in the faith and now serve God around the heavenly throne.

Thursday, November 3
Martín de Porres, renewer of society, died 1639

Martín was the son of a Spanish knight and Ana Velázquez, a freed black slave from Panama. Martín apprenticed himself to a barber-surgeon in Lima, Peru, and was known for his work as a healer. Martín was a lay brother in the Order of Preachers (Dominicans) and engaged in many charitable works. He was a gardener as well as a counselor to those who sought him out. He was noted for his care of all the poor, regardless of race. His own religious community described him as the "father of charity." His work included the founding of an orphanage, a hospital, and a clinic for dogs and cats. He is recognized as an advocate for Christian charity and interracial justice.

○ denotes suggestions that relate to the hymn of the day.
● denotes songs that are available on iTunes®.

TIME AFTER PENTECOST

NOVEMBER

PREPARING FOR NOVEMBER

All Saints

Year A concludes in only three Sundays this month. Advent begins November 27. Because Advent often includes considerable preparation, make sure and look ahead to *Sundays and Seasons* 2012 to begin Advent planning. Read a good commentary on Mark this month too, like *Binding the Strong Man* by Ched Myers (Orbis, 2008), Donald Juel's commentary on Mark in the Augsburg Commentary on the New Testament series, or Lamar Williamson's new *Mark* commentary in the Interpretation series.

Worship planning for this month will involve planning at least two festivals: All Saints Sunday (Nov. 6) and Christ the King Sunday (Nov. 20). In the United States the Day of Thanksgiving (which Canadians celebrated Oct. 10) is a third observance that may need additional planning. These preparatory reflections for November will be structured around these three festivals, plus the commemorations of veterans (Nov. 11), and Elizabeth of Hungary (Nov. 17).

All Saints Sunday, though often observed, is not always given the gravity it deserves, at least in the North American context. On this Sunday, we are reminded that the church is a communion not only of the living and local, but of the dead and distant as well. It is the day we celebrate that even death cannot divide us from the body of Christ, because Jesus Christ has conquered death.

The day therefore has a dual focus. We commemorate those who have died. But we remember them not for themselves and in themselves, but because of what God has done through them. "When the church praises the saints, it praises God himself, who has triumphed through them. Those who are still in the church on earth are supported and encouraged by the fellowship of a throng of witnesses, who fought their way with effort and pain, and who now in the company of the redeemed are watching and supporting the church on earth in its present struggle" (Philip Pfatteicher, *New Book of Festivals and Commemorations: A Proposed Common Calendar of Saints* [Minneapolis: Fortress, 2008], p. 533).

Did you know that Luther chose the eve of All Saints Day, October 31, to post his Ninety-five Theses on the Wittenberg church door, because he knew many people would come to church that next day and would see his posting? Many churches and communities in Europe, though possibly more secular than their North American counterparts, still make a trip to cemeteries on All Saints Eve to place candles, votives, and flowers at the graveside. Some church graveyards are so lit by these candles on the eve of All Saints that they glow. Talk about a great cloud of witnesses!

Most churches have had at least a few funerals in the past year. All Saints Sunday is an opportunity to commemorate those who have died and provide further support and counsel to those who grieve. Consider preparing for All Saints Sunday the same way you prepare for a baptism. Purchase candles that can be lit for the faithful departed and then given to families at the conclusion of the service. Contact all the families of those who have lost loved ones in the past year, and let them know you will be lifting them up in prayer and remembering their loved ones during the service. Review your congregation's practices around caring for the grieving. Consider making use of the Stephen Ministries quarterly follow-up resource *Journeying through Grief*, http://www.stephenministries.org/griefresources/default.cfm/775.

Sing the sturdy and beautiful "For all the saints" (ELW 422), possibly organizing the choir to sing stanzas responsively with the assembly, or even organizing a smaller ensemble or children's choir to sing stanzas of the hymn.

In preparation for All Saints Sunday, it may also be helpful to review and consider the difference between the festival, All Saints Day (Nov. 1), and the commemoration of the faithful departed (Nov. 2). Churches often combine these two into one on All Saints Sunday, but in the history of the church these were separate, and offered opportunity to remember the saints, and then the next day to commemorate the faithful departed, two items that are related but also discrete from each other in some ways.

Veterans and Elizabeth of Hungary

The church, and to a certain extent the larger culture, can easily overlook what is for many an important national holiday. Veterans Day (U.S.A.) is existentially significant especially to those who served in the armed forces or who have loved ones or friends who are veterans. However, the church as a whole has made a commitment to care for those in the armed services, especially through military chaplaincy programs, through prayer, and in our prayers for peace and order in society. On the Sunday closest to Veterans Day, consider simply inviting all veterans to stand and be recognized, or especially include in the prayers of intercession petitions for veterans. Worship leaders uncomfortable with too close an association between national and church observances can still find creative ways to minister to veterans without condoning all forms of militarism.

Second, as a lead up to Thanksgiving, consider lifting up for the consideration of worshipers the life of Elizabeth of Thuringia, Princess of Hungary, 1231. Elizabeth (who married Ludwig, Landgrave of Thuringia) is remembered as being profoundly generous to the poor, at one time during a famine even giving away much of her own wealth and grain to the poor. She did this while her husband was away, and was criticized for it, but when her husband returned he gave approval for her actions.

Elizabeth also founded hospitals and nursed many patients and children herself. After the death of her husband, she became a follower of St. Francis of Assisi, built a hospice, and cared for the sick and dying. Elizabeth lived much of her life in the Wartburg castle, where Luther translated the New Testament into German. She also lived for many years in Eisenach, the childhood home of Luther and J.S. Bach. Philip of Hesse was one of her descendants.

Elizabeth's life and ministry offers many opportunities for lifting up the life of a saint as role model and witness for the church. Consider offering a meditation on Elizabeth in sermons this month. Publish a brief biography of her in the church newsletter or bulletin. This might also be an opportunity to offer a historical comparison between Luther and Elizabeth, since they lived and ministered in the same place. In fact, meditating on the life of Elizabeth might function as a sort of continuation of the Reformation theme throughout the month of November. Finally, the life of Elizabeth is a holy and generous launching place for preparations for the celebration of Thanksgiving. Celebrate and give thanks for ministries in and through the congregation that heal the sick, comfort the dying, and feed the poor.

The saintly life of Elizabeth of Thuringia also sheds light on the lectionary gospels for November 13 and 20, both from Matthew 25. The central spiritual insight of these readings is epitomized in these words of Christ: "Truly I tell you, just as you did it to one of the least of these who are members of my family, you did it to me" (Matt. 25:40).

Christ the King

Christ the King Sunday is confusing. Much preaching on this day might tend to end up saying, "Christ is a king, but not like any other king you know." As we have already observed, not all kings and queens lord their power over others. Elizabeth the princess certainly did not. However, in our minds, kings consolidate power, lord their authority over their subjects, and create unjust and inequitable distribution of wealth and resources. God never considered the giving of kings to Israel a blessing. Instead, it was a response to their hardness of heart.

One could do worse in preparing to preach on Christ the King Sunday, than to meditate on 1 Samuel 8 in addition to the Sunday readings. The key passage here is the Lord's word to Samuel, "They have not rejected you, but they have rejected me from being king over them" (1 Sam. 8:7). Now there is a quote on which to hang your hat come Christ the King Sunday. The only reason we call Christ a king is not because he is an earthly ruler like other kings, but because he has come in his birth, ministry, death, and resurrection, to reestablish himself as king and lord, and precisely as a servant of all, giver of life, and conqueror of death. If preaching and teaching on this day simply meditated on the creative tensions, even paradoxes, of this situation, it would be a Sunday well spent.

Thanksgiving

The Lord be with you.
And also with you.
Lift up your hearts.
We lift them to the Lord.
Let us give thanks to the Lord our God.
It is right to give our thanks and praise.

In the Pattern for Worship for Holy Communion (*Evangelical Lutheran Worship*, pp. 91–93), the rubrics indicate that "before the Lord's supper is shared, the presiding minister leads us into thanksgiving. With the whole creation, we join the angels' song." In previous seasons, we have spent time with the "Holy, holy, holy," the song the angels sing with the whole of creation. But here, in the last week of the church year, the Thursday before the advent of Advent, we are given one last opportunity to give thanks. Christians are to live lives of constant thanksgiving. Our thankfulness should be so transparent, so frequent, so full-bodied, that the whole world would perceive Christians as ones who give thanks with a grateful heart for all that the Lord has done. Keep this in mind not only for Thanksgiving Day, but for every Sunday and day of the church year.

In order to maintain the integrity of the Christian dimensions of the Day of Thanksgiving, root all the liturgical preparations, preaching focus, and congregational practice in the important dialogue that opens the great thanksgiving. The presiding minister invites the assembly to give thanks. The assembly confesses in faith that it is right to give thanks. There are many beautiful settings of the great thanksgiving, including the settings in *Evangelical Lutheran Worship*, but for a Thanksgiving Eve or Day service, consider using an alternative version, such as Jonathan Rundman's in his *Heartland Liturgy*, or, if the choir is ambitious, offer selections such as those on the album *The Great Thanksgiving* (Sony, 1995; http://www.amazon.com/Great-Thanksgiving-Johann-Sebastian-Bach/dp/B0000029NJ).

Thanksgiving is a moment when congregations are even more naturally generous than usual. Tap into this. Call the local food pantry and ask what their special needs are for their shelves. Print their list of needs on pieces of paper, then staple them onto the outside of paper grocery bags you have collected in advance for this purpose. Place these bags in the narthex on a table and invite the congregation in the week preceding Thanksgiving to take the bags home, fill them with the items listed, and return the bags by or on Thanksgiving. At the special Thanksgiving worship, consecrate the gathered food pantry items, and consider creating a special display at the front of the sanctuary that exhibits the congregation's thank-offering. Also invite special financial gifts for the hungry, since many food pantries are well stocked during Thanksgiving but need financial support to offer food year round.

Does your congregation know the classic thanksgiving campfire song, "Give thanks" (W&P 41, http://www.atthewell.com/thanks/)? To increase involvement in this special opportunity to center in on the spiritual practice of giving thanks, teach it to the confirmation or Sunday school classes to sing as a special youth anthem.

Seasonal Checklist

- Consider using harvest decorations during November, from All Saints Sunday through Thanksgiving.
- Publicize any special food collections and arrange for delivery to the appropriate agency after the collection.
- Provide a book of remembrance for All Saints Sunday and the month of November in which names of loved ones may be written and perhaps remembered aloud in prayer. If candles are lit, order these in advance and prepare to display them appropriately.
- Incorporate the names of those who have died into a baptismal remembrance or into the prayers of intercession on All Saints Sunday.
- Continue planning for Advent 2011.
- Omit the Kyrie.
- Use the hymn of praise ("This is the feast").
- Use the Nicene Creed for the festivals of All Saints and Christ the King; use the Apostles' Creed for other Sundays in November.

Confession and Forgiveness

All may make the sign of the cross, the sign marked at baptism,
as the presiding minister begins.

Blessed be the holy Trinity, + one God,
who forgives our sin, heals every illness,
saves us from death, enfolds us with tender care,
and crowns us with steadfast love.
Amen.

Let us confess our sin
in the presence of God and of one another.

Silence is kept for reflection.

God of abundant mercy,
we confess that we are more ready
to be forgiven than to forgive others.
We hold too closely your gifts to us.
We trample your vineyard, our good earth.
Have mercy, O God;
turn us again to you and toward others;
and grant that we may live for you and die in you,
for the sake of Jesus Christ, our redeemer and Lord.
Amen.

God is generous and faithful,
forgiving sins without number,
welcoming all to the feast,
giving us a place among the saints.
Through the humble obedience of + Christ Jesus,
who went to the cross for our sake,
you are forgiven and made whole.
The Spirit of God is at work in you,
enabling you to live for one another.
Amen.

Greeting

Grace and peace from our God and Father,
hope in our Lord Jesus Christ,
and the consolation of the Holy Spirit
be with you all.
And also with you.

Offering Prayer

Merciful God, as grains of wheat scattered upon the hills
were gathered together to become one bread,
so let your church be gathered together
from the ends of the earth into your kingdom,
for yours is the glory through Jesus Christ, now and forever.
Amen.

Invitation to Communion

Come, you that are blessed by God.
Come to the banquet.

Prayer after Communion

God our shepherd,
you have gathered us again from scattered places
and nourished us with rich food in word and sacrament.
Go with us now, that we may seek the lost,
bind up the injured, and strengthen the weak,
until you gather us and all the saints into your eternal feast
with Jesus Christ, our Savior and Lord.
Amen.

Sending of Communion

Gracious God, you took the form of a servant,
offering yourself as food, comfort, and strength
to a sick and hurting world.
Anoint with a servant heart those
who take your word and sacrament
to our sisters and brothers
in their homes/in prisons/in hospitals.
Grant grace, mercy, healing, and hope to those
who feast on your body and blood
and receive your words of new life.
May we all recognize that we have a place and a home
in the body of our Lord Jesus Christ.
Amen.

Blessing

The peace of God,
which surpasses all understanding,
✠ guard your hearts and your minds in Christ Jesus.
Amen.

Dismissal

Go in peace. The Lord is near.
Thanks be to God.

Remembering Those Who Have Died

Remembering Those Who Have Died may be used at any time of the year. It is especially appropriate on a significant anniversary of a loved one's death, such as one month following death or on the date of death in a succeeding year. It is also useful during the month of November, when the church remembers all the saints.

Gathering

The leader begins with one or both of the following, or in similar words.

Blessed be the God and Father of our Lord Jesus Christ,
the source of all mercy and the God of all consolation,
who comforts us in all our sorrows
so that we can comfort others in their sorrows
with the consolation we ourselves have received from God.

or

When we were baptized in Christ Jesus, we were baptized
into his death.
We were buried therefore with him by baptism into death,
so that as Christ was raised from the dead
by the glory of the Father,
we too might live a new life.
For if we have been united with him in a death like his,
we shall certainly be united with him
in a resurrection like his.

Word

The following or another appropriate psalm may be sung or spoken.
Psalm 121

One or more of the following or other appropriate scripture passages may be read.
Isaiah 49:15-16
John 11:25-26
1 Thessalonians 4:13-14
2 Timothy 2:8, 11
Hebrews 12:1-2

Reflection on the readings may follow. Informal conversation among those present may be appropriate.

Prayer

The leader continues with one or more of the following or other appropriate prayers.

O God, we remember with thanksgiving
those who have loved and served you on earth,
who now rest from their labors, especially *name/s*.
Keep us in union with all your saints,
and bring us with them to the joyous feast of heaven;
through Jesus Christ, our Savior and Lord.
Amen.

O God, our help in ages past and our hope for years to come:
We give you thanks for all your faithful people
who have followed the light of your word
throughout the centuries
into our time and place.
Here individual names may be spoken.
As we remember these people,
strengthen us to follow Christ through this world
until we are carried into the harvest of eternal life,
where suffering and death will be no more.
Hear our prayer in the name
of the good and gracious shepherd,
Jesus Christ, our Savior and Lord.
Amen.

Lord Jesus, by your death you took away the sting of death.
Strengthen us to follow in faith where you have led the way,
that we may at length fall asleep in you
and wake in your likeness;
to you, the author and giver of life, be all honor and glory,
now and forever.
Amen.

O Lord, support us all the day long of this troubled life,
until the shadows lengthen and the evening comes
and the busy world is hushed, the fever of life is over,
and our work is done.
Then, in your mercy, grant us a safe lodging, and a holy rest,
and peace at the last,
through Jesus Christ our Lord.
Amen.

The Lord's Prayer is prayed by all. The leader may introduce the prayer with these or similar words.

Gathered into one by the Holy Spirit, let us pray as Jesus taught us.

Our Father . . .

Sending

A hymn or acclamation may be sung.

The leader concludes with a blessing.
Almighty God bless us,
defend us from all evil,
and bring us to everlasting life.
Amen.

The greeting of peace may be shared by all.

NOTES ON THE SERVICE

This order is informal and flexible in nature, and may be adapted to the context and circumstances. The service may take place in the home or at the place where the person's body has been interred. Family members, friends, or the pastor may lead the service or share its leadership as desired.

Before or after the sentences at the Gathering, the leader may note the occasion for the service. Following the reading/s, those present may share in reflection and conversation.

Service music and hymns may include the following.

223	All of Us Go Down to the Dust
423	Shall We Gather at the River
426	Sing with All the Saints in Glory
619	I Know That My Redeemer Lives, sts. 1-2, 7-8
632	O God, Our Help in Ages Past, sts. 1-2, 5

Additional psalms, readings, and hymns are listed in the propers for the funeral service (Occasional Services for the Assembly, p. 336).

Elements of this service may also be included in the worship of the assembly on All Saints Day. Before the service or after the hymn of the day, the presiding minister may say these or similar words:

In joyful expectation of the resurrection to eternal life, we remember this day those who have gone before us in faith and who now rest from their labors, especially those family members and friends who are dear to us [and who have died since last All Saints Day].

Either the first or the second prayer from this service or a similar prayer is then prayed. The names of those who are being remembered may be read as indicated. A bell may be tolled following the reading of each name.

From Evangelical Lutheran Worship: Occasional Services for the Assembly (Augsburg Fortress, 2009).

November 6, 2011

All Saints Sunday

All Saints celebrates the baptized people of God, living and dead, who are the body of Christ. As November heralds the dying of the landscape in many northern regions, the readings and liturgy call us to remember all who have died in Christ and whose baptism is complete. At the Lord's table we gather with the faithful of every time and place, trusting that the promises of God will be fulfilled and that all tears will be wiped away in the new Jerusalem.

Prayer of the Day

Almighty God, you have knit your people together in one communion in the mystical body of your Son, Jesus Christ our Lord. Grant us grace to follow your blessed saints in lives of faith and commitment, and to know the inexpressible joys you have prepared for those who love you, through Jesus Christ, our Savior and Lord, who lives and reigns with you and the Holy Spirit, one God, now and forever.

Gospel Acclamation

Alleluia. They are before the ǀ throne of God,* and the one who is seated on the throne will ǀ shelter them. *Alleluia.* (Rev. 7:15)

Readings and Psalm

Revelation 7:9-17

The book of Revelation is written to seven churches in western Asia Minor during a time of great oppression. Today's reading is a response to the question asked in 6:17: "Who is able to stand?" The writer gives the faithful the assurance of God's protection and a vision of victory.

Psalm 34:1-10, 22

Fear the LORD, you saints of the LORD; for those who fear the LORD lack nothing. (Ps. 34:9)

1 John 3:1-3

A saint is one who has been set apart by God for God's purposes. God, out of divine love, set us apart to be the children of God. Our holy hope is that we shall see God as God really is.

Matthew 5:1-12

In the beatitudes, Jesus provides a unique description of those who are blessed with God's favor. His teaching is surprising and shocking to those who seek wealth, fame, and control over others.

Preface   All Saints

Color   White

Prayers of Intercession

The prayers are prepared locally for each occasion. The following examples may be adapted or used as appropriate.

Clinging to the promise of abundant life and resurrection, let us pray for the church, the world, and all of God's creation.

A brief silence.

God of the generations, God of the saints in every time and place, make your whole church bold to proclaim the good news of your salvation. Hear us, O God.

Your mercy is great.

God of the universe, nourish the land with sun and rain. Fill all who hunger and thirst for your righteousness with good things, that we and your whole creation may be blessed. Hear us, O God.

Your mercy is great.

God of all nations, of all tribes and peoples and languages, send your Spirit among all your children. Inspire all peacemakers and those who work for justice. Hear us, O God.

Your mercy is great.

God of compassion, tenderly care for those in need of your hope and comfort. Wipe away the tears from their eyes. Give shelter to all who call upon your name (*especially*). Hear us, O God.

Your mercy is great.

God of love and strength, bless the poor in spirit, the meek, the merciful, and the persecuted. Make us pure of heart, transparent in our love for one another. Hear us, O God.

Your mercy is great.

Here other intercessions may be offered.

God of the living and the dead, accept the praise we bring with all the saints and angels, with our brothers and sisters in Christ throughout the world. We remember today all the faithful departed who are with the Lord forever (*especially*). Bring us, together with them, before your throne. Hear us, O God.

Your mercy is great.

Receive these our prayers, O God, and give us all we need for this day and the days to come, through Jesus Christ, our Lord.

Amen.

Ideas and Images for the Day

All Saints Sunday and the appointed readings are pregnant with themes of stark contrast: death and life, condemnation and redemption, sorrow and joy, suffering and relief, present life and future life. By virtue of baptism we are made saints while we are still sinners. We give thanks this day for the saints who have gone before us, for moments of faithfulness in their lives, and the fullness of eternal life in which they now partake and we have yet to enjoy.

1. To increase an awareness of the connection between us and the saints of every time and place, include in worship the rite of Affirmation of Baptism from *Evangelical Lutheran Worship* (pp. 234–237). To further the experience, consider sprinkling the assembly with water from the font as a reminder of baptism.

2. Invite the school-age children (even teens!) to come to the font with their parents. Remind them they are saints of God by virtue of their baptism. Have parents dip their thumb in the font and make the sign of the cross on their child's forehead, saying, "You are a saint of God" or something similar. Have each child, in turn, do the same to their parents.

3. In the weeks prior to All Saints Sunday, place blank white half-sheets of paper or cardstock in the pews or seats. Each week, invite worshipers to take as many sheets as they wish and write the name of someone in the church on earth or the church triumphant who is or was important in their faith life and why (one per half-sheet). Collect the sheets and during the week prior to All Saints Sunday, display them around the nave. Let worshipers be symbolically surrounded by the saints who were formative in their lives and in the life of the congregation.

4. We often identify saints as those who, in some way, exemplify the kind of faithful Christian life we want to emulate. Call attention to the saints who will be commemorated on Monday, November 7: John Christian Frederick Heyer (1793–1873), Bartholomaeus Ziegenbalg (1682–1719) and Ludwig Nommensen (1834–1918), missionaries. Not everyone's vocation is to be a missionary, but we are all called to faithful Christian vocation. Whether it is in the home as a stay-at-home parent, in the public workforce, or in some other capacity, the living Lord Jesus equips us for faithful saintliness through word and sacrament.

Hymns for Worship
Gathering

Holy God, we praise your name   ELW 414, LBW 535
Shall we gather at the river   ELW 423, WOV 690, TFF 179
For all your saints, O Lord   ELW 427, LBW 176

Hymn of the Day

In our day of thanksgiving   ELW 429   ST. CATHERINE'S COURT
Rejoice in God's saints   ELW 418, WOV 689
    LAUDATE DOMINUM
For all the saints   ELW 422, LBW 174   SINE NOMINE

Offering

Sing with all the saints in glory   ELW 426, WOV 691
In heaven above   ELW 630, LBW 330

Communion

Blest are they   ELW 728, WOV 764
Behold the host arrayed in white   ELW 425, LBW 314
Lord, thee I love with all my heart   ELW 750, LBW 325

Sending

Give Thanks for Saints   ELW 428
O God, our help in ages past   ELW 632, LBW 320

Additional Hymns and Songs

Oh, when the saints go marching in   TFF 180
Sing alleluia forth in duteous praise   HS91 838, H82 619
Oh, what their joy   LBW 337

Music for the Day
Psalmody and Acclamations

Cherwien, David. "Psalm 34," Refrain 1, from PSCY.
Harbor, Rawn. "Taste and See the Goodness of the Lord (Psalm 34)." TFF 5.
Helgen, John. *Gospel Acclamations for Autumn.*

Keesecker, Thomas. "Psalm 34:1-10, 22" from PWA, Evangelical Lutheran Worship Edition.

Makeever, Ray. "I Will Bless You, O God (Psalm 34)" from *Dancing at the Harvest*.

Moore, James E. "Taste and See." ELW 493.

Choral

Lang, Rupert. "The Kontakion." SSAATTBB, org, assembly. B&H 9790051471423.

Martinson, Joel. "By All Your Saints" from *Augsburg Easy Choirbook*, vol. 2. 2 pt mxd, org. AFP 9780800677510.

Nelson, Ronald A. "Jesus at the Door." 2 pt mxd, pno. GIA G-6764.

Organ, Anne Krentz. "Blessed Are the Peacemakers." SATB, kybd. AFP 9780800664343.

Schalk, Carl. "I Saw a New Heaven and a New Earth" from *The Augsburg Choirbook*. SATB. AFP 9780800656782.

Children's Choir

Christopherson, Dorothy. "Psalm 34" from *ChildrenSing Psalms*. U, kybd. AFP 9780800663872.

Spiritual. "Chatter With the Angels" from *LifeSongs*. U, kybd.

Wold, Wayne. "I Sing a Song of the Saints of God." UE, U/2 pt, kybd. AFP 9780800632045.

Keyboard / Instrumental

○ Dahl, David P. "Laudate Dominum" from *Hymn Interpretations for Organ*. Org. AFP 9780800658243.

○ Organ, Anne Krentz. "St. Catherine's Court" from *Eight for Eighty-Eight*, vol. 3. Pno, inst. AFP 9780800623494.

○ Sadowski, Kevin J. "St. Catherine's Court" from *Twelve Hymn Preludes*. Org. CPH 97-6830U1.

○ Wold, Wayne L. "Sine nomine" from *A November to Remember*. Org. AFP 9780800659837.

Handbell

○ Birling, Andrew. "For All the Saints." 3 oct, L2. HOP 2218.

Honoré, Jeffrey. "Marching to Zion." 3 or 5 oct, L4. AFP 9780800674885.

○ McKechnie, D. Linda. "Resounding Alleluias." 3-5 oct, org or kybd, opt SATB, opt Bb or C inst, L3. CG CGA1141 (SATB). CGB558 (Full Score). CGB559 (HB).

Praise Ensemble

● Cull, Bob. "Open Our Eyes." MAR/WRD. W&P 113.

● Haas, David. "Blest Are They." GIA G-2958. ELW 728.

● Howard, Adrian/Pat Turner. "Salvation Belongs to Our God." Restoration Music.

● Moen, Don. "God Will Make a Way." INT.

● Tomlin, Chris/John Newton/John Rees/Edwin Excell/Louie Giglio. "Amazing Grace (My Chains Are Gone)." WT.

● Zschech, Darlene. "Shout to the Lord." Hillsong/INT. ELW 821.

Global

African American spiritual. "Wade in the Water" from *This Far by Faith*. SATB.

Harbor, Rawn. "Taste and See the Goodness of the Lord (Psalm 34)" from *This Far by Faith*. U.

○ denotes suggestions that relate to the hymn of the day.
● denotes songs that are available on iTunes®.
306

November 6, 2011
Time after Pentecost — Lectionary 32

Today the prophet Amos calls for justice to roll down like waters. Paul urges us to encourage one another with the promised coming of the Lord. Jesus tells the parable of the wise and foolish bridesmaids. Surrounded by the faithful of every time and place, we celebrate Christ's coming in our midst in the word of life and the feast of victory—the marriage feast of the lamb.

Today the church remembers with thanksgiving all the saints.

Prayer of the Day

O God of justice and love, you illumine our way through life with the words of your Son. Give us the light we need, and awaken us to the needs of others, through Jesus Christ, our Savior and Lord.

Gospel Acclamation

Alleluia. Keep awake [1] and be ready,* for you do not know on what day your [1] Lord is coming. *Alleluia.* (Matt. 24:42, 44)

Readings and Psalm

Amos 5:18-24

In the days of Amos people thought that the day of the Lord would be a time of great victory, but Amos announced that it would be a day of darkness, not light. He said liturgy is no substitute for obedience. The Lord demands justice and righteousness in the community.

or Wisdom 6:12-16

Wisdom is part of the structure of the universe and is easily accessible to those who want to find her. Wisdom actually seeks people out. People who are wise are free from care.

Psalm 70

You are my helper and my deliverer; O LORD, do not tarry. (Ps. 70:5)

or Wisdom 6:17-20

The beginning of wisdom is the most sincere desire for instruction. (Wis. 6:17)

1 Thessalonians 4:13-18

Some of the Thessalonians are worried that dead Christians will be excluded from the resurrection to eternal life when Christ comes again. Paul reassures them with the word of hope that all Christians, living or dead, will be raised into everlasting life with Christ.

Matthew 25:1-13

Jesus tells a parable about his own second coming, emphasizing the need for readiness at all times.

Semicontinuous reading and psalm

Joshua 24:1-3a, 14-25

In this farewell speech, Joshua exhorts the people to serve only the Lord. Joshua erected a stone monument to serve as a witness to the solemn promise the people had made to serve the Lord.

Psalm 78:1-7

We will recount to generations to come the power of the LORD. (Ps. 78:4)

Preface   Sundays

Color   Green

Prayers of Intercession

The prayers are prepared locally for each occasion. The following examples may be adapted or used as appropriate.

Clinging to the promise of abundant life and resurrection, let us pray for the church, the world, and all of God's creation.

A brief silence.

God of the living and of the dead, the bridegroom brings life with his coming. Keep us ever vigilant and ready to receive him. As we await the Lord, let justice roll down like waters, and righteousness like an ever-flowing stream. Hear us, O God.

Your mercy is great.

Maker of all things, nurture the world you have created. Preserve its goodness. Bring to fulfillment the labor of all who tend the earth, its plants, and its creatures. Hear us, O God.
Your mercy is great.

Governor of the nations, bless all peoples in their diversity. Strengthen those who work for peace and justice. Restore those who live amid the horror of war. Shield veterans of armed conflict. Hear us, O God.
Your mercy is great.

Compassionate God, soothe the sick, give hope to the hopeless, and send us out as relief for those in any need (*especially*). Hear us, O God.
Your mercy is great.

God of abundance, you have blessed this community of faith. Bring to fruitful harvest all we have sown. Use our presence in our neighborhood for good. Hear us, O God.
Your mercy is great.

Here other intercessions may be offered.

God of all consolation, comfort those who grieve as we remember the faithful departed who are with the Lord forever (*especially*). Raise us from all that grieves our hearts and restore our hope. Hear us, O God.
Your mercy is great.

Receive these our prayers, O God, and give us all we need for this day and the days to come, through Jesus Christ, our Lord.
Amen.

Ideas and Images for the Day

All relationships require trust to grow and become mature. Relationships rooted in trust can bring out the best in us. Relationships rooted in anything else can bring out the worst. Today's readings give us the chance to consider the trust required in the relationship between God and God's people. Moreover, we are invited to give thought to the consequences of replacing trust with something else: hubris stemming from trust in one's identity or work (in Amos) or hubris stemming from trust in others to sustain us rather than God (in Matthew). Paul reminds us that our relationship with God is cause for joy even in the midst of sorrow, since we believe (trust) God's promise of eternal life through the living Lord Jesus.

1. The ELCA social statement "Human Sexuality: Gift and Trust" provides a way of understanding relationships through the lens of trust. "Trust is a critical element that holds together couples and relationships, households and families, social structures and institutions." Consider how this social statement may provide fodder for elucidating the right place of trust in relationships both human and divine.

2. The relationship between children and parents is, by its very nature, one of trust. Children must trust their parents to provide for their every need. They are born unable to provide for themselves. Hence, Luther said parents are apostles, bishops, and priests to their children, "for it is they who make them acquainted with the gospel." Caspar David Friedrich's oil on canvas painting *Stages of Life* (1835), http://uofugeron.files.wordpress.com/2009/03/caspar_david_friedrich_013.jpg, provides a representation of deep familial interconnectedness and trust from one generation to the next.

3. The purpose of group-building exercises is to build relationships by developing trust among members of a group. Youth groups commonly employ a myriad of activities to facilitate this process. One of the most effective is the "trust fall." In relinquishing control or self-reliance, participants find themselves supported and protected in the arms of those gathered around them.

4. Teach the children to sing "I am trusting you, Lord Jesus" (LS 170). Invite them to sing it at an appropriate time during worship.

Hymns for Worship

Gathering

Blessed assurance   ELW 638, WOV 699, TFF 118
Through the night of doubt and sorrow   ELW 327, LBW 355
Oh, happy day when we shall stand   ELW 441, LBW 351

Hymn of the Day

Soul, adorn yourself with gladness   ELW 488, LBW 224
   SCHMÜCKE DICH
Wake, awake, for night is flying   ELW 436, LBW 31
   WACHET AUF
Rejoice, rejoice, believers   ELW 244, LBW 25
   HAF TRONES LAMPA FÄRDIG

Offering

Arise, my soul, arise!   ELW 827, LBW 516
Come, we that love the Lord   ELW 625, WOV 742

Communion

When long before time   ELW 861, WOV 799
For the bread which you have broken   ELW 494, LBW 200
Wait for the Lord   ELW 262

Sending

Soon and very soon   ELW 439, WOV 744, TFF 38
In peace and joy I now depart   ELW 440, LBW 349

Additional Hymns and Songs

Come away to the skies   WOV 669
Let justice roll like a river   W&P 85
This is the three-fold truth   HS91 797

Music for the Day
Psalmody and Acclamations

Messner, Sally. "Wisdom 6:17-20" and "Psalm 78:1-7" from PWA, Evangelical Lutheran Worship Edition.

Nicholson, Paul. "Psalm 78," Refrain 1, from PSCY.

Organ, Anne Krentz. "Psalm 70" from PWA, Evangelical Lutheran Worship Edition.

Raabe, Nancy. "Psalm 70" from PSCY.

Schalk, Carl F. *Gospel Acclamations for Autumn.*

Weidler, Scott C. "Wisdom 6:17-20" from PSCY.

Choral

○ Bouman, Paul. "Rejoice, Rejoice, Believers." SATB, org, opt assembly. MSM 50-0004.

○ Christiansen, F. Melius. "Wake, Awake." SSAATTBB. AFP 9780800645069.

Helgen, John. "Keep Your Lamps Trimmed and Burning." U, pno. AFP 9780800677497.

Leavitt, John. "Love the Lord." SATB, kybd, opt C inst. AFP 9780800664299.

Thomas, André. "Keep Your Lamps." SATB, conga drm. HIN HMC-577.

Children's Choir

Bach, J. S. "Prepare to Receive Him." UE, U, kybd. GIA G-3348.

Exner, Max. "Give Me Oil in My Lamp." 2/3 pt, kybd. CG CGA659.

Makeever, Ray. "It Won't Be Long" from *Dancing at the Harvest.* U, kybd.

Keyboard / Instrumental

Helman, Michael. "Fanfare" from *Organ Music for the Seasons*, vol. 1. Org. AFP 9780800657239.

○ Hotton, Martin. "Wachet auf" from *Organ Music for the Seasons*, vol. 3. Org. AFP 9780800675646.

○ Manz, Paul O. "Haf trones lampa färdig" from *Augsburg Organ Library: Advent.* Org. AFP 9780800658953.

○ Organ, Anne Krentz. "Haf trones lampa färdig" from *Introductions and Alternate Accompaniments*, vol. 1. Pno. AFP 9780800623593.

Handbell

Helman, Michael. "Let Us Break Bread Together." 3-5 oct hb, opt 3-5 oct hc, L3. GIA G-7044.

○ Honoré, Jeffrey, "Wake, Awake." 3 or 5 oct, L3. CPH 97-7060.

○ Larson, Katherine Jordahl. "Wake, Awake, for Night Is Flying." 4-5 oct, L4. AFP 9780800655105.

Praise Ensemble

● Baloche, Paul. "Open the Eyes of My Heart." INT.

● Evans, Darrell. "Let the River Flow." VIN/INT.

● Grul, Daniel/John Ezzy/Steve McPherson. "Jesus, Lover of My Soul." Hillsong/INT.

Haugen, Marty. "Let Justice Roll Like a River." GIA G-3491. W&P 85.

Kendrick, Graham. "The Trumpets Sound, the Angels Sing." Make Way Music. ELW 531. Various editions.

● Millard, Bart. "I Can Only Imagine." Simpleville Music.

Global

Bell, John. "Send Out Your Light" from *Come, All You People: Shorter Songs for Worship.* SAB. GIA G-4391.

South African trad. "Sizohamba naye/We Will Go with God" from *Global Songs 2.* SATB. AFP 9780800656744.

Monday, November 7

John Christian Frederick Heyer, died 1873; Bartholomaeus Ziegenbalg, died 1719; Ludwig Nommensen, died 1918; missionaries

Three missionaries are commemorated on this date. Heyer was the first missionary sent out by American Lutherans. Ordained in 1820, he established Sunday schools and taught at Gettysburg College and Seminary. Heyer became a missionary in the Andhra region of India. During a break in his mission work he received the M.D. degree from what would later be Johns Hopkins University.

Bartholomaeus Ziegenbalg (ZEEG-en-balg) was a missionary to the Tamils of Tranquebar on the southeast coast of India. The first convert to Christianity was baptized about ten months after Ziegenbalg began preaching. His missionary work was opposed by the local Hindus and also by Danish authorities in that area. Ziegenbalg was imprisoned for his work on a charge of converting the natives. Today, the Tamil Evangelical Lutheran Church carries on his work.

Ludwig Ingwer Nommensen was born in Schleswig-Holstein, Germany. In the early 1860s he went to Sumatra to serve as a Lutheran missionary. His work was among the Batak people, who had previously not seen Christian missionaries. Though he encountered some initial difficulties, the missions began to succeed following the conversion of several tribal chiefs. Nommensen translated the scriptures into Batak while honoring much of the native culture.

○ denotes suggestions that relate to the hymn of the day.
● denotes songs that are available on iTunes®.

Friday, November 11

Martin, Bishop of Tours, died 397

Martin's pagan father enlisted him in the army at age fifteen. One winter day, a beggar approached Martin for aid, and he cut his cloak in half and gave a portion to the beggar. Later, Martin understood that he had seen the presence of Christ in that beggar, and this ended his uncertainty about Christianity. He soon asked for his release from his military duties, but he was imprisoned instead. After his release from prison he began preaching, particularly against the Arians. In 371 he was elected bishop of Tours. As bishop he developed a reputation for intervening on behalf of prisoners and heretics who had been sentenced to death.

Søren Aabye Kierkegaard, teacher, died 1855

Kierkegaard (KEER-keh-gore), a nineteenth-century Danish theologian whose writings reflect his Lutheran heritage, was the founder of modern existentialism. Though he was engaged to a woman he deeply loved, he ended the relationship because he believed he was called to search the hidden side of life. Many of his works were published under a variety of names, so that he could reply to arguments from his own previous works. Kierkegaard's work attacked the established church of his day—its complacency, its tendency to intellectualize faith, and its desire to be accepted by polite society.

November 13, 2011
Time after Pentecost — Lectionary 33

Our readings during November speak of the end times. Zephaniah proclaims that the coming day of the Lord will be filled with wrath and distress. Paul says it will come like a thief in the night and urges us to be awake and sober. Jesus tells the parable of the talents, calling us to use our gifts, while we still have time, for the greater and common good. In a world filled with violence and despair, we gather around signs of hope—word, water, bread and wine—eager to welcome the good news of Christ's coming among us.

Prayer of the Day

Righteous God, our merciful master, you own the earth and all its peoples, and you give us all that we have. Inspire us to serve you with justice and wisdom, and prepare us for the joy of the day of your coming, through Jesus Christ, our Savior and Lord.

Gospel Acclamation

Alleluia. Abide in me as I a- ¹ bide in you;* those who abide in me ¹ bear much fruit. *Alleluia.* (John 15:4, 5)

Readings and Psalm
Zephaniah 1:7, 12-18

Zephaniah (like the prophet Amos in last week's first reading) presents the day of the Lord as one of judgment and wrath. Descriptions of the last day in the New Testament include details taken from Old Testament accounts of the day of the Lord.

Psalm 90:1-8 [9-11] 12

So teach us to number our days that we may apply our hearts to wisdom. (Ps. 90:12)

1 Thessalonians 5:1-11

Though we do not know and cannot calculate the day of Christ's return, we live faithfully in the here and now as we anticipate the day when we will be given eternal salvation through our Lord Jesus Christ.

Matthew 25:14-30

Jesus tells a parable about his second coming, indicating that it is not sufficient merely to maintain things as they are. Those who await his return should make good use of the gifts that God has provided them.

Semicontinuous reading and psalm
Judges 4:1-7

Deborah was a prophetess and judge, who, with her general, Barak, led a victorious holy war against a stronger Canaanite force from the north.

Psalm 123

Our eyes look to you, O God, until you show us your mercy. (Ps. 123:2)

Preface   Sundays

Color   Green

Prayers of Intercession

The prayers are prepared locally for each occasion. The following examples may be adapted or used as appropriate.

Clinging to the promise of abundant life and resurrection, let us pray for the church, the world, and all of God's creation.

A brief silence.

Everlasting God, stir your church to be ever vigilant and awake. Deliver us from every fear and distraction, that we might be found faithful on the day of the Lord. Hear us, O God.

Your mercy is great.

Ruler of the universe, keep us faithful in our stewardship of your creation. Inspire our serving, our care-taking, and the use of our talents, that we may be trustworthy in all things. Hear us, O God.

Your mercy is great.

Almighty God, deliver all nations from the day of wrath. Bear up the peacemakers with your mighty arm. Hear us, O God.

Your mercy is great.

God of all mercy, defend the weak, the ill, and those in any need (*especially*), that they might be delivered from their distress and restored to sing your praises. Hear us, O God.
Your mercy is great.
O God, the strength of those who hope in you, as the days darken and the earth in many places becomes dormant, deliver us from every fear. Shine the light of your love into our lives, that we might build each other up. Hear us, O God.
Your mercy is great.
Here other intercessions may be offered.
O God, giver of all life, raise us from every grief (*especially*). Meet us with your merciful embrace and bear us along in the hope of your salvation. Hear us, O God.
Your mercy is great.
Receive these our prayers, O God, and give us all we need for this day and the days to come, through Jesus Christ, our Lord.
Amen.

Ideas and Images for the Day

What does it mean to be awake to the grace of God? Paired with the reading from 1 Thessalonians, Jesus' parable of the talents invites a full-hearted response to God's lavish gifts of faith and purpose. The people of God are meant to be engaged, alert, and ready to share what God so lavishly gives. While this story has sometimes been interpreted in the context of judgment, a careful reading also spotlights the beauty of the faith-generated response to God's generous grace.

1. See *Kingdom, Grace, Judgment: Paradox, Outrage, and Vindication in the Parables of Jesus,* by Robert Farrar Capon (Grand Rapids, MI: Eerdmans, 2002). The parable of the talents is interpreted by Capon as having a single message: God wants us to *do business* with God's grace, not play it safe. Jesus' story is not about God's demand for high productivity. After all, the gifts of faith, grace, and love are not a reward for hard work or good behavior. We are simply meant to jump into the game to do our best. The word of judgment to the last servant is only because he did not try; he did not act in faith.

2. Ask the children what they would do with a gift of a thousand balloons (share them with the congregation, their family, or friends at school, for example). Have them consider the kindness and smiles they would be sharing. If someone so generous gave them a gift of so many balloons, we might guess that he or she would want us to share them, and not keep them to ourselves.

Compare this lavish gift with God's gifts of kindness and love, which we are generously given so we can be generous in sharing.

3. For several weeks before this Sunday, initiate a food drive. Gather the food in a prominent location in the narthex or worship space. As you teach this parable of Jesus, invite the community to consider how you are collectively "in charge of many things" (Matt. 25:21, 23), such as caring for those in the wider community who need food. This response in service is enacting the point of the parable: to do what you can, to take action in faith.

4. "You miss 100 percent of the shots you never take." —Wayne Gretzky

5. In the folk story of Stone Soup, when everyone pitches in a little something, everyone benefits. As people of God, we can be generous with who we are and what we have, and count it as faithfulness to Christ's calling. What is your contribution to Christ's soup that feeds the world? What is the most natural thing you can offer because it is part of your own life-giving joy?

Hymns for Worship
Gathering
Lord of glory, you have bought us   ELW 707, LBW 424
Christ is made the sure foundation   ELW 645, LBW 367, WOV 747
Light dawns on a weary world   ELW 726

Hymn of the Day
Lord of light   ELW 688, LBW 405   *ABBOT'S LEIGH*
If God my Lord be for me   ELW 788, LBW 454   *IST GOTT FÜR MICH*
God, whose giving knows no ending   ELW 678, LBW 408   *RUSTINGTON*

Offering
As saints of old   ELW 695, LBW 404
Let us talents and tongues employ   ELW 674, WOV 754

Communion
O Christ the same   ELW 760, WOV 778
When peace like a river   ELW 785, LBW 346
Christ, Be Our Light   ELW 715

Sending
Go, my children, with my blessing   ELW 543, WOV 721
On Jordan's stormy bank I stand   ELW 437, TFF 49

Additional Hymns and Songs

The day is near   GC 768
Once he came in blessing   LBW 312
Lord, whose then shall they be   HFG 11

Music for the Day
Psalmody and Acclamations

Cherwien, David. "Psalm 90," Refrain 2, from PSCY.

Hobby, Robert A. "Psalm 123" from PWA, Evangelical Lutheran Worship Edition.

Jennings, Carolyn. "Psalm 123" from PSCY.

Organ, Anne Krentz. "Psalm 90:1-8 [9-11] 12" from PWA, Evangelical Lutheran Worship Edition.

Schalk, Carl F. *Gospel Acclamations for Autumn.*

Choral

Ferguson, John. "O God, Our Help in Ages Past." SATB, org, br, opt assembly. GIA G-3892.

Hillert, Richard. "Festival Canticle: Worthy Is Christ." U, opt desc, org. CPH 98-2305.

Parker, Alice. "Through Every Age, Eternal God." SATB. GIA G-5090.

Schulz-Widmar, Russell. "Here, O My Lord." 2 pt, kybd, opt violin or oboe. AFP 9780800664220.

Walter, Johann. "Rise Up, Rise Up!" from *Chantry Choirbook.* SATB. AFP 9780800657772.

Children's Choir

Lovelace, Austin. "Let Us Talents and Tongues Employ." 2 pt, kybd, opt gtr, bng. CG CGA619.

Patterson, Mark. "I Will Give My Heart to the Lord" from *Young ChildrenSing.* U, kybd. AFP 9780800676803.

Wright, Vicki Hancock. "Do Unto Others." U, kybd. CG CGA1091.

Keyboard / Instrumental

DeJong, Kenneth L. "Processia Nova" from *Organ Music for the Seasons,* vol. 4. Org. AFP 9780800637507.

o Frahm, Frederick. "Ist Gott für mich" from *Faith Alive,* vol. 1. Org. AFP 9780800675738.

o Manz, Paul O. "Abbot's Leigh" from *Three Hymn Improvisations.* Org. MSM 10-867.

o Raabe, Nancy M. "Rustington" from *Introductions and Alternate Accompaniments,* vol. 7. Pno. AFP 9780800623654.

Handbell

o Afdahl, Lee. "Abbot's Leigh." 3-5 oct, L2+. HOP 2103.

Mathis, William. "Let Us Talents and Tongues Employ and We Come to the Hungry Feast." 3-5 oct hb, opt 4 oct hc, L3. AFP 9780800658885.

Sherman, Arnold. "The Gift of Grace." 3-5 oct hb, opt C inst, L3. HOP 2231.

Praise Ensemble

● Brown, Brenton. "Lord, Reign in Me." VIN.

● Farrell, Bernadette. "Christ, Be Our Light." ELW 715.

● Hanson, Handt. "Lord, Let My Heart Be Good Soil." ELW 512. Various editions.

● Jabusch, Willard. "The King of Glory." W&P 136. Various editions.

● Redman, Matt. "Let Everything That Has Breath." Thankyou Music.

● Zschech, Darlene. "The Potter's Hand." Hillsong/INT.

Global

Chen-Chang, Yang. "In All the Seasons Seeking God" from *Sound the Bamboo.* U. GIA G-6830.

Dexter, Noel. "The Right Hand of God" from *Global Songs 2.* SATB. AFP 9780800656744. ELW 889.

Thursday, November 17
Elizabeth of Hungary, renewer of society, died 1231

This Hungarian princess lived her entire life in east-central Germany, and is often called Elizabeth of Thuringia. Married to a duke, she gave large sums of money, including her dowry, for relief of the poor and sick. She founded hospitals, cared for orphans, and used the royal food supplies to feed the hungry. Though she had the support of her husband, her generosity and charity did not earn her friends within the royal court. At the death of her husband, she was driven out. She joined a Franciscan order and continued her charitable work, though she suffered abuse at the hands of her confessor and spiritual guide. Her lifetime of charity is particularly remarkable when one remembers that she died at the age of twenty-four. She founded two hospitals, and many more are named for her.

o denotes suggestions that relate to the hymn of the day.
● denotes songs that are available on iTunes®.

November 20, 2011

Christ the King
Last Sunday after Pentecost — Lectionary 34

On this final Sunday of the church year our gospel is Jesus' great story of judgment. In the end, the faithful are those who served Christ by ministering to those who are poor, hungry, naked, sick, or estranged. In the first reading God is the shepherd who seeks the lost, weak, and injured and feeds them with justice. We gather this day to celebrate the reign of Christ and his victory over death, yet awaiting the consummation of all things yet to come. Acknowledging Christ as our merciful ruler, we go forth that his reign may be known in our loving words and deeds.

Prayer of the Day

O God of power and might, your Son shows us the way of service, and in him we inherit the riches of your grace. Give us the wisdom to know what is right and the strength to serve the world you have made, through Jesus Christ, our Savior and Lord, who lives and reigns with you and the Holy Spirit, one God, now and forever.

Gospel Acclamation

Alleluia. Blessed is the one who comes in the name ¹ of the Lord.* Blessed is the coming kingdom of our an- ¹ cestor David. *Alleluia.* (Mark 11:9)

Readings and Psalm
Ezekiel 34:11-16, 20-24

Since Israel's kings proved to be bad shepherds, Ezekiel declares that the Lord will assume the role of shepherd in Israel. The Lord will also set over them a shepherd-messiah, "my servant David," who will feed and care for the people.

Psalm 95:1-7a

We are the people of God's pasture and the sheep of God's hand. (Ps. 95:7)

Ephesians 1:15-23

In this passage, God is praised for revealing ultimate divine power in raising Jesus from the dead. The resurrected, exalted Christ is Lord both of the church and the entire universe, now and in the age to come.

Matthew 25:31-46

Jesus compares himself to a king who moves among his subjects to see how he is treated: what is done for the least of those who belong to his family is truly done for him.

Semicontinuous reading and psalm
Ezekiel 34:11-16, 20-24

See above.

Psalm 100

We are God's people and the sheep of God's pasture. (Ps. 100:3)

Preface   Ascension *or* Sundays

Color   White *or* Green

Prayers of Intercession

The prayers are prepared locally for each occasion. The following examples may be adapted or used as appropriate.

Clinging to the promise of abundant life and resurrection, let us pray for the church, the world, and all of God's creation.

A brief silence.

Ruler of the universe, bring your wisdom to the churches of the world. Strengthen their proclamation of the gracious reign of Christ to all people everywhere. Hear us, O God.

Your mercy is great.

God of creation, make us wise and mindful caretakers of the land, air, and water. Turn us away from patterns of careless and neglectful stewardship of your good earth. Hear us, O God.

Your mercy is great.

God of power, guide the nations into ways of justice and truth. Where conflicts prevail, may peace be forthcoming. Strengthen the weak. Temper the strong. Hear us, O God.

Your mercy is great.

Shepherding God, you are the source of life and health. Surround those who struggle with illness or other difficulties of life and bring them to wholeness and healing (*especially*). Hear us, O God.

Your mercy is great.

God of glory, guide our lives in service to you through love and care for all your children. Strengthen us to seek justice for all people and to reach out in welcome to the stranger in our midst. Hear us, O God.

Your mercy is great.

Here other intercessions may be offered.

Life-giving God, strengthen us to face our mortality with humility and courage, and to trust in your promise of life from death. Support those who grieve (*especially*). Hear us, O God.

Your mercy is great.

Receive these our prayers, O God, and give us all we need for this day and the days to come, through Jesus Christ, our Lord.

Amen.

Ideas and Images for the Day

Our lives are designed to embody the presence of Christ. The biggest barrier to accepting this is not a lack of faith, but a lack of imagination. On this final Sunday of the liturgical year, we receive a parable from Jesus challenging and inspiring our imaginations to grasp our whole vocation in baptism: to both embody Christ as a servant as we go about our daily routine and to engage every part of our world as Christ's redeemed creation.

1. Take a moment in worship to allow the simple, natural response of your community's children to bring home the point of Jesus' parable. Ask, "If you saw me on the street and I was hungry and I needed food, what would you do for me?" (Give you food.) Affirm enthusiastically their clear response. Continue with the other moments in the story: "If you knew I was freezing cold and didn't have clothes? If I was thirsty? If I was a stranger and I didn't have a friend? If I was sick? If I was in jail and feeling scared because I had no visitors?" Affirm for the entire community the blessed simplicity of faithful response.

2. How does the natural giftedness of your congregation reflect faithful service for your wider community? If your congregation vanished, would anyone miss you? Where is your congregation restless to have a gospel influence in the wider community? If money were no object, what would your church desire to do in the community? To what extent does money compel or restrain us to act faithfully?

3. The Christmas story is about incarnation. But the story of God-with-us is not merely that God is among us in the person of Jesus Christ (Emmanuel). The scandal of the gospel is that God, through the Holy Spirit, is incarnate in every particle of creation and all the people of God. Are we willing to imagine that God's presence is so pervasive and complete that we are each part of God's conspiracy of holiness?

4. God's renewable recycling program: Step 1: God loves us (all of us) and is with us in Jesus Christ (Emmanuel). Step 2: God gave us the Holy Spirit of Jesus Christ to seal the deal. Step 3: Through the Holy Spirit of Christ, we love God back by loving the world.

5. "Paul put it like this: 'For everything God created is good' (1 Tim. 4:4). . . . This is why it is impossible for a Christian to have a secular job. If you follow Jesus and you are doing what you do in his name, then it is no longer secular work; it is sacred. You are there; God is there. The difference is our awareness." Rob Bell, *Velvet Elvis* (Grand Rapids, MI: Zondervan, 2005), p. 85.

Hymns for Worship
Gathering

Christ is alive! Let Christians sing   ELW 389, LBW 363
Crown him with many crowns   ELW 855, LBW 170
Jesus shall reign   ELW 434, LBW 530

Hymn of the Day

O Christ, what can it mean for us   ELW 431   *ALL SAINTS NEW*
Lord of glory, you have bought us   ELW 707, LBW 424
    HYFRYDOL
Lo! He comes with clouds descending   ELW 435, LBW 27
    HELMSLEY

Offering

The trumpets sound, the angels sing   ELW 531, W&P 139
Soon and very soon   ELW 439, WOV 744

Communion

O Christ the same   ELW 760, WOV 778
Thine the amen   ELW 826, WOV 801
The King shall come   ELW 260, LBW 33

Sending

The head that once was crowned   ELW 432, LBW 173
Rejoice, for Christ is king!   ELW 430, LBW 171

Additional Hymns and Songs

For he alone is worthy   TFF 284
Strange King   DH 61
King of kings   W&P 80

Music for the Day
Psalmody and Acclamations

"All People That on Earth Do Dwell." ELW 883.

Makeever, Ray. "Come with Joy (Psalm 100)" from *Dancing at the Harvest.*

Organ, Anne Krentz. "Psalm 95:1-7a" from PWA, Evangelical Lutheran Worship Edition.

Pelz, Walter L. "Psalm 100" from PWA, Evangelical Lutheran Worship Edition.

Roberts, William Bradley. "Psalm 100" from PSCY.

Schalk, Carl F. *Gospel Acclamations for Autumn.*

Sedio, Mark. "Psalm 95," Refrain 2, from PSCY.

Choral

Fedak, Alfred V. "Christus Paradox." SATB, org. GIA G-5463.

Jennings, Carolyn. "Climb to the Top of the Highest Mountain." SATB, opt children's choir or solo, org. KJO C-8118.

Mendelssohn, Felix/ed. Olaf C. Christiansen. "The Lord Is a Mighty God (Psalm 95)." 2 pt mxd, kybd. KJO C-0009.

Nelson, Ronald A. "Oh, Sing to the Lord (Cantad al Señor)." SATB, pno, 2 tpts, perc, assembly. SEL 410-602.

Children's Choir

Brink, Emily. "Come Now, You Blessed" from *LifeSongs.* UE, U, kybd.

Carter, Sydney. "When I Needed a Neighbor" from *LifeSongs.* LE, U, kybd.

Patterson, Mark. "Let All the World in Every Corner Sing" from *ChildrenSing.* U, kybd. AFP 9780800677695.

Keyboard / Instrumental

○ Callahan, Charles. "Partita on Hyfrydol." Org. CPH 97-5940U1.

○ Cherwien David. "Hyfrydol" from *Groundings.* Org. AFP 9780800659806.

○ Miller, Aaron David. "Hyfrydol" from *Improvisations for Organ and Instrument.* Org, inst. AFP 9780800621599.

○ Osterland, Karl. "Helmsley" from *Augsburg Organ Library: Advent.* Org. AFP 9780800658953.

Handbell

Geschke, Susan. "O Worship the King." 3-5 oct, L1. CG CGB519.

○ Hanna, Donna. "Prelude on Hyfrydol." 3-5 oct, L2. GIA G-7210.

Praise Ensemble

● Foote, Billy. "You Are My King (Amazing Love)." WT/Sixsteps Music.

● Foote, Billy/Charles Horne. "Sing to the King." WT/Sixsteps Music.

● Founds, Rick. "Lord, I Lift Your Name on High." MAR. ELW 857

● Kendrick, Graham. "Amazing Love." Make Way Music.

● Moody, Dave. "All Hail King Jesus." WRD. W&P 3. Various editions.

● Tomlin, Chris. "We Fall Down." WT.

Global

Bell, John, arr. "The Love of God Comes Close" from *Love and Anger: Songs of Lively Faith and Social Justice.* U. GIA G-4947.

Trad. South African. "Amen. Alleluia!" from *Global Songs 2.* SATB. AFP 9780800656744.

Wednesday, November 23
Clement, Bishop of Rome, died around 100

Clement was the third bishop of Rome and served at the end of the first century. He is best remembered for a letter he wrote to the Corinthian congregation, still having difficulty with divisions in spite of Paul's canonical letters. Clement's writing echoes Paul's. "Love . . . has no limits to its endurance, bears everything patiently. Love is neither servile nor arrogant. It does not provoke schisms or form cliques, but always acts in harmony with others." Clement's letter is also a witness to early understandings of church government and the way each office in the church works for the good of the whole.

Miguel Agustín Pro, martyr, died 1927

Miguel Agustín Pro grew up among oppression in Mexico, where revolutionaries accused the church of siding with the rich. He was a Jesuit priest who served during a time of intense anticlericalism, and therefore he carried out much of his ministry in private settings. He worked on behalf of the poor and homeless. Miguel and his two brothers were arrested, falsely accused of throwing a bomb at the car of a government official, and executed by a firing squad. Just before the guns fired, he yelled, "¡Viva Cristo Rey!" which means "Long live Christ the king!"

○ denotes suggestions that relate to the hymn of the day.
● denotes songs that are available on iTunes®.

November 24, 2011
Day of Thanksgiving (U.S.A.)

At harvest time we join the psalmist in offering thanksgiving to God: "You crown the year with your goodness, and your paths overflow with plenty." We are grateful for the abundance of the good things of God's creation. Paul reminds us that our thanksgiving overflows into generosity. As the body of Christ in the world, we give ourselves away as bread for the hungry.

November 24 is the commemoration of three pastors in North America: Justus Falckner, who died in 1723; Jehu Jones, who died in 1852; and William Passavant, who died in 1894.

Prayer of the Day

Almighty God our Father, your generous goodness comes to us new every day. By the work of your Spirit lead us to acknowledge your goodness, give thanks for your benefits, and serve you in willing obedience, through Jesus Christ, our Savior and Lord.

Gospel Acclamation

Alleluia. God is able to provide you with every blessing | in abundance,* so that by always having enough of everything, you may share abundantly in ev- | 'ry good work. *Alleluia.* (2 Cor. 9:8)

Readings and Psalm

Deuteronomy 8:7-18

Times of abundance tempt us to forget the Lord and rely on our own power and resources. But the Lord is the one who took Israel out of Egypt, led and fed them in the wilderness, brought them into the land, and gave them power to be productive. To thank this God is to remember and proclaim God's deeds.

Psalm 65

You crown the year with your goodness, and your paths overflow with plenty. (Ps. 65:11)

2 Corinthians 9:6-15

Christian fellowship involves sharing with those in need. Here Paul is gathering a collection for the church in Jerusalem from all the Gentile churches he helped found. We can be extravagant in our giving because God is extravagant, not stingy, in providing for our lives.

Luke 17:11-19

A Samaritan leper becomes a model for thanksgiving. He does not take for granted the kindness shown to him, but takes time to thank Jesus and glorify God.

Preface   Weekdays

Color   of the season

Prayers of Intercession

The prayers are prepared locally for each occasion. The following examples may be adapted or used as appropriate.

Clinging to the promise of abundant life and resurrection, let us pray for the church, the world, and all of God's creation.

A brief silence.

Giver and sustainer of life, your church sings your praise, our hearts full with thanksgiving for your saving deeds. Make us ever thankful, gracious, and generous. Hear us, O God.

Your mercy is great.

Generous God, you brought us into a good land. Make us faithful stewards of the marvelous gifts of your creation. We praise you for your bounty showered upon us. Hear us, O God.

Your mercy is great.

Pilgrim God, you journey with every nation and people. Guide us into ways of peace and justice, that all would have reason to give you thanks and praise. Hear us, O God.

Your mercy is great.

Gracious Lord, you deliver us from every need and every peril by your mighty hand. Reach out and raise up those who suffer in any way (*especially*), that they would sing your praises. Hear us, O God.

Your mercy is great.

God of all mercies, on this day of Thanksgiving we are overwhelmed by your generosity. Strengthen and encourage us that others would come to know you through our sharing of your abundance. Hear us, O God.

Your mercy is great.

Here other intercessions may be offered.

Loving Savior, the generations rise and fall before you. We praise you for the gift of our forebears (*especially Justus Falckner, Jehu Jones, and William Passavant, pastors in North America, and Isaac Watts, hymnwriter*). As you gather every generation to your breast, strengthen those who grieve with your promise of abundant life. Hear us, O God.

Your mercy is great.

Receive these our prayers, O God, and give us all we need for this day and the days to come, through Jesus Christ, our Lord.

Amen.

Ideas and Images for the Day

How do we define an abundant life? Is it by how much *we* have? Do we define it in comparison or contrast to what others have? Too often, our definition of an abundant life keeps us turned inward because it is characterized by the amount of money we have in the bank, the number of friends by our side, or gadgets in our pocket. Perhaps today's readings provide us an opportunity to redefine what constitutes an abundant life. Each reading orients our perspective outward and gives us pause to consider the correlation between an abundant life and a life lived in faithful relationship to God.

1. In 2 Corinthians Paul writes of the indescribable gift of God's grace. This grace is God's good work and is made abundant because of God's love for humanity. How is God at work in us to make that abundant grace known? How does God use our gifts and talents to share "abundantly in every good work"?

2. A common Thanksgiving symbol of abundance is the cornucopia. In the weeks leading to Thanksgiving Day, enlist the children of the congregation to construct a large cornucopia for use during worship. Place the cornucopia in a conspicuous location and invite the congregation to reflect on what gifts God has given them that can be shared with others. Give everyone slips of paper or note cards on which they may write their reflections. Invite young children to draw their reflections. At an appropriate time, ask the congregation to deposit those reflections in the cornucopia.

3. God gives abundantly to God's people through varied ministries in the church. Consider calling attention to those saints in light commemorated closest to Thanksgiving Day. Henry Melchior Muhlenberg (Oct. 7) and Teresa of Avila (Oct. 15) fall closest to Canada's Monday, October 10, 2011, Day of Thanksgiving. These two saints were led by the Holy Spirit to put the gospel into action through the work of reconciliation (Muhlenberg) and reformation (Teresa of Ávila). Both individuals worked to build up the church. Muhlenberg did so through the establishment of the Ministerium of North America; Teresa by establishing seventeen reformed monasteries in Spain.

4. In the United States, three diverse pastors are commemorated on Thanksgiving Day this year: Justus Falckner (1672–1723), Jehu Jones (1786–1852), and William A. Passavant (1821–1894). These three men each shared their specific Spirit-given gifts in service of our Lord. They expressed the good news through hymnody (Falckner), work for racial justice (Jones), and other expressions of social welfare such as the establishment of orphanages and hospitals (Passavant).

5. Invite the congregation to consider how they may share their Spirit-given gifts in the community in which you live. To help worshipers consider ways they may be led to use their gifts as rostered leaders visit http://elcic.ca/Its-Your-Call/default.cfm or http://www.elca.org/Growing-In-Faith/Vocation/Become-a-Leader.aspx.

Hymns for Worship

Gathering

Come, ye thankful people, come   ELW 693, LBW 407
We praise you, O God   ELW 870, LBW 241, TFF 100
For the beauty of the earth   ELW 879, LBW 561

Hymn of the Day

Now thank we all our God   ELW 839/840, LBW 533/534
NUN DANKET ALLE GOTT
Praise and thanksgiving   ELW 689, LBW 409   BUNESSAN
For the fruit of all creation   ELW 679, WOV 760
AR HYD Y NOS   LBW 563   SANTA BARBARA

Offering

To God our thanks we give   ELW 682
Have you thanked the Lord?   ELW 829, TFF 270

Communion

Sing to the Lord of harvest   ELW 694, LBW 412
The numberless gifts of God's mercies   ELW 683
Great is thy faithfulness   ELW 733, WOV 771

Sending

Let all things now living ELW 881, LBW 557
O God, beyond all praising ELW 880, WOV 797

Additional Hymns and Songs

Give thanks TFF 292, W&P 41
Living thanksgiving DH 99
All things bright and beautiful WOV 767, HS91 827

Music for the Day
Psalmody and Acclamations

Krentz, Michael. "Psalm 65" from PWA, Evangelical Lutheran Worship Edition.
Long, Larry J. "Psalm 65," Refrain 2, from PSCY.

Choral

o Bach, J. S. "Now Thank We All Our God" from *Bach for All Seasons*. SATB, kybd. AFP 9780800658540.

Johnson, Ralph M. "For Such a Time as This." SATB, opt assembly, org, opt br. AFP 9780800676568.

Patterson, Mark. "When in Our Music God Is Glorified." U, opt desc, pno, opt hb. AFP 9780800638108.

Willan, Healey. "Sing to the Lord of Harvest." SATB, opt children's choir, opt assembly, org. CPH 98-1454.

Children's Choir

Bedford, Michael. "Thanks Be to God" from *Seasonal Songs for Young Singers*. U, kybd, hb. CG CGA1160.

Patterson, Mark. "Lord, We Give Thanks" from *ChildrenSing*. U, kybd. AFP 9780800677695.

Patterson, Mark. "Now We Give Thanks" from *Young ChildrenSing*. U, kybd. AFP 9780800676803.

Keyboard / Instrumental

o Bach, J. S. "Nun danket alle Gott" from *Timeless Music for Weddings and Special Occasions*. Org, tpt. HOP 8160.

o Burkhardt, Michael. "Bunessan" and "Nun danket alle Gott" from *Praise and Thanksgiving Hymn Improvisations*, set 4. Org. MSM 10-754.

o Carter, John. "Nun danket alle Gott" from *Hymns for Piano*, vol. 2. Pno. HOP 8197.

o Stoldt, Frank. "Ar hyd y nos" from *Augsburg Organ Library: November*. Org. AFP 9780800658960.

Handbell

o Barrow, Lee. "Nun Danket." 3-5 oct hb, opt 3 oct hc, L3+. BP HB337.

o Mary Kay Parrish. "Now Thank We All Our God." 4-6 oct, L4. AGEHR AG46022.

o Quintana, Ariel. "Morning Has Broken (Bunessan)." 4-5 oct, L4. Fred Bock BGH1014.

Praise Ensemble

● Chisholm, Thomas/William Runyan. "Great Is Thy Faithfulness." HOP.

● Jernigan, Dennis. "You Are My All in All (Jesus, Lamb of God)." Shepherd's Heart Music. W&P 76.

● Moen, Don/Paul Baloche. "Thank You Lord." INT.

● Picking, Tim. "Thanks Be to God." INT. Various editions.

● Schwartz, Stephen. "All Good Gifts" from *Godspell*. Quartet Music and New Cadenza Music.

● Smith, Henry. "Give Thanks." INT.

Global

Solis, Melchizedek M. "In Great Thanksgiving" from *Sound the Bamboo*. 2 pt. GIA G-6830.

Trad. Southern/East Africa. "Siyabonga/Thank You, Jesus" from *Agape: Songs of Hope and Reconciliation*. SATB. Lutheran World Federation. AFP 9780191000133.

Thursday, November 24

Justus Falckner, died 1723; Jehu Jones, died 1852; William Passavant, died 1894; pastors in North America

A native of Saxony, Falckner was the son of a Lutheran pastor and, seeing the stresses his father endured, did not plan on becoming a pastor himself, though he studied theology in Halle. Instead, he joined with his brother in the real estate business in Pennsylvania. Through this business he became acquainted with a Swedish pastor in America, and finally he decided to become ordained. He served congregations in New York and New Jersey. Not only was he the first Lutheran ordained in North America, but he published a catechism that was the first Lutheran book published on the continent.

Jones was a native of Charleston, South Carolina. Ordained by the New York Ministerium in 1832, he became the Lutheran church's first African American pastor. Upon returning to South Carolina he was arrested under a law prohibiting free blacks from reentering the state, so he was unable to join the group of Charlestonians he had been commissioned to accompany to Liberia. For nearly twenty years Jones carried out missionary work in Philadelphia in the face of many difficulties. There he led in the formation of the first African American Lutheran congregation, St. Paul's, and the construction of its church building.

William Passavant created and nurtured a new level of organized social ministry in western Pennsylvania. It was the seed of the system of social services that is now known as Lutheran Services in America. Passavant and his legacy sought to serve the poorest of the poor, providing shelter, medical, and living assistance.

---

o denotes suggestions that relate to the hymn of the day.
● denotes songs that are available on iTunes®.

Friday, November 25

Isaac Watts, hymnwriter, died 1748

Isaac Watts was born in England to a family of nonconformists, people who thought the Church of England had not carried its reforms far enough. As a youth, Watts complained to his father about the quality of hymnody in the metrical psalter of his day. That was the start of his hymnwriting career. He wrote about six hundred hymns, many in a two-year period beginning when he was twenty years old. Some of Watts's hymns are based on psalms, a nonconformist tradition. When criticized for writing hymns not taken from scripture, he responded that if we can pray prayers that are not from scripture but written by us, then surely we can sing hymns that we have made up ourselves. Ten of Watts's hymn texts are in *Evangelical Lutheran Worship*, including "O God, Our Help in Ages Past" (ELW 632).

Resources

*   denotes new or newer print resource
∞   denotes electronic or Web resource

Lectionaries

Lectionary for Worship Year A. Minneapolis: Augsburg Fortress, 2007. The Revised Common Lectionary. Includes first reading, psalm citation, second reading, and gospel for each Sunday and lesser festival. Each reading is "sense-lined" for clearer proclamation of the scriptural texts. New Revised Standard Version. Available in study (includes reader helps) and ritual editions.

Revised Common Lectionary Daily Readings. Consultation on Common Texts. Minneapolis: Fortress Press, 2005.

Readings for the Assembly (A). Gordon Lathrop and Gail Ramshaw, eds. Minneapolis: Augsburg Fortress, 1995. The Revised Common Lectionary. Emended NRSV with inclusive language.

Worship Books

Evangelical Lutheran Worship. Minneapolis: Augsburg Fortress, 2006. Ten holy communion settings, more than 650 hymns, complete psalter, daily prayer resources, and more. Available in pew, leaders ritual, leaders desk, gift, pocket, and enlarged print editions.

Evangelical Lutheran Worship Accompaniment Edition: Liturgies. Minneapolis: Augsburg Fortress, 2006. Complete keyboard accompaniments for all ten holy communion settings and additional music within liturgies.

Evangelical Lutheran Worship Accompaniment Edition: Service Music and Hymns (2 vols). Minneapolis: Augsburg Fortress, 2006. Full accompaniments to all hymns and songs in the pew edition, #151–893. Simplified Keyboard and Guitar editions also available.

* *Evangelical Lutheran Worship Occasional Services for the Assembly*. Minneapolis: Augsburg Fortress, 2009. Rites and prayers for use on particular occasions in the worshiping assemblies of congregations and synods, such as ministry rites, dedications, and blessings.

* *Evangelical Lutheran Worship Pastoral Care:* Occasional Services, Readings, and Prayers. Minneapolis: Augsburg Fortress, 2008. An essential tool for caregivers conducting the church's ministry of care outside the worshiping assembly.

Libro de Liturgia y Cántico. Minneapolis: Augsburg Fortress, 1998. A complete Spanish-language worship resource including liturgies and hymns, some with English translations. Leader edition (2001) with additional psalms and indexes.

Ritos Ocasionales. Minneapolis: Augsburg Fortress, 2000. Spanish language translation of rites from Occasional Services.

This Far by Faith: An African American Resource for Worship. Minneapolis: Augsburg Fortress, 1999. A supplement of worship orders, psalms, service music, and hymns representing African American traditions and developed by African American Lutherans.

With One Voice: A Lutheran Resource for Worship. Minneapolis: Augsburg Fortress, 1995. Pew, leader, and accompaniment editions; instrumental parts; organ accompaniment for the liturgy.

Worship Planning Tools, Indexes, Calendars

∞ www.sundaysandseasons.com. A subscription-based online worship planning tool. Browse, select, and download content for worship planning and worship folder preparation. Complements *Sundays and Seasons*.

∞ *Evangelical Lutheran Worship* Liturgies CD-ROM. Minneapolis: Augsburg Fortress, 2006. Liturgical material from pew edition in editable text files; assembly singing lines provided as graphics. For use in desktop publishing.

Indexes to Evangelical Lutheran Worship. Minneapolis: Augsburg Fortress, 2007. Indexes the hymns and songs in *Evangelical Lutheran Worship*. Includes extensive lectionary, scripture, and topical indexes.

Choral Literature for Sundays and Seasons. Bradley Ellingboe, ed. Minneapolis: Augsburg Fortress, 2004. A comprehensive listing of time-tested choral works, indexed to the readings for each Sunday and principal festival of the three-year lectionary. Includes information on voicing, instrumentation, composers, and publishers.

Choosing Contemporary Music: Seasonal, Topical, Lectionary Indexes. Minneapolis: Augsburg Fortress, 2000. Provides references to multiple collections of contemporary praise and liturgical songs. Includes extensive scripture and topic indexes.

* ∞ *Words for Worship: 2011, Year A*. Minneapolis: Augsburg Fortress, 2010. CD-ROM includes lectionary readings, worship texts, seasonal rites, and more for use in worship folders and other self-published materials.

* *Calendar of Word and Season 2011: Liturgical Wall Calendar*. Minneapolis: Augsburg Fortress, 2010. Features artwork by DeAnne L. Parks. Date blocks identify seasonal or festival color. Includes Revised Common Lectionary readings for Sundays and festivals. A reference tool for home, sacristy, office.

* *Church Year Calendar 2011*. Minneapolis: Augsburg Fortress, 2010. A one-sheet calendar of lectionary citations and liturgical colors for each Sunday and festival of the liturgical year. Appropriate for bulk purchase and distribution.

* *Worship Planning Calendar 2011*. Minneapolis: Augsburg Fortress, 2010. A two-page per week calendar helpful for worship planners, with space to record appointments and notes for each day. Specially designed to complement *Sundays and Seasons*. Features daily readings from the daily lectionary developed by the Consultation on Common Texts.

* Westermeyer, Paul. *Hymnal Companion to Evangelical Lutheran Worship*. Minneapolis: Augsburg Fortress, 2010. Background and insightful commentary on all 650 hymns, both text and music, together with biographical information on hymn writers and composers. Expanded indexes.

Worship Support

Brugh, Lorraine, and Gordon Lathrop. *The Sunday Assembly.* Minneapolis: Augsburg Fortress, 2008. A resource to guide leaders in their understanding and interpretation of the *Evangelical Lutheran Worship* resources. The first of three volumes in a series of pastoral guides, Using *Evangelical Lutheran Worship*, focusing on holy communion.

Bushkofsky, Dennis, and Craig Satterlee. *The Christian Life: Baptism and Life Passages.* Minneapolis: Augsburg Fortress, 2008. The second of three volumes in a series of pastoral guides, Using *Evangelical Lutheran Worship*, containing detailed information on holy baptism and its related rites, as well as marriage, healing, and funeral.

* Ramshaw, Gail, and Mons Teig. *Keeping Time: The Church's Years.* Minneapolis: Augsburg Fortress, 2009. The third of three volumes in a series of pastoral guides, Using *Evangelical Lutheran Worship*, containing detailed information on Sundays, seasons, festivals, and commemorations, as well as daily prayer.

Adams, William Seth. *Shaped by Images: One Who Presides.* New York: Church Hymnal Corporation, 1995. An excellent review of the ministry of presiding at worship.

Huck, Gabe, and Gerald T. Chinchar. *Liturgy with Style and Grace*, 3rd. ed. Chicago: Liturgy Training Publications, 1998. The first three chapters offer a practical, well-written overview of the purpose of worship, the elements of worship, and liturgical leadership.

Huffman, Walter C. *Prayer of the Faithful: Understanding and Creatively Leading Corporate Intercessory Prayer*, rev. ed. Minneapolis: Augsburg Fortress, 1992. A helpful treatment of communal prayer, the Lord's Prayer, and the prayers of the people.

* ∞ *Fed and Forgiven: Communion Preparation and Formation.* Minneapolis: Augsburg Fortress, 2009. A comprehensive set of resources for leading children, youth, and adults into the sacrament of holy communion. Leader Guide with CD-ROM for all ages. Learner Resources for PreK-K, Grades 1-3, Grades 4-6, and adults. Supplementary DVD.

* Mueller, Craig. *Soli Deo Gloria: Choir Devotions for Year A.* Minneapolis: Augsburg Fortress, 2010.

* Wold, Wayne L. *Soli Deo Gloria: Choir Devotions for Year C.* Minneapolis: Augsburg Fortress, 2009.

———. *Tune My Heart to Sing.* Minneapolis: Augsburg Fortress, 1997. Devotions for choirs based on the lectionary.

Worship Handbook Series. Minneapolis: Augsburg Fortress, 2001–. Brief guides to liturgical ministries and celebrations for those who lead and participate in worship.

Acolytes and Servers. Gerald Spice.
Assisting Ministers and Readers. Gerald Spice.
Christian Burial. Karen Bockelman.
Marriage. Karen Bockelman.
Ministers of Communion from the Assembly. Donald Luther.
Musicians in the Assembly. Robert Buckley Farlee.
Preparing the Assembly's Worship. Craig Mueller.
Presiding in the Assembly. Craig Satterlee.
Sponsors and Baptism. Elaine Ramshaw.
Ushers and Greeters. Gerald Spice.
Welcome to Worship. Karen Bockelman.

Choirbooks

Augsburg Choirbook, The. Minneapolis: Augsburg Fortress, 1998. Kenneth Jennings, ed. Sixty-seven anthems primarily from twentieth-century North American composers.

Augsburg Choirbook for Advent, Christmas, and Epiphany. Minneapolis: Augsburg Fortress, 2007. Thirty-three anthems, mostly easy-to-medium difficulty, for the Christmas cycle.

Augsburg Choirbook for Men. Minneapolis: Augsburg Fortress, 2004. Fourteen anthems for two- to four-part male chorus.

Augsburg Choirbook for Women. Minneapolis: Augsburg Fortress, 2006. Diverse selections for choirs of all ages and abilities from high school through adult.

Augsburg Easy Choirbook, vol. 1. Minneapolis: Augsburg Fortress, 2003. Fourteen unison and two-part mixed anthems for the church year.

Augsburg Easy Choirbook, vol. 2. Minneapolis: Augsburg Fortress, 2005. Sixteen anthems for the church year; accessible, quality music for the smaller, less-experienced choir.

Bach for All Seasons. Minneapolis: Augsburg Fortress, 1999. Richard Erickson and Mark Bighley, eds. Offers movements from cantatas and oratorios presented with carefully reconstructed keyboard parts and fresh English texts. Instrumental parts available.

Chantry Choirbook. Minneapolis: Augsburg Fortress, 2000. Choral masterworks of European composers spanning five centuries, many with new English translations, and indexed for use in the liturgical assembly throughout the year.

GladSong Choirbook. Minneapolis: Augsburg Fortress, 2005. Eleven titles for fall, Advent, and Christmas use, plus Reformation, Thanksgiving, All Saints, Christ the King, Epiphany, and communion.

Hear Our Prayer. Minneapolis: Augsburg Fortress, 2007. A collection of sung prayer responses to be used between the petitions of the prayers of intercession or as a call or closing to prayer.

Let the Peoples Sing, vol. 1: Sacred Choral Music from the Caribbean. Minneapolis: Augsburg Fortress, 2002. Marian Dolan, ed. Nine texts and tunes.

Let the Peoples Sing, vol. 2: Sacred Choral Music of the Baltics. Minneapolis: Augsburg Fortress, 2003. Marian Dolan, ed. Twelve choral pieces from Estonia, Latvia, and Lithuania.

Let the Peoples Sing, vol. 3: An International Christmas. Minneapolis: Augsburg Fortress, 2005. Marian Dolan, ed. A collection of Advent, Christmas, and Epiphany choral music representing countries as diverse as India, Korea, Palestine, Venezuela, and Sweden.

Wade in the Water: Easy Choral Music for All Ages. Minneapolis: Augsburg Fortress, 2007. A collection of two- and three-part choral music for the less-experienced singer.

Hymn and Song Collections

As Sunshine to a Garden: Hymns and Songs. Rusty Edwards. Minneapolis: Augsburg Fortress, 1999. Forty-six collected hymns from the author of "We all are one in mission."

Bread of Life: Mass and Songs for the Assembly. Minneapolis: Augsburg Fortress, 2000. Jeremy Young's complete eucharistic music based on *With One Voice* Setting 5 and twelve of his worship songs.

* *Come Beloved of the Maker: Hymns of Susan Palo Cherwien*. Minneapolis: Augsburg Fortress, 2010. Thirty-four hymn texts by Cherwien, following up on her previous collection, *O Blessed Spring*. Each text is presented by itself as well as with a harmonized tune.

Dancing at the Harvest: Songs by Ray Makeever. Minneapolis: Augsburg Fortress, 1997. More than 100 songs and service music items.

Earth and All Stars: Hymns and Songs for Young and Old. Herbert F. Brokering. Minneapolis: Augsburg Fortress, 2003. A collection of hymn texts by the popular writer.

Justice like a Base of Stone. Bret Hesla. Minneapolis: Augsburg Fortress, 2006. A collection of peace and justice songs in a variety of styles, easily taught to the congregation. Also audio CD.

O Blessed Spring: Hymns of Susan Palo Cherwien. Minneapolis: Augsburg Fortress, 1997. New hymn texts set to both new and familiar hymn tunes.

Pave the Way: Global Songs 3. Bread for the Journey. Minneapolis: Augsburg Fortress, 2004. Eighteen songs from around the world, with performance notes.

*∞ *Singing Our Prayer: A Companion to Holden Prayer Around the Cross. Shorter Songs for Contemplative Worship*. Minneapolis: Augsburg Fortress, 2010. A collection of short, simple songs for worship. Available in full score and assembly editions, as well as an audio CD.

Worship & Praise. Minneapolis: Augsburg Fortress, 1999. A collection of songs in various contemporary and popular styles, with helps for using them in Lutheran worship.

Psalm Collections

∞ *Psalter for Worship Year A*, Evangelical Lutheran Worship Edition. Minneapolis: Augsburg Fortress, 2007. Settings of psalm refrains by various composers with *Evangelical Lutheran Worship* psalm tones. Coordinate with Celebrate and Today's Readings inserts. Revised Common Lectionary. Includes a CD-ROM with psalm texts, refrains, and tones.

* ∞ *Psalm Settings for the Church Year*. Mark Mummert, ed. Minneapolis: Augsburg Fortress, 2008. A new collection of psalm settings in a wide variety of styles and structures. Contains all psalms used in the Revised Common Lectionary. 2 vols.

Anglican Chant Psalter, The. Alec Wyton, ed. New York: Church Publishing, 1987.

∞ Bruxvoort Colligan, Richard. *The Psalm Project: Sharing the Road, Songs for Lent*. Minneapolis: Augsburg Fortress, 2007. Fifteen contemporary worship songs that bring the Psalms to life. Songbook and audio CD.

* *ChildrenSing Psalms*. Marilyn Comer, ed. Minneapolis: Augsburg Fortress, 2009. Selected psalms for all seasons, keyed to the lectionary.

Daw, Carl P., and Kevin R. Hackett. *Hymn Tune Psalter*. Revised Common Lectionary edition. New York: Church Publishing, 2007.

Grail Gelineau Psalter, The. Chicago: GIA Publications, Inc., 1972. 150 psalms and eighteen canticles.

Guimont, Michel. *Lectionary Psalms*. Chicago: GIA Publications, Inc., 1998. Responsorial psalm settings for the three-year Roman Catholic lectionary.

* Hopson, Hal H. *The People's Psalter*. Fenton, MO: MorningStar Music, 2008.

Plainsong Psalter, The. James Litton, ed. New York: Church Publishing, 1988.

Portland Psalter, The. Robert A. Hawthorne. 2 vols. New York: Church Publishing. Book One contains settings for RCL psalms; Book Two contains settings for lesser festivals and the Easter Vigil.

Psalter: Psalms and Canticles for Singing, The. Louisville, KY: Westminster John Knox Press, 1993. Various composers.

∞ *St. Martin's Psalter, Year A*. Thomas Pavlechko, arr. Tryon, NC: St. James Music Press. Revised Common Lectionary. Matches refrains with hymn-based psalm tones.

Selah Psalter, The. Richard Leach and David P. Schaap, eds. Kingston, NY: Selah Publishing Co., 2001. Sixty-six psalms in a variety of styles.

Preparing Music for Worship

Cherwien, David. *Let the People Sing! A Keyboardist's Creative and Practical Guide to Engaging God's People in Meaningful Song*. St. Louis: Concordia Publishing House, 1997. Emphasis on the organ.

∞ *Evangelical Lutheran Worship* Liturgies Audio CD, vols. 1, 2, 3. Minneapolis: Augsburg Fortress, 2006, 2010. Complete recordings of Holy Communion Settings One—Ten and Daily Prayer.

∞ *Evangelical Lutheran Worship* Hymns Audio CD, vols. 1 and 2. Minneapolis: Augsburg Fortress, 2006, 2007. Recordings of four dozen hymns and songs from Evangelical Lutheran Worship, both new and familiar. Performed by choirs from St. Olaf and Lenoir Rhyne colleges.

Evangelical Lutheran Worship Simplified Keyboard Accompaniment Edition: Service Music and Hymns. Minneapolis: Augsburg Fortress, 2007.

Evangelical Lutheran Worship Guitar Accompaniment Edition (2 vols). Minneapolis: Augsburg Fortress, 2007. "Lead sheet"-style accompaniments for every piece in the service music section and every hymn in the pew edition.

Farlee, Robert Buckley, gen. ed. *Leading the Church's Song*. Minneapolis: Augsburg Fortress, 1998. Articles by various contributors, with musical examples and audio CD, giving guidance on the interpretation and leadership of various genres of congregational song.

∞ *Favorite Hymns Accompanied*. John Ferguson, organist. Minneapolis: Augsburg Fortress, 2005. A 2-CD set of 52 hymns from all seasons of the year, most widely known, played without singing.

* *Field Guide to Contemporary Worship*. Andrew Boesenecker and James Graeser. Minneapolis: Augsburg Fortress, 2010. A guide for anyone thinking about starting a contemporary worship service. Covers the nuts and bolts of instrumentation, arranging, working with mics and speakers, and more.

Handbells in the Liturgy: A Practical Guide for the Use of Handbells in Liturgical Worship Traditions. St. Louis: Concordia Publishing House, 1996.

Haugen, Marty. *Instrumentation and the Liturgical Ensemble*. Chicago: GIA Publications, Inc., 1991.

Highben, Zebulon M., and Kristina M. Langlois, eds. *With a Voice of Singing: Essays on Children, Choirs, and Music in the Church.* Minneapolis: Kirk House Publishers, 2007.

Hopson, Hal H. *The Creative Use of Handbells in Worship; The Creative Use of Choir in Worship; The Creative Use of Instruments in Worship; The Creative Use of Descants in Worship; The Creative Use of Organ in Worship.* Carol Stream, IL: Hope Publishing Co.

* *Introductions and Alternate Accompaniments* to hymns and songs in *Evangelical Lutheran Worship.* Minneapolis: Augsburg Fortress, 2007–2009. Two 10-volume series, one for organ and one for piano, covering every *Evangelical Lutheran Worship* hymn and song. Various composers.

Let It Rip! at the Piano (vol. 1 & 2) and *Pull Out the Stops* (vol. 1 & 2). Minneapolis: Augsburg Fortress, 2000–2005. Collections for piano and organ respectively, each containing introductions and varied musical accompaniments by various composers for more than 100 widely used hymns and songs. Emphasis on current musical styles including blues, gospel, new age, jazz, and rolling contemporary.

Musicians Guide to Evangelical Lutheran Worship. Minneapolis: Augsburg Fortress, 2007. An introduction to the music, including specific suggestions for each liturgical music item, service music item, and hymn.

Piano Plus: Hymns for Piano and Treble Instrument, Advent/Christmas. Minneapolis: Augsburg Fortress, 2006. *Through the Year*, 2009. Arrangements by various composers that range in difficulty from simple cradle songs to jazz, and span numerous world cultures and several centuries.

Weidler, Scott, and Dori Collins. *Sound Decisions.* Chicago: Evangelical Lutheran Church in America, 1997. Theological principles for the evaluation of contemporary worship music.

Westermeyer, Paul. *The Church Musician*, rev. ed. Minneapolis: Augsburg Fortress, 1997. Foundational introduction to the role and task of the church musician as the leader of the people's song.

———. *Te Deum: The Church and Music.* Minneapolis: Fortress Press, 1998. A historical and theological introduction to the music of the church.

Wold, Wayne. *Preaching to the Choir: The Care and Nurture of the Church Choir.* Minneapolis: Augsburg Fortress, 2003. Practical helps for the choir director.

Visual and Media Ministry Resources

∞ *Icon Three: Visual Images for Every Sunday.* Minneapolis: Augsburg Fortress, 2007. 260 images by artist Julie Lonneman presented in both black-and-white and colorized versions on CD-ROM. Suitable for use in self-published materials or for projection using presentation software.

∞ *Icon Two for Projection.* Minneapolis: Augsburg Fortress, 2005. 250 colorized images based on the Revised Common Lectionary by liturgical artist Lucinda Naylor suitable for projection using presentation software.

∞ *Icon Two: Visual Images for Every Sunday.* Minneapolis: Augsburg Fortress, 2004. 250 images by liturgical artist Lucinda Naylor based on the church year and lectionary gospel readings for use in self-published materials.

∞ *Graphics for Worship 2.0.* Minneapolis: Augsburg Fortress. A collection of 358 graphics by Tanja Butler, Steve Erspamer, Jane Pitz, Nicholas Markell, Barbara Zuber, and others.

Crowley, Eileen D. *A Moving Word: Media Art in Worship.* Minneapolis: Augsburg Fortress, 2006. An exploration of how visual elements in worship can enhance the assembly's understanding of the gospel.

∞ Jensen, Richard. *Envisioning the Word: The Use of Visual Images in Preaching*, with CD-ROM. Minneapolis: Fortress Press, 2005. A discussion of how vital, if controversial, image making has always been in Christian tradition, followed by a demonstration of how preaching with images is both profoundly traditional and necessary to contemporary proclamation.

∞ Wilson, Kent V. *For the Sake of the Gospel: A Media Ministry Primer* (with DVD). Minneapolis: Augsburg Fortress, 2006. A case for the why, how, and what of media ministry with practical helps and examples.

∞ Wilson, Len, and Jason Moore. *Digital Storytellers: The Art of Communicating the Gospel in Worship* (with DVD). Nashville, Abingdon Press, 2002. Representing the word of God as image and art in a digital culture.

Preparing Environment and Art

Chinn, Nancy. *Spaces for Spirit: Adorning the Church.* Chicago: Liturgy Training Publications, 1998. Imaginative thinking about ways to treat visual elements in the worship space.

Christopherson, D. Foy. *A Place of Encounter: Renewing Worship Spaces.* Minneapolis: Augsburg Fortress, 2004. An exploration of principles for planning and renewing worship spaces.

Clothed in Glory: Vesting the Church. David Philippart, ed. Chicago: Liturgy Training Publications, 1997. Photos and essays about liturgical paraments and vestments.

Giles, Richard. *Re-Pitching the Tent: Reordering the Church Building for Worship and Mission.* Collegeville, MN: The Liturgical Press, 1999.

Huffman, Walter C., S. Anita Stauffer, and Ralph R. Van Loon. *Where We Worship.* Minneapolis: Augsburg Publishing House, 1987. Written by three Lutheran worship leaders, this volume sets forth the central principles for understanding and organizing space for worship. Study book and leader guide.

Mazar, Peter. *To Crown the Year: Decorating the Church through the Seasons.* Chicago: Liturgy Training Publications, 1995. A contemporary guide for decorating the worship space throughout the seasons of the year.

Stauffer, S. Anita. *Altar Guild and Sacristy Handbook.* Minneapolis: Augsburg Fortress, 2000. Revised and expanded edition of this classic on preparing the table and the worship environment.

Seasons and Liturgical Year

* *Worship Guidebook for Lent and the Three Days.* Minneapolis: Augsburg Fortress, 2009. A collection of insights, images, and practical tips to help deepen your congregation's worship life during the days from Ash Wednesday to Easter. A companion to *Music Sourcebook for Lent and the Three Days.*

* ∞ *Music Sourcebook for Lent and the Three Days*. Minneapolis: Augsburg Fortress, 2010. This collection greatly expands the repetoire of resources for the song of the assembly and its leaders during the days from Ash Wednesday to Easter.
* *Keeping Time: The Church's Years*. Minneapolis: Augsburg Fortress, 2009. A resource to guide leaders in their understanding and interpretation of the *Evangelical Lutheran Worship* resources. The third of three volumes in a series of pastoral guides, Using *Evangelical Lutheran Worship*, containing detailed information on Sundays, seasons, festivals, and commemorations, as well as daily prayer.

Hynes, Mary Ellen. *Companion to the Calendar*. Chicago: Liturgy Training Publications, 1993. An excellent overview of the seasons, festivals and lesser festivals, and many commemorations Written from an ecumenical/Roman Catholic perspective, including commemorations unique to the Lutheran calendar.

* Pfatteicher, Philip. *New Book of Festivals and Commemorations: A Proposed Common Calendar of the Saints*. Minneapolis: Fortress Press, 2008.

Prayer in the Paschal Triduum, rev. ed. Chicago: Liturgy Training Publications, 1992. For worship committees, an excellent introduction to worship during the Three Days.

Ramshaw, Gail. *The Three-Day Feast: Maundy Thursday, Good Friday, Easter*. Minneapolis: Augsburg Fortress, 2004. A little history and a lot of suggestions about how these services can enrich the assembly's worship life.

Children

* *ChildrenSing Psalms*. Marilyn Comer, ed. Minneapolis: Augsburg Fortress, 2009. Collection of psalms for all seasons keyed to the lectionary.
* ∞ *Fed and Forgiven: Communion Preparation and Formation*. Minneapolis: Augsburg Fortress, 2009. A comprehensive set of resources for leading children, youth, and adults into the sacrament of holy communion. Leader Guide with CD-ROM for all ages. Learner Resources for PreK-K, Grades 1-3, Grades 4-6, and adults. Supplementary DVD.

Kids Celebrate Worship Series. Minneapolis: Augsburg Fortress, 2006–. A series of seasonal and topical 8-page booklets that introduce children and their families to worship and *Evangelical Lutheran Worship*. Pre-reader and young reader versions. Includes ideas and helps for parents, pastors, educators, and children's choir directors. For use in worship, Sunday school, or home.
Our Worship Book (2006). A kid-friendly introduction to *Evangelical Lutheran Worship*.
Sunday Worship (2006). Focuses on the gathering, word, meal, sending pattern of Holy Communion.
Advent & Christmas (2006). Introduction to the Advent-Christmas season with activities.
Lent & Easter (2006). Introduction to the seasons of Lent and Easter with activities.
Three Amazing Days (2006). Introduction to Maundy Thursday, Good Friday, and the Easter Vigil.

Holy Communion (2007). Introduction to the sacrament of holy communion.
Baptism (2007). Introduction to the sacrament of holy baptism and baptismal living.
Our Prayers (2007). Focuses on how and when the assembly prays in worship, and prayer in the home.
The Bible (2007). Introduction to the ways in which scripture is used in worship.

∞ *Kids Celebrate: Worship Bulletins for Children, Lectionary Year A*. Minneapolis: Augsburg Fortress, 2004. A full year's worth of reproducible bulletins that engage children in the weekly gathering of God's people. Includes CD-ROM.

LifeSongs (children's songbook, leader book, and audio CDs). Minneapolis: Augsburg Fortress, 1999. A well-rounded selection of age-appropriate songs, hymns, and liturgical music that builds a foundation for a lifetime of singing the faith.

Patterson, Mark. *Young ChildrenSing, ChildrenSing, and ChildrenSing with Instruments*. Minneapolis: Augsburg Fortress, 2004–2006. Short anthems for young singers.

Ramshaw, Gail. *Every Day and Sunday, Too*. Minneapolis: Augsburg Fortress, 1996. An illustrated book for parents and children. Daily life is related to the central actions of the liturgy.
———. *Sunday Morning*. Chicago: Liturgy Training Publications, 1993. A book for children and adults on the primary words of Sunday worship.

∞ Vandermeer, Harriet; illustrated by Elizabeth Steele Halstead. *Rings, Kings, and Butterflies: Lessons on Christian Symbols for Children* (with CD-ROM). Minneapolis: Augsburg Fortress, 2006. An illustrated explanation of Christian seasons and symbols. Ideas for children's messages, and activities for teachers and parents.

Daily Prayer Resources

* Briehl, Susan and Tom Witt. *Holden Prayer Around the Cross: Handbook to the Liturgy*. Minneapolis: Augsburg Fortress, 2009. Practical suggestions for planning and leading flexible orders for contemplative prayer. Includes fourteen liturgies in the Prayer Around the Cross format.
*∞ *Singing Our Prayer: A Companion to Holden Prayer Around the Cross. Shorter Songs for Contemplative Worship*. Minneapolis: Augsburg Fortress, 2010. A collection of short, simple songs for worship. Available in full score and assembly editions, as well as an audio CD.

Book of Common Worship: Daily Prayer. Louisville, KY: Westminster John Knox Press, 1993. Presbyterian.

* *Bread for the Day 2011: Daily Bible Readings and Prayers*. Minneapolis: Augsburg Fortress, 2010. Daily scripture texts for individual or group prayer based on the daily lectionary in *Evangelical Lutheran Worship*.

Cherwien, David. *Stay with Us, Lord: Liturgies for Evening*. Minneapolis: Augsburg Fortress, 2001. Settings for Evening Prayer and Holy Communion, available in full music and congregational editions.

Haugen, Marty. *Holden Evening Prayer*. Chicago: GIA Publications, Inc., 1990.

Haugen, Marty and Susan Briehl. *Unfailing Light.* Chicago: GIA Publications, Inc., 2004.

Makeever, Ray. *Joyous Light Evening Prayer.* Minneapolis: Augsburg Fortress, 2000.

Revised Common Lectionary Daily Readings. Consultation on Common Texts. Minneapolis: Fortress Press, 2005.

Worship Studies, series

Worship Matters Series. Minneapolis: Augsburg Fortress, 2004–. The series explores a range of worship-related topics.

Christopherson, D. Foy. *A Place of Encounter: Renewing Worship Spaces* (2004).

Crowley, Eileen D. *A Moving Word: Media Art in Worship* (2006).

Dahill, Lisa. *Truly Present: Practicing Prayer in the Liturgy* (2005).

Lathrop, Gordon. *Central Things: Worship in Word and Sacrament* (2005).

Quivik, Melinda. *A Christian Funeral: Witness to the Resurrection* (2005).

Ramshaw, Gail. *A Three-Year Banquet: The Lectionary for the Assembly* (2004).

———. *The Three-Day Feast: Maundy Thursday, Good Friday, Easter* (2004).

Rimbo, Robert A. *Why Worship Matters* (2004). Foreword by Mark S. Hanson.

Torvend, Samuel. *Daily Bread, Holy Meal: Opening the Gifts of Holy Communion* (2004).

Wengert, Timothy, ed. *Centripetal Worship: The Evangelical Heart of Lutheran Worship* (2007). With contributions from Mark Mummert, Dirk Lange, Melinda Quivik, and Russell Mitman.

Ylvisaker, John. *What Song Shall We Sing?* (2005).

Welcome to Christ. Minneapolis: Augsburg Fortress, 1997–2003. A Lutheran approach to incorporating adult catechumens.

A Lutheran Catechetical Guide.

A Lutheran Introduction to the Catechumenate.

Lutheran Rites for the Catechumenate.

Sponsors Guide.

Worship Studies, individual titles

The Christian Life: Baptism and Life Passages. Minneapolis: Augsburg Fortress, 2008.

* *Keeping Time: The Church's Years.* Minneapolis: Augsburg Fortress, 2009.

The Sunday Assembly. Minneapolis: Augsburg Fortress, 2008. Three volumes of pastoral guides to Evangelical Lutheran Worship.

Gathered and Sent: An Introduction to Worship. Participant book by Karen Bockelman. Leader guide by Roger Prehn. Minneapolis: Augsburg Fortress, 1999. Basic worship study course for inquirers and general adult instruction in congregations.

Inside Out: Worship in an Age of Mission. Thomas Schattauer, gen. ed. Minneapolis: Fortress Press, 1999. Lutheran seminary teachers address the mission of the church as it pertains to various aspects of worship.

Lathrop, Gordon. *Holy Ground: A Liturgical Cosmology.* Minneapolis: Fortress Press, 2003. Explores how the symbols and interactions of the liturgy lead to a new understanding and experience of the world.

———. *Holy People: A Liturgical Ecclesiology.* Minneapolis: Fortress Press, 1999. The concept of "church" is defined using the activities of worship.

———. *Holy Things: A Liturgical Theology.* Minneapolis: Fortress Press, 1998. A call for worship leaders to discern what is central in the liturgy and to lift those up through liturgical reform.

Ramshaw, Gail. *Christian Worship.* Minneapolis: Fortress Press, 2009. An engaging textbook on 100,000 Sundays of Christians at worship.

Senn, Frank. *Christian Liturgy: Catholic and Evangelical.* Minneapolis: Fortress Press, 1997. A comprehensive historical introduction to the liturgy of the Western church with particular emphasis on Lutheran traditions.

———. *The People's Work: A Social History of the Liturgy.* Minneapolis: Fortress Press, 2006. The first book to document the full history of ordinary Christians' liturgical expression.

Use of the Means of Grace: A Statement on the Practice of Word and Sacrament, The. Chicago: Evangelical Lutheran Church in America, 1997. Also available in Spanish and Mandarin versions.

What Do You Seek? Welcoming the Adult Inquirer. Minneapolis: Augsburg Fortress, 2000. An introduction to a congregational process for welcoming Christians through affirmation of their baptism.

Web Sites

∞ www.sundaysandseasons.com. A subscription-based online worship planning tool. Browse, select, and download content for worship planning and worship folder preparation. Complements *Sundays and Seasons.*

∞ www.alcm.org. Association of Lutheran Church Musicians. Links to conferences and resources available through this pan-Lutheran musicians' organization. Also a bulletin board and placement service.

∞ www.elca.org/Growing-In-Faith/Worship.aspx. Worship and Liturgical Resources, Evangelical Lutheran Church in America. Contains links to articles and essays on a variety of worship-related topics. Includes a section on frequently asked questions about church year, language, lectionary, liturgy, worship planning, worship space, and many other topics. Monthly WorshipNews e-newsletter.

∞ www.newproclamation.com. An online sermon preparation resource that combines in-depth exegesis with homiletic advice from practicing preachers.

∞ www.worship.ca. Lift Up Your Hearts: The worship and spirituality site of the Evangelical Lutheran Church in Canada. Contains a variety of resources and news about events related to Lutheran worship.

∞ www.workingpreacher.org. A resource for preachers from the Center for Biblical Preaching at Luther Seminary.

Preaching Resources

Brueggemann, Walter, et al. *Texts for Preaching: A Lectionary Commentary Based on the NRSV.* Cycles A, B, C. Louisville, KY: Westminster John Knox Press, 1993–95.

Craddock, Fred, et al. *Preaching through the Christian Year.* Three volumes for Cycles A, B, C. Valley Forge, PA: Trinity Press International, 1992, 1993. In three volumes, various authors comment on the Sunday readings and psalms as well as various festival readings.

Elements of Preaching series. O. Wesley Allen, series editor. Minneapolis: Fortress, 2008—. Guides to the art and craft of preaching. Authors include Ronald Allen, Teresa Fry Brown, Mary Foskett, Jennifer Lord, Marvin McMickle, James Nieman, Melinda Quirik.

Hedahl, Susan K. *Who Do You Say that I Am? 21st Century Preaching.* Minneapolis: Augsburg Fortress, 2003. An exploration of Lutheran preaching. A Lutheran Voices title.

Homily Service: An Ecumenical Resource for Sharing the Word. Silver Spring, MD: The Liturgical Conference. A quarterly/seasonal publication with commentary on the Sunday readings, ideas, and illustrations for preaching. customerservice@taylorandfrancis.com. 800/354-1420, ext. 216. www.homily-servicejournal.com.

* *New Proclamation, Year A.* Minneapolis: Augsburg Fortress, 2010–2011. Various authors. A sound and useful series of commentaries on year A readings. In two volumes, Advent–Holy Week and Easter–Christ the King. www.newproclamation.com.

Ramshaw, Gail. *Treasures Old and New: Images in the Lectionary.* Minneapolis: Fortress Press, 2002. A creative unfolding of forty images drawn from the lectionary readings.

∞ Sloyan, Gerard. *Preaching from the Lectionary: An Exegetical Commentary with CD-ROM.* Minneapolis: Fortress Press, 2003. Exegetical analysis of each text from the three-year Revised Common Lectionary.

Stiller, Brian. *Preaching Parables to Postmoderns.* Minneapolis: Fortress Press, 2005. An introduction to postmodern sensibilities and how it informs preaching the parables.

∞ www.homileticsonline.com. An online sermon preparation resource including illustrations and visuals.

∞ www.workingpreacher.org. A resource for preachers from the Center for Biblical Preaching at Luther Seminary.

Periodicals

Assembly. Notre Dame Center for Pastoral Liturgy. Chicago: Liturgy Training Publications. Published six times a year. Each issue examines a particular aspect of worship. 800/933-1800.

Catechumenate: A Journal of Christian Initiation. Chicago: Liturgy Training Publications. Published six times a year with articles on congregational preparation of older children and adults for the celebration of baptism and eucharist. 800/933-1800.

CrossAccent. Journal of the Association of Lutheran Church Musicians. Publication for church musicians and worship leaders in North America. www.alcm.org.

Faith & Form. Journal of the Interfaith Forum on Religion, Art and Architecture. www.faithandform.com.

Liturgy. Quarterly journal of The Liturgical Conference. Each issue explores a worship-related issue from an ecumenical perspective. customerservice@taylorandfrancis.com. 800/354-1420, ext. 216.

Pastoral Liturgy. Published six times a year by Liturgy Training Publications. A liturgy magazine for the whole parish. 800/933-1800.

Worship. Collegeville, MN: The Order of St. Benedict, published through The Liturgical Press six times a year. One of the primary journals of liturgical renewal among the churches. 800/858-5450.

Key to Music Publishers

ABP	Abingdon	BRN	Bourne	HOP	Hope	MSM	MorningStar Music
AFP	Augsburg Fortress	CC	Changing Church/	HWG	H. W. Gray (Warner)	NM	National Music
AG	Agape (Hope)		Prince of Peace	INT	Integrity (Word)	NOV	Novello (Shawnee)
AGEHR	(Lorenz)	CG	Choristers Guild (Lorenz)	JEF	Jeffers	OCP	Oregon Catholic Press
ALF	Alfred	CPH	Concordia	KJO	Kjos	OXF	Oxford University Press
AMC	Arista	DUR	Durand (Presser)	KV	Kevin Mayhew	PRE	Presser
AMSI	Arts Masters Studio Inc.	EAR	EarthSongs	LAK	Lake State	RR	Red River Music
	(Lorenz)	ECS	E. C. Schirmer	LG	Lawson Gould	SEL	Selah
AUR	Aureole	FEL	Fellowship Ministries		(Hal Leonard)	SHW	Shawnee
B&H	Boosey & Hawkes	FLA	Flammer (Shawnee)	LOR	Lorenz	SMP	Sacred Music Press
BAR	Bärenreiter	GAL	Galaxy	LP	The Liturgical Press		(Lorenz)
BBM	Brentwood-Benson	GIA	GIA Publications	MAR	Maranatha	VIN	Vineyard Music
	Music	GS	G. Schirmer (Hal	MCF	McAfee Music Corp	WAL	Walton
BP	Beckenhorst Press		Leonard)		(Warner)	WRD	Word Music
BRB	Broude Brothers	HAL	Hal Leonard	MFS	Mark Foster	WT	WorshipTogether.com
BRD	Broadman	HIN	Hinshaw Music Co.				

Music for Worship Key

acc	accompaniment	fc	finger cymbals	narr	narrator	synth	synthesizer
bar	baritone	fl	flute	ob	oboe	tamb	tambourine
bng	bongos	glock	glockenspiel	oct	octave	tba	tuba
br	brass	gtr	guitar	opt	optional	tbn	trombone
bsn	bassoon	hb	handbells	orch	orchestra	tpt	trumpet
cant	cantor	hc	handchimes	org	organ	timp	timpani
ch	chimes	hp	harp	perc	percussion	trbl	treble
cl	clarinet	hpd	harpsichord	picc	piccolo	tri	triangle
cont	continuo	hrn	horn	pno	piano	U	unison
cym	cymbal	inst	instrument	pt	part	UE	upper elementary
DB	double or string bass	kybd	keyboard	qnt	quintet	vc	violoncello
dbl	double	LE	lower elementary	qrt	quartet	vcs	voices
desc	descant	M	medium	rec	recorder	vla	viola
div	divisi	MH	medium high	sax	saxophone	vln	violin
drm	drum	ML	medium low	sop	soprano	ww	woodwind
eng hrn	English horn	mxd	mixed	str	strings	xyl	xylophone

Key to Hymn and Psalm Collections

* Indicates resources whose hymns or psalm refrains are, at least in part, included in the online worship planning tool Sundays and Seasons.com.

ASF	A Singing Faith: The Hymns of Jane Parker Huber. Westminster/ John Knox Press.
BC	Borning Cry. Second ed. New Generation Publishers.
DH*	Dancing at the Harvest. Augsburg Fortress.
ELW*	Evangelical Lutheran Worship. Augsburg Fortress.
GC	Gather Comprehensive. GIA Publications.
GC2	Gather Comprehensive—Second Edition. GIA Publications.
GS2*	Global Songs 2: Bread for the Journey. Augsburg Fortress.
H82	The Hymnal 1982 (Episcopal). The Church Pension Fund.
HCW	Hosanna! Music Come & Worship. Integrity.

HFG	Hymns for the Gospels. GIA Publications.
HS91	Hymnal Supplement 1991. GIA Publications.
LBW*	Lutheran Book of Worship. Augsburg Fortress.
LLC	Libro de Liturgia y Cántico. Augsburg Fortress.
LS*	LifeSongs. Augsburg Fortress.
LSB	Lutheran Service Book (Lutheran Church – Missouri Synod). Concordia Publishing House.
NCH	The New Century Hymnal. The Pilgrim Press.
NSR	New Songs of Rejoicing. Selah.
OBS*	O Blessed Spring: Hymns of Susan Palo Cherwien. Augsburg Fortress.
PH	The Presbyterian Hymnal. Westminster/John Knox Press.

PSCY*	Psalm Settings for the Church Year. Augsburg Fortress.
PWA*	Psalter for Worship Year A, Evangelical Lutheran Worship Edition.
RS	RitualSong: A Hymnal and Service Book for Roman Catholics. GIA Publications.
SCR	Spirit Calls, Rejoice! Changing Church Forum.
SIC	Singing in Celebration. Westminster/John Knox Press.
TFF*	This Far by Faith. Augsburg Fortress.
W&P*	Worship & Praise. Augsburg Fortress.
WLP	Wonder, Love, and Praise. Church Publishing.
WOV*	With One Voice. Augsburg Fortress.

A Note on Music Listings

Please note that some choral and instrumental music in the day listings may be out of print. We are unable to research whether musical pieces from other publishers are still available.

Why do we still list music if it is out of print? Primarily because many music planners may have that piece in their files, and can consider it for use. If a planner wishes to use a piece that has gone out of print, that may still be possible. For Augsburg Fortress resources, call 800/421-0239 or e-mail copyright@augsburgfortress.org to inquire about onetime reprint rights or to see whether a piece may be available by print on demand.

Selected Publishers

Arts Masters Studio, Inc.
Contact the Lorenz Corp.

Abingdon Press
201 Eighth Avenue South
PO Box 801
Nashville TN 37202-0801
800/251-3320 Customer Service
800/836-7802 Fax
www.abingdonpress.com

Alfred Publishing Co., Inc.
PO Box 10003
Van Nuys CA 91410-0003
818/892-2452
818/830-6252 Fax
www.alfred.com

American Lutheran Publicity Bureau
PO Box 327
Delhi NY 13753-0327
607/746-7511
www.alpb.org

Augsburg Fortress
PO Box 1209
Minneapolis MN 55440-1209
800/328-4648 Ordering
800/421-0239 Permissions
612/330-3300 General
www.augsburgfortress.org

Beckenhorst Press
PO Box 14273
Columbus OH 43214
614/451-6461 General
614/451-6627 Fax
www.beckenhorstpress.com

Brentwood-Benson Music
960 East Mark St.
Winona MN 55987
www.brentwood-benson.com

Broadman Holman Genevox
See LifeWay Christian Resources

Boosey & Hawkes, Inc
35 East 21st Street
New York NY 10010-6212
212/358-5300
212/358-5305 Fax
www.boosey.com

Changing Church Forum, Inc.
13901 Fairview Drive
Burnsville MN 55337
800/874-2044
952/435-8065 Fax
www.changingchurch.org

Chester Music
Contact Hal Leonard Corp.—Music Dispatch

Concordia Publishing House
3558 South Jefferson
Saint Louis MO 63118
800/325-3040 Customer Service
800/490-9889 Fax
www.cph.org

E.C. Schirmer Music Co.
138 Ipswich Street
Boston MA 02215-3534
617/236-1935 General
617/236-0261 Fax
www.ecspublishing.com

Dakota Road Music
29225 468th Avenue
Beresford SD 57004
605/957-2333
www.dakotaroadmusic.com

GIA Publications, Inc.
7404 South Mason Avenue
Chicago IL 60638
800/442-1358 General
708/496-3828 Fax
www.giamusic.com

Hinshaw Music, Inc.
PO Box 470
Chapel Hill NC 27514-0470
919/933-1691 General
919/967-3399 Fax
www.hinshawmusic.com

Hal Leonard Corp.
PO Box 13819
7777 West Bluemound Road
Milwaukee WI 53213
414/774-3630 General
414/774-3259 Fax
www.halleonard.com

Hope Publishing Co.
380 South Main Place
Carol Stream IL 60188
800/323-1049 General
630/665-2552 Fax
www.hopepublishing.com

Hosanna! Music
See Integrity Music

Integrity Music
1000 Cody Road
Mobile, AL 36695
800/533-6912 Customer Service
www.integritymusic.com
www.integritydirect.com

Kevin Mayhew Ltd.
Buxhall, Stowmarket
Suffolk IP14 3BW
England
01449-737978 General
01449-737834 Fax
sales@kevinmayhewltd.com

Lead Worship
P.O. Box 2101
Lindale TX 75771
903/882-5755
903/882-5059 Fax
www.leadworship.com

LifeWay Christian Resources
One LifeWay Plaza
Nashville TN 37234
800/251-3225 Broadman & Holman
800/884-7712 Genevox
customerservice@lifeway.com

The Liturgical Conference
PO Box 31
Evanston IL 60204
847/866-3875
www.liturgicalconference.org

The Liturgical Press
St. John's Abbey
PO Box 7500
Collegeville MN 56321-7500
800/858-5450 General
320/363-2213 General
320/363-3299 Fax
sales@litpress.org

Liturgy Training Publications
1800 North Hermitage Avenue
Chicago IL 60622-1101
800/933-4779 Customer Service
800/933-7094 Fax
orders@ltp.org

The Lorenz Corporation
501 East Third Street
Dayton OH 45402
800/444-1144 General
937/223-2042 Fax
www.lorenz.com

Ludwig Music Publishing Co.
557 East 140th Street
Cleveland OH 44110-1999
800/851-1150 General
216/851-1958 Fax
info@ludwigmusic.com

Maranatha!
PO Box 1077
Dana Point CA 92629
800/245-7664

MorningStar Music Publishers
1727 Larkin Williams Road
Fenton MO 63026
800/647-2117 Ordering
636/305-0121 Fax
morningstar@morningstarmusic.com

musicnotes.com
800/944-4667
www.musicnotes.com

New Creation Ministries
P.O. Box 80010
Broadmoor Postal Outlet
Sherwood Park AB T8A 5T4
Canada
info@new-creation.net
www.new-creation.net

Oregon Catholic Press
OCP Publications
PO Box 18030
Portland OR 97218-0030
800/548-8749 General
800/462-7329 Fax
liturgy@ocp.org

Oxford University Press
2001 Evans Road
Cary NC 27513
800/445-9714 Customer Service
919/677-1303 Fax
custserv@oup-usa.org

Praise Charts
Suite 123
#505-8840 210th St.
Langley BC V1M 2Y2
Canada
800/695-6293 Customer Service
www.praisecharts.com

Red River Music
316 Dublin
Tyler TX 75703
877/547-4837
903/839-0809 Fax

Selah Publishing Co.
PO Box 98066
Pittsburgh PA 15227
800/852-6172 Ordering
412/886-1022 Fax
www.selahpub.com

Shawnee Press
PO Box 690
49 Waring Drive
Delaware Water Gap PA 18327-1690
570/476-0550 General
570/476-5247 Fax
shawnee-info@shawneepress.com

Thankyou Music
26-28 Lottbridge Drive
Eastbourne BN23 6NT
UK
01440-1323437712
01440-1323411970 Fax
www.thankyoumusic.co.uk

Theodore Presser Co.
588 North Gulph Road
King of Prussia PA 19406
610/525-3636
610/527-7841 Fax
www.presser.com

Vineyard Music
12650 Directors Drive
Suite 500
Stafford TX 77477
281/565-8463
281/565-8467 Fax

Word Music Inc.
3319 West End Avenue
Suite 200
Nashville TN 37203
888/324-9673
888/324-4329 Fax
questions@wordmusic.com

WorshipTogether.com
101 Winners Circle
Brentwood TN 37027
888/711-0198
www.worshiptogether.com

About the Art

In creating the cover art for *Sundays and Seasons*, **Nicholas Wilton** believed that symbols of things were needed as, like poetry, we are trying to express something about the spiritual. Working metaphorically, for him, is far more universal and engaging than literally depicting something specific. His artist statement at nicholaswiltonpaintings.com says, "My process combines intuitive painting with fundamental principles of color harmony, juxtaposition of form, and excavated texture. The resulting work, often called 'contemporary organic' addresses the spiritual potency of nature, and celebrates the fragile balance between the natural and developed world in which we live."

Joel Nickel (introductory images, seasonal images, Vigil of Easter) seeks to locate his artwork somewhere between expressionism and abstract geometric design. His artistic heroes are mostly expressionists (Klee, Kandinsky, Dix, Nolde, Grosz, Picasso, etc.), whose existential visions he believes dovetail nicely with the dynamic tensions present in biblical texts. Joel believes that graphic art for church use ought to have visual power tied to text and contemporary context.

Peggy Adams Parker (Advent–Transfiguration) thinks of her biblical images as visual explorations of the text. She begins by imagining what it would be like for her to enter the scene: how would she hold her body if she were Sarah laughing at God's prophecy or Mary cradling her new born child? She finds that often a small gesture such as the slump of shoulders helps convey the essence of a story. Peggy tries to understand and depict each story as a recognizable human experience, hoping to draw the viewer into the narrative.

According to **Robyn Sand Anderson** (Ash Wednesday–Day of Pentecost), creating a simplified visual design from a grouping of scriptural verses is somewhat like reading the entire Gospel of John and coming up with one to two summarizing sentences: It is like solving a puzzle, a challenge she enjoys. Robyn believes that the beauty of art speaks a universal language across time and culture. She is grateful for the artistic gifts God has given her, which bring great joy into her life.

Work by **Meg Bussey** (Holy Trinity–Lectionary 22, Day of Thanksgiving) on illustrations for this volume with brush and ink meant doing a sketch and developing a composition in charcoal or pencil, then turning to the brush and ink and drawing each idea out repeatedly until it seemed to be filled with the right kind of liveliness. She believes that the most successful images convey gestures that somehow intuitively signal God's presence.

The art style of **Paula Wiggins** (Lectionary 23–Christ the King) emphasizes simplicity and economy of line. She enjoys the challenge of portraying emotional range in a character by the tilt of a head or the raising of a hand. Paula believes that most of the time, not much else is needed to tell a story. Her artwork for this project involved developing 2-4 different sketches to explore each subject before creating the final illustration. This process enabled Paula to remain aware of the multivalent meanings of the gospel texts she was interpreting.